# BALTIMORE AND OHIO RAILROAD EMPLOYEES

## 1842 AND 1852

⊁ PAGES 1-44 ⊱

## 1855 AND 1857

⋈ PAGES 45-348 ⋈

*Edna A. Kanely*

HERITAGE BOOKS
2008

# HERITAGE BOOKS
*AN IMPRINT OF HERITAGE BOOKS, INC.*

**Books, CDs, and more—Worldwide**

For our listing of thousands of titles see our website at
www.HeritageBooks.com

Published 2008 by
HERITAGE BOOKS, INC.
Publishing Division
100 Railroad Ave. #104
Westminster, Maryland 21157

Copyright © 1982 Edna A. Kanely

Other books by the author:
*Directory of Maryland Church Records*
Edna A. Kanely, Under the Auspices of the Genealogical Council of Maryland
*Directory of Ministers and Maryland Churches They Served, 1634-1990*

All rights reserved. No part of this book may be reproduced or transmitted in any form or by any means, electronic or mechanical, including photocopying, recording or by any information storage and retrieval system without written permission from the author, except for the inclusion of brief quotations in a review.

International Standard Book Numbers
Paperbound: 978-1-58549-493-4
Clothbound: 978-0-7884-7270-1

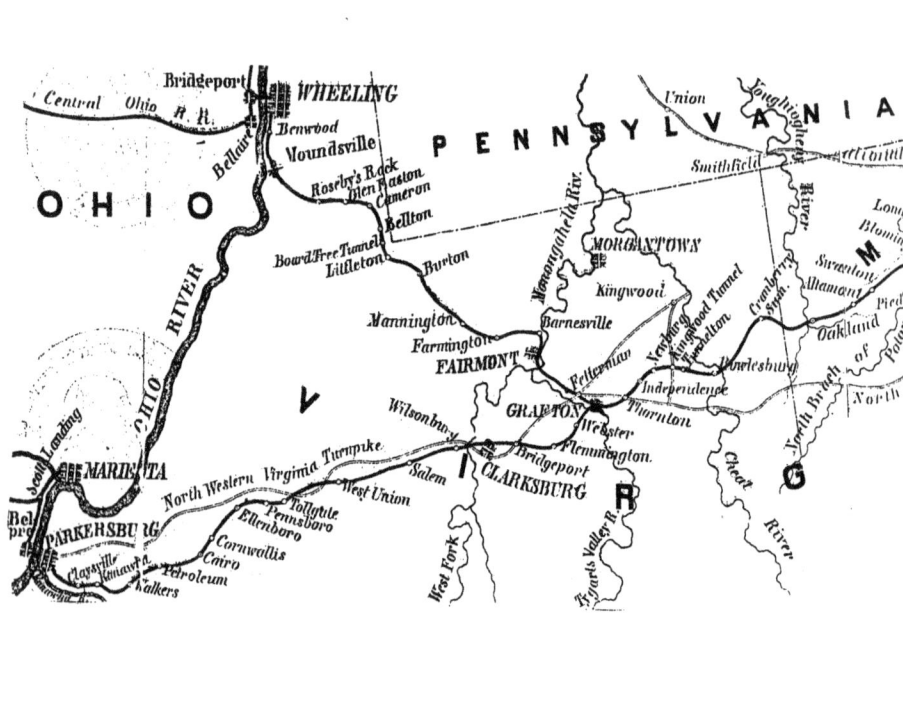

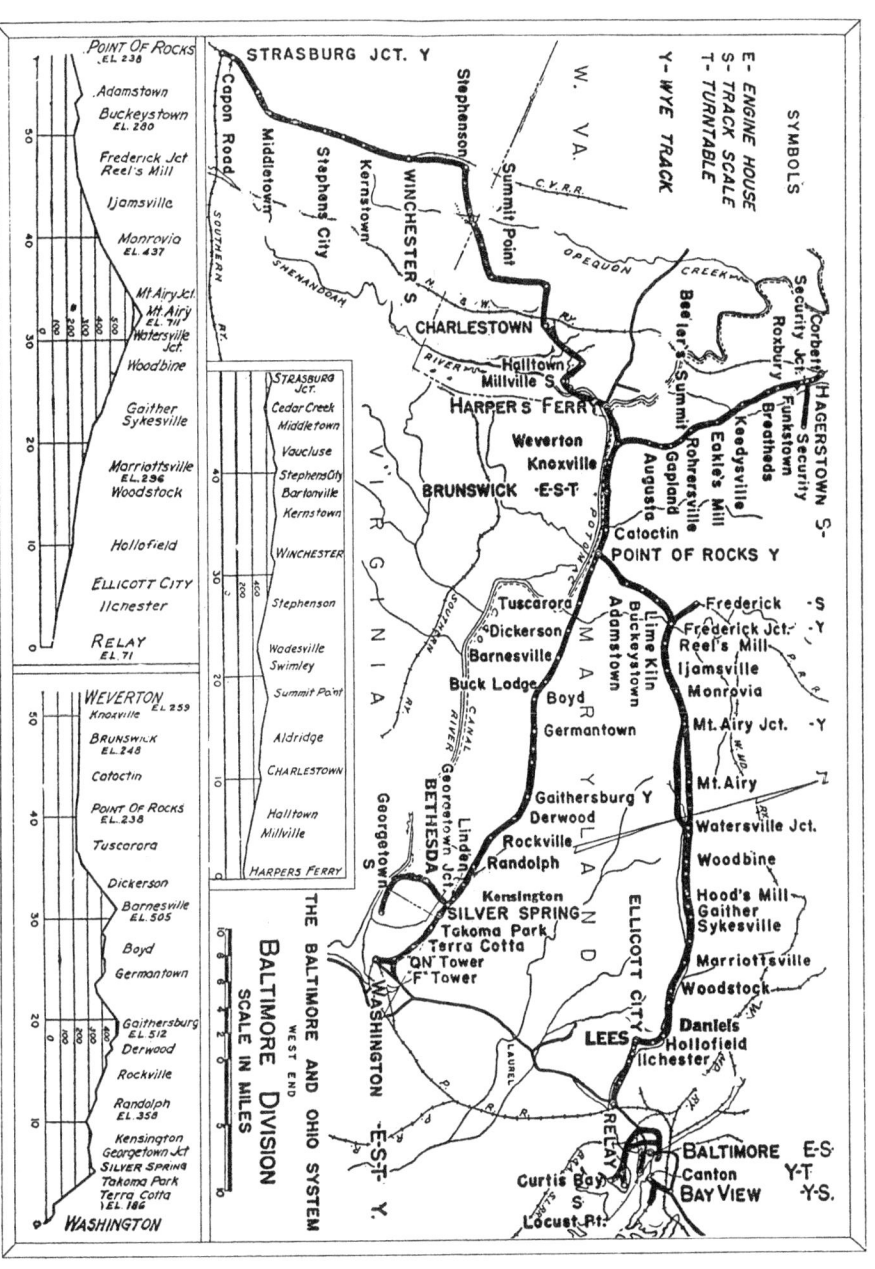

BALTIMORE AND OHIO RAILROAD EMPLOYEES

by Edna A. Kanely

"By the work one knows the workman."

The first chartered and fully organized railroad company in the United States was the Baltimore and Ohio Railroad; incorporated by an act of the Maryland Legislature on February 28, 1827. The president and directors of the company were "invested with all the rights and powers necessary to the construction and repair of a rail road from the City of Baltimore to some suitable point on the Ohio river, to be by them determined".[1]

The State of Virginia by a legislative act on March 8, 1827 "granted to the said company the same rights and privileges within the territory of Virginia as are granted to them within the territory of Maryland."[2] The Pennsylvania Legislature in February 1828 "proceeding upon the ground that the best route adapted for said road, would pass through a large portion of that State also incorporated the said company".[3]

Everybody wanted stock in the new company. Individual contributions amounted to $3,000,000. "The State of Maryland and the City of Baltimore each subscribed and paid half a million dollars."[4]

After surveys and cost estimates were studied, the B & O Board decided to run the first rail from Baltimore to Ellicott's Mills on the Patapsco, a place of industrial activity and business importance for freight and travel, also a romantic spot for pleasure excursions from the city.

Construction began on July 4, 1828. There was a great celebration in Baltimore with a magnificent parade of military and civic organizations, trades and professions, and bands. "The 'first stone' was laid by the venerable Charles Carroll of Carrollton, then over ninety years of age, on the south-western line of the City".[5]

A car was built, similar to a "country market wagon", without a top, mounted upon wheels, drawn by a single horse. As soon as a mile of track had been laid west of Mt Clare, the public was invited to try the new mode of travel. "In this car Charles Carroll of Carrollton, Alexander Brown, William Patterson, Philip E. Thomas, and others of the directors of the Company, with some leading citizens of Baltimore, made trips backwards and forwards, drawn by a single horse, with the same elation that we now see among the boys who are lucky enough to

[1] Baltimore & Ohio Railroad Co, Memorial of the Baltimore and Ohio Railroad Company to the Legislature of Virginia...1844 (Baltimore?: 1844), 3.
[2] Ibid.
[3] Ibid. 3-4.
[4] Ibid. 5
[5] A Citizen of Baltimore (Smith), A History and Description of the Baltimore and Ohio Rail Road...;(Baltimore: John Murphy & Co., 1853), 19.

secure a ride on the platform of a passenger car as it passes along the streets"? so stated John H. B. Latrobe in a lecture to the Maryland Institute on March 23, 1868. The cost of a round trip was 12½ cents. "This was the first money ever earned on a railroad constructed for general purposes in America."[7]

Less than two years after laying of the corner stone, on May 22, 1830, the first division of the road (from Baltimore to Ellicott's Mills) was opened for transportation of passengers, but the cars were not ready until the early part of June; from that time on traveling to and from Ellicott's Mills continued uninterrupted, horse and mule power being used for drawing the cars.

The use of a small steam engine (the Tom Thumb) was tried in the summer of 1830. Mr. Peter Cooper of New York had come to Baltimore and built the boiler and engine in the car-shop at Mt Clare. The 13 mile trip to Ellicott's Mills was made in 57 minutes.

Horses and mules continued to pull the cars from place to place as tracks were extended to Washington and to Frederick. In 1832 a report prepared by Mr. Gillingham, the Superintendent of Machinery, stated that using locomotive power cost $16 per day whereas the same work done by horse power averaged $33 a day. Steam engines gradually replaced the horses.

It was not until 1831 that the B & O was empowered by the City Council of Baltimore to lay tracks along Pratt Street from Mt Clare to the Basin and then to the City Block, running parallel with the water front. By Fall of that year, transportation of passengers and freight commenced on this section of the road. An inner depot had been built on Charles Street below Pratt Street.

By 1835 tracks had been laid to Washington on the southwest (which became known as the Washington Branch) and to Harpers Ferry on the west, the latter a distance of 82 miles from Baltimore. In 1842 the railroad reached Cumberland, Md.-- 97 miles from Harpers Ferry, 178 miles from Baltimore--this track became known as the "main stem". Service was begun on November 3, 1842. Twenty-five days later, a special locomotive left Washington with a copy of President Tyler's message to the Congress and reached Cumberland in 5 hours 50 minutes. Normal passenger travel over the same route was estimated to take less than 10 hours--averaging 25 or 30 miles an hour.

On January 1, 1853, after 25 years of effort, 25 years of achievement, the B & O finally reached its goal. The first train traveled from Baltimore to Wheeling, W. Va., a brisk river town on the banks of the Ohio, in 19 hours. It was estimated that after the new road bed had settled, travel time for freight and passengers would be reduced to 16 hours.

[6]Latrobe, John H. B., The Baltimore and Ohio Railroad. Personal Recollections. A Lecture Delivered Before the Maryland Institute, March 23d, 1868 (Baltimore: Sun Book and Job Printing Establishment, 1868?), 12.

[7]Ibid.

# B & O RR EMPLOYEES

During this period, real locomotives were being developed, cars were being improved, and service on the B & O was getting better with greater comfort, faster trains and more rolling stock. All of this due to the ingenuity, competency and skill of many dedicated employees.

In 1842, about the time the railroad reached Cumberland, the B & O published a List of Persons with Their Pay, in the Service of the Baltimore and Ohio Railroad Company (April 1, 1842); also in 1852, the year before the first train reached Wheeling, List of Officers and Employees in the Service of the Baltimore and Ohio R. Road Co. with Their Salaries, Duties &c. September 1852.

The 1842 list identifies the following departments and sub-divisions to which employees were assigned:

|  | Abbreviations |
|---|---|
| Office Department | Ofc Dept |
| Engineer Department | Engr Dept |
|   officers of general duty | gen duty |
|   office duty | ofc duty |
|   construction of road west of Harpers Ferry | |
|     first division | 1st div |
|     second division | 2d div |
| Department of Repairs of Rail-Way and of Machinery | Repairs of Rwy & Mach Dept |
|   main stem (including lateral branch to Frederick--total length of road 83½ miles) | main stem |
|     1st sub-division (length 21 miles) | 1st s-div |
|     2d sub-division (length 19 miles) | 2d s-div |
|     3d sub-division (length 15 miles) | 3d s-div |
|     4th sub-division (length 15½ miles) | 4th s-div |
|     5th sub-division (length 15 miles) | 5th s-div |
|   Washington Branch | Wash br |
|     1st sub-division (length 15 miles) | |
|     2d sub-division (length 16 miles) | |
|   Mount Clare Depot (preparing materials for construction and repairs of railway, bridges, water stations, depots and switches) | Mt Clare |
|   construction and repairs of machinery in the Machine Shop | Mt Clare mach shop |
| Transportation Department | Trans Dept |
|   main stem | |
|   Washington Branch | |

The 1852 list identifies the following departments:

| | |
|---|---|
| Secretary's Office | Secy Ofc |
| Road Department | Rd Dept |
| Machinery Department | Mach Dept |
| Transportation Department | Trans Dept |
| Washington Branch | |

Listed alphabetically are the names of employees taken from the 1842 and 1852 documents, with job title and salary, name of department and sub-division to which they were assigned, followed by a list of abbreviations used other than those shown above.

# B & O RR EMPLOYEES

| Year-Ref | Name | | Description |
|---|---|---|---|
| 1842-4 | Adair, | James | rough carp 94¢ per da. Repairs of Rwy & Mach Dept main stem 2d s-div |
| 1842-4 | | John | watch bridge, Elysville 80¢ per da. Repairs of Rwy & Mach Dept main stem 2d s-div |
| 1842-4 | | Robert | rough carp 94¢ per da. Repairs of Rwy & Mach Dept main stem 2d o-div |
| 1852-30 | | " | local agt main stem Marriottsville 10¢ per ton plus comm. Trans Dept |
| 1842-4 | | William | rough carp 94¢ per da. Repairs of Rwy & Mach Dept main stem 2d s-div |
| 1852-26 | Addison, E. R. | | eng'man $2.50 per da. Trans Dept |
| 1852-14 | | J. O.* | timekpr Martinsburg sta $40 per mo. Mach Dept appointed Mar 1850 |
| 1852-25 | Adolph, John | | laborer Locust Pt $300 per yr. Trans Dept |
| 1852-17 | Agnew, J. L.* | | clk Cumberland $41.65 per mo. Trans Dept entered co serv Sept 1851 |
| 1852-26 | Aldridge, John | | eng'man $2.50 per da. Trans Dept |
| 1842-13 | Alexander, Thomas | | master painter $1.42 per da. Repairs of Rwy & Mach Dept Mt Clare mach shop |
| 1842-10 | Allen, William | | helper & tube cleaning $1 per da. Repairs of Rwy & Mach Dept Mt Clare mach shop |
| 1842-10 | Aller, Jeremiah | | finisher(app) 50¢ per da. Repairs of Rwy & Mach Dept Mt Clare mach shop |
| 1852-32 | Alvey, Samuel | | pass brakeman $30 per mo. Wash br appointed 1852 |
| 1852-28 | Ambrose, Robert | | fireman $400 per yr. Trans Dept |
| 1842-5 | Amburger, Michael | | laborer 75¢ per da. Repairs of Rwy & Mach Dept main stem 3d s-div |
| 1852-27 | Anderson, James | | eng'man $2.50 per da. Trans Dept |
| 1852-21 | R. | | ton conduc $480 per yr. Trans Dept |
| 1852-33 | Archibald, Thomas | | fireman $33.33 per mo. Wash br appointed 1851 |
| 1852-30 | Armstrong, E. M. | | local agt w of Cumberland New Creek 10¢ per ton plus comm. Trans Dept appointed 1851 |
| 1842-16 | Arnold, Davis | | ostler & ton driv Balto $30 per mo. Trans Dept main stem |
| 1852-32 | | Wm. | pass brakeman $30 per mo. Wash br appointed 1847 |
| 1842-1 | Atkinson, J. I. | | secy $2,000 per annum Ofc Dept |
| 1852-3 | | J. I.* | treas & secy $2,500 per annum 17 yrs in co serv, from $1,000 to present amt |
| 1842-2 | | T. C. | vaneman $1 per da. Engr Dept cons of rd w of Harper's Ferry 1st div |
| 1852-7 | | Thomas C. | asst master of rd $900 per annum Rd Dept appointed Oct 1851 |

# B & O RR EMPLOYEES

| | | |
|---|---|---|
| 1842-2 | Atkinson, Thomas Ch. | div engr $4.38 per da. Engr Dept cons of rd w of harper's Ferry 2d div |
| 1842-2 | William G. | axeman $1 per da. Engr Dept cons of rd w of Harper's Ferry 2d div |
| 1852-21 | Bailey, Otho | ton conduc $480 per yr. Trans Dept |
| 1842-5 | Baily, Jacob | laborer 75¢ per da. Repairs of Rwy & Mach Dept main stem 3d s-div |
| 1842-5 | Otho | rough carp 94¢ per da. Repairs of Rwy & Mach Dept main stem 4th s-div |
| 1852-25 | Bainhart, A. | laborer load & unload cars Harper's Ferry $330 per yr. Trans Dept |
| 1852-21 | Baitges, Geo. | ton brakeman $360 per yr. Trans Dept |
| 1842-15 | Baker, Hezekiah | fireman Balto $35 per mo. Trans Dept main stem |
| 1852-30 | Isaac | local agt main stem Paw Paw 10¢ per ton plus comm. Trans Dept |
| 1852-17 | John H.* | chief clk Mt Clare $750 per annum Trans Dept entered co serv 1847 as asst collec $500 per annum |
| 1852-27 | Baldwin, John | eng'man $2 per da. Trans Dept |
| 1842-5 | Rignal | nailor 80¢ per da. Repairs of Rwy & Mach Dept main stem 4th s-div |
| 1842-5 | William | laborer 75¢ per da. Repairs of Rwy & Mach Dept main stem 4th s-div |
| 1852-33 | Ball, J. | cleaning ton eng Cumberland $300 per yr. Wash br |
| 1852-12 | James* | foreman Cumberland sta $800 per annum wi house. Mach Dept appointed May 1846 at $600 per annum |
| 1842-12 | Ballinger, Samuel | carp $1.37½ per da. Repairs of Rwy & Mach Dept Mt Clare mach shop |
| 1842-13 | Barneclo, J. W. | timekpr $45 per mo. Repairs of Rwy & Mach Dept Mt Clare mach shop |
| 1842-16 | Barnes, William | agt City Block Balto $22.50 per mo. Trans Dept Wash br |
| 1852-25 | Barney, Patrick | laborer Locust Pt $300 per yr. Trans Dept |
| 1852-27 | Barrett, James | eng'man $2.50 per da. Trans Dept |
| 1852-30 | Barry, Philip | local agt main stem Green Spring Run 10¢ per ton plus comm. Trans Dept |
| 1842-12 | Bartlett, Henry | coach mkr $1.37½ per da. Repairs of Rwy & Mach Dept Mt Clare mach shop |
| 1852-21 | Bassard, Daniel | ton brakeman $360 per yr. Trans Dept |

# B & O RR EMPLOYEES

1852-21 Batson, John — ton brakeman $360 per yr. Trans Dept
1842-10 Bauckman, Rudolph — smith $1.42 per da. Repairs of Rwy & Mach Dept Mt Clare mach shop
1842-15 Baughman, George — fireman Balto $35 per mo. Trans Dept main stem
1842-8 Beale, Theophilus — carp $1.37½ per da. Repairs of Rwy & Mach Dept Mt Clare
1842-7 Beall, Thomas — laborer 75¢ per da. Repairs of Rwy & Mach Dept Wash br 2d s-div
1842-16 Beck, James R. — brakeman Balto $30 per mo. Trans Dept Wash br
1852-30 Beckenbaugh, W. W. — local agt main stem Duffields 10¢ per ton plus comm. Trans Dept appointed in 1852
1852-27 Beckett, Thos. — eng'man $2 per da. Trans Dept
1852-16 Beckham, F.* — agt Harper's Ferry $900 per annum Trans Dept appointed in 1833 at $600 per annum
1842-14 Beekham, Fontaine — gen agt Harper's Ferry $58.33 per mo. Trans Dept main stem
1842-2 Bell, Hanson — axeman 75¢ per da. Engr Dept cons of rd w of Harper's Ferry 2d div
1852-24 " Isaac — burden car driv $360 per yr. Trans Dept
1852-21 Bennett, Wm. — ton brakeman $360 per yr. Trans Dept
1852-28 " " — fireman $400 per yr. Trans Dept
1842-14 Berry, Charles — eng'man Balto $2 per da. Trans Dept main stem
1852-27 " " — eng'man $2.50 per da. Trans Dept
1842-10 " Jesse — finisher (app) 66 2/3¢ per da. Repairs of Rwy & Mach Dept Mt Clare mach shop
1852-21 Best, S. A. — ton brakeman $360 per yr. Trans Dept
1842-2 Bester, Norman S. — vaneman $1.25 per da. Engr Dept cons of rd w of Harper's Ferry 2d div
1842-16 Bevan, John — ostler & ton driv Balto $30 per mo. Trans Dept main stem
1842-11 Biddle, Peregrine — master carp $55 per mo. Repairs of Rwy & Mach Dept Mt Clare mach shop
1852-13 " * — foreman of carp shops for cons & repairs of burden cars, at Mt Clare $50 per mo. Mach Dept appointed May 1840
1842-9 Billson, Henry — finisher $1.42 per da. Repairs of Rwy & Mach Dept Mt Clare mach shop
1852-25 Bishop, P. — tender filler Mt Clare $325 per yr. Trans Dept
1842-17 " Patrick — laborer Balto $25 per mo. Trans Dept Wash br
1842-15 Black, Evan — watchman Mt Clare Depot $30 per mo. Trans Dept main stem

## B & O RR EMPLOYEES

| | | |
|---|---|---|
| 1842-12 | Blackston, William | carp $1.25 per da. Repairs of Rwy & Mach Dept Mt Clare mach shop |
| 1842-4 | Blakley, Christopher | rough carp 94¢ per da. Repairs of Rwy & Mach Dept main stem 2d s-div |
| 1852-27 | Blessing, Geo. | eng'man $2.50 per da. Trans Dept |
| 1842-15 | Blucher, Mathias | eng'man $2 per da. Balto Trans Dept main stem |
| 1852-21 | Blue, J. P. | ton brakeman $360 per yr. Trans Dept |
| 1852-28 | Boardman, Sidney | fireman $400 per yr. Trans Dept |
| 1852-6 | Bollman, Wendel* | master of rd $1,500 per yr. Rd Dept appointed Sept 1849 at $1200 |
| 1842-11 | Booth, George W. | coach mkr $1.50 per da. Repairs of Rwy & Mach Dept Mt Clare mach shop |
| 1852-25 | Boseley, Jos. | laborer Locust Pt $300 per yr. Trans Dept |
| 1842-9 | Bosley, Edward | finisher $1.33 1/3 per da. Repairs of Rwy & Mach Dept Mt Clare mach shop |
| 1852-8 | Boteler, Beverly W.* | clk & timekpr at Mt Clare $50 per mo. Rd Dept appointed 1 Apr 1847 at $45 per mo. |
| 1852-30 | W. H. | local agt main stem Point Rocks 10¢ per ton plus comm. Trans Dept appointed in 1852 |
| 1852-26 | Bowman, Wm. | car coupler Mt Clare $325 per yr Trans Dept |
| 1842-15 | Boyce, Thomas | watchman Pratt St Depot $25 per mo. Trans Dept main stem |
| 1842-13 | Boyd, Alexander | trimmer $1.25 per da. Repairs of Rwy & Mach Dept Mt Clare mach shop |
| 1852-25 | Boyer, Thomas | laborer load & unload cars at Pratt St $360 per yr. Trans Dept |
| 1842-4 | Bradshaw, Jas. | nailor 80¢ per da. Repairs of Rwy & Mach Dept main stem 2d s-div |
| 1842-6 | Branny, Patrick | nail & exam track 80¢ per da. Repairs of Rwy & Mach Dept Wash br 1st s-div |
| 1852-25 | Brien, John | laborer Locust Pt $300 per yr. Trans Dept |
| 1852-28 | Briggs, J. | eng'man stationary eng Locust Pt $414 per yr. Trans Dept |
| 1842-15 | James | eng'man City Block $30 per mo. Trans Dept main stem |
| 1842-5 | Britt, John | rough carp 94¢ per da. Repairs of Rwy & Mach Dept main stem 5th s-div |
| 1852-28 | Brown, Anthony | fireman $400 per yr. Trans Dept |
| 1852-19 | B. F.* | pass conduc $58.33 per mo. Trans Dept entered co serv in 1847 as baggage master at $30 per mo. |
| 1842-10 | David | smith $1.58 per da. Repairs of Rwy & Mach Dept Mt Clare mach shop |

# B & O RR EMPLOYEES

1842-15 Brown, John — laborer Harper's Ferry $25 per mo. Trans Dept main stem
1842-14 " Joseph — way ton conduc Harper's Ferry $40 per mo. Trans Dept main stem
1852-16 " * — supv of trains e of Cumberland $1,000 per annum Trans Dept entered co serv in 1834 as yard driv at $30 per mo.
1842-3 " Robert — stone cutter on repairs city track $1.06¼ per da. Repairs of Rwy & Mach Dept main stem 1st s-div
1852-9 " Vachel* — supv 2d s-div $45 per mo. Rd Dept appointed 1 Oct 1849
1842-16 " William — ostler & ton driv Balto $30 per mo. Trans Dept main stem
1852-27 Bryan, Wm. — eng'man $2.50 per da. Trans Dept
1842-3 Bryon, Patrick — laborer 75¢ per da. Repairs of Rwy & Mach Dept main stem 1st s-div
1842-1 Bryson, G. H. — vaneman $1.50 per da. Engr Dept cons of rd w of Harper's Ferry 1st div
1852-5 " James F.* — asst clk $750 per annum Secy Ofc appointed 13 Dec 1848
1842-9 " John — finisher $1.33 1/3 per da. Repairs of Rwy & Mach Dept Mt Clare mach shop
1852-30 Bruce, C. K. — local agt main stem Great Cacapon 10¢ per ton plus comm. Trans Dept
1842-15 Budd, Henry — watchman Frederick $24 per mo. Trans Dept main stem
1852-26 " — watchman Frederick $240 per yr. Trans Dept
1842-10 Buddy, William — boiler mkr $1.58 per da. Repairs of Rwy & Mach Dept Mt Clare mach shop
1852-28 Burchfield, James — fireman $400 per yr. Trans Dept
1852-21 " — ton conduc $480 per yr. " "
1842-5 Burgoyne, John — rough carp 94¢ per da. Repairs of Rwy & Mach Dept main stem 5th s-div
1842-11 Burke, Samuel — helper 92¢ per da. Repairs of Rwy & Mach Dept Mt Clare mach shop
1842-15 Burrall, George — porter, etc. Frederick $25 per mo. Trans Dept main stem
1842-8 Burton, John F. — laborer (boy) 56¼¢ per da. Repairs of Rwy & Mach Dept Mt Clare
1842-8 " William D. — master carp $1.75 per da. Repairs of Rwy & Mach Dept Mt Clare
1852-30 Bussard, Henry — local agt main stem Mt Airy 10¢ per ton plus comm. Trans Dept
1852-27 " L. J. — eng'man $2.50 per da. Trans Dept
1852-20 " M. — regulator of trains Mt Clare westward $40 per mo. Trans Dept appointed in 1849

## B & O RR EMPLOYEES

| | | |
|---|---|---|
| 1852-28 | Bussard, Marshall | fireman $400 per yr. Trans Dept |
| 1842-14 | " Matthew | ton breakman Harper's Ferry $35 per mo. Trans Dept main stem |
| 1852-28 | Butler, George | fireman $400 per yr. Trans Dept |
| 1842-15 | " Ormond | eng'man Balto $2 per da. Trans Dept main stem |
| 1852-20 | Butt, H. S. | regulator at Cumberland $35 per mo. Trans Dept appointed 1849 |
| 1852-23 | " P. | tender filler Cumberland $300 per yr. Trans Dept |
| 1852-21 | " " | ton conduc $480 per yr. Trans Dept |
| 1852-25 | Byrne, Dennis | laborer load & unload cars Pratt St $360 per yr. Trans Dept |
| 1852-25 | Calahan, Christian | laborer Locust Pt $300 per yr. Trans Dept |
| 1852-25 | " John | laborer Locust Pt $300 per yr. Trans Dept |
| 1852-24 | Campbell, John | blacksmith $336 per yr. Trans Dept |
| 1852-24 | " M. | regulator ton trains $360 per yr. Trans Dept |
| 1842-14 | Canby, Samuel | local agt Ellicott's Mills $20 per mo. Trans Dept main stem |
| 1852-21 | Carder, Levi | ton brakeman $360 per yr. Trans Dept |
| 1842-10 | Carley, James | smith & spring mkr $1.42 per da. Repairs of Rwy & Mach Dept Mt Clare mach shop |
| 1842-16 | Carnihan, Frederick | ostler & pass driv Balto $30 per mo. Trans Dept main stem |
| 1842-5 | Carr, Edward | supv $45 per mo. Repairs of Rwy & Mach Dept main stem 5th s-div |
| 1852-10 | " " * | supv 7th s-div $45 per mo. Rd Dept appointed 1 Apr 1839 |
| 1842-11 | " Greenbury | coar mkr $1 per da. Repairs of Rwy & Mach Dept Mt Clare mach shop |
| 1852-26 | " John | cleaning eng Mt Clare $300 per yr. Trans Dept |
| 1852-28 | " " | fireman $400 per yr. Trans Dept |
| 1842-3 | " Roseby | supv $60 per mo. Repairs of Rwy & Mach Dept main stem 1st s-div |
| 1852-9 | " " * | laying track w of Cumberland |
| 1852-32 | Carroll, John | laborer unload cars $340 per yr. Wash br |
| 1852-26 | " M. | car coupler Mt Clare $325 per yr. Trans Dept |
| 1842-6 | Cassady, James | rough carp 94¢ per da. Repairs of Rwy & Mach Dept Wash br 1st s-div |
| 1852-28 | Caster, Benj. | fireman $400 per yr. Trans Dept |
| 1842-10 | Cathrell, Michael | boiler mkr $1.25 per da. Repairs of Rwy & Mach Dept Mt Clare mach shop |
| 1852-19 | Cauly, Samuel* | agt at Ellicott's Mills $35 per mo. Trans Dept appointed 1847 |
| 1842-4 | Cavey, Brice | nailor 80¢ per da. Repairs of Rwy & Mach Dept main stem 2d s-div |
| 1852-21 | Chance, Edward | ton brakeman $360 per yr. Trans Dept |

## B & O RR EMPLOYEES

| | | | |
|---|---|---|---|
| 1842-2 | Chiffelle, Thomas P. | | res engr $3 per da. Engr Dept cons of rd w of Harper's Ferry 2d div |
| 1842-11 | Chisty, Michael | | helper 92¢ per da. Repairs of Rwy & Mach Dept Mt Clare mach shop |
| 1842-7 | Cladermaker, John | | laborer 75¢ per da. Repairs of Rwy & Mach Dept Wash br 2d s-div |
| 1842-3 | Clark, Barny | | laborer 75¢ per da. Repairs of Rwy & Mach Dept main stem 1st s-div |
| 1852-9 | Clarke, James* | | engr & supt of ballast train $75 per mo. Rd Dept appointed 1 Oct 1850 |
| 1852-7 | " | * | foreman of mach shop $60 per mo. Rd Dept appointed 1 Feb 1850 at $50 per mo. |
| 1842-9 | " | John | finisher $1.42 per da. Repairs of Rwy & Mach Dept Mt Clare mach shop |
| 1852-20 | Clay, George | | regulator of trains Mt Clare $40 per mo. Trans Dept appointed 1850 |
| 1852-24 | Clerk, Lawrence | | stableman $300 per yr. Trans Dept |
| 1852-28 | Cleary, Cornelius | | fireman $400 per yr Trans Dept |
| 1842-7 | Coffmon, John | | laborer 75¢ per da. Repairs of Rwy & Mach Dept Wash br 2d s-div |
| 1852-25 | Coffy, Matthew | | laborer load & unload cars Cumberland $360 per yr. Trans Dept |
| 1852-15 | Cole, Lewis M.* | | master of trans $1,500 per annum Trans Dept entered co serv in 1843 as clk at $400 per annum |
| 1842-10 | Colleir, Henry | | smith $1.58 per da. Repairs of Rwy & Mach Dept Mt Clare mach shop |
| 1842-10 | Collier, William J. | | smith & tube mkr $1.25 per da. Repairs of Rwy & Mach Dept Mt Clare mach shop |
| 1842-14 | Collins, Elijah | | ton breakman Balto $30 per mo. Trans Dept main stem |
| 1852-27 | " | " | eng'man $2.50 per da. Trans Dept |
| 1842-16 | " | John | brakeman Balto $30 per mo. Trans Dept Wash br |
| 1852-31 | " | " * | ton conduc $40 per mo. Wash br appointed in May 1851 |
| 1852-31 | " | R. | day watch & porter $360 per yr. Wash br |
| 1842-17 | " | Reuben | yard driv & mail carrier Wash $33 per mo. Trans Dept Wash br |
| 1852-28 | " | Upton | fireman $400 per yr. Trans Dept |
| 1852-28 | " | Wm. | fireman $400 per yr. " " |
| 1842-2 | " | colored man | axeman 75¢ per da. Engr Dept cons of rd w of Harper's Ferry 1st div |
| 1842-2 | " | " " | vaneman 75¢ per da. Engr Dept cons of rd w of Harper's Ferry 1st div |

| | | |
|---|---|---|
| 1842-16 | Compton, Jackson | pass breakman Balto $30 per mo. Trans Dept main stem |
| 1842-7 | Connor, Owen | laborer 75¢ per da. Repairs of Rwy & Mach Dept Wash br 1st s-div |
| 1852-30 | Cookus, P. H. | local agt main stem North Mountain 10¢ per ton plus comm. Trans Dept |
| 1852-26 | Corbin, P. B. | cleaning eng Mt Clare $300 per yr. Trans Dept |
| 1842-7 | Cosgrove, Patrick | laborer 75¢ per da. Repairs of Rwy & Mach Dept Wash br 1st s-div |
| 1842-8 | Counselman, Charles | carp $1.37½ per da. Repairs of Rwy & Mach Dept Mt Clare |
| 1852-28 | J. | fireman $400 per yr. Trans Dept |
| 1842-9 | Courtney, William | finisher $1.42 per da. Repairs of Rwy & Mach Dept Mt Clare mach shop |
| 1842-10 | Courts, George | helper $1 per da. Repairs of Rwy & Mach Dept Mt Clare mach shop |
| 1852-28 | Covel, W. H. | fireman $400 per yr. Trans Dept |
| 1842-14 | Coville, Joel | way ton conduc Balto $40 per mo. Trans Dept main stem |
| 1852-21 | Cowell, Joel* | way conduc $600 per yr. Trans Dept |
| 1842-12 | Crabbins, Benjamin | carp $1.25 per da. Repairs of Rwy & Mach Dept Mt Clare mach shop |
| 1852-27 | Crawford, Lewis | eng'man $2.50 per da. Trans Dept |
| 1852-33 | Criswell, Wm. | car cleaner $27.50 per mo. Wash br |
| 1852-10 | Cromwell, George* | supv 9th s-div $45 per mo. Rd Dept appointed 1 Mar 1851 |
| 1842-12 | Oliver | coach mkr $1.37½ per da. Repairs of Rwy & Mach Dept Mt Clare mach shop |
| 1842-1 | Cronise, J. S. | clk $500 per annum Ofc Dept |
| 1852-30 | Jacob | local agt main stem Monrovia 10¢ per ton plus comm. Trans Dept |
| 1842-11 | Cunningham, Edward | helper 92¢ per da. Repairs of Rwy & Mach Dept Mt Clare mach shop |
| 1852-23 | Cutting, N. | tender filler Monocacy $330 per yr. Trans Dept |
| 1842-11 | Cyphert, Mark | helper 92¢ per da. Repairs of Rwy & Mach Dept Mt Clare mach shop |
| 1852-27 | Darby, Grafton | eng'man $2 per da. Trans Dept |
| 1852-26 | Davies, Gilbert | watchman Martinsburg $360 per yr. Trans Dept |
| 1852-19 | Davis, H. C.* | conduc $58.33 per mo. Trans Dept entered co serv in 1846 as ton brakesman at $25 per mo. |
| 1852-12 | John C.* | gen foreman at Mt Clare $1,000 per annum wi house Mach Dept appointed Feb 1851 |
| 1842-17 | William B. | pass eng'man Balto $2 per da. Trans Dept Wash br |
| 1842-10 | Zack | finisher $1.25 per da. Repairs of Rwy & Mach Dept Mt Clare mach shop |

B & O RR EMPLOYEES

| | | |
|---|---|---|
| 1842-4 | Day, Owen | laborer 75¢ per da. Repairs of Rwy & Mach Dept main stem 2d s-div |
| 1842-4 | Robert | laborer 75¢ per da. Repairs of Rwy & Mach Dept main stem 2d s-div |
| 1842-9 | DeBrink, Henry | finisher $1.33 1/3 per da. Repairs of Rwy & Mach Dept Mt Clare mach shop |
| 1852-28 | Delany, Daniel | fireman $400 per yr. Trans Dept |
| 1852-27 | Delay, Denton | eng'man $2.50 per da. Trans Dept |
| 1852-28 | " | fireman $400 per yr. " " |
| 1852-21 | " | ton brakeman $360 per yr." " |
| 1842-7 | Demsey, William | laborer 75¢ per da. Repairs of Rwy & Mach Dept Wash br 2d s-div |
| 1842-9 | Denmead, Thomas | finisher $1.58 per da. Repairs of Rwy & Mach Dept Mt Clare mach shop |
| 1852-12 | " * | gen foreman at Martinsburg sta $1,000 per annum wi house Mach Dept appointed Mar 1850 |
| 1852-24 | Dennis, Daniel | burden car driv $360 per yr. Trans Dept |
| 1842-11 | DeShields, Eleva | helper 92¢ per da. Repairs of Rwy & Mach Dept Mt Clare mach shop |
| 1842-15 | Deteman, Herman | eng'man Frederick $2 per da. Trans Dept main stem |
| 1852-25 | Devine, John | tender filler Mt Clare $325 per yr. Trans Dept |
| 1852-24 | Dibb, James | burden car driv $360 per yr. Trans Dept |
| 1852-20 | Dickenson, Peter* | agt at Locust Pt $50 per mo. Trans Dept appointed in 1851 |
| 1842-9 | Diffey, Owen | finisher $1.42 per da. Repairs of Rwy & Mach Dept Mt Clare mach shop |
| 1852-27 | Diffy, Alex'r. | eng'man $2.50 per da. Trans Dept |
| 1842-12 | Dill, Exra | carp $1.25 per da. Repairs of Rwy & Mach Dept Mt Clare mach shop |
| 1852-28 | Dillen, Ezekiel | fireman $400 per yr. Trans Dept |
| 1852-27 | Dillon, Daniel | eng'man $2 per da. Trans Dept |
| 1842-15 | David | eng'man Balto $2 per da. Trans Dept |
| 1852-28 | Diske, James | fireman $400 per yr. Trans Dept |
| 1842-5 | Dixson, Thomas | laborer 75¢ per da. Repairs of Rwy & Mach Dept main stem 5th s-div |
| 1852-26 | Doffler, Jacob | cleaning eng Frederick $300 per yr. Trans Dept |
| 1852-28 | Dolan, Patrick | fireman $400 per yr. Trans Dept |
| 1852-21 | Doll, Daniel | ton conduc $480 per yr. Trans Dept |
| 1842-7 | Donavan, David | laborer 75¢ per da. Repairs of Rwy & Mach Dept Wash br 1st s-div |
| 1852-28 | Donden, A. | fireman $400 per yr. Trans Dept |
| 1842-15 | Done, Benjamin | car cleaner Balto $25 per mo. Trans Dept main stem |

# B & O RR EMPLOYEES 13

| | | |
|---|---|---|
| 1852-26 | Donley, Edward | cleaning eng Mt Clare $300 per yr. Trans Dept |
| 1852-26 | Wm. | cleaning eng Mt Clare $300 per yr. Trans Dept |
| 1842-3 | Donly, James | rough carp on Repairs Rd 94¢ per da. Repairs of Rwy & Mach Dept main stem 1st s-div |
| 1852-21 | Donnely, James | ton conduc $480 per yr. Trans Dept |
| 1852-27 | Donovan, John | eng'man $2.50 per da. Trans Dept |
| 1852-32 | Dore, Benj. | pass brakeman $30 per mo. Wash br appointed in 1839 |
| 1842-13 | Dorsey, Thos. | carp, making seat for new pass cars by the piece. about $1.37½ per da. Repairs of Rwy & Mach Dept Mt Clare mach shop |
| 1842-4 | Dougherty, Jno. | nailor 80¢ per da. Repairs of Rwy & Mach Dept main stem 3d s-div |
| 1842-5 | Douglas, William | nailor 80¢ per da. Repairs of Rwy & Mach Dept main stem 5th s-div |
| 1842-3 | Doulon, James | nailor who exam track prev to pass of sev trains 80¢ per da. Repairs of Rwy & Mach Dept main stem 1st s-div |
| 1852-27 | Douty, Moses | eng'man $2.50 per da. Trans Dept |
| 1852-21 | Dowden, A. | ton brakeman $360 per yr. Trans Dept |
| 1852-20 | Drill, J. M. | timekpr Mt Clare $35 per mo. Trans Dept appointed Nov 1851 |
| 1842-4 | Duffey, Thos. | nailor 80¢ per da. Repairs of Rwy & Mach Dept main stem 2d s-div |
| 1852-21 | Duke, Wm. | ton brakeman $360 per yr. Trans Dept |
| 1842-10 | Dulaney, Charles | boiler mkr $1.25 per da. Repairs of Rwy & Mach Dept Mt Clare mach shop |
| 1842-9 | Duncan, Harrison W. | finisher $1.33 1/3 per da. Repairs of Rwy & Mach Dept Mt Clare mach shop |
| 1852-28 | Thomas | fireman $400 per yr. Trans Dept |
| 1842-10 | Dunkerly, Richard | finisher $1.25 per da. Repairs of Rwy & Mach Dept Mt Clare mach shop |
| 1842-14 | Dunlop, John | clk, etc. Mt Clare Depot $40 per mo. Trans Dept main stem |
| 1852-15 | " * | agt Mt Clare $1,000 per annum Trans Dept entered co serv in 1838 as weight master at $25 per mo. |
| 1842-9 | Dunn, Michael | finisher $1.33 1/3 per da. Repairs of Rwy & Mach Dept Mt Clare mach shop |
| 1842-10 | Durr, William | coach mkr $1.50 per da. Repairs of Rwy & Mach Dept Mt Clare mach shop |
| 1852-8 | Dushane, John (of V.)* | storekpr $40 per mo. Rd Dept appointed 5 Sep 1851 |

B & O RR EMPLOYEES

| | | | |
|---|---|---|---|
| 1842-11 | Duvall, George | | helper 92¢ per da. Repairs of Rwy & Mach Dept Mt Clare mach shop |
| 1842-9 | | James H. | finisher $1.58 per da. Repairs of Rwy & Mach Dept Mt Clare mach shop |
| 1842-4 | | Lewis | laborer 75¢ per da. Repairs of Rwy & Mach Dept main stem 2d s-div |
| 1842-8 | | Richard | helper 92¢ per da. Repairs of Rwy & Mach Dept Mt Clare |
| 1852-25 | Dyall, John | | sawyer Locust Pt $345 per yr. Trans Dept |
| 1842-2 | Edgerton, Erastus | | res engr $2.50 per da. Engr Dept cons of rd w of Harper's Ferry 2d div |
| 1842-9 | Edwards, William | | finisher $1.33 1/3 per da. Repairs of Rwy & Mach Dept Mt Clare mach shop |
| 1852-12 | " | * | asst foreman Martinsburg $55 per mo. Mach Dept appointed Mar 1850 |
| 1852-25 | Egan, John | | tender filler Mt Clare $325 per yr. Trans Dept |
| 1852-30 | Ellicott (Elliott?), George | | local agt main stem Ilchester 10¢ per ton plus comm. Trans Dept |
| 1842-3 | Elliot, Charles A. | | supt deliv of iron at Balto $1.50 per da. Engr Dept |
| 1852-25 | Elliott, Robert | | laborer Locust Pt $300 per yr. Trans Dept |
| 1842-9 | Emmerson, Nathaniel | | finisher & ex eng'man $1.42 per da. Repairs of Rwy & Mach Dept Mt Clare mach shop |
| 1852-15 | England, J. T.* | | track agt Pratt St Depot $1,000 per annum Trans Dept appointed as collec 1837 at $600 per annum |
| 1842-14 | | Joseph J. | collec agt Balto $50 per mo. Trans Dept main stem |
| 1842-15 | Ensor, George | | watchman Mt Clare Depot $30 per mo. Trans Dept main stem |
| 1852-26 | | " | watchman Mt Clare Depot $300 per yr. Trans Dept |
| 1842-12 | | Hiram | carp $1.37½ per da. Repairs of Rwy & Mach Dept Mt Clare mach shop |
| 1842-9 | Essender, John | | finisher $1.42 per da. Repairs of Rwy & Mach Dept Mt Clare mach shop |
| 1842-5 | Fable, Solomon | | laborer 75¢ per da. Repairs of Rwy & Mach Dept main stem 4th s-div |
| 1852-31 | Fairbanks, John | | ton brakesman $30 per mo. Wash br appointed in 1850 |
| 1842-14 | | William | conduc etc. Balto & Ellicott's Mills $40 per mo. Trans Dept main stem |
| 1852-18 | Falconer, Jonathan* | | clk Pratt St Ton Ofc $35 per mo. Trans Dept entered co serv in Aug 1849 |

| | | | |
|---|---|---|---|
| 1842-5 | Fearhearke, Adolphus | | supv $45 per mo. Repairs of Rwy & Mach Dept main stem 4th s-div |
| 1852-21 | Feller, Thos. | | ton brakeman $360 per yr. Trans Dept |
| 1842-2 | Fenby, P. F. | | axeman $1.50 per da. Engr Dept cons of rd w of Harper's Ferry 1st div |
| 1852-18 | Fennel, Maurice* | | clk & collec Pratt St Ton Ofc $50 per mo. Trans Dept entered co serv Sept 1848 $35 per mo. |
| 1842-15 | Ferguson, John | | weighmaster, laborer, etc. Pratt St Depot $35 per mo. Trans Dept main stem |
| 1842-10 | | William | finisher $1.25 per da. Repairs of Rwy & Mach Dept Mt Clare mach shop |
| 1852-19 | Fergusson, John* | | weighmaster Pratt St Depot $50 per mo. Trans Dept entered co serv 1830 as laborer $25 per mo. |
| 1842-14 | Ferry, Dennis | | conduc of pass Harper's Ferry $58.33 per mo. Trans Dept main stem |
| 1842-16 | | Edward | conduc of ton Balto $45 per mo. Trans Dept Wash br |
| 1852-31 | | "     * | pass conduc $58.35 per mo. Wash br entered co serv 1832 as driv main stem $30 per mo. |
| 1842-15 | Fisher, Barney | | fireman Balto $35 per mo. Trans Dept main stem |
| 1852-27 | | " | eng'man $2 per da. Trans Dept |
| 1852-27 | | Hugh | eng'man $2 per da.   "     " |
| 1852-28 | | Lewis | fireman $400 per yr.  "     " |
| 1842-7 | | Uriah | laborer 75¢ per da. Repairs of Rwy & Mach Dept Wash br 1st s-div |
| 1852-24 | | " | stableman $300 per yr. Trans Dpt |
| 1852-33 | Flaxcomb, Charles | | fireman $33.33 per mo. Wash br appointed in 1851 |
| 1842-15 | | William | eng'man Harper's Ferry $2 per da. Trans Dept main stem |
| 1852-32 | | " | eng'man ton train $2.50 per da. Wash br appointed in 1851 |
| 1852-29 | Flohr, William | | fireman $400 per yr. Trans Dept |
| 1852-8 | Flury, Henry* | | foreman Cumberland Depot $45 per mo. Rd Dept appointed 1846 at $40 per mo. |
| 1842-14 | Foley, Daniel J. | | gen agt Pratt St Depot $66.66 per mo. Trans Dept main stem |
| 1852-24 | | Michael | stableman $300 per yr Trans Dept |
| 1852-16 | Ford, J. B.* | | agt Cumberland $1,200 per annum Trans Dept appointed clk in 1846 at $600 per annum |
| 1842-10 | Fornst, Leonard | | smith & spring mkr $1.42 per da. Repairs of Rwy & Mach Dept Mt Clare mach shop |
| 1842-12 | Fowble, Thomas | | coach mkr $1.37½ per da. Repairs of Rwy & Mach Dept Mt Clare mach shop |

# B & O RR EMPLOYEES

| Date | Name | Position/Notes |
|---|---|---|
| 1852-21 | Fowler, Wm | ton brakeman $360 per yr. Trans Dept |
| 1852-29 | Franklin, William | fireman $400 per yr. Trans Dept |
| 1852-29 | Frazier, Henry | fireman $400 per yr. " " |
| 1852-24 |         John | burden car driv $360 per yr. Trans Dept |
| 1852-24 |         R. | burden car driv $360 per yr. Trans Dept |
| 1852-24 | Freeman, D. | pass car driv $360 per yr. Trans Dept |
| 1852-24 | French, John | pass car driv $360 per yr. Trans Dept |
| 1852-29 |         Robert | fireman $400 per yr. Trans Dept |
| 1852-30 |         Wm. | local agt main stem South Br 10¢ per ton plus comm. Trans Dept |
| 1842-2 | Frick, J. C. | vaneman $1.25 per da. Engr Dept cons of rd w of Harper's Ferry 1st div |
| 1852-21 | Fryer, Jesse | ton brakeman $360 per yr. Trans Dept |
| 1852-27 | Fulton, Joseph | eng'man $2.50 per da. Trans Dept |
| 1842-11 | Galloway, Vincent | helper 92¢ per da. Repairs of Rwy & Mach Dept Mt Clare mach shop |
| 1842-17 |         William | ton eng'man Balto $2 per da. Trans Dept Wash br |
| 1852-27 |         " | eng'man $2 per da. Trans Dept |
| 1852-32 |         " | eng'man pass train $2 per da. Wash br appointed in 1835 |
| 1842-16 | Garland, Benj. | ostler & ton driv Balto $30 per mo. Trans Dept main stem |
| 1852-20 | Garly, Darius | despatcher of ton trains at Martinsburg $50 per mo. Trans Dept appointed in 1850 |
| 1842-15 | Gates, Jonathan | fireman Balto $35 per mo. Trans Dept main stem |
| 1842-13 | Getteir, George | oiler of cars $1.12½ per da. Repairs of Rwy & Mach Dept Mt Clare mach shop |
| 1852-21 | Getzendanner, C. | ton conduc $480 per yr. Trans Dept |
| 1842-5 | Gibbs, George W. | nailor 80¢ per da. Repairs of Rwy & Mach Dept main stem 5th s-div |
| 1852-21 | Gibson, J. S. | ton conduc $480 per yr. Trans Dept |
| 1852-24 | Gillan, John | stableman $300 per yr. Trans Dpt |
| 1852-29 | Gillingham, George | fireman $400 per yr. Trans Dept |
| 1842-15 | Ginneman, George | fireman Harper's Ferry $35 per mo. Trans Dept main stem |
| 1842-13 | Gist, Thomas | oiler of cars $1.12½ per da. Repairs of Rwy & Mach Dept Mt Clare mach shop |
| 1852-27 |         " | eng'man $2.50 per da. Trans Dept |
| 1842-12 | Gitchall, Augustus | carp $1.25 per da. Repairs of Rwy & Mach Dept Mt Clare mach shop |
| 1842-5 | Gitz, Charles | nailor 80¢ per da. Repairs of Rwy & Mach Dept main stem 4th s-div |

## B & O RR EMPLOYEES

| | | |
|---|---|---|
| 1852-21 | Golden, Wm. | ton brakeman $360 per yr. Trans Dept |
| 1842-7 | Goodman, Samuel | nailor 80¢ per da. Repairs of Rwy & Mach Dept Wash br 2d s-div |
| 1852-27 | Goodrick, Leroy | eng'man $2 per da. Trans Dept |
| 1852-19 | Gorsuch, H. P.* | conduc $58.33 per mo. Trans Dept entered co serv 1847 as brakesman at $30 per mo. |
| 1852-29 | Gough, James | fireman $400 per yr. Trans Dept |
| 1842-14 | Graves, George H. | St supv Balto $50 per mo. Trans Dept main stem |
| 1852-26 | Gray, H. | cleaning eng Mt Clare $300 per yr. Trans Dept |
| 1842-15 | Greenwood, Jacob | manag laborer Harper's Ferry $30 per mo. Trans Dept main stem |
| 1852-21 | Gregg, Sam'l. | ton conduc $480 per yr. Trans Dept |
| 1852-21 | Thos. | ton brakeman $360 per yr. Trans Dept |
| 1852-26 | Wm. | watchman Pratt St $360 per yr. Trans Dept |
| 1852-25 | Grendall, Jos. | laborer Locust Pt $300 per yr. Trans Dept |
| 1852-30 | Grimes, John | local agt main stem Hood's Mill 10¢ per ton plus comm. Trans Dept |
| 1852-23 | Grove, D. | tender filler Monocacy $330 per yr. Trans Dept |
| 1852-10 | Groves, Solomon* | supv 8th s-div $45 per mo. Rd Dept appointed 1 Apr 1838 |
| 1842-3 | Haffay, James | laborer 75¢ per da. Repairs of Rwy & Mach Dept main stem 1st s-div |
| 1852-30 | Hagans, E. M. | local agt w of Cumberland Cranberry Summit 10¢ per ton plus comm. Trans Dept appointed in 1852 |
| 1852-30 | L. A. | local agt w of Cumberland Cheat Riv 10¢ per ton plus comm. Trans Dept appointed in 1852 |
| 1852-24 | Hagerty, P. | blacksmith $336 per yr. Trans Dept |
| 1852-32 | Halfpenny, Samuel | laborer Locust Pt sawing wd $1 per da. Wash br |
| 1842-4 | Hall, Jesse | nailor 80¢ per da. Repairs of Rwy & Mach Dept main stem 3d s-div |
| 1842-4 | Joshua | rough carp 94¢ per da. Repairs of Rwy & Mach Dept main stem 3d s-div |
| 1852-24 | M. | pass car driv $360 per yr. Trans Dept |
| 1852-27 | Wm. | eng'man $2.50 per da. Trans Dept |
| 1852-30 | Hamill, G. C. | local agt main stem Kerneysville 10¢ per ton plus comm. Trans Dept appointed in 1851 |
| 1852-33 | Hamilton, John | cleaning ton eng Cumberland $300 per yr. Wash br |
| 1842-15 | N. | fireman Harper's Ferry $35 per mo. Trans Dept main stem |

| | | |
|---|---|---|
| 1852-30 | Hammond, A. C. | local agt main stem Cherry Run 10¢ per ton plus comm. Trans Dept appointed in 1851 |
| 1842-3 | Hanlan, Thomas | rough carp on Repairs Rd 94¢ per da. Repairs of Rwy & Mach Dept main stem 1st s-div |
| 1842-8 | Hanlun, John | helper 92¢ per da. Repairs of Rwy & Mach Dept Mt Clare |
| 1852-25 | Hanly, Patrick | tender filler Mt Clare $325 per yr. Trans Dept |
| 1852-24 | Hannixman, H. | burden car driv $360 per yr. Trans Dept |
| 1842-12 | Harbaugh, Jerome | coach mkr $1.37½ per da. Repairs of Rwy & Mach Dept Mt Clare mach shop |
| 1842-16 | Harding, William | ostler & ton driv Balto $30 per mo. Trans Dept main stem |
| 1842-10 | Hardison, James H. | stationary eng'man $1.12½ per da. Repairs of Rwy & Mach Dept Mt Clare mach shop |
| 1852-27 | Hardy, C. W. | eng'man $2.50 per da. Trans Dept |
| 1852-32 | D. | regulator Wash $360 per yr. Wash br |
| 1852-20 | Samuel | regulator of trains Mt Clare $40 per mo. Trans Dept appointed in Jan 1852 |
| 1852-24 | Hargeden, Brian | stableman $300 per yr. Trans Dpt |
| 1852-10 | Harman, J. M.* | supv 5th s-div $45 per mo. Rd Dept appointed 1 Nov 1842 |
| 1842-7 | James | laborer 75¢ per da. Repairs of Rwy & Mach Dept Wash br 1st s-div |
| 1842-10 | Harney, Joshua | smith $1.58 per da. Repairs of Rwy & Mach Dept Mt Clare mach shop |
| 1852-24 | Harris, Wm. | burden car driv $360 per yr. Trans Dept |
| 1842-5 | Hartman, Nicholas | rough carp 94¢ per da. Repairs of Rwy & Mach Dept main stem 4th s-div |
| 1852-21 | Harvey, C. W.* | way conduc $600 per yr. Trans Dept |
| 1852-18 | Harwood, J. K.* | ticket clk $50 per mo. Trans Dept entered co serv in Jan 1848 |
| 1852-8 | Haskell, Thomas* | foreman of bridges $50 per mo. Rd Dept appointed 1 Dec 1850 at $45 per mo. |
| 1842-4 | Hatfield, Thomas | laborer 75¢ per da. Repairs of Rwy & Mach Dept main stem 2d s-div |
| 1852-23 | Hayden, B. | pass car driv $360 per yr. Trans Dept |
| 1842-16 | Barney | ostler & pass driv Balto $30 per mo. Trans Dept main stem |
| 1842-15 | Michael | laborer Mt Clare $30 per mo. Trans Dept main stem |
| 1852-12 | Hayes, Samuel J.* | master of mach $1,500 per annum Mach Dept appointed Feb 1851 |

## B & O RR EMPLOYEES 19

| | | |
|---|---|---|
| 1842-15 | Hays, John | laborer Harper's Ferry $25 per mo. Trans Dept main stem |
| 1842-17 | Lloyd | fireman Balto $35 per mo. Trans Dept Wash br |
| 1842-11 | Hayse, James | helper 92¢ per da. Repairs of Rwy & Mach Dept Mt Clare mach shop |
| 1842-9 | Samuel | foreman in mach shop $60 per mo. Repairs of Rwy & Mach Dept Mt Clare mach shop |
| 1842-1 | Hazlehurst, F. M. | vaneman $1.50 per da. Engr Dept cons of rd w of Harper's Ferry 1st div |
| 1842-1 | Henry R. | div engr $4.38 per da. Engr Dept cons of rd w of Harper's Ferry 1st div |
| 1842-2 | R. P. | vaneman $1.50 per da. Engr Dept cons of rd w of Harper's Ferry 2d div |
| 1852-23 | Helvesten, Jas. | tender filler Monocacy $330 per yr. Trans Dept |
| 1842-4 | Henderson, John | laborer 75¢ per da. Repairs of Rwy & Mach Dept main stem 2d s-div |
| 1842-7 | Henninger, John | laborer 75¢ per da. Repairs of Rwy & Mach Dept Wash br 2d s-div |
| 1842-16 | Henry, Samuel | ostler & pass driv Balto $30 per mo. Trans Dept main stem |
| 1842-12 | William L. | carp $1.25 per da. Repairs of Rwy & Mach Dept Mt Clare mach shop |
| 1852-10 | Herr, John F.* | supv 14th s-div $50 per mo. Rd Dept appointed 28 Mar 1852 |
| 1852-25 | Hicker, Wm. | teamster Locust Pt $330 per yr. Trans Dept |
| 1852-30 | Higgins, M. P. | local agt main stem Sir John's Run 10¢ per ton plus comm. Trans Dept appointed in 1851 |
| 1842-10 | Hilbert, John | helper 92¢ per da. Repairs of Rwy & Mach Dept Mt Clare mach shop |
| 1842-5 | Hillert, John | laborer 75¢ per da. Repairs of Rwy & Mach Dept main stem 4th s-div |
| 1842-5 | Hillery, Howard | laborer 75¢ per da. Repairs of Rwy & Mach Dept main stem 3d s-div |
| 1842-11 | Hissey, Archibald | helper 80¢ per da. Repairs of Rwy & Mach Dept Mt Clare mach shop |
| 1842-12 | Hobbs, Samuel | carp $1.25 per da. Repairs of Rwy & Mach Dept Mt Clare mach shop |
| 1852-26 | Thos. | watchman Mt Clare $300 per yr. Trans Dept |
| 1842-2 | Hodges, Charles R. | vaneman $1.50 per da. Engr Dept cons of rd w of Harper's Ferry 2d div |

## B & O RR EMPLOYEES

| | | | |
|---|---|---|---|
| 1842-2 | Hoffman, George | | vaneman $1 per da. Engr Dept cons of rd w of Harper's Ferry 1st div |
| 1852-32 | | John | laborer Locust Pt sawing wd $1 per da. Wash br |
| 1842-8 | | Nicholas | bricklayer $1.75 per da. Repairs of Rwy & Mach Dept Mt Clare |
| 1842-11 | Hoffnogler, William | | moulder $1.58 per da. Repairs of Rwy & Mach Dept Mt Clare mach shop |
| 1852-33 | Hogan, John | | cleaning ton eng Cumberland $300 per yr. Wash br |
| 1842-12 | Holland, Samuel | | carp $1.25 per da. Repairs of Rwy & Mach Dept Mt Clare mach shop |
| 1842-8 | Holley, Albert | | manag helper 94¢ per da. Repairs of Rwy & Mach Dept Mt Clare |
| 1842-12 | Hollingsworth, Jarret | | coach mkr $1.37½ per da. Repairs of Rwy & Mach Dept Mt Clare mach shop |
| 1852-29 | Holten, John | | fireman $400 per yr. Trans Dept |
| 1852-13 | Hoofnagle, William* | | foreman of foundry $1,000 per annum Mach Dept appointed in Jan 1845 at $2.25 per da. |
| 1852-29 | Hooper, Charles | | fireman $400 per yr. Trans Dept |
| 1842-12 | | James B. | carp $1.25 per da. Repairs of Rwy & Mach Dept Mt Clare mach shop |
| 1842-7 | | Samuel | rough carp 94¢ per da. Repairs of Rwy & Mach Dept Wash br 2d s-div |
| 1852-19 | Hoover, G. W.* | | conduc $40 per mo. Trans Dept entered co serv in 1844 as brakesman at $30 per mo. |
| 1842-16 | | George W. | ostler, etc. Balto $30 per mo. Trans Dept main stem |
| 1842-10 | Hopkins, John | | smith $1.42 per da. Repairs of Rwy & Mach Dept Mt Clare mach shop |
| 1842-5 | Hough, P. H. | | carp $1.12½ per da. Repairs of Rwy & Mach Dept main stem 5th s-div |
| 1852-21 | | Thos. | ton brakeman $360 per yr. Trans Dept |
| 1852-26 | Houston, John | | car coupler Mt Clare $325 per yr. Trans Dept |
| 1842-16 | | Rodney | pass breakman Harper's Ferry $30 per mo. Trans Dept main stem |
| 1842-3 | Howard, Thomas | | laborer 75¢ per da. Repairs of Rwy & Mach Dept main stem 1st s-div |
| 1852-21 | Howser, Israel | | ton brakeman $360 per yr. Trans Dept |
| 1852-17 | Huggins, A. L.* | | clk at Cumberland $50 per mo. Trans Dept entered co serv in 1850 |
| 1842-9 | Hughes, Hugby | | finisher $1.42 per da. Repairs of Rwy & Mach Dept Mt Clare mach shop |

B & O RR EMPLOYEES                                            21

| | | |
|---|---|---|
| 1852-33 | Hughes, J. | car cleaner $27.50 per mo. Wash br |
| 1842-11 | " William | watchman $1 per da. Repairs of Rwy & Mach Dept Mt Clare mach shop |
| 1842-12 | " " | carp charged wi exam of pass cars $50 per mo. Repairs of Rwy & Mach Dept Mt Clare mach shop |
| 1852-13 | " " H.* | foreman of repairs of pass cars, Mt Clare $55 per mo. Mach Dept appointed May 1840 |
| 1852-31 | Humphreys, O. T.* | pass conduc $58.35 per mo. Wash br appointed St supv in 1845 at $41.65 per mo. |
| 1842-11 | Hunt, Stephen | helper 92¢ per da. Repairs of Rwy & Mach Dept Mt Clare mach shop |
| 1852-27 | Hurdle, Geo. W. | eng'man $2 per da. Trans Dept |
| 1852-32 | Hussel, Casper | eng'man pass train $2 per da. Wash br appointed in 1851 |
| 1842-7 | Hyle, Joseph | laborer 75¢ per da. Repairs of Rwy & Mach Dept Wash br 2d s-div |
| 1842-9 | Hynes, James | finisher $1.25 per da. Repairs of Rwy & Mach Dept Mt Clare mach shop |
| 1842-12 | Icor, George | coach mkr $1.37½ per da. Repairs of Rwy & Mach Dept Mt Clare mach shop |
| 1842-4 | Iglehart, Michael | laborer 75¢ per da. Repairs of Rwy & Mach Dept main s tem 2d s-div |
| 1852-5 | Ing, Charles* | bookkpr $750 per annum Secy Ofc appointed 9 May 1849 at $600 |
| 1852-5 | " William* | clk $600 per yr. Secy Ofc appointed 12 Feb 1852 |
| 1842-15 | Irvin, Thomas | laborer Pratt St Depot $25 per mo. Trans Dept main stem |
| 1852-16 | Jacobs, B. L.* | agt Martinsburg $700 per annum Trans Dept appointed clk in 1846 at $41 per mo. |
| 1852-21 | " F. A. | ton conduc $480 per yr. Trans Dept |
| 1842-17 | " John | fireman Balto $35 per mo. Trans Dept Wash br |
| 1852-26 | " John C. | supt eng $65 per mo. Trans Dept |
| 1852-30 | Janney, G. W. | local agt main s tem Berlin 10¢ per ton plus comm. Trans Dept appointed in 1851 |
| 1842-10 | Jarvis, Elijah | smith $1.42 per da. Repairs of Rwy & Mach Dept Mt Clare mach shop |
| 1842-17 | Jeffers, Alex. | fireman Balto $35 per mo. Trans Dept Wash br |
| 1842-13 | Jenkins, George W. | trimmer $1.42 per da. Repairs of Rwy & Mach Dept Mt Clare mach shop |
| 1842-11 | Jessop, William | helper 92¢ per da. Repairs of Rwy & Mach Dept Mt Clare mach shop |

| | | | |
|---|---|---|---|
| 1852-29 | Johnson, | Benjamin | fireman $400 per yr. Trans Dept |
| 1852-30 | | C. | local agt w of Cumberland Oakland 10¢ per ton plus comm. Trans Dept appointed in 1851 |
| 1852-33 | | George | fireman $33.33 per mo. Wash br appointed in 1852 |
| 1852-21 | | " | ton brakeman $360 per yr. Trans Dept |
| 1852-32 | | Park | laborer Locust Pt sawing wd $1 per da. Wash br |
| 1852-25 | | Robert | laborer load & unload cars Pratt St $360 per yr. Trans Dept |
| 1852-22 | | Wm. | ton brakeman $360 per yr. Trans Dept |
| 1852-29 | Jones, | Basil | fireman $400 per yr. Trans Dept |
| 1842-15 | | " J. | fireman Balto $35 per mo. Trans Dept main stem |
| 1842-7 | | Henry | laborer 75¢ per da. Repairs of Rwy & Mach Dept Wash br 2d s-div |
| 1842-15 | | John P. | eng'man Balto $2 per da. Trans Dept main stem |
| 1842-5 | | Thomas | laborer 75¢ per da. Repairs of Rwy & Mach Dept main stem 5th s-div |
| 1852-27 | | Wm. | eng'man $2 per da. Trans Dept |
| 1852-7 | Jordan, | James B.* | foreman at Mt Clare $83.35 per mo. Rd Dept appointed in July 1842 at $45 per mo. |
| 1852-21 | | John T. | ton conduc $480 per yr. Trans Dept |
| 1842-4 | Jordon, | Jeremiah | laborer 75¢ per da. Repairs of Rwy & Mach Dept main stem 1st s-div |
| 1842-8 | Jurdon, | James B. | master smith $1.66 2/3 per da. Repairs of Rwy & Mach Dept Mt Clare |
| 1852-29 | Keiser, | J. | fireman $400 per yr. Trans Dept |
| 1852-23 | Keller, | C. | tender filler Cumberland $300 per yr. Trans Dept |
| 1852-30 | | D. T. | local agt main stem Patterson's Creek 10¢ per ton plus comm. Trans Dept |
| 1852-29 | Kelley, | H. | fireman $400 per yr. Trans Dept |
| 1842-10 | Kelling, | Lewis | helper 92¢ per da. Repairs of Rwy & Mach Dept Mt Clare mach shop |
| 1842-11 | Kelly, | Luke | moulder $1.25 per da. Repairs of Rwy & Mach Dept Mt Clare mach shop |
| 1842-13 | Kennard, | William | helper 92¢ per da. Repairs of Rwy & Mach Dept Mt Clare mach shop |
| 1842-16 | Kennedy, | John | ostler & ton driv Balto $30 per mo. Trans Dept main stem |
| 1852-24 | | " | burden car driv $360 per yr. Trans Dept |
| 1852-22 | Kerns, | Henry | ton brakeman $360 per yr. Trans Dept |
| 1852-24 | Kesslachr, | John | pass car driv $360 per yr. Trans Dept |

## B & O RR EMPLOYEES 23

| | | |
|---|---|---|
| 1852-33 | Killpatrick, J. | tender filler $27.50 per mo. Wash br |
| 1852-27 | King, Joshua | eng'man $2.50 per da. Trans Dept |
| 1852-24 | Wm. | burden car driv $360 per yr. Trans Dept |
| 1852-27 | Kinley, Thos. | eng'man $2.50 per da. Trans Dept |
| 1842-11 | Kinly, William | moulder $1.42 per da. Repairs of Rwy & Mach Dept Mt Clare mach shop |
| 1852-22 | Kinney, Thos. | ton conduc $480 per yr. Trans Dept |
| 1842-12 | Kinsey, Stacy | carp $1.25 per da. Repairs of Rwy & Mach Dept Mt Clare mach shop |
| 1852-32 | Kipley, James | pass brakeman $30 per mo. Wash br appointed in 1846 |
| 1852-24 | Kircher, F. | stableman $480 per yr. Trans Dpt |
| 1852-22 | Kissinger, Otho | ton conduc $480 per yr. Trans Dept |
| 1842-16 | Kneller, John C. | clk Wash $35 per mo. Trans Dept Wash br |
| 1842-8 | Knight, Francis | laborer 75¢ per da. Repairs of Rwy & Mach Dept Mt Clare |
| 1852-24 | M. | pass car driv $360 per yr. Trans Dept |
| 1852-30 | Kohlenberg, A. | local agt main stem Davis' warehouse 10¢ per ton plus comm. Trans Dept appointed in 1851 |
| 1852-30 | Kohlenburg, D. H. | local agt main stem Buckeystown 10¢ per ton plus comm. Trans Dept appointed in 1851 |
| 1852-21 | Koonce, David* | way conduc $600 per yr. Trans Dept |
| 1852-25 | Koontz, Charles | laborer load & unload cars Frederick $300 per yr. Trans Dept |
| 1852-18 | George* | clk at Mt Clare $50 per mo. Trans Dept entered co serv in 1850 at $35 per mo. |
| 1852-27 | Henry | eng'man $2.25 per da. Trans Dept |
| 1842-15 | John | manag laborer Frederick $33.33 per mo. Trans Dept main stem |
| 1852-25 | " | laborer load & unload cars Frederick $360 per yr. Trans Dept |
| 1852-25 | Kulp, Geo. | laborer Locust Pt $300 per yr. Trans Dept |
| 1842-15 | Kuzer, Daniel | fireman Frederick $35 per mo. Trans Dept main stem |
| 1842-7 | Kyan, Michael | laborer 75¢ per da. Repairs of Rwy & Mach Dept Wash br 1st s-div |
| 1842-7 | Patrick | laborer 75¢ per da. Repairs of Rwy & Mach Dept Wash br 1st s-div |
| 1852-26 | Lamb, Wm. | cleaning eng Martinsburg $300 per yr. Trans Dept |
| 1842-12 | Lannan, John | carp $1.25 per da. Repairs of Rwy & Mach Dept Mt Clare mach shop |

B & O RR EMPLOYEES

| | | | |
|---|---|---|---|
| 1852-9 | Lanthus, James* | | supv 1st s-div $55 per mo. Rd Dept appointed 1 Nov 1851 |
| 1852-26 | Lathe, Eli | | cleaning eng Mt Clare $300 per yr. Trans Dept |
| 1852-26 | | Wm. | cleaning eng Mt Clare $300 per yr. Trans Dept |
| 1852-24 | Lather, Daniel | | burden car driv $360 per yr. Trans Dept |
| 1842-2 | Latimer, R. B. | | vaneman $1.50 per da. Engr Dept cons of rd w of Harper's Ferry 1st div |
| 1842-1 | Latrobe, Benjamin H. | | engr of loc & cons $3,000 per annum Engr Dept |
| 1842-1 | | J. H. B. | counsel $1,000 per annum Ofc Dpt |
| 1852-3 | | John H. B. | "    "    "    "   elect 1 Oct 1832 |
| 1842-12 | Laughy, James | | carp $1.25 per da. Repairs of Rwy & Mach Dept Mt Clare mach shop |
| 1852-26 | Lawder, B. H. | | watchman Cumberland $360 per yr. Trans Dept |
| 1852-26 | Layman, James | | cleaning eng Mt Clare $300 per yr. Trans Dept |
| 1852-26 | | Wm. | cleaning eng Mt Clare $300 per yr. Trans Dept |
| 1842-16 | Lee, John | | ostler & ton driv Balto $30 per mo. Trans Dept main stem |
| 1842-15 | | Samuel | regulator Mt Clare $35 per mo. Trans Dept main stem |
| 1852-17 | | "    * | St supv upper div $33.33 per mo. Trans Dept entered co serv in 1845 as regulator at $30 per mo. |
| 1852-30 | Lemmon, J. M. | | local agt main stem Sleepy Creek 10¢ per ton plus comm. Trans Dept appointed in 1851 |
| 1842-11 | | William | helper 80¢ per da. Repairs of Rwy & Mach Dept Mt Clare mach shop |
| 1852-23 | Lemon, W. | | tender filler Monocacy $330 per yr. Trans Dept |
| 1852-24 | Lenoy, Wm. | | Burden car driv $360 per yr. Trans Dept |
| 1842-12 | Letsinger, Henry T. | | mill wright $1.37½ per da. Repairs of Rwy & Mach Dept Mt Clare mach shop |
| 1842-11 | | Richard | prin pattern mkr $1.75 per da. Repairs of Rwy & Mach Dept Mt Clare mach shop |
| 1852-33 | Lettle, Joseph | | fireman $33.33 per mo. Wash br appointed in 1851 |
| 1852-17 | Levering, R.* | | clk to agt at Harper's Ferry $41.65 per mo. Trans Dept entered co serv in Sept 1850 |
| 1852-22 | Lewis, Lawson | | ton conduc $480 per yr. Trans Dept |
| 1852-27 | Light, Jacob | | eng'man $2 per da. Trans Dept |
| 1842-3 | Linch, Michael | | boss of hands removing slips, etc 87½¢ per da. Repairs of Rwy & Mach Dept main stem 1st s-div |

| | | |
|---|---|---|
| 1852-27 | Linthicum, Charles | eng'man $2.50 per da. Trans Dept |
| 1852-25 | J. | laborer load & unload cars Martinsburg $330 per yr. Trans Dept |
| 1852-13 | Litchfield, Samuel* | foreman of turn shops at Mt Clare $50 per mo. Mach Dept appointed in Feb 1851 |
| 1852-33 | Lloyd, J. | mail carrier, Wash $35 per mo. Wash br appointed in 1832 |
| 1842-5 | James | laborer 75¢ per da. Repairs of Rwy & Mach Dept main stem 5th s-div |
| 1842-5 | William | laborer 75¢ per da. Repairs of Rwy & Mach Dept main stem 5th s-div |
| 1852-25 | Lockeridge, John | laborer load & unload cars Pratt St $360 per yr. Trans Dept |
| 1842-11 | Lockman, Christian | helper 92¢ per da. Repairs of Rwy & Mach Dept Mt Clare mach shop |
| 1842-13 | Logan, James H. | cabinet mkr, making seat for new pass cars by the piece about $1.37½ per da. Repairs of Rwy & Mach Dept Mt Clare mach shop |
| 1842-13 | Joseph | cabinet mkr, making seat for new pass cars by the piece about $1.37½ per da. Repairs of Rwy & Mach Dept Mt Clare mach shop |
| 1842-12 | Logsdon, John | coach mkr $1.37½ per da. Repairs of Rwy & Mach Dept Mt Clare mach shop |
| 1852-22 | Long, George | ton conduc $480 per yr. Trans Dept |
| 1852-24 | J. | regulator ton trains $360 per yr. Trans Dept |
| 1842-3 | Loughlan, Patrick | rough carp on Repairs Rd 94¢ per da. Repairs of Rwy & Mach Dept main stem 1st s-div |
| 1852-25 | Loughridge, Daniel | tender filler Mt Clare $325 per yr. Trans Dept |
| 1842-12 | Louthers, Jacob | carp $1.25 per da. Repairs of Rwy & Mach Dept Mt Clare mach shop |
| 1852-33 | Wm. | eng'man ton train $2.25 per da. Wash br appointed in 1852 |
| 1842-12 | Low, Malchi | carp $1.25 per da. Repairs of Rwy & Mach Dept Mt Clare mach shop |
| 1852-29 | Lower, John P. | fireman $400 per yr. Trans Dept |
| 1842-9 | Lowry, George N. | finisher $1.50 per da. Repairs of Rwy & Mach Dept Mt Clare mach shop |
| 1852-27 | Lowthens, Wm. | eng'man $2.25 per da. Trans Dept |
| 1842-10 | Lowthers, William | finisher $1.25 per da. Repairs of Rwy & Mach Dept Mt Clare mach shop |
| 1852-29 | Loyall, Alfred | fireman $400 per yr. Trans Dept |
| 1852-24 | Ludlow, Thomas | stableman $300 per yr. Trans Dpt |
| 1842-12 | Lyborn, Henry | carp $1.37½ per da. Repairs of Rwy & Mach Dept Mt Clare mach shop |

1842-12 Lyons, Richard H.    carp $1.25 per da. Repairs of Rwy & Mach Dept Mt Clare mach shop
1852-27    Robert    eng'man $2.50 per da. Trans Dept
1852-29 McAbee, J. B.    fireman $400 per yr. Trans Dept
1852-26    John    cleaning eng Martinsburg $300 per yr. Trans Dept
1852-27    Zack    eng'man $2.50 per da. Trans Dept
1842-15 Macabee, William    fireman Harper's Ferry $35 per mo. Trans Dept main stem
1842-11 McAlvany, Benjamin    helper 92¢ per da. Repairs of Rwy & Mach Dept Mt Clare mach shop
1842-13 McAntte, Philip    helper 92¢ per da. Repairs of Rwy & Mach Dept Mt Clare mach shop
1842-4 McAvoy, John    laborer 75¢ per da. Repairs of Rwy & Mach Dept main stem 1st s-div
1842-3 McCann, James    nailor who exam track prev to pass of sev trains 80¢ per da. Repairs of Rwy & Mach Dept main stem 1st s-div
1852-20    " *    attend switch at Relay House 92¢ per da. Trans Dept appointed in 1840
1852-33    "    attend switches at Relay $300 per yr. Wash br
1842-6 McCurdy, James    boss over hands cleaning ditches 80¢ per da. Repairs of Rwy & Mach Dept Wash br 1st s-div
1852-20    "    nt watch at Pratt St Depot $30 per mo. Trans Dept appointed in 1851
1852-25 McDonald, L.    tender filler Mt Clare $325 per yr. Trans Dept
1842-13 McGew, James    master painter $1.37½ per da. Repairs of Rwy & Mach Dept Mt Clare mach shop
1852-30 McGrew, J. A.    local agt w of Cumberland Tunnelton 10¢ per ton plus comm. Trans Dept appointed in 1852
1842-9 McGurk, James    finisher $1.33 1/3 per da. Repairs of Rwy & Mach Dept Mt Clare mach shop
1852-26 Mack, Edward    cleaning eng Cumberland $300 per yr. Trans Dept
1842-1 McKean, John A.    ofc clk $600 per annum Engr Dept
1842-12 McKeane, James D.    attend plaining mach $1.25 per da. Repairs of Rwy & Mach Dept Mt Clare mach shop
1842-16 McKee, Barney    brakeman Balto $30 per mo. Trans Dept Wash br
1852-20    Bernard*    mail carrier $115 per mo. Trans Dept raised from $62.50 per mo.
1852-24    James    stableman $300 per yr. Trans Dpt
1842-4 McKew, Hugh    laborer 75¢ per da. Repairs of Rwy & Mach Dept main stem 1st s-div
1852-24 McKewen, Wm.    burden car driv $360 per yr. Trans Dept

B & O RR EMPLOYEES 27

| | | |
|---|---|---|
| 1842-13 | McKnew, Thomas | day watchman 62½¢ per da. Repairs of Rwy & Mach Dept Mt Clare mach shop |
| 1852-19 | McLaughlin, T. J.* | conduc $58.33 per mo. Trans Dept made pass conduc in 1851 |
| 1842-2 | McLeod, Robert | res engr $3 per da. Engr Dept cons of rd w of Harper's Ferry 2d div |
| 1852-9 | McMachin, John H.* | foreman at Wash $70 per mo. Rd Dept appointed in Sept 1844 at $45 per mo. |
| 1842-9 | McMahan, William | finisher $1.50 per da. Repairs of Rwy & Mach Dept Mt Clare mach shop |
| 1842-11 | McQuinn, William | helper 92¢ per da. Repairs of Rwy & Mach Dept Mt Clare mach shop |
| 1842-10 | Madden, David | smith & tube mkr $1.42 per da. Repairs of Rwy & Mach Dept Mt Clare mach shop |
| 1842-14 | Mainsell, Robert | clk etc. Pratt St Depot $41.66 per mo. Trans Dept main stem |
| 1842-2 | Manning, Charles P. | res engr $2.25 per da. Engr Dept cons of rd w of Harper's Ferry 2d div |
| 1852-27 | Hugh | eng'man $2.50 per da. Trans Dept |
| 1852-4 | Saml.* | asst secy $1,200 per annum Secy Ofc appointed 11 Dec 1851 |
| 1852-26 | Mantz, Francis | watchman Monocacy $300 per yr. Trans Dept |
| 1852-9 | Peter* | supv 4th s-div $45 per mo. Rd Dept appointed 18 Apr 1852 |
| 1852-8 | Marfield, William* | foreman at Martinsburg $45 per mo. Rd Dept appointed 1 Aug 1848 |
| 1842-6 | Mark, Lemuel | boss over hands cleaning ditches 94¢ per da. Repairs of Rwy & Mach Dept Wash br 1st s-div |
| 1852-24 | Marshall, L. | regulator ton trains $360 per yr. Trans Dept |
| 1852-27 | Martin, Eastman | eng'man $2.50 per da. Trans Dept |
| 1852-26 | Henry | car coupler Mt Clare $325 per yr. Trans Dept |
| 1842-12 | Matchin, Thomas | carp $1.25 per da. Repairs of Rwy & Mach Dept Mt Clare mach shop |
| 1852-8 | Mathews, George* | foreman of carp shop $45 per mo. Rd Dept appointed 1 Mar 1850 |
| 1842-2 | Matthews, Charles H. | res engr $2.50 per da. Engr Dept cons of rd w of Harper's Ferry 1st div |
| 1842-12 | George H. | carp $1.25 per da. Repairs of Rwy & Mach Dept Mt Clare mach shop |
| 1852-24 | Mattingly, J. | regulator ton trains $360 per yr. Trans Dept |
| 1842-12 | Maunox, John | carp $1.25 per da. Repairs of Rwy & Mach Dept Mt Clare mach shop |

| | | |
|---|---|---|
| 1842-4 | Mauter, Barney | laborer 75¢ per da. Repairs of Rwy & Mach Dept main stem 3d s-div |
| 1842-10 | Maver, John | smith & tube mkr $1.25 per da. Repairs of Rwy & Mach Dept Mt Clare mach shop |
| 1842-1 | Mayo, S. | porter $300 per annum Ofc Dept |
| 1852-24 | Meara, Daniel | cart driv $300 per yr. Trans Dept |
| 1852-27 | Medcalf, Thomas | eng'man $2.50 per da. Trans Dept |
| 1842-9 | Meekes, John W. | finisher $1.25 per da. Repairs of Rwy & Mach Dept Mt Clare mach shop |
| 1852-22 | Megaha, Sam'l. | ton brakeman $360 per yr. Trans Dept |
| 1852-29 | Meller, Mark | fireman $400 per yr. Trans Dept |
| 1852-4 | Mentzel, William* | collec $750 per annum appointed 1 Mar 1850 |
| 1842-16 | Menzer, Jacob | ostler & ton driv Balto $30 per mo. Trans Dept main stem |
| 1852-17 | Menzies, James* | clk to master of trans $62.50 per mo. Trans Dept entered co serv in 1847 at $50 per mo. |
| 1852-23 | Merath, Joseph | pass card riv $360 per yr. Trans Dept |
| 1842-13 | Merryman, Oliver P. | cabinet mkr, making seat for new pass cars by the piece about $1.37½ per da. Repairs of Rwy & Mach Dept Mt Clare mach shop |
| 1852-23 | Messinger, Wm. | ton brakeman $360 per yr. Trans Dept |
| 1852-27 | Miller, Charles | eng'man $2.50 per da. Trans Dept |
| 1852-26 | Harrison | cleaning eng Martinsburg $300 per yr. Trans Dept |
| 1852-17 | J. B.* | supv of horses $66.66 per mo. Trans Dept entered co serv in 1840 at $50 per mo. |
| 1842-16 | Jacob B. | supv of stock Balto $50 per mo. Trans Dept main stem |
| 1842-12 | Oliver M. | carp $1.25 per da. Repairs of Rwy & Mach Dept Mt Clare mach shop |
| 1852-26 | Rob't. | car coupler Mt Clare $350 per yr. Trans Dept |
| 1852-23 | Millington, A. | tender filler Cumberland $300 per yr. Trans Dept |
| 1842-7 | Mitcheale, Thomas | boss over men clearing ditch 94¢ per da. Repairs of Rwy & Mach Dept Wash br 2d s-div |
| 1842-7 | Mitchell, George | laborer 75¢ per da. Repairs of Rwy & Mach Dept Wash br 2d s-div |
| 1842-8 | P. G. | smith $1.42 per da. Repairs of Rwy & Mach Dept Mt Clare |
| 1852-8 | Perry* | foreman of smith shop $60 per mo. Rd Dept appointed in July 1850 at $45 per mo. |
| 1852-22 | Mitten, George A. | ton conduc $480 per yr. Trans Dept |

| | | | |
|---|---|---|---|
| 1852-33 | Mobbley, Wm. | | fireman $33.33 per mo. Wash br Appointed 1851 |
| 1852-27 | Mobley, Horace | | eng'man $2.50 per da. Trans Dept |
| 1842-10 | Moony, John | | finisher $1.12½ per da. Repairs of Rwy & Mach Dept Mt Clare mach shop |
| 1852-25 | Moor, John | | laborer Locust Pt $300 per yr. Trans Dept |
| 1842-2 | Moore, John J. | | vaneman $1.25 per da. Engr Dept cons of rd w of Harper's Ferry 2d div |
| 1852-22 | Morris, John | | ton brakeman $360 per yr. Trans Dept |
| 1852-29 | | Robert | fireman $400 per yr. Trans Dept |
| 1852-22 | | " | ton brakeman $360 per yr. Trans Dept |
| 1852-30 | Morrison, J. G. | | local agt main stem Knoxville 10¢ per ton plus comm. Trans Dept |
| 1852-10 | Mudge, Wm. R. | | supv 10th s-div $45 per mo. Rd Dept appointed 17 Sept 1851 |
| 1852-22 | Mullinix, Bazil | | ton brakeman $360 per yr. Trans Dept |
| 1852-22 | | J. H. | ton conduc $480 per yr. Trans Dept |
| 1852-29 | | Thomas | fireman $400 per yr. Trans Dept |
| 1852-22 | | W. H. | ton conduc $480 per yr. Trans Dept |
| 1852-33 | Munroe, James* | | baggage porter Balto $120 per yr. Wash br |
| 1852-22 | | R. | ton brakeman $360 per yr. Trans Dept |
| 1842-1 | Murray, James | | asst engr, mach & repairs $2,000 per annum Engr Dept. |
| 1852-26 | | P. | cleaning eng Martinsburg $300 per yr. Trans Dept |
| 1852-29 | | Patrick | fireman $400 per yr. Trans Dept |
| 1842-4 | | Robert | supv $50 per mo. Repairs of Rwy & Mach Dept main stem 2d s-div |
| 1852-24 | Muson, T. | | regulator ton trains $360 per yr. Trans Dept |
| 1852-22 | Musseton, Plummer | | ton brakeman $360 per yr. Trans Dept |
| 1842-4 | Mussetta, Plummer | | rough carp 94¢ per da. Repairs of Rwy & Mach Dept main stem 3d s-div |
| 1842-2 | Myers, Jon G. | | vaneman $1 per da. Engr Dept cons of rd w of Harper's Ferry 2d div |
| 1842-17 | | Joseph | attend on pass cars Balto $30 per mo. Trans Dept Wash br |
| 1842-7 | Nally, Henry | | laborer 75¢ per da. Repairs of Rwy & Mach Dept Wash br 2d s-div |
| 1842-7 | | John | laborer 75¢ per da. Repairs of Rwy & Mach Dept Wash br 2d s-div |
| 1842-7 | | Levi | nailor 80¢ per da. Repairs of Rwy & Mach Dept Wash br 2d s-div |

## B & O RR EMPLOYEES

| | | |
|---|---|---|
| 1842-7 | Neale, Levi | laborer 75¢ per da. Repairs of Rwy & Mach Dept Wash br 2d s-div |
| 1852-29 | Neer, John W. | fireman $400 per yr. Trans Dept |
| 1842-2 | Neilson, Jomes C. | res engr $3 per da. Engr Dept cons of rd w of Harper's Ferry 1st div |
| 1842-11 | Nickman, John | helper 92¢ per da. Repairs of Rwy & Mach Dept Mt Clare mach shop |
| 1842-1 | Niernsee, John R. | ofc draftsman $3 per diem Engr Dept |
| 1842-9 | Night, N. A. | finisher $1.42 per da. Repairs of Rwy & Mach Dept Mt Clare mach shop |
| 1852-22 | Niswann, Stephen | ton conduc $480 per yr. Trans Dept |
| 1852-30 | Nixdorff, Sam | local agt main stem Ijamsville 10¢ per ton plus comm. Trans Dept appointed in 1851 |
| 1852-29 | Norris, Benjamin | fireman $400 per yr. Trans Dept |
| 1852-25 |        John | laborer load & unload cars Harper's Ferry $330 per yr. Trans Dept |
| 1842-3 | Obrian, David | nailor who exam track prev to pass of sev trains 80¢ per da. Repairs of Rwy & Mach Dept main stem 1st s-div |
| 1842-3 |        William | laborer on repairs city track 75¢ per da. Repairs of Rwy & Mach Dept main stem 1st s-div |
| 1852-23 | O'Brian, J. | tender filler Cumberland $300 per yr. Trans Dept |
| 1852-24 | O'Brien, Michael | blacksmith $360 per yr. Trans Dept |
| 1852-25 | Ogh, Jacob | sawyer Locust Pt $345 per yr. Trans Dept |
| 1842-4 | O'Neale, James | laborer 75¢ per da. Repairs of Rwy & Mach Dept main stem 1st s-div |
| 1842-11 | Osborne, Edward | moulder $1.17 per da. Repairs of Rwy & Mach Dept Mt Clare mach shop |
| 1842-7 | Osburn, William | laborer 75¢ per da. Repairs of Rwy & Mach Dept Wash br 1st s-div |
| 1852-22 | O'Toole, Wm. | ton conduc $480 per yr. Trans Dept |
| 1842-7 | Owen, John H. | laborer 75¢ per da. Repairs of Rwy & Mach Dept Wash br 2d s-div |
| 1842-16 | Owens, Benjamin | ostler & ton driv Balto $30 per mo. Trans Dept main stem |
| 1842-7 |        Thomas | supv $50 per mo. Repairs of Rwy & Mach Dept Wash br 2d s-div |
| 1852-10 |        "   * | supv 13th s-div $60 per mo. Rd Dept trans fr Wash br 1 Nov 1851 |

## B & O RR EMPLOYEES

1852-10 Owens, W. W.* — supv 12th s-div $45 per mo. Rd Dept appointed 1 Oct 1851

1842-14 " William — mail conduc Frederick $40 per mo. Trans Dept main stem

1852-18 " " * — pass conduc bet Balto & Cumberland $58.35 per mo. Trans Dept entered co serv in 1832 as depot laborer at $35 per mo.

1852-30 Owings, Basil — local agt main stem Woodbine 10¢ per ton plus comm. Trans Dept

1852-22 Palmer, Sam'l. — ton conduc $480 per yr. Trans Dept

1852-25 Parker, Edward — tender filler Mt Clare $325 per yr. Trans Dept

1852-3 " William — gen supt $5,000 per annum elect 14 Feb 1849

1842-9 Parsons, John — finisher $1.42 per da. Repairs of Rwy & Mach Dept Mt Clare mach shop

1852-31 " Thomas H.* — agt Wash $1,000 per annum Wash br entered co serv in 1847

1842-14 Pattengall, Samuel — main conduc Balto $40 per mo. Trans Dept main stem

1842-5 Pattingall, John — nailor 80¢ per da. Repairs of Rwy & Mach Dept main stem 4th s-div

1842-15 Peck, Stephen — porter Pratt St Depot $25 per mo. Trans Dept main stem

1842-4 Penington, James — laborer 75¢ per da. Repairs of Rwy & Mach Dept main stem 2d s-div

1852-22 Pentony, A. — ton brakeman $360 per yr. Trans Dept

1852-29 " Adam — fireman $400 per yr. Trans Dept

1842-11 Perkins, Otis B. — prin pattern mkr $1.50 per da. Repairs of Rwy & Mach Dept Mt Clare mach shop

1842-9 " Thatcher — foreman in mach shop $83.33 1/3 per mo. Repairs of Rwy & Mach Dept Mt Clare mach shop

1852-23 Perl, Samuel — ton brakeman $360 per yr. Trans Dept

1852-21 Permal, Jon'a* — way conduc $600 per yr. Trans Dept

1842-10 Perry, Isrial — drilling & helping $1 per da. Repairs of Rwy & Mach Dept Mt Clare mach shop

1852-23 Peterman, I. — tender filler Monocacy $330 per yr. Trans Dept

1852-22 Phebus, John — ton conduc $480 per yr. Trans Dept

1842-8 Phelps, Walter W. — pattern mkr $1.62½ per da. Repairs of Rwy & Mach Dept Mt Clare

1842-4 Phillips, James — laborer 75¢ per da. Repairs of Rwy & Mach Dept main stem 1st s-div

1852-31 Picken, J. — nt watchman $360 per yr. Wash br

1852-22 Piett, Rich'd. — ton brakeman $360 per yr. Trans Dept

| | | |
|---|---|---|
| 1852-29 | Pinnen, Thomas | fireman $400 per yr. Trans Dept |
| 1842-4 | Plummer, Jesse | supv $45 per mo. Repairs of Rwy & Mach Dept main stem 3d s-div |
| 1852-9 | " * | supv 3d s-div $45 per mo. Rd Dept appointed 1 July 1835 |
| 1852-29 | Robert N. | fireman $400 per yr. Trans Dept |
| 1852-10 | W. W. | supv Wash br $50 per mo. Rd Dept appointed 1 Nov 1851 |
| 1842-6 | William W. | supv $50 per mo. Repairs of Rwy & Mach Dept Wash br 1st s-div |
| 1842-4 | Poe, Henry | laborer 75¢ per da. Repairs of Rwy & Mach Dept main stem 1st s-div |
| 1852-27 | Pollock, Wm. | eng'man $2 per da. Trans Dept |
| 1842-5 | Pool, Amos | laborer 75¢ per da. Repairs of Rwy & Mach Dept main stem 3d s-div |
| 1842-11 | George | helper 92¢ per da. Repairs of Rwy & Mach Dept Mt Clare mach shop |
| 1842-5 | Solomon | laborer 75¢ per da. Repairs of Rwy & Mach Dept main stem 3d s-div |
| 1842-7 | Porter, Amos | laborer 75¢ per da. Repairs of Rwy & Mach Dept Wash br 2d s-div |
| 1852-10 | W. E.* | supv 11th s-div $50 per mo. Rd Dept appointed 1 Mar 1852 |
| 1852-17 | Posey, Henry C.* | clk Frederick Depot $20 per mo. Trans Dept entered co serv in May 1851 |
| 1842-7 | Poulton, Alexander | nail & exam track 80¢ per da. Repairs of Rwy & Mach Dept Wash br 1st s-div |
| 1842-11 | Powell, George | moulder $1.42 per da. Repairs of Rwy & Mach Dept Mt Clare mach shop |
| 1842-11 | Morris | master foundryman $2 per da. Repairs of Rwy & Mach Dept Mt Clare mach shop |
| 1842-11 | Thomas | watchman $1 per da. Repairs of Rwy & Mach Dept Mt Clare mach shop |
| 1842-10 | Powill, Samuel | smith Frederick $30 per mo. Repairs of Rwy & Mach Dept Mt Clare mach shop |
| 1852-22 | Pownal, J. A. | ton conduc $480 per yr. Trans Dept |
| 1852-22 | Joseph | ton conduc $480 per yr. Trans Dept |
| 1852-29 | Prescott, Charles | fireman $400 per yr. Trans Dept |
| 1852-22 | Prince, Thos. C. | ton conduc $480 per yr. Trans Dept |
| 1842-15 | Probay, James | yard driv Frederick $30 per mo. Trans Dept main stem |
| 1852-33 | Proby, James* | mail driv Cumberland $300 per yr. Wash br |
| 1842-13 | Pryor, Benj. | help to carp 92¢ per da. Repairs of Rwy & Mach Dept Mt Clare mach shop |

| | | |
|---|---|---|
| 1842-12 | Pryor, Edward W. | carp $1.25 per da. Repairs of Rwy & Mach Dept Mt Clare mach shop |
| 1842-7 | Pumphrey, Judson | boss over men clearing ditch 94¢ per da. Repairs of Rwy & Mach Dept Wash br 2d s-div |
| 1852-27 | Purdy, John | eng'man $2 per da. Trans Dept |
| 1842-9 | " H. | finisher $1.50 per da. Repairs of Rwy & Mach Dept Mt Clare mach shop |
| 1842-16 | Pywell, Robert R. | brakeman Balto $30 per mo. Trans Dept Wash br |
| 1852-10 | Quigg, James* | supv 15th s-div $50 per mo. Rd Dept appointed 1 June 1852 |
| 1852-16 | Quynn, J. T.* | agt Frederick $50 per mo. Trans Dept appointed in 1846 as conduc at $40 per mo. |
| 1842-14 | John J. | clk, etc. Frederick $33.33 per mo. Trans Dept main stem |
| 1852-22 | Randall, John | ton conduc $480 per yr. Trans Dept |
| 1842-2 | Randolph, J. L. | res engr $2 per da. Engr Dept cons of rd w of Harper's Ferry 1st div |
| 1842-2 | Raney, Allen | supt cons of water sta & trav supv (trav expenses pd when oper w of Harper's Ferry) $60 per mo. Engr Dept |
| 1852-22 | Rasinger, Martin | ton brakeman $360 per yr. Trans Dept |
| 1852-22 | Ray, Josiah | ton conduc $480 per yr. Trans Dept |
| 1852-29 | Rea, Samuel | fireman $400 per yr. Trans Dept |
| 1842-7 | Ream, Mathias | laborer 75¢ per da. Repairs of Rwy & Mach Dept Wash br 1st s-div |
| 1842-13 | Reaves, James | master painter $1.37½ per da. Repairs of Rwy & Mach Dept Mt Clare mach shop |
| 1842-11 | Reavis, William | helper 92¢ per da. Repairs of Rwy & Mach Dept Mt Clare mach shop |
| 1842-12 | Reed, Thomas | asst attend plaining mach 92¢ per da. Repairs of Rwy & Mach Dept Mt Clare mach shop |
| 1842-15 | Reel, Otho | eng'man Frederick $2 per da. Trans Dept main stem |
| 1852-22 | Reinhard, A. H. | ton conduc $480 per yr. Trans Dept |
| 1842-5 | Relger, Christian | laborer 75¢ per da. Repairs of Rwy & Mach Dept main stem 4th s-div |
| 1852-14 | Rennie, D. P.* | draughtsman in Mach Dept Mt Clare $66.66 per mo. Mach Dept appointed June 1847 $40 per mo. |
| 1842-2 | Reynolds, Michael | axeman $1 per da. Engr Dept cons of rd w of Harper's Ferry 1st div |
| 1852-22 | Rhodes, E. | ton brakeman $360 per yr. Trans Dept |

## B & O RR EMPLOYEES

| | | |
|---|---|---|
| 1852-23 | Rhodes, Nich's | sawyer Cumberland $336 per yr. Trans Dept |
| 1852-27 | Richardson, George | eng'man $2 per da. Trans Dept |
| 1842-10 | Thomas | boiler mkr $1.50 per da. Repairs of Rwy & Mach Dept Mt Clare mach shop |
| 1852-13 | " * | foreman of boiler shops at Mt Clare $50 per mo. Mach Dept appointed in Feb 1851 |
| 1842-10 | Ricketts, Daniel | smith $1.42 per da. Repairs of Rwy & Mach Dept Mt Clare mach shop |
| 1852-27 | Riddle, Adam | eng'man $2 per da. Trans Dept |
| 1852-29 | " | fireman $400 per yr. Trans Dept |
| 1842-1 | George R. | res engr $3 per da. Engr Dept cons of rd w of Harper's Ferry 1st div |
| 1852-22 | Rigney, Edward | ton brakeman $360 per yr. Trans Dept |
| 1852-3 | John T.* | clk of gen supt, also clk to chief engr $600 for former, $250 for latter appointed 1 Jan 1852 entered co serv 8 Aug 1844 at $500 |
| 1842-8 | **Riley, Alex.** | laborer 75¢ per da. Repairs of Rwy & Mach Dept Mt Clare |
| 1852-22 | John | ton brakeman $360 per yr. Trans Dept |
| 1842-3 | Richard | laborer on repairs city track 75¢ per da. Repairs of Rwy & Mach Dept main stem 1st s-div |
| 1852-33 | Wm. | cleaning ton eng Cumberland $300 per yr. Wash br |
| 1842-11 | Rinehart, George | helper 92¢ per da. Repairs of Rwy & Mach Dept Mt Clare mach shop |
| 1852-29 | **Ritchie, William** | fireman $400 per yr. Trans Dept |
| 1852-29 | **Ritzeel, Jacob** | fireman $400 per yr. " " |
| 1842-2 | **Rivers, Philip** | vaneman $1 per da. Engr Dept cons of rd w of Harper's Ferry 1st div |
| 1842-9 | Roads, Frederick C. | finisher $1.50 per da. Repairs of Rwy & Mach Dept Mt Clare mach shop |
| 1842-2 | Robert (colored) | axeman 75¢ per da. Engr Dept cons of rd w of Harper's Ferry 1st div |
| 1852-25 | Robinson, A. | laborer load & unload cars Pratt St $360 per yr. Trans Dept |
| 1852-24 | J. | regulator pass trains $420 per yr. Trans Dept |
| 1842-8 | Roby, William | helper 92¢ per da. Repairs of Rwy & Mach Dept Mt Clare |
| 1852-22 | Rockwell, Thos. | ton brakeman $360 per yr. Trans Dept |
| 1852-30 | Roderick, Lewis | local agt main stem Catoctin switch 10¢ per ton plus comm. Trans Dept |
| 1842-8 | Rodman, Francis | laborer 75¢ per da. Repairs of Rwy & Mach Dept Mt Clare |

## B & O RR EMPLOYEES

| | | |
|---|---|---|
| 1842-4 | Rogan, Edward | laborer 75¢ per da. Repairs of Rwy & Mach Dept main stem 1st s-div |
| 1842-5 | Roger, Michael | laborer 75¢ per da. Repairs of Rwy & Mach Dept main stem 4th s-div |
| 1842-12 | Roop, Jacob | carp $1.25 per da. Repairs of Rwy & Mach Dept Mt Clare mach shop |
| 1852-22 | Rowland, Jona. | ton brakeman $360 per yr. Trans Dept |
| 1842-3 | Rowles, Thomas | supt mech work at Harper's Ferry $2.50 per da. Engr Dept |
| 1852-29 | Royston, Thomas | fireman $400 per yr. Trans Dept |
| 1842-8 | Russell, Thomas | laborer 75¢ per da. Repairs of Rwy & Mach Dept Wash br 2d s-div |
| 1852-23 | Ryan, P. | tender filler Cumberland $300 per yr. Trans Dept |
| 1842-4 | Salmon, Charles | rough carp 94¢ per da. Repairs of Rwy & Mach Dept main stem 3d s-div |
| 1842-11 | Sanders, Henry | helper 92¢ per da. Repairs of Rwy & Mach Dept Mt Clare mach shop |
| 1842-10 | Saville, John | finisher $1.25 per da. Repairs of Rwy & Mach Dept Mt Clare mach shop |
| 1842-9 | Sawtwell, Edward | finisher & ex eng'man $1.42 per da. Repairs of Rwy & Mach Dept Mt Clare mach shop |
| 1852-28 | Schaeffer, Henry | eng'man $2 per da. Trans Dept |
| 1852-27 | John | eng'man $2 per da. " " |
| 1852-29 | Schaid, Peter | fireman $400 per yr. Trans Dept |
| 1852-22 | Schollay, John A. | ton conduc $480 per yr. Trans Dept |
| 1852-32 | Scott, James | pass brakeman $30 per mo. Wash br appointed in 1851 |
| 1842-9 | Scotti, John | finisher $1.42 per da. Repairs of Rwy & Mach Dept Mt Clare mach shop |
| 1842-10 | Sears, Thomas | boiler mkr $1.25 per da. Repairs of Rwy & Mach Dept Mt Clare mach shop |
| 1842-12 | Sefton, Jeremiah | coach mkr $1.37½ per da. Repairs of Rwy & Mach Dept Mt Clare mach shop |
| 1852-26 | Senseny, Wm. | cleaning eng Cumberland $300 per yr. Trans Dept |
| 1842-10 | Sexton, Daniel | finisher (app) 75¢ per da. Repairs of Rwy & Mach Dept Mt Clare mach shop |
| 1842-3 | Shanks, Gilbert | nailor who exam track prev to pass of sev trains 80¢ per da. Repairs of Rwy & Mach Dept main stem 1st s-div |
| 1852-29 | Shannon, Edward | fireman $400 per yr. Trans Dept |
| 1852-26 | Grafton | watchman Harper's Ferry $300 per yr. Trans Dept |

| Date | Name | Position |
|---|---|---|
| 1842-7 | Sharp, Benjamin | laborer 75¢ per da. Repairs of Rwy & Mach Dept Wash br 2d s-div |
| 1842-7 | Shavung, Francis | laborer 75¢ per da. Repairs of Rwy & Mach Dept Wash br 2d s-div |
| 1852-10 | Shepherd, Jacob* | supv 6th s-div $45 per mo. Rd Dept appointed 1 Nov 1851 |
| 1852-25 | Sheppard, Hayward | laborer load & unload cars Harper's Ferry $330 per yr. Trans Dept |
| 1842-14 | N. A. | clk, etc. Pratt St Depot $41.66 per mo. Trans Dept main stem |
| 1852-18 | " " * | clk at Pratt St Ton Ofc $50 per mo. Trans Dept entered co serv in Sept 1836 as clk at $45 per mo. |
| 1852-25 | Shields, John | laborer load & unload cars Pratt St $360 per yr. Trans Dept |
| 1852-24 | Shipley, B. | burden car driv $360 per yr. Trans Dept |
| 1852-26 | James | cleaning eng Mt Clare $300 per yr. Trans Dept |
| 1852-26 | L. | cleaning eng Mt Clare $300 per yr. Trans Dept |
| 1852-22 | N. H. | ton brakeman $360 per yr. Trans Dept |
| 1842-3 | Samuel T. | supt masonry at Paw Paw tunnel $2 per da. Engr Dept |
| 1852-26 | Thos. | cleaning eng Mt Clare $300 per yr. Trans Dept |
| 1842-17 | Washington | pass eng'man Balto $2 per da. Trans Dept Wash br |
| 1842-11 | William | watchman $1 per da. Repairs of Rwy & Mach Dept Mt Clare mach shop |
| 1852-23 | " | ton brakeman $360 per yr. Trans Dept |
| 1842-8 | " | smith $1.42 per da. Repairs of Rwy & Mach Dept Mt Clare |
| 1852-13 | " H.* | foreman of smith shop Mt Clare $55 per mo. Mach Dept appointed July 1850 |
| 1852-24 | Shorts, --- | burden car driv $360 per yr. Trans Dept |
| 1842-5 | William | laborer 75¢ per da. Repairs of Rwy & Mach Dept main stem 5th s-div |
| 1842-11 | Shryack, Jacob S. | coach mkr $1.50 per da. Repairs of Rwy & Mach Dept Mt Clare mach shop |
| 1842-10 | Shurdon, Luther | smith & tube mkr $1.25 per da. Repairs of Rwy & Mach Dept Mt Clare mach shop |
| 1842-11 | Sides, George | helper 92¢ per da. Repairs of Rwy & Mach Dept Mt Clare mach shop |
| 1842-8 | Henry | carp (app) $1 per da. Repairs of Rwy & Mach Dept Mt Clare |

| | | | |
|---|---|---|---|
| 1852-23 | Silous, I. | | tender filler Monocacy $360 per yr. Trans Dept |
| 1852-14 | Sindall, S.* | | clk Mt Clare $58.33 per mo. Mach Dept appointed Oct 1847 at $50 per mo. |
| 1842-14 | Slack, Cornelius | | clk, etc. Mt Clare $41.66 per mo. Trans Dept main stem |
| 1842-16 | " | W. B. | conduc of pass Balto $58.33 per mo. Trans Dept Wash br |
| 1852-31 | " | " * | pass conduc $700 per annum Wash br appointed in 1833 |
| 1842-1 | Small, | Edward | bookkpr $700 per annum Ofc Dept |
| 1852-29 | | Eli | fireman $400 per yr. Trans Dept |
| 1842-2 | | John Jr. | res engr $3 per da. Engr Dept cons of rd w of Harper's Ferry 1st div |
| 1842-2 | | William | vaneman $1 per da. Engr Dept cons of rd w of Harper's Ferry 2d div |
| 1852-23 | Smith, C. | | tender filler Monocacy $330 per yr. Trans Dept |
| 1842-10 | | Christian | helper & ex eng'man $1 per da. Repairs of Rwy & Mach Dept Mt Clare mach shop |
| 1842-7 | | Elijah | laborer 75¢ per da. Repairs of Rwy & Mach Dept Wash br 2d s-div |
| 1852-23 | | H. | sawyer Cumberland $336 per yr. Trans Dept |
| 1842-5 | | Henry | laborer 75¢ per da. Repairs of Rwy & Mach Dept main stem 3d s-div |
| 1842-15 | | John | eng'man Harper's Ferry $2 per da. Trans Dept main stem |
| 1852-28 | | " | eng'man $2 per da. Trans Dept |
| 1842-11 | | Patrick | helper 92¢ per da. Repairs of Rwy & Mach Dept Mt Clare mach shop |
| 1842-8 | | William | laborer 75¢ per da. Repairs of Rwy & Mach Dept Wash br 2d s-div |
| 1842-14 | | " | eng'man Harper's Ferry $2 per da. Trans Dept main stem |
| 1852-30 | | " H. | local agt w of Cumberland Fetterman's 10¢ per ton plus comm. Trans Dept appointed in 1852 |
| 1842-12 | Snuggrass, Hiram | | coach mkr $1.37½ per da. Repairs of Rwy & Mach Dept Mt Clare mach shop |
| 1852-32 | Soder, Alex. | | pass brakeman $30 per mo. Wash br appointed in 1852 |
| 1852-24 | Soffron, Conrad | | stableman $300 per yr. Trans Dpt |
| 1842-16 | Sollars, Benj. | | blacksmith Balto $37.50 per mo. Trans Dept main stem |
| 1852-24 | Sollers, Benj. | | blacksmith $480 per yr. Trans Dept |
| 1852-26 | Solman, Anthony | | watchman Pratt St $300 per yr. Trans Dept |
| 1842-2 | Soynster, James | | axeman $1 per da. Engr Dept cons of rd w of Harper's Ferry 2d div |

B & O RR EMPLOYEES

| | | |
|---|---|---|
| 1852-22 | Spicknell, W. H. | ton brakeman $360 per yr. Trans Dept |
| 1852-28 | Spurrier, Thos. | eng'man $2.50 per da. Trans Dept |
| 1852-22 |         Wm. | ton brakeman $360 per yr. Trans Dept |
| 1842-10 | Stabler, Joseph | smith & spring mkr $1.42 per da. Repairs of Rwy & Mach Dept Mt Clare mach shop |
| 1842-4 | Stacks, James | laborer 75¢ per da. Repairs of Rwy & Mach Dept main stem 1st s-div |
| 1842-17 | Staggers, John | blacksmith Balto $25 per mo. Trans Dept Wash br |
| 1852-19 | Stansbury, D. R.* | conduc $58.33 per mo. Trans Dept entered co serv in 1849 at $30 per mo. |
| 1842-2 | Staunton, John | axeman 75¢ per da. Engr Dept cons of rd w of Harper's Ferry 2d div |
| 1842-7 | Stearm, John | laborer 75¢ per da. Repairs of Rwy & Mach Dept Wash br 1st s-div |
| 1842-14 | Steiner, David | gen agt Frederick $66.66 per mo. Trans Dept main stem |
| 1852-26 | Stephens, Thos. | cleaning eng Cumberland $300 per yr. Trans Dept |
| 1852-31 | Stephenson, J. A.* | clk at Wash $600 per annum Wash br appointed in 1851 |
| 1842-16 | Stettinius, Samuel | gen agt Wash $83.33 per mo. Trans Dept Wash br |
| 1852-16 | Stewart, A.* | supv of trains w of Cumberland $60 per mo. Trans Dept entered co serv in Oct 1851 at $50 per mo. |
| 1842-10 | Stoany, Edward | boiler mkr $1.66 2/3 per da. Repairs of Rwy & Mach Dept Mt Clare mach shop |
| 1852-32 | Stokes, Charles | laborer unload cars $360 per yr. Wash br |
| 1842-11 |         Martin | helper 92¢ per da. Repairs of Rwy & Mach Dept Mt Clare mach shop |
| 1852-28 | Story, Walter | eng'man $2.50 per da. Trans Dept |
| 1842-10 | Strany, John | boiler mkr $1.25 per da. Repairs of Rwy & Mach Dept Mt Clare mach shop |
| 1852-29 | Street, Washington | fireman $400 per yr. Trans Dept |
| 1852-22 | Stribling, Francis | ton conduc $480 per yr. Trans Dept |
| 1852-24 | Stuart, Charles | burden car driv $360 per yr. Trans Dept |
| 1852-22 | Stubbins, Chas. | ton conduc $480 per yr. Trans Dept |
| 1852-29 | Summers, William | fireman $400 per yr. Trans Dept |
| 1852-22 | Suter, Samuel | ton conduc $480 per yr. Trans Dept |
| 1852-18 | Swain, J. K.* | clk Pratt St Ton Ofc $50 per mo. Trans Dept entered co serv in Sept 1851 |
| 1852-30 | Swann, C. A. | local agt main stem Hancock 10¢ per ton plus comm. Trans Dept |

| | | | |
|---|---|---|---|
| 1842-2 | Swann, Charles A. | | vaneman $1.50 per da. Engr Dept cons of rd w of Harper's Ferry 1st div |
| 1852-3 | | Thomas | president $3,000 per annum elect 11 Oct 1848 |
| 1842-17 | Swigart, Joseph | | watchman Wash $25 per mo. Trans Dept Wash br |
| 1852-22 | Swigent, Henry | | ton brakeman $360 per yr. Trans Dept |
| 1852-30 | Sykes, James | | local agt main stem Sykesville 10¢ per ton plus comm. Trans Dept |
| 1852-28 | Taft, John H. | | eng'man $2 per da. Trans Dept |
| 1842-10 | Taylor, Edward | | finisher $1.12½ per da. Repairs of Rwy & Mach Dept Mt Clare mach shop |
| 1842-5 | | Jesse | laborer 75¢ per da. Repairs of Rwy & Mach Dept main stem 3d s-div |
| 1842-2 | | John C. | res engr $2.50 per da. Engr Dept cons of rd w of Harper's Ferry 2d div |
| 1842-2 | | William | axeman 75¢ per da. Engr Dept cons of rd w of Harper's Ferry 2d div |
| 1852-7 | Tegmeyer, John H.* | | asst master of rd $1,200 per annum Rd Dept appointed Jan 1851 |
| 1852-24 | Thomas, J. H. | | burden car driv $360 per yr. Trans Dept |
| 1842-13 | | Robert | master painter $1.37½ per da. Repairs of Rwy & Mach Dept Mt Clare mach shop |
| 1842-15 | | Warner | laborer Plane # 1 & 4 87¢ per da. Trans Dept main stem |
| 1842-11 | Thompson, Edward | | moulder (app) 50¢ per da. Repairs of Rwy & Mach Dept Mt Clare mach shop |
| 1852-22 | | J. W. | ton brakeman $360 per yr. Trans Dept |
| 1842-4 | | Jas. | nailor 80¢ per da. Repairs of Rwy & Mach Dept main stem 2d s-div |
| 1842-5 | | Smallwood | rough carp 94¢ per da. Repairs of Rwy & Mach Dept main stem 4th s-div |
| 1852-22 | | William | ton conduc $480 per yr. Trans Dept |
| 1842-3 | Thomson, John | | rough carp on Repairs Rd 87½¢ per da. Repairs of Rwy & Mach Dept main stem 1st s-div |
| 1852-18 | Thumelat, J. E.* | | clk Pratt St Ton Ofc $50 per mo. Trans Dept entered co serv in 1846 |
| 1842-17 | Tingstrow, Peter | | porter at Ticket Ofc Wash $25 per mo. Trans Dept Wash br |
| 1842-15 | Titlow, James | | laborer Frederick $25 per mo. Trans Dept main stem |
| 1852-23 | Tobin, Patrick | | ton brakeman $360 per yr. Trans Dept |

## B & O RR EMPLOYEES

| | | |
|---|---|---|
| 1842-7 | Toucheir, John | pump water & attend track in Washington City 80¢ per da. Repairs of Rwy & Mach Dept Wash br 2d s-div |
| 1852-19 | Townsend, W. M.* | agt Relay House $33.33 per mo. Trans Dept appointed in 1847 |
| 1842-12 | Tracy, Jarrot | wheel wright $1.25 per da. Repairs of Rwy & Mach Dept Mt Clare mach shop |
| 1842-10 | John P. | helper $1 per da. Repairs of Rwy & Mach Dept Mt Clare mach shop |
| 1842-10 | Trigg, William | smith & tube mkr $1.25 per da. Repairs of Rwy & Mach Dept Mt Clare mach shop |
| 1852-26 | Turner, Geo. | cleaning eng Mt Clare $300 per yr. Trans Dept |
| 1852-11 | Uncles, Benj.* | supt of repairs of water sta $60 per mo. Rd Dept appointed Sept 1842 at $45 per mo. |
| 1842-7 | Vermileon, Nicholas | rough carp 94¢ per da. Repairs of Rwy & Mach Dept Wash br 2d s-div |
| 1852-19 | Walker, William* | weighmaster Mt Clare $35 per mo. Trans Dept entered co serv in 1850 as ton brakesman at $25 per mo. |
| 1852-23 | Walling, H. | ton brakeman $360 per yr. Trans Dept |
| 1852-22 | Waltermyer, Jacob | ton conduc $480 per yr. Trans Dept |
| 1842-7 | Walters, John | laborer 75¢ per da. Repairs of Rwy & Mach Dept Wash br 1st s-div |
| 1842-11 | Waltmire, John | helper 92¢ per da. Repairs of Rwy & Mach Dept Mt Clare mach shop |
| 1842-7 | Ward, James | laborer 75¢ per da. Repairs of Rwy & Mach Dept Wash br 1st s-div |
| 1842-4 | John | nailor 80¢ per da. Repairs of Rwy & Mach Dept main stem 3d s-div |
| 1842-6 | " | rough carp 94¢ per da. Repairs of Rwy & Mach Dept Wash br 1st s-div |
| 1852-28 | Ware, Henry | eng'man $2 per da. Trans Dept |
| 1852-23 | Warfield, Charles | ton conduc $480 per yr. Trans Dept |
| 1842-2 | Warner, Edward | vaneman $1.50 per da. Engr Dept cons of rd w of Harper's Ferry 2d div |
| 1842-16 | Thadeus | ostler & pass driv Balto $30 per mo. Trans Dept main stem |
| 1852-29 | Washburn, L. | fireman $400 per yr. Trans Dept |
| 1842-15 | Watts, Albert | eng'man Balto $2 per da. Trans Dept main stem |
| 1842-11 | Allen | helper 92¢ per da. Repairs of Rwy & Mach Dept Mt Clare mach shop |

| | | |
|---|---|---|
| 1842-12 | Wattson, Charles | carp $1.25 per da. Repairs of Rwy & Mach Dept Mt Clare mach shop |
| 1852-23 | Ways, John | ton conduc $480 per yr. Trans Dept |
| 1852-33 | Weaver, Christian | cleaning ton eng Cumberland $300 per yr. Wash br |
| 1852-28 | Webb, John | eng'man $2 per da. Trans Dept |
| 1852-29 | Weckathon, William | fireman $400 per yr. Trans Dept |
| 1852-23 | Weddle, James | ton brakeman $360 per yr. Trans Dept |
| 1842-3 | Welch, Michael | stone cutter on repairs city track $1.12½ per da. Repairs of Rwy & Mach Dept main stem 1st s-div |
| 1842-5 | Welcom, John | laborer 75¢ per da. Repairs of Rwy & Mach Dept main stem 4th s-div |
| 1842-12 | Weller, Edward | coach mkr $1.37½ per da. Repairs of Rwy & Mach Dept Mt Clare mach shop |
| 1852-29 | Welsh, William | fireman $400 per yr. Trans Dept |
| 1852-20 | Wescott, C. F. | regulator coal trains Cumberland $35 per mo. Trans Dept appointed in 1851 |
| 1842-14 | Charles J. | ton breakman Frederick $30 per mo. Trans Dept main stem |
| 1842-7 | Wesley, Joseph | laborer 75¢ per da. Repairs of Rwy & Mach Dept Wash br 2d s-div |
| 1852-23 | West, Joseph | ton conduc $480 per yr. Trans Dept |
| 1852-23 | Whally, Geo. | ton conduc $480 per yr. Trans Dept |
| 1842-9 | Wheary, John | finisher $1.50 per da. Repairs of Rwy & Mach Dept Mt Clare mach shop |
| 1852-17 | Wheeler, John D.* | St supv lower div $50 per mo. Trans Dept entered co serv in 1847 at $41.65 per mo. |
| 1842-12 | White, Charles W. | carp $1.25 per da. Repairs of Rwy & Mach Dept Mt Clare mach shop |
| 1842-13 | Orlando G. | trimmer $1.25 per da. Repairs of Rwy & Mach Dept Mt Clare mach shop |
| 1842-5 | Whitter, Ignatius | laborer 75¢ per da. Repairs of Rwy & Mach Dept main stem 4th s-div |
| 1852-32 | Wholly, W. | eng'man pass train $2 per da. Wash br appointed in 1849 |
| 1852-30 | Wickard (Wickan?), Jacob | local agt main stem Little Cacapon 10¢ per ton plus comm. Trans Dept |
| 1842-5 | Wicker, John | laborer 75¢ per da. Repairs of Rwy & Mach Dept main stem 4th s-div |
| 1842-16 | Wilde, J. W. F. | conduc of pass Wash $58.33 per mo. Trans Dept Wash br |
| 1852-23 | Wilking, C. | pass car driv $360 per yr. Trans Dept |

## B & O RR EMPLOYEES

| | | |
|---|---|---|
| 1842-15 | Wilkins, Charles | fireman Balto $35 per mo. Trans Dept main stem |
| 1852-23 | Willard, Perry | ton brakeman $360 per yr. Trans Dept |
| 1842-15 | Williams, S. M. | watchman Harper's Ferry $30 per mo. Trans Dept main stem |
| 1852-20 | Samuel | bridge toll collec Harper's Ferry $30 per mo. Trans Dept |
| 1852-28 | Uriah | eng'man $2.50 per da. Trans Dept |
| 1842-10 | William | smith $1.42 per da. Repairs of Rwy & Mach Dept Mt Clare mach shop |
| 1852-28 | " | eng'man $2.50 per da. Trans Dept |
| 1842-16 | Wills, Thomas | ostler & pass driv Balto $30 per mo. Trans Dept main stem |
| 1842-1 | Wilson, James | asst porter $240 per annum Ofc Dept |
| 1842-8 | " | laborer 75¢ per da. Repairs of Rwy & Mach Dept Wash br 2d s-div |
| 1842-8 | John | pattern mkr $1.62½ per da. Repairs of Rwy & Mach Dept Mt Clare |
| 1842-14 | Joseph | ton breakman Balto $35 per mo. Trans Dept main stem |
| 1842-8 | Robert | painter $1.50 per da. Repairs of Rwy & Mach Dept Mt Clare |
| 1842-13 | Samuel | master painter $1.37½ per da. Repairs of Rwy & Mach Dept Mt Clare mach shop |
| 1842-12 | William M. | carp $1.25 per da. Repairs of Rwy & Mach Dept Mt Clare mach shop |
| 1852-28 | Winn, Wm. | eng'man $2 per da. Trans Dept |
| 1852-24 | Wise, John | burden car driv $360 per yr. Trans Dept |
| 1842-14 | Wonderly, John | conduc of pass Balto $58.33 per mo. Trans Dept main stem |
| 1842-14 | Woodside, W. S. | supt of trans Balto $166.66 per mo. Trans Dept main stem |
| 1852-4 | William S.* | paymaster $1,500 per annum, $300 trav exp allow entered co serv in 1830 at $45 per mo. |
| 1842-16 | Woodward, Benj. F. | pass breakman Frederick $30 per mo. Trans Dept main stem |
| 1842-16 | Horace | pass breakman Balto $30 per mo. Trans Dept main stem |
| 1852-28 | " | eng'man $60 per mo. Trans Dept |
| 1852-29 | Worbly, Horace | fireman $400 per yr. Trans Dept |
| 1852-29 | Wright, George | fireman $400 per yr. " " |
| 1852-23 | Nelson | pass car driv $360 per yr. Trans Dept |
| 1852-30 | Young, J. B. | local agt w of Cumberland Independence 10¢ per ton plus comm. Trans Dept appointed in 1852 |
| 1852-23 | James | ton brakeman $360 per yr. Trans Dept |
| 1842-16 | Zepp, Henry | ostler & ton driv Balto $30 per mo. Trans Dept main stem |
| 1852-28 | " | eng'man $2.50 per da. Trans Dept |

| | | | |
|---|---|---|---|
| 1852-28 | Zepp, Jere'h. | | eng'man $2 per da. Trans Dept |
| 1842-15 | | Thomas | fireman Frederick $35 per mo. Trans Dept main stem |
| 1852-28 | | " | eng'man $2.50 per da. Trans Dept |
| 1842-4 | Zept, Ephrim | | laborer 75¢ per da. Repairs of Rwy & Mach Dept main stem 2d s-div |
| 1842-4 | | William | laborer 75¢ per da. Repairs of Rwy & Mach Dept main stem 2d s-div |
| 1842-5 | Ziegler, Jacob | | laborer 75¢ per da. Repairs of Rwy & Mach Dept main stem 4th s-div |
| 1852-29 | Zimmerman, Daniel | | fireman $400 per yr. Trans Dept |

## ABBREVIATIONS

\* indicates that further information regarding job duties of the individual is given in the printed List (a copy of the List is in the Maryland Historical Society Library).

1842-10)  identifies the List and page number on which the
1852-4  )  individual name appears (a copy of the List is in the Maryland Historical Society Library).

agt - agent
amt - amount
app - apprentice
asst - assistant
attend -(attending
           (attendant
Balto - Baltimore
bet - between
bkkpr - bookkeeper
carp - carpenter
clk - clerk
co - company
collec -(collecting
        (collector
comm - commission
conduc - conductor
cons - construction
da - day
deliv - delivery
Dept) - Department
Dpt )
driv - driver
e - east
eng - engine
eng'man - engineman

engr - engineer
ex - extra
exam -(examine
        (examination
fr - from
gen - general
kpr - keeper
load - loading
loc - location
mach -(machinery
        (machine
manag - managing
mech - mechanical
mkr - maker
mo - month
Mt - Mount
nail - nailing
nt - night
oper - operating
pass -(passenger
        (passage
pd - paid
Pt - Point
prev - previous
prin - principal

pump - pumping
rd - road
res - resident
riv - river
secy - secretary
serv - service
sev - several
St - Street
sta - station
supt - superintendent
supv - supervisor
timekpr - timekeeper
ton - tonnage
trans - transportation
trav - traveling
treas - treasurer
turn - turning
unload - unloading
w - west
watch - watching
wd - wood
wi - with
yr - year

## BIBLIOGRAPHY

Baltimore and Ohio Railroad Co. List of Persons with Their Pay in the Service of the Baltimore and Ohio Rail Road Company April 1, 1842. Baltimore?: 1842

_____. Memorial of the Baltimore and Ohio Railroad Company to the Legislature of Virginia...1844. (Baltimore?: 1844)

Baltimore and Ohio Railway Co.  List of Officers and Employees
    in the Service of the Baltimore and Ohio R. Road Co. with
    Their Salaries, Duties, &c.  September-1852.  Baltimore:
    James Lucas, 1852.

A Citizen of Baltimore (Smith).  A History and Description of
    the Baltimore and Ohio Rail Road; with An Appendix...Balti-
    more: John Murphy & Co., 1853.

Hungerford, Edward.   The Story of the Baltimore and Ohio Rail-
    road 1827-1927.  New York: G. P. Putnam's Sons, 1928.

Latrobe, John H. B.  The Baltimore and Ohio Railroad.  Personal
    Recollections.  A Lecture Delivered Before the Maryland
    Institute, March 23d, 1868.  Baltimore: The Sun Book and Job
    Printing Establishment, (1868).

Laws and Ordinances Relating to the Baltimore and Ohio Railroad
    Company.  Baltimore: John Murphy & Co., 1850.

White, Roy Barton.  At Baltimore on December 7, 1842--being
    extracts from a Railroad Minute Book...(Princeton: 1943).

THE FIRST PASSENGER COACH ON THE B. & O. R. R.

## BALTIMORE AND OHIO RAILROAD EMPLOYEES
### 1855 and 1857

"By the work one knows the workman."

The Baltimore and Ohio Railroad Company organized in 1827 began construction in 1828; reached Ellicotts Mills, 13 miles from Baltimore, in 1830; Washington, D.C. to the southwest (the Washington branch) in 1835; also in 1835, Harpers Ferry to the west, 82 miles from Baltimore. By 1842 the railroad had arrived in Cumberland, Md., 178 miles from Baltimore (the main stem).

In the beginning, horses were used to draw the railroad cars, the load for one horse being one car carrying 25 passengers with a relay every 6 or 7 miles. It was estimated that a speed of 10 miles per hour could be maintained with proper relays. Even after the line was completed to Frederick, relays of horses took cars back and forth to Baltimore.

However, locomotive steam power was tried early in railroad history. The combined cylindrical and conical wheel, the friction wheel, had been invented and other improvements made. Peter Cooper of New York constructed the "Tom Thumb",[1] a single engine with a single working cylinder of $3\frac{1}{2}$" diameter placed on 30" wheels, an engine weighing no more than one ton with a boiler smaller than a boiler of a kitchen range; the first locomotive for railroad purposes. It worked smoothly on August 28, 1830, when an open coach attached to the engine made its first ride between Baltimore and Ellicotts Mills filled with directors of the B&O RR and their friends. The trip was exciting and a high rate of speed of 15 to 18 miles per hour was attained. The engine returned to Baltimore over the 13 miles in record time of 57 minutes.

The first division of the road west of Cumberland to Piedmont was opened in 1851; in 1853 the road had reached Wheeling, 379 miles from Baltimore.[2]

The Virginia legislature granted the B&O a charter on February 14, 1851 authorizing construction of a railroad from the Ohio River at Parkersburg to Grafton. The road was opened for travel in May 1857, known as the Parkersburg branch.

The Marietta and Cincinnati Railroad Company was organized in 1847 and construction of the road from Marietta to Cincinnati was completed in 1857. The Ohio and Mississippi Railroad was given a charter in 1848 and the road from Cincinnati to St. Louis was also completed in 1857.[3]

In 1857 a special B&O train conveying the Secretary of State, representing personally the President of the United States, Mr. James Buchanan,[4] members of his cabinet together with foreign ministers, governors of many states and other distinguished people took part in a great railroad celebration held in Cincinnati. The time table for the special train required the train to leave Camden Station in Baltimore on June 1, 1857 at 6 a.m., arrive at Grafton 9 p.m., lie in Grafton over night, leave the next morning at 6 a.m. and arrive in Parkersburg at 10:20 a.m. There was a grand celebration at Marietta; at 9 a.m. the day following, the train left for Cincinnati, reaching there the same evening.[5]

Vast numbers of people, fire companies, militia, bands with music, parades, banqueting, speeches and entertainment contributed to the great railroad celebration held in Cincinnati on June 3 and 4, 1857; followed by similar festivities in St. Louis. During the following month occurred the great Railroad Excursion from the West to the City of Baltimore.[6]

B & O RR EMPLOYEES

A great many miles of track had been laid, bridges constructed, tunnels built, cars and locomotives made to carry riders over land, mountains and rivers--many years of hard work! Construction of a railroad from Baltimore to the Ohio River and then to Wheeling[7] and Cincinnati, "the Queen City of the West",[8] was a great achievement made possible by the dedication of men who envisioned a means of transportation new, faster and better than the world had ever known; a boon to commerce and trade, an easier way to travel, an improvement in communication, employment and opportunity.

Peter Arras, an immigrant born in Winterkasten, Germany, in 1791, one of two leaders of a group of 162 people making the journey to America, wrote in 1831, "If anyone wants to work he can earn a good living as a day laborer. The people that came with us found jobs and earn 75 cents a day, they are building a railroad track from Baltimore to Ohio. An ordinary man can live as well as a rich man." and "There is work to be had if you want to work. A day laborer can earn more here than a farmer can in Germany. Lich and G ro Repper are working as hand laborers, they work with railroad tracks, they each earn $1.00 a day, they are building a new track to Friedrickstown,..."[9]

1. Baltimore and Ohio Railroad Passenger Department, An Historical and Geographical Treatise on the Baltimore and Ohio Railroad (Baltimore?), p.11
2. Baltimore and Ohio Railroad Company. Table of Distances and Epitome of the Route by the Baltimore and Ohio Railroad, and its Connecting Lines, between Baltimore, Cincinnati, St. Louis, &c (Baltimore: Wiley, Printer, 1860), p.24
3. -----. 1828 Then and Now 1880 (Baltimore: John D. Lucas, 1880), p.1
4. Hungerford, Edward, The Story of the Baltimore and Ohio Railroad 1827-1927 (New York: G. P. Putnam's Sons, 1928), v.1, p.306
5. Baltimore and Ohio Railroad Company. 1828 Then and Now 1880 (Baltimore: John D. Lucas, 1880), p.1
6. Ibid.
7. Hungerford, Edward, The Story of the Baltimore and Ohio Railroad 1827-1927 (New York: G. P. Putnam's Sons, 1928), v.1, p.289
8. Ibid. v.1, p.290
9. Letter written by Peter Arras from Friedrickstown dated November 7, 1831 (Furnished through the courtesy of Mr. Theron H. Arras, 2769 Shrewsbury Road, Columbus, Ohio 43221)

## B & O RR EMPLOYEES

In 1855 the B&O published "List of Officers & Employees in the Service of the Baltimore & Ohio R. Road Co. with their Occupation and Salary as Appearing on the Company's Pay Rolls for the Month of February 1855". The departments to which employees were assigned are listed below:

Officers' Pay-roll -- Hanover St. p.1;  Departments p.1
Transportation Dept. -- Washington Branch Road p.4-5; Main Stem p.6-36
Road Way Dept. -- p.37-75
Machinery Dept. -- p.76-96
errata

In 1858 was published "A List of the Officers and Employees of the Baltimore and Ohio Rail Road, with the Amount of Their Pay for the Month of November 1857". The departments and sub-divisions to which employees were assigned are listed below:

Roll of General Officers (not connected with either of the three operating
  departments)-- p.3
General Transportation Offices at Baltimore -- Master of Transportation's
  Office p.7; General Freight Agent's Office p.7; General Ticket Agent's
  Office p.7; Clerk of Errors' Office p.7; Supervisors of Trains on the
  Road p.7

Camden Station -- p.8
Mount Clare Station -- p.9
Horse Power Expense Roll at
  Baltimore -- p.9-10
Locust Point -- p.11
Washington Junction -- p.11
Ellicotts Mills -- p.11
Switch above Ellicotts Mills -- p.12
Putney's Switch -- p.12
Plane No. 1 -- p.12
Monocacy -- p.12
Frederick Station -- p.12
Point of Rocks -- p.12
Harper's Ferry -- p.13
Martinsburg -- p.13
Hancock -- p.13
Cumberland -- p.14

Piedmont Station -- p.14
Rowlesburg Station -- p.14
Newburg Station -- p.14
Independence Station -- p.14
Grafton Station -- p.15
Fetterman Station -- p.15
Fairmont Station -- p.15
Farmington Station -- p.15
Mannington Station -- p.15
Cameron Station -- p.15
Moundsville Station -- p.16
Benwood Station -- p.16
Transfer Steamer Brown Dick--Ohio
  River between Benwood and Bellaire
  -- p.16
Freight Transfer Force at Bellaire
  opposite Benwood -- p.17
Wheeling Station -- p.17

Passenger Train Conductors -- (Th. Mail and Ex., West End, Fred'k Accom'n,
  Ellicotts Mills, Street Car) p.18
Passenger Train Brakemen -- (Th. Mail and Ex., West End) p.18
Baggage Masters -- (Th. Mail and Ex., West End, Fred'k Accom'n, Ellicotts
  Mills) p.19
Passenger Enginemen -- (1st, 2d, 3d, 4th div) p.19
Passenger Firemen -- (1st, 2d, 3d, 4th div) p.20
Tonnage Conductors -- (1st div, Locust Point, Camden Station, 2d div, 3d and
  4th div, Board Tree Tunnel) p.21-23
Tonnage Brakemen -- (1st div, Camden Station, 2d div, 3d and 4th div, Board
  Tree Tunnel) p.24-27
Tonnage Enginemen -- (1st, 2d, 3d, 4th div, Board Tree Tunnel) p.28-31
Tonnage Firemen -- (1st, 2d, 3d, 4th div, Board Tree Tunnel) p.31-34
Board Tree Tunnel -- p.34
Edwards' Wood Train -- (3d and 4th div) p.35
J. R. Shrode's Wood Train -- (4th div) p.35-36
Telegraph Operators -- p.36

Washington Branch Road, Transportation Rolls -- Washington City Station
p.37-38
Northwestern Virginia Road, Transportation Rolls --
   Parkersburg Station p.39-41        Athey's Wood Train p.41
General Officers of the Road Department -- p.45
Road Department, Main Stem --
     (beginning and termination of each division)*

| | | | | | |
|---|---|---|---|---|---|
| 1st at | City Block | | 20 miles | -- p.46-47- | (This division includes Locust |
| 2d " | 20th mile post | | 40 " | -- p.47-48 | Point branch and Mount Clare |
| 3d " | 40th | " | 60 " | -- p.49 | Station) |
| 4th " | 60th | " | 80 " | -- p.50 | - (Includes Frederick branch) |
| 5th " | 80th | " | 100 " | -- p.50-51- | (Includes Martinsburg Station) |
| 6th " | 100th | " | 120 " | -- p.52 | |
| 7th " | 120th | " | 140 " | -- p.53 | |
| 8th " | 140th | " | 160 " | -- p.54 | |
| 9th " | 160th | " | 180 " | -- p.55 | - (Includes Cumberland Station) |
| 10th " | 180th | " | 200 " | -- p.56 | |
| 11th " | 200th | " | 220 " | -- p.57-58- | (Includes Piedmont Station) |
| 12th " | 220th | " | 240 " | -- p.58-59 | |
| 13th " | 240th | " | 260 " | -- p.59-60 | |
| 14th " | 260th | " | 280 " | -- p.61 | |
| 15th " | 280th | " | 300 " | -- p.62 | |
| 16th " | 300th | " | 320 " | -- p.63 | |
| 17th " | 320th | " | 340 " | -- p.64-65 | |
| 18th " | 340th | " | 360 " | -- p.66-67 | |
| 19th " | 360th | " | 379 " | -- p.67-68- | (Includes Wheeling Station) |

   Mt. Clare Station -- p.69-71
   Mt. Clare, repairing tracks in yard
     -- p.71
   Camden Station, repairing tracks
     -- p.71
   Locust Pt., loading materials -- p.72
   Martinsburg Depot -- p.72
   Cumberland Depot -- p.72
   Piedmont Depot -- p.72
   Repairs of telegraph line -- p.72
   Repairs of water stations -- p.73
   Repairs of bridges, etc. -- p.73-74
   Putting in switches on line of road
     -- p.74
   Ballast train for second track --
     -- p.75-77
   laying second track -- p.77-81
   Board Tree Tunnel -- p.81-85
   McGuire's Tunnel -- p.86-87
   Welling Tunnel -- p.87-91
   Littleton Tunnel -- p.91-92
   Quarrying and hauling stone for
     Board Tree and Littleton Tunnels
     -- p.93-94
   Repairs of bridges -- p.94
Washington Branch Road, Road Dept. -- p.95
Northwestern Virginia Road, Road Dept. --
   1st sub-div -- p.96-97
   2d sub-div -- p.97-98
   3d sub-div - p.98
   4th sub-div -- p.99
   5th sub-div -- p.100
   Ballast train -- p.101
   Bridges -- p.102
   Pumping water -- p.102
   Railway depots -- p.102-103
   Tunnels -- p.103-104
   Building sand and wood houses --
     p.104
Machinery Dept. Rolls -- General Officers of the Machinery Dept. p.107;
   Supervisors of Machinery on the Road p.107
Machinery Dept. --
   Baltimore -- p.108-122
   Martinsburg -- p.123-126
   Piedmont -- p.127-130
   Newburg -- p.130
   Grafton -- p.131-132
   Fetterman -- p.133
   Board Tree Tunnel -- p.133
   Cameron -- p.133
   Wheeling -- p.134-136
   Cumberland -- p.136-137
Northwestern Virginia Road, Machinery Dept. -- Parkersburg p.139

\* The 29th Annual Report of the President and Directors to the Stockholders
   of the Baltimore and Ohio Railroad Co. - October 1, 1855 (Baltimore: John
   Murphy & Co., 1855), p.59

The alphabetical listing which follows gives names of employees taken from the 1855 and 1857 documents, with year, page number, name, job title and salary, name of department and sub-division to which each employee was assigned. In many instances the name of the same individual appears more than once, his time being recorded on the B&O Rolls according to the nature of his employment, whether in the shop as a "machinist" or on the road as an "engineman". Also, it often occurs that the same engineman, fireman, brakeman, &c ran part of a month east of Cumberland and part west; consequently, his name appears twice on the Rolls.

After the alphabetical listing of names and job titles, is a list of the abbreviations used in this compilation.

| | | | |
|---|---|---|---|
| 1857-31 | Abbott, David | ton fire 17 da @ $1.75 - $29.75. | 1st div |
| 1857-33 | George | ton fire 16½ da @ $1.75 - $28.85. | 3d div |
| 1857-31 | Granville | ton fire 8½ da @ $1.75 - $14.85. | 1st div |
| 1855-13 | James | conduc & brak 8 da @ $40 per mo - $13.35. Trans Dept main stem |
| 1857-31 | John J. | ton fire 7 da @ $1.25; 9 da @ $33.35 per mo - $24.25. 1st div |
| 1857-31 | Joseph | ton fire 1¼ da @ $1.75 - $2.20. 1st div |
| 1855-74 | Abigail, Richard | lab 24 da @ $1 - $24.00. Rd Way Dept |
| 1857-95 | " | fore 23 da @ $1.25 - $28.75. Wash br, Rd Dept |
| 1857-39 | Acton, Edward | watch, Wharf boat 30 da @ $30 per mo - $30.00. NW Va rd, Parkersburg sta |
| 1855-7 | Adair, John | pass conduc 28 da @$62.50 per mo - $62.50. Trans Dept main stem |
| 1857-59 | " | horse & cart 25 da @ $1.12 - $28.10. Rd Dept main stem 12th s-div |
| 1857-59 | " | horse hire 25 da @ $1 - $25.00. Rd Dept main stem 12th s-div |
| 1857-58 | " | supv @ $50 per mo - $50.00. Rd Dept main stem 12th s-div |
| 1855-78 | Adams, Charles | mach 31½ da @ $2 - $63.00. Mach Dept |
| 1857-134 | " | fore mach @ $70 per mo - $70.00. Mach Dept, Wheeling |
| 1855-79 | Henry | help 29 da @ $1.15 - $33.35. Mach Dept |
| 1857-120 | " | carp help 17 3/4 da @ $1.15 - $24.40. Mach Dept, Balto |
| 1855-89 | J. B. | mach 22¼ da @ $1.70 - $37.80. Mach Dept |
| 1855-68 | Michael | tend to masons 19 3/4 da @ $1 - $19.75. Rd Way Dept |
| 1857-85 | " | lab 11 da @ $1 - $11.00. grad, Board Tree Tun |
| 1855-32 | T. | lab 24 da @ $30 per mo - $30.00. Trans Dept main stem |
| 1857-85 | Thomas | lab 14½ da @ $.80 - $11.60. grad, Board Tree Tun |
| 1855-72 | W. W. | help 23½ da @ $.50 - $11.75. Rd Way Dept |
| 1857-108 | Addison, E. R. | mast mech @ $83.35 per mo - $83.35. Mach Dept, Balto |
| 1855-86 | J. O. | clk @ $50 per mo - $50.00. Mach Dept |
| 1855-18 | Theodore | ton eng'man 16¾ da @ $3 - $48.75. Trans Dept main stem |
| 1857-28 | " | ton eng'man 19 3/4 da @ $3 - $59.25. 1st div |
| 1855-21 | William | fire 13 da @ $1.75 - $22.75. Trans Dept main stem |

# B & O RR EMPLOYEES

| | | |
|---|---|---|
| 1855-18 | Addison, William | ton eng'man 12½ da @ $2.50 - $30.60. Trans Dept main stem 1st div |
| 1857-28 | " | ton eng'man 24½ da @ $2.50 - $61.25. 1st div |
| 1855-78 | Adison, E. R. | fore @ $83.35 per mo - $83.35. Mach Dept |
| 1855-35 | Adler, W. H. | reg 24 da @ $35 per mo - $35.00. Trans Dept main stem |
| 1855-5 | Adolph, John | lab 18¼ da @ $1 - $18.25. Trans Dept, Wash br |
| 1857-54 | Adwalt, John | lab 19 da @ $1 - $19.00. Rd Dept main stem 8th s-div |
| 1857-19 | Ady, John | bag mast 5 da @ $45 per mo - $7.50. w end |
| 1857-18 | " | pass train brak 22½ da @ $33.35 per mo - $25.00. w end |
| 1857-118 | Aff, H. | blksmith help 18¾ da @ $1.15 - $21.00. Mach Dept, Balto |
| 1857-21 | Afflick, James | ton conduc 13 da @ $50 per mo - $26.00. 1st div |
| 1855-85 | Aft, Hubert | help 14¼ da @ $1.15 - $16.40. Mach Dept |
| 1855-70 | Agin, Patrick | lab 9½ da @ $1 - $9.50. Rd Way Dept |
| 1857-16 | Agnew, J. P. | clk 30 da @ $50 per mo - $50.00. Benwood sta |
| 1855-50 | " | watch cuts 28 da @ $1 - $28.00. Rd Way Dept |
| 1857-67 | John L. | watch 30 da @ $1 - $30.00. Rd Dept main stem 18th s-div |
| 1857-39 | Ailoms, William | agt 30 da @ $100 per mo - $100.00. NW Va rd, Parkersburg sta |
| 1857-53 | Airnold, Lewis | lab 25 da @ $1 - $25.00. Rd Dept main stem 7th s-div |
| 1855-85 | Airs, George | help 23 da @ $1.15 - $26.45. Mach Dept |
| 1855-93 | Albaugh, Daniel | help 28½ da @ $1.20 - $34.20. Mach Dept |
| 1857-55 | Edward | watch 31 da @ $1 - $31.00. Rd Dept main stem 9th s-div |
| 1857-76 | George | fire 24 da @ $1.25 - $30.00. ballast train for 2d track |
| 1855-60 | " | fore 24 da @ $1 - $24.00. Rd Way Dept |
| 1857-64 | Silas J. | fore 27 da @ $1.25 - $33.75. Rd Dept main stem 17th s-div |
| 1855-60 | William | ton brak 23½ da @ $40 per mo - $37.20. 1st div |
| 1857-64 | " | fore 24 da @ $1.25 - $30.00. Rd Way Dept |
| 1855-45 | Alborgh, D. | fore 27 da @ $1.25 - $33.75. Rd Dept main stem 17th s-div |
| 1857-48 | Albright, Jacob | lab 14 3/4 da @ $1 - $14.75. Rd Way Dept |
| 1857-116 | Julius | lab 30 da @ $1.05 - $31.50. Rd Dept main stem 2d s-div |
| 1855-45 | M. | blksmith 18 da @ $1.80 - $32.40. Mach Dept, Balto |
| 1855-38 | Albrites, Jacob | lab 15½ da @ $1 - $15.50. Rd Way Dept |
| 1855-76 | Alderdice, Jno. | nail 28 da @ $1.05 - $29.40. Rd Way Dept |
| 1855-10 | Alderton, W. | carp 27½ da @ $1.55 - $42.25. Mach Dept |
| 1855-39 | Aldridge, A. | conduc & brak 20¾ da @ $50 per mo - $45.20. Trans Dept main stem |
| 1857-47 | Alfred | lab 11 da @ $1 - $11.00. Rd Way Dept |
| 1857-55 | Edward | lab 23¼ da @ $1 - $23.25. Rd Dept main stem 2d s-div |
| 1857-32 | " | fire 11 da @ $1.31 - $14.40. Rd Dept main stem 9th s-div |
| | | ton fire 2 da @ $1.75 - $3.50. 2d div |

# B & O RR EMPLOYEES 51

| Ref | Name | Details |
|---|---|---|
| 1857-47 | Aldridge, John N. | lab 25½ da @ $1 - $25.50. Rd Dept main stem 2d s-div |
| 1857-110 | " L. G. | mach 4½ da @ $1.60 - $7.20. Mach Dept, Balto |
| 1855-9 | " Wm. | conduc & brak 13½ da @ $50 per mo - $28.10. Trans Dept main stem |
| 1857-32 | Aldrige, John | ton fire 11 da @ $1.75 - $19.25. 2d div |
| 1855-31 | Aler, Jerry | saw wd 40 cords @ $.35 - $14.00. Trans Dept main stem |
| 1855-76 | " John T. | mach 23⅓ da @ $1.72 - $40.00. Mach Dept |
| 1857-122 | " Martin | eng clean 24 da @ $.75 - $18.00. Mach Dept, Balto |
| 1855-95 | " " | pat mkr 23½ da @ $1.50 - $35.25. Mach Dept |
| 1857-115 | " Samuel | pat mkr 18¼ da @ $1.55 - $28.30. Mach Dept, Balto |
| 1855-86 | " " | mach 24 da @ $1.60 - $38.40. Mach Dept |
| 1857-123 | " W. H. | fore mach @ $50 per mo - $50.00. Mach Dept, Martinsburg |
| 1857-122 | Alexander, J. | fore eng clean 25 3/4 da @ $1.25 - $32.20. Mach Dept, Balto |
| 1855-40 | " Joseph | lab 22 da @ $1 - $22.00. Rd Way Dept |
| 1857-50 | Alford, Henry | lab 23 3/4 da @ $1 - $23.75. Rd Dept main stem 4th s-div |
| 1855-21 | " " | fire 13 3/4 da @ $1.75 - $24.05. Trans Dept main stem |
| 1857-34 | Alfred, Henry | ton fire 7 da @ $1.75 - $12.25. Board Tree Tun |
| 1857-33 | Allbaugh, E. | ton fire 14½ da @ $1.75 - $25.35. 3d div |
| 1855-9 | Allen, A. M. | conduc & brak 1 da @ $40 per mo - $1.65. Trans Dept main stem |
| 1857-40 | " Charles | ton brak 12½ da @ $40 per mo - $19.60. NW Va rd, Parkersburg sta |
| 1857-20 | " George | pass fire 30½ da @ $40 per mo - $40.65. 1st div |
| 1855-38 | " " | lab 24 da @ $1 - $24.00. Rd Way Dept |
| 1857-48 | " " | lab 24½ da @ $1 - $24.50. Rd Dept main stem 2d s-div |
| 1857-134 | " James | mach 20 da @ $1.50 - $30.00. Mach Dept, Wheeling |
| 1855-76 | " " | mach 27 da @ $1.72 - $46.45. Mach Dept |
| 1857-110 | " John | mach 18 da @ $1.72 - $30.95. Mach Dept, Balto |
| 1855-82 | " " | help 22 da @ $1 - $32.00. Mach Dept |
| 1857-112 | " Thomas | mach help 19½ da @ $1.15 - $22.40. Mach Dept, Balto |
| 1855-9 | " William | conduc & brak 16¾ da @ $40 per mo - $27.10. Trans Dept main stem |
| 1857-62 | Allenbee, Joseph | fore 24 da @ $1.25 - $30.00. Rd Way Dept |
| 1857-102 | " " | fore @ $60 per mo - $60.00. NW Va RR bridges |
| 1855-50 | Allows, Wm. | watch cuts 28 da @ $1 - $28.00. Rd Way Dept |
| 1857-64 | Althouse, William | lab 24 3/4 da @ $1 - $24.75. Rd Dept main stem 17th s-div |
| 1855-42 | Aman, Andrew | lab 19 da @ $1 - $19.00. Rd Way Dept |
| 1855-10 | " " | conduc & brak 15½ da @ $40 per mo - $25.85. Trans Dept main stem |
| 1855-74 | Ambrose, Henry | lab 24 da @ $1 - $24.00. Rd Way Dept |
| 1857-95 | | lab 24 da @ $1 - $24.00. Wash br, Rd Dept |
| 1855-51 | | lab @ $35 per mo - $35.00. Rd Way Dept |

## B & O RR EMPLOYEES

| ID | Name | | Description |
|---|---|---|---|
| 1857-28 | Ambrose, James L. | | ton eng'man 18 3/4 da @ $3 - $56.25. 1st div |
| 1855-22 | | T. L. | fire 10 da @ $1.75 - $17.50. Trans Dept main stem |
| 1855-93 | Ameallia, John | | carp 23½ da @ $1.50 - $35.25. Mach Dept |
| 1857-103 | Ames, John | | lab 23½ da @ $1 - $23.50. NW Va RR Tun |
| 1855-79 | Amey, Peter | | help 16 da @ $1.15 - $18.40. Mach Dept |
| 1857-110 | Amos, James | | mach 20½ da @ $1.25 - $25.60. Mach Dept, Balto |
| 1857-127 | Anderson, D. L. | | mach 13¼ da @ $1.60 - $21.20. Mach Dept, Piedmont |
| 1855-17 | | D. N. | ton eng'man 17½ da @ $3 - $51.75. Trans Dept main stem |
| 1855-79 | | G. W. | coach mkr 21 da @ $1.55 - $32.55. Mach Dept |
| 1855-65 | | George | lab 7 da @ $2.50 - $17.50. Rd Way Dept |
| 1855-90 | | " | mach 2 3/4 da @ $1.50 - $4.10. Mach Dept |
| 1855-17 | | " | ton eng'man 7½ da @ $3 - $22.50. Trans Dept main stem |
| 1855-86 | | " | train inspec @ $34.50 per mo - $34.50. Mach Dept |
| 1857-29 | | " | ton eng'man 33½ da @ $3 - $100.50. 3d div |
| 1857-125 | | George H. | inspec cars @ $34.50 per mo - $34.50. Mach Dept, Martinsburg |
| 1857-136 | | J. F. | mach app 26 3/4 da @ $.75 - $20.05. Mach Dept, Cumb |
| 1855-84 | | J. W. | blksmith 24 da @ $1.45 - $34.80. Mach Dept |
| 1855-94 | | James | app 32¼ da @ $.45 - $14.45. Mach Dept |
| 1857-107 | | " | supv of mach on rd @ $83.35 per mo. Mach Dept, Board Tree Tun |
| 1857-49 | | Jesse | lab 25 da @ $1 - $25.00. Rd Dept main stem 3d s-div |
| 1855-13 | | John | conduc & brak 26 da @ $40 per mo - $43.35. Trans Dept main stem |
| 1857-125 | | " | inspec eng 31 da @ $1.50 - $46.50. Mach Dept, Martinsburg |
| 1857-71 | | John W. | chair mkr 18 da @ $1.25 - $22.50. Mt Clare sta, Balto |
| 1857-113 | | Milton | mach app 23½ da @ $.45 - $10.55. Mach Dept, Balto |
| 1855-33 | | R. | greas cars 28 da @ $30 per mo - $30.00. Trans Dept main stem |
| 1855-18 | | Richard | ton eng'man 21½ da @ $3 - $64.50. Trans Dept main stem |
| 1857-19 | | " | pass eng'man 37 da @ $3 - $111.00. 2d div |
| 1857-33 | | Wm. | ton fire 5½ da @ $1.75 - $9.60. 3d div |
| 1857-84 | Andren, George W. | | eng'man 3½ da @ $3 - $10.50. grad, Board Tree Tun |
| 1855-17 | Andrews, G. W. | | ton eng'man 12 3/4 da @ $3 - $38.25. Trans Dept main stem |
| 1857-30 | | George | ton eng'man 17½ da @ $3 - $52.50. 4th div |
| 1857-35 | | Jacob | lab 21 3/4 da @ $1 - $21.75. Edwards' wd train 3d & 4th div |
| 1857-25 | | " | ton brak 3½ da @ $40 per mo - $5.60. 3d & 4th div |
| 1857-116 | | James | blksmith 18½ da @ $1.85 - $33.75. Mach Dept, Balto |
| 1857-113 | | William | iron mould 13 3/4 da @ $1.50 - $20.60. Mach Dept, Balto |
| 1855-85 | Anlis, John | | help 23½ da @ $1 - $23.50. Mach Dept |
| 1857-47 | Apelbee, Washington | | lab 25 da @ $1 - $25.00. Rd Dept main stem 2d s-div |

# B & O RR EMPLOYEES

| |  |  |
|---|---|---|
| 1855-56 | Apell, Casper | lab 24 3/4 da @ $1.50 - $37.15. Rd Way Dept |
| 1855-83 | Apler, Peter | mach (includ boil mkr, work of sht iron, &c) 24 da @ $1.65 - $39.60. Mach Dept |
| 1857-115 | " | boil mkr 26 3/4 da @ $1.65 - $44.15. Mach Dept, Balto |
| 1857-56 | Apple, George | lab 24 da @ $1 - $24.00. Rd Dept main stem 10th s-div |
| 1855-39 | Appleby, W. | lab 16 da @ $1 - $16.00. Rd Way Dept |
| 1857-19 | Archer, Thomas | bag mast 30 da @ $45 per mo - $45.00. thr mail & exp |
| 1857-18 | Wm. | pass train brak 14 da @ $33.35 per mo - $15.55. thr mail & exp |
| 1857-85 | Armicost, James | bricklay 7½ da @ $2.25 - $16.85. grad, Board Tree Tun |
| 1855-42 | Armstead, J. | lab 24 da @ $1 - $24.00. Rd Way Dept |
| 1857-120 | Armstrong, Henry | carp help 17½ da @ $1.15 - $20.10. Mach Dept, Balto |
| 1855-52 | James | lab 10 3/4 da @ $1 - $10.25. Rd Way Dept |
| 1857-53 | James D. | lab 24 da @ $1 - $24.00. Rd Dept main stem 7th s-div |
| 1855-10 | John | conduc & brak 3 da @ $40 per mo - $5.00. Trans Dept main stem |
| 1857-22 | Richard | ton conduc 24½ da @ $50 per mo - $49.00. 3d & 4th div |
| 1857-88 | T. D. | horse hire 158 da @ $1 - $158.00. grad, Welling Tun |
| 1857-87 | " | supt @ $75 per mo - $75.00. grad, Welling Tun |
| 1855-66 | Thomas | lab 25½ da @ $2 - $51.00. Rd Way Dept |
| 1855-91 | William | cop'smith 14½ da - $24.60. Mach Dept |
| 1857-33 | " | ton fire 30 da @ $1.75 - $52.50. 3d div |
| 1857-39 | William J. | clk 30 da @ $55 per mo - $55.00. NW Va rd, Parkersburg sta |
| 1855-79 | Arnold, Adam | help 30 da @ $1 - $30.00. Mach Dept |
| 1857-121 | " | lab @ $30 per mo - $30.00. Mach Dept, Balto |
| 1857-40 | H. | pass eng'man 26 da @ $3 - $78.00. NW Va rd, Parkersburg sta |
| 1855-17 | Harding | ton eng'man 12¼ da @ $3 - $36.75. Trans Dept main stem |
| 1855-10 | John | conduc & brak 10½ da @ $40 per mo - $17.50. Trans Dept main stem |
| 1857-122 | " | eng clean 29 da @ $1.15 - $33.35. Mach Dept, Balto |
| 1857-92 | Simon | lab 23 3/4 da @ $33.35 per mo - $26.70. grad, Littleton Tun |
| 1855-4 | Wm. | brak 28 da @ $1.12 - $33.35. Trans Dept, Wash br |
| 1855-57 | " | lab 19½ da @ $1 - $19.50. Rd Way Dept |
| 1857-10 | Arrington, A. | stab'man 25 da @ $1 - $25.00. hp exp, Balto |
| 1857-48 | Austin | nail 30 da @ $1.05 - $31.50. Rd Dept main stem 2d s-div |
| 1855-73 | " | fore 24 da @ $1.25 - $30.00. Rd Way Dept |
| 1855-38 | Thomas | fore 23 da @ $1.25 - $28.75. Rd Way Dept |
| 1857-48 | " | lab 25¼ da @ $1 - $25.25. Rd Dept main stem 2d s-div |
| 1855-79 | Arther, William | tin 28 da @ $2.25 - $63.00. Mach Dept |
| 1857-111 | Arthur, John | mach help 22½ da @ $1 - $22.50. Mach Dept, Balto |
| 1855-93 | William | clk @ $40 per mo - $40.00. Mach Dept |

## B & O RR EMPLOYEES

| ID | Name | Details |
|---|---|---|
| 1857-119 | Arthur, William | fore tin 27 da @ $2.25 - $60.75. Mach Dept, Balto |
| 1857-134 | " | mach app 19 da @ $.45 - $8.55. Mach Dept, Wheeling |
| 1855-17 | " | watch 30 da @ $30 per mo - $30.00. Wheeling sta |
| 1855-21 | Artis, G. W. | fire 9 da @ $1.75 - $15.75. Trans Dept main stem |
| 1857-30 | Artiz, George | ton eng'man 21½ da @ $3 - $64.50. Board Tree Tun |
| 1857-29 | Ash, George | ton eng'man 10 da @ $3 - $30.00. 3d div |
| 1857-40 | Ash, J. P. | ton conduc 23 da @ $50 per mo - $46.00. NW Va rd, Parkersburg sta |
| 1857-40 | J. W. | ton brak 7 da @ $40 per mo - $11.20. NW Va rd, Parkersburg sta |
| 1857-41 | Morgan | ton fire 28½ da @ $1.75 - $49.85. NW Va rd, Parkersburg sta |
| 1855-76 | Ashby, John | ton brak 24 3/4 da @ $40 per mo - $38.80. 3d & 4th div |
| 1857-114 | Ashton, Jno. | mach 21 da @ $1.65 - $34.65. Mach Dept |
| 1857-113 | " Thomas | cupalo tend 18 da @ $1.50 - $27.00. Mach Dept, Balto |
| 1855-58 | Asmear, John | mach app 23 da @ $.75 - $17.25. Mach Dept, Balto |
| 1857-58 | Assler, Casper | fore 24 da @ $1.25 - $30.00. Rd Way Dept |
| 1855-8 | Athey, Elijah | horse & cart 26½ da @ $1.50 - $39.75. Rd Dept main stem 11th s-div |
| 1857-54 | George W. | conduc 19 3/4 da @ $50 per mo - $41.15. Trans Dept main stem |
| 1855-13 | " Thomas | lab 20 da @ $1 - $20.00. Rd Dept main stem 8th s-div |
| 1857-41 | " | conduc & brak 26½ da @ $40 per mo - $44.15. Trans Dept main stem |
| 1855-44 | W. L. | conduc 25 da @ $60 per mo - $60.00. NW Va rd, Athey's wd train |
| 1855-8 | W. L. | lab 15½ da @ $1 - $15.50. Rd Way Dept |
| 1857-22 | Atkins, William | conduc 15½ da @ $50 per mo - $32.30. Trans Dept main stem |
| 1855-1 | Atkinson, J. I. | ton conduc 21½ da @ $50 per mo - $42.50. 3d & 4th div |
| 1857-3 | " " | treas & secy $2500 per annum - $208.33. Ofc Hanover St |
| 1855-79 | Joseph | treas $208.33 per mo. Gen Ofc |
| 1857-120 | " | coach mkr 22 3/4 da @ $1.45 - $33.00. Mach Dept |
| 1855-1 | Thomas C. | carp 18 da @ $1.50 - $27.00. Mach Dept, Balto |
| 1857-135 | Atwell, Thomas | asst mast of rd $1300 per annum - $108.33 |
| 1857-61 | Atwood, Perry | carp 19 3/4 da @ $1.45 - $28.65. Mach Dept, Wheeling |
| 1857-22 | " | conduc 5 da @ $1.94 - $9.70. Rd Dept main stem 14th s-div |
| 1855-66 | " William | ton conduc 31 da @ $50 per mo - $62.00. 3d & 4th div |
| 1857-121 | Aubery, T. | lab 20⅞ da @ $1.75 - $35.85. Rd Way Dept |
| 1857-25 | Aulick, Edwin | paint 12 3/4 da @ $1.60 - $20.40. Mach Dept, Balto |
| 1857-13 | Ault, Michael | ton brak 22½ da @ $40 per mo - $36.00. 3d & 4th div |
| 1857-65 | Auston, A. | toll collec 30 da @ $27.50 - $27.50. Harpers Ferry |
| 1855-33 | Autt, N. | lab 19½ da @ $1 - $19.25. Rd Dept main stem 17th s-div |
| | | toll collec 28 da @ $27.50 per mo - $27.50. Trans Dept main stem |

B & O RR EMPLOYEES                                                          55

| ID | Name | Description |
|---|---|---|
| 1857-124 | Averly, Christian | blksmith help 20 da @ $1 - $20.00. Mach Dept, Martinsburg |
| 1857-59 | Axmear, John | fore 26½ da @ $1.25 - $33.15. Rd Dept main stem 13th s-div |
| 1857-134 | Ayres, George | mach 21 3/4 da @ $1.75 - $38.05. Mach Dept, Wheeling |
| 1857-93 | Baham, John | blksmith 23 da @ $1.50 - $34.50. quarry & haul stone for Board Tree & Littleton Tun |
| 1857-49 | Bailey, William | lab 25 da @ $1 - $25.00. Rd Dept main stem 3d s-div |
| 1855-52 | Bails, A. | bricklay 3 da @ $1.50 - $4.50. Rd Way Dept |
| 1855-52 | " William | bricklay 3 da @ $1.50 - $4.50. Rd Way Dept |
| 1857-25 | Baily, Jerome | ton brak 29½ da @ $40 per mo - $47.20. 3d & 4th div |
| 1857-25 | " Thomas | ton brak 35 da @ $40 per mo - $56.00. 3d & 4th div |
| 1855-29 | Bainbridge, W. | prepar fuel 11½ da @ $1 - $11.50. Trans Dept main stem |
| 1857-22 | Bains, Jacob | ton conduc 2 3/4 da @ $1 - $50 per mo - $5.50. 3d & 4th div |
| 1855-88 | Baker, Adam | lab 30 3/4 da @ $1 - $30.75. Mach Dept |
| 1857-124 | " Francis | sht iron work 18 da @ $1.25 - $22.50. Mach Dept, Martinsburg |
| 1857-137 | " Henry | lab 23½ da @ $1 - $23.25. Mach Dept, Cumb |
| 1857-130 | " Jacob | lab 25 da @ $1 - $25.00. Mach Dept, Piedmont |
| 1857-10 | " James | bur brak 27½ da @ $1.15 - $31.60. hp exp, Balto |
| 1855-22 | " " | fire 18 da @ $1.75 - $31.50. Trans Dept main stem |
| 1855-76 | " " | mach 16½ da @ $2 - $32.50. Mach Dept |
| 1855-68 | " " | mason 3 da @ $2 - $6.00. Rd Way Dept |
| 1857-108 | " " | fore mach @ $70 per mo - $70.00. Mach Dept, Balto |
| 1857-35 | " " | lab 20½ da @ $1 - $20.50. J. R. Shrode's wd train 4th div |
| 1857-29 | " " | ton eng'man 37 da @ $3 - $111.60. 2d div |
| 1855-22 | " John | fire 19 da @ $33.35 per mo - $26.40. Trans Dept main stem |
| 1855-84 | " " | help 23½ da @ $1.15 - $26.75. Mach Dept |
| 1857-115 | " " | boil mkr help 18 3/4 da @ $1.15 - $21.55. Mach Dept, Balto |
| 1857-78 | " " | eng'man 26 da @ $2.50 - $65.00. lay 2d track |
| 1857-35 | " " | lab 19½ da @ $1 - $19.50. J. R. Shrode's wd train 4th div |
| 1857-24 | " " | ton brak 19½ da @ $40 per mo - $31.20. 1st div |
| 1857-124 | " John A. | blksmith help 19½ da @ $1 - $19.50. Mach Dept, Martinsburg |
| 1857-55 | " Joseph | lab 22½ da @ $1 - $22.25. Rd Dept main stem 9th s-div |
| 1857-131 | " " | rig @ $45 per mo - $45.00. Mach Dept, Grafton |
| 1857-9 | " N. R. | clk 30 da @ $54.15 per mo - $54.15. Mt Clare sta |
| 1857-74 | " Samuel | lab 18 3/4 da @ $1.12 - $21.10. repair bridges &c |
| 1855-6 | " Wilson | clk 28 da @ $1.65 per mo - $41.65. Trans Dept main stem |
| 1857-132 | Baldwin, Benjamin F. | lab 5 da @ $1.25 - $6.25. Mach Dept, Grafton |
| 1857-109 | " George | mach 16 3/4 da @ $1.60 - $26.80. Mach Dept, Balto |

# B & O RR EMPLOYEES

| ID | Name | Description |
|---|---|---|
| 1855-15 | Baldwin, J. E. | pass eng'man 33 da @ $3 - $99.00. Trans Dept main stem |
| 1855-50 | James | watch cuts 28 da @ $1 - $28.00. Rd Way Dept |
| 1857-113 | Jeff. | iron mould 17 3/4 da @ $1.65 - $29.30. Mach Dept, Balto |
| 1857-28 | John | ton eng'man 14¼ da @ $2.50; 10½ da @ $2.25 - $59.25. 1st div |
| 1855-16 | L. E. | pass fire 25 da @ $40 per mo - $35.70. Trans Dept main stem |
| 1855-22 | Samuel | fire 3 da @ $1.75 - $5.25. Trans Dept main stem |
| 1857-73 | " | carp 6 da @ $1.65 - $9.90. repair water sta, M.S. & P.B. |
| 1857-15 | T. J. | yd fire 25 da @ $35 per mo - $35.00. Grafton sta |
| 1857-131 | William | clk @ $40 per mo - $40.00. Mach Dept, Grafton |
| 1857-117 | Bales, Jefferson | blksmith 17⅞ da @ $1.50 - $25.85. Mach Dept, Balto |
| 1857-13 | " | watch 30 da @ $.15 - $4.50. Martinsburg |
| 1857-51 | Ball, J. T. | watch 30 da @ $1 - $30.00. Rd Dept main stem 5th s-div |
| 1855-8 | James | conduc 23 da @ $55 per mo - $53.05. Trans Dept main stem |
| 1855-93 | James T. | fore @ $83.33 per mo - $83.33. Mach Dept |
| 1857-22 | John | ton conduc 25 da @ $55 per mo - $55.00. 3d & 4th div |
| 1857-87 | Bamber, Thomas | bricklay 15⅜ da @ $2.25 - $34.30. grad, Wellin Tun |
| 1857-70 | Banes, Anthony | lab 30 3/4 da @ $1 - $30.75. Mt Clare sta, Balto |
| 1855-50 | Banett, Joseph | watch cuts 28 da @ $1 - $28.00. Rd Way Dept |
| 1855-18 | Banford, Adam | ton eng'man 13 da @ $2.50 - $32.50. Trans Dept main stem |
| 1855-30 | Banks, Lewis | prepar fuel 17 da @ $30 per mo - $18.20. Trans Dept main stem |
| 1855-81 | " | mach 24 3/4 da @ $1.72 - $42.60. Mach Dept |
| 1857-108 | Mart. | mach 18 da @ $1.80 - $32.40. Mach Dept, Balto |
| 1855-52 | Bannett, David | lab 28 da @ $1 - $28.00. Rd Way Dept |
| 1855-75 | Bannon, Patrick | fire 12 da @ $33 per mo - $15.25. ballast train for 2d track |
| 1857-57 | " | lab 11½ da @ $1 - $11.50. Rd Way Dept |
| 1857-82 | Bantz, F. M. | lab 21½ da @ $1.12 - $24.20. grad, Board Tree Tun |
| 1855-14 | Peter S. | tak nos &c 30 da @ $.45 - $10.10. Mach Dept |
| 1855-92 | Barbeer, L. | app 32½ da @ $.45 - $10.10. Mach Dept |
| 1855-40 | Barber, Wm. | lab 21½ da @ $1 - $21.50. Rd Way Dept |
| 1857-109 | Barbour, Wm. | mach 17 da @ $1.60 - $27.20. Mach Dept, Balto |
| 1855-82 | Barger, Frank | app 23½ da @ $.55 - $12.80. Mach Dept |
| 1855-8 | Bark, Martin | conduc 6 da @ $50 per mo - $12.50. Trans Dept main stem |
| 1855-38 | Barker, Abram | lab 23 da @ $1 - $23.00. Rd Way Dept |
| 1857-22 | John | ton conduc 16 da @ $40 per mo; 7½ da @ $50 per mo - $40.60. 3d & 4th div |
| 1857-52 | " | lab 24 da @ $1 - $24.00. Rd Dept main stem 6th s-div |
| 1855-42 | Joseph | fore 23½ da @ $1.25 - $23.50. Rd Way Dept |

# B & O RR EMPLOYEES

| Year-ID | Name | Description |
|---|---|---|
| 1857-53 | Barker, Joseph | fore 21 da @ $1.25 - $26.25. Rd Dept main stem 7th s-div |
| 1855-22 | W. C. | fire 15 3/4 da @ $1.75 - $27.55. Trans Dept main stem |
| 1855-70 | Barkley, George | fore @ $60 per mo - $60.00. Rd Way Dept |
| 1857-47 | Barley, John | lab 17 da @ $1 - $17.00. Rd Dept main stem 1st s-div |
| 1857-25 | " | ton brak 25 da @ $1.60 per mo - $40.00. 3d & 4th div |
| 1857-47 | Thomas | eng'man 24 da @ $2.25 - $54.00. Rd Dept main stem 1st s-div |
| 1857-58 | Barman, Patrick | lab 24½ da @ $1 - $24.50. Rd Dept main stem 12th s-div |
| 1857-65 | Barnes, J. M. | conduc 17½ da @ $2 - $35.00. Rd Dept main stem 17th s-div |
| 1857-60 | John | lab 27 da @ $1 - $27.00. Rd Dept main stem 13th s-div |
| 1855-43 | Peter | lab 7 da @ $1 - $7.00. Rd Way Dept |
| 1857-21 | Samuel | ton conduc 21 da @ $50 per mo - $42.00. 1st div |
| 1855-42 | Wm. | lab 20 3/4 da @ $1 - $20.75. Rd Way Dept |
| 1857-32 | Barnett, David | ton fire 9 da @ $1.75 - $15.75. 2d div |
| 1857-128 | Joseph | blksmith 16¾ da @ $1.65 - $26.80. Mach Dept, Piedmont |
| 1855-32 | William | saw wd 18 3/4 cords @ $.50 - $9.35. Trans Dept main stem |
| 1857-13 | Barnhart, A. H. | lab 25 da @ $30 per mo - $30.00. Harpers Ferry |
| 1857-22 | Barns, J. W. | ton conduc 5 da @ $50 per mo - $10.00. 3d & 4th div |
| 1855-76 | Barnsticks, M. | help 25 3/4 da @ $1.15 - $29.60. Mach Dept |
| 1857-112 | Barresticker, M. | mach help 20¼ da @ $1.15 - $23.20. Mach Dept, Balto |
| 1857-89 | Barret, John | lab 11½ da @ $1.12 - $12.95. grad, Welling Tun |
| 1857-113 | Barrett, James | mach app 26½ da @ $.45 - $11.90. Mach Dept, Balto |
| 1855-56 | John | lab 16 da @ $1 - $16.00. Rd Way Dept |
| 1855-61 | " | lab 21 da @ $1 - $21.00. Rd Way Dept |
| 1857-96 | " | fore 25 da @ $1.25 - $31.25. NW Va RR, Rd Dept 1st s-div |
| 1857-66 | " | lab 17½ da @ $1 - $17.50. Rd Dept main stem 18th s-div |
| 1857-28 | " | ton eng'man 19 da @ $3 - $57.00. 1st div |
| 1857-77 | Joseph | quarry 4 da @ $1 - $4.00. ballast train for 2d track |
| 1855-60 | Leonard | lab 28 da @ $1 - $28.00. Rd Way Dept |
| 1855-50 | M. | watch cuts 28 da @ $1 - $28.00. Rd Way Dept |
| 1855-52 | Matthew | lab 28 da @ $1 - $28.00. Rd Way Dept |
| 1857-65 | " | watch 30 da @ $1 - $30.00. Rd Dept main stem 17th s-div |
| 1857-61 | " | lab 10½ da @ $1 - $10.50. NW Va RR, Rd Dept 14th s-div |
| 1857-96 | Michael | lab 25 da @ $1 - $25.00. Rd Dept main stem 1st s-div |
| 1855-91 | Miles | help 24½ da @ $1 - $24.50. Mach Dept |
| 1857-67 | " | lab 21 3/4 da @ $1 - $21.75. Rd Dept main stem 18th s-div |

B & O RR EMPLOYEES

| Name | Years | Details |
|---|---|---|
| Barrett, Patrick | 1855-61 | lab 15½ da @ $1 - $15.50. Rd Way Dept |
| " | 1857-132 | clean eng 29 da @ $1 - $29.00. Mach Dept, Grafton |
| " | 1857-91 | lab 20 da @ $1 - $20.00. grad, Welling Tun |
| " | 1857-96 | lab 9½ da @ $1 - $9.50. NW Va RR, Rd Dept 1st s-div |
| " | 1857-66 | lab 24½ da @ $1 - $24.50. Rd Dept main stem 18th s-div |
| " Thomas | 1855-95 | app 23 da @ $.85 -$19.55. Mach Dept |
| " | 1857-113 | iron mould 17 3/4 da @ $1.55 - $27.50. Mach Dept, Balto |
| " | 1857-67 | lab 17½ da @ $1 - $17.50. Rd Dept main stem 18th s-div |
| " | 1857-127 | mach 17¼ da @ $1.60 - $27.60. Mach Dept, Piedmont |
| " William | 1855-61 | lab 17½ da @ $1 - $17.50. Rd Way Dept |
| " | 1857-79 | lab 26 da @ $1 - $26.00. lay 2d track |
| " | 1857-66 | lab 23½ da @ $1 - $23.50. Rd Dept main stem 18th s-div |
| Barrick, William | 1855-38 | lab 24 da @ $1 - $24.00. Rd Way Dept |
| Barrickman, Jacob | 1857-104 | fore 24½ da @ $1.50 - $36.75. NW Va RR Tun |
| Barron, Samuel | 1857-134 | mach 24 da @ $1.75 - $42.00. Mach Dept, Wheeling |
| Barry, Daniel | 1855-50 | watch cuts 28 da @ $1 - $28.00. Rd Way Dept |
| " | 1857-63 | lab 20 3/4 da @ $1 -$20.75. Rd Dept main stem 16th s-div |
| " E. T. | 1855-10 | conduc & brak 14 da @ $50 per mo - $29.15. Trans Dept main stem |
| " John | 1857-83 | lab 8½ da @ $1.12 - $9.55. grad, Board Tree Tun |
| " P. | 1855-6 | agt 28 da @ $75 per mo - $75.00. Trans Dept main stem |
| " Patrick | 1855-55 | lab 21 da @ $1 - $21.00. Rd Way Dept |
| " | 1857-63 | lab 22 3/4 da @ $1 - $22.75. Rd Dept main stem 16th s-div |
| " Philip | 1857-16 | agt 30 da @ $75 per mo - $75.00. Moundsville sta |
| " Thomas | 1857-33 | ton fire 12½ da @ $1.75 - $21.45. 3d div |
| Bartell, Henry | 1857-125 | carp 18 3/4 da @ $1.30 - $24.35. Mach Dept, Martinsburg |
| Bartgis, G. W. L. | 1855-9 | conduc 24 da @ $50 per mo - $50.00. Trans Dept main stem |
| Bartholow, George | 1857-25 | ton brak 26 da @ $40 per mo - $41.60. 2d div |
| Bartlett, J. | 1857-85 | carp 23 da @ $1.75 - $40.25. grad, Board Tree Tun |
| " Rodger | 1855-84 | help 25½ da @ $1 - $25.50. Mach Dept |
| " Thomas | 1857-92 | lab 34 da @ $1 - $34.00. grad, Littleton Tun |
| Barton, William L. | 1857-62 | lab 23 3/4 da @ $1 - $23.75. Rd Dept main stem 15th s-div |
| Baset, F. | 1855-65 | plumb 12 da @ $1.25 - $15.00. Rd Way Dept |
| Basford, Zebidee | 1855-84 | mach (includ boil mkr, work in sht iron, &c) 22 da @ $1.72 - $37.85. Mach Dept |
| Basite, Francis | 1857-53 | watch 30 da @ $1 - $30.00. Rd Dept main stem 7th s-div |
| " Frk. | 1857-110 | mach 32 da @ $1.90 - $60.80. Mach Dept, Balto |
| Bassett, Freeman | 1855-76 | mach 25½ da @ $1.90 - $48.45. Mach Dept |
| " | 1857-115 | boil mkr 9 da @ $1.72 - $15.50. Mach Dept, Balto |

## B & O RR EMPLOYEES 59

| | | |
|---|---|---|
| 1855-30 | Bassferd, Alfred | lab 15 da @ $1 - $15.00. Trans Dept main stem |
| 1855-42 | Bassford, L. | fore 23 da @ $1.25 - $28.75. Rd Way Dept |
| 1857-24 | Bast, Charles | ton brak 13½ da @ $40 per mo - $21.60. 1st div |
| 1857-21 | Solomon | ton conduc 25 da @ $60 per mo - $60.00. 1st div |
| 1855-10 | T. | conduc & brak 7 da @ $50 per mo - $14.60. Trans Dept main stem |
| 1855-4 | Bateman, James | brak 28 da @ $33.35 per mo - $33.35. Trans Dept, Wash br |
| 1855-84 | John | help 23¾ da @ $1.15 - $26.75. Mach Dept |
| 1857-115 | " | boil mkr help 18½ da @ $1.15 - $21.25. Mach Dept, Balto |
| 1857-22 | " | ton conduc 25⅜ da @ $60 per mo - $50.50. 3d & 4th div |
| 1855-53 | Thomas | carp 22 da @ $1.25 - $27.50. Rd Way Dept |
| 1857-73 | " | carp 24 da @ $1.37 - $33.00. repair bridges &c |
| 1855-65 | Battegan, John | carp 24 da @ $1.62½ - $39.00. Rd Way Dept |
| 1855-61 | Battel, James | lab 22 da @ $1 - $22.00. Rd Way Dept |
| 1857-61 | Baucher, John | lab 27 da @ $1 - $27.00. Rd Dept main stem 14th s-div |
| 1855-88 | Baugtman, A. | lab 19 da @ $1 - $19.00. Mach Dept |
| 1857-120 | Daniel | carp 17 3/4 da @ $1.50 - $26.60. Mach Dept, Balto |
| 1857-69 | Baum, Chris. | carp 19 3/4 da @ $1.60 - $31.60. Mt Clare sta, Balto |
| 1855-53 | Bawcher, John | lab 14½ da @ $1 - $14.50. Rd Way Dept |
| 1857-51 | Baxten, James | watch 30 da @ $1 - $30.00. Rd Dept main stem 5th s-div |
| 1855-51 | Baxter, James | lab 28 da @ $1 - $28.00. Rd Way Dept |
| 1857-19 | Baxton, Upton | bag mast 30 da @ $45 per mo - $45.00. thr mail & exp |
| 1855-33 | Bayless, H. W. | watch 28 da @ $40 per mo - $40.00. Trans Dept main stem |
| 1857-31 | Bayliss, George | ton fire 9 3/4 da @ $1.75 - $17.05. 1st div |
| 1855-95 | Bazell, John | mould 25 3/4 da @ $1.72 - $44.30. Mach Dept |
| 1857-113 | " | fore iron mould @ $66.70 per mo - $66.70. Mach Dept, Balto |
| 1855-86 | Beall, Alfred | mach 23 3/4 da @ $1.35 - $32.05. Mach Dept |
| 1857-123 | " | mach 20¼ da @ $1.70 - $34.40. Mach Dept, Martinsburg |
| 1855-73 | Benj. | fore 24 da @ $1.25 - $30.00. Rd Way Dept |
| 1855-74 | George | lab 22 da @ $1 - $22.00. Rd Way Dept |
| 1857-95 | H. | nail 25 da @ $1.05 - $26.25. Wash br, Rd Dept |
| 1855-78 | Richard | timekpr @ $35 per mo - $35.00. Mach Dept |
| 1855-73 | Bealt, Jesse | fore 21 da @ $1.25 - $26.25. Rd Way Dept |
| 1857-95 | Beans, Elias | fore 27 da @ $1.25 - $33.75. Wash br, Rd Dept |
| 1857-73 | Beard, Andrew | carp 25 da @ $1.65 - $41.25. repair water sta, M.S. & P.B. |
| 1857-32 | | ton fire 22½ da @ $1.75 - $39.35. 2d div |
| 1857-52 | | lab 23 da @ $1 - $23.00. Rd Dept main stem 6th s-div |

# B & O RR EMPLOYEES

| |  | |  |
|---|---|---|---|
| 1857-124 | Beard, Geo. W. | | blksmith help 19 da @ $1 - $19.00. Mach Dept, Martinsburg |
| 1855-69 | Beatty, Martin | | lab 23 da @ $1 - $23.00. Rd Way Dept |
| 1857-89 | Beaty, Martin | | lab 25 3/4 da @ $1.25 - $32.20. grad, Welling Tun |
| 1857-56 | Beck, Charles | | nail 28½ da @ $1 -$28.50. Rd Dept main stem 10th s-div |
| 1857-120 | Beck, Francis | | carp 17¼ da @ $1.50 - $25.85. Mach Dept, Balto |
| 1855-8 | " James | | conduc 19½ da @ $40.60. Mach Dept, Balto |
| 1855-8 | " " | | conduc 24 da @ $50 per mo - $50.00. Trans Dept main stem |
| 1857-76 | " " | | fore @ $60 per mo - $60.00. ballast train for 2d track |
| 1855-22 | Beckcomb, Wm. | | fire 14½ da @ $1.75 - $25.35. Trans Dept main stem |
| 1855-75 | Becker, Adam | | lab 22 da @ $1 - $22.00. Rd Way Dept |
| 1857-113 | Beckett, Oliver | | mach app 21 3/4 da @ $.45 - $9.80. Mach Dept, Balto |
| 1855-15 | " T. | | pass eng'man 27 da @ $3 - $81.00. Trans Dept main stem |
| 1857-111 | " " | | mach 4 da @ $1.25 - $6.00. Mach Dept, Balto |
| 1855-4 | " Thomas | | ton eng'man 1 da @ $2.50 - $2.50. Trans Dept, Wash br |
| 1857-38 | " " | | pass eng'man 15 da @ $3 - $45.00. Wash br rd, Wash city sta |
| 1855-6 | Beckham, F. | | agt 28 da @ $75 per mo - $75.00. Trans Dept main stem |
| 1857-13 | " " | | agt 30 da @ $75 per mo - $75.00. Harpers Ferry |
| 1855-41 | Beckley, Jno. | | lab 28 da @ $1 - $28.00. Rd Way Dept |
| 1857-49 | Becraft, George | | lab 25 da @ $1 - $25.00. Rd Dept main stem 3d s-div |
| 1855-49 | Bedford, Hammond | | lab 24 da @ $1 - $24.00. Rd Dept main stem 3d s-div |
| 1855-22 | Bedford, Charles | | fire 14 da @ $1.75 - $24.50. Trans Dept main stem |
| 1857-32 | " " | | ton fire 29¼ da @ $1.75 - $51.20. 2d div |
| 1855-6 | " J. D. | | clk 28 da @ $58.65 per mo - $58.65. Trans Dept main stem |
| 1857-8 | " " | | rec clk 30 da @ $58.35 per mo - $58.35. Camden sta |
| 1857-135 | Beeid, Daniel | | carp 19½ da @ $1.50 - $29.25. Mach Dept, Wheeling |
| 1855-7 | Beeler, L. F. | | clk 28 da @ $58.35 per mo -$58.35. Trans Dept main stem |
| 1857-17 | " " | | clk 30 da @ $58.35 per mo - $58.35. Wheeling sta |
| 1855-41 | Beerd, Edw. | | lab 8¼ da @ $1 - $8.25. Rd Way Dept |
| 1857-24 | Befelt, William | | ton brak 18 3/4 da @ $40 per mo - $30.00. 1st div |
| 1855-26 | Beggar, Frederick | | clean eng 28½ da @ $1 - $28.50. Trans Dept main stem |
| 1857-124 | Beidheimer, Ferdinand | | blksmith 20½ da @ $1.55 - $31.75. Mach Dept, Martinsburg |
| 1857-108 | Beeler, Lewis | | mach 17¼ da @ $1.72 - $29.65. Mach Dept, Balto |
| 1857-139 | Beleville, William | | carp 31¼ da @ $1.60 - $50.00. NW Va RR, Mach Dept, Parkersburg |
| 1857-129 | Belew, W. N. | | fore yd lab 19 da @ $1.50 - $28.50. Mach Dept, Piedmont |
| 1857-118 | Belfry, James | | blksmith help 17 3/4 da @ $1 - $17.75. Mach Dept, Balto |
| 1855-34 | Bell, E. | | lamp trim 27½ da @ $1 -$27.50. Trans Dept main stem |

| | | | |
|---|---|---|---|
| 1857-10 | Bell, Edward | bur reg 25 da @ $40 per mo - $40.00. hp exp, Balto |
| 1857-130 | Elisha | lab 17½ da @ $1 - $17.50. Mach Dept, Piedmont |
| 1857-130 | James | lab 23 da @ $1 - $23.00. Mach Dept, Piedmont |
| 1857-52 | John | lab 16 da @ $1 - $16.00. Rd Dept main stem 6th s-div |
| 1857-128 | Joseph | mach help 5 da @ $.40 - $2.00. Mach Dept, Piedmont |
| 1855-71 | Samuel | bricklay 11 3/4 da @ $2 - $23.50. Rd Way Dept |
| 1857-135 | Thaddeus | paint 18¼ da @ $2 - $36.50. Mach Dept, Wheeling |
| 1855-64 | William | watch 28 da @ $1 - $28.00. Rd Way Dept |
| 1857-130 | " | lab 21 da @ $1 - $21.00. Mach Dept, Piedmont |
| 1857-127 | William A. | mach help 24½ da @ $.40 - $9.80. Mach Dept, Piedmont |
| 1857-67 | Belliter, T. | lab 18½ da @ $1 - $18.50. Rd Dept main stem 18th s-div |
| 1857-56 | Bellman, Andrew | lab 26 da @ $1 - $26.00. Rd Dept main stem 10th s-div |
| 1857-39 | Belt, T. H. Jr. | agt 30 da @ $100 per mo - $100.00. NW Va Rd, Parkersburg sta |
| 1855-68 | Belt, Thomas H. Jr. | clk @ $75 per mo - $75.00. Rd Way Dept |
| 1857-49 | Benard, Jonathan | fore 25 da @ $1.25 - $31.25. Rd Dept main stem 3d s-div |
| 1857-127 | Bender, George | nt fore mach @ $60 per mo - $60.00. Mach Dept, Piedmont |
| 1855-90 | George H. | mach 18 da @ $1.68 - $30.30. Mach Dept |
| 1855-34 | John | greas cars 28 da @ $1 - $28.00. Trans Dept main stem |
| 1857-128 | Reuben | mach help 28½ da @ $.40 - $11.40. Mach Dept, Piedmont |
| 1855-37 | Bennett, John | lab 24½ da @ $1 - $24.50. Rd Way Dept |
| 1855-82 | Benkins, Isaac | help 23½ da @ $1 - $23.50. Mach Dept |
| 1857-70 | Benner, Ferd. | mach 29 da @ $1.75 - $50.15. Mt Clare sta, Balto |
| 1855-20 | Bennet, Jesse | fire 15 da @ $1.75 - $26.25. Trans Dept main stem |
| 1857-132 | Bennett, Edgar | clean eng 7 da @ $1 - $7.00. Mach Dept, Grafton |
| 1855-44 | L. | lab 3½ da @ $1 - $3.50. Rd Way Dept |
| 1855-68 | Michael | lab 22 3/4 da @ $1 - $22.75. Rd Way Dept |
| 1857-24 | Robert | ton brak 20 da @ $40 per mo - $32.00. 1st div |
| 1857-132 | Rolley | clean eng 28 da @ $1 - $28.00. Mach Dept, Grafton |
| 1857-25 | William | ton brak ½ da @ $40 per mo -$.80. 2d div |
| 1855-33 | Benning, F. | swit 28 da @ $1 -$28.00. Trans Dept main stem |
| 1857-14 | " | watch 30 da @ $1 -$30.00. Cumb |
| 1857-49 | Bennit, Rezen | lab 25 da @ $1 -$25.00. Rd Dept main stem 3d s-div |
| 1857-21 | Bentley, Alonzo | ton conduc 19¾ da @ $40 per mo; 4 da @ $59 per mo -$38.80. 2d div |
| 1855-76 | Bently, Geo. | mach 22¼ da @ $1.55 -$34.50. Mach Dept |
| 1855-10 | Benton, R. H. | conduc & brak 24 da @ $40 per mo - $40.00. Trans Dept main stem |
| 1855-86 | Bentz, Charles | mach 31½ da @ $1.35 - $42.50. Mach Dept |

## B & O RR EMPLOYEES

| | | | |
|---|---|---|---|
| 1857-124 | Bentz, Charles | sht iron work 25 da @ $1.35 - $33.75. Mach Dept, Martinsburg |
| 1855-35 | Berger, F. A. | rec 28 da @ $50 per mo - $50.00. Trans Dept main stem |
| 1857-22 | Frank A. | ton conduc 31¼ da @ $60 per mo - $75.00. 3d & 4th div |
| 1855-30 | Berk, Charles | lab 21 da @$1.-$21.00. Trans Dept main stem |
| 1855-30 | John | lab 18 da @ $1 - $18.00. Trans Dept main stem |
| 1857-125 | " | nt watch 28 da @ $1.15 - $32.20. Mach Dept, Martinsburg |
| 1855-30 | Joseph | lab 20 da @ $1 - $20.00. Trans Dept main stem |
| 1855-30 | Theodore | lab 18 da @ $1 - $18.00. Trans Dept main stem |
| 1855-30 | William | lab 20 da @ $1 - $20.00. Trans Dept main stem |
| 1857-64 | Berker, Joseph | lab 28 da @$1 - $28.00. Rd Dept main stem 17th s-div |
| 1857-64 | Shilby | lab 26 da @ $1 - $26.00. Rd Dept main stem 17th s-div |
| 1855-50 | Berkley, George | fore 8 da @$1.37 - $11.00. Rd Dept main stem 5th s-div |
| 1855-86 | Berlin, John | mach 21 da @ $1.35 - $28.35. Mach Dept |
| 1857-114 | Bermingham, Cain | iron mould help 18 3/4 da @ $1.10 - $20.65. Mach Dept, Balto |
| 1855-51 | Berran, Charles | lab @ $30 per mo -$30.00. Rd Way Dept |
| 1857-64 | Berrett, John | lab 13½ da @ $1 - $13.50. Rd Dept main stem 17th s-div |
| 1855-87 | Berry, Charles | mach 1 da @ $1.50 - $1.50. Mach Dept |
| 1855-15 | " | pass eng'man 30 da @ $3 - $90.00. Trans Dept main stem |
| 1855-79 | D. | paint 23 da @ $1.65 - $37.95. Mach Dept |
| 1857-55 | Betts, Adam | lab 20 3/4 da @ $1 - $20.75. Rd Dept main stem 9th s-div |
| 1855-30 | James | prepar fuel 28 da @$30 per mo - $30.00. Trans Dept main stem |
| 1857-9 | Bevan, John | prepar fuel 12 da @ $30 per mo - $12.85. Trans Dept main stem |
| 1855-29 | Beyer, Richard | asst 30 da @ $35 per mo - $35.00. hp exp, Balto |
| 1855-87 | Biahimer, F. | haul & saw firewd 7 da @ $1 - $7.00. Trans Dept main stem |
| 1857-18 | Biays, J. P. | blksmith 24 da @ $1.50 - $36.00. Mach Dept |
| 1857-22 | Bice, George | pass train conduc 30 da @$50 per mo - $50.00. w end |
| 1857-22 | Bickfoot, Jesse | ton conduc 11 da @ $60 per mo -$22.00. 3d & 4th div |
| 1857-110 | Bidason, Zac. | ton conduc 15 3/4 da @ $50 per mo - $31.50. 3d & 4th div |
| 1857-25 | Biddenger, J. | mach 18½ da @ $1.50 - $27.75. Mach Dept, Balto |
| 1857-91 | Biddle, Andrew | ton brak 27 da @ $40 per mo -$43.20. 3d & 4th div |
| 1857-79 | Perry | stone mason 12½ da @ $2 - $25.00. grad, Littleton Tun |
| 1857-119 | " | carp @ $55 per mo - $55.00. Mach Dept |
| 1857-7 | S. R. | carp 25 da @ $1.50 -$37.50. Mach Dept, Balto |
| 1855-81 | Biderson, Z. | watch @ $35 per mo. Mast of Trans Ofc |
| 1855-81 | Bier, Lewis | mach 37½ da @ $1.25 - $46.90. Mach Dept |
| | | mach 25 3/4 da @ $1.65 - $42.50. Mach Dept |

| | | |
|---|---|---|
| 1857-25 | Biggs, Jacob | ton brak 19½ da @ $40 per mo -$31.20. 3d & 4th div |
| 1855-33 | Bigham, H. | watch 28 da @$30 per mo -$30.00. Trans Dept main stem |
| 1855-18 | Bigner, Jos. | ton eng'man ½ da @ $2.50 - $1.25. Rd Way Dept |
| 1855-75 | Billman, Jno. | lab 21½ da @$1 - $21.50. Rd Way Dept |
| 1857-31 | Billmire, George | ton fire 2 da @ $1.75 - $3.50. 1st div |
| 1855-108 | Bilson, H. | fore mach 25 da @ $2.50 - $62.50. Mach Dept, Balto |
| 1855-76 | " | mach 25 3/4 da @ $2.30 - $59.25. Mach Dept |
| 1857-114 | Bineman, John | iron mould help 17 3/4 da @ $1.15 - $20.40. Mach Dept, Balto |
| 1855-96 | Binerman, John | lab 24 da @ $1.15 - $27.60. Mach Dept |
| 1857-40 | Birchfield, James | ton brak 4 da @ $40 per mo -$6.40. NW Va rd, Parkersburg sta |
| 1857-25 | " | ton brak 14 da @ $40 per mo - $22.40. 3d & 4th div |
| 1857-31 | Birely, George | ton fire 21½ da @ $1.75 - $37.20. 1st div |
| 1857-12 | W. M. | clk 30 da @ $33.35 per mo - $33.35. Fred sta |
| 1855-86 | Birmingham, John | lab 24 da @ $1 - $24.00. grad, McGuire's Tun |
| 1855-47 | W. | lab 26 da @$1 - $26.00. Rd Way Dept |
| 1855-56 | Wm. | lab 23½ da @ $1 - $23.50. Rd Dept main stem 10th s-div |
| 1857-92 | Biset, Andy | fill tend 30 da @ $1 - $11.00. grad, Littleton Tun |
| 1857-133 | Bishop, F. | lab 30 da @ $1 - $30.00. Mach Dept, Fetterman |
| 1855-51 | George | lab @ $45 per mo - $45.00. Rd Way Dept |
| 1855-35 | P. | swit 32-4 ex da @ $40 per mo - $38.80. Trans Dept main stem |
| 1855-13 | William | conduc & brak 13½ da @ $40 per mo -$22.50. Trans Dept main stem |
| 1857-62 | Bishops, George | pump water @ $45 per mo - $45.00. Rd Dept main stem 15th s-div |
| 1857-20 | Bissett, Jeremiah | pass fire 1 da @ $40 per mo - $1.35. 4th div |
| 1857-33 | " | ton fire 4¼ da @ $1.75 - $7.45. 4th div |
| 1855-20 | Jerry | fire 15 da @$1.75 - $26.25. Trans Dept main stem |
| 1857-134 | " | mach help 2½ da @ $1 -$2.25. Mach Dept, Wheeling |
| 1855-45 | Bissy, William | lab 22½ da @ $1 - $22.25. Rd Way Dept |
| 1855-6 | Bixler, Benjamin M. | clk 28 da @ $33.35 per mo - $33.35. Trans Dept main stem |
| 1857-3 | Benjamin M. | clk @ $54.16 per mo. Gen Ofc |
| 1855-92 | Blackiston, John T. | carp @ $50 per mo - $50.00. Mach Dept |
| 1857-128 | Blackstone, John T. | fore carp @ $60 per mo - $60.00. Mach Dept, Piedmont |
| 1855-16 | Blackwell, G. | pass fire 30 da @ $40 per mo - $42.85. Trans Dept main stem |
| 1857-123 | George | mach 4 3/4 da @ $1.25 - $5.95. Mach Dept, Martinsburg |
| 1857-19 | " | pass eng'man 4½ da @ $3 - $13.50. 2d div |
| 1857-20 | " | pass fire 9 da @ $40 per mo - $12.00. 2d div |
| 1857-29 | " | ton eng'man 9 da @ $3 - $27.00. 2d div |

| ID | Name | Details |
|---|---|---|
| 1855-15 | Blackwell, W. | pass eng'man 22 da @ $3 - $66.00. Trans Dept main stem |
| 1857-19 | " Wm. | pass eng'man 38 da @ $3 - $114.00. 2d div |
| 1857-20 | Blair, F. P. | pass fire 18 da @ $40 per mo - $24.00. 2d div |
| 1855-64 | " Samuel | lab 23 3/4 da @ $1 - $23.75. Rd Way Dept |
| 1857-93 | | smith help 25 da @ $1 - $25.00. quarry & haul stone for Board Tree & Littleton Tun |
| 1857-80 | Blake, Thomas | lab 20½ da @ $1 - $20.50. lay 2d track |
| 1857-24 | " Van Buren | ton brak 24 da @ $40 per mo - $38.40. 1st div |
| 1857-126 | Blakely, Edward | clean eng 27 da @ $1.15 - $31.05. Mach Dept, Martinsburg |
| 1855-86 | Blakeney, Edward | train inspec @ $34.50 per mo - $34.50. Mach Dept |
| 1857-52 | Blamer, James | lab 29 da @ $1 - $29.00. Rd Dept main stem 6th s-div |
| 1855-42 | " Samuel | lab 20½ da @ $1 - $20.50. Rd Way Dept |
| 1857-52 | | lab 22 3/4 da @ $1 - $22.75. Rd Dept main stem 6th s-div |
| 1855-26 | Blanchfield, John | clean eng 23½ da @ $1 - $23.50. Trans Dept main stem |
| 1855-52 | Blaner, Gutlop | lab 14 3/4 da @ $.75 - $11.05. Rd Way Dept |
| 1855-24 | Blank, Jacob | ton brak 18 3/4 da @ $40 per mo - $30.00. 1st div |
| 1855-18 | Blessing, George | ton eng'man 18 3/4 da @ $3 - $56.25. Trans Dept main stem |
| 1857-29 | " | ton eng'man 16½ da @ $3 - $49.50. 2d div |
| 1857-55 | Blomker, William | lab 24 da @ $1 - $24.00. Rd Dept main stem 9th s-div |
| 1857-45 | Bloneker, William | nail 24 da @ $1 - $24.00. Rd Way Dept |
| 1857-63 | Board, Thomas | watch 30 da @ $1 - $30.00. Rd Dept main stem 16th s-div |
| 1857-109 | Boardman, Lyman | mach 17 3/4 da @ $1.25 - $22.20. Mach Dept, Balto |
| 1855-6 | Bochus, L. C. | clk 28 da @ $50 per mo - $50.00. Trans Dept main stem |
| 1857-51 | Boden, Henry | lab 28 da @ $1 - $28.00. Rd Way Dept |
| 1857-51 | " | watch 30 da @ $1 - $30.00. Rd Dept main stem 5th s-div |
| 1855-13 | Boggard, J. | conduc & brak 10 da @ $40 per mo - $16.65. Trans Dept main stem |
| 1857-100 | Bogle, Peter | fore 25 da @ $1.75 - $43.75. NW Va RR, Rd Dept 5th s-div |
| 1855-86 | Bohda, H. | mach 23½ da @ $1.55 - $36.45. Mach Dept |
| 1855-55 | Bohen, James | lab 3 da @ $1 - $3.00. Rd Way Dept |
| 1857-57 | " | lab 27½ da @ $1 -$27.50. Rd Dept main stem 11th s-div |
| 1857-14 | Bohm, L. C. | clk 30 da @ $50 per mo - $50.00. Cumb |
| 1857-76 | Boice, John | quarry 23½ da @ $1 - $23.50. ballast train for 2d track |
| 1857-71 | Bolden, Patrick | lab 23½ da @ $1 - $23.25. Mt Clare, repair tracks in yd |
| 1855-71 | " Robert | help 23 da @ $1.15 - $26.45. Rd Way Dept |
| 1857-70 | " " | chair mkr 18 da @ $1.25 - $22.50. Mt Clare sta, Balto |
| 1855-72 | " Wm. | mach 24 da @ $1.73 - $41.50. Rd Way Dept |
| 1857-69 | " " | mach 31 da @ $1.73 - $53.65. Mt Clare sta, Balto |

# B & O RR EMPLOYEES

| ID | Name | Description |
|---|---|---|
| 1857-116 | Bolkman, Henry | boil mkr help 15 3/4 da @ $1 - $15.75. Mach Dept, Balto |
| 1855-84 | R. | blksmith 21 da @ $1.85 - $38.85. Mach Dept |
| 1857-116 | Richard | blksmith 17½ da @ $1.85 - $31.90. Mach Dept, Balto |
| 1855-73 | Bollman, A. | driv 21½ da @ $.60 - $12.75. Rd Way Dept |
| 1855-70 | Andrew | app 22 3/4 da @ $.75 - $17.05. Mt Clare sta, Balto |
| 1855-22 | Edward | carp 23 3/4 da @ $1.60 - $38.00. Rd Way Dept |
| 1857-69 | " | carp 17 3/4 da @ $1.60 - $28.40. Mt Clare sta, Balto |
| 1855-72 | James | mach 22 da @ $1.50 - $33.00. Rd Way Dept |
| 1857-70 | " | mach 29½ da @ $1.73 - $51.00. Mt Clare sta, Balto |
| 1855-13 | Lewis | conduc & Brak 18 3/4 da @ $40 per mo - $31.25. Trans Dept main stem |
| 1857-70 | Thos. W. | app 22 da @ $.60 - $13.20. Mt Clare sta, Balto |
| 1855-1 | W. | mast of rd @ $2500 per annum - $208.33 |
| 1857-45 | Wendell | mast of rd @ $208.33 per mo. Rd Dept |
| 1857-74 | Bolta, Charles | track lay 6⅞ da @ $.75 - $4.70. put swit on line of rd |
| 1857-74 | Frene | track lay 22 3/4 da @ $1.12 - $25.60. put swit on line of rd |
| 1857-74 | George | track lay 23 da @ $1.37 - $31.60. put swit on line of rd |
| 1857-72 | Boman, Christopher | lab 30 da @ $1.50 - $45.00. repair tele line |
| 1857-72 | William | lab 30 da @ $1.50 - $45.00. repair tele line |
| 1857-75 | Bond, Bartlett | fire 13 da @ $1.75 - $22.75. ballast train for 2d track |
| 1857-81 | Battle | brak 1 da @ $1.50 - $1.50. lay 2d track |
| 1855-22 | John | fire 7 da @ $1.75 - $12.25. Trans Dept main stem |
| 1857-132 | " | blksmith 19 3/4 da @ $1.60 - $31.60. Mach Dept, Grafton |
| 1855-89 | Bone, William | help 22½ da @ $1 - $22.50. Mach Dept |
| 1857-137 | " | eng clean 18 da @ $1 - $18.00. Mach Dept, Cumb |
| 1857-118 | Bonig, Henry | blksmith help 18 da @ $1 - $18.00. Mach Dept, Balto |
| 1857-29 | Boogher, Alfred | ton eng'man 2 da @ $2.50 - $5.00. 3d div |
| 1857-61 | John | lab 18½ da @ $1 - $18.50. Rd Dept main stem 14th s-div |
| 1855-22 | Boohher, Alfred | fire 12⅔ da @ $1.75 - $21.85. Trans Dept main stem |
| 1857-126 | Boosee, Theodore | greas cars 30 da @ $1 - $30.00. Mach Dept, Martinsburg |
| 1857-127 | Booth, James | mach help 24⅔ da @ $.65 - $15.90. Mach Dept, Piedmont |
| 1857-127 | Joseph | mach 19½ da @ $2 - $39.00. Mach Dept, Piedmont |
| 1855-79 | Samuel | paint 17 3/4 da @ $1.65 - $29.30. Mach Dept |
| 1855-73 | Borchelt, Wm. | track lay 22½ da @ $1.50 - $33.75. Rd Way Dept |
| 1857-112 | Borland, August | mach help 33 da @ $1.25 - $41.25. Mach Dept, Balto |
| 1855-85 | O. | help 22½ da @ $1.15 - $25.60. Mach Dept |
| 1857-117 | Otis | blksmith 17 3/4 da @ $1.45 - $25.75. Mach Dept, Balto |

66    B & O RR EMPLOYEES

| ID | Name | Description |
|---|---|---|
| 1857-40 | Borst, Freeman | pass eng'man 25½ da @ ℔ - $76.50. NW Va rd, Parkersburg sta |
| 1857-18 | Bosh, John | blksmith help 18 da @ $1 - $18.00. Mach Dept, Balto |
| 1855-8 | Bosler, Samuel | conduc 16¼ da @ $50 per mo - $33.85. Trans Dept main stem |
| 1855-78 | Bosley, Edward | fore @ $70 per mo - $70.00. Mach Dept |
| 1857-127 | " | mast mech @ $83.35 per mo - $83.35. Mach Dept, Piedmont |
| 1855-44 | Boswell, James | lab 6 da @ $1 - $6.00. Rd Way Dept |
| 1857-54 | " | lab 14 da @ $1 - $14.00. Rd Dept main stem 8th s-div |
| 1855-44 | " John | lab 8 3/4 da @ $1 - $8.75. Rd Way Dept |
| 1857-45 | Boteler, B. W. | chief clk @ $75 per mo. Rd Dept |
| 1855-72 | " Charles | app 22½ da @ $.60 - $13.35. Rd Way Dept |
| 1857-69 | " George M. | carp 17 3/4 da @ $1.73 - $30.70. Mt Clare sta, Balto |
| 1855-71 | " George W. | carp 23 3/4 da @ $1.60 - $38.00. Rd Way Dept |
| 1857-119 | " J. P. | carp 18 da @ $1.60 - $28.80. Mach Dept, Balto |
| 1855-72 | " R. W. | clk @ $65 per mo - $65.00. Rd Way Dept |
| 1857-71 | Bothe, H. | track lay 23 da @ $1 - $23.00. Camden sta, repair tracks |
| 1857-132 | Bouce, James | blksmith help 16½ da @ $1.04 - $17.50. Mach Dept, Grafton |
| 1855-31 | Boucher, Thomas | prepar fuel 15½ da @ $1 - $15.50. Trans Dept main stem |
| 1855-39 | Bouerd, J. | lab 24 da @ $1.25 - $30.00. Rd Way Dept |
| 1857-127 | Bouldin, Jehu L. | mach help 20 da @$.45 - $9.00. Mach Dept, Piedmont |
| 1855-42 | Bourlincy, Geo. | lab 22½ da @ $1 - $22.25. Rd Way Dept |
| 1857-119 | Bowen, Granill | carp 13½ da @ $1.65 - $22.25. Mach Dept, Balto |
| 1857-110 | " Jos. | mach 17 da @ $1.55 - $26.35. Mach Dept, Balto |
| 1855-79 | " S. | carp 24 da @$1.55 -$37.20. Mach Dept, Balto |
| 1857-80 | Bower, Amos | timekpr 25 da @ $2 -$50.00. lay 2d track |
| 1857-116 | " George | blksmith 17½ da @$1.45 -$25.00. Mach Dept, Balto |
| 1855-79 | Bowers, Adam | lab 24 da @$1.15 -$27.60. Mach Dept |
| 1857-124 | " Frederick | sht iron work 21 da @ $1.25 - $26.25. Mach Dept, Martinsburg |
| 1857-36 | " H. J. | tele oper 30 da @$30 per mo - $30.00. Mannington |
| 1855-24 | " Henry | pass & bur driv 26½ da @ $30 per mo - $33.10. Trans Dept main stem |
| 1857-117 | " " | blksmith help 18 da @ $1 -$18.50. Mach Dept, Balto |
| 1857-50 | " James | lab 25½ da @ $1 -$25.00. Rd Dept main stem 4th s-div |
| 1855-34 | " John | lab 4 da @ $1 - $4.00. Trans Dept main stem |
| 1855-85 | " " | help 21 3/4 da @ $1.15 - $25.00. Mach Dept |
| 1855-89 | " " | help 25 da @ $1 -$25.00. Mach Dept |
| 1857-118 | " " | blksmith help 2¼ da @ $1 -$2.25. Mach Dept, Balto |
| 1857-125 | " John A. | lab 26½ da @ $1.25 - $33.10. Mach Dept, Martinsburg |

| | | |
|---|---|---|
| 1857-90 | Bowers, Joseph | lab 10½ da @ $1.12 - $11.80. grad, Welling Tun |
| 1857-73 | Oliver | lab 23 da @ $1.12 -$25.90. repair water sta, M.S. & P.B. |
| 1855-44 | U. | lab 17½ da @ $1 - $17.50. Rd Way Dept |
| 1855-84 | William | mach (includ boil mkr, work in sht iron, &c) 23 da @$1.55 - $35.65. Mach Dept |
| 1857-115 | " | boil mkr 21 da @ $1.65 - $34.65. Mach Dept, Balto |
| 1857-24 | " | ton brak 5¼ da @ $40 per mo - $8.40. 1st div |
| 1855-18 | Bowert, Jno. A. | ton eng'man 15¼ da @ $2.50 - $38.10. Trans Dept main stem |
| 1857-123 | Bowman, Adam | mach 15½ da @$1.15 -$17.80. Mach Dept, Martinsburg |
| 1857-24 | D. C. | ton brak 20¼ da @ $40 per mo - $32.40. 1st div |
| 1857-55 | George | lab 19 da @ $1 -$19.00. Rd Dept main stem 9th s-div |
| 1855-65 | William | carp 24 da @ $1.62½ - $39.00. Rd Way Dept |
| 1855-35 | " | clean cars 28 da @ $30 per mo - $30.00. Trans Dept main stem |
| 1857-83 | Boyal, C. | lab 6 da @ $1.12 - $6.75. grad, Board Tree Tun |
| 1857-119 | Boyce, John | blksmith app 25 da @ $.75 - $18.75. Mach Dept, Balto |
| 1855-86 | Robert | app 32 3/4 da @ $.55 - $18.00. Mach Dept |
| 1857-117 | " | blksmith 17¼ da @ $1.50 - $25.85. Mach Dept, Balto |
| 1855-32 | T. | lab 24 da @ $30 per mo - $30.00. Trans Dept main stem |
| 1857-25 | Boyd, Frank | ton brak 28 da @ $40 per mo - $44.80. 3d & 4th div |
| 1857-91 | Frederick | lab 22¼ da @ $1 -$22.25. grad, Welling Tun |
| 1855-44 | Robert | lab 8 da @ $1 - $8.00. Mach Dept |
| 1857-22 | Solomon | ton conduc 26 da @ $60 per mo - $52.00. 3d & 4th div |
| 1857-128 | Boyer, Oliver | carp 18½ da @ $1.50 - $27.75. Mach Dept, Piedmont |
| 1857-14 | Boylan, G. | 30 da @ $30 per mo (Oct. omit 31 da @ $30 per mo) - $60.00. Rowlesburg sta |
| 1855-24 | Boyle, Charles | pass & bur driv 24 da @ $1 - $24.00. Trans Dept main stem |
| 1857-9 | " | pass driv 25 da @ $30 per mo - $30.00. hp exp, Balto |
| 1855-64 | Josh. | lab 17 da @ $1 - $17.00. Rd Way Dept |
| 1857-10 | Michael | bur brak 27½ da @ $1.15 -$31.60. hp exp, Balto |
| 1857-9 | " | lab 25 da @ $30 per mo -$30.00. Mt Clare sta |
| 1857-101 | Patrick | lab 20 da @ $1 -$20.00. NW Va RR ballast train |
| 1857-62 | " | lab 24 da @ $1 - $24.00. Rd Dept main stem 15th s-div |
| 1857-68 | William | lab 20¼ da @ $1 - $20.25. Rd Dept main stem 19th s-div |
| 1857-65 | Boyles, Charles | lab 30 da @ $1 - $30.00. Rd Dept main stem 17th s-div |
| 1857-97 | Cornelius | lab 26 da @ $1 - $26.00. NW Va RR, Rd Dept 2d s-div |
| 1857-64 | Emory | fore 25 da @ $1.25 - $31.25. Rd Dept main stem 17th s-div |
| 1855-31 | James | saw wd 10 cords @ $.35 - $3.50. Trans Dept main stem |
| 1855-16 | Boyston, T. | pass fire 2 da @ $1.75; 10 3/4 da @ $1.25 - $17.55. Trans Dept main stem |

B & O RR EMPLOYEES

| | | |
|---|---|---|
| 1857-66 | Brabson, Thomas | lab 23¾ da @ $1 - $23.25. Rd Dept main stem 18th s-div |
| 1855-95 | Brackman, J. E. | pat mkr 23½ da @ $1.80 - $42.30. Mach Dept |
| 1855-79 | Bradbun, Isaac | paint 22 da @ $1.65 - $36.30. Mach Dept |
| 1857-135 | Bradenburg, Daniel | blksmith 20⅔ da @ $1.75 - $35.45. Mach Dept, Wheeling |
| 1857-117 | Bradencoff, John | blksmith 18 da @ $1.35 - $24.30. Mach Dept, Balto |
| 1857-28 | Bradford, J. D. | ton eng'man 15½ da @ $3 - $46.50. 1st div |
| 1855-49 | Bradley, John | watch cuts 23 da @ $1 - $28.00. Rd Way Dept |
| 1857-53 | " | watch 30 da @ $1 - $30.00. Rd Dept main stem 7th s-div |
| 1857-132 | Bradshaw, Geo. W. | clean eng 28½ da @ $1 - $28.50. Mach Dept, Grafton |
| 1855-87 | H. | help 21 da @ $1.10 - $23.10. Mach Dept |
| 1857-124 | Harrison | blksmith help 16½ da @ $1 - $16.25. Mach Dept, Martinsburg |
| 1857-86 | James | fore 25 da @ $1.50 - $37.50. grad, McGuire's Tun |
| 1855-70 | John | supv @ $60 per mo - $60.00. Rd Way Dept |
| 1857-87 | " | horse hire 22 da @ $2 - $44.00. grad, McGuire's Tun |
| 1857-86 | " | supt @ $75 per mo -$75.00. grad, McGuire's Tun |
| 1855-79 | Brady, James | carp 16 da @$1.55 -$24.80. Mach Dept |
| 1857-120 | James H. | carp 16 3/4 da @ $1.55 - $25.95. Mach Dept, Balto |
| 1855-13 | John | conduc & brak 18½ da @ $40 per mo - $30.40. Trans Dept main stem |
| 1857-20 | " | pass fire 39 da @ $40 per mo - $52.00. 4th div |
| 1855-75 | Joseph | lab 21 da @ $1 -$21.00. Rd Way Dept |
| 1855-37 | Michael | nail 28 da @ $1 -$28.00. Rd Way Dept |
| 1855-55 | Patrick | lab 21½ da @ $1 - $21.50. Rd Way Dept |
| 1857-63 | " | lab 23 da @ $1 - $23.00. Rd Dept main stem 16th s-div |
| 1857-104 | Thomas | lab 17⅞ da @ $1 - $17.25. NW Va RR Tun |
| 1857-20 | " | pass fire 6 3/4 da @ $1.75 - $11.80. 2d div |
| 1857-41 | Brainard, George | ton fire 5 da @ $1.75 - $8.75. NW Va rd, Parkersburg sta |
| 1857-102 | Braithwaite, John | carp 24 da @ $1.65 - $39.60. NW Va RR bridges |
| 1857-124 | Braman, William | fore sht work 16 da @ $1.90 - $30.40. Mach Dept, Martinsburg |
| 1855-48 | Branagan, E. | lab 7½ da @ $1 -$7.50. Rd Way Dept |
| 1857-77 | Branan, John | quarry 8 da @ $1 -$8.00. ballast train for 2d track |
| 1857-96 | Thomas | lab 21 da @ $1 - $21.00. NW Va RR, Rd Dept 1st s-div |
| 1857-64 | Brand, Charles | fore 28 da @ $1.25 -$35.00. Rd Dept main stem 17th s-div |
| 1857-64 | Henry | lab 27 da @ $1 -$27.00. Rd Dept main stem 17th s-div |
| 1855-88 | Brandenburg, C. | lab 24 da @ $1 - $24.00. Mach Dept |
| 1855-60 | Branes, Charles | fore 21 da @ $1.25 -$26.25. Rd Way Dept |
| 1855-68 | Branley, Michael | lab 24 da @ $1.12½ - $27.00. Rd Way Dept |

B & O RR EMPLOYEES  69

| | | | |
|---|---|---|---|
| 1855-68 | Brannan, Edward | lab 24 da @ $1 -$24.00. Rd Way Dept |
| 1857-80 | James | lab 23¼ da @ $1 -$23.25. lay 2d track |
| 1857-39 | John | watch, Wharf Boat 30 da @ $30 per mo - $30.00. NW Va rd, Parkersburg sta |
| 1857-84 | John J. | help 25¾ da @ $.87 - $22.10. grad, Board Tree Tun |
| 1855-67 | Michael | mason 10 da @ $2 - $20.00. Rd Way Dept |
| 1855-94 | P. | lab 2 3/4 da @ $1 - $2.75. Mach Dept |
| 1857-78 | Patrick | lab 23½ da @ $1 - $23.50. lay 2d track |
| 1857-104 | " | lab 22 3/4 da @ $1.12 - $22.75. NW Va RR Tun |
| 1855-66 | Peter | lab 20 da @ $1.50 -$30.00. Rd Way Dept |
| 1857-84 | " | fore 15 da @ $50 per mo - $25.00. grad, Board Tree Tun |
| 1857-104 | " | lab 20½ da @ $1.12 - $23.05. NW Va RR Tun |
| 1857-104 | Theodore | lab 23¾ da @ $1.12 -$26.15. NW Va RR Tun |
| 1855-50 | Thomas | watch cuts 28 da @ $1 -$28.00. Rd Way Dept |
| 1857-17 | " | lab 25 da @ $1 -$25.00. frt transfer force at Bellaire, opp Benwood |
| 1857-86 | William | mach 19 3/4 da @ $1.90 - $37.55. Mach Dept |
| 1857-92 | Brannon, Patrick | lab 24½ da @ $1 - $24.50. grad, Littleton Tun |
| 1855-65 | Brant, John | lab 12 da @ $1.12½ - $13.50. Rd Way Dept |
| 1855-75 | Brantner, George | lab 22 da @ $1 - $22.00. Rd Way Dept |
| 1857-50 | " | fore 25 da @ $1.25 - $31.25. Rd Dept main stem 5th s-div |
| 1855-22 | Samuel | fire 13¼ da @ $1.75 - $23.20. Trans Dept main stem |
| 1857-29 | " | ton eng'man 21½ da @ B - $64.50. 2d div |
| 1857-13 | William | watch 30 da @ $40 per mo - $40.00. Martinsburg |
| 1855-74 | Brany, Patrick | spik 28 da @ $1.05 - $29.40. Rd Way Dept |
| 1857-95 | " | nail 30 da @ $1 -$31.50. Wash br, Rd Dept |
| 1855-40 | Brashears, L. | fore 14½ da @ $1.37½ - $19.65. Rd Way Dept |
| 1857-50 | Lorenzo Z. | fore 23 3/4 da @ $1.37 - $32.65. Rd Dept main stem 4th s-div |
| 1855-10 | Braski, G. W. | conduc & brak 10½ da @ $3 - $40 per mo - $29.15. Trans Dept main stem |
| 1855-17 | Bratt, Arthur | ton eng'man 10½ da @ $3 - $31.50. Trans Dept main stem |
| 1855-87 | " | blksmith 21½ da @ $2 - $43.00. Mach Dept |
| 1857-124 | Samuel | fore blksmith 20¾ da @ $2 - $40.50. Mach Dept, Martinsburg |
| 1857-125 | Thomas | app 20 da @ $.50 - $10.00. Mach Dept, Martinsburg |
| 1855-86 | " | mach 24 da @ $1.65 - $39.60. Mach Dept, Balto |
| 1857-109 | Brawdest, George | mach 9½ da @ $1.60 - $15.20. Mach Dept |
| 1857-48 | Breese, H. C. | lab 22 da @ $1 - $22.00. Rd Dept main stem 2d s-div |
| 1857-37 | Brenan, Thomas | eng'man 25 da @ $50 per mo - $50.00. Wash br rd, Wash city sta |
| 1857-63 | | lab 26 da @ $1 - $26.00. Rd Dept main stem 16th s-div |

| ID | Name | Description |
|---|---|---|
| 1857-139 | Brennan, Bridget | clean pass cars 30 da @ $.50 - $15.00. NW Va RR, Mach Dept, Parkersburg |
| 1857-132 | Brennard, Patrick | clean eng 14 da @ $1 - $14.00. Mach Dept, Grafton |
| 1855-46 | Brennen, John | fire 19½ da @ $1.75 - $44.10. NW Va rd, Athey's wd train |
| 1857-124 | Bresiens, Hamond | lab 22 da @ $- - $22.00. Rd Way Dept |
| 1855-89 | Brian, John O. | mach app 11½ da @ $.50 - $5.60. Mach Dept, Martinsburg |
| 1857-120 | | help 18½ da @ $1 - $18.50. Mach Dept |
| 1857-36 | Briceland, William E. | carp 17⅞ da @ $1.50 - $25.85. Mach Dept, Balto |
| 1855-8 | Brickford, J. F. | lab 5 da @ $1 - $5.00. J. R. Shrode's wd train 4th div |
| 1857-113 | Briggs, George | conduc 24 da @ $40 per mo - $40.00. Trans Dept main stem |
| 1855-30 | | mach app 4 da @ $.65 - $2.60. Mach Dept, Balto |
| 1857-11 | J. M. | prepar fuel 24 da @ $50 per mo - $50.00. Trans Dept main stem |
| 1857-120 | Brigham, B. T. | eng'man 25 da @ $50 per mo - $50.00. Locust Pt |
| 1857-11 | Brill, John | carp 14 3/4 da @ $1.50 - $22.10. Mach Dept, Balto |
| 1855-96 | Brimigham, C. | lab 2 da @ $1 - $2.00. Locust Pt |
| 1857-11 | Bringer, John | lab 24½ da @ $1.10 - $26.95. Mach Dept |
| 1857-72 | Brinker, Casper | lab 23¼ da @ $1 - $23.25. Locust Pt |
| 1855-54 | Brinkman, Frederick | carp 23¼ da @ $1.12 - $26.15. Cumb depot |
| 1855-45 | Brinkmon, F. | lab 24 da @ $1 - $24.00. Rd Dept main stem 8th s-div |
| 1857-58 | Brion, John O. | lab 20 da @ $1 - $20.00. Rd Way Dept |
| 1855-28 | Brisleham, C. | lab 25 3/4 da @ $1 - $25.75. Rd Dept main stem 12th s-div |
| 1855-95 | Brison, James | reg eng 24 da @ $1.15 - $27.60. Trans Dept main stem |
| 1857-114 | " | core mkr 20 d= @ $1.25 - $25.00. Mach Dept |
| 1857-77 | Bristlin, Michael | core mkr 17¼ ca @ $1.25 - $21.55. Mach Dept, Balto |
| 1855-46 | Bristlow, M. | fore 25 da @ $1.25 - $31.25. lay 2d track |
| 1857-126 | Britney, Gregory | lab 20 da @ $1.12½ - $22.50. Rd Way Dept |
| 1857-101 | Britt, Benjamin | clean eng 22½ da @ $1.15 - $25.85. Mach Dept, Martinsburg |
| 1855-42 | John | fore 26 da @ $1.25 - $32.50. NW Va RR ballast train |
| 1855-51 | " | lab 20½ da @ $1 - $20.50. Rd Way Dept |
| 1857-53 | " | lab 28 da @ $1 - $28.00. Rd Way Dept |
| 1857-132 | Joseph | watch 30 da @ $1 - $30.00. Rd Dept main stem 7th s-div |
| 1857-133 | Brittingham, John | blksmith help 29¼ da @ $1 - $29.25. Mach Dept, Grafton |
| 1857-46 | Broaderick, Wm. | rig @ $45 per mo - $45.00. Mach Dept, Cameron |
| 1857-131 | Brobson, John | lab 22 3/4 da @ $1 - $22.75. Rd Dept main stem 1st s-div |
| 1855-50 | Brobston, Thomas | mach app 25 da @ $.45 - $11.25. Mach Dept, Grafton |
| 1855-41 | Brockey, Wm. | watch cuts 28 da @ $1 - $28.00. Rd Way Dept |
| | | lab 22½ da @ $1 - $22.50. Rd Way Dept |

B & O RR EMPLOYEES 71

| ID | Name | Description |
|---|---|---|
| 1855-34 | Brockman, H. | lab 24 da @ $30 per mo - $30.00. Trans Dept main stem |
| 1857-14 | Brockmare, H. | lab 25 da @ $30 per mo - $30.00. Cumb |
| 1857-130 | Broctor, Thomas | lab 13½ da @ $1 - $13.50. Mach Dept, Piedmont |
| 1857-9 | Broderick, Thomas | lab 18 da @ $30 per mo - $21.60. Mt Clare sta |
| 1857-9 | " | watch 8 da @ $1.25 - $10.00. Mt Clare sta |
| 1857-9 | Brodigan, Pat. | pass driv 25 da @ $30 per mo - $30.00. hp exp, Balto |
| 1855-31 | Brodrick, T. | prepar fuel 15½ da @ $1 - $15.50. Trans Dept main stem |
| 1855-18 | Broklaw, Theo. | ton eng'man 24 3/4 da @ $2.50 - $61.85. Trans Dept main stem |
| 1855-78 | Broochy, John | help 24 da @ $1 - $24.00. Mach Dept |
| 1855-82 | Brookaven, Joseph | lab 19 da @ $1 - $19.00. Mach Dept |
| 1857-64 | Brooke, Allen M. | lab 10 da @ $1 - $10.00. Rd Dept main stem 17th s-div |
| 1857-22 | Brookman, Francis | ton conduc 24 da @ $50 per mo - $48.00. 3d & 4th div |
| 1855-54 | " | nail 22½ da @ $1 - $22.50. Rd Way Dept |
| 1857-55 | Brookover, Brice | lab 25 da @ $1 - $25.00. Rd Dept main stem 9th s-div |
| 1857-65 | Brooks, Alfred | fire 18 da @ $1.25 - $22.50. Rd Dept main stem 17th s-div |
| 1855-8 | " | conduc 18 3/4 da @ $50 per mo - $39.05. Trans Dept main stem |
| 1857-3 | Chauncy | pres @ $333.33 per mo. Gen Ofc |
| 1857-110 | J. | mach 17½ da @ $1.50 - $25.85. Mach Dept, Balto |
| 1855-41 | James | lab 20 da @ $1 - $20.00. Rd Way Dept |
| 1857-52 | " | lab 25½ da @ $1 - $25.50. Rd Dept main stem 6th s-div |
| 1855-22 | Samuel | fire 7 da @ $1.75 - $12.25. Trans Dept main stem |
| 1855-96 | William | app 10 da @ $.65 - $6.50. Mach Dept |
| 1855-8 | Brosins, George | conduc 7½ da @ $50 per mo - $15.60. Trans Dept main stem |
| 1855-8 | W. | conduc 16⅞ da @ $50 per mo - $33.85. Trans Dept main stem |
| 1857-32 | Brosius, B. F. | ton fire 34 da @ $1.75 - $59.50. 2d div |
| 1855-21 | Isaac | fire 10⅛ da @ $1.75 - $17.95. Trans Dept main stem |
| 1857-133 | John | clean eng 30 da @ $1 - $30.00. Mach Dept, Fetterman |
| 1857-130 | Broske, George | lab 5¼ da @ $1 - $5.25. Mach Dept, Piedmont |
| 1857-29 | Broski, George W. | ton eng'man 12 da @ $3 - $36.00. 3d div |
| 1855-18 | Brouchby, Henry | ton eng'man 12½ da @ $2.50 - $30.60. Trans Dept main stem |
| 1857-122 | Brouchey, John | lab 21 da @ $1.15 - $24.15. Mach Dept, Balto |
| 1857-111 | Joseph | mach help 18 da @ $1.15 - $20.70. Mach Dept, Balto |
| 1855-79 | Browers, T. W. | mech 28 da @ $1.25 - $35.00. Mach Dept |
| 1855-65 | Browl, John | lab 13½ da @ $1 - $13.50. Rd Way Dept |
| 1857-125 | Brown, Anthony | lab 7¼ da @ $1.25 - $9.05. Mach Dept, Martinsburg |
| 1857-29 | " | ton eng'man 14 da @ $2.25 - $31.50. 2d div |

B & O RR EMPLOYEES

| ID | Name | Details |
|---|---|---|
| 1855-7 | Brown, B. F. | pass conduc 28 da @ $62.50 per mo - $62.50. Trans Dept main stem |
| 1855-79 | Benjamin | paint 1 da @ $1.45 - $1.45. Mach Dept |
| 1855-20 | C. M. | fire 1½ da @ $1.75 - $2.60. Trans Dept main stem |
| 1855-90 | Edward | mach @ $60 per mo - $60.00. Mach Dept |
| 1857-47 | " | fore 27 da @ $1.25 - $33.75. Rd Dept main stem 1st s-div |
| 1857-121 | George | paint 17½ da @ $1.50 - $25.85. Mach Dept, Balto |
| 1855-90 | George H. | mach 25 da @ $1.77 - $44.30. Mach Dept |
| 1855-79 | George L. | carp 20½ da @ $1.50 - $30.75. Mach Dept |
| 1855-25 | James | bur driv 23 da @ $40 per mo - $38.35. Trans Dept main stem |
| 1855-38 | " | lab 25 da @ $_ - $25.00. Rd Way Dept |
| 1855-57 | " | lab 21 da @ $1 - $21.00. Rd Way Dept |
| 1857-10 | " | bur reg 25 da @ $40 per mo - $40.00. hp exp, Balto |
| 1857-73 | " | carp 19¼ da @ $1.25 - $24.05. repair bridges &c |
| 1857-17 | " | lab 25 da @ $1 - $25.00. frt transfer force at Bellaire, opp Benwood |
| 1857-59 | " | lab 24 da @ $1 - $24.00. Rd Dept main stem 12th s-div |
| 1857-21 | " | ton conduc 27½ da @ $50 per mo - $55.50. 2d div |
| 1855-10 | John | conduc & brak 15 da @ $40 per mo - $27.00. Trans Dept main stem |
| 1855-91 | " | help 27 da @ $1 - $27.00. Mach Dept |
| 1855-64 | " | lab 23 da @ $1 - $23.00. Rd Way Dept |
| 1857-124 | " | blksmith help 30 da @ $1 - $30.00. Mach Dept, Martinsburg |
| 1857-47 | " | lab 18½ da @ $1 - $18.25. Rd Dept main stem 2d s-div |
| 1857-59 | " | lab 25 da @ $1 - $25.00. Rd Dept main stem 12th s-div |
| 1857-18 | " | pass train brak 23 da @ $33.35 per mo - $25.55. w end |
| 1855-4 | John F. | brak 28 da @ $33.35 - $33.35. Trans Dept, Wash br |
| 1857-39 | John M. | mess 30 da @ $20 per mo - $20.00. NW Va rd, Parkersburg sta |
| 1857-37 | John W. | brak 30 da @ $33.33 per mo - $33.35. Wash br rd, Wash city sta |
| 1857-3 | John Wilson | clk @ $50 per mo. Gen Ofc |
| 1857-7 | Joseph | gen supv trains (whole line) @ $125 per mo. Supv Trains on Rd |
| 1855-75 | M. | lab 24½ da @ $1 - $24.50. Rd Way Dept |
| 1857-50 | Martin | lab 26 da @ $1 - $26.00. Rd Dept main stem 5th s-div |
| 1857-100 | Michael | lab 23½ da @ $1 - $23.50. NW Va RR, Rd Dept 5th s-div |
| 1857-68 | " | lab 18 da @ $1 - $16.00. Rd Dept main stem 19th s-div |
| 1855-71 | Thomas | help 24 da @ $1.06 - $25.45. Rd Way Dept |
| 1855-72 | " | mach 2½ da @ $1.25 - $3.10. Rd Way Dept |
| 1857-113 | " | iron mould 17 da @ $1.55 - $26.35. Mach Dept, Balto |
| 1857-46 | " | lab 24 da @ $1 - $24.00. Rd Dept main stem 1st s-div |

| ID | Name | Description |
|---|---|---|
| 1857-70 | Brown, Thomas | rig 31 da @ $1.50 - $46.50. Mt Clare sta, Balto |
| 1857-133 | Brown, Thomas A. | mach 24½ da @ $1.72 - $42.15. Mach Dept, Feterman |
| 1857-119 | Brown, Thomas W. | carp 21 da @ $1.25 - $26.25. Mach Dept, Balto |
| 1857-100 | " " | watch 30 da @ $1 - $30.00. NW Va RR, Rd Dept 5th s-div |
| 1855-79 | W. A. | coach mkr 23½ da @ $1.65 - $38.75. Mach Dept |
| 1855-10 | W. H. | conduc & brak 3 da @ $50 per mo - $6.25. Trans Dept main stem |
| 1855-28 | William | reg eng 20 da @ $1.15 - $23.00. Trans Dept main stem |
| 1857-70 | " | mach 18¾ da @ $1.73 - $31.60. Mt Clare sta, Balto |
| 1857-120 | William A. | carp 20¾ da @ $1.75 - $35.15. Mach Dept, Balto |
| 1855-38 | Zachariah | fore 24 da @ $1.25 - $30.00. Rd Way Dept |
| 1857-93 | Browman, Adam | driv 21½ da @ $1 - $21.50. quarry & haul stone for Board Tree & Littleton Tun |
| 1857-73 | Browning, Darias | carp 21 3/4 da @ $1.50 - $32.60. repair bridges &c |
| 1855-27 | James | reg eng 28 da @ $50 per mo - $50.00. Trans Dept main stem |
| 1857-125 | " | put away eng &c @ $30.00. Rd Dept main stem 11th s-div |
| 1857-58 | Browns, W. | watch 30 da @ $1 - $30.00. Rd Dept main stem 11th s-div |
| 1857-128 | Bruce, James D. | blksmith help 25 da @ $.65 - $16.25. Mach Dept, Piedmont |
| 1855-91 | John W. | blksmith 23½ da @ $2.50 - $58.75. Mach Dept |
| 1857-128 | " " | fore blksmith 25 da @ $2.50 - $62.50. Mach Dept, Piedmont |
| 1855-76 | Bruer, Chas. | mach 22 3/4 da @ $1.55 - $35.25. Mach Dept |
| 1857-115 | Brunback, Joseph | boil mkr help 18 3/4 da @ $1.25 - $23.45. Mach Dept, Balto |
| 1857-118 | Brundige, W. H. | blksmith help 17¼ da @ $1 - $17.25. Mach Dept, Balto |
| 1857-110 | Zebr. | mach 20½ da @ $1.50 - $30.75. Mach Dept, Balto |
| 1857-127 | Bruner, Chas. A. | mach help 23 da @ $.45 - $10.35. Mach Dept, Piedmont |
| 1857-83 | Brunty, Hugh | lab 13½ da @ $1.12 - $15.20. grad, Board Tree Tun |
| 1857-86 | Bruschal, Thies | stone mason 19½ da @ $2 - $39.00. grad, McGuire's Tun |
| 1857-66 | Bryan, Daniel O. | lab 22 da @ $1 -$22.00. Rd Dept main stem 18th s-div |
| 1855-79 | Patrick | driv 24 da @ $1 - $24.00. Mach Dept |
| 1855-15 | W. | pass eng'man 19 da @ $3 - $57.00. Trans Dept main stem |
| 1857-139 | Bryant, Samuel | supv of mach 21 da @ $83.35 per mo - $83.35. NW Va RR, Mach Dept, Parkersburg |
| 1857-95 | Bryson, B. A. | lab 21 da @ $1 -$21.00. Wash br, Rd Dept |
| 1855-7 | " | pass conduc 28 da @ $62.50 per mo - $62.50. Trans Dept main stem |
| 1857-18 | James | pass train conduc 30 da @ $75 per mo - $75.00. thr mail & exp |
| 1855-94 | Buan, Stephen | fin 14¾ da @ $1.75 - $24.95. Mach Dept |
| 1855-89 | Bubert, George | help 23 da @ $1 - $23.00. Mach Dept |
| 1857-118 | Buckalew, W. | blksmith help 17¼ da @ $1 - $17.25. Mach Dept, Balto |
| 1857-41 | | lab 1 da @ $1 - $1.00. NW Va rd, Athey's wd train |

B & O RR EMPLOYEES

| Year-No | Name | Description |
|---|---|---|
| 1855-58 | Buckaloo, John | lab 20 da @ $1 - $20.00. Rd Way Dept |
| 1857-13 | Buckey, George | fire 15 da @ $1.25 - $18.75. Martinsburg |
| 1857-29 | Buckingham, James | ton eng'man 16 3/4 da @ $3 - $50.25. 2d div |
| 1855-79 | Buckingham, J. G. | carp 25½ da @ $1.50 - $38.25. Mach Dept |
| 1855-79 | Buckingham, J. W. | carp 20½ da @ $1.55 - $31.80. Mach Dept |
| 1857-110 | Buckingham, John | mach 17¼ da @ $1.50 - $25.85. Mach Dept, Balto |
| 1857-119 | Buckingham, John W. | carp 17 3/4 da @ $1.65 - $29.30. Mach Dept, Balto |
| 1857-7 | Buckler, John | clk @ $41.65 per mo. Gen Tick Agt Ofc |
| 1855-16 | Buckley, J. | pass fire 28 da @ $40 per mo - $40.00. Trans Dept main stem |
| 1857-19 | Buckley, James | pass eng'man 39 da @ $3 - $117.00. 2d div |
| 1855-93 | Buckley, John | help 16 3/4 da @ $1.25 - $20.95. Mach Dept |
| 1857-81 | Buckley, Patrick | lab 23 da @$1.12 - $25.90. grad, Board Tree Tun |
| 1855-89 | Buckley, T. | help 22½ da @ $1.10 - $24.75. Mach Dept |
| 1857-70 | Buckley, Thomas | lab 9 3/4 da @ $1 - $9.75. Rd Way Dept |
| 1857-81 | Buckley, Timothy | lab 15 3/4 da @ $1 -$15.75. lay 2d track |
| 1857-137 | Buckley, " | lab 27 da @ $1 - $27.00. Mach Dept, Cumb |
| 1857-22 | Buckston, George | ton conduc 33½ da @ $60 per mo - $67.00. 3d & 4th div |
| 1857-89 | Bucraft, Jack | brak 25 da @ $1 - $25.00. grad, Welling Tun |
| 1855-31 | Bucraft, George | saw wd 44½ cords @ $.35 - $15.55. Trans Dept main stem |
| 1855-31 | Bucraft, H. | saw wd 137½ cords @ $.35 - $48.15. Trans Dept main stem |
| 1855-33 | Budd, H. | watch 28 da @ $20 per mo -$20.00. Trans Dept main stem |
| 1855-88 | Buel, John | lab 19½ da @ $1 -$19.50. Mach Dept |
| 1855-52 | Bullikan, John | carp 14 da @ $1.50 - $21.00. Rd Way Dept |
| 1857-35 | Bullinger, Adam | lab 3½ da @ $1 - $3.50. Edwards' wd train 3d & 4th div |
| 1855-84 | Bumback, Joseph | help 25 3/4 da @ $1 - $25.75. Mach Dept |
| 1855-17 | Bunall, Otho | ton eng'man 14½ da @ $2.50 - $36.25. Trans Dept main stem |
| 1857-116 | Bunkins, Wm. | brass mould 12 3/4 da @ $1.85 - $23.60. Mach Dept, Balto |
| 1857-19 | Burall, Otho | pass eng'man 3 da @ $3 - $9.00. 4th div |
| 1855-37 | Burch, Thomas | fore 25½ da @ $1 -$25.50. Rd Way Dept |
| 1855-93 | Burd, Daniel | carp 21½ da @ $1.50 - $32.25. Mach Dept |
| 1857-115 | Buren, Conrad | boil mkr 16½ da @ $1.35 - $22.25. Mach Dept |
| 1855-75 | Burey, Anty. | lab 18 da @$1 -$18.00. Rd Way Dept |
| 1857-109 | Burgee, Edward | mach 17¼ da @ $1.60 - $27.60. Mach Dept, Balto |
| 1855-88 | Burger, George | carp 20½ da @ $1.25 -$25.30. Mach Dept |
| 1857-125 | Burger, " | carp 20½ da @ $1.25 - $25.60. Mach Dept, Martinsburg |
| 1857-116 | Burger, John | blksmith 17½ da @ $1.90 - $32.80. Mach Dept, Balto |

| | | | |
|---|---|---|---|
| 1855-95 | Burgess, B. | pat mkr 24¾ da @$2.25 - $54.55. Mach Dept |
| 1857-114 | Burgess, Benjamin | fore pat mkr 18½ da @ $2.25 - $41.65. Mach Dept, Balto |
| 1855-13 | Burgh, S. S. | conduc & brak 14¾ da @$40 per mo - $23.75. Trans Dept main stem |
| 1857-25 | Burgoyne, Harrison | ton brak 25 da @ $40 per mo - $40.00. 3d & 4th div |
| 1857-62 | Burins, Charles | watch 30 da @ $1 - $30.00. Rd Dept main stem 15th s-div |
| 1857-60 | Buriss, Patrick | watch 30 da @ $1 - $30.00. Rd Dept main stem 13th s-div |
| 1857-92 | Burk, Alexander | lab 11¼ da @ $1 - $11.25. grad, Littleton Tun |
| 1857-58 | " Edw. | lab 26 da @ $1 - $26.00. Rd Dept main stem 12th s-div |
| 1857-48 | " James | lab 24 da @ $1 - $24.00. Rd Dept main stem 2d s-div |
| 1855-41 | " John | lab 15 da @ $1 - $15.00. Rd Way Dept |
| 1855-74 | " " | fore 24 da @ $1.25 - $30.00. Rd Dept main stem 6th s-div |
| 1857-52 | " " | lab 26 da @ $1 -$26.00. NW Va RR, Rd Dept 1st s-div |
| 1857-96 | " " | lab 27 da @ $1.12 - $30.35. grad, Welling Tun |
| 1857-88 | " John 1st | lab 10 da @ $1.12 - $11.25. grad, Welling Tun |
| 1857-89 | " John 2d | lab 24 da @ $30 per mo - $30.00. Trans Dept main stem |
| 1855-33 | " M. | lab 26½ da @$1 -$26.50. Rd Dept main stem 11th s-div |
| 1857-57 | " " | fore 24 da @$1.25 - $30.00. Rd Way Dept |
| 1855-55 | " Martin | lab 18½ da @$1 -$18.50. Rd Dept main stem 19th s-div |
| 1857-68 | " " | lab 10¼ da @ $1 - $10.25. Rd Way Dept |
| 1855-59 | " Mike | lab 9 da @ $1 - $9.00. Rd Way Dept |
| 1855-65 | " Patrick | lab 23½ da @ $1 - $23.50. Rd Way Dept |
| 1857-88 | " " | lab 24 da @ $1.12 - $27.00. grad, Welling Tun |
| 1857-96 | " " | lab 26 da @ $1 - $26.00. NW Va RR, Rd Dept 1st s-div |
| 1857-62 | " " | lab 25 da @ $1 - $25.00. Rd Dept main stem 15th s-div |
| 1857-67 | " " | lab 22 da @$1 - $22.00. Rd Dept main stem 19th s-div |
| 1857-97 | " Peter | watch 30 da @ $1 -$30.00. NW Va RR, Rd Dept 1st s-div |
| 1857-60 | " Stephen | watch 30 da @ $1 -$30.00. NW Va RR, Rd Dept 1st s-div |
| 1855-56 | " Thomas | lab 26½ da @$1 -$26.50. Rd Dept main stem 13th s-div |
| 1855-60 | " " | lab 2½ da @ $1 -$2.50. Rd Way Dept |
| 1857-57 | " William | lab 17 3/4 da @$1 -$17.75. Rd Way Dept |
| 1857-89 | Burke, Anthony | lab 22 3/4 da @ $1 - $22.75. Rd Dept main stem 11th s-div |
| 1855-60 | " Frank | lab 26 da @ $1 - $26.00. Rd Dept main stem 11th s-div |
| 1857-118 | | lab 5½ da @ $1.12 - $6.20. grad, Welling Tun |
| | | fore 25¼ da @ $1 - $25.25. Rd Way Dept |
| | | blksmith help 18 da @ $1 - $18.00. Mach Dept, Balto |

| | | |
|---|---|---|
| 1857-46 | Burke, James | lab 25 da @$1 -$25.00. Rd Dept main stem 1st s-div |
| 1855-26 | John | clean eng 24 da @$1 - $24.00. Trans Dept main stem |
| 1857-47 | " | lab 27 da @ $1 -$27.00. Rd Dept main stem 1st s-div |
| 1857-93 | " | smith help 21 da @ $1 - $21.00. quarry & haul stone for Board Tree & Littleton Tun |
| 1857-31 | " | ton fire 2 da @ $1.75 -$3.50. 1st div |
| 1857-31 | John Sr | ton fire 17¼ da @ $1.75 - $30.20. 1st div |
| 1857-130 | Michael | lab 26 da @$1 - $26.00. Mach Dept, Piedmont |
| 1857-62 | " | lab 24¼ da @ $1 - $24.25. Rd Dept main stem 15th s-div |
| 1855-91 | Mike | help 30 da @ $1 -$30.00. Mach Dept |
| 1855-59 | Patrick | lab 15 3/4 da @ $1 - $15.75. Rd Way Dept |
| 1857-78 | " | lab 26½ da @ $1 - $26.50. lay 2d track |
| 1857-62 | " | lab 24½ da @ $1 -$24.50. Rd Dept main stem 15th s-div |
| 1855-26 | Stephen | clean eng 26 da @ $1 -$26.00. Trans Dept main stem |
| 1855-58 | " | lab 15½ da @ $1 - $15.50. Rd Way Dept |
| 1857-125 | " | lab 28 da @$1 - $28.00. Mach Dept, Martinsburg |
| 1855-62 | Thomas | lab 11¼ da @ $1 - $11.25. Rd Way Dept |
| 1857-31 | William | ton fire 24½ da @$33.35 per mo - $32.65. 1st div |
| 1855-95 | Burkin, William | mould 24 da @ $1.55 - $37.20. Mach Dept |
| 1857-103 | Burkley, John | lab 21¼ da @ $1.12 -$23.90. NW Va RR Tun |
| 1855-13 | Burley, L. | conduc & brak 5¼ da @ $40 per mo - $8.75. Trans Dept main stem |
| 1857-22 | Lindsey | ton conduc 32 da @ $50 per mo - $64.00. 3d & 4th div |
| 1855-17 | Burnell, P. J. | ton eng'man 23 da @ $2 - $46.00. Trans Dept main stem |
| 1857-127 | Burnep, Robert | mach 17½ da @ $1.75 - $30.60. Mach Dept, Piedmont |
| 1855-84 | Burnes, Daniel | app 23½ da @ $.75 - $17.65. Mach Dept |
| 1857-83 | Hugh | lab 25½ da @$1.12 - $28.70. grad, Board Tree Tun |
| 1855-38 | P. | lab 24½ da @ $1 - $24.50. Rd Way Dept |
| 1857-64 | Patrick | lab 24½ da @ $1 - $24.50. Rd Dept main stem 17th s-div |
| 1857-122 | " | tend fill @ $30 per mo - $30.00. Mach Dept, Balto |
| 1857-64 | Walker | lab 24 3/4 da @ $1 - $24.75. Rd Dept main stem 17th s-div |
| 1855-79 | Burnett, G. G. | paint 24½ da @$1.50 - $36.75. Mach Dept |
| 1857-121 | George G. | paint 19¼ da @ $1.55 - $29.85. Mach Dept, Balto |
| 1857-123 | James | mach 24 da @ $1 - $24.00. Mach Dept, Martinsburg |
| 1855-44 | Levi | lab 15 da @ $1 - $15.00. Rd Way Dept |
| 1857-121 | Burns, Adam | lab 22 da @ $1.15 -$25.30. Mach Dept, Balto |
| 1855-54 | Dennis | lab 15 3/4 da @ $1 - $15.75. Rd Way Dept |
| 1857-71 | " | load mat 24 da @ $1 - $24.00. Mt Clare, repair tracks in yd |

| ID | Name | Description |
|---|---|---|
| 1855-67 | Burns, Hugh | lab 22 3/4 da @ $1 -$22.75. Rd Way Dept |
| 1855-36 | James | lab 24¼ da @ $25 per mo - $25.25. Trans Dept main stem |
| 1857-90 | " | lab 10 da @ $1.12 - $1.25. grad, Welling Tun |
| 1857-35 | " | lab 22 da @ $1 - $22.00. J. R. Shrode's wd train 4th div |
| 1857-98 | " | lab 24 3/4 da @ $1 -$24.75. NW Va RR, Rd Dept 3d s-div |
| 1855-94 | John | fin 21¼ da @ $1.50 - $32.25. Mach Dept |
| 1855-55 | " | lab 21 da @ $1 -$21.00. Rd Way Dept |
| 1855-66 | " | lab 25½ da @ $1 - $25.50. Rd Way Dept |
| 1857-116 | " | blksmith 17 3/4 da @ $1.50 - $26.60. Mach Dept, Balto |
| 1857-90 | " | lab 10 da @ $1.12 -$11.25. grad, Welling Tun |
| 1857-103 | " | lab 20½ da @ $1.12 - $23.05. NW Va RR Tun |
| 1857-63 | " | lab 27 da @ $1 -$27.00. Rd Dept main stem 16th s-div |
| 1855-88 | Joseph | store kpr @ $35 per mo - $35.00. Mach Dept |
| 1855-73 | M. A. | lab 21 da @ $1.06 - $22.25. Rd Way Dept |
| 1855-28 | Martin | prepar fuel 12 da @ $1 - $12.00. Trans Dept main stem |
| 1857-139 | Michael | watch 30 da @ $1 - $30.00. NW Va RR, Mach Dept, Parkersburg |
| 1855-54 | " | lab 24 da @ $1 -$24.00. Rd Way Dept |
| 1857-75 | " | lab 20 da @ $1.15 -$22.70. ballast train for 2d track |
| 1857-130 | " | lab @ $35 per mo -$35.00. Mach Dept, Piedmont |
| 1855-91 | Mike | help 35 da @ $1 - $35.00. Mach Dept |
| 1857-122 | " | lab 19 3/4 da @ $1 -$19.75. Mach Dept, Balto |
| 1855-66 | P. | lab 20½ da @ $1.50 - $30.75. Rd Way Dept |
| 1855-68 | Patrick | lab 24 da @ $1 - $24.00. Rd Way Dept |
| 1857-15 | " | lab 25 da @ $1 -$25.00. Grafton sta |
| 1857-80 | Peter | lab 17¼ da @ $1 - $17.25. lay 2d track |
| 1857-45 | " | lab 15½ da @ $1 -$15.50. Rd Way Dept |
| 1857-76 | Pierce | dril 24¼ da @ $1.10 - $26.65. ballast train for 2d track |
| 1857-71 | Robert L. | load mat 24 da @ $1 - $24.00. Mt Clare, repair tracks in yd |
| 1857-120 | Thomas | carp 18 da @ $1.55 -$27.90. Mach Dept, Balto |
| 1855-54 | " | lab 24 da @ $1 -$24.00. Rd Way Dept |
| 1857-98 | " | fore 24 3/4 da @ $1 - $30.95. NW Va RR, Rd Dept 3d s-div |
| 1855-69 | William | lab 18½ da @ $1 - $18.55. Rd Way Dept |
| 1855-35 | " | watch 28 da @ $1.25 -$35.00. Trans Dept main stem |
| 1857-101 | " | lab 23½ da @ $1 - $23.50. NW Va RR ballast train |
| 1857-110 | " | mach 14½ da @ $1.50 - $21.75. Mach Dept, Balto |
| 1855-18 | Burrall, Jno. | ton eng'man 10¼ da @ $2.50 - $25.60. Trans Dept main stem |

| | | | |
|---|---|---|---|
| 1855-92 | Burris, James | carp 23 da - $32.35. Mach Dept | |
| 1855-52 | " | lab 28 da @ $.75 - $21.00. Rd Way Dept | |
| 1857-128 | John | carp 19 da @ $1.50 - $28.50. Mach Dept, Piedmont | |
| 1857-135 | Patrick | blksmith 13½ da @ $1.70 -$22.95. Mach Dept, Wheeling | |
| 1855-52 | Burton, Isaac | lab 28 da @ $1 - $28.00. Rd Way Dept | |
| 1857-131 | J. T. | fore mach @ $60 per mo -$60.00. Mach Dept, Grafton | |
| 1857-108 | Jackson | mach 19¾ da @$1.72 -$33.10. Mach Dept, Balto | |
| 1855-69 | R. H. | driv 6½ da @ $1 - $6.50. Rd Way Dept | |
| 1857-21 | William | ton conduc 24½ da @ $50 per mo -$49.00. 2d div | |
| 1855-4 | " | brak 28 da @ $33.35 - $33.35. Trans Dept, Wash br | |
| 1855-10 | Busch, William | conduc & saw firewd 7½ da @ $40 per mo -$6.65. Trans Dept main stem | |
| 1855-29 | Bush, Frederick | haul & saw firewd 7½ da @ $1 - $7.50. Trans Dept main stem | |
| 1857-131 | Henry | mach 21 da @$1.50 -$31.50. Mach Dept, Grafton | |
| 1857-54 | Bussard, D. | lab 22 da @ $1 -$22.00. Rd Way Dept | |
| 1857-118 | David | blksmith help 25 da @$1.25 -$31.25. Mach Dept, Balto | |
| 1857-9 | Marsh | watch 30 da @$1.25 -$37.50. Mt Clare sta | |
| 1855-35 | Marshall | watch 28 da @$1.25 -$35.00. Trans Dept main stem | |
| 1855-22 | Mat. | fire 1 da @$33.35 per mo - $1.40. Trans Dept main stem | |
| 1857-28 | Matthew | ton eng'man 24 da @$2 -$48.00. 1st div | |
| 1855-35 | Bussel, John | reg 24 da @ $50 per mo - $50.00. Mt Clare sta | |
| 1857-9 | Busy, Anthony | reg 25 da @$50 per mo - $50.00. Trans Dept main stem | |
| 1857-50 | Butler, A. | lab 24 3/4 da @ $1 -$24.75. Rd Dept main stem 4th s-div | |
| 1857-51 | Abel | lab 25 da @ $1 -$25.00. Rd Dept main stem 5th s-div | |
| 1855-25 | Albert | bur driv 24 da @$40 per mo -$40.00. Trans Dept main stem | |
| 1855-76 | Armond | mach 23¾ da @ $1.72 - $40.00. Mach Dept | |
| 1857-109 | C. J. | mach 18½ da @$1.72 - $31.80. Mach Dept, Balto | |
| 1857-10 | Charles | bur brak 27½ da @ $1.15 -$31.60. hp exp, Balto | |
| 1855-18 | " | ton eng'man 7 da @$2.50 -$17.50. Trans Dept main stem | |
| 1855-48 | " | eng'man 24 da @$2 -$48.00. Rd Way Dept | |
| 1857-75 | Edw. | eng'man 8 da @$2.30 - $18.40. ballast train for 2d track | |
| 1857-81 | George | eng'man 5 da @ $2.25 - $11.25. lay 2d track | |
| 1857-110 | " | mach 16¾ da @$1.50 - $24.35. Mach Dept, Balto | |
| 1857-86 | " | bricklay 19½ da @ $2.25 - $43.85. grad, McGuire's Tun | |
| 1855-17 | " | ton eng'man 21 da @ $3 - $63.00. Trans Dept main stem | |
| 1857-86 | " | bricklay 20½ da @ $2.25 -$46.10. grad, McGuire's Tun | |
| 1857-30 | " | ton eng'man 23½ da @ $3 -$70.50. Board Tree Tun | |

B & O RR EMPLOYEES 79

| | | | |
|---|---|---|---|
| 1855-96 | Butler, John | | lab 24½ da @ $1.10 - $26.95. Mach Dept |
| 1857-114 | " | | iron mould help 15 3/4 da @$1 - $17.35. Mach Dept, Balto |
| 1857-75 | " | | lab 22 da @ $.97 - $21.85. ballast train for 2d track |
| 1857-113 | | Mike | polish 15¾ da @ $2 -$30.50. Mach Dept, Balto |
| 1857-114 | | Richard | iron mould help 18 da @ $1 - $18.00. Mach Dept, Balto |
| 1855-95 | | " | eng'man @ $45 per mo - $45.00. Mach Dept |
| 1857-115 | | Robert | stat'ry eng'man @ $45 per mo - $45.00. Mach Dept, Balto |
| 1857-72 | | William | carp 15 3/4 da @$1.50 - $23.60. Piedmont depot |
| 1857-61 | | " | eng'man 5 da @ $3 - $15.00. Rd Dept main stem 14th s-div |
| 1857-29 | | | ton eng'man 28 da @ $3 - $84.00. 3d div |
| 1855-33 | Butt, H. S. | | disp 28 da @ $50 per mo - $50.00. Trans Dept main stem |
| 1857-14 | | | disp 30 da @ $50 per mo - $50.00. Cumb |
| 1857-52 | | Joseph | lab 21½ da @ $1 - $21.50. Rd Dept main stem 6th s-div |
| 1855-17 | | P. | ton eng'man 10 3/4 da @ $2 - $21.50. Trans Dept main stem |
| 1857-22 | | Proverb | ton conduc 26 da @ $50 per mo - $52.00. 3d & 4th div |
| 1855-52 | | Samuel | lab 22½ da @ $1 - $22.50. Rd Dept main stem 6th s-div |
| 1857-43 | | Thomas | lab 7 da @ $1 - $7.00. Rd Way Dept |
| 1857-53 | | " | lab 23 da @ $1 - $23.00. Rd Dept main stem 7th s-div |
| 1857-52 | | William | lab 25¼ da @ $1 - $25.25. Rd Dept main stem 6th s-div |
| 1855-79 | Butterly, Jas. | | help 27 da @ $1.15 - $31.05. Mach Dept |
| 1855-75 | Buxter, Jas. | | fore 25 da @ $1.25 - $31.25. Rd Way Dept |
| 1857-31 | Buxton, John | | ton fire 21¼ da @ $1.75 - $37.20. 1st div |
| 1855-7 | | U. | bag mast 28 da @ $45 per mo - $45.00. Trans Dept main stem |
| 1855-43 | Buzzard, George | | lab 4½ da @ $1 - $4.50. Rd Way Dept |
| 1855-31 | | John | saw wd 96½ cords @ $.35 - $23.25. Trans Dept main stem |
| 1857-53 | | William | fore 24½ da @ $1.25 - $30.60. Rd Dept main stem 7th s-div |
| 1855-76 | Buzzel, George | | ton eng'man 28 da @ $3 - $84.00. 4th div |
| 1855-13 | Byers, Frederick | | help 24 da @ $1.15 - $27.60. Mach Dept |
| 1857-13 | | Thomas | tak nos 30 da @ $40 per mo - $40.00. Martinsburg |
| 1855-84 | Bypert, Mark | | mach (includ boil mkr, work in sht iron,&c) 24½ da @ $1.50 - $36.75. Mach Dept |
| 1855-35 | Byrne, Andrew | | port 28 da @ $27.50 per mo - $27.50. Trans Dept main stem |
| 1857-11 | | Andy | bag'man 30 da @ $1.25 - $37.50. Wash Junc |
| 1857-133 | | James | mach 20 da @ $1.72 - $34.40. Mach Dept, Fetterman |
| 1855-70 | Byrnes, Patrick | | track lay 23 da @ $1.50 - $34.50. Rd Way Dept |
| 1855-76 | Byron, Edw. | | mach 24½ da @ $1.75 - $42.45. Mach Dept |
| 1857-113 | Byson, Edward | | polish 18¾ da @ $2.25 - $41.05. Mach Dept, Balto |

| | | | |
|---|---|---|---|
| 1855-10 | Bywards, James | conduc & brak 21 da @ $40 per mo - $38.50. Trans Dept main stem |
| 1857-122 | Cadwalder, L. | lab 21 da @ $1.15 - $24.15. Mach Dept, Balto |
| 1857-77 | Cady, Tim. | lab 22½ da @ $1 - $22.50. lay 2d track |
| 1855-10 | Cage, A. J. | conduc & brak 11 da @ $40 per mo - $19.35. Trans Dept main stem |
| 1857-25 | Cage, Andrew | ton brak 2 da @ $40 per mo - $3.20. 2d div |
| 1857-88 | Cahil, Mat. | lab 22 da @ $1.12 - $24.75. grad, Welling Tun |
| 1855-62 | Cahill, Michael | lab 10 da @ $1 - $10.00. Rd Way Dept |
| 1857-59 | Cahill, Andrew | nail 30 da @ $1.05 - $31.50. Rd Dept main stem 12th s-div |
| 1855-67 | Martin | tend to masons 22 da @ $1 -$22.00. Rd Way Dept |
| 1857-40 | Matthew | ton eng'man 23 da @ $3 - $69.00. NW Va rd, Parkersburg sta |
| 1855-68 | Partly | tend to masons 20½ da @ $1 -$20.50. Rd Way Dept |
| 1857-88 | Patrick | fore 26½ da @ $1.75 - $45.50. grad, Welling Tun |
| 1857-92 | | lab 24 3/4 da @ $1 -$24.75. grad, Littleton Tun |
| 1855-10 | Caid, A. J. | conduc & brak 18 da @ $50 per mo - $40.50. Trans Dept main stem |
| 1855-64 | Cain, Anthony | lab 23½ da @ $1 - $23.50. Rd Way Dept |
| 1857-93 | " | lab 24¼ da @ $1 - $24.25. quarry & haul stone for Board Tree & Littleton Tun |
| 1857-47 | Edward | lab 24 da @ $1 -$24.00. Rd Dept main stem 2d s-div |
| 1855-40 | John | lab 24 da @ $1 - $24.00. Rd Way Dept |
| 1857-49 | " | lab 22 da @ $1 -$22.00. Rd Dept main stem 3d s-div |
| 1855-62 | Michael | lab 16½ da @ $1 -$16.50. Rd Way Dept |
| 1857-93 | " | smith help 23 da @ $1 - $23.00. quarry & haul stone for Board Tree & Littleton Tun |
| 1857-61 | Owen | lab 21½ da @ $1 - $21.50. Rd Way Dept |
| 1857-66 | " | lab 25 da @ $1 - $25.00. Rd Dept main stem 18th s-div |
| 1855-48 | Patrick | dril 20½ da @ $1.10 - $22.55. Rd Way Dept |
| 1855-64 | " | lab 23½ da @ $1 - $23.50. Rd Way Dept |
| 1857-93 | " | lab 21¼ da @ $1 - $21.25. quarry & haul stone for Board Tree & Littleton Tun |
| 1857-97 | Peter | smith help 22½ da @ $1 - $22.50. quarry & haul stone for Board Tree & Littleton Tun |
| 1857-53 | Roger | lab 26 da @ $1 - $26.00. NW Va RR, Rd Dept 2d s-div |
| 1857-46 | Caiton, Patrick | lab 24 da @ $1 -$24.00. Rd Dept main stem 7th s-div |
| 1857-129 | Caitore, Patrick | lab 25 da @ $1 - $25.00. Rd Dept main stem 1st s-div |
| 1857-101 | Calery, Bernard | clean eng 25 da @ $1 - $25.00. Mach Dept, Piedmont |
| 1855-58 | Call, Tim | lab 23½ da @ $1 - $23.50. NW Va RR ballast train |
| 1857-93 | Callaghan, John | fore 24 da @ $1.50 - $36.00. Rd Way Dept |
| 1857-61 | Callahan, James | smith help 23 da @ $1 -$23.00. quarry & haul stone for Board Tree & Littleton Tun |
| 1855-55 | Callahar, Patrick | lab 25½ da @ $1 - $25.50. Rd Dept main stem 14th s-div |
| | Callan, Richard | fore 24 da @ $1.25 - $30.00. Rd Way Dept |

B & O RR EMPLOYEES 81

| | | | |
|---|---|---|---|
| 1857-68 | Callehan, Bartley | lab 21½ da @ $1 - $21.50. Rd Dept main stem 19th s-div |
| 1857-82 | Timothy | bricklay 21 da @ $2 - $42.00. grad, Board Tree Tun |
| 1857-67 | William | fore 26 da @ $1.25 - $32.50. Rd Dept main stem 19th s-div |
| 1857-131 | Callendine, James | mach 26½ da @ $1.75 - $46.35. Mach Dept, Grafton |
| 1857-130 | Callery, Barney | lab 18½ da @ $1 - $18.50. Mach Dept, Piedmont |
| 1857-129 | Callery, Patrick | clean eng 28 da @ $1 - $28.00. Mach Dept, Piedmont |
| 1857-58 | Callett, John | watch 19 da @ $1 - $19.00. Rd Dept Main Stem 11th s-div |
| 1857-79 | Callihan, Wm. | lab 24 3/4 da @ $1 - $24.75. lay 2d track |
| 1857-63 | Callon, Richard | fore 25 da @$1.25 - $31.25. Rd Dept main stem 16th s-div |
| 1857-33 | Callory, Barney | ton fire 1 da @ $1.75 - $1.75. 4th div |
| 1857-74 | Calner, Daniel | lab 11½ da @ $.90 - $10.35. repair bridges &c |
| 1857-80 | Calnomer, Martin | lab 20 3/4 da @ $1 - $20.75. lay 2d track |
| 1855-90 | Calvin, John | app 24 da @ $.45 - $10.80. Mach Dept |
| 1855-64 | " Thomas | blksmith 23 da @ $1.50 - $34.50. Rd Way Dept |
| 1857-89 | " | swit tend 21½ da @ $1.25 - $26.85. grad, Welling Tun |
| 1857-109 | Gamble, John | mach 17 3/4 da @ $1.55 - $27.50. Mach Dept, Balto |
| 1855-84 | Cameday, William | help 25¾ da @ $1 - $25.25. Mach Dept |
| 1857-99 | Camp, G. W. | watch 30 da @ $1 - $30.00. NW Va RR, Rd Dept 4th s-div |
| 1857-87 | Campbell, Alexander | supt @ $60 per mo - $60.00. grad, McGuire's Tun |
| 1857-83 | Daniel | lab 23½ da @ $1.12 - $26.45. grad, Board Tree Tun |
| 1857-40 | Dennis | pass fire 22 da @ $40 per mo - $29.35. NW Va rd, Parkersburg sta |
| 1855-5 | H. | driv 24 da @ $30 per mo - $30.00. Trans Dept, Wash br |
| 1857-33 | Jacob | ton fire 15¾ da @ $1.75 - $26.70. 4th div |
| 1857-41 | " | ton fire 2 da @ $1.75 - $3.50. NW Va rd, Parkersburg sta |
| 1855-37 | James | lab 26 da @ $1 - $26.00. Rd Way Dept |
| 1855-76 | " | mach 23 3/4 da @ $1.55 - $36.80. Mach Dept |
| 1857-46 | " | fore 26 da @ $1.25 - $32.50. Rd Dept main stem 1st s-div |
| 1857-101 | " | lab 22 da @ $1 - $22.00. NW Va RR ballast train |
| 1855-69 | James G. | supt of quarry @ $65 per mo - $65.00. Rd Way Dept |
| 1857-74 | " | fore @ $75 per mo - $75.00. repair bridges &c |
| 1857-10 | John | blksmith 25 da @ $46 per mo - $46.00. hp exp, Balto |
| 1857-135 | " | blksmith 19½ da @ $1.80 - $35.10. Mach Dept, Wheeling |
| 1857-79 | Michael | lab 6½ da @ $1 - $6.50. lay 2d track |
| 1855-24 | Campell, John | pass & bur driv 24 da @ $34.50 per mo - $34.50. Trans Dept main stem |
| 1857-78 | Can, James | lab 23½ da @ $1 - $23.50. lay 2d track |
| 1857-99 | Cane, Michael | watch 30 da @ $1 - $30.00. NW Va RR, Rd Dept 4th s-div |

| | | | |
|---|---|---|---|
| 1855-55 | Cane, Timothy | lab 20¾ da @ $1 - $20.25. Rd Way Dept | |
| 1857-35 | Canning, Michael | lab 22 3/4 da @ $1 - $22.75. Edwards' wd train 3d & 4th div | |
| 1857-62 | Cannon, John | lab 23½ da @ $1 - $23.50. Rd Dept main stem 15th s-div | |
| 1855-52 | " Patrick | lab 28 da @ $1 - $28.00. Rd Way Dept | |
| 1855-59 | " | lab 25½ da @ $1 - $25.50. Rd Dept main stem 13th s-div | |
| 1857-100 | Canton, Michael | watch 30 da @ $1 - $30.00. NW Va RR, Rd Dept 5th s-div | |
| 1855-53 | Cantz, Jacob | lab 13 da @ $1 - $13.00. Rd Way Dept | |
| 1857-94 | Capite, Christian | carp 24 da @ $1.75 - $42.00. repair bridges | |
| 1855-65 | Capito, C. | carp 16½ da @ $1.65 - $27.20. Rd Way Dept | |
| 1857-17 | Capstack, J. | watch 30 da @ $30 per mo - $30.00. Wheeling sta | |
| 1857-136 | Capstock, Jonathan | watch 10 da @ $1 - $10.00. Mach Dept, Wheeling | |
| 1857-54 | Carady, Patrick | lab 24½ da @ $1 - $24.50. Rd Dept main stem 8th s-div | |
| 1857-11 | Carback, Frank | lab 2 da @ $1 - $2.00. Locust Pt | |
| 1855-46 | Card, Adw. | lab 23 da @ $1 - $23.00. Rd Way Dept | |
| 1855-30 | Carey, John | lab 6 da @ $1 - $6.00. Trans Dept main stem | |
| 1857-17 | " M. | lab 25 da @ $1 - $25.00. frt transfer force at Bellaire, opp Benwood (W.S.River) | |
| 1857-135 | " Mike | lab 19 da @ $1 - $19.00. Mach Dept, Wheeling | |
| 1855-91 | " Thomas | blksmith 24 da @ $39.00. Mach Dept | |
| 1855-85 | Carles, James | help 21¼ da @ $1.10 - $23.35. Mach Dept | |
| 1855-92 | Carlin, Francis | carp @ $32 per mo - $32.00. Mach Dept | |
| 1857-56 | " Frank | lab 23 3/4 da @ $1 - $23.75. Rd Dept main stem 10th s-div | |
| 1857-21 | Carlisle, J. A. | ton conduc 19 da @ $50 per mo - $38.00. 2d div | |
| 1855-10 | " Jas. H. | conduc & brak 19 3/4 da @ $50 per mo - $41.65. Trans Dept main stem | |
| 1857-32 | " Robert | ton fire 19½ da @ $1.75 - $34.10. 2d div | |
| 1857-25 | " Robert | ton brak 21½ da @ $40 per mo - $34.40. 2d div | |
| 1857-58 | Carlon, Peter | lab 26 da @ $1 - $26.00. Rd Dept main stem 12th s-div | |
| 1857-127 | Carlougher, Hanson | oil house kpr @ $35 per mo - $35.00. Mach Dept, Piedmont | |
| 1855-96 | Carly, Mike | lab 23 da @ $1.10 - $25.30. Mach Dept | |
| 1855-10 | Carmack, John | conduc & brak 4 da @ $30 per mo - $5.00. Trans Dept main stem | |
| 1857-134 | Carmichael, Duncan | boil mkr 21½ da @ $1.75 - $37.60. Mach Dept, Wheeling | |
| 1857-134 | " Robert | boil mkr 21½ da @ $1.75 - $37.60. Mach Dept, Wheeling | |
| 1857-131 | Carmichal, Duncan | boil mkr 4 da @ $1.75 - $7.00. Mach Dept, Grafton | |
| 1857-131 | " Robert | boil mkr 4 da @ $1.75 - $7.00. Mach Dept, Grafton | |
| 1857-49 | Carmit, Walter | lab 25 da @ $1 - $25.00. Rd Dept main stem 3d s-div | |
| 1855-70 | Carmody, John | lab 14 3/4 da @ $1 - $14.75. Rd Way Dept | |
| 1857-85 | Carnay, Patrick | lab 8 da @ $1.12 - $9.00. grad, Board Tree Tun | |

| | | |
|---|---|---|
| 1855-37 | Carne, M. | lab 24 da @ $1 - $24.00. Rd Way Dept |
| 1855-34 | Carney, C. | 28 da @ $1.10 - $30.80. Trans Dept main stem |
| 1857-16 | C. J. | clk 30 da @ $40 per mo - $40.00. Moundsville sta |
| 1857-130 | Darbey | lab 19¼ da @ $1.15 - $22.15. Mach Dept, Piedmont |
| 1857-84 | James | lab 26 da @ $1.12 - $29.25. grad, Board Tree Tun |
| 1857-84 | Michael | lab 28 3/4 da @ $1.12 - $32.35. grad, Board Tree Tun |
| 1857-27 | " | ton brak 26 da @ $40 per mo - $41.60. Board Tree Tun |
| 1857-26 | " | ton brak 2 da @ $40 per mo - $3.20. 3d & 4th div |
| 1855-91 | Mike | help 23¼ da @ $1 - $23.25. Mach Dept |
| 1857-88 | Patrick | lab 19½ da @ $1.12 - $21.95. grad, Welling Tun |
| 1857-68 | " | lab 22½ da @ $1 - $22.50. Rd Dept main stem 19th s-div |
| 1857-68 | Thomas | lab 22½ da @ $1 - $22.50. Rd Dept main stem 19th s-div |
| 1857-50 | Carns, William | lab 21 da @ $1 -$21.00. Rd Dept main stem 4th s-div |
| 1855-63 | Carons, Jno. | lab 22 da @ $1 - $22.00. Rd Way Dept |
| 1855-26 | Carothers, John | clean eng 24½ da @ $1 - $24.50. Trans Dept main stem |
| 1857-21 | Carpenter, R. H. | ton conduc 28½ da @$50 per mo - $57.00. 2d div |
| 1857-102 | Carr, Alpheus | lab 8¼ da @ $1 - $8.25. NW Va RR, rwy depot |
| 1855-69 | Anthony | lab 22½ da @ $1 - $22.50. Rd Way Dept |
| 1855-85 | Benjamin | help 24 da @$1.10 - $26.40. Mach Dept |
| 1857-31 | " | ton fire 16¼ da @ $1.75 - $28.45. 1st div |
| 1857-31 | Charles | ton fire 4½ da @ $1.75 - $7.85. 1st div |
| 1857-114 | Greasly | core mkr 17¼ da @ $1.25 - $21.55. Mach Dept, Balto |
| 1855-95 | Green | core mkr 24 da @ $1.25 - $30.00. Mach Dept |
| 1857-78 | Hugh | lab 15 da @ $1 - $15.00. lay 2d track |
| 1855-27 | James | clean eng 25 da @$1 -$25.00. Trans Dept main stem |
| 1855-90 | " | help 3 da @ $1 -$3.00. Mach Dept |
| 1857-130 | " | blksmith help 30½ ga @ $1 - $30.00. Mach Dept, Newburg |
| 1857-108 | " | mach 15½ da @ $2 - $31.00. Mach Dept, Balto |
| 1857-131 | " | mach help 9¼ da @ $1 - $9.25. Mach Dept, Grafton |
| 1855-27 | John | get out eng 27 da @$1.15 - $31.05. Trans Dept main stem |
| 1857-129 | " | clean eng 22 1/8 da @ $1.15 - $25.45. Mach Dept, Piedmont |
| 1857-131 | " | mach 26 3/4 da @ $1.65 - $44.15. Mach Dept, Grafton |
| 1857-84 | Matthew | lab 21 da @ $1.12 - $23.60. grad, Board Tree Tun |
| 1857-85 | Michael | lab 12 3/4 da @ $1 - $12.75. grad, Board Tree Tun |
| 1857-102 | Nicholas | lab 8¼ da @ $1 - $8.25. NW Va RR, rwy depot |
| 1857-78 | R. T. | horse & cart 21 da @ $1 - $21.00. lay 2d track |

84                    B & O RR EMPLOYEES

| Ref | Name | Description |
|---|---|---|
| 1857-77 | Carr, R. T. | supt @ $75 per mo - $75.00. lay 2d track |
| 1855-46 | Roseby T. | supv 24 da @$60 per mo - $60.00. Rd Way Dept |
| 1855-60 | Thomas | lab 22 da @ $1 - $22.00. Rd Way Dept |
| 1857-129 | " | clean eng 15 da @ $1 - $15.00. Mach Dept, Piedmont |
| 1857-103 | " | fore 22 da @ $1.50 - $33.00. NW Va RR Tun |
| 1857-40 | W. | ton conduc 25 da @ $55 per mo - $55.00. NW Va rd, Parkersburg sta |
| 1855-8 | William | conduc 21 da @ $50 per mo - $43.75. Trans Dept main stem |
| 1855-43 | " | lab 23 da @$1 -$23.00. Rd Way Dept |
| 1857-102 | Carrack, Richard | lab 3 3/4 da @$.75 - $2.80. NW Va RR, rwy depot |
| 1857-60 | Carrick, Edw. | lab 30½ da @ $1 - $30.50. Rd Dept main stem 13th s-div |
| 1855-95 | James | mould 22 da @$1.72 - $37.85. Mach Dept |
| 1855-49 | " | watch cuts 28 da @ $1 -$28.00. Rd Way Dept |
| 1857-61 | Martin | lab 30 da @ $1 - $30.00. Rd Dept main stem 14th s-div |
| 1857-35 | Richard | lab 14½ da @ $1 - $4.50. Edwards' wd train 3d & 4th div |
| 1855-68 | Carrigan, Matthew | mason 2 da @ $2 -$4.00. Rd Way Dept |
| 1857-74 | Michael | stonecut 25 da @$2 - $50.00. repair bridges &c |
| 1857-89 | Carrol, Michael | lab 20 3/4 da @$1.12 - $23.35. grad, Welling Tun |
| 1857-110 | Carroll, Edward | lab 16 da @ $1.50 - $24.00. Mach Dept, Balto |
| 1857-121 | George | carp app 10 3/4 da @ $.65 - $7.00. Mach Dept, Balto |
| 1857-52 | " | lab 22 da @ $1 - $22.00. Rd Dept main stem 6th s-div |
| 1855-5 | J. | lab 24 da @ $30 per mo - $30.00. Trans Dept, Wash br |
| 1857-76 | James | lab 2 da @ $.97 - $1.95. ballast train for 2d track |
| 1857-108 | " | mach 18 da @ $1.65 - $29.70. Mach Dept, Balto |
| 1855-42 | John | lab 22 da @ $1 -$22.00. Rd Way Dept |
| 1855-57 | " | lab 20¼ da @ $1 - $20.25. Rd Way Dept |
| 1857-82 | " | lab 5 da @ $1.12 - $5.60. grad, Board Tree Tun |
| 1857-52 | " | lab 25 da @$1 -$25.00. Rd Dept main stem 6th s-div |
| 1857-58 | " | lab 25½ da @ $1 - $25.50. Rd Dept main stem 12th s-div |
| 1857-37 | " | lab 25 da @$30 per mo - $30.00. Wash br rd, Wash city sta |
| 1855-20 | Joseph | fire 17 da @$1.75 - $9.75. Trans Dept main stem |
| 1855-17 | Michael | ton eng'man 7 da @ $2.50 - $17.50. Trans Dept main stem |
| 1857-84 | Patrick | lab 26 3/4 da @$1.12 -$30.10. grad, Board Tree Tun |
| 1857-101 | Philip | lab 6 da @ $1 - $6.00. NW Va RR ballast train |
| 1857-108 | S. S. | mach 20 3/4 da @ $1.72 - $35.70. Mach Dept, Balto |
| 1857-8 | T. | rec clk 30 da @$58.35 per mo - $58.35. Camden sta |
| 1857-76 | Thomas | dril 16½ da @ $1.02 - $16.90. ballast train for 2d track |

# B & O RR EMPLOYEES

| | | |
|---|---|---|
| 1857-11 | Carroll, Thomas | lab 25 da @ $30 per mo - $30.00. Locust Pt |
| 1857-76 | Wm. | lab ½ da @ $.97 - $.45. ballast train for 2d track |
| 1857-103 | Wm. P. | carp 25 da @ $1.65 - $41.25. NW Va RR depot |
| 1855-96 | Carson, James | lab 24 da @$1.10 - $26.40. Mach Dept |
| 1857-114 | " | iron mould help 23½ da @ $1.10 - $25.85. Mach Dept, Balto |
| 1857-54 | William | lab 25 da @ $1 - $25.00. Rd Dept main stem 8th s-div |
| 1857-99 | Cartcamp, Casper | lab 16 3/4 da @ $1 - $16.75. NW Va RR, Rd Dept 4th s-div |
| 1855-91 | Carter, Daniel | help 21½ da @ $1 - $21.50. Mach Dept |
| 1857-37 | George | port 30 da @ $25 per mo - $25.00. Wash br rd, Wash city sta |
| 1857-91 | John | stone mason 18½ da @ $2 - $37.00. grad, Littleton Tun |
| 1855-28 | Levi | reg eng 26 da @ $1.25 - $32.50. Trans Dept main stem |
| 1855-33 | Margaret | saloon 28 da @ $16 per mo - $16.00. Trans Dept main stem |
| 1855-40 | Carus, William | lab 18½ da @ $1 - $18.50. Rd Way Dept |
| 1855-46 | Carvenaugh, T. | lab 5 3/4 da @ $1 - $5.75. Rd Way Dept |
| 1857-128 | Cary, Michael | blksmith 18 3/4 da @ $1.75 - $32.80. Mach Dept, Piedmont |
| 1855-37 | Nathan | lab 24 da @ $1 - $24.00. Rd Way Dept |
| 1857-48 | Reubin | lab 24 3/4 da @ $1 - $24.75. Rd Dept main stem 2d s-div |
| 1855-70 | Richard | lab 16¼ da @ $1 - $16.25. Rd Way Dept |
| 1855-84 | Casey, Abraham | blksmith 24½ da @ $1.90 - $46.10. Mach Dept |
| 1857-96 | James | lab 21 3/4 da @ $1 - $21.75. NW Va RR, Rd Dept 1st s-div |
| 1857-101 | John | lab 20 da @ $1 - $20.00. NW Va RR ballast train |
| 1857-81 | Patrick | lab 19⅞ da @ $1.12 - $21.65. grad, Board Tree Tun |
| 1857-85 | Richard | watch 30 da @ $1 - $30.00. grad, Board Tree Tun |
| 1857-67 | Cashion, Michael | fore 25½ da @ $1.25 - $31.85. Rd Dept main stem 19th s-div |
| 1857-72 | Caskcamp, Harman | carp 31 da @ $1.50 - $51.50. Martinsburg depot |
| 1855-22 | Caskey, James | fire 16¼ da @ $1.75 - $28.85. Trans Dept main stem |
| 1857-84 | " | eng'man 5½ da @ $3 - $16.50. grad, Board Tree Tun |
| 1857-30 | Caskie, James | ton eng'man 4½ da @ $2.50 - $11.25. 4th div |
| 1857-65 | Casky, James | engr 18½ da @ $3 - $55.50. Rd Dept main stem 17th s-div |
| 1857-74 | Casler, John | stonecut 2 da @ $2 - $4.00. repair bridges &c |
| 1855-62 | Caslim, Michael | fore 26 da @ $1.25 - $32.50. Rd Way Dept |
| 1855-46 | Wm. | lab 22 da @ $1 - $22.00. Rd Way Dept |
| 1857-61 | Cassady, Thomas | lab 24 3/4 da @ $1 - $24.50. Rd Dept main stem 14th s-div |
| 1855-71 | Cassell, Henry | bricklay 11 3/4 da @ $2 - $23.50. Rd Way Dept |
| 1857-69 | " | bricklay 22 da @ $2.25 - $49.50. Mt Clare sta, Balto |
| 1857-137 | Cassiday, James | lab 23 da @ $1 - $23.00. Mach Dept, Cumb |

85

86  B & O RR EMPLOYEES

| ID | Name | Record |
|---|---|---|
| 1855-57 | Cassidy, Edward | fore 23 da @ $1.25 - $28.75. Rd Way Dept |
| 1857-100 | " James | supv @ $50 per mo @ $1 - $50.00. NW Va RR, Rd Dept 5th s-div |
| 1855-26 | " James | clean eng 14 da @ $1 - $14.00. Trans Dept main stem |
| 1857-119 | " Michael | carp 18 da @ $1.50 - $27.00. Mach Dept, Balto |
| 1855-54 | " Thomas | fore 24 da @ $1.25 - $30.00. Rd Way Dept |
| 1857-100 | " Thomas | fore 26 da @ $1.25 - $32.50. NW Va RR, Rd Dept 5th s-div |
| 1855-44 | " | lab 20½ da @ $1 - $20.50. Rd Way Dept |
| 1855-56 | " | lab 16 da @ $1 - $16.00. Rd Way Dept |
| 1857-77 | Cassity, John | quarry 24 da @ $1 - $24.00. ballast train for 2d track |
| 1855-63 | Castello, P. | lab 20½ da @ $1 - $20.50. Rd Way Dept |
| 1855-31 | Castey, John | prepar fuel 15% da @ $1 - $15.50. Trans Dept main stem |
| 1855-58 | Castle, James | fore 26 da @ $1.25 - $32.50. Rd Way Dept |
| 1855-59 | " John | lab 23½ da @ $1 - $23.50. Rd Way Dept |
| 1857-132 | " Peter | clean eng 27 da @ $1 - $27.00. Mach Dept, Grafton |
| 1855-37 | Casty, M. | nail 27½ da @ $1 - $27.50. Rd Way Dept |
| 1857-64 | Casy, Robert | lab 21 3/4 da @ $1 - $21.75. Rd Dept main stem 17th s-div |
| 1857-100 | " Thomas | lab 21¼ da @ $1 - $21.25. NW Va RR, Rd Dept 5th s-div |
| 1855-80 | Cathcart, George H. | carp 23¼ da @ $1.60 - $37.20. Mach Dept |
| 1857-120 | " " | carp 20¼ da @ $1.65 - $33.40. Mach Dept, Balto |
| 1855-94 | Catin, William | app 23 3/4 da @ $.60 - $14.25. Mach Dept |
| 1857-35 | Catlett, Carter | lab 8 da @ $1.60 - $12.80. J. R. Shrode's wd train 4th div |
| 1857-35 | " " | lab 16 da @ $1 - $16.00. J. R. Shrode's wd train 4th div |
| 1857-26 | " George | ton brak 8 da @ $40 per mo - $12.80. 3d & 4th div |
| 1855-43 | Caton, Martin | fore 24 da @ $1.25 - $30.00. Rd Way Dept |
| 1857-80 | " Patrick | lab 13 da @ $1 - $13.00. lay 2d track |
| 1855-44 | " Thomas | lab 22½ da @ $1 - $22.50. Rd Way Dept |
| 1855-26 | " William | clean eng 4½ da @ $1 - $4.50. Trans Dept main stem |
| 1857-33 | Caugherin, John | ton fire 18¼ da @ $1.75 - $31.95. 3d div |
| 1857-66 | Caulahan, Bernard | lab 25½ da @ $1 - $25.50. Rd Dept main stem 18th s-div |
| 1857-51 | Caulehan, Martin | watch 30 da @ $1 - $30.00. Rd Dept main stem 5th s-div |
| 1857-56 | Cautz, Charles | fore 25 da @ $1.25 - $31.25. Rd Dept main stem 10th s-div |
| 1857-61 | " Francis | lab 24 da @ $1 - $24.00. Rd Dept main stem 14th s-div |
| 1857-61 | " Jacob | lab 25 da @ $1 - $25.00. Rd Dept main stem 14th s-div |
| 1857-46 | Cavana, Dennis | lab 25 da @ $1 - $25.00. Rd Dept main stem 1st s-div |
| 1857-103 | Cavanaugh, Frank | lab 23 da @ $1.12 - $25.90. NW Va RR Tun |

| | | |
|---|---|---|
| 1855-54 | Cavanaugh, John | lab 23 3/4 da @ $1 - $23.75. Rd Way Dept |
| 1857-47 | " | lab 28 da @ $1 - $28.00. Rd Dept main stem 1st s-div |
| 1855-62 | Cavenagh, M. | lab 12¼ da @ $1 - $12.25. Rd Way Dept |
| 1855-53 | Cavenaugh, Charles | lab 24 da @ $1.25 - $30.00. Rd Way Dept |
| 1857-56 | " | fore 24 da @ $1.25 - $30.00. Rd Dept main stem 10th s-div |
| 1857-78 | John | lab 26¼ da @ $1 - $26.25. lay 2d track |
| 1857-69 | " | lab 17 3/4 da @ $1 - $17.75. Mt Clare sta, Balto |
| 1857-56 | " | watch 30 da @ $1 - $30.00. Rd Dept main stem 10th s-div |
| 1855-54 | Michael | lab 23 3/4 da @ $.87½ - $1 - $23.75. Rd Way Dept |
| 1857-56 | " | nail 23 3/4 da @ $1 - $23.75. Rd Dept main stem 10th s-div |
| 1855-37 | Cavener, D. | lab 25 da @ $1 - $25.00. Rd Way Dept |
| 1855-37 | John | lab 24 da @ $1 - $24.00. Rd Way Dept |
| 1855-54 | Matthias | lab 16 3/4 da @ $1 - $16.75. Rd Way Dept |
| 1857-96 | Caveney, Patrick | lab 20½ da @ $1 - $20.50. NW Va RR, Rd Dept 1st s-div |
| 1857-98 | Cavenny, Thomas | lab 18½ da @ $1 - $18.50. NW Va RR, Rd Dept 3d s-div |
| 1857-101 | Caveny, John | lab 24 da @ $1 - $24.00. NW Va RR ballast train |
| 1857-62 | Thomas | lab 9½ da @ $1 - $9.50. Rd Dept main stem 15th s-div |
| 1857-46 | Cavey, Joseph | lab 23 da @ $1 - $23.00. Rd Dept main stem 1st s-div |
| 1857-46 | Nathan | fore 27 da @ $1.25 - $33.75. Rd Dept main stem 1st s-div |
| 1857-46 | William | lab 26½ da @ $1 - $26.50. Rd Dept main stem 1st s-div |
| 1855-38 | Caveys, R. | lab 28 da @ $1 - $28.00. Rd Way Dept |
| 1855-71 | Cavner, John | carp 21 da @ $1 - $21.00. Rd Way Dept |
| 1857-48 | Cavry, William | lab 25½ da @ $1 - $25.50. Rd Dept main stem 2d s-div |
| 1857-62 | Cawty, Christian | lab 22½ da @ $1 - $22.50. Rd Dept main stem 15th s-div |
| 1857-76 | Cestler, Chris. | blksmith 14 3/4 da @ $1.25 - $18.40. ballast train for 2d track |
| 1855-29 | Cha, John | haul & saw firewd 13 da @ $1 - $13.00. Trans Dept main stem |
| 1857-73 | Chaddock, Richard | mason 12½ da @ $2 - $25.00. repair water sta, M.S. & P.B. |
| 1857-120 | Chalmers, James J. | carp 14 3/4 da @ $1.55 - $22.85. Mach Dept, Balto |
| 1857-13 | Chambers, Anthony | haul wd 6½ da @ $1 - $6.50. Martinsburg |
| 1855-84 | B. | blksmith 24 da @ $1.45 - $34.80. Mach Dept |
| 1857-116 | Brown | blksmith 17½ da @ $1.45 - $25.00. Mach Dept, Balto |
| 1857-113 | George | mach app 14⅓ da @ $.45 - $6.40. Mach Dept, Balto |
| 1855-61 | William | lab 24 da @ $1 - $24.00. Rd Way Dept |
| 1857-91 | | stone mason 19 da @ $2 - $38.00. grad, Littleton Tun |
| 1855-10 | Chance, Edward | conduc 9 da @ brak 24 da @ $50 per mo - $50.00. Trans Dept main stem |
| 1857-9 | | coup 9 da @ $30 per mo - $10.80. Mt Clare sta |

# B & O RR EMPLOYEES

| Ref | Name | Details |
|---|---|---|
| 1857-24 | Chance, Edward | ton brak 12½ da @ $40 per mo - $20.00. 1st div |
| 1855-25 | " M. | clean eng 28½ da @ $1 - $42.75. Trans Dept main stem |
| 1857-56 | Chanch, Adam | lab 25 da @ $1 - $25.00. Rd Dept main stem 10th s-div |
| 1855-96 | Chaney, B. | lab 24 da @ $1.15 -$27.60. Mach Dept |
| 1855-96 | " Henry | lab 17 da @ $1.15 - $19.55. Mach Dept |
| 1857-114 | " " | iron mould app 23 da @ $.75 - $17.25. Mach Dept, Balto |
| 1857-126 | " Louis | clean eng 30 da @ $1 - $30.00. Mach Dept, Martinsburg |
| 1857-116 | " Thomas | boil mkr app 26 da @ $.45 - $11.70. Mach Dept, Balto |
| 1857-25 | Chaplain, Washington | ton brak 2 da @ $58.35 per mo - $3.20. 3d & 4th div |
| 1855-7 | Chapline, A. H. | clk 28 da @ $58.35 per mo - $58.35. Trans Dept main stem |
| 1855-7 | " N. Z. | clk 28 da @ $41.65 per mo - $41.65. Trans Dept main stem |
| 1857-16 | " " | clk 30 da @ $50 per mo - $50.00. Benwood sta |
| 1857-110 | Chapman, E. F. | mach 17 da @ $1.55 - $26.35. Mach Dept, Balto |
| 1857-27 | " Washington | ton brak 29 da @ $40 per mo - $46.40. Board Tree Tun |
| 1857-25 | " " | ton brak 1 da @ $40 per mo - $1.60. 3d & 4th div |
| 1857-55 | Charles, John | lab 22 da @ $1 - $22.00. Rd Dept main stem 9th s-div |
| 1857-131 | Chase, Joseph | mach help 17 da @ $1.25 - $21.25. Mach Dept, Grafton |
| 1857-110 | Chaulk, Samuel | mach 16½ da @ $1.40 - $23.10. Mach Dept, Balto |
| 1857-31 | Cheney, Nathan | ton fire 24 da @ $1.75 - $42.00. 1st div |
| 1855-71 | Chenoweth, William | carp 24 da @ $1.60 - $38.40. Rd Way Dept |
| 1857-72 | " " | fore @ $50 per mo - $50.00. Martinsburg depot |
| 1855-72 | Chenowith, R. | help 32 da @ $1 - $32.00. Rd Way Dept |
| 1857-71 | " Robert | clean cast 27⅞ da @ $1.20 - $28.00. Mt Clare sta, Balto |
| 1855-26 | Cheny, Lewis | clean eng 28 da @ $1 - $28.00. Trans Dept main stem |
| 1857-22 | Chilester, Zac | ton conduc 8 da @ $40 per mo; 3 da @ $50 per mo - $18.80. 3d & 4th div |
| 1855-89 | Chippenger, V. B. | tin 17⅞ da @ $1.50 - $25.85. Mach Dept |
| 1855-67 | Chisham, William | tend to masons 22½ da @ $1 - $22.50. Rd Way Dept |
| 1855-33 | Chisholm, H. | ofcr 28 da @ $41.65 per mo - $41.65. Trans Dept main stem |
| 1855-31 | Christ, David | prepar fuel 13 da @ $1 - $13.00. Trans Dept main stem |
| 1855-57 | Christall, Thos. | lab 19 3/4 da @ $1 -$19.75. Rd Way Dept |
| 1857-58 | Christie, Anthony | lab 25½ da @ $1 - $25.50. Rd Dept main stem 12th s-div |
| 1857-90 | Christman, George | lab 9½ da @ $1.12 - $10.70. grad, Welling Tun |
| 1855-89 | Christy, Anthony | help 22½ da @ $1.10 - $24.75. Mach Dept |
| 1857-84 | " Michael | lab 10 da @ $1.12 - $11.25. grad, Board Tree Tun |
| 1857-91 | " " | bricklay 10½ da @ $2 - $21.00. grad, Littleton Tun |
| 1857-28 | Church, John | ton eng'man 20½ da @ $3 -$61.50. 1st div |

| ID | Name | | Description |
|---|---|---|---|
| 1855-18 | Church, T. T. | | ton eng'man 13 3/4 da @ $3 - $41.25. Trans Dept main stem |
| 1855-5 | Clagett, John | | brak 4 da @ $30 per mo - $5.00. Trans Dept, Wash br |
| 1855-10 | Claggett, John | | conduc & brak 7 3/4 da @ $40 per mo - $12.90. Trans Dept main stem |
| 1855-49 | Clancello, Otto | | watch cuts 28 da @ $1 - $28.00. Rd Way Dept |
| 1857-93 | Clancy, Michael | | smith help 24¼ da @ $1 - $24.25. quarry & haul stone for Board Tree & Littleton Tun |
| 1857-94 | Claney, John | | lab 22 da @ $1 - $22.00. quarry & haul stone for Board Tree & Littleton Tun |
| 1855-18 | Clark, Andrew | | ton eng'man 8 da @ $2.50 - $20.00. Trans Dept main stem |
| 1857-139 | " | | lab 27 3/4 da @ $1.25 - $34.65. NW Va RR, Mach Dept, Parkersburg |
| 1857-59 | Clark, Anthony | | lab 26½ da @ $1 - $26.50. Rd Dept main stem 13th s-div |
| 1855-61 | Clark, Barney | | fore 24 da @ $1.25 - $30.00. Rd Way Dept |
| 1857-100 | " | | fore 26 da @ $1.25 - $32.50. NW Va RR, Rd Dept 5th s-div |
| 1855-10 | Clark, C. A. | | conduc & Brak 1 da @ $40 per mo - $1.65. Trans Dept main stem |
| 1855-36 | Clark, Edward | | lab 25 da @ $25 per mo - $26.05. Trans Dept main stem |
| 1857-100 | " | | lab 24 3/4 da @ $1 - $24.75. NW Va RR, Rd Dept 5th s-div |
| 1855-22 | Clark, Geo. | | fire 8 3/4 da @ $1.75 - $15.30. Trans Dept main stem |
| 1855-80 | Clark, Geo. W. | | carp 22 da @ $1.55 - $34.10. Mach Dept |
| 1857-22 | Clark, J. C. | | ton conduc 13½ da @ $50 per mo - $27.00. 3d & 4th div |
| 1855-72 | Clark, James | | fore @ $75 per mo - $75.00. Rd Way Dept |
| 1855-58 | " | | lab 18½ da @ $1 - $18.50. Rd Way Dept |
| 1855-63 | " | | lab 18¼ da @ $1 - $18.25. Rd Way Dept |
| 1855-6 | " | | supt of trains 28 da @ $75 per mo - $75.00. Trans Dept main stem |
| 1857-45 | " | | asst mast of rd @ $100 per mo - $22.00. Mach Dept, NW Va rd |
| 1857-134 | Clark, James B. | | mach help 22 da @ $1 - $22.00. Mach Dept, Wheeling |
| 1855-72 | Clark, James C. | | lab @ $20 per mo - $20.00. Rd Way Dept |
| 1855-76 | Clark, John | | help 24½ da @ $1.15 - $28.15. Mach Dept |
| 1855-72 | " | | help 24 da @ $1.12½ - $27.00. Rd Way Dept |
| 1855-58 | " | | lab 17½ da @ $1 - $17.50. Rd Way Dept |
| 1855-69 | " | | lab 23 da @ $1 - $23.00. Rd Way Dept |
| 1857-70 | " | | help 21 da @ $1.12 - $23.60. Mt Clare sta, Balto |
| 1857-135 | " | | lab 30½ da @ $1 - $30.50. Mach Dept, Wheeling |
| 1857-39 | " | | lab 25 da @ $30 per mo - $30.00. NW Va rd, Parkersburg sta |
| 1857-100 | " | | lab 25¼ da @ $1 - $25.25. NW Va RR, Rd Dept 5th s-div |
| 1857-60 | " | | lab 24 da @ $1 - $24.00. Rd Dept main stem 13th s-div |
| 1857-39 | " | | lab 25½ da @ $1 - $25.50. Rd Dept main stem 13th s-div |
| 1857-25 | " | | no. 2 mach 18 da @ $2.12 - $38.15. NW Va rd, Parkersburg sta |
| | ton brak 39 da @ $40 per mo - $62.40. 3d & 4th div | | |

B & O RR EMPLOYEES

90  B & O RR EMPLOYEES

| ID | Name | Entry |
|---|---|---|
| 1857-134 | Clark, John M. | mach 20 3/4 da @ $1.50 - $31.10. Mach Dept, Wheeling |
| 1857-17 | " " | stat'ry eng'man 30 da @ $65 per mo - $65.00. frt transfer force at Bellaire, opp Benwood |
| 1857-111 | " John S. | mach help 20 da @ $1.15 - $23.00. Mach Dept, Balto |
| 1857-119 | " John W. | carp 18½ da @ $1.55 - $28.70. Mach Dept, Balto |
| 1855-94 | " L. | Lab 14 3/4 da @ $1 - $14.75. Mach Dept |
| 1857-86 | " Lauglin | Lab 19⅞ da @ $1 - $19.25. grad, McGuire's Tun |
| 1855-26 | " Lawrence | clean eng 16 da @ $1 - $16.00. Trans Dept main stem |
| 1857-136 | " Lawrence | watch 30 da @ $1 - $30.00. Mach Dept, Wheeling |
| 1857-92 | " Martin | lab 10½ da @ $1 - $10.50. grad, Littleton Tun |
| 1857-90 | " " | Lab 10½ da @ $1.12 - $11.80. grad, Welling Tun |
| 1857-131 | " Michael | boil kpr 4½ da @ $1 - $4.50. Mach Dept, Grafton |
| 1857-25 | " " | ton brak 8 da @ $40 per mo - $12.80. 3d & 4th div |
| 1857-8 | " Owen | swit'man, Bailey's 31 da @ $1.25 - $37.50. Camden sta |
| 1855-37 | " P. | fore 25 da @ $1.25 - $31.25. Rd Way Dept |
| 1855-56 | " Patrick | Lab 14½ da @ $1 - $14.50. Rd Way Dept |
| 1857-133 | " " | clean eng 30 da @ $1 - $30.00. Mach Dept, Fetterman |
| 1857-56 | " " | lab 24 da @ $1 - $24.00. Rd Dept main stem 10th s-div |
| 1857-60 | " " | lab 25½ da @ $1 - $25.50. Rd Dept main stem 13th s-div |
| 1857-62 | " " | lab 18½ da @ $1 - $18.50. Rd Dept main stem 15th s-div |
| 1857-66 | " " | lab 24 da @ $1 - $24.00. Rd Dept main stem 18th s-div |
| 1855-10 | " Peter | conduc & brak 16½ da @ $40 per mo - $27.50. Trans Dept main stem |
| 1857-25 | " " | ton brak 24 3/4 da @ $40 per mo - $39.60. 2d div |
| 1857-84 | " Philip | lab 5½ da @ $1.12 - $6.20. grad, Board Tree Tun |
| 1855-18 | " Samuel | ton eng'man 13½ da @ $2.50 - $33.75. Trans Dept main stem |
| 1857-103 | " " | carp 22½ da @ $1.60 - $36.00. NW Va RR depot |
| 1855-72 | " Thomas | mach 14 3/4 da @ $1.73 - $25.50. Rd Way Dept |
| 1855-31 | " " | prepar fuel 28 da @ $1 - $28.00. Trans Dept main stem |
| 1857-135 | " " | put away eng &c 30½ da @ $1 - $30.50. Mach Dept, Wheeling |
| 1857-83 | " Timothy | lab 19½ da @ $1.12 - $21.95. grad, Board Tree Tun |
| 1855-8 | " William | brak 20 da @ $33.35 per mo - $23.00. Trans Dept main stem |
| 1857-78 | Clarke, August | lab 13 3/4 da @ $1 - $13.75. lay 2d track |
| 1855-28 | " Dan. | reg eng 19½ da @ $1.15 - $22.15. Trans Dept main stem |
| 1855-26 | " John | clean eng 29½ da @ $1 - $29.50. Trans Dept main stem |
| 1857-78 | " " | lab 23 3/4 da @ $1 - $23.75. lay 2d track |
| 1857-123 | " Nehemiah | mach 29 3/4 da @ $1.50 - $44.60. Mach Dept, Martinsburg |
| 1855-33 | " O. | swit 33 da @ $1.25 - $41.25. Trans Dept main stem |

B & O RR  EMPLOYEES  91

| Code | Name | Description |
|---|---|---|
| 1857-33 | Clarke, Patrick | ton fire 2 da @ $1.75 - $3.50. 3d div |
| 1855-70 | Clarrty, B. | lab 22 3/4 da @ $1 - $2.75. Rd Way Dept |
| 1857-103 | Clasby, Frank | lab 22 3/4 da @ $.60 - $13.65. NW Va RR Tun |
| 1855-18 | Claspy, Frank | ton eng'man 13 da @ $2.50 - $32.50. Trans Dept main stem |
| 1855-49 | Clastenman, John | watch cuts 28 da @ $1 - $28.00. Rd Way Dept |
| 1855-79 | Clautice, George | carp 25 da @ $1.25 - $31.25. Mach Dept |
| 1857-120 | " | carp 16 3/4 da @ $1.55 - $25.95. Mach Dept, Balto |
| 1855-18 | Clay, George | ton eng'man 15½ da @ $3 - $46.50. Trans Dept main stem |
| 1857-28 | " | ton eng'man 17½ da @ $3 - $51.75. 1st div |
| 1857-39 | John | pass brak 30 da @ $33.35 per mo - $33.35. NW Va rd, Parkersburg sta |
| 1855-48 | Cleary, D. | train hand 20¼ da @ $1 - $20.25. Rd Way Dept |
| 1855-18 | Cleaveland, Erastus | ton eng'man 11½ da @ $2.25 - $25.85. Trans Dept main stem |
| 1857-16 | Cleaver, C. | fire 30 da @ $40 per mo - $40.00. transfer steam Brown Dick--Ohio Riv, bet Benwood & Bellaire |
| 1857-16 | Joseph | deck hand 30 da @ $20 per mo - $20.00. transfer steam Brown Dick--Ohio Riv, bet Benwood & Bellaire |
| 1857-135 | Cleaves, Charles | carp 19 da @ $1.45 - $27.55. Mach Dept, Wheeling |
| 1855-94 | Clegg, Charles | lab 23 3/4 da @ $1 - $23.75. Mach Dept |
| 1857-35 | " | lab 14½ da @ $1 - $14.50. J. R. Shrode's wd train 4th div |
| 1857-17 | Clemens, S. A. | coop 25 da @ $1.25 - $31.25. frt transfer force at Bellaire, opp Benwood (E.S.River) |
| 1857-98 | Clemmer, James | watch 30 da @ $1 - $30.00. NW Va RR, Rd Dept 2d s-div |
| 1857-98 | John | watch 30 da @ $1 - $30.00. NW Va RR, Rd Dept 2d s-div |
| 1855-37 | Clenoy, Thomas | lab 24½ da @ $1 - $24.50. Rd Way Dept |
| 1857-21 | Clevenger, John | ton conduc 16½ da @ $50 per mo - $33.00. 1st div |
| 1855-95 | Cline, Eli | mould 17 da @ $1.72 - $29.25. Mach Dept |
| 1857-113 | " | iron mould 13 3/5 da @ $1.72 - $23.20. Mach Dept, Balto |
| 1855-8 | Elias | conduc 14½ da @ $50 per mo - $30.20. Trans Dept main stem |
| 1855-75 | Geo. | lab 23 da @ $1 - $23.00. Rd Way Dept |
| 1855-26 | Jacob | clean eng 26 3/4 da @ $1 - $26.75. Trans Dept main stem |
| 1857-90 | Owen | lab 11 da @ $1.12 - $12.35. grad, Welling Tun |
| 1855-28 | Wm. H. | reg eng 25 3/4 da @ $1.50 - $38.60. Trans Dept main stem |
| 1857-32 | Clinger, Samuel | ton fire 20 da @ $1.75 - $35.00. 2d div |
| 1857-52 | Clinton, A. D. | lab 21 3/4 da @ $1 - $21.75. Rd Dept main stem 6th s-div |
| 1857-39 | G. D. | mach engr 30 da @ $45 per mo - $45.00. NW Va rd, Parkersburg sta |
| 1855-22 | T. | fire 15¾ da @ $1.75 - $26.70. Trans Dept main stem |
| 1855-13 | | conduc & brak 6 da @ $40 per mo - $10.00. Trans Dept main stem |

| |  |  |
|---|---|---|
| 1855-32 | Clinton, T. L. | tele oper 28 da @ $30 per mo - $30.00. Trans Dept main stem |
| 1855-20 | " William | fire 16 da @ $1.75 - $28.00. Trans Dept main stem |
| 1857-131 | " " | mach help 8½ da @ $1 - $8.50. Mach Dept, Grafton |
| 1857-34 | " " | ton fire 3 da @ $1.75 - $5.25. Board Tree Tun |
| 1857-34 | " " | watch 13 da @ $1 - $13.00. Board Tree Tun |
| 1857-118 | Cloak, Laurence | blksmith help 18 da @ $1 - $18.00. Mach Dept, Balto |
| 1857-56 | Closterman, John | watch 30 da @ $1 - $30.00. Rd Dept main stem 10th s-div |
| 1857-120 | Clothworthy, William | carp help 18 da @ $1.15 - $20.70. Mach Dept, Balto |
| 1855-40 | Coader, John | lab 25 da @ $1 - $25.00. Rd Way Dept |
| 1857-84 | Coalman, John | fore @ $50 per mo - $50.00. grad, Board Tree Tun |
| 1855-57 | Coan, William | lab 21 da @ $1 - $21.00. Rd Way Dept |
| 1855-28 | Cobb, Gardner | ton eng'man 17½ da @ $3 - $52.50. 1st div |
| 1857-11 | Cochran, Cor. | lab 2 da @ $1 - $2.00. Locust Pt |
| 1857-51 | " James | lab 25 da @ $1 - $25.00. Rd Dept main stem 5th s-div |
| 1857-39 | " Kells | lab 25 da @ $30 per mo - $30.00. NW Va rd, Parkersburg sta |
| 1857-77 | " Michael | quarry 24½ da @ $1 - $24.50. ballast train for 2d track |
| 1855-82 | Cocks, Wm. | app 23½ da @ $.45 - $10.55. Mach Dept |
| 1857-57 | Coffee, Michael | lab 22½ da @ $1 - $22.50. Rd Way Dept |
| 1857-58 | " " | lab 25 da @ $1 - $25.00. Rd Dept main stem 12th s-div |
| 1857-96 | " Martin | fore 25 da @ $1.25 - $31.25. NW Va RR, Rd Dept 1st s-div |
| 1855-62 | " Patrick | lab 16½ da @ $1 - $16.50. Rd Way Dept |
| 1857-67 | " " | lab 20¼ da @ $1 - $20.25. Rd Dept main stem 19th s-div |
| 1855-6 | Coffield, E. C. | clk 27 da @ $1.65 per mo - $41.65. Trans Dept main stem |
| 1855-66 | " Patrick | lab 28 da @ $1 - $28.00. Rd Way Dept |
| 1857-98 | Cofty, Patrick | lab 20¼ da @ $1 - $20.25. N W Va RR, Rd Dept 3d s-div |
| 1857-113 | Cofran, James H. | mach app 23 3/4 da @ $.45 - $10.70. Mach Dept, Balto |
| 1855-8 | " L. R. | conduc 24 da @ $55 per mo - $55.00. Trans Dept main stem |
| 1857-22 | " " | ton conduc 25 da @ $60 per mo - $60.00. 3d & 4th div |
| 1857-57 | Cogans, John | lab 25 da @ $1 - $25.00. Rd Dept main stem 11th s-div |
| 1857-83 | Coggey, Stephen | lab 21½ da @ $1.12 - $24.20. grad, Board Tree Tun |
| 1855-64 | Coghlan, Jno. | lab 22½ da @ $1 - $22.50. Rd Way Dept |
| 1855-57 | Cogley, Daniel | lab 18¼ da @ $1 - $18.25. Rd Way Dept |
| 1857-58 | " " | lab 23 da @ $1 - $23.00. Rd Way Dept |
| 1855-57 | " Martin | lab 26 da @ $1 - $26.00. Rd Dept main stem 12th s-div |
| 1857-58 | " " | lab 18 3/4 da @ $1 - $18.75. Rd Way Dept |
| | | fore 26 da @ $1.25 - $32.50. Rd Dept main stem 12th s-div |

| | | | |
|---|---|---|---|
| 1857-17 | Cohagan, Tim. | coop 25½ da @ $35 per mo - $35.70. Wheeling sta |
| 1855-36 | Cohagen, Timothy | lab 25 da @ $35 per mo - $36.45. Trans Dept main stem |
| 1855-18 | Cohen, Mendez | ton eng'man 28 da @ $65 per mo - $65.00. Trans Dept main stem |
| 1855-46 | Cohen, Patrick | lab 21½ da @ $1 - $21.50. Rd Way Dept |
| 1857-93 | Coin, Bernard | smith help 6½ da @ $1 - $6.50. quarry & haul stone for Board Tree & Littleton Tun |
| 1857-78 | Coine, Patrick | lab 26½ da @ $1 - $26.50. lay 2d track |
| 1857-77 | Coirley, James | quarry 21 da @ $1 - $21.00. ballast train for 2d track |
| 1855-31 | Colbert, A. | saw wd 76 cords @ $.35 - $26.60. Trans Dept main stem |
| 1855-28 | " Arch. | reg eng 19 3/4 da @ $1.15 - $22.70. Trans Dept main stem |
| 1855-32 | " J. W. | saw wd 97 cords @ $.35 - $33.95. Trans Dept main stem |
| 1855-32 | " William | saw wd 38 cords @ $.35 - $13.30. Trans Dept main stem |
| 1855-8 | Colby, H. D. | brak 8 da @ $33.35 per mo - $9.50. Trans Dept main stem |
| 1857-101 | Colcamp, Henry | fore 26 da @ $1.25 - $32.50. NW Va RR ballast train |
| 1857-37 | Cole, Alexander | brak 7 da @ $33.33 per mo - $7.80. Wash br rd, Wash city sta |
| 1855-25 | " Alfred | bur driv 24 da @ $30 per mo - $30.00. Trans Dept main stem |
| 1855-80 | " David | carp 20 da @ $1.50 - $30.00. Mach Dept |
| 1857-139 | " Edward | dry sand 30 da @ $1 - $30.00. NW Va RR, Mach Dept, Parkersburg |
| 1857-90 | " James M. | lab ¼ da @ $1.12 - $.55. grad, Welling Tun |
| 1855-80 | " John R. | carp 21½ da @ $1.50 - $32.25. Mach Dept |
| 1857-119 | " " | carp 13 da @ $1.55 - $27.90. Mach Dept, Balto |
| 1857-139 | " " | mach 26 da @ $.55 - $14.30. NW Va RR, Mach Dept, Parkersburg |
| 1857-7 | " Joseph | gen tick agt @ $166.65 per mo. Gen Tick Agt Ofc |
| 1855-1 | " L. M. | gen tick agt $1500 per annum - $125.00 |
| 1855-85 | " Lewis M. | blksmith 24 da @$1.30 - $31.20. Mach Dept |
| 1857-116 | " Philip | blksmith 18 da @ $1.50 - $27.00. NW Va RR depot |
| 1857-103 | Coleman, Edward | lab 17 3/4 da @ $1 - $17.75. NW Va RR depot, Balto |
| 1855-53 | " Henry | carp 24 da @ $1.50 - $36.00. Rd Way Dept |
| 1855-53 | " Jacob | carp 13 da @ $1.37½ - $17.85. Rd Way Dept |
| 1855-91 | " John | help 15 da @ $1.10 - $16.50. Mach Dept |
| 1855-63 | " " | lab 21½ da @ $1 - $21.50. Mach Dept |
| 1855-43 | " W. | lab 6 da @ $1 - $6.00. Rd Way Dept |
| 1857-18 | " Wm. H. | lab 28 3/4 da @ $1 - $28.75. Rd Way Dept |
| 1855-66 | Colemon, John | pass train brak 12 da @ $33.35 per mo - $13.35. thr mail & exp |
| 1857-51 | Colgan, John | lab 21 da @ $1.75 - $30.75. Rd Way Dept |
| 1857-57 | Collaghan, Tim. | watch 30 da @ $1 - $30.00. Rd Dept main stem 5th s-div |
| | | lab 26 da @ $1 - $26.00. Rd Dept main stem 11th s-div |

| | | |
|---|---|---|
| 1855-62 | Collahan, William | fore 24 da @ $1.25 - $30.00. Rd Way Dept |
| 1855-84 | Collier, Henry | blksmith 23 da @$2.30 - $52.90. Mach Dept |
| 1857-116 | " | blksmith 9 da @ $2.30 - $20.70. Mach Dept, Balto |
| 1855-78 | James | help 15 3/4 da @ $1 - $15.75. Mach Dept |
| 1855-77 | " | mach 24½ da @ $1.65 - $40.40. Mach Dept |
| 1855-93 | Collin, James | mach 21½ da @ $1.65 - $35.45. Mach Dept |
| 1855-8 | Collins, Charles | conduc 19 3/4 da @ $55 per mo - $38.75. Trans Dept main stem |
| 1855-52 | " | lab 28 da @ $1 - $28.00. Rd Way Dept |
| 1857-18 | Charles W. | pass train conduc 9 da @ $62.50 per mo - $18.75. w end |
| 1857-132 | George C. | carp @ $50 per mo - $50.00. Mach Dept, Grafton |
| 1855-48 | James | dril 20 da @ $1.10 - $22.00. Rd Way Dept |
| 1855-57 | " | lab 20¼ da @ $1 - $20.25. Rd Way Dept |
| 1855-62 | " | lab 12¼ da @ $1 - $12.25. Rd Way Dept |
| 1855-95 | " | mould 21 da @ $1.72 - $36.10. Mach Dept |
| 1855-67 | " | tend to masons 22½ da @ $1 - $22.50. Rd Way Dept |
| 1857-113 | " | iron mould 17 da @ $1.72 - $29.25. Mach Dept, Balto |
| 1857-98 | " | lab 23½ da @ $1 - $23.50. NW Va RR, Rd Dept 3d s-div |
| 1857-58 | " | lab 25½ da @ $1 - $25.50. Rd Dept main stem 12th s-div |
| 1855-4 | John | conduc 28 da @ $62.50 per mo - $62.50. Trans Dept, Wash br |
| 1857-37 | " | pass train conduc 30 da @$75 per mo - $75.00. Wash br rd, Wash city sta |
| 1855-71 | M. | carp 23 da @ $1 - $23.00. Rd Way Dept |
| 1857-39 | Martin | lab 25 da @ $30 per mo - $30.00. NW Va rd, Parkersburg sta |
| 1857-74 | Matthew | lab 15¼ da @ $1.12 - $17.15. repair bridges &c |
| 1857-37 | R. | bag mast 30 da @ $40 per mo - $40.00. Wash br rd, Wash city sta |
| 1857-37 | " | bag rm 30 da @ $40 per mo - $40.00. Wash br rd, Wash city sta |
| 1855-5 | Reuben | bag mast 28 da @$40 per mo - $40.00. Trans Dept, Wash br |
| 1855-62 | Thomas | lab 8 da @ $1 - $8.00. Rd Way Dept |
| 1857-67 | " | lab 11½ da @ $1 - $11.50. Rd Dept main stem 19th s-div |
| 1855-18 | Upton | ton eng'man 13½ da @ $2.25 - $30.35. Trans Dept main stem |
| 1855-18 | William | ton eng'man 29¼ da @ $2.25 - $65.80. Trans Dept main stem |
| 1857-29 | " | ton eng'man 23½ da @ $2.25 - $52.85. 2d div |
| 1857-65 | Collman, John | lab 24¼ da @ $1 - $24.25. Rd Dept main stem 17th s-div |
| 1855-60 | M. | fore 23½ da @ $1 - $23.25. Rd Way Dept |
| 1857-100 | Colpin, Martin | lab 20 da @ $1 - $20.00. NW Va RR, Rd Dept 5th s-div |
| 1857-20 | Colson, Thomas | pass fire 13 da @ $40 per mo - $17.35. 1st div |
| 1857-38 | " | pass fire 11½ da @ $40 per mo - $15.35. Wash br rd, Wash city sta |

| Years | Name | Description |
|---|---|---|
| 1857-69 | Coltin, John | carp 17¾ da @ $1.60 - $27.60. Mt Clare sta, Balto |
| 1857-74 | Colton, Frederick | stonecut 23 da @ $2 - $46.00. repair bridges &c |
| 1857-136 | Colvin, John | mach app 25 3/4 da @ $.75 - $19.30. Mach Dept, Cumb |
| 1855-76 | Comegys, Edward | help 24 da @ $1 -$24.00. Mach Dept |
| 1857-111 | " Lemuel | mach help 18 da @ $1.15 - $20.70. Mach Dept, Balto |
| 1857-69 | " Wm. | port 26½ da @ $1.15 - $30.45. Mt Clare sta, Balto |
| 1857-70 | " " | help 29 3/4 da @ $1.25 - $37.20. Mt Clare sta, Balto |
| 1855-58 | Comer, John | lab 20½ da @ $1 - $20.50. Rd Way Dept |
| 1857-133 | Comford, James | blksmith 29¾ da @ $1.50 - $43.85. Mach Dept, Cameron |
| 1855-66 | Comfort, John | lab 23 da @ $1 - $23.00. Rd Way Dept |
| 1857-89 | " " | watch 30 da @ $1 - $30.00. grad, Welling Tun |
| 1857-89 | " Martin | tool boy 27½ da @ $.87 - $24.05. grad, Welling Tun |
| 1855-48 | " Peter | train hand 15½ da @ $1 - $15.50. Rd Way Dept |
| 1857-102 | " " | lab 19½ da @ $1 - $19.25. NW Va RR, rwy depot |
| 1855-89 | Commerford, E. | mach 19½ da @ $1.70 - $33.15. Mach Dept |
| 1855-54 | Commons, John | lab 21 3/4 da @ $1 - $21.75. Rd Way Dept |
| 1857-56 | " " | lab 25 da @ $1 - $25.00. Rd Dept main stem 10th s-div |
| 1855-69 | Compbell, Alex. | fore @ $36 per mo - $36.00. Rd Way Dept |
| 1855-94 | Comptin, Samuel | cop'smith 24½ da @ $1.60 - $38.80. Mach Dept |
| 1855-42 | Compton, George | lab 19 da @ $1 - $19.00. Rd Way Dept |
| 1857-134 | " John | mach help 2¼ da @ $1 - $2.25. Mach Dept, Wheeling |
| 1855-43 | " P. | lab 10½ da @ $1 - $10.50. Rd Way Dept |
| 1857-53 | " Peter | lab 11 da @ $1 - $11.00. Rd Dept main stem 7th s-div |
| 1857-135 | " Samuel | cop'smith 28 da @ $2 -$56.00. Mach Dept, Wheeling |
| 1855-43 | " W. | lab 9½ da @ $1 - $9.50. Rd Way Dept |
| 1857-110 | " William | mach 18 da @ $1.50 - $27.00. Mach Dept, Balto |
| 1855-74 | Comray, Richd. | lab 23 da @ $1 - $23.00. Rd Way Dept |
| 1857-79 | Comsey, Thos. | fore 24½ da @ $1.35 - $33.05. lay 2d track |
| 1857-100 | Conaroy, Hugh | lab 25 3/4 da @ $1 - $25.75. NW Va RR, Rd Dept 5th s-div |
| 1857-22 | Conaway, Solomon | ton conduc 31½ da @ $50 per mo - $63.00. 3d & 4th div |
| 1857-97 | Concanon, Michael | lab 26 da @ $1 - $26.00. NW Va RR, Rd Dept 2d s-div |
| 1855-88 | Conchuan, H. | carp 23 da @ $1.35 - $31.05. Mach Dept |
| 1857-29 | Condell, Charles | ton eng'man 22 3/4 da @ $3 - $68.25. 2d div |
| 1857-88 | Condrey, Patrick | lab 18 1/4 da @ $1.12 - $21.10. grad, Welling Tun |
| 1857-57 | Condry, James | lab 25 da @ $1 - $25.00. Rd Dept main stem 11th s-div |
| 1857-85 | " Patrick | lab 4½ da @ $1.12 - $5.05. grad, Board Tree Tun |

96                           B & O RR EMPLOYEES

| | | | |
|---|---|---|---|
| 1855-50 | Cone, John | watch cuts 28 da @ $1 - $28.00. Rd Way Dept |
| 1857-66 | | lab 17 da @ $1 - $17.00. Rd Dept main stem 18th s-div |
| 1857-103 | Coneley, John | lab 24 da @ $1.12 - $27.00. NW Va RR Tun |
| 1857-103 | Joseph | lab 18 da @ $1.12 - $20.25. NW Va RR Tun |
| 1855-50 | Patrick | watch cuts 28 da @ $1 - $28.00. Rd Way Dept |
| 1857-103 | Thomas | lab 20 da @ $1.12 - $52.50. NW Va RR Tun |
| 1857-103 | " | lab 23 da @ $1.12 - $25.90. NW Va RR Tun |
| 1857-99 | Conell, H. | lab 24 da @ $1 - $24.00. N W Va RR, Rd Dept 4th s-div |
| 1855-62 | Conelly, John | lab 12 da @ $1 - $12.00. Rd Way Dept |
| 1857-101 | Coner, Thomas | lab 24 da @ $1 - $24.00. NW Va RR ballast train |
| 1855-75 | Congan, Jno. | lab 19½ da @ $1 - $19.50. Rd Way Dept |
| 1855-63 | Conghron, M. | lab 17¼ da @ $1 - $17.25. Rd Way Dept |
| 1857-130 | Conlan, Edward | lab 19½ da @ $1 - $19.50. Mach Dept, Piedmont |
| 1855-65 | Conley, John | carp 19 da @ $1.50 - $28.50. Rd Way Dept |
| 1855-96 | " | lab 24 da @ $1.10 - $26.40. Mach Dept |
| 1857-114 | " | iron mould help 18 da @ $1.10 - $19.80. Mach Dept, Balto |
| 1857-127 | " | mach help 19 3/4 da @ $1.15 - $22.70. Mach Dept, Piedmont |
| 1855-67 | Martin | tend to masons 17 3/4 da @ $1 - $17.75. Rd Way Dept |
| 1857-102 | " | pump water 30 da @ $1 - $30.00. NW Va RR |
| 1857-139 | Michael | fill tend 15 da @ $1 - $15.00. NW Va RR, Mach Dept, Parkersburg |
| 1855-47 | Mike | lab 22 3/4 da @ $1 - $22.75. Rd Way Dept |
| 1857-115 | " | boil mkr help 20 da @ $1.10 - $22.00. Mach Dept, Balto |
| 1857-101 | Morgan | lab 23 da @ $1 - $3.00. NW Va RR ballast train |
| 1857-132 | Patrick | cupola tend 20½ da @ $1.25 - $25.60. Mach Dept, Grafton |
| 1857-101 | " | engr 7 da @ $3 - $21.00. NW Va RR ballast train |
| 1857-101 | Peter | lab 24 da @ $1 - $24.00. NW Va RR ballast train |
| 1855-64 | Tim | lab 24½ da @ $1 - $24.50. Rd Way Dept |
| 1857-101 | " | lab 23 da @ $1 - $23.00. NW Va RR ballast train |
| 1857-110 | William | mach 20½ da @ $1.50 - $30.75. Mach Dept, Balto |
| 1857-89 | Conly, John | lab 10½ da @ $1.12 - $11.80. grad, Welling Tun |
| 1855-84 | Mike | help 23½ da @ $1.10 - $25.85. Mach Dept |
| 1857-139 | Patrick | watch cuts 28 da @ $1 - $28.00. Rd Way Dept |
| 1857-41 | " | clean eng 4 da @ $1 - $4.00. NW Va RR, Mach Dept, Parkersburg |
| 1857-89 | Thomas | lab 12 da @ $1 - $12.00. NW Va rd, Athey's wd train |
| 1857-96 | " | lab 27½ da @ $1.12 - $30.95. grad, Welling Tun |
| | " | lab 25 da @ $1 - $25.00. NW Va RR, Rd Dept 1st s-div |

B & O RR EMPLOYEES

| Year | Name | Details |
|---|---|---|
| 1857-87 | Conn, Caleb | lab 23½ ½ @$1 - $23.50. grad, McGuire's Tun |
| 1857-86 | Ephraim | lab 20 3/4 da @ $1 - $20.75. grad, McGuire's Tun |
| 1855-73 | Robt. | lab 24½ da @ $1 - $24.25. Rd Way Dept |
| 1855-80 | Thos. | trim 24 da @ $1.50 - $36.00. Mach Dept |
| 1857-47 | Connel, James | lab 24 da @ $1 - $24.00. Rd Dept main stem 1st s-div |
| 1857-78 | Connell, Bartley | lab 25½ da @ $1 - $25.50. lay 2d track |
| 1855-41 | C. | lab 18 3/4 da @ $1 - $18.75. Rd Way Dept |
| 1857-52 | Cornelius | lab 24 da @ $1 - $24.00. Rd Dept main stem 6th s-div |
| 1855-57 | John | fore 24 da @ $1.25 - $30.00. Rd Way Dept |
| 1857-59 | " | fore 25 da @ $1.25 - $31.25. Rd Dept main stem 12th s-div |
| 1855-41 | P. | lab 9½ da @ $1 - $9.50. Rd Way Dept |
| 1855-41 | T. | lab 14 da @ $1 - $14.00. Rd Way Dept |
| 1857-80 | Tim | lab 19 3/4 da @ $1 - $19.75. lay 2d track |
| 1855-41 | Connelly, D. | lab 17 da @ $1 - $17.00. Rd Way Dept |
| 1857-79 | Mat. | lab 26 3/4 da @ $1 - $26.75. lay 2d track |
| 1857-93 | Michael | smith help 21 3/4 da @ $1 - $21.75. quarry & haul stone for Board Tree & Littleton Tun |
| 1857-78 | Nicholas | lab 25¼ da @ $1 - $25.25. lay 2d track |
| 1855-17 | Patrick | ton eng'man 19½ da @ $2 - $38.50. Trans Dept main stem |
| 1857-99 | " | lab 24½ da @ $1 - $24.50. NW Va RR, Rd Dept 4th s-div |
| 1857-79 | Tim. | lab 23 3/4 da @ $1 - $23.75. lay 2d track |
| 1855-56 | Connely, Thomas | lab 18 da @ $1 - $18.00. Rd Way Dept |
| 1855-58 | Connens, Peter | lab 25½ da @ $1 - $25.50. Rd Dept main stem 12th s-div |
| 1857-136 | Conner, B. M. | mach app 24 3/4 da @ $.55 - $13.60. Mach Dept, Cumb |
| 1857-67 | Bernard | fore 25 da @ $1.25 - $31.25. Rd Dept main stem 19th s-div |
| 1855-73 | Constantine | fore 23 da @ $1.25 - $28.75. Rd Way Dept |
| 1857-95 | " | pump water 30 da @ $1 - $30.00. Wash br, Rd Dept |
| 1855-52 | Dennis | lab 14½ da @ $.75 - $10.90. Rd Way Dept |
| 1857-95 | James | lab 23 da @ $1 - $23.00. Wash br, Rd Dept |
| 1855-89 | Jesse | help 26½ da @ $1.10 - $29.15. Mach Dept |
| 1855-46 | John | lab 18 da @ $1 - $18.00. Rd Way Dept |
| 1857-134 | Joseph L. | mast mech asst @ $60 per mo - $60.00. Mach Dept, Wheeling |
| 1857-139 | Michael | blksmith help 26½ da @ $.90 - $23.60. NW Va RR, Mach Dept, Parkersburg |
| 1857-78 | " | lab 26 da @ $1 - $26.00. lay 2d track |
| 1857-80 | " | lab 20½ da @ $1 - $20.50. lay 2d track |
| 1857-33 | Richard | ton fire 1 da @ $1.75 - $1.75. 4th div |
| 1857-20 | Robert | pass fire 24½ da @ $40 per mo - $32.65. 2d div |

| | | |
|---|---|---|
| 1855-89 | Conner, Theodore | help 26 da @ $1.10 - $28.60. Mach Dept |
| 1855-37 | Thomas | fore 25½ da @ $1 - $25.50. Rd Way Dept |
| 1855-59 | " | lab 15¼ da @ $1 - $15.25. Rd Way Dept |
| 1857-135 | " | lab 19½ da @ $1 - $19.50. Mach Dept, Wheeling |
| 1857-50 | " | lab 24½ da @ $1 - $24.50. Rd Dept main stem 4th s-div |
| 1857-121 | " | paint 17¼ da @ $1.65 - $28.45. Mach Dept, Balto |
| 1857-126 | " | prepar fuel 30 da @ $1 -$30.00. Mach Dept, Martinsburg |
| 1857-80 | William | lab 20 3/4 da @ $1 - $20.75. lay 2d track |
| 1857-131 | " | mach app 15½ da @ $.65 - $10.05. Mach Dept, Grafton |
| 1857-63 | Conners, David | lab 21¼ da @ $1 - $21.25. Rd Dept main stem 16th s-div |
| 1857-98 | Dimerick | lab 25 da @ $1 - $25.00. NW Va RR, Rd Dept 3d s-div |
| 1857-46 | Edward | lab 25 da @ $1 - $25.00. Rd Dept main stem 1st s-div |
| 1857-99 | James | lab 25 da @ $1 - $25.00. NW Va RR, Rd Dept 4th s-div |
| 1857-90 | John | lab 9 da @ $1.12 - $10.15. grad, Welling Tun |
| 1857-74 | " | lab 12 da @ $.90 - $10.80. repair bridges &c |
| 1857-63 | " | lab 24½ da @ $1 - $24.50. Rd Dept main stem 16th s-div |
| 1857-78 | Michael | lab 25 3/4 da @ $1 - $25.75. lay 2d track |
| 1857-90 | " | stone mason 3 da @ $2 - $6.00. grad, Welling Tun |
| 1857-52 | Patrick | lab 14 da @ $1 - $14.00. Rd Dept main stem 6th s-div |
| 1857-99 | Thomas | lab 25 da @ $1 - $25.00. NW Va RR, Rd Dept 4th s-div |
| 1855-51 | Connocton, Michael | lab 20½ da @ $1 - $20.50. Rd Way Dept |
| 1855-47 | Connolly, B. | lab 17¼ da @ $1 -$17.25. Rd Way Dept |
| 1857-38 | Isaac | brak 11 da @ $30 per mo - $13.20. Wash br rd, Wash city sta |
| 1855-47 | John | lab 15¼ da @ $1 - $15.25. Rd Way Dept |
| 1857-101 | Patrick | engr 11 da @ $3 - $33.00. NW Va RR ballast train |
| 1857-38 | Thomas | brak 25 da @ $30 per mo - $30.00. Wash br rd, Wash city sta |
| 1857-98 | " | lab 22½ da @ $1 - $22.50. N W Va RR, Rd Dept 3d s-div |
| 1857-98 | Connoloy, Michael | lab 26 da @ $1 - $26.00. NW Va RR, Rd Dept 3d s-div |
| 1855-54 | Connoly, Martin | nail 24 da @ $1 - $24.00. Rd Way Dept |
| 1857-56 | " | fore 25 da @ $1.25 - $31.25. Rd Dept main stem 10th s-div |
| 1855-62 | Connor, B. | lab 9 da @ $1 - $9.00. Rd Way Dept |
| 1855-13 | B. A. | conduc & brak 15½ da @ $40 per mo - $25.85. Trans Dept main stem |
| 1855-47 | James | lab 20¼ da @ $1 - $20.25. Rd Way Dept |
| 1857-97 | John | lab 4 da @ $1 - $4.00. NW Va RR, Rd Dept 1st s-div |
| 1855-93 | Joseph | mach 28 3/4 da @ $1.75 - $50.35. Mach Dept |
| 1855-59 | M. | lab 13½ da @ $1 - $13.50. Rd Way Dept |
| 1855-63 | " | lab 31¼ da @ $1 - $31.25. Rd Way Dept |

B & O RR EMPLOYEES    99

| | | | |
|---|---|---|---|
| 1855-48 | Connor, M. | train hand 20 3/4 da @ $1 - $20.75. Rd Way Dept | |
| 1855-57 | Peter | lab 20 3/4 da @ $1 - $20.75. Rd Way Dept | |
| 1855-10 | R. L. | conduc & brak 15½ da @ $40 per mo - $25.85. Trans Dept main stem | |
| 1855-29 | Thomas | haul & saw firewd 13 da @ $1 - $13.00. Trans Dept main stem | |
| 1855-94 | " | lab 23 3/4 da @ $1.10 - $26.15. Mach Dept | |
| 1855-41 | " | lab 23 da @ $1 - $23.00. Rd Way Dept | |
| 1855-62 | " | lab 16½ da @ $1 - $16.50. Rd Way Dept | |
| 1855-63 | " | lab 21 da @ $1 - $21.00. Rd Way Dept | |
| 1857-98 | " | lab 24 3/4 da @ $1 - $24.75. NW Va RR, Rd Dept 3d s-div | |
| 1857-82 | Connors, John | bricklay 7 da @ $2 - $14.00. grad, Board Tree Tun | |
| 1857-99 | " | lab 25 da @ $1 - $25.00. NW Va RR, Rd Dept 4th s-div | |
| 1857-96 | Michael | lab 22½ da @ $1 - $22.50. NW Va RR, Rd Dept 1st s-div | |
| 1857-103 | Patrick | lab 22 3/4 da @ $1.12 - $25.60. NW Va RR Tun | |
| 1857-84 | Walter | lab 25 da @ $1.12 - $28.10. grad, Board Tree Tun | |
| 1855-18 | Connover, J. A. | ton eng'man 12 3/4 da @ $2.50 - $31.85. Trans Dept main stem | |
| 1855-49 | Conway, Patrick | watch cuts 28 da @ $1 - $28.00. Rd Way Dept | |
| 1857-83 | Conoley, John | lab 10 3/4 da @ $1.12 - $12.10. grad, Board Tree Tun | |
| 1855-22 | Conrad, H. | fire 1 da @ $1.75 - $1.75. Trans Dept main stem | |
| 1855-69 | Mannice | lab 11 da @ $1.75 - $19.25. Rd Way Dept | |
| 1857-51 | Henry | lab 21 da @ $1 - $21.00. Rd Dept main stem 5th s-div | |
| 1857-80 | Conrey, John | lab 26 da @ $.80 - $20.80. lay 2d track | |
| 1857-47 | Conroy, D. | lab 5½ da @ $1 - $5.50. Rd Way Dept | |
| 1857-122 | Daniel | lab 18 da @ $1 - $18.00. Mach Dept, Balto | |
| 1857-72 | Patrick | lab 4½ da @ $1 - $4.50. Piedmont depot | |
| 1857-97 | Conry, Martin | lab 25 da @ $1 - $25.00. NW Va RR, Rd Dept 2d s-div | |
| 1857-79 | Michael | lab 24 3/4 da @ $1 - $24.75. lay 2d track | |
| 1857-101 | " | lab 20½ da @ $1 - $20.50. NW Va RR ballast train | |
| 1855-59 | Contz, C. | lab 23 da @ $1 - $23.00. Rd Way Dept | |
| 1857-99 | Comuss, John | lab 24 3/4 da @ $1 - $24.00. NW Va RR, Rd Dept 4th s-div | |
| 1857-110 | Conway, Frank | mach 11 3/4 da @ $1.50 - $17.60. Mach Dept, Balto | |
| 1855-50 | J. E. | watch cuts 28 da @ $1 - $28.00. Rd Way Dept | |
| 1855-94 | James | blksmith 21 3/4 da @ $1.65 - $35.90. Mach Dept | |
| 1857-41 | Jerry | lab 4 da @ $1 - $4.00. NW Va rd, Athey's wd train | |
| 1855-82 | Jesse | app 23 3/4 da @ $.55 - $13.05. Mach Dept | |
| 1857-108 | " | mach 12 da @ $1.50 - $18.00. Mach Dept, Balto | |
| 1855-94 | John | blksmith 19 3/4 da @ $1.45 - $28.65. Mach Dept | |

| ID | Name | Description |
|---|---|---|
| 1855-26 | Conway, John | clean eng 24 da @$1 - $24.00. Trans Dept main stem |
| 1855-95 | " | mould 23 da @ $1.55 - $35.65. Mach Dept |
| 1857-113 | " | iron mould 15½ da @ $1.55 -$24.05. Mach Dept, Balto |
| 1857-130 | " | lab 18 da @ $1 -$18.00. Mach Dept, Piedmont |
| 1857-57 | Patrick | lab 22½ da @ $.50 - $11.25. Rd Dept main stem 11th s-div |
| 1857-58 | Richard | watch 30 da @ $1 -$24.00. Wash br, Rd Dept |
| 1857-95 | S. | conduc & brak 12 da @ $40 per mo - $20.00. Trans Dept main stem |
| 1855-13 | Solomon | lab 24 da @ $1 - $24.00. Rd Dept main stem 2d s-div |
| 1857-48 | William | mach 21 da @ $1.60 -$33.60. Mach Dept |
| 1855-82 | " | mach 19 3/4 da @ $1.35 - $26.65. Mach Dept |
| 1855-86 | " | mach 17½ da @ $1.60 -$27.60. Mach Dept, Balto |
| 1857-109 | Coogan, Pat. | mach 26 3/4 da @ $1.55 - $41.45. Mach Dept, Martinsburg |
| 1857-123 | Coogen, Pat. | pav 24½ da @ $1.12 - $27.30. Mt Clare, repair tracks in yd |
| 1857-71 | Coogle, Benjamin | lab 25 da @ $1 - $25.00. Rd Way Dept |
| 1855-73 | Cook | lab 20 da @ $1 - $20.00. NW Va rd, Athey's wd train |
| 1857-41 | A. J. | @ $20 per mo - $20.00. ballast train for 2d track |
| 1857-75 | A. S. | boil mkr 8 3/4 da - $16.95. Mach Dept |
| 1855-92 | Adison | blksmith 18 3/4 da @ $1.45 - $27.20. Mach Dept, Balto |
| 1857-117 | Benjamin | blksmith 24 da @ $1.45 - $34.80. Mach Dept |
| 1855-84 | " | clean eng 26 da @ $1.15 - $29.90. Mach Dept, Martinsburg |
| 1857-125 | Charles | lab 21½ da @ $1 - $21.50. Rd Dept main stem 11th s-div |
| 1857-57 | E. T. | blksmith help 15 3/4 da @ $1 - $15.75. Mach Dept, Balto |
| 1855-25 | E. W. | clean eng 22 3/4 da @ $1.15 - $26.15. Trans Dept main stem |
| 1857-122 | Frank | blksmith help 24 3/4 da @ $1 - $24.75. Mach Dept, Balto |
| 1857-118 | Jacob | prepar fuel 17 da @ $30 per mo - $18.20. Trans Dept main stem |
| 1855-30 | James | lab 30 da @ $1 -$30.00. Mach Dept, Martinsburg |
| 1857-126 | Jasper | carp 24 da @ $1.45 - $34.80. Mach Dept |
| 1855-90 | Lewis | lab 14½ da @ $1 - $14.50. Mach Dept |
| 1855-88 | Robert | mach 24 da @$1 -$24.00. Mach Dept |
| 1855-85 | William | mach help 19½ da @ $1 - $19.50. Mach Dept, Grafton |
| 1857-131 | " | blksmith 24¼ da @ $1.45 - $35.15. Mach Dept |
| 1855-84 | " | blksmith 18 da @ $1.55 - $27.90. Mach Dept, Balto |
| 1857-116 | | lab 9½ da @ $.97 - $9.25. ballast train for 2d track |
| 1857-76 | | quarry 8 da @ $1 - $8.00. ballast train for 2d track |
| 1857-77 | | |

B & O RR EMPLOYEES 101

| ID | Name | Entry |
|---|---|---|
| 1855-30 | Cooke, J. | prepar fuel 9 da @ $1 - $9.00. Trans Dept main stem |
| 1857-90 | Cooley, James | lab 15 3/4 da @ $1 - $15.75. grad, Welling Tun |
| 1857-91 | Cooly, Martin | lab 22½ da @ $1 - $22.50. grad, Welling Tun |
| 1857-67 | Cooly, Thomas | lab 22 3/4 da @ $1 - $22.75. Rd Dept main stem 18th s-div |
| 1855-31 | Cooney, Patrick | prepar fuel 14½ da @ $1 - $14.50. Trans Dept main stem |
| 1857-85 | Coonrod, Henry | stone mason 12 da @ $2 - $24.00. grad, Board Tree Tun |
| 1857-53 | Cooper, A. P. | lab 24 da @ $1.25 - $30.00. Rd Dept main stem 7th s-div |
| 1857-76 | " George | fire 24 da @ $1.75 - $42.00. ballast train for 2d track |
| 1857-11 | " John | lab 2 da @ $1 - $2.00. Locust Pt |
| 1857-81 | " Jonas | lab 24 3/4 da @ $4.12 - $27.85. grad, Board Tree Tun |
| 1857-53 | Cope, George | lab 23½ da @ $1 - $23.50. Rd Dept main stem 7th s-div |
| 1857-95 | Copeland, William | lab 23 da @ $1 - $23.00. Wash br, Rd Dept |
| 1855-65 | Copely, John | lab 24 da @ $1.12 3/4 - $27.00. Rd Way Dept |
| 1857-75 | Cople, Patrick | lab 19 da @ $1.05 - $19.85. ballast train for 2d track |
| 1857-54 | Copley, Patrick | lab 21½ da @ $1 - $21.50. Rd Dept main stem 8th s-div |
| 1855-46 | Coppinger, John | lab 4½ da @ $1 - $4.50. Rd Way Dept |
| 1857-86 | Coran, William | lab 23 da @ $1 -$23.00. grad, McGuire's Tun |
| 1855-5 | Corbine, Robert | brak 23 da @ $30 per mo - $28.75. Trans Dept, Wash br |
| 1857-102 | Cordial, M. | carp 22 da @ $1.60 - $35.20. NW Va RR, rwy depot |
| 1855-42 | Cordial, Peter | lab 20 da @ $1 - $20.00. Rd Way Dept |
| 1855-31 | Corgan, Bernard | saw wd 67½ cords @ $.35 - $23.60. Trans Dept main stem |
| 1857-86 | Cormel, Philip | lab 17⅜ da @ $1 - $17.25. grad, McGuire's Tun |
| 1857-47 | Cornell, M. | lab 30 da @ $1 - $30.00. Rd Dept main stem 1st s-div |
| 1857-8 | " Patrick | rec clk 30 da @ $41.65 per mo - $41.65. Camden sta |
| 1857-75 | Corner, Edward | lab 9 3/4 da @ $1.15 - $11.40. ballast train for 2d track |
| 1855-68 | Cornwell, Chas. | lab 22 da @ $1 - $22.00. Rd Way Dept |
| 1855-18 | Corpreul, Moses | ton eng'man 2 da @$2.50 - $5.00. Trans Dept main stem |
| 1857-128 | Corprew, Andrew | fore boil mkr 25 da @ $2.50 - $62.50. Mach Dept, Piedmont |
| 1857-130 | Corregan, Michael | lab 19½ da @ $.75 - $14.45. Mach Dept, Piedmont |
| 1857-90 | Correll, George | fore 23 3/4 da @ $1.75 - $41.55. grad, Welling Tun |
| 1855-93 | Corrick, Edw. | mach 16⅔ da @ $1.60 - $26.00. Mach Dept |
| 1855-56 | Corrigan, Matthew | lab 15¼ da @ $1 - $15.25. Rd Way Dept |
| 1857-86 | " Rodger | stone mason 20 3/4 da @ $2 - $41.50. grad, McGuire's Tun |
| 1855-65 | Corse, William D. | lab 25 3/4 da @ $1.12 - $28.95. grad, Welling Tun |
| 1855-91 | Cosgrove, Adam | paint 2½ da @ $1.50 - $3.75. Rd Way Dept |
|  |  | help 26 da @ $1 - $26.00. Mach Dept |

B & O RR EMPLOYEES

| | | | |
|---|---|---|---|
| 1857-85 | Cosgrove, Festy | lab 9¼ da @ $1 - $9.25. grad, Board Tree Tun |
| 1855-82 | John | app 23½ da @ $5.55 - $12.90. Mach Dept |
| 1855-73 | " | lab 23½ da @ $1 - $23.50. Rd Way Dept |
| 1857-20 | " | lab 18 da @ $1 - $18.00. Mt Clare, repair tracks in yd |
| 1857-45 | L. | pass fire 31½ da @ $1.25 - $39.35. 4th div |
| 1855-54 | Lawrence | lab 8½ da @ $1 - $8.50. Rd Way Dept |
| 1857-45 | M. | watch 27½ da @ $1 - $27.50. Rd Dept main stem 8th s-div |
| 1855-54 | Michael | lab 11½ da @ $1 - $11.50. Rd Way Dept |
| 1857-68 | " | lab 24 da @ $1 - $24.00. Rd Dept main stem 8th s-div |
| 1857-60 | Patrick | lab 16 da @ $1 - $16.00. Rd Dept main stem 19th s-div |
| 1857-97 | Costalo, James | lab 26 da @ $1 - $26.00. Rd Dept main stem 13th s-div |
| 1857-93 | Costelle, Edward | lab 25 da @ $1 - $25.00. NW Va RR, Rd Dept 2d s-div |
| 1855-63 | Costello, M. | smith help 13 da @ $1 - $13.00. quarry & haul stone for Board Tree & Littleton Tun |
| 1857-89 | " | lab 23 da @ $1 - $23.00. Rd Way Dept |
| 1857-75 | Patrick | lab 10½ da @ $1.12 - $11.80. grad, Welling Tun |
| 1857-84 | Costelow, Edward | lab 17⅞ da @ $.97 - $16.80. ballast train for 2d track |
| 1857-99 | Costlin, John | lab 22 3/4 da @ $1.12 - $25.60. grad, Board Tree Tun |
| 1857-99 | Costlo, Matthew | watch 30 da @ $1 - $30.00. NW Va RR, Rd Dept 4th s-div |
| 1857-99 | Miles | lab 28 da @ $1 - $28.00. NW Va RR, Rd Dept 4th s-div |
| 1857-77 | Patrick | fore 25 da @ $1.25 - $31.25. NW Va RR, Rd Dept 4th s-div |
| 1857-136 | Costol, Edward | quarry 8 da @ $1 - $8.00. ballast train for 2d track |
| 1857-61 | Costolo, James | fill tend @ $30 per mo - $30.00. Mach Dept, Wheeling |
| 1855-56 | Cotcamp, William | lab 27½ da @ $1 - $27.50. Rd Dept main stem 14th s-div |
| 1857-97 | Cotter, F. S. | lab 13¼ da @ $1 - $13.25. Rd Way Dept |
| 1857-17 | Cottingham, George | watch 30 da @ $1 - $30.00. NW Va RR, Rd Dept 1st s-div |
| 1855-9 | Cottman, George | lab 6 da @ $1 - $6.00. frt transfer force at Bellaire, opp Benwood |
| 1857-125 | Coubwright, J. | conduc 8½ da @ $50 per mo - $17.70. Trans Dept main stem |
| 1855-13 | Couchman, Henry | carp 19 da @ $1.40 - $26.60. Mach Dept, Martinsburg |
| 1857-81 | Coughlan, M. | conduc & brak 12 da @ $40 per mo - $20.00. Trans Dept main stem |
| 1855-56 | Coughlen, Joseph | lab 20½ da @ $1 - $20.50. lay 2d track |
| 1855-55 | Coughlin, Jas. | lab 12 da @ $1.75 - $21.00. Rd Way Dept |
| 1857-57 | Patrick | lab 7 da @ $1 - $7.00. Rd Way Dept |
| 1857-104 | " | lab 21½ da @ $1 - $21.50. Rd Dept main stem 11th s-div |
| | William | miner 22½ da @ $1.12 - $25.05. NW Va RR Tun |
| 1857-94 | Couglin, John | lab 20 da @ $1 - $20.00. quarry & haul stone for Board Tree & Littleton Tun |
| 1855-91 | Coulan, Edward | help 24 3/4 da @ $1 - $24.75. Mach Dept |

| ID | Name | Description |
|---|---|---|
| 1855-53 | Coulehan, Mart. | lab 24 da @ $1.25 - $30.00. Rd Way Dept |
| 1857-68 | " Wm. | watch 30 da @ $1 -$30.00. Rd Dept main stem 19th s-div |
| 1855-63 | Couleman, Wm. | lab 18 da @ $1 - $18.00. Rd Way Dept |
| 1857-86 | Couley, Coleman | lab 23 3/4 da @ $1.12 - $26.70. grad, McGuire's Tun |
| 1857-122 | Coulter, John | lab 20½ da @ $1 - $20.50. Mach Dept, Balto |
| 1857-94 | Counahan, Michael | lab 9½ da @ $1 - $9.50. quarry & haul stone for Board Tree & Littleton Tun |
| 1857-9 | Counselman, G. F. | watch 25 da @ $15 per mo - $35.00. hp exp, Balto |
| 1855-25 | " J. W. | clean eng 22½ da @ $1.50 - $35.25. Trans Dept main stem |
| 1857-113 | " R. | mach app 5½ da @ $.65 - $3.60. Mach Dept, Balto |
| 1857-9 | " Wm. H. | supv of stock 30 da @ $75 per mo - $75.00. hp exp, Balto |
| 1855-71 | Couregys, Samuel | carp 26¾ da @ $1.15 - $30.20. Rd Way Dept |
| 1857-118 | Coursey, James | blksmith help 17½ da @ $1 - $17.25. Mach Dept, Balto |
| 1857-40 | Courtney, J. | ton eng'man 3 da @ $2.25 - $6.75. NW Va rd, Parkersburg sta |
| 1857-52 | " James | watch 30 da @ $1 - $30.00. Rd Dept main stem 6th s-div |
| 1857-76 | " Jerry | dril 19½ da @ $1.10 - $21.45. ballast train for 2d track |
| 1855-22 | " John | fire 18½ da @ $1.75 - $32.35. Trans Dept main stem |
| 1857-139 | " " | lab 2 da @ $1.20 - $2.40. NW Va RR, Mach Dept, Parkersburg |
| 1857-39 | " Patrick | yd eng'man 6½ da @ $1.92 - $12.50. NW Va rd, Parkersburg sta |
| 1857-98 | " Samuel | lab 25 da @ $1. - $25.00. NW Va RR, Rd Dept 3d s-div |
| 1857-52 | " William | lab 27½ da @ $1 - $27.50. Rd Dept main stem 6th s-div |
| 1855-76 | Courts, Edward | lab 24½ da @ $1 - $24.25. Rd Dept main stem 6th s-div |
| 1857-109 | " " | mach 22 3/4 da @ $1.55 - $35.25. Mach Dept |
| 1855-10 | Covel, Joel | conduc & brak 24 da @ $50 per mo - $50.00. Trans Dept main stem |
| 1857-21 | Covell, Joel | ton conduc 25 da @ $60 per mo - $60.00. 1st div |
| 1857-49 | " John | lab 22 da @ $1 - $22.00. Rd Dept main stem 3d s-div |
| 1855-28 | " Joseph | reg eng 20 da @ $1.15 - $23.00. Trans Dept main stem |
| 1855-94 | Coville, William | ton eng'man 17½ da @ $3 - $52.50. 1st div |
| 1857-19 | Cowell, Robert | app 34 da @ $.50 - $17.00. Mach Dept |
| 1855-49 | Cowman, Richard | bag mast 30 da @ $35 per mo - $15.00. Ellicotts Mills |
| 1857-104 | Cox, Barney | watch cuts 28 da @ $1 - $28.00. Rd Way Dept |
| 1857-53 | " " | lab 20 da @ $1 - $20.00. N W Va RR Tun |
| 1857-121 | " C. E. | watch 30 da @ $1 - $30.00. Rd Dept main stem 7th s-div |
| 1855-16 | " G. W. | paint 18 da @ $1.65 - $29.70. Mach Dept, Balto |
| 1857-40 | " George | fire 14 da @ $1.75; 12 3/4 da @ $1.25 - $40.45. Trans Dept main stem @ $3 - $7.50. NW Va rd, Parkersburg sta |

| ID | Name | Description |
|---|---|---|
| 1857-29 | Cox, George W. | ton eng'man 5½ da @ $3 - $16.50. 3d div |
| 1855-31 | James | saw wd 10 cords @ $.35 - $3.50. Trans Dept main stem |
| 1855-82 | John | app 22 3/4 da @ $.65 - $14.80. Mach Dept |
| 1857-98 | " | lab 18 da @ $1 - $18.00. Rd Way Dept |
| 1855-41 | Michael | watch 30 da @ $1 - $30.00. NW Va RR, Rd Dept 3d s-div |
| 1855-80 | Perry | lab 19 da @ $1 - $19.00. Rd Way Dept |
| 1857-103 | " | trim 23 3/4 da @ $1.65 - $39.20. Mach Dept |
| 1857-121 | Thomas | car trim 22⅜ da @ $1.90 - $42.30. Mach Dept, Balto |
| 1855-43 | Coy, Henry | fore 20½ da @ $1.50 - $30.75. NW Va RR Tun |
| 1855-44 | Coyle, Edward | car trim 16 da @ $1.65 - $26.40. Mach Dept, Balto |
| | M. | lab 20½ da @ $1 - $20.50. Rd Way Dept |
| 1857-119 | Coyne, Jerry | lab 21½ da @$1 - $21.50. Rd Way Dept |
| 1857-97 | Crabbin, Patrick | carp 18 da @ $1.50 - $27.00. Mach Dept, Balto |
| 1855-92 | Crabtree, B. | lab 26½ da @ $1 - $26.50. N W Va RR, Rd Dept 2d s-div |
| 1855-8 | " | carp 21½ da - $30.15. Mach Dept |
| 1857-55 | Dennis | conduc 12½ da @ $50 per mo - $25.50. Trans Dept main stem |
| 1855-44 | M. | lab 26½ da @ $1 -$26.50. Rd Dept main stem 9th s-div |
| 1855-45 | N. | lab 6 da @ $1 - $6.00. Rd Way Dept |
| 1857-50 | Craemer, Michael | lab 13½ da @ $1 - $13.50. Rd Way Dept |
| 1857-86 | Craft, Anthony | lab 25½ da @$1 - $25.50. Rd Dept main stem 5th s-div |
| 1857-32 | George | bricklay 21¼ da @ $2 - $42.50. grad, McGuire's Tun |
| 1855-10 | Craig, J. A. | ton fire 3/4 da @ $1.75 - $1.30. 2d div |
| 1855-76 | Jas. | conduc & brak 7 da @ $40 per mo - $12.15. Trans Dept main stem |
| 1855-18 | Morgan | mach 12¼ da @ $1.50 - $18.35. Mach Dept |
| 1855-34 | Crain, Mark | ton eng'man 16 3/4 da @ $2.50 - $41.85. Trans Dept main stem |
| 1857-112 | Cramblitt, Henry | clean pass car 28 da @ $30 per mo - $30.00. Trans Dept main stem |
| 1855-53 | Cramer, Frederick | mach help 13½ da @ $1 - $13.50. Mach Dept, Balto |
| 1857-61 | " | fore 24 da @ $1.25 - $30.00. Rd Way Dept |
| 1855-17 | Jno. | fore 27 da @ $1.25 - $33.75. Rd Dept main stem 14th s-div |
| 1857-75 | Thomas | ton eng'man 6 3/4 da @ $3 - $20.25. Trans Dept main stem |
| 1857-76 | " | eng'man 18 da @ $2.50 - $45.00. ballast train for 2d track |
| 1857-95 | William | eng'man 8 da @ $2.50 - $20.00. ballast train for 2d track |
| 1857-130 | Crammer, Jeremiah | lab 24 da @ $1 - $24.00. Wash br, Rd Dept |
| 1857-47 | Crane, Jeremiah | lab 23 da @ $1 - $23.00. Mach Dept, Piedmont |
| 1857-100 | Martin | lab 23 3/4 da @ $1 -$23.75. Rd Dept main stem 1st s-div |
| | | lab 10 da @ $1 - $10.00. NW Va RR, Rd Dept 5th s-div |

| | | |
|---|---|---|
| 1857-100 | Crane, Patrick | lab 23½ da @ $1 - $23.50. NW Va RR, Rd Dept 5th s-div |
| 1857-59 | Crannen, Wm. | lab 30 da @ $1 - $30.00. Rd Dept main stem 12th s-div |
| 1857-23 | Crapston, John | ton conduc 21 da @$50 per mo - $42.00. Board Tree Tun |
| 1857-10 | Crat, Frederick | bur driv 23 da @ $1.15 - $26.45. hp exp, Balto |
| 1857-135 | Craven, Elmer | lab 20½ da @ $1 - $20.50. Mach Dept, Wheeling |
| 1857-48 | Cravil, Joel | lab 20 3/4 da @ $1 - $20.75. Rd Dept main stem 2d s-div |
| 1857-25 | Crawfis, Henry | ton brak 17 da @ $40 per mo - $27.20. 3d & 4th div |
| 1857-27 | Crawford, Hiram | ton brak 5 da @$40 per mo - $8.00. Board Tree Tun |
| 1855-45 | Crawfish, H. | lab 8½ da @ $1 -$8.50. Rd Way Dept |
| 1855-79 | Crawford, A. | carp 25¼ da @ $1.60 - $40.44. Mach Dept |
| 1855-10 | Andrew | conduc & brak 21 da @ $50 per mo - $45.40. Trans Dept main stem |
| 1857-119 | C. | carp 21 da @$1.60 - $33.60. Mach Dept, Balto |
| 1855-10 | " | conduc & brak 2½ da @ $40 per mo - $4.15. Trans Dept main stem |
| 1857-16 | George | cook 30 da @ $15 per mo - $15.00. transfer steam Brown Dick--Ohio Riv, bet Benwood & Bellaire |
| 1855-65 | James | carp 14½ da @ $1.65 - $23.90. Rd Way Dept |
| 1855-54 | " | lab 11 da @ $1 - $11.00. Rd Way Dept |
| 1857-102 | " | pump water @ $45 per mo - $45.00. NW Va RR |
| 1855-26 | John | ton brak 19 da @$40 per mo - $30.40. 3d & 4th div |
| 1855-22 | Levi | fire 5 3/4 da @ $1.75 - $10.05. Trans Dept main stem |
| 1855-18 | Lewis | ton eng'man 24 da @ $2 - $48.00. Trans Dept main stem |
| 1857-28 | " | ton eng'man 24½ da @ $3 - $72.75. 1st div |
| 1855-34 | Nathaniel | ton brak 3 da @ $40 per mo - $4.80. 3d & 4th div |
| 1857-133 | S. B. | prepar sand 28 da @ $1 - $28.00. Trans Dept main stem |
| 1855-34 | Samuel B. | mach help 24½ da @ $1 - $24.50. Mach Dept, Fetterman |
| 1855-54 | William | kpr of oil house 28 da @ $1 - $28.00. Trans Dept main stem |
| 1857-96 | " | lab 11¼ da @ $1 - $11.25. Rd Way Dept |
| 1855-82 | Crayton, Robert | fore 26 da @ $1.25 - $32.50. NW Va RR, Rd Dept 1st s-div |
| 1857-108 | Creamer, John | mach 23 da @ $1.60 - $36.80. Mach Dept |
| 1857-29 | " | mach 18 da @ $1.60 - $28.80. Mach Dept, Balto |
| 1855-82 | Lewis | ton eng'man 16 da @ $3 - $48.00. 2d div |
| 1857-108 | " | mach 23 da @$1.60 - $36.80. Mach Dept |
| 1855-75 | Michl. | lab 18⅞ da @ $1.60 - $29.20. Mach Dept, Balto |
| 1855-94 | R. | lab 23 da @$1 - $23.00. Rd Way Dept |
| 1857-134 | Rudolph | app 21½ da @ $.45 - $9.65. Mach Dept |
| | | mach app 35½ da @ $.65 - $23.05. Mach Dept, Wheeling |

| ID | Name | Details |
|---|---|---|
| 1857-81 | Creamer, Thomas | eng'man 1 da @ $2.50 - $2.50. lay 2d track |
| 1857-122 | Cree, Peter | lab 21 da @ $1.15 - $24.15. Mach Dept, Balto |
| 1857-31 | Creek, Albert | ton fire 4 da @$1.75 - $7.00. 1st div |
| 1855-10 | " George | conduc & brak 1 da @ $40 per mo - $1.65. Trans Dept main stem |
| 1855-30 | Creighton, Thomas | prepar fuel 28 da @ $30 per mo - $30.00. Trans Dept main stem |
| 1857-122 | " " | tend fill @ $30 per mo - $30.00. Mach Dept, Balto |
| 1857-119 | Creuger, George W. | carp 15 3/4 da @ $1.50 - $23.60. Mach Dept, Balto |
| 1857-22 | Crigler, E. M. | ton conduc 26 da @ $50 per mo - $52.00. 3d & 4th div |
| 1855-87 | Crim, Henry | blksmith 23½ da @ $1.50 - $35.25. Mach Dept |
| 1857-124 | " " | blksmith 17¾ da @ $1.70 - $29.30. Mach Dept, Martinsburg |
| 1857-125 | " Joseph | carp 19½ da @ $1.25 - $24.35. Mach Dept, Martinsburg |
| 1857-129 | Crimer, Henry | fill tend 29 da @ $1 - $29.00. Mach Dept, Piedmont |
| 1855-20 | Criswell, D. | fire 27 da @ $1.75 - $47.25. Trans Dept main stem |
| 1857-33 | " Daniel | ton fire 11 da @ $1.75 - $19.25. 4th div |
| 1857-78 | Croby, Mat. | lab 14¼ da @ $1 - $14.25. lay 2d track |
| 1855-45 | Crock, James | lab 13½ da @ $1 - $13.50. Rd Way Dept |
| 1857-79 | Croe, Francis | lab 24 3/4 da @ $1 - $24.75. lay 2d track |
| 1855-86 | Croft, James | mach 20½ da @ $1.45 - $29.75. Mach Dept |
| 1855-28 | Crofton, George | prepar fuel 24 da @ $1.25 - $30.00. Trans Dept main stem |
| 1857-101 | " " | fore @ $50 per mo - $50.00. NW Va RR ballast train |
| 1855-28 | " M. | prepar fuel 6 da @ $1 - $6.00. Trans Dept main stem |
| 1855-52 | Crogan, Hugh | lab 15½ da @ $1 - $15.50. Rd Way Dept |
| 1857-61 | " " | fore 28½ da @ $1.25 - $35.60. Rd Dept main stem 14th s-div |
| 1855-52 | " James | lab 24 da @ $1.25 - $30.00. Rd Way Dept |
| 1855-52 | " John | lab 15½ da @ $1 - $15.50. Rd Way Dept |
| 1857-61 | " " | lab 17 da @ $1 - $17.00. Rd Dept main stem 14th s-div |
| 1855-52 | " Peter | lab 15½ da - $15.50. Rd Way Dept |
| 1857-40 | " T. H. | ton conduc 24½ da @ $50 per mo - $50.00. Rd Way Dept |
| 1857-84 | Grohan, Thomas | lab 22¼ da @ $1.12 - $25.05. grad, Board Tree Tun |
| 1857-32 | Croll, Edward | ton fire 21 3/4 da @ $1.75 - $38.05. 2d div |
| 1857-127 | Wm. M. | mach 20¼ da @ $1.60 - $32.40. Mach Dept, Piedmont |
| 1855-89 | Cromwell, Andrew | mach 10½ da @ $1.60 - $16.80. Mach Dept |
| 1857-136 | " " | fore mach @ $50 per mo - $50.00. Mach Dept, Cumb |
| 1855-51 | " G. W. | lab 56 da @ $.90 - $50.40. Rd Way Dept |
| 1855-45 | " George W. | supv @ $45 per mo - $45.00. Rd Way Dept |
| 1857-55 | " " | horse & cart 25 da @ $1.25 - $31.25. Rd Dept main stem 9th s-div |

## B & O RR EMPLOYEES 107

| | | | |
|---|---|---|---|
| 1857-55 | Cromwell, George W. | horse hire 60 da @ $.90 - $54.00. Rd Dept main stem 9th s-div |
| 1857-55 | " Jacob | supv @ $45 per mo - $45.00. Rd Dept main stem 9th s-div |
| 1857-19 | " William E. | bag mast 30 da @ $45 per mo - $45.00. thr mail & exp |
| 1857-128 | Cronern, Daniel | mach help 2¼ da @ $.75 - $18.00. Mach Dept, Piedmont |
| 1855-46 | Crook, William | lab 15½ da @ $1 - $15.50. Rd Way Dept |
| 1857-113 | Crookes, J. | mach app 19 3/4 da @ $.65 - $12.85. Mach Dept, Balto |
| 1855-72 | Crosby, Michael | help 22½ da @ $1 - $22.50. Rd Way Dept |
| 1857-78 | Cross, John | help 24 da @ $1 - $24.00. lay 2d track |
| 1855-53 | " | carp 24 da @ $1.62½ - $39.00. Rd Way Dept |
| 1857-73 | " Samuel | carp 25 da @ $1.62 - $40.60. repair bridges &c |
| 1857-102 | " W. R. | carp 21 da @ $1.65 - $34.65. NW Va RR bridges |
| 1857-128 | " Wm. R. | carp 8 3/4 da @ $1.50 - $13.10. Mach Dept, Piedmont |
| 1855-92 | Crouch, Edw. | carp 20 da - $29.25. Mach Dept |
| 1857-70 | Crow, John | app 22⅞ da @ $.60 - $13.35. Mt Clare sta, Balto |
| 1855-65 | " | carp 21 da @ $1.62½ - $34.10. Rd Way Dept |
| 1855-61 | " T. | lab 13 da @ $1 - $13.00. Rd Way Dept |
| 1857-94 | Crowl, G. W. | carp 25 da @ $1.75 - $43.75. repair bridges |
| 1855-13 | Crowley, D. | conduc & brak 12 da @ $40 per mo - $20.00. Trans Dept main stem |
| 1855-88 | " Jerre | lab 24 3/4 da @ $1 - $24.75. Mach Dept |
| 1855-48 | " John | train hand 9½ da @ $1 - $9.50. Rd Way Dept |
| 1855-46 | Crozier, James | lab 5 3/4 da @ $1 - $5.75. Rd Way Dept |
| 1855-43 | " | lab 21½ da @ $1 - $21.50. Rd Way Dept |
| 1855-95 | Crude, Joseph | mould 30 da @ $1.60 - $48.00. Mach Dept |
| 1857-113 | Cruise, Charles | iron mould 17 3/4 da @ $1.60 - $28.40. Mach Dept, Balto |
| 1857-17 | Crum, Isaac | lab 25 da @ $1 - $25.00. frt transfer force at Bellaire, opp Benwood |
| 1857-28 | " James | ton eng'man 20½ da @ $3 - $61.50. 1st div |
| 1857-12 | " William | lab 25 da @ $1.20 - $30.00. Monocacy |
| 1857-21 | Crumb, William | ton conduc 9 3/4 da @ $50 per mo - $19.50. 1st div |
| 1855-39 | Crumet, George | lab 17 da @ $1 - $17.00. Rd Way Dept |
| 1857-31 | Crumit, George | ton fire 26½ da @ $1.75 - $46.35. 1st div |
| 1855-40 | Crumwell, G. | lab 14 da @ $1 - $14.00. Rd Way Dept |
| 1857-49 | Cruse, Joseph | lab 22 da @ $1 - $22.00. Rd Dept main stem 3d s-div |
| 1857-120 | " Patrick | carp 20¼ da @ $1.65 - $33.40. Mach Dept, Balto |
| 1857-113 | " Thomas | mach app 24 da @ $.65 - $15.60. Mach Dept, Balto |
| 1857-88 | | lab 23 da @ $1.12 - $25.85. grad, Welling Tun |
| 1857-61 | | lab 24½ da @ $1 - $24.50. Rd Dept main stem 14th s-div |

# B & O RR EMPLOYEES

| | | | |
|---|---|---|---|
| 1857-69 | Cruzen, Edward | mach 18¾ da @ $1.65 - $30.10. Mt Clare sta, Balto |
| 1855-54 | Jno. | lab 24 da @ $.70 - $16.80. Rd Way Dept |
| 1857-66 | Cubboard, John | lab 25 da @ $1 - $25.00. Rd Dept main stem 18th s-div |
| 1857-113 | Cubley, P. | mach app 23 da @ $1 - $23.00. Mach Dept, Balto |
| 1857-99 | Cuff, Anthony | lab 29 da @ $1 - $29.00. NW Va RR, Rd Dept 4th s-div |
| 1857-99 | Lawrence | lab 28 da @ $1 - $28.00. Rd Dept 4th s-div |
| 1857-60 | Michael | lab 26 da @ $1 - $26.00. Rd Dept main stem 13th s-div |
| 1857-68 | Patrick | lab 20 da @ $1 - $20.00. Rd Dept main stem 19th s-div |
| 1855-62 | Thomas | fore 25¼ da @ $1.25 - $31.50. Rd Way Dept |
| 1855-66 | Culings, Mart. | lab 24 da @ $1 - $24.00. Rd Way Dept |
| 1855-70 | Culitan, Daniel | lab 14 3/4 da @ $1 - $14.75. Rd Way Dept |
| 1855-80 | Cullison, John M. | carp 22 3/4 da @ $1.50 - $34.10. Mach Dept |
| 1857-116 | Culp, Mike S. | blksmith 18 da @ $1.50 - $27.00. Mach Dept, Balto |
| 1857-126 | Cumiskey, Thomas | greas cars 30 da @ $1 - $30.00. Mach Dept, Martinsburg |
| 1855-94 | Cummerford, James | blksmith 19¾ da @ $1.40 - $26.95. Mach Dept |
| 1857-130 | Cummings, George | lab 19 da @ $1 - $19.00. Mach Dept, Piedmont |
| 1855-24 | Jacob | pass & bur driv 26½ da @ $30 per mo - $33.10. Trans Dept main stem |
| 1857-10 | " | bur driv 27 da @ $1.15 - $31.05. hp exp, Balto |
| 1857-92 | John | lab 15¼ da @ $1 - $15.25. grad, Littleton Tun |
| 1857-130 | Lewis | lab 19¼ da @ $1 - $19.25. Mach Dept, Piedmont |
| 1857-130 | Morris | lab 21 da @ $1 - $21.00. Mach Dept, Piedmont |
| 1855-47 | P. | lab 22 3/4 da @ $1 - $22.75. Rd Way Dept |
| 1857-122 | Patrick | lab 19 da @ $1 - $19.00. Mach Dept, Balto |
| 1857-94 | Cummins, John | lab 16¼ da @ $1 - $16.25. quarry & haul stone for Board Tree & Littleton Tun |
| 1857-78 | Thomas | lab 30 da @ $1 - $30.00. lay 2d track |
| 1855-69 | Cunaboy, M. | lab 18 da @ $1 - $18.00. Rd Way Dept |
| 1857-61 | Cuniff, Patrick | lab 29 da @ $1 - $29.00. Rd Dept main stem 14th s-div |
| 1857-61 | Peter | lab 26 da @ $1 - $26.00. Rd Dept main stem 14th s-div |
| 1857-63 | Cunningham, Benj. | lab 22½ da @ $1 - $22.50. Rd Dept main stem 16th s-div |
| 1857-126 | David | lab 30 da @ $1 - $30.00. Mach Dept, Martinsburg |
| 1855-50 | Cunningham, B. | watch cuts 28 da @ $1 - $28.00. Rd Way Dept |
| 1855-30 | D. | prepar fuel 28 da @ $30 per mo - $30.00. Trans Dept main stem |
| 1855-81 | E. | mach 20¾ da @ $1.60 - $32.40. Mach Dept |
| 1855-76 | Edward | mach 24 da @ $1.25 - $30.00. Mach Dept |
| 1857-123 | " | mach 23½ da @ $1.60 - $37.60. Mach Dept, Martinsburg |
| 1857-65 | " | watch 30 da @ $1 - $30.00. Rd Dept main stem 17th s-div |

# B & O RR EMPLOYEES 109

| Ref | Name | | Entry |
|---|---|---|---|
| 1857-64 | Cunningham, George | | lab 28 da @ $1 - $28.00. Rd Dept main stem 17th s-div |
| 1855-62 | | J. | lab 10 3/4 da @ $1 - $10.75. Rd Way Dept |
| 1857-65 | | Joseph | watch 30 da @$1 - $30.00. Rd Dept main stem 17th s-div |
| 1855-69 | | Michael | lab 16 da @$1 - $16.00. Rd Way Dept |
| 1855-66 | | Patrick | lab 21 da @ $1 - $21.00. Rd Way Dept |
| 1857-60 | | " | lab 28 da @ $1 - $28.00. Rd Dept main stem 13th s-div |
| 1857-77 | | " | quarry 22 da @ $1 - $22.00. ballast train for 2d track |
| 1857-100 | | Peter | lab 22 da @ $1 - $22.00. NW Va RR, Rd Dept 5th s-div |
| 1855-64 | | Thomas | lab 22½ da @ $1 - $22.50. Rd Way Dept |
| 1857-66 | | " | lab 24 da @ $1 - $24.00. Rd Dept main stem 18th s-div |
| 1855-59 | | W. | lab 14 3/4 da @ $1 - $14.75. Rd Way Dept |
| 1855-69 | | William | lab 20 da @ $1 - $20.00. Rd Way Dept |
| 1857-15 | | " | lab 5½ da @ $1 - $5.50. Grafton sta |
| 1857-62 | | " | lab 24 da @ $1 - $24.00. Rd Dept main stem 15th s-div |
| 1857-64 | | " | lab 13 da @ $1 - $13.00. Rd Dept main stem 17th s-div |
| 1855-72 | Curby, Hiram | | help 23 3/4 da @ $.50 - $11.85. Rd Way Dept |
| 1855-71 | Curley, Jno. P. | | smith 24 da @ $2 - $48.00. Rd Way Dept |
| 1857-75 | Curley, Daniel | | dril 22 da @ $1.04 - $23.00. ballast train for 2d track |
| 1855-70 | | James | lab 22½ da @ $1 - $22.50. Rd Way Dept |
| 1855-43 | | John | lab 17½ da @ $1 - $17.50. Rd Way Dept |
| 1857-75 | | " | lab 17 da @ $1.15 - $19.40. ballast train for 2d track |
| 1857-76 | | " | lab 12 da @ $.97 - $11.70. ballast train for 2d track |
| 1857-85 | | Patrick | lab 11½ da @ $1 - $11.50. grad, Board Tree Tun |
| 1857-75 | | Thomas | lab 17 da @ $1 - $17.00. ballast train for 2d track |
| 1857-86 | | " | lab 22½ da @ $1 - $22.50. grad, McGuire's Tun |
| 1857-101 | | " | lab 13 da @ $1 - $13.00. NW Va RR ballast train |
| 1857-58 | | " | lab 26 da @ $1 - $26.00. Rd Dept main stem 12th s-div |
| 1857-103 | Curly, Barry | | lab 23 da @ $1 - $23.00. NW Va RR Tun |
| 1855-68 | Curn, John | | lab 22 3/4 da @ $1 - $22.75. Rd Way Dept |
| 1857-77 | Curran, James | | quarry 8 da @ $1 - $8.00. ballast train for 2d track |
| 1857-82 | | Peter | lab 25½ da @ $1.12 - $28.70. grad, Board Tree Tun |
| 1857-100 | | Terrence | lab 26 da @ $1 - $26.00. NW Va RR, Rd Dept 5th s-div |
| 1857-94 | Currant, Timothy | | lab 17½ da @ $1 - $17.50. quarry & haul stone for Board Tree & Littleton Tun |
| 1857-92 | Curren, John | | lab 25⅞ da @ $1.12 - $28.40. grad, Littleton Tun |
| 1855-32 | Curriff, Patrick | | saw wd 75⅝ cords @ $.45 - $34.00. Trans Dept main stem |
| 1855-32 | | Peter | saw wd 37 3/4 cords @ $.45 - $17.00. Trans Dept main stem |

| | | | |
|---|---|---|---|
| 1857-88 | Currin, James | lab 24¼ da @ $1.12 - $27.30. grad, Welling Tun |
| 1855-47 | Curtain, Timothy | lab 8 da @ $1 - $8.00. Rd Way Dept |
| 1855-6 | Curtis, J. W. | clk 28 da @ $35 per mo - $35.00. Trans Dept main stem |
| 1857-13 | " John W. | clk 30 da @ $50 per mo -$50.00. Martinsburg |
| 1855-84 | " Peter | help 24 da @$1.15 - $27.60. Mach Dept |
| 1857-115 | | boil mkr help 18 da @$1.15 - $20.70. Mach Dept, Balto |
| 1855-18 | Custer, Benjamin | ton eng'man 12 da @$2.50 - $30.00. Trans Dept main stem |
| 1857-29 | " | ton eng'man 21¼ da @ $3 - $63.75. 2d div |
| 1857-119 | Custis, John | tin 23 da @ $1.60 - $36.80. Mach Dept, Balto |
| 1857-47 | Custy, Michael | lab 29 da @ $1 - $29.00. Rd Dept main stem 1st s-div |
| 1857-120 | Cutler, S. | carp 4½ da @ $1.50 - $6.75. Mach Dept, Balto |
| 1855-28 | Cutting, N. | reg eng 13 da @$1.50 - $19.50. Trans Dept main stem |
| 1857-125 | " Nathaniel | lab @ $34.50 per mo - $34.50. Mach Dept, Martinsburg |
| 1855-38 | Cyne, Peter | lab 25 da @$1 - $25.00. Rd Way Dept |
| 1855-67 | Cynelt, Patrick | lab 20 da @$1 - $20.00. Rd Way Dept |
| 1857-115 | Cypert, Mark | boil mkr 17 da @ $1.50 - $25.50. Mach Dept, Balto |
| 1855-59 | Cyrns, Joseph | lab 24 da @$.75 - $18.00. Rd Way Dept |
| 1857-137 | Cyrus, Emanuel | eng clean 17½ da @ $1 - $17.50. Mach Dept, Cumb |
| 1857-101 | Dabet, Owen | lab 12 da @ $1 - $12.00. NW Va RR ballast train |
| 1857-124 | Dace, Jeremiah | mach 5½ da @$1 - $5.50. Mach Dept, Martinsburg |
| 1855-90 | Daddyeman, John | app 24¼ da @ $.55 - $13.35. Mach Dept |
| 1855-89 | " W. | clk @ $40 per mo - $40.00. Mach Dept |
| 1857-136 | Daddysman, George | mach app 20½ da @ $.45 - $9.20. Mach Dept, Cumb |
| 1857-126 | " William | clk & storekpr @ $40 per mo - $40.00. Mach Dept, Cumb |
| 1857-15 | Daffin, Charles | yd eng'man 25 da @$35 per mo - $35.00. Grafton sta |
| 1857-14 | Dahler, John | lab 11 da @ $30 per mo - $13.20. Cumb |
| 1855-37 | Dailey, Michael | lab 24½ da @ $1 - $24.50. Rd Way Dept |
| 1857-75 | Daily, Patrick | fore 19 da @ $35 per mo - $25.60. ballast train for 2d track |
| 1855-93 | Daly, James | car repair 14 da @ $1.25 - $17.50. Mach Dept |
| 1855-93 | " John | fin 19½ da - $31.20. Mach Dept |
| 1855-54 | " | track lay 15 da @$1.25 -$18.75. Rd Way Dept |
| 1857-20 | " | pass fire 23½ da @ $1.75 - $11.10. 4th div |
| 1857-25 | " | ton brak 1½ da @ $40 per mo - $2.40. 2d div |
| 1855-27 | " John H. P. | get out eng 25 da @ $1.15 - $28.75. Trans Dept main stem |
| 1855-93 | " John 2d | car repair @ $32 per mo - $32.00. Mach Dept |
| 1855-27 | " Patrick | get out eng 27 da @ $1.50 - $40.50. Trans Dept main stem |

| ID | Name | Description |
|---|---|---|
| 1857-20 | Daily, Patrick | pass fire 26½ da @ $1.75 - $45.95. 3d div |
| 1857-24 | " William J. | ton brak 4½ da @ $40 per mo - $7.20. 1st div |
| 1857-128 | Daken, Reuben | boil mkr 14½ da @$1.50 - $21.35. Mach Dept, Piedmont |
| 1855-85 | Dales, Daniel | help 23 da @$1.10 - $25.30. Mach Dept |
| 1857-88 | Daley, Charles | lab 26 da @$1.12 - $29.25. grad, Welling Tun |
| 1855-15 | " D. | pass eng'man 24 da @$1 -$2.50. grad, $60.00. Trans Dept main stem |
| 1855-34 | " George | watch 22 da @$1 -$22.00. Trans Dept main stem |
| 1857-84 | " Hugh | lab 16 da @ $1.12 - $18.00. grad, Board Tree Tun |
| 1855-44 | " John | lab 13 da @ $1 - $13.00. Rd Way Dept |
| 1855-47 | " " | lab 7½ da @ $1 - $7.25. Rd Way Dept |
| 1855-67 | " " | tend to masons 27 da @ $1 - $27.00. Rd Way Dept |
| 1857-113 | " " | iron mould 17 3/4 da @$1.60 - $28.40. Mach Dept, Balto |
| 1857-82 | " " | lab 31½ da @ $1.12 - $35.15. grad, Board Tree Tun |
| 1857-84 | " " | lab 39 da @ $1.12 - $43.85. grad, Board Tree Tun |
| 1857-127 | " " | mach 17 3/4 da @ $1.75 - $31.05. Mach Dept, Piedmont |
| 1857-130 | " John F. | lab 19½ da @ $1 - $19.50. Mach Dept, Piedmont |
| 1857-85 | " Martin | lab 7½ da @ $1.12 - $8.45. grad, Board Tree Tun |
| 1857-87 | " Patrick | lab 18 3/4 da @ $1.12 - $21.10. grad, Welling Tun |
| 1857-88 | " " | lab 28 da @$1.12 - $31.50. grad, Welling Tun |
| 1855-10 | Dalrymple, A. | conduc & brak 8½ da @ $40 per mo - $13.75. Trans Dept main stem |
| 1855-44 | Dalton, James | lab 11½ da @ $1 - $14.50. Rd Way Dept |
| 1855-61 | Daly, John | fore 23 da @ $1.25 - $28.75. Rd Way Dept |
| 1857-66 | " " | fore 25 da @ $1.25 - $31.25. Rd Dept main stem 18th s-div |
| 1857-91 | " Patrick | stone mason 24½ da @ $2 - $48.50. grad, Littleton Tun |
| 1857-63 | Dancer, Jesse | watch 30 da @ $1 - $30.00. Rd Dept main stem 16th s-div |
| 1857-54 | Danehart, John | lab 24 da @ $1 - $24.00. Rd Dept main stem 8th s-div |
| 1855-30 | Daniel, John | prepar fuel 15 da @$30 per mo - $16.05. Trans Dept main stem |
| 1857-54 | Dansen, James | fore 12 da @ $1.12 - $13.50. Rd Dept main stem 8th s-div |
| 1855-8 | Danson, T. T. | brak 28 da @ $33.35 per mo - $33.35. Trans Dept main stem |
| 1857-36 | Danvarin, C. | tele oper mess 30 da @ $8 per mo - $8.00. Camden sta |
| 1857-61 | Danzell, Charles | watch 30 da @ $1 - $30.00. Rd Dept main stem 14th s-div |
| 1857-108 | Darbey, Montr'y | mach 18 da @ $1.72 - $30.95. Mach Dept, Balto |
| 1855-7 | Darby, D. | asst supt of trans 28 da @ $75 per mo - $75.00. Trans Dept main stem |
| 1857-13 | " Darius | disp 30 da @$60 per mo - $60.00. Martinsburg |
| 1855-18 | " Grafton | ton eng'man 12 da @ $3 - $36.00. Trans Dept main stem |
| 1857-19 | " " | pass eng'man 22 da @$3 - $66.00. 2d div |

| | | |
|---|---|---|
| Darby, M. | 1855-82 | mach 23½ da @ $1.65 - $38.75. Mach Dept |
| Dare, Jerry | 1857-20 | pass fire 15 da @ $40 per mo - $20.00. 2d div |
| " Wm. H. | 1857-69 | carp 19 da @ $1.73 - $32.85. Mt Clare sta, Balto |
| Dargin, John | 1857-88 | lab 29½ da @ $1.12 - $33.15. grad, Welling Tun |
| Dargon, Cornelius | 1857-56 | lab 23 da @ $1 - $23.00. Rd Dept main stem 10th s-div |
| Darlin, Patk. | 1857-75 | lab 20 da @ $1 - $20.00. Rd Way Dept |
| Darly, Grafton | 1857-30 | ton eng'man 1 da @ $3 - $3.00. 4th div |
| Darr, Norval | 1857-50 | lab 24 da @ $1 - $24.00. Rd Dept main stem 4th s-div |
| Darrah, William E. | 1857-131 | mach 18 3/4 da @ $1.80 - $33.75. Mach Dept, Grafton |
| Daton, Edward | 1857-130 | lab 3½ da @ $1 - $3.50. Mach Dept, Piedmont |
| Daub, Henry | 1857-135 | sht iron work 27¾ da @ $1.55 - $42.25. Mach Dept, Wheeling |
| Daugherty, Charles | 1857-66 | lab 22½ da @ $1 - $22.50. Rd Dept main stem 18th s-div |
| " James P. | 1857-132 | fill tend @ $30 per mo - $30.00. Mach Dept, Grafton |
| " Wm. | 1857-121 | paint help 17½ da @ $1.15 - $20.10. Mach Dept, Balto |
| " " | 1857-118 | blksmith help 16 da @ $1 - $16.00. Mach Dept, Balto |
| Davenport, Daniel | 1855-22 | fire 13 da @ $1.75 - $22.75. Trans Dept main stem |
| Davette, A. | 1855-60 | fore 2¼ da @ $1 -$24.50. Rd Way Dept |
| Davidson, C. A. | 1855-8 | bag mast 28 da @ $45 per mo - $45.00. Trans Dept main stem |
| " John | 1855-26 | clean eng 11 da @ $1 - $11.00. Trars Dept main stem |
| " William | 1857-24 | ton brak 15 3/4 da @ $40 per mo - $25.20. 1st div |
| Davis, Alfred G. | 1855-6 | St supv 28 da @ $50 per mo - $50.00. Trans Dept main stem |
| " C. B. | 1857-18 | pass train brak 30 da @ $40 per mo - $40.00. thr mail & exp |
| " Caleb | 1855-9 | conduc 11¼ da @ $50 per mo - $23.45. Trans Dept main stem |
| " Col. | 1855-7 | bag mast 28 da @ $45 per mo - $45.00. Trans Dept main stem |
| " Cyrus | 1857-17 | brak 30 da @ $30 per mo - $30.00. frt transfer force at Bellaire, opp Benwood |
| " E. G. | 1857-28 | ton eng'man 20½ da @ $3 - $61.50. 1st div |
| " E. R. | 1857-21 | ton conduc 1 da @ $40 per mo; 2 3/4 da @ $50 per mo - $7.10. 2d div |
| " Edw. | 1855-63 | lab 21¼ da @ $1 - $21.25. Rd Way Dept |
| " " | 1857-68 | lab 25 da @ $1 - $25.00. Rd Dept main stem 19th s-div |
| " " | 1857-24 | ton brak 13 3/4 da @ $40 per mo - $22.00. 1st div |
| " Eli | 1855-40 | lab 24 da @ $1 - $24.00. Rd Way Dept |
| " " | 1857-49 | lab 21 da @ $1 - $21.00. Rd Dept main stem 3d s-div |
| " Elias | 1857-103 | carp 25 da @$1.50 - $37.50. NW Va RR depot |
| " G. | 1855-33 | disp 28 da @ $40 per mo - $40.00. Trans Dept main stem |
| " " | 1857-39 | disp 30 da @ $50 per mo - $50.00. NW Va rd, Parkersburg sta |
| " G. B. | 1855-18 | ton eng'man 10½ da @ $2.50 - $26.25. Trans Dept main stem |

| | | |
|---|---|---|
| 1855-39 | Davis, George | lab 15 da @ $1 - $15.00. Rd Way Dept |
| 1855-31 | " | saw wd 57 cords @ $.35 - $19.95. Trans Dept main stem |
| 1857-52 | " | blksmith 21½ da @ $1.12 - $24.15. Rd Dept main stem 6th s-div |
| 1857-55 | " | lab 18 3/4 da @ $1 - $18.75. Rd Dept main stem 9th s-div |
| 1855-18 | George W. | ton eng'man ½ da @ $1.25 - $1.25. Trans Dept main stem |
| 1855-eratta | " " | eng'man instead of $1.25, $62½ rec'd |
| 1855-6 | H. G. | agt 28 da @ $75 per mo - $75.00. Trans Dept main stem |
| 1857-14 | " " | agt 30 da @ $100 per mo - $100.00. Piedmont sta |
| 1855-63 | James | lab 22 da @ $1 - $22.00. Rd Way Dept |
| 1857-17 | " | lab & watch 30 da @ $30 per mo - $30.00. frt transfer force at Bellaire, opp Benwood |
| 1857-68 | " | lab 22 3/4 da @ $1 - $22.75. Rd Dept main stem 19th s-div |
| 1855-94 | John | carp 17¼ da @ $1.40 - $24.15. Mach Dept |
| 1857-55 | " | lab 27½ da @ $1 - $27.50. Rd Dept main stem 9th s-div |
| 1857-109 | " | mach 17 3/4 da @ $1.25 - $22.20. Mach Dept, Balto |
| 1857-123 | " | mach 23¼ da @ $1 - $23.25. Mach Dept, Martinsburg |
| 1855-82 | John E. | lab 26½ da @ $1.25 - $33.15. Mach Dept |
| 1857-108 | " " | rig 21½ da @ $1.25 - $26.90. Mach Dept, Balto |
| 1855-57 | John W. | lab 20 da @ $1 - $20.00. Rd Way Dept |
| 1855-57 | " " | lab 21 da @ $1 - $21.00. Rd Way Dept |
| 1855-57 | " " | supv @ $45 per mo - $45.00. Rd Way Dept |
| 1855-82 | Joseph | lab 27½ da @ $1.15 - $31.60. Mach Dept |
| 1855-45 | " | lab 6½ da @ $1 - $6.50. Rd Way Dept |
| 1857-111 | " | mach help 18 da @ $1 - $18.00. Mach Dept, Balto |
| 1857-119 | Joseph P. | blksmith app 25 da @ $.45 - $11.25. Mach Dept, Balto |
| 1857-17 | Joshua | lab 24 da @ $1 - $24.00. frt transfer force at Bellaire, opp Benwood |
| 1857-60 | Mathew | lab 28 da @ $1 - $28.00. Rd Dept main stem 13th s-div |
| 1855-62 | Michael | lab 10 da @ $1 - $10.00. Rd Way Dept |
| 1857-35 | " | fire 3½ da @ $1.75 - $6.10. J. R. Shrode's wd train 4th div |
| 1857-34 | " | ton fire 19 3/4 da @ $1.75 - $34.55. 4th div |
| 1857-17 | Morris | lab 17 da @ $1 - $17.00. frt transfer force at Bellaire, opp Benwood |
| 1857-113 | Oliver | mach app 26½ da @ $.45 - $11.90. Mach Dept, Balto |
| 1855-59 | Patrick | lab 10 3/4 da @ $1 - $10.75. Rd Way Dept |
| 1855-1 | Peter | port $300 per annum - $25.00. Ofc Hanover St |
| 1857-99 | " | lab 24 da @ $1 - $24.00. NW Va RR, Rd Dept 4th s-div |
| 1857-3 | " | mess @ $25 per mo. Gen Ofc |
| 1855-92 | Richard | fore @ $60 per mo - $60.00. Mach Dept |
| 1855-52 | " | lab 6 da @ $.87½ - $5.25. Rd Way Dept |

## B & O RR EMPLOYEES

| |  | |  |
|---|---|---|---|
| 1857-127 | Davis, Richard | | fore mach @ $65 per mo - $65.00. Mach Dept, Piedmont |
| 1855-77 | Robert | | mach 23 da @ $1.25 - $28.75. Mach Dept |
| 1857-38 | " | T. B. | ton eng'man 23 da @ $2.50 - $57.50. Wash br rd, Wash city sta |
| 1855-7 | " | T. G. | pass conduc 28 da @ $62.50 per mo - $62.50. Trans Dept main stem |
| 1857-116 | " | Tyler | blksmith 18 da @ $1.55 - $27.90. Mach Dept, Balto |
| 1855-8 | " | " | bag mast 28 da @ $35 per mo - $35.00. Mach Dept, Balto |
| 1857-19 | " | " | bag mast 30 da @ $35 per mo - $35.00. Trans Dept main stem |
| 1857-40 | " | W. | ton conduc 17 3/4 da @ $50 per mo - $35.50. NW Va rd, Parkersburg sta |
| 1855-33 | " | William | watch 25 da @ $30 per mo - $30.00. Trans Dept main stem |
| 1857-49 | " | " | lab 25 da @ $1 - $25.00. Rd Dept main stem 3d s-div |
| 1855-72 | " | William J. | help 24 da @ $1.12½ - $27.00. Rd Way Dept |
| 1857-70 | " | William T. | bolt cut 17 da @ $1.12 - $19.10. Mt Clare sta, Balto |
| 1857-131 | " | Zachariah | mach 16¾ da @ $1.70 - $27.60. Mach Dept, Grafton |
| 1855-94 | Zack. | | fin 30⅞ da @ $1.75 - $52.95. Mach Dept |
| 1857-51 | Davlin, Patrick | | lab 30 da @ $1 - $30.00. Rd Dept main stem 5th s-div |
| 1857-56 | Dawson, Abraham | | lab 24 da @ $1 - $24.00. Rd Dept main stem 10th s-div |
| 1855-64 | " | J. | lab 14½ da @ $1.12½ - $16.30. Rd Way Dept |
| 1855-43 | " | James | fore 24 da @ $1.25 - $30.00. Rd Way Dept |
| 1857-26 | " | Thomas | ton brak 26 da @ $40 per mo - $41.60. 3d & 4th div |
| 1855-47 | " | Wm. | lab 18 3/4 da @ $1 - $18.75. Rd Way Dept |
| 1855-39 | Day, George | | lab 19½ da @ $1 - $19.50. Rd Way Dept |
| 1857-48 | " | " | lab 12 da @ $1 - $12.00. Rd Dept main stem 2d s-div |
| 1855-65 | " | M. O. | lab 24½ da @ $1 - $24.25. Rd Way Dept |
| 1857-78 | " | Thomas O. | lab 24½ da @ $1 - $24.50. lay 2d track |
| 1857-104 | Dayhoof, J. | | carp 17½ da @ $1.25 - $21.90. NW Va RR, build sand & wd houses |
| 1857-73 | " | Jno. | lab 1½ da @ $1 - $1.50. repair bridges &c |
| 1857-19 | Dayton, James M. | | bag mast 8 da @ $45 per mo - $12.00. thr mail & exp |
| 1857-26 | " | John | ton brak 20 da @ $40 per mo - $32.00. 3d & 4th div |
| 1857-18 | Daytor, J. H. | | pass train brak 8 da @ $3.35 per mo - $8.90. w end |
| 1855-43 | Dean, Edward | | lab 12 da @ $1 - $12.00. Rd Way Dept |
| 1857-58 | Deanan, John | | lab 25 da @ $1 - $25.50. Rd Dept main stem 12th s-div |
| 1857-96 | Deats, Charles | | lab 18 3/4 da @ $1 - $18.75. NW Va RR, Rd Dept 1st s-div |
| 1857-35 | Deck, Abraham | | lab 14 da @ $1 - $14.00. J. R. Shrode's wd train 4th div |
| 1857-124 | " | J. B. | blksmith 29⅞ da @ $1.25 - $36.55. Mach Dept, Martinsburg |
| 1855-22 | " | " | fire 18 3/4 da @ $1.75 - $32.80. Trans Dept main stem |
| 1857-116 | " | John | boil mkr help 23 da @ $1 - $23.00. Mach Dept, Balto |

B & O RR EMPLOYEES 115

| ID | Name | Details |
|---|---|---|
| 1857-72 | Decorse, William | paint 4 da @ $1.62 - $.50. Piedmont depot |
| 1857-11 | Dee, James | boil mkr help 16 3/4 da @ $1 - $16.75. Mach Dept, Balto |
| 1857-83 | Deeds, George | lab 15¾ da @ $1.12 - $17.15. grad, Board Tree Tun |
| 1855-88 | Deemin, Edward | shop inspec @ $34.50 per mo - $34.50. Mach Dept |
| 1855-77 | Deems, George | mach 19¼ da @ $1.65 - $31.75. Mach Dept |
| 1857-110 | Deems, George " | mach 25¼ da @ $1.65 - $41.65. Mach Dept, Balto |
| 1855-32 | Deets, George | tele oper 28 da @ $16.65 per mo - $16.65. Trans Dept main stem |
| 1857-18 | Deford, A. J. | pass train brak 30 da @ $33.35 per mo - $33.35. w end |
| 1857-9 | " Richard | clk 30 da @ $50 per mo - $50.00. Mt Clare sta |
| 1857-29 | Degrange, George W. | ton eng'man 13½ da @ $3 - $40.50. 2d div |
| 1857-32 | " Nathan | ton fire 3¾ da @ $1.75 - $5.70. 2d div |
| 1857-76 | " Nathaniel | fire 8½ da @ $1.75 - $14.85. ballast train for 2d track |
| 1857-119 | DeGraw, William | blksmith app 25 da @ $.55 - $13.75. Mach Dept, Balto |
| 1855-22 | Degroff, Abram | fire 11¼ da @ $1.75 - $19.70. Trans Dept main stem |
| 1855-63 | Dehan, Jno. | lab 19 3/4 da @ $1 - $19.75. Rd Way Dept |
| 1857-62 | Deighn, Malichi | watch 29 da @ $1 - $29.00. Rd Dept main stem 15th s-div |
| 1857-113 | Deighn, George | mach app 24 da @ $.45 - $10.80. Mach Dept, Balto |
| 1857-47 | Delander, J. A. | fore 24½ da @ $1.25 - $30.60. Rd Dept main stem 2d s-div |
| 1855-41 | Delaney, John | lab 18 3/4 da @ $1 - $18.75. Rd Way Dept |
| 1857-49 | " M. | watch cuts 28 da @ $1 - $28.00. Rd Way Dept |
| 1857-55 | " Michael | lab 23 da @ $1 - $23.00. Rd Dept main stem 6th s-div |
| 1857-100 | " Patrick | watch 30 da @ $1 - $30.00. NW Va RR, Rd Dept 5th s-div |
| 1855-41 | " " | lab 21 da @ $1 - $21.00. Rd Way Dept |
| 1857-52 | DeLawder, J. A. | lab 27 3/4 da @ $1 - $27.75. Rd Dept main stem 6th s-div |
| 1855-39 | " Lloyd | lab 25½ da @ $1 - $25.50. Rd Way Dept |
| 1855-53 | Delay, John | carp 17 3/4 da @ $1.37½ - $24.40. Rd Way Dept |
| 1855-20 | Delfert, John | fire 4 3/4 da @ $1.75 - $8.30. Trans Dept main stem |
| 1857-55 | Delgarn, J. W. | lab 22½ da @ $1 - $22.50. Rd Dept main stem 9th s-div |
| 1855-10 | Delgram, John W. | conduc & brak 21½ da @ $50 per mo - $45.30. Trans Dept main stem |
| 1857-21 | Delhouse, Christy | ton conduc 25 da @ $60 per mo - $60.00. 2d div |
| 1857-90 | Dellaway, Joshua | lab 12 da @ $1.12 - $13.50. grad, Welling Tun |
| 1857-103 | Delno, Phil. | carp 20 da @ $1.60 - $32.00. NW Va RR depot |
| 1857-121 | Delran, M. | paint 15 3/4 da @ $1.65 - $26.00. Mach Dept, Balto |
| 1855-50 | Deluo, Philip | watch cuts 30 da @ $1 - $30.00. Rd Way Dept |
| 1855-80 | Demich, M. | carp 21¼ da @ $1.50 - $31.85. Mach Dept |
| 1855-39 | " | lab 24 da @ $1 - $24.00. Rd Way Dept |

| | | |
|---|---|---|
| 1857-49 | Demick, Michael | lab 25 da @ $1 - $25.00. Rd Dept main stem 3d s-div |
| 1857-91 | Dempsey, John | lab 17½ da @ $1 - $17.50. grad, Welling Tun |
| 1857-88 | Patrick | lab 21¼ da @ $1.12 - $23.90. grad, Welling Tun |
| 1857-112 | T. | mach help 3 da @ $1 - $3.00. Mach Dept, Balto |
| 1857-20 | Thomas | pass fire 12 da @ $40 per mo - $16.00. 1st div |
| 1857-38 | " | pass fire 15½ da @ $40 per mo - $20.65. Wash br rd, Wash city sta |
| 1855-25 | Wm. | clean eng 16½ da @ $1.15 - $19.00. Trans Dept main stem |
| 1857-10 | " | harness mkr 25 da @ $35 per mo - $35.00. hp exp, Balto |
| 1855-5 | Demsey, Thomas | eng clean 27 3/4 da @ $1.15 - $31.90. Trans Dept, Wash br |
| 1857-84 | Dennie, Charles | lab 28 da @ $1.12 - $31.50. grad, Board Tree Tun |
| 1857-71 | Denroot, Phil. | track lay 23 da @ $1.25 - $28.75. Camden sta, repair tracks |
| 1857-99 | Denry, Patrick | lab 24 da @ $1 - $24.00. NW Va RR, Rd Dept 4th s-div |
| 1857-72 | Derew, John | lab 22½ da @ $1 - $22.50. Locust Pt, load mat |
| 1857-25 | Derff, James C. | ton brak 1½ da @ $40 per mo - $2.40. 2d div |
| 1857-25 | James O. | ton brak 16¼ da @ $40 per mo - $26.00. 2d div |
| 1855-26 | Dergan, Corn. | clean eng 28½ da @ $1 - $28.50. Trans Dept main stem |
| 1857-102 | Derkin, James | pump water 30 da @ $1 - $30.00. NW Va RR |
| 1855-18 | Derkirdge, G. W. | ton eng'man 20 da @ $2.50 - $50.00. Trans Dept main stem |
| 1857-92 | Dermody, Martin | lab 12¼ da @ $1 - $12.25. grad, Littleton Tun |
| 1855-57 | Derr, Adam | fire 11¼ da @ $1.75 - $19.65. Rd Way Dept |
| 1855-20 | " | fire 11 da @ $1.75 - $19.25. Trans Dept main stem |
| 1857-33 | " | ton fire 2 da @ $1.75 - $3.50. 3d div |
| 1857-32 | Jeremiah | ton fire 11¼ da @ $1.75 - $19.70. 2d div |
| 1855-35 | John | 28 da @ $35 per mo - $35.00. Trans Dept main stem |
| 1857-20 | " | pass fire 24 da @ $40 per mo - $32.00. 2d div |
| 1855-73 | Dessey, George | tin 15¼ da @ $1.73 - $26.40. Rd Way Dept |
| 1857-69 | " | tin 12 da @ $1.73 - $20.75. Mt Clare sta, Balto |
| 1855-90 | Detman, William | carp 22 da @ $1.40 - $30.80. Mach Dept |
| 1857-73 | Detterman, Barney | lab 24 da @ $1.12 - $27.00. repair water sta, M.S. & P.B. |
| 1857-97 | Devan, John | lab 26½ da @ $1 - $26.50. NW Va RR, Rd Dept 2d s-div |
| 1857-64 | Patrick | lab 25 da @ $1 -$25.00. Rd Dept main stem 17th s-div |
| 1857-114 | Deven, George | iron mould app 22 da @ $.55 - $12.10. Mach Dept, Balto |
| 1855-52 | Deveney, John | lab 17 da @ $1 - $17.00. Rd Way Dept |
| 1857-61 | " | lab 26½ da @ $1 - $26.50. Rd Dept main stem 14th s-div |
| 1857-99 | Deviken, Patrick | lab 24 da @ $1 - $24.00. NW Va RR, Rd Dept 4th s-div |
| 1857-83 | Devine, Barney | lab 24 da @ $1.12 - $27.00. grad, Board Tree Tun |

B & O RR EMPLOYEES 117

| ID | Name | Description |
|---|---|---|
| 1857-84 | Devine, Daniel | lab 17 da @ $1.12 - $19.10. grad, Board Tree Tun |
| 1857-89 | " John | lab 25½ da @ $1.12 - $28.70. grad, Welling Tun |
| 1857-51 | " " | lab 25 da @ $1 - $25.00. Rd Dept main stem 5th s-div |
| 1857-111 | " John W. | mach help 19 3/4 da @ $1 - $19.75. Mach Dept, Balto |
| 1857-121 | " Michael | paint app 18 da @ $.75 - $13.50. Mach Dept, Balto |
| 1857-88 | " Mike | fore 23 da @ $1.75 - $40.25. grad, Welling Tun |
| 1857-114 | " Patrick | iron mould app 23 da @ $.45 - $10.35. Mach Dept, Balto |
| 1857-128 | Devithe, William | boil mkr 23½ da @ $1.50 - $35.25. Mach Dept, Piedmont |
| 1857-78 | Devries, R. T. | lab 23 da @ $1 - $23.00. lay 2d track |
| 1857-18 | Dewalt, Wm. H. | pass train conduc 30 da @ $50 per mo - $50.00. thr mail & exp |
| 1857-109 | Dewsenberry, Charles | mach 15 3/4 da @ $1.50 - $23.60. Mach Dept, Balto |
| 1857-111 | Dibbs, James | mach help 24 da @ $1 - $24.00. Mach Dept, Balto |
| 1857-35 | " | coup 24 da @ $30 per mo - $30.00. Trans Dept main stem |
| 1857-9 | " | coup 6 da @ $30 per mo - $7.20. Mt Clare sta |
| 1857-31 | Dickenson, George | ton fire 3 da @ $1.75 - $5.25. 1st div |
| 1855-9 | Dickerhoof, J. | conduc 3 3/4 da @ $50 per mo - $7.80. Trans Dept main stem |
| 1855-92 | Dickerhoop, A. | carp @ $40 per mo - $40.00. Mach Dept |
| 1857-108 | Dickerson, Harvey | mach 16½ da @ $1.50 - $24.75. Mach Dept, Balto |
| 1855-6 | " P. | agt 28 4/5 da @ $33.35 per mo - $26.70. Trans Dept main stem |
| 1855-55 | " Peter | agt ½ mo @ $33.35 per mo - $33.35. Rd Way Dept |
| 1855-4 | " " | agt 28 1/5 da @ $33.35 per mo - $6.65. Trans Dept, Wash br |
| 1855-48 | Dickey, John | blksmith 24 da @ $1.25 - $30.00. Rd Way Dept |
| 1855-92 | Dickinson, H. | app 23 da @ $.55 - $12.65. Mach Dept |
| 1855-37 | Dickson, Charles | lab 20 da @ $1 - $20.00. Rd Way Dept |
| 1855-56 | " Owen | spik 28 da @ $1.06 - $29.70. Rd Way Dept |
| 1855-34 | " Thomas | port 28 da @ $30 per mo - $30.00. Trans Dept main stem |
| 1857-82 | Diel, John | bricklay 17 3/4 da @ $2 - $35.50. grad, Board Tree Tun |
| 1855-86 | Dieterlan, Frederick | mach 21 3/4 da @ $1.60 - $34.80. Mach Dept |
| 1855-54 | Diffenbaugh, S. | lab 22 da @ $1 - $22.00. Rd Dept main stem 8th s-div |
| 1855-18 | Diffey, Alexander | ton eng'man 28 da @ $83.35 per mo - $83.35. Trans Dept main stem |
| 1857-7 | " | asst supv trains (1st two div) @ $83.35 per mo. Supv Trains on Rd |
| 1857-118 | " | blksmith app 25 da @ $.55 - $13.75. Mach Dept, Balto |
| 1857-45 | " | distrib mat @ $20 per mo. Rd Dept |
| 1857-75 | " John | lab 8 3/4 da @ $.97 - $8.50. ballast train for ?? track |
| 1857-134 | " Owen | mach 19 da @ $1.60 - $30.40. Mach Dept, Wheeling |
| 1857-113 | " Victor | mach app 24 da @ $.55 - $13.20. Mach Dept, Balto |

## B & O RR EMPLOYEES

| | | | |
|---|---|---|---|
| 1857-25 | Dike, George | ton brak 28 da @ $40 per mo - $44.80. 2d div | |
| 1857-84 | Dill, James | eng'man 20 3/4 da @ $3 - $62.25. grad, Board Tree Tun | |
| 1857-57 | Dill, Leonard | lab 27½ da @ $1 - $27.50. Rd Dept main stem 11th s-div | |
| 1857-58 | " | watch 30 da @ $.75 - $22.50. Rd Dept main stem 11th s-div | |
| 1857-57 | Dillan, William | lab 27½ da @ $1 - $27.50. Rd Dept main stem 11th s-div | |
| 1857-100 | Dillan, Peter | lab 23½ da @ $1 - $23.50. NW Va RR, Rd Dept 5th s-div | |
| 1855-43 | Dillen, M. | lab 21½ da @ $1 - $21.50 - Rd Way Dept | |
| 1855-46 | Dillon, David | gather iron 2 da @ $2.50 - $5.00. Rd Way Dept | |
| 1855-18 | " | ton eng'man 9½ da @ $2.50 - $23.10. Trans Dept main stem | |
| 1857-29 | " | ton eng'man 25 3/4 da @ $3 - $77.25. 2d div | |
| 1857-94 | John | fore 26 da @ $1.50 - $39.00. quarry & haul stone for Board Tree & Littleton Tun |
| 1855-56 | William | lab 14¼ da @ $1 - $14.25. Rd Way Dept | |
| 1855-80 | Dinen, E. R. | carp 24 da @ $1.75 - $42.00. Mach Dept | |
| 1855-76 | Dinsmore, Jas. | lab 26 da @ $1.72 - $44.70. Mach Dept | |
| 1857-110 | " | mach 30½ da @ $1.72 - $52.45. Mach Dept, Balto | |
| 1857-90 | Dirkin, Daniel | lab 11 da @ $1.12 - $12.35. grad, Welling Tun | |
| 1857-28 | Disney, Leonard | ton eng'man 20½ da @ $2.50 - $51.25. 1st div | |
| 1857-31 | Wilson | ton fire 18 3/4 da @ $1.75 - $32.80. 1st div | |
| 1857-102 | Ditman, William | carp 18 da @ $1.40 - $25.20. NW Va RR, rwy depot | |
| 1855-24 | Divan, Edward | pass & bur driv 24 da @ $1 - $24.00. Trans Dept main stem | |
| 1857-9 | Divans, Elias | reg 25 da @ $50 per mo - $50.00. Mt Clare sta | |
| 1855-35 | Divens, E. | reg 24 da @ $50 per mo - $50.00. Trans Dept main stem | |
| 1857-120 | E. R. | carp 22 da @ $1.90 - $41.80. Mach Dept, Balto | |
| 1857-24 | Edw. T. | ton brak 25 da @ $40 per mo - $40.00. Camden sta | |
| 1855-7 | J. | asst supv 28 da @ $1 - $35 per mo - $35.00. Trans Dept main stem | |
| 1857-66 | Divers, Hugh | lab 25 da @ $1 - $25.00. Rd Dept main stem 18th s-div | |
| 1857-66 | Divine, Barry | lab 23½ da @ $1 - $23.50. Rd Dept main stem 18th s-div | |
| 1855-25 | John | clean eng 25 3/4 da @ $1.15 - $29.60. Trans Dept main stem | |
| 1855-18 | " | ton eng'man 8 da @ $2.50 - $20.00. Trans Dept main stem | |
| 1857-40 | Mark | ton eng'man 15 da @ $3 - $45.00. NW Va rd, Parkersburg sta | |
| 1857-66 | Patrick | lab 25½ da @ $1 - $25.50. Rd Dept main stem 18th s-div | |
| 1855-46 | Diviney, John | lab 24 da @ $1 - $24.00. Rd Dept main stem 1st s-div | |
| 1855-67 | Divins, Hugh | lab 21½ da @ $1 - $21.50. Rd Way Dept | |
| 1855-61 | Dixon, Augustus | bricklay 23 da @ $2.25 - $51.75. Mt Clare sta, Balto | |
| 1857-31 | George | ton fire 19 da @ $1.75 - $33.25. 1st div | |

# B & O RR EMPLOYEES 119

| | | | |
|---|---|---|---|
| 1857-65 | Dixon, John | watch 30 da @ $1 - $30.00. Rd Dept main stem 17th s-div |
| 1855-35 | Thomas | 28 da @ $35 per mo - $35.00. Trans Dept main stem |
| 1857-17 | " | port 30 da @ $30 per mo - $30.00. Wheeling sta |
| 1857-12 | " | swit tend 30 da @ $35 per mo - $35.00. Pt of Rocks |
| 1855-42 | Dockery, Pat. | lab 14½ da @ $1 - $14.50. Rd Way Dept |
| 1857-13 | Dockerty, Bridget | keep pass rm 30 da @ $5 per mo - $5.00. Hancock |
| 1857-53 | Dockney, Patrick | lab 21½ da @ $1 - $21.50. Rd Dept main stem 7th s-div |
| 1855-32 | Dodd, Francis | saw wd 22½ cords @ $.50 - $11.25. Trans Dept main stem |
| 1855-7 | Dodson, A. | clk 28 da @ $50 per mo - $50.00. Trans Dept main stem |
| 1857-17 | Adam | agt 30 da @ $75 per mo - $75.00. frt transfer force at Bellaire, opp Benwood |
| 1857-41 | Garrison | lab 8 da @ $1 - $8.00. NW Va rd, Athey's wd train |
| 1855-7 | J. M. | clk 28 da @ $41.65 per mo - $41.65. Trans Dept main stem |
| 1857-17 | T. M. | clk 30 da @ $58.35 per mo - $58.35. Wheeling sta |
| 1857-41 | Van | lab 1 da @ $1 - $1.00. NW Va rd, Athey's wd train |
| 1857-20 | Wm. | pass fire 29 da @ $40 per mo - $38.65. 1st div |
| 1857-125 | Doeman, Edward | flue clean @ $34.50 per mo - $34.50. Mach Dept, Martinsburg |
| 1855-26 | Doffler, Jacob | clean eng 28 da @ $1 - $28.00. Trans Dept main stem |
| 1857-126 | " | clean eng 30 da @ $1 - $30.00. Mach Dept, Martinsburg |
| 1857-83 | Dogan, Patrick | lab 25 da @ $1.12 - $28.10. grad, Board Tree Tun |
| 1857-84 | Dogarty, Patrick | lab 7 da @ $1.12 - $7.85. grad, Board Tree Tun |
| 1857-81 | Dohaney, Patrick | lab 19 3/4 da @ $1 - $19.75. lay 2d track |
| 1855-35 | Dohiry, Bridget | 28 da @ $5 per mo - $5.00. Trans Dept main stem |
| 1857-74 | Dohrmer, Herman | track lay 22 3/4 da @ $1 - $22.75. put swit on line of rd |
| 1857-58 | Doil, John | lab 29½ da @ $1 - $29.50. Rd Dept main stem 12th s-div |
| 1855-61 | Dolan, Andrew | lab 22 da @ $1 - $22.00. Rd Way Dept |
| 1857-83 | Barney | lab 6 da @ $1.12 - $6.75. grad, Board Tree Tun |
| 1857-111 | Edward | mach help 17⅞ da @ $1.15 - $19.85. Mach Dept, Balto |
| 1855-37 | James | nail 28 da @ $1 - $28.00. Rd Way Dept |
| 1857-47 | " | lab 27 da @ $1 - $27.00. Rd Dept main stem 1st s-div |
| 1857-79 | John | lab 27 da @ $.65 - $17.55. lay 2d track |
| 1855-62 | Michael | lab 9 3/4 da @ $1 - $9.75. Rd Way Dept |
| 1855-34 | " | watch 28 da @ $1 - $28.00. Trans Dept main stem |
| 1857-96 | " | lab 24½ da @ $1 - $24.50. Rd Dept 1st s-div |
| 1857-68 | " | lab 20½ da @ $1 - $20.50. Rd Dept main stem 19th s-div |
| 1857-98 | " | watch 30 da @ $1 - $30.00. NW Va RR, Rd Dept 2d s-div |
| 1857-96 | Patrick | fore 24½ da @ $1.25 - $30.60. NW Va RR, Rd Dept 1st s-div |

120    B & O RR EMPLOYEES

| | | |
|---|---|---|
| 1857-58 | Dolan, Patrick | lab 25 3/4 da @ $1 - $25.75. Rd Dept main stem 12th s-div |
| 1857-16 | " Peter | fire stat'ry eng 30 da @ $25 per mo - $25.00. Berwood sta |
| 1855-62 | " Thomas | lab 19 da @ $1 - $19.00. Rd Way Dept |
| 1857-67 | " " | lab 20 3/4 da @ $1 - $20.75. Rd Dept main stem 19th s-div |
| 1855-62 | " Timothy | fore 22½ da @ $1.25 - $28.10. Rd Way Dept |
| 1857-130 | " Wm. | lab 19 da @ $1 - $19.00. Mach Dept, Piedmont |
| 1855-43 | Dolen, Thomas | lab 17 3/4 da @ $1 - $14.75. Rd Way Dept |
| 1855-35 | Doll, D. | reg 24 da @ $50 per mo - $50.00. Trans Dept main stem |
| 1857-9 | " Daniel | reg 25 da @ $50 per mo - $50.00. Mt Clare sta |
| 1857-21 | " George | ton conduc 25 3/4 da @ $50 per mo - $51.50. 2d div |
| 1855-58 | " Jacob | lab 20 da @ $1 - $20.00. Rd Way Dept |
| 1855-69 | Doman, John | lab 21 da @ $1 - $21.00. Rd Way Dept |
| 1857-91 | Donaho, Michael | lab 20¼ da @ $1 - $20.25. grad, Welling Tun |
| 1855-90 | " Mike | help 27½ da @ $1 - $27.50. Mach Dept |
| 1855-76 | " Patrick | help 23⅜ da @ $1.15 - $26.75. Mach Dept |
| 1857-111 | " " | mach help 18 da @ $1.15 - $20.70. Mach Dept, Balto |
| 1857-101 | Donahoe, Andrew | lab 24 da @ $1 - $24.00. NW Va RR ballast train |
| 1857-101 | " " | lab 22 da @ $1 - $22.00. NW Va RR ballast train |
| 1855-90 | " James | lab 8½ da @ $1.12 - $9.55. grad, Welling Tun |
| 1855-24 | " John | pass & bur driv 26½ da @ $30 per mo - $33.10. Trans Dept main stem |
| 1857-10 | " " | bur brak 9½ da @ $1.15 - $10.90. hp exp, Balto |
| 1857-90 | Donahue, John | lab 11½ da @ $1.12 - $12.95. grad, Welling Tun |
| 1855-46 | " M. | lab 20¼ da @ $1 - $20.25. Rd Way Dept |
| 1857-101 | " Martin | lab 21½ da @ $1 - $21.50. NW Va RR ballast train |
| 1857-97 | " Mat. | lab 25 da @ $1 - $25.00. NW Va RR, Rd Dept 2d s-div |
| 1857-80 | " Michael | lab 21½ da @ $1 - $21.50. lay 2d track |
| 1857-128 | " " | boil mkr 14 3/4 da @ $1.25 - $18.45. Mach Dept, Piedmont |
| 1857-130 | " " | lab 16 3/4 da @ $1 - $16.75. Mach Dept, Piedmont |
| 1857-99 | " Morgan | lab 25 da @ $1 - $25.00. NW Va RR, Rd Dept 4th s-div |
| 1857-104 | " Tim. | lab 22¼ da @ $1 - $22.25. NW Va RR Tun |
| 1855-46 | Donaley, M. | lab 21 da @ $1 - $21.00. Rd Way Dept |
| 1855-50 | Donce, L. | watch cuts 28 da @ $1 - $28.00. Rd Way Dept |
| 1855-60 | Done, George | fore 25¼ da @ $1 - $25.25. Rd Way Dept |
| 1857-113 | " John H. | mach app 24 3/4 da @ $.55 - $13.60. Mach Dept, Balto |
| 1855-1 | " " | mast of trans $4000 per annum - $333.33 |
| 1855-53 | Donegan, Daniel | lab 24 da @ $1.25 - $30.00. Rd Way Dept |

| | | | |
|---|---|---|---|
| 1857-56 | Donegan, Daniel | fore 25 da @ $1.25 - $31.25. Rd Dept main stem 10th s-div |
| 1857-98 | Donlan, Patrick | fore 24 da @ $1.25 - $30.00. NW Va RR, Rd Dept 3d s-div |
| 1857-62 | Donlavy, Owen | watch 30 da @ $1 - $30.00. Rd Dept main stem 15th s-div |
| 1857-64 | Donley, Derby | lab 4 3/4 da @ $1 - $4.75. grad, Welling Tun |
| 1857-90 | Donley, Michael | lab 19 3/4 da @ $1 - $19.75. grad, Welling Tun |
| 1857-99 | Donnell, John O. | lab 2 3/4 da @ $1 - $23.25. NW Va RR, Rd Dept 4th s-div |
| 1855-20 | Donnelly, James | fire 17 da @ $1.75 - $29.75. Trans Dept main stem |
| 1857-113 | " | mach app 15 da @ $.55 - $8.25. Mach Dept, Balto |
| 1857-23 | " | ton conduc 24 da @ $50 per mo - $48.00. Board Tree Tun |
| 1857-22 | " | ton conduc 2 da @ $50 per mo - $4.00. 3d & 4th div |
| 1857-47 | William | lab 27 da @ $1 - $27.00. Rd Dept main stem 1st s-div |
| 1855-63 | Donoghue, Jno. | lab 22 da @ $1 - $22.00. Rd Way Dept |
| 1855-27 | Donoho, Pat. | clean eng 24 da @ $1 - $24.00. Trans Dept main stem |
| 1855-59 | Donohoe, M. | lab 10 da @ $1 - $10.00. Rd Way Dept |
| 1857-84 | Donohue, James | blksmith 24½ da @ $1.50 - $36.75. grad, Board Tree Tun |
| 1857-94 | " | lab 9 3/4 da @ $1 - $9.75. quarry & haul stone for Board Tree & Littleton Tun |
| 1857-67 | " | lab 20 3/4 da @ $1 - $20.75. Rd Dept main stem 19th s-div |
| 1855-63 | John | lab 22 da @ $1 - $22.00. Rd Way Dept |
| 1857-13 | " | clk 30 da @ $41.65 per mo - $41.65. Harpers Ferry |
| 1857-93 | " | lab 24 da @ $1 - $24.00. quarry & haul stone for Board Tree & Littleton Tun |
| 1857-68 | " | lab 24 da @ $1 - $24.00. Rd Dept main stem 19th s-div |
| 1855-63 | M. | lab 16¼ da @ $1 - $16.25. Rd Way Dept |
| 1855-27 | Michael | clean eng 27½ da @ $1 - $27.50. Trans Dept main stem |
| 1857-68 | " | lab 15½ da @ $1 - $15.50. Rd Dept main stem 19th s-div |
| 1857-13 | Patrick | watch 30 da @ $1 - $30.00. Martinsburg |
| 1857-81 | Donolly, John | lab 23½ da @ $1.12 - $26.45. grad, Board Tree Tun |
| 1857-83 | Dooley, Michael | lab 6 da @ $1.12 - $6.75. grad, Board Tree Tun |
| 1857-67 | Dooley, Patrick | lab 22¼ da @ $1 - $22.25. Rd Dept main stem 19th s-div |
| 1857-21 | Samuel | ton conduc 29 3/4 da @ $50 per mo - $59.50. 2d div |
| 1855-63 | Thos. | lab 20½ da @ $1 - $20.25. Rd Way Dept |
| 1855-80 | Dooling, Thos. | lab 24¼ da @ $1.15 - $27.90. Mach Dept |
| 1857-87 | Dooly, Michael | lab 18 3/4 da @ $1 - $18.75. grad, McGuire's Tun |
| 1857-93 | Owen | smith help 21 da @ $1 - $21.00. quarry & haul stone for Board Tree & Littleton Tun |
| 1857-103 | Doonan, Edward | lab 20 da @ $1 - $20.00. NW Va RR Tun |
| 1857-90 | John | lab 8½ da @ $1.12 - $9.55. grad, Welling Tun |
| 1857-98 | Peter | watch 30 da @ $1 - $30.00. NW Va RR, Rd D$_e$pt 3d s-div |

## B & O RR EMPLOYEES

| | | |
|---|---|---|
| 1855-80 | Dooner, John | lab 21 da @ $1 - $21.00. Mach Dept |
| 1857-90 | Doovey, John | lab 12 da @ $1.12 - $13.50. grad, Welling Tun |
| 1857-129 | Dorithy, Thomas | clean eng 28 da @ $1 - $28.00. Mach Dept, Piedmont |
| 1855-14 | Dorman, George | conduc & brak 1 da @ $40 per mo - $1.65. Trans Dept main stem |
| 1857-27 | Dormire, Elmore | ton brak 5 da @ $40 per mo - $8.00. Board Tree Tun |
| 1855-58 | Dorsey, B. | lab 19½ da @ $1 - $19.50. Rd Way Dept |
| 1857-57 | " | lab 27½ da @ $1 - $27.50. Rd Dept main stem 11th s-div |
| 1857-60 | Bartley | lab 26½ da @ $1 - $26.50. Rd Dept main stem 13th s-div |
| 1855-39 | Beal | lab 27½ da @ $1 - $27.50. Rd Way Dept |
| 1857-7 | E. R. | clk @ $75 per mo. Gen Frt Agt Ofc |
| 1855-87 | Edward | help 9½ da @ $1 - $9.50. Mach Dept |
| 1857-102 | " | carp 23½ da @ $1.60 - $37.60. NW Va RR, rwy depot |
| 1857-24 | Evan | ton brak 14½ da @ $40 per mo; 2½ da @ $50 per mo - $28.20. 1st div |
| 1857-48 | Frederick | 25½ da @ $1 - $25.50. Rd Dept main stem 2d s-div |
| 1857-95 | Hammond | lab 23 da @ $1 - $23.00. Wash br, Rd Dept |
| 1855-71 | J. | carp 22 da @ $1 - $22.00. Rd Way Dept |
| 1857-31 | Jackson | ton fire 4 da @ $1.75 - $7.00. 1st div |
| 1857-20 | James | pass fire 11½ da @ $40 per mo - $19.35. 4th div |
| 1857-100 | " | watch 30 da @ $1 - $30.00. NW Va RR, Rd Dept 5th s-div |
| 1857-7 | Jerry | mess @ $25 per mo - Mast of Trans Ofc |
| 1857-57 | John | lab 13½ da @ $1 - $13.50. Rd Dept main stem 11th s-div |
| 1855-56 | Thomas | lab 2 da @ $1 - $2.00. Rd Way Dept |
| 1857-120 | " | carp 18 da @ $1.65 - $29.70. Mach Dept, Balto |
| 1857-57 | " | lab 26½ da @ $1 - $26.50. Rd Dept main stem 11th s-div |
| 1857-84 | William L. | lab 16½ da @ $1.12 - $18.55. grad, Board Tree Tun |
| 1857-121 | William L. | carp trim help 18½ da @ $1.15 - $21.00. Mach Dept, Balto |
| 1857-94 | Dory, John | lab 8 da @ $1 - $8.00. quarry & haul stone for Board Tree & Littleton Tun |
| 1855-88 | Dotson, William | carp 19 da @ $1.30 - $24.70. Mach Dept |
| 1857-89 | Dougherty, Patrick | lab 6½ da @ $1.12 - $7.30. grad, Welling Tun |
| 1857-15 | R. | lab 25 da @ $1 - $25.00. Grafton sta |
| 1857-99 | William C. | fore 25 da @ $1.25 - $31.25. NW Va RR, Rd Dept 4th s-div |
| 1857-19 | Douglas, Alanson | pass eng'man 3 3/4 da @ $3 - $11.25. 3d div |
| 1857-29 | Uriah | ton eng'man 31 da @ $3 - $93.00. 3d div |
| 1855-90 | Douglass, A. | mach 6 da @ $1.50 - $9.00. Mach Dept |
| 1855-15 | " | pass eng'man 17½ da @ $3 - $51.75. Trans Dept main stem |
| 1857-40 | " | pass eng'man 11 da @ $3 - $33.00. NW Va rd, Parkersburg sta |

B & O RR EMPLOYEES 123

| ID | Name | Details |
|---|---|---|
| 1857-133 | Doulin, James | blksmith help 21½ da @ $1 - $24.50. Mach Dept, Fetterman |
| 1855-78 | Douns, T. | help 23¼ da @ $1.15 - $26.75. Mach Dept |
| 1855-64 | Doutan, Thos. | carp 16 da @ $1 - $16.00. Rd Way Dept |
| 1855-59 | Douzell, Charles | lab 20½ da @ $1 - $20.50. Rd Way Dept |
| 1855-4 | Dove, Benjamin | bag mast 28 da @ $35 per mo - $35.00. Trans Dept, Wash br |
| 1855-37 | " | bag mast 30 da @ $35 per mo - $35.00. Wash br rd, Wash city sta |
| 1857-121 | Dover, John | paint help 14⅞ da @ $1.15 - $16.40. Mach Dept, Balto |
| 1857-83 | Dowd, Patrick | lab 11 3/4 da @$1.12 - $13.20. grad, Board Tree Tun |
| 1855-10 | Dowden, A. | conduc & brak 1 da @ $40 per mo - $1.65. Trans Dept main stem |
| 1855-40 | " | ton eng'man 25 da @ $50 per mo - $50.00. NW Va rd, Parkersburg sta |
| 1857-113 | Dowing, J. L. | mach app 20 3/4 da @ $.55 - $11.40. Mach Dept, Balto |
| 1857-96 | Dowlin, Thomas | lab 20⅞ da @ $1 - $20.25. NW Va RR, Rd Dept 1st s-div |
| 1857-75 | Dowling, Thomas | lab 17 3/4 da @ $1.15 - $20.20. ballast train for 2d track |
| 1857-47 | Dowlon, James | lab 24 da @ $1 - $24.00. Rd Dept main stem 1st s-div |
| 1855-14 | Dowman, T. W. | conduc & brak 16½ da @ $40 per mo - $27.50. Trans Dept main stem |
| 1855-47 | Downey, James | lab 22 3/4 da @$1 - $22.75. Rd Way Dept |
| 1857-36 | " M. | tele oper 30 da @ $30 per mo - $30.00. Piedmont |
| 1855-14 | Downing, A. Patrick | fore 24 da @ $1.25 - $30.00. Rd Dept main stem 1st s-div |
| 1857-139 | " Alexander | conduc & brak 1 da @ $40 per mo - $1.65. Trans Dept main stem |
| 1855-94 | " | lab 16 3/4 da @ $1 - $16.75. Mach Dept |
| 1857-40 | " | lab 13 da @ $1.12 - $14.55. NW Va R?, Mach Dept, Parkersburg |
| 1857-113 | Downs, Samuel | pass fire 4 da @ $40 per mo - $5.35. NW 7a rd, Parkersburg sta |
| 1857-118 | Dowry, Theodore | iron mould 16 3/4 da @ $1.65 - $27.65. Mach Dept, Balto |
| 1857-85 | Doyal, Michael | blksmith help 24 da @ $1.15 - $27.60. Mach Dept, Balto |
| 1857-111 | Doyer, Peter | lab 7½ da @ $1.12 - $8.15. grad, Board Tree Tun |
| 1855-42 | Doyle, Edward | mach help 18 da @ $1 - $18.00. Mach Dept, Balto |
| 1857-53 | " Edward B. | lab 19 da @ $1 - $19.00. Rd Way Dept |
| 1855-52 | " James | lab 24½ da @ $1 - $24.50. Rd Dept main stem 7th s-div |
| 1857-117 | " " | lab 16 da @ $1 - $16.00. Rd Way Dept |
| 1855-49 | " John | blksmith help 16 3/4 da @ $1.10 - $18.45. Mach Dept, Balto |
| 1857-69 | " " | watch cuts 28 da @ $1 - $28.00. Rd Way Dept |
| 1857-61 | " " | lab 18 da @ $1 - $18.00. Mt Clare sta, Balto |
| 1857-129 | " Martin | watch 30 da @ $1 - $30.00. Rd Dept main stem 14th s-div |
| 1857-88 | " Michael | clean eng 16 da @ $1 - $16.00. Mach Dept, Piedmont |
| 1857-79 | " " | lab 17 da @ $1.12 - $19.10. grad, Welling Tun |
| | " " | lab 21½ da @ $1 - $21.50. lay 2d track |

| |  |  |
|---|---|---|
| 1855-52 | Doyle, Terry | lab 15 da @ $1 - $15.00. Rd Way Dept |
| 1855-43 | " Thomas | lab 5 da @ $1 - $5.00. Rd Way Dept |
| 1857-52 | Draner, John | lab 18½ da @ $1 - $18.50. Rd Dept main stem 6th s-div |
| 1857-74 | Drenner, Henry | lab 22 da @ $1 - $22.00. Rd Dept main stem 6th s-div |
| 1857-74 | Drescoll, John | track lay 22 3/4 da @ $1.12 - $25.60. put swit on line of rd |
| 1855-45 | Dresher, C. | track lay 22 3/4 da @ $1.12 - $25.60. put swit on line of rd |
| 1857-37 | Drew, Arthur | lab 16 da @ $1 - $16.00. Rd Way Dept |
| 1857-122 | Drill, J. M. | lab 25 da @ $30 per mo - $30.00. Wash br rd, Wash city sta |
| 1855-6 | " " | clk 28 da @ $58.65 per mo - $58.65. Trans Dept main stem |
| 1857-7 | | gen frt clk @ $75 per mo. Gen Frt Agt Ofc |
| 1855-49 | Dripingham, J. | watch cuts 28 da @ $1 - $28.00. Rd Way Dept |
| 1857-54 | Droall, Simon | lab 23 da @ $1 - $23.00. Rd Dept main stem 8th s-div |
| 1857-125 | Droman, Albert | carp 18½ da @ $1.35 - $24.95. Mach Dept, Martinsburg |
| 1857-100 | Drury, John | lab 26½ da @ $1 - $26.50. NW Va RR, Rd Dept 5th s-div |
| 1855-86 | Duble, J. | train inspec @ $34.50 per mo - $34.50. Mach Dept |
| 1857-125 | " Jonathan | inspec cars @ $34.50 per mo -$34.50. Mach Dept, Martinsburg |
| 1855-38 | Duce, James | lab 17 da @ $1 - $17.00. Rd Way Dept |
| 1857-74 | Duckett, Buck | lab 18½ da @ $1.12 - $20.80. repair bridges &c |
| 1857-76 | Dudee, James | dril 22½ da @ $1.10 - $24.75. ballast train for 2d track |
| 1857-76 | " Phil. | dril 23½ da @ $1.10 - $25.55. ballast train for 2d track |
| 1857-79 | Dudley, Chris. | lab 18¼ da @ $1 - $18.25. lay 2d track |
| 1855-16 | " J. | pass fire 9 da @ $1.25 - $11.25. Trans Dept main stem |
| 1857-48 | Duffey, Edward | lab 25 da @ $1 -$25.00. Rd Dept main stem 2d s-div |
| 1857-68 | " " | lab 22 da @ $1 -$22.00. Rd Dept main stem 19th s-div |
| 1855-44 | " James | fore 20 da @ $1.25 -$25.00. Rd Way Dept |
| 1857-77 | " John | quarry 8 da @ $1 - $8.00. ballast train for 2d track |
| 1857-101 | " Michael | lab 12 da @ $1 - $12.00. NW Va RR ballast train |
| 1855-46 | " Patrick | lab 6 da @ $1 - $6.00. Rd Way Dept |
| 1855-52 | " " | lab 15½ da @ $1 - $15.50. Rd Way Dept |
| 1857-61 | | lab 18½ da @ $1 - $18.50. Rd Dept main stem 14th s-div |
| 1855-38 | Duffey, Michael | lab 25 3/4 da @ $1 - $25.75. lay 2d track |
| 1857-100 | Duffy, Edward | lab 24 da @ $1 - $24.00. NW Va RR, Rd Dept 5th s-div |
| 1855-117 | " Hugh | watch 30 da @ $1 - $30.00. NW Va RR, Mach Dept, Balto |
| 1855-31 | " James M. | blksmith help 15 da @ $1.15 - $17.25. Mach Dept, Balto |
| | | prepar fuel 16 3/4 da @ $1 - $16.75. Trans Dept main stem |

B & O RR EMPLOYEES    125

| ID | Name | Description |
|---|---|---|
| 1857-102 | Duffy, Michael | pump water 30 da @ $1 -$30.00. NW Va RR |
| 1857-66 | " Patrick | lab 18 da @ $1 - $18.00. Rd Dept main stem 18th s-div |
| 1857-8 | " Thomas | lab 24 da @ $30 per mo - $28.80. Camden sta |
| 1857-129 | Dugan, Edward | clean eng 31 da @ $1 - $31.00. Mach Dept, Piedmont |
| 1855-45 | " J. W. | lab 11 da @ $1 - $11.00. Rd Way Dept |
| 1855-25 | " John | ton brak 9½ da @ $40 per mo - $15.20. 2d div |
| 1855-36 | " " | lab 25 da @ $25 per mo - $26.05. Trans Dept main stem |
| 1857-16 | " " | lab 25 da @ $28 per mo - $28.00. Benwood sta |
| 1857-52 | " Timothy | lab 26¼ da @ $1 - $26.25. Rd Dept main stem 6th s-div |
| 1855-74 | " Timy. | lab 23¼ da @ $1 - $23.25. Rd Way Dept |
| 1857-18 | Duke, A. W. | pass train brak 30 da @ $33.35 per mo - $33.35. thr mail & exp |
| 1855-7 | Dukehart, J. P. | pass conduc 28 da @ $62.50 per mo - $62.50. Trans Dept main stem |
| 1857-18 | " " " | pass train conduc 30 da @ $75 per mo - $75.00. thr mail & exp |
| 1855-84 | Dulaney, Charles | mach (includ boil mkr, work sht iron, &c) 23 3/4 da @ $1.72 - $40.85. Mach Dept |
| 1857-115 | " " | boil mkr 17 3/4 da @ $1.72 - $30.55. Mach Dept, Balto |
| 1857-117 | " James | blksmith help 2 da @ $1 - $2.00. Mach Dept, Balto |
| 1857-118 | " " | blksmith help 18 da @ $1.15 - $20.70. Mach Dept, Balto |
| 1855-95 | Dulis, John | mould 22 da @ $1.60 - $35.20. Mach Dept |
| 1855-13 | Duly, John | conduc & brak 13½ da @ $40 per mo - $22.50. Trans Dept main stem |
| 1857-26 | Dumire, A. | ton brak 4 da @ $40 per mo - $6.40. 3d & 4th div |
| 1855-9 | " Elmore | conduc 4 3/4 da @ $50 per mo - $9.90. Trans Dept main stem |
| 1855-20 | Dumphsey, John | fire 15 da @ $1.75 - $26.25. Trans Dept main stem |
| 1857-91 | Dumpley, John | lab 12.00. grad, Littleton Tun |
| 1855-60 | Dunahoe, John | lab 20 da @ $1 - $20.00. Rd Way Dept |
| 1855-60 | Dunbar, Anthony | lab 22½ da @ $1 - $22.50. Rd Way Dept |
| 1857-36 | " Mike | tele oper 30 da @ $30 per mo - $30.00. Altamont |
| 1855-55 | Duncan, G. S. | fore 19 da @ $1.25 - $23.75. Rd Way Dept |
| 1857-57 | " James | fore 25 da @ $1.25 -$31.25. Rd Dept main stem 11th s-div |
| 1855-18 | Dungan, Jesse | ton eng'man 8 3/4 da @ $2.50 - $21.85. Trans Dept main stem |
| 1857-117 | " John | blksmith 18 da @ $1.25 - $22.50. Mach Dept, Balto |
| 1857-108 | " Phenius | mach 18½ da @ $1.25 - $23.15. Mach Dept, Balto |
| 1857-112 | " S. | mach app 24 da @ $.45 - $10.80. Mach Dept, Balto |
| 1857-100 | Dunkird, Frederick | watch 30 da @ $1 - $30.00. NW Va RR, Rd Dept 5th s-div |
| 1857-108 | Dunkley, George | mach 17¼ da @ $1.50 - $25.85. Mach Dept, Balto |
| 1857-108 | " Richard | mach 6 3/4 da @ $1.40 - $9.45. Mach Dept, Balto |
| 1855-16 | Dunlap, J. | pass fire 3 da @ $40 per mo - $4.30. Trans Dept main stem |

126    B & O RR EMPLOYEES

| | | | |
|---|---|---|---|
| 1857-36 | Dunlap, J. R. | tele oper 30 da @ $30 per mo - $30.00. Grafton |
| 1857-90 | " Robert | lab 25 da @ $1 -$25.00. grad, Welling Tun |
| 1855-20 | " William | fire 9½ da @ $1.75 - $16.60. Trans Dept main stem |
| 1855-91 | " " | help 2½ da @ $1 - $2.50. Mach Dept |
| 1857-29 | " " | ton eng'man 31¼ da @ $2.50 - $78.10. 3d div |
| 1855-59 | Dunlavy, Owen | lab 14 3/4 da @ $1 -$14.75. Rd Way Dept |
| 1857-19 | Dunn, E. | bag mast 30 da @ $45 per mo - $45.00. thr mail & exp |
| 1855-37 | " " | lab 25 da @ $1 -$25.00. Rd Way Dept |
| 1857-46 | " John | lab 27 da @ $1 -$27.00. Rd Dept main stem 1st s-div |
| 1855-82 | " Michael | lab 24½ da @ $1.12 -$27.55. grad, Board Tree Tun |
| 1855-75 | " " | fore 25 da @ $1.25 -$31.25. Rd Way Dept |
| 1857-50 | " P. | fore 25 da @ $1.25 -$31.25. Rd Dept main stem 5th s-div |
| 1855-47 | " Patrick | lab 20¼ da @ $1 -$20.25. Rd Way Dept |
| 1855-37 | " " | lab 25 da @ $1 -$25.00. Rd Way Dept |
| 1857-79 | " " | lab 24½ da @ $1 -$24.50. lay 2d track |
| 1857-60 | " Simon | watch 30 da @ $1 -$30.00. Rd Dept main stem 13th s-div |
| 1857-95 | " Terence | lab 22½ da @ $1 - $22.50. Wash br, Rd Dept |
| 1855-46 | " Thomas | lab 22½ da @ $1 -$22.50. Rd Dept main stem 1st s-div |
| 1855-55 | " " | lab 6 da @ $1 -$6.00. Rd Way Dept |
| 1857-132 | " William | iron mould help 25 da @ $1 - $25.00. Mach Dept, Grafton |
| 1857-47 | Durff, James O. | watch 27 da @ $1 - $27.00. Rd Dept main stem 1st s-div |
| 1855-57 | Durken, Jas. | pass train b'mk 2 da @ $33.35 per mo - $2.20. thr mail & exp |
| 1855-57 | Durkin, Patk. | fore 20½ da @ $1.25 - $25.60. Rd Way Dept |
| 1857-98 | " John | lab 21½ da @$1 -$21.50. Rd Way Dept |
| 1855-64 | " Patrick | fore 21 3/4 da @$1.25 - $27.20. NW Va RR, Rd Dept 3d s-div |
| 1857-98 | " Peter | lab 22 da @ $1 -$22.00. Rd Way Dept |
| 1857-98 | " Thomas | lab 23½ da @ $1 -$23.50. NW Va RR, Rd Dept 3d s-div |
| 1857-83 | " " | lab 22 da @ $1 - $22.00. NW Va RR, Rd Dept 3d s-div |
| 1857-64 | " " | lab 23¾ da @ $1.12 - $25.90. grad, Board Tree Tun |
| 1855-22 | Durst, T. W. | lab 26 da @ $1 -$26.00. Rd Dept main stem 17th s-div |
| 1855-76 | Dusenbury, C. | fire 10½ da @ $1.75 -$18.35. Trans Dept main stem |
| 1857-108 | Dushane, J. T. | lab 24 da @ $1 -$24.00. Mach Dept |
| 1855-72 | " John | mach 18¾ da @ $1.60 - $29.20. Mach Dept, Balto |
| 1855-72 | " John T. | stock kpr @ $11.65 per mo - $11.65. Rd Way Dept |
| 1857-120 | Dusten, George C. | app 20 3/4 da @ $.50 - $10.35. Mach Dept |
| | | carp 6 da @ $1.50 -$9.00. Mach Dept, Balto |

B & O RR EMPLOYEES 127

| Year-Page | Name | Details |
|---|---|---|
| 1855-91 | Duvall, Benjamin | blksmith 20½ da - $38.30. Mach Dept |
| 1857-48 | " | watch 23 da @ $1 - $23.00. Rd Dept main stem 2d s-div |
| 1855-39 | " D. | lab 24 da @ $1 - $24.00. Rd Way Dept |
| 1857-49 | " Daniel | lab 25 da @ $1 - $25.00. Rd Dept main stem 3d s-div |
| 1855-22 | " Fred | fire 11¼ da @ $1.75 - $19.70. Trans Dept main stem |
| 1857-30 | " Frederick | ton eng'man 30½ da @ $3 - $91.50. Board Tree Tun |
| 1857-30 | " " | ton eng'man 1 da @ $3 - $3.00. 4th div |
| 1857-115 | " George | boil mkr 19 3/4 da @$1.72 - $34.00. Mach Dept, Balto |
| 1855-4 | " Henry | bag mast 28 da @ $35.00 per mo - $35.00. Trans Dept, Wash br |
| 1857-37 | " " | bag mast 30 da @ $35.00 per mo - $35.00. Wash br rd, Wash city sta |
| 1857-110 | " Isaac | mach 20½ da @ $1.60 - $32.80. Mach Dept, Balto |
| 1855-22 | " J. C. | fire 13 3/4 da @ $1.75 - $24.05. Trans Dept main stem |
| 1855-5 | " " " | ton fire 1 da @ $33.33 per mo - $1.40. Trans Dept, Wash br |
| 1855-22 | " J. W. | fire ½ da @ $1.75 - $.85. Trans Dept main stem |
| 1855-47 | " John C. | supv @ $45 per mo - $45.00. Rd Way Dept |
| 1855-49 | " " | fire 25 da @ $1.25 - $31.25. Rd Dept main stem 3d s-div |
| 1855-22 | " M. J. | fire 17½ da @ $1.75 - $30.20. Trans Dept main stem |
| 1855-72 | " Mark | help 12 3/4 da @$1.06 - $13.50. Rd Way Dept |
| 1857-70 | " Richard | help 18 da @$1.06 - $19.10. Mt Clare sta, Balto |
| 1857-113 | " William | mach app 27½ da @ $.65 - $17.90. Mach Dept, Balto |
| 1857-92 | Duvanne, Patrick | lab 4 da @ $1 - $4.00. grad, Littleton Tun |
| 1857-81 | Dwine, Bartty | lab 19 da @ $1.12 - $21.35. grad, Board Tree Tun |
| 1857-92 | Dwire, Patrick | lab 25 da @ $.75 - $18.75. grad, Littleton Tun |
| 1857-118 | Dwyer, Henry | blksmith app 24 da @ $.55 - $13.20. Mach Dept, Balto |
| 1855-43 | Dyche, Alex. | lab 17 da @ $1 - $17.00. Rd Way Dept |
| 1855-18 | " James | ton eng'man 20 da @ $3 - $60.00. Trans Dept main stem |
| 1857-30 | " " | ton eng'man 4½ da @ $3 - $13.50. Board Tree Tun |
| 1855-43 | " Lewis | fore 24 da @$1.25 - $30.00. Rd Way Dept |
| 1857-53 | " " | fore 23 da @ $1.25 - $27.50. Rd Dept main stem 7th s-div |
| 1857-54 | " Wesley | lab 22 da @ $1 - $22.00. Rd Dept main stem 8th s-div |
| 1855-82 | Dyer, Levi | mach 23¼ da @ $1.72 - $40.40. Mach Dept |
| 1855-85 | Dyser, George | help 26⅔ da @ $1.10 - $28.85. Mach Dept |
| 1857-116 | " " | blksmith 24½ da @ $1.25 - $30.60. Mach Dept, Balto |
| 1855-85 | Eader, Jacob | help 25 da @ $1 - $25.00. Mach Dept |
| 1857-50 | " John | lab 20½ da @ $1 - $20.50. Rd Dept main stem 4th s-div |

## B & O RR EMPLOYEES

| ID | Name | Entry |
|---|---|---|
| 1855-51 | Eader, Lazarus | watch cuts 24 da @ $1 - $24.00. Rd Way Dept |
| 1857-84 | Eagan, Andrew | lab 27 da @ $1.12 - $30.35. grad, Board Tree Tun |
| 1855-71 | Eagan, John | carp 23½ da @ $1 - $23.25. Rd Way Dept |
| 1855-55 | " | lab 24 da @ $1 - $24.00. Rd Way Dept |
| 1857-63 | " | lab 22½ da @ $1 - $22.25. Rd Dept main stem 16th s-div |
| 1857-49 | Eagan, Michael | watch cuts 28 da @ $1 - $28.00. Rd Way Dept |
| 1857-69 | " | lab 18 da @ $1 - $18.00. Mt Clare sta, Balto |
| 1857-103 | " | lab 10½ da @ $1.12 - $11.80. NW Va RR Tun |
| 1857-60 | " | lab 28½ da @ $1 - $28.50. Rd Dept main stem 13th s-div |
| 1855-58 | Eagan, Patrick | lab 22 da @ $1 - $22.00. Rd Way Dept |
| 1857-59 | " | lab 30 da @ $1 - $30.00. Rd Dept main stem 13th s-div |
| 1857-65 | " | lab 24 da @ $1 - $24.00. Rd Dept main stem 17th s-div |
| 1857-69 | Eagard, John | lab 18 da @ $1 - $18.00. Mt Clare sta, Balto |
| 1855-63 | Eagon, Peter | lab 21 3/4 da @ $1 - $21.75. Rd Way Dept |
| 1857-71 | Baney, Jerry | chair mkr 15 3/4 da @ $1 - $15.75. Mt Clare sta, Balto |
| 1857-79 | Earl, Thomas | eng'man 24½ da @ $2.25 - $55.10. lay 2d track |
| 1855-22 | Earle, Thomas | fire 1½ da @ $1.75 - $2.60. Trans Dept main stem |
| 1855-75 | Earley, William | lab 20 da @ $1 - $20.00. Rd Way Dept |
| 1857-50 | Early, James | fore 24 da @ $1.25 - $30.00. Rd Way Dept |
| 1857-74 | " | fore 25 da @ $1.25 - $31.25. Rd Dept main stem 5th s-div |
| 1857-26 | Earnest, Jno. | blksmith 12⅞ da @ $1.50 - $18.35. repair bridges &c |
| 1855-44 | Earsome, Joseph | ton brak 3 da @ $40 per mo - $4.80. 3d & 4th div |
| 1855-79 | Easton, J. | lab 13 da @ $1 - $13.00. Rd Way Dept |
| 1855-80 | Eaton, Jno. | driv 24 da @ $1.75 - $42.00. Mach Dept |
| 1857-22 | Eavans, James | lab 22 da @ $1 -$22.00. Mach Dept |
| 1857-22 | Eavans, Samuel | ton conduc 22 3/4 da @ $50 per mo - $45.50. 3d & 4th div |
| 1855-64 | Eavans, Danl. | ton conduc 26 da @ $55 per mo - $57.20. 3d & 4th div |
| 1857-47 | Eavins, John | carp 17½ da @ $1.12½ - $19.70. Rd Way Dept |
| 1855-94 | Ebbers, S. | lab 25½ da @ $1 - $25.50. Rd Dept main stem 2d s-div |
| 1855-10 | Ebbert, Adam | blksmith 24 3/4 da @ $1.25 - $30.95. Mach Dept |
| 1857-21 | " | conduc & brak 17 3/4 da @ $50 per mo - $36.95. Trans Dept main stem |
| 1855-65 | Eberle, Paul | ton conduc 18½ da @ $50 per mo - $36.50. 1st div |
| 1857-72 | Eberly, Chris. | lab 8 da @ $1 - $8.00. Rd Way Dept |
| 1855-35 | Ebert, A. | carp 23 da @ $1.37 - $31.60. Martinsburg depot |
| 1855-53 | Ebertee, Paul | car exam 28 da @ $30 per mo - $30.00. Trans Dept main stem |
| | | lab 7 da @ $1 - $7.00. Rd Way Dept |

| | | |
|---|---|---|
| 1857-127 | Eborall, Frederick | mach 32¼ da @ $1.70 - $54.80. Mach Dept, Piedmont |
| 1857-22 | Echerd, John | ton conduc 35 da @ $50 per mo - $70.00. 3d & 4th div |
| 1857-49 | Echson, Charles | lab 22 da @ $1 - $22.00. Rd Dept main stem 3d s-div |
| 1855-54 | Eckhart, Jno. | track lay 15 da @ $1.25 - $18.75. Rd Way Dept |
| 1855-14 | Eckland, J. C. | conduc & brak 23 da @ $40 per mo -$38.35. Trans Dept main stem |
| 1855-48 | Eckman, George | lab 23 3/4 da @ $1 -$23.75. Rd Dept main stem 2d s-div |
| 1857-73 | Edelers, Balders | lab 8½ da @ $1.12 -$9.55. repair water sta, M.S. & P.B. |
| 1857-116 | Eden, Alfred | boil mkr help 15 3/4 da @ $1.10 - $17.35. Mach Dept, Balto |
| 1857-116 | Edmand, Alfred | blksmith 18 3/4 da @ $1.80 - $33.75. Mach Dept, Balto |
| 1855-85 | Edmonds, B. | blksmith 24 3/4 da @ $1.72 - $42.60. Mach Dept |
| 1855-10 | " | conduc & brak 17 3/4 da @ $50 per mo -$40.15. Trans Dept main stem |
| 1857-21 | Edmunds, Barton | ton conduc 16 3/4 da @ $50 per mo; 11 da @ $60 per mo - $59.90. 2d div |
| 1855-28 | Esom. | reg eng 23½ da @ $1.15 -$27.00. Trans Dept main stem |
| 1855-44 | Edwards, A. | lab 12½ da @ $1 - $12.50. Rd Way Dept |
| 1857-111 | Charles | mach help 17 3/4 da @ $1 - $17.75. Mach Dept, Balto |
| 1855-22 | Elihu | fire 24 da @ $33.35 per mo -$33.35. Trans Dept main stem |
| 1855-28 | " | ton eng'man 2 da @ $2.50 - $5.00. 1st div |
| 1857-111 | Elisha | mach help 14 3/4 da @ $1.25 - $18.45. Mach Dept, Balto |
| 1855-10 | G. B. | conduc & brak 18 3/4 da @ $40 per mo - $31.25. Trans Dept main stem |
| 1857-31 | George | ton fire 13½ da @ $1.75 - $23.60. 1st div |
| 1857-35 | George B. | ton fire 5½ da @ $1.75 - $9.60. 1st div |
| 1855-9 | J. W. | conduc 25 da @ $60 per mo - $60.00. Edwards wd train 3d & 4th div |
| 1855-20 | John | conduc 24 da @ $45 per mo - $45.00. Trans Dept main stem |
| 1855-24 | " | fire 5 da @ $1.75 - $8.75. Trans Dept main stem |
| 1855-20 | Jonathan | ton brak 8¼ da @ $40 per mo; 1 da @ $50 per mo - $15.20. 1st div |
| 1855-86 | William | fire 10 da @ $1.75 - $17.50. Trans Dept main stem |
| 1855-34 | " | fore @ $83.35 per mo - $83.35. Mach Dept |
| 1857-123 | " | watch 24 da @ $1 -$24.00. Trans Dept main stem |
| 1857-79 | Edwin, Henry | mast mech @ $83.35 per mo -$83.35. Mach Dept, Martinsburg |
| 1857-93 | Egan, Philip | lab 26 3/4 da @ $1 - $26.75. lay 2d track |
| 1855-14 | Eichelberger, E. | smith help 20 da @ $1 - $20.00. quarry & haul stone for Board Tree & Littleton Tun |
| 1855-44 | Eighelton, John | conduc & brak 13½ da @ $40 per mo - $22.50. Trans Dept main stem |
| 1855-72 | Elder, Benjamin | lab 24 da @ $1 -$24.00. Rd Way Dept |
| 1855-70 | " | mach 9 2/7 da @ $1.25 - $11.55. Rd Way Dept |
| 1855-71 | James | help 20 3/4 da @ $1.25 - $25.95. Mt Clare sta, Balto |
| | | carp 22½ da @ $1.25 - $27.80. Rd Way Dept |

B & O RR EMPLOYEES

| Date | Name | Description |
|---|---|---|
| 1857-69 | Elder, James | carp 18 da @ $1.25 - $22.50. Mt Clare sta, Balto |
| 1855-34 | " Samuel | watch 28 da @ $20 per mo - $20.00. Trans Dept main stem |
| 1855-36 | " Thomas | lab 25 da @ $20 per mo - $20.70. Trans Dept main stem |
| 1857-55 | Eleicamp, Henry | fore 27 3/4 da @ $1.33 - $37.00. Rd Dept main stem 9th s-div |
| 1855-73 | Elijah, Robt. | fore 24 da @ $1.25 - $30.00. Rd Way Dept |
| 1855-80 | Eline, J. A. | carp 24 da @ $1.50 - $36.00. Mach Dept |
| 1857-119 | " Jacob A. | carp 18 da @ $1.50 - $27.00. Mach Dept, Balto |
| 1855-31 | Ellenberger, N. | saw wd 28½ cords @ $.35 - $9.95. Trans Dept main stem |
| 1857-26 | Ellery, A. | ton brak 6 da @ $40 per mo - $9.60. 3d & 4th div |
| 1855-45 | Ellicomb, H. | fore 26 da @ $1.25 - $34.65. Rd Way Dept |
| 1855-17 | Elliot, Thomas | ton eng'man 6½ da @ $2.50 - $16.25. Trans Dept main stem |
| 1855-34 | Elliott, A. | watch 28 da @ $1 - $28.00. Trans Dept main stem |
| 1855-34 | " C. A. | fore of lab 28 da @ $45 per mo - $45.00. Trans Dept main stem |
| 1855-22 | " Charles | fire 12½ da @ $1.75 - $21.85. Trans Dept main stem |
| 1857-135 | " Charles T. | lab 6¼ da @ $1 - $6.25. Mach Dept, Wheeling |
| 1857-24 | " Curtis | ton brak 4 da @ $40 per mo - $6.40. 1st div |
| 1855-40 | " John | nail 26 da @ $1.05 - $27.30. Rd Way Dept |
| 1857-50 | " " | nail 30 da @ $1.05 - $31.50. Rd Dept main stem 4th s-div |
| 1855-30 | " Robert | prepar fuel 19½ da @ $1.15 - $22.40. Trans Dept main stem |
| 1857-20 | " T. C. | pass fire 6 da @ $40 per mo - $8.00. 3d div |
| 1857-30 | " Thomas | ton eng'man 25 3/4 da @ $2.50 - $64.35. 4th div |
| 1855-40 | " Thomas C. | ton fire 22½ da @ $1.75 - $39.35. 4th div |
| 1857-50 | " William | fore 24 da @ $1.25 - $30.00. Rd Way Dept |
| 1857-60 | Ellip, Joseph | fore 27 da @ $1.25 - $33.75. Rd Dept main stem 4th s-div |
| 1855-17 | Ellis, Daniel | eng'man 8 da @ $3 - $24.00. Rd Dept main stem 13th s-div |
| 1857-30 | " " | ton eng'man 12 da @$3 - $36.00. Trans Dept main stem |
| 1857-40 | " " | ton eng'man 5 da @ $3 - $15.00. Board Tree Tun |
| 1857-29 | " " | ton eng'man 2 da @ #3 - $6.00. NW Va rd, Parkersburg sta |
| 1857-110 | " Isaac | ton eng'man 5 da @ $3 - $15.00. 3d div |
| 1855-17 | " Joseph | mach 18 da @ $1.60 - $28.80. Mach Dept, Balto |
| 1857-29 | " " | ton eng'man 19¼ da @ $3 - $57.75. Trans Dept main stem |
| 1855-18 | " Wm. | ton eng'man 20½ da @ $3 - $61.50. 3d div |
| 1855-19 | " Wm. H. | ton eng'man 5 da @ $3 - $15.00. Trans Dept main stem |
| 1857-35 | Elmas, Peter | lab 8¾ da @ $1 -$8.25. Edwards wd train 3d & 4th div |
| 1857-74 | Elrick, John | blksmith 25 da @ $1.50 - $37.50. repair bridges &c |

| | | |
|---|---|---|
| 1857-61 | Elurler, Paul | lab 27 da @ $1 - $27.00. Rd Dept main stem 14th s-div |
| 1857-112 | Elwell, Edward | mach app 22¼ da @ $.55 - $12.25. Mach Dept, Balto |
| 1857-24 | Emery, John W. | ton brak 21½ da @ $40 per mo - $34.40. 1st div |
| 1857-119 | Emich, Andrew | carp 18 da @ $1.50 - $27.00. Mach Dept, Balto |
| 1857-135 | Emory, Frederick | boil mkr help 23¼ da @ $1 - $23.25. Mach Dept, Wheeling |
| 1855-27 | Engelhart, Conrad | get out eng 28 da @ $1.50 - $42.00. Trans Dept main stem |
| 1855-74 | Engelt, Michl. | fore 24½ da @ $1.25 - $30.60. Rd Way Dept |
| 1855-6 | England, J. T. | agt 28 da @ $100 per mo - $100.00. Trans Dept main stem |
| 1857-8 | " " | agt 30 da @ $100 per mo - $100.00. Camden sta |
| 1857-40 | Englehard, C. | ton eng'man 27½ da @ $2.50 -$68.10. NW Va rd, Parkersburg sta |
| 1855-16 | Englehart, W. | pass fire 12 3/4 da @ $1.75 - $22.30. Trans Dept main stem |
| 1857-24 | Engleman, Palmer | ton brak 14 3/4 da @ $40 per mo - $23.60. 1st div |
| 1857-92 | Engler, John | lab 24½ da @ $1 - $24.50. grad, Littleton Tun |
| 1857-72 | Englert, Margaret | clean sta house @ $8 per mo - $8.00. Martinsburg depot |
| 1857-50 | Englerth, Michael | fore 26½ da @ $1.25 - $33.00. Rd Dept main stem 5th s-div |
| 1857-54 | Engleton, John | lab 25 da @ $1 - $25.00. Rd Dept main stem 8th s-div |
| 1857-24 | English, J. T. | ton brak 5 3/4 da @ $40 per mo - $9.20. 1st div |
| 1855-73 | John | lab 20 da @ $1 - $20.00. Rd Way Dept |
| 1857-69 | " | lab 16 da @ $1 - $16.00. Mt Clare sta, Balto |
| 1855-86 | Ennis, John | app 33 da @ $.65 - $21.45. Mach Dept |
| 1857-116 | John A. | blksmith 15¼ da @ $1.45 - $22.10. Mach Dept, Balto |
| 1857-48 | Ensey, Nathan | lab 22 3/4 da @ $1 - $22.75. Rd Dept main stem 2d s-div |
| 1857-129 | Ensor, Columbus | paint 16¼ da @ $1.50 - $24.35. Mach Dept, Piedmont |
| 1855-35 | George | watch 28 da @ $1.25 - $35.00. Trans Dept main stem |
| 1855-80 | H. | coach mkr 28¼ da @ $1.65 - $46.60. Mach Dept |
| 1857-120 | Hiram | carp 30 da @ $1.65 - $49.50. Mach Dept, Balto |
| 1857-24 | James | ton brak 14¼ da @ $40 per mo - $22.80. 1st div |
| 1855-95 | John | flask mkr 26¼ da @ $1.55 - $40.70. Mach Dept |
| 1857-119 | " | carp 18 da @ $1.60 - $28.80. Mach Dept, Balto |
| 1857-128 | Washington | mach help 38¼ da @ $.40 - $15.30. Mach Dept, Piedmont |
| 1857-72 | Entler, Henry | Martinsburg depot |
| 1855-44 | Eny, George | lab 25½ da @ $1 - $25.50. Rd Way Dept |
| 1855-44 | Philip | lab 23½ da @ $1 - $23.50. Rd Way Dept |
| 1857-120 | Epards, George H. | carp help 21 da @ $1.15 - $24.15. Mach Dept, Balto |
| 1857-120 | Sylvester | carp help 20 da @ $1.15 - $23.00. Mach Dept, Balto |
| 1857-111 | Ernshaw, Thomas | mach help 18 da @ $1.25 - $22.50. Mach Dept, Balto |

## B & O RR EMPLOYEES

| ID | Name | Details |
|---|---|---|
| 1857-40 | Erserne, Joseph | ton brak 19 da @ $40 per mo - $30.40. NW Va rd, Parkersburg sta |
| 1855-31 | Erusole, John | saw wd 10 3/4 cords @ $.35 - $3.75. Trans Dept main stem |
| 1857-74 | Ervalt, Henry | lab 22½ da @ $1.12 - $25.30. repair bridges &c |
| 1855-63 | Ervin, James | lab 18½ da @ $1 - $18.50. Rd Way Dept |
| 1855-55 | Erwin, Philip | lab 24 da @ $1 - $24.00. Rd Way Dept |
| 1857-63 | " | watch 30 da @ $1 - $30.00. Rd Dept main stem 16th s-div |
| 1857-15 | Eskey, Thomas | carry mail 30 da @ $4.50 per mo - $4.50. Mannington sta |
| 1855-94 | Eskey, William | blksmith 13¾ da @ $1.40 - $18.55. Mach Dept |
| 1857-10 | Esler, Edward | bur driv 27½ da @ $1.15 - $31.60. hp exp, Balto |
| 1857-127 | Essender, John | mach 19⅞ da @ $1.75 - $33.70. Mach Dept, Piedmont |
| 1855-90 | " John J. | mach 23 3/4 da @ $1.84 - $43.85. Mach Dept |
| 1857-120 | " Thomas | carp 18 da @ $1.65 - $29.70. Mach Dept, Balto |
| 1855-80 | Essinger, Tho | coach mkr 23½ da @ $1.65 - $38.75. Mach Dept |
| 1855-54 | Esterhaws, Geo. | track lay 15 da @ $1.25 - $18.75. Rd Way Dept |
| 1855-54 | " Henry | track lay 15 da @ $1.12½ - $16.90. Rd Way Dept |
| 1857-71 | Esterhouse, H. | track lay 21 da @ $1.12 - $23.60. Camden sta, repair tracks |
| 1857-55 | Evalt, John | lab 24 da @ $1 - $24.00. Rd Dept main stem 9th s-div |
| 1857-116 | Evans, Daniel | boil mkr help 19¼ da @ $1.15 - $22.15. Mach Dept, Balto |
| 1855-91 | " Edward | help 27½ da @ $1 - $27.50. Mach Dept |
| 1857-127 | " | mach help 32½ da @ $1.25 - $40.60. Mach Dept, Piedmont |
| 1857-90 | " George | lab 8 da @ $1.12 - $9.00. grad, Welling Tun |
| 1855-27 | " Hugh | get out eng 28 da @ $1.50 - $42.00. Trans Dept main stem |
| 1855-27 | " Isaac | clean eng 12 da @ $1 - $12.00. Trans Dept main stem |
| 1857-16 | " | fire 5 da @ $33.35 per mo - $6.65. Benwood sta |
| 1857-34 | " | ton fire 14½ da @ $1.75 - $25.35. 4th div |
| 1857-110 | " Jacob | mach 18¼ da @ $1.50 - $27.35. Mach Dept, Balto |
| 1857-16 | " James M. | conduc 25 da @ $50 per mo - $50.00. Benwood sta |
| 1855-9 | " Samuel | conduc 14 da @ $50 per mo - $28.70. Trans Dept main stem |
| 1855-93 | " Wm. | mach 10¾ da @ $1.60 - $16.40. Mach Dept |
| 1857-10 | " | bur driv 28 da @ $1.15 - $32.20. hp exp, Balto |
| 1855-76 | Evansham, T. | bolt cut 24 da @ $1.25 - $30.00. Mach Dept |
| 1855-84 | Evens, Daniel | help 25 da @ $1 - $25.00. Rd Way Dept |
| 1855-66 | Everhart, John | lab 23½ da @ $1.75 - $41.10. Rd Way Dept |
| 1857-85 | " Wm. M. | fore @ $50 per mo - $50.00. grad, Board Tree Tun |
| 1857-37 | Everley, Christian | brak 30 da @ $3.33 per mo - $33.35. Wash br rd, Wash city sta |
| 1855-52 | " | carp 22 3/4 da @ $1.20 - $27.30. Rd Way Dept |

| | | | |
|---|---|---|---|
| 1855-52 | Everley, Christian | lab 21 3/4 da @ $1. Rd Way Dept |
| 1857-100 | Evers, Patrick | fore 23 da @ $1.25 - $28.75. NW Va RR, Rd Dept 5th s-div |
| 1855-62 | Eversham, Thomas | lab 9 da @ $1 - $9.00. Rd Way Dept |
| 1855-86 | Eversole, Jacob | blksmith 9½ da - $14.85. Mach Dept |
| 1857-125 | " | mach 24 3/4 da @ $1.40 - $34.65. Mach Dept |
| 1855-53 | " James | fore wheel 21 3/4 da @ $1.80 - $39.15. Mach Dept, Martinsburg |
| 1857-52 | " John | carp 10 da @ $1.62½ - $16.25. Rd Way Dept |
| 1857-124 | " Owen | lab 24 da @ $1 - $24.00. Rd Dept main stem 6th s-div |
| 1857-121 | Evoy, J. | mach 19½ da @ $1 - $19.25. Mach Dept, Martinsburg |
| 1857-59 | Ewing, Edward | paint help 18 da @ $1.15 - $20.70. Mach Dept, Balto |
| 1855-41 | Fabel, John | lab 23 da @ $1 - $23.00. Rd Dept main stem 13th s-div |
| 1855-73 | Faces, Geo. | lab 18½ da @ $1 - $18.50. Rd Way Dept |
| 1857-57 | Fagan, John | blksmith 21¼ da @ $1.50 - $31.85. repair bridges &c |
| 1857-57 | " John B. | lab 27 da @ $1 - $27.00. Rd Dept main stem 11th s-div |
| 1857-57 | " Owen | lab 15 3/4 da @ $1 - $15.75. Rd Dept main stem 11th s-div |
| 1855-77 | Fagman, Robert | lab 26½ da @ $1 - $26.50. Rd Dept main stem 11th s-div |
| 1855-31 | Faha, Peter | mach 22½ da @ $1.75 - $38.95. Mach Dept |
| 1857-91 | Fahay, Patrick | prepar fuel 28 da @ $1 - $28.00. Trans Dept main stem |
| 1857-82 | Fahey, Daniel | lab 7 da @ $1 - $7.00. grad, Welling Tun |
| 1855-47 | " John | lab 30½ da @ $1.12 - $34.30. grad, Board Tree Tun |
| 1855-56 | " Michael | lab 21½ da @ $1 - $21.50. Rd Way Dept |
| 1857-92 | " " | lab 15 3/4 da @ $1 - $15.75. Rd Way Dept |
| 1857-91 | " Patrick | lab 25 da @ $1 - $25.00. grad, Littleton Tun |
| 1857-103 | " Peter | lab 15 da @ $1 - $15.00. grad, Welling Tun |
| 1857-81 | " Thomas | lab 20½ da @ $1.12 - $22.80. NW Va RR Tun |
| 1857-62 | Fahnestock, J. | lab 27 da @ $1.62 - $43.85. grad, Board Tree Tun |
| 1855-1 | " " | lab 23½ da @ $1 - $23.50. Rd Dept main stem 15th s-div |
| 1857-7 | | clk of errors $1000 per annum - $83.33. Ofc Hanover St |
| 1855-59 | Fahy, Thomas | clk errors @ $100 per mo. Clk of Errors Ofc |
| 1855-31 | Failey, Patrick | lab 24 da @ $1 - $24.00. Rd Way Dept |
| 1855-94 | Fair, Henry | prepar fuel 15½ da @ $1 - $15.50. Trans Dept main stem |
| 1857-21 | Fairbank, A. J. | carp 22½ da @ $1.45 - $32.25. Mach Dept |
| 1857-38 | " | ton conduc 26 3/4 da @ $50 per mo - $57.50. Locust Pt |
| 1855-10 | Fairbanks, A. J. | ton conduc 25 da @ $50 per mo - $50.00. Wash br rd, Wash city sta |
| 1855-5 | " John | conduc & brak 24½ da @ $50 per mo - $50.50. Trans Dept main stem |
| | | ton conduc 24 da @ $50 per mo - $50.00. Trans Dept, Wash br |

## B & O RR EMPLOYEES

| | | | |
|---|---|---|---|
| 1857-127 | Fairbanks, John | mach 17 3/4 da @ $1.60 - $28.40. Mach Dept, Piedmont |
| 1855-9 | Fairfax, J. B. | conduc 8½ da @ $50 per mo - $17.70. Trans Dept main stem |
| 1857-22 | Faith, Henry | ton conduc 7 da @ $50 per mo - $14.00. 3d & 4th div |
| 1857-70 | Falconar, Jonathan | lab 19 3/4 da @ $1 - $19.75. Mt Clare sta, Balto |
| 1855-6 | Falconer, Jona. | clk 28 da @ $1.65 per mo - $41.65. Trans Dept main stem |
| 1857-8 | Faley, Michael | rec clk 30 da @ $1.65 per mo - $41.65. Camden sta |
| 1857-74 | Falkman, Francis | lab 24 da @ $1.12 - $27.00. repair bridges &c |
| 1857-55 | Falkner, Henry | watch 31 da @ $1 - $31.00. Rd Dept main stem 9th s-div |
| 1855-51 | Falkner, John | lab @ $31 per mo - $31.00. Rd Way Dept |
| 1857-26 | Fallan, Pat. | ton brak 16 da @ $40 per mo - $25.60. 3d & 4th div |
| 1855-47 | Fallen, Michael | lab 23 da @ $1 - $23.00. Rd Way Dept |
| 1857-17 | Fallen, Pat. | lab 20 da @ $1 - $20.00. frt transfer force at Bellaire, opp Benwood |
| 1857-76 | Fallen, William | dril 21 da @ $1.10 - $23.10. ballast train for 2d track |
| 1857-88 | Fallin, John | lab 29 da @ $1.12 - $32.60. grad, Welling Tun |
| 1855-51 | Fallon, James | watch cuts 28 da @ $1 - $28.00. Rd Way Dept |
| 1857-104 | Fallon, John | miner 12 da @ $1 - $12.00. NW Va RR Tun |
| 1855-47 | " " | lab 20¼ da @ $1 - $20.25. Rd Way Dept |
| 1857-68 | " Michael | watch 20 da @ $1 - $20.00. Rd Dept main stem 19th s-div |
| 1857-89 | " Patrick | lab 23 da @ $1.12 - $25.85. grad, Welling Tun |
| 1857-56 | " Thomas | lab 21 da @ $1 - $21.00. Rd Dept main stem 10th s-div |
| 1857-132 | Falls, John | fill tend @ $30 per mo - $30.00. Mach Dept, Grafton |
| 1857-80 | Fank, Thomas | lab 20 3/4 da @ $1 - $20.75. lay 2d track |
| 1857-60 | Fannan, James | conduc 8 da @ $1.94 - $15.50. Rd Dept main stem 13th s-div |
| 1857-85 | Fannan, John | lab 11 da @ $1 -$11.00. grad, Board Tree Tun |
| 1855-69 | Fannell, Michael | lab 23½ da @ $1 - $23.00. Rd Way Dept |
| 1857-79 | Fannell, John | lab 24 3/4 da @ $1 -$24.75. lay 2d track |
| 1857-139 | " Owen | mach 29 3/4 da @ $1.57 - $46.70. NW Va RR, Mach Dept, Parkersburg |
| 1857-139 | " Stephen | mach 24 3/4 da @ $1.57 - $38.85. NW Va RR, Mach Dept, Parkersburg |
| 1857-139 | " Thomas | mach 22 3/4 da @ $1.33 - $34.80. NW Va RR, Mach Dept, Parkersburg |
| 1857-139 | " William | lab 27 da @ $.90 - $24.30. NW Va RR, Mach Dept, Parkersburg |
| 1857-22 | Fanner, Henry | blksmith 25½ da @ $1.57 - $38.85. NW Va RR, Mach Dept, Parkersburg |
| 1857-80 | Fannon, Wm. | ton conduc 13½ da @ $50 per mo - $27.00. 3d & 4th div |
| 1857-75 | Fannor, Michael | lab 20 3/4 da @ $1.25 - $25.95. lay 2d track |
| 1857-73 | Fant, John | fore @ $50 per mo - $50.00. ballast train for 2d track |
| 1857-117 | Farbourg, Jacob | carp 25 da @ $1.60 - $40.00. repair water sta, M.S. & P.B. |
| | | blksmith 17½ da @ $1.70 - $29.30. Mach Dept, Balto |

| | | | |
|---|---|---|---|
| 1857-139 | Farely, Barton | clean eng 31 da @ $1 - $31.00. NW Va RR, Mach Dept, Parkersburg |
| 1855-51 | Farley, James | watch cuts 28 da @ $1 - $28.00. Rd Way Dept |
| 1855-20 | " Michael | fire 11½ da @ $1.75 -$20.10. Trans Dept main stem |
| 1857-139 | " " | put away eng &c 27 da @ $1.50 - $40.50. NW Va RR, Mach Dept, Parkersburg |
| 1857-93 | Farrall, Patrick | lab 24 da @ $1 - $24.00. quarry & haul stone for Board Tree & Littleton Tun |
| 1857-60 | " Robert | lab 28 da @ $1 - $28.00. Rd Dept main stem 13th s-div |
| 1857-56 | Farrel, James | nail 27⅔ da @ $1 -$27.25. Rd Dept main stem 10th s-div |
| 1855-67 | " John | mason 17 3/4 da @ $2 - $35.50. Rd Way Dept |
| 1857-8 | " Mathew | lab 24 da @ $30 per mo - $28.80. Camden sta |
| 1855-64 | " Patk. | lab 21½ da @ $1 - $21.50. Rd Way Dept |
| 1857-84 | Farrell, James | lab 23¼ da @ $1 - $26.15. grad, Board Tree Tun |
| 1857-56 | " John | lab 24 da @ $1 -$24.00. Rd Dept main stem 10th s-div |
| 1857-86 | " " | stone mason 18 3/4 da @ $2 - $37.50. grad, McGuire's Tun |
| 1857-135 | " Owen | clean eng 29⅔ da @ $1 - $29.25. Mach Dept, Wheeling |
| 1857-68 | " Patrick | fore 20 da @ $1.25 - $25.00. Rd Dept main stem 19th s-div |
| 1857-75 | " " | lab 11½ da @ $.97 - $11.20. ballast train for 2d track |
| 1857-83 | " " | lab 8 da @ $1.12 - $9.00. grad, Board Tree Tun |
| 1857-97 | " " | lab 4 da @ $1 - $4.00 - NW Va RR, Rd Dept 1st s-div |
| 1857-77 | " " | quarry 8 da @ $1 - $8.00. ballast, train for 2d track |
| 1857-83 | " Thomas | lab 25½ da @ $1.12 - $28.70. grad, Board Tree Tun |
| 1857-83 | " Timothy | lab 24 3/4 da @ $1.12 -$27.85. grad, Board Tree Tun |
| 1857-83 | Farrely, Philip | lab 22½ da @ $1.12 -$25.30. grad, Board Tree Tun |
| 1857-124 | Farris, Moses | blksmith help 18½ da @ $1 - $18.50. Mach Dept, Martinsburg |
| 1855-51 | Farity, James | lab 21 da @ $1 - $21.00. Rd Way Dept |
| 1857-79 | Farwick, Patrick | lab 4 da @ $1 - $4.00. lay 2d track |
| 1857-22 | Fast, Thomas | ton conduc 12½ da @ $50 per mo -$25.00. 3d & 4th div |
| 1857-58 | Fatchie, John | lab 21½ da @ $1 - $21.50. Rd Dept main stem 11th s-div |
| 1855-72 | Fath, Henry | help 24 da @ $1 -$24.00. Rd Way Dept |
| 1855-57 | Fathey, John | lab 20½ da @ $1 -$20.50. Rd Way Dept |
| 1857-97 | Faucer, Michael | lab 26 da @ $1 -$26.00. NW Va RR, Rd Dept 2d s-div |
| 1857-98 | Faughner, Patrick | watch 30 da @ $1 -$30.00. NW Va RR, Rd Dept 3d s-div |
| 1857-98 | " Tim. | watch 30 da @ $1 - $30.00. NW Va RR, Rd Dept 3d s-div |
| 1857-127 | Faulkenstine, Jno. | mach 18½ da @ $1.50 - $27.75. Mach Dept, Piedmont |
| 1855-66 | Fauner, Henry | lab 28½ da @ $1 - $28.50. Rd Way Dept |
| 1857-21 | Fauver, Isaac | ton conduc 27⅖ da @ $50 per mo -$54.50. 2d div |
| 1857-25 | Fayman, John | ton brak 22 da @ $40 per mo - $35.20. 2d div |

| | | |
|---|---|---|
| 1855-54 | Feaga, P. H. | fore carp @ $45 per mo - $45.00. Rd Way Dept |
| 1857-72 | Feagan, P. H. | fore @ $50 per mo -$50.00. Cumb depot |
| 1855-50 | Feagen, M. | watch cuts 28 da @ $1 - $28.00. Rd Way Dept |
| 1857-67 | Feaghan, Matthew | watch 30 da @ $1 - $30.00. Rd Dept main stem 18th s-div |
| 1857-89 | Featherston, Barney | watch 18 da @ $1 - $18.00. grad, Welling Tun |
| 1857-90 | Barry | watch 12 da @ $1 - $12.00. grad, Welling Tun |
| 1857-87 | Patrick | lab 15½ da @ $1.12 - $16.85. grad, Welling Tun |
| 1855-6 | Fechtig, L. R. | clk 28 da @ $50 per mo - $50.00. Trans Dept main stem |
| 1857-14 | Fecktig, L. R. | clk 30 da @ $50 per mo - $50.00. Cumb |
| 1857-121 | Fedderman, Rd. | paint 16½ da @ $1.60 - $26.40. Mach Dept, Balto |
| 1855-76 | Fee, Caleb | help 24¼ da @ $1 -$24.25. Mach Dept |
| 1857-111 | Jacob | mach help 17 3/4 da @ $1.25 - $22.20. Mach Dept, Balto |
| 1855-80 | Jos. | mach help 18 da @ $1.15 -$20.70. Mach Dept, Balto |
| 1855-58 | Feeney, John | lab 23½ da @ $1.15 - $27.00. Mach Dept |
| 1855-7 | Feeny, S. O. | lab 21 da @ $1 - $21.00. Rd Way Dept |
| 1857-51 | Feister, John | clk 28 da @ $1.65 per mo - $41.65. Trans Dept main stem |
| 1855-72 | Fell, Casper | lab 25 da @ $1 -$25.00. Rd Dept main stem 5th s-div |
| 1857-70 | | help 19½ da @ $1.12½ - $21.95. Rd Way Dept |
| 1857-124 | Feller, Charles | bolt cut 19½ da @$1.12 -$21.95. Mt Clare sta, Balto |
| 1855-76 | Fellows, George | mach 25¼ da @ $1 - $25.25. Mach Dept, Martinsburg |
| 1857-51 | " | lab 24 da @ $1 - $24.00. Rd Way Dept |
| 1855-47 | Fenanty, L. | lab 25 da @ $1 - $25.00. Rd Dept main stem 5th s-div |
| 1857-75 | Fenerman, Henry | lab 23 da @ $1 - $23.00. Rd Way Dept |
| 1857-51 | Fenn, Valentine | lab 14 da @ $1.15 - $16.10. ballast train for 2d track |
| 1857-115 | Fennell, James | lab 24 da @ $1 - $24.00. Rd Dept main stem 5th s-div |
| 1855-6 | M. | boil mkr 30 da @ $1.30 - $39.00. Mach Dept, Balto |
| 1857-8 | " | clk 28 da @ $62.50 per mo - $62.50. Trans Dept main stem |
| 1857-78 | Fennerty, John | rec clk 30 da @ $58.35 per mo - $58.35. Camden sta |
| 1857-81 | " | lab 24½ da @ $1 - $24.50. lay 2d track |
| 1857-77 | Fentone, John | lab 15½ da @ $1 - $15.50. lay 2d track |
| 1855-32 | Ferguson, J. | lab 24 da @ $1 - $24.00. lay 2d track |
| 1857-8 | " | weigh mast 24 da @ $50 per mo - $50.00. Trans Dept main stem |
| 1857-59 | James | mark 25 da @$50 per mo - $50.00. Camden sta |
| 1855-61 | William | watch 30 da @ $1 -$30.00. Rd Dept main stem 12th s-div |
| 1857-46 | " | lab 11 da @ $1 - $11.00. Rd Way Dept |
| | " | lab 25 da @ $1 - $25.00. Rd Dept main stem 1st s-div |

| | | |
|---|---|---|
| 1855-51 | Fergusson, James | lab @ $30 per mo - $30.00. Rd Way Dept |
| 1855-32 | " W. | lab 24 da @$30 per mo - $30.00. Trans Dept main stem |
| 1855-90 | " William | mach 24 da @$1.62½ da - $39.00. Mach Dept |
| 1855-30 | Fernan, Henry | prepar fuel 16 3/4 da @ $1 - $16.75. Trans Dept main stem |
| 1855-66 | Fernarney, John | lab 20½ da @ $1 - $20.50. Rd Way Dept |
| 1857-91 | Ferrel, James | lab 18 da @ $1 - $18.00. grad, Littleton Tun |
| 1855-50 | Ferrell, John | watch cuts 28 da @ $1 - $28.00. Rd Way Dept |
| 1857-92 | " Patrick | lab 10 da @ $1 - $10.00. grad, Littleton Tun |
| 1855-52 | Ferrett, John | lab 11¼ da @ $1 - $11.50. Rd Way Dept |
| 1855-69 | " | lab 22 da @ $1 - $22.00. Rd Way Dept |
| 1857-86 | Ferrick, John | lab 24 da @ $1 - $24.00. grad, McGuire's Tun |
| 1857-38 | Ferrider, John | ton fire 1½ da @ $33.33 per mo - $1.65. Wash br rd, Wash city sta |
| 1857-63 | Ferroll, John | watch 30 da @ $1 - $30.00. Rd Dept main stem 16th s-div |
| 1855-26 | Fetch, John | clean eng 14 3/4 da @ $1 - $14.75. Trans Dept main stem |
| 1857-114 | Fetterman, Edward | iron mould help 18 da @ $1.10 -$19.80. Mach Dept, Balto |
| 1855-67 | Fibben, Michael | lab 24 da @ $1 - $24.00. Rd Way Dept |
| 1855-82 | Fiefer, Wm. | app 23¼ da @ $.65 - $15.10. Mach Dept |
| 1855-47 | Fihaley, Thomas | lab 18½ da @ $1 - $18.50. Rd Way Dept |
| 1855-38 | Filay, Roger | lab 15½ da @ $1 - $15.50. Rd Way Dept |
| 1857-82 | Filbin, John | lab 28¼ da @ $1.12 - $31.80. grad, Board Tree Tun |
| 1857-82 | " Martin | lab 21½ da @ $1.12 - $24.20. grad, Board Tree Tun |
| 1857-82 | " Michael | lab 19½ da @ $1.12 - $21.95. grad, Board Tree Tun |
| 1857-61 | Filbut, Miles | lab 22½ da @ $1 - $22.50. Rd Dept main stem 14th s-div |
| 1857-63 | Fimple, Isaac | lab 24½ da @ $1 - $24.50. Rd Dept main stem 16th s-div |
| 1857-137 | Fine, Alfred | lab 7 3/4 da @ $1 - $7.75. Mach Dept, Cumb |
| 1857-86 | Finegan, John | lab 22½ da @ $1 - $22.50. grad, McGuire's Tun |
| 1857-136 | " Michael | fill tend @ $30 per mo - $30.00. Mach Dept, Wheeling |
| 1857-132 | " | greas cars @ $30 per mo - $30.00. Mach Dept, Grafton |
| 1857-75 | | lab 15 da @ $1.05 - $15.85. ballast train for 2d track |
| 1857-81 | Finehan, Patrick | lab 22½ da @ $1.12 - $25.05. grad, Board Tree Tun |
| 1857-96 | Fineran, Hugh | lab 24 da @ $1 - $24.00. NW Va RR, Rd Dept 1st s-div |
| 1857-32 | Fink, Albert | ton fire 7 da @ $1.75 - $12.25. 2d div |
| 1857-87 | " John | bricklay 18½ da @ $2.25 - $41.05. grad, Welling Tun |
| 1855-20 | " Michael | fire 10 da @ $1.75 - $17.50. Trans Dept main stem |
| 1855-54 | Finlon, Thomas | watch 27½ da @ $1 - $27.50. Rd Dept main stem 8th s-div |
| 1855-70 | Finnarin, Hugh | lab 15 3/4 da @ $1 - $15.75. Rd Way Dept |

| ID | Name | Details |
|---|---|---|
| 1855-70 | Finnaughty, Patrick | lab 14 3/4 da @ $1 - $14.75. Rd Way Dept |
| 1855-74 | Finnegan, Barney | lab 23½ da @ $1 -$23.50. Rd Way Dept |
| 1857-95 | " | lab 24 da @ $1 - $24.00. Wash br, Rd Dept |
| 1857-74 | " Hugh | lab 23 da @ $1 - $23.00. Wash br, Rd Dept |
| 1855-68 | " Jno. | lab 22½ da @ $1 - $22.50. Rd Way Dept |
| 1855-98 | " Patrick | tend to masons 23½ da @ $1 - $23.50. Rd Way Dept |
| 1857-65 | " " | lab 22½ da @ $1 - $22.50. NW Va RR, Rd Dept 3d s-div |
| 1857-39 | Finnell, John | lab 26¼ da @ $1 - $26.25. Rd Dept main stem 17th s-div |
| 1857-39 | Finnelle, Thomas | bag mast 5 da @ $35 per mo - $5.85. NW Va rd, Parkersburg sta |
| 1857-40 | " Thomas | bag mast 30 da @ $35 per mo - $35.00. NW Va rd, Parkersburg sta |
| 1857-81 | Finneman, Martin | ton brak 27 da @ $40 per mo - $43.20. NW Va rd, Parkersburg sta |
| 1857-88 | Finnerty, John | lab 20 3/4 da @ $1 - $20.75. lay 2d track |
| 1857-129 | " | lab 24½ da @ $1.12 -$27.55. grad, Welling Tun |
| 1855-76 | Finnery, John | clean eng 20 da @ $1 - $20.00. Mach Dept, Piedmont |
| 1855-48 | Finngane, Jno. | lab 20 da @ $1 - $20.00. Rd Way Dept |
| 1857-117 | Finton, Michael | train hand 12½ da @ $1 - $12.75. Rd Way Dept |
| 1857-41 | Fishan, John | blksmith help 17¼ da @ $1 - $17.25. Mach Dept, Balto |
| 1855-45 | Fisher, A. C. | ton fire 17 da @ $1.75 -$29.75. NW Va rd, Parkersburg sta |
| 1855-45 | " Adam | lab 11 3/4 da @ $1 -$11.75. Rd Way Dept |
| 1855-15 | " B. | pass eng'man 30½ da @ $2 - $61.00. Trans Dept main stem |
| 1857-19 | " Barney | pass eng'man 28 da @ $2.25 -$63.00. 1st div |
| 1855-45 | " Byron | lab 20 da @ $1 - $20.00. Rd Way Dept |
| 1855-45 | " D. | lab 17 da @ $1 - $17.00. Rd Way Dept |
| 1855-29 | " Francis | fill tend 28 da @ $1 - $28.00. Trans Dept main stem |
| 1857-55 | " George | lab 24 da @ $1 - $24.00. Rd Dept main stem 9th s-div |
| 1855-74 | " H. | lab 19½ da @ $1 -$19.50. Rd Way Dept |
| 1855-15 | " " | pass eng'man 28 da @ $2 - $56.00. Trans Dept main stem |
| 1857-95 | " Hierons | lab 24 da @ $1 - $24.00. Wash br, Rd Dept |
| 1857-19 | " Hugh | pass eng'man 28 da @ $2.25 -$63.00. 1st div |
| 1857-70 | " Jacob | lab 29 da @ $1 - $29.00. Mt Clare sta, Balto |
| 1855-45 | " Julius | lab 21 da @ $1 -$21.00. Rd Way Dept |
| 1857-55 | " " | lab 27 da @ $1 -$27.00. Rd Dept main stem 9th s-div |
| 1855-16 | " L. | pass fire 31½ da @ $40 per mo - $45.00. Trans Dept main stem |
| 1857-20 | " Lewis | pass fire 27 da @$40 per mo -$36.00. 1st div |
| 1855-25 | " Robert | clean eng ½ da @ $1.15 -$.55. Trans Dept main stem |
| 1855-76 | " " | help 24½ da @ $1 -$24.50. Mach Dept |
| 1857-111 | " " | mach help 21 3/4 da @ $1 -$21.75. Mach Dept, Balto |

B & O RR EMPLOYEES 139

| ID | Name | Description |
|---|---|---|
| 1857-122 | Fisher, Robert Jr. | eng clean 18½ da @ $1.15 - $21.25. Mach Dept, Balto |
| 1855-80 | Uriah | lab 27 da @ $1.15 - $31.05. Mach Dept |
| 1857-121 | " | car trim help 22½ da @ $1.15 - $25.85. Mach Dept, Balto |
| 1855-69 | William | driv 7½ da @ $1 - $7.50. Rd Way Dept |
| 1857-113 | " | mach app 22¼ da @ $.45 - $10.00. Mach Dept, Balto |
| 1857-74 | " | track lay 23¼ da @ $1.25 - $29.05. put swit on line of rd |
| 1857-125 | Fisk, Christian | app 3½ da @ $.50 - $17.25. Mach Dept, Martinsburg |
| 1857-89 | Fistle, Frederick | mason 1 da @ $2 - $2.00. grad, Welling Tun |
| 1857-90 | " | stone mason 6 3/4 da @ $2 - $13.50. grad, Welling Tun |
| 1857-88 | Fitz, Patrick | lab 18¼ da @ $1.12 - $20.55. grad, Welling Tun |
| 1855-50 | Fitzgard, P. | watch cuts 12 da @ $1 - $12.00. Rd Way Dept |
| 1857-116 | Fitzgerald, Edward | boil mkr help 16½ da @$1 - $16.50. Mach Dept, Balto |
| 1855-54 | John | nail 22 da @ $1 - $22.00. Rd Way Dept |
| 1857-65 | " | lab 26 da @ $1 - $26.00. Rd Dept main stem 17th s-div |
| 1855-31 | " | prepar fuel 6 da @ $1 - $6.00. Trans Dept main stem |
| 1857-62 | Patrick | watch 30 da @ $1 - $30.00. Rd Dept main stem 15th s-div |
| 1857-11 | Fitzgigin, F. | lab 23 da @ $1 - $23.00. Locust Pt |
| 1855-67 | Fitzhenry, Thomas | lab 16½ da @ $1 - $16.50. Rd Way Dept |
| 1857-97 | " | lab 26 da @ $1 - $26.00. NW Va RR, Rd Dept 2d s-div |
| 1855-49 | Fitzpatrick, James | watch cuts 28 da @ $1 - $28.00. Rd Way Dept |
| 1857-113 | " | iron mould 13 3/4 da @ $1.50 - $20.60. Mach Dept, Balto |
| 1857-53 | " | watch 30 da @ $1 - $30.00. Rd Dept main stem 7th s-div |
| 1855-54 | John | lab 24 da @ $1 - $24.00. Rd Way Dept |
| 1857-63 | " | lab 23 da @ $1 - $23.00. Rd Dept main stem 16th s-div |
| 1855-38 | M. | lab 24 da @ $1 - $24.00. Rd Way Dept |
| 1857-46 | Michael | lab 25 da @ $1 - $25.00. Rd Dept main stem 1st s-div |
| 1855-67 | Patrick | lab 24 da @ $1 - $24.00. Rd Way Dept |
| 1857-100 | Thomas | lab 24½ da @ $1 - $24.25. NW Va RR, Rd Dept 5th s-div |
| 1857-53 | " | lab 18 da @ $1 - $18.00. Rd Dept main stem 7th s-div |
| 1855-96 | Fitzsimmons, E. | lab 24 da @ $1.10 - $26.40. Mach Dept |
| 1857-80 | Flagerty, John | lab 20 3/4 da @ $1 - $20.75. lay 2d track |
| 1857-83 | Flagherty, Bartley | lab 19½ da @ $1.12 - $21.95. grad, Board Tree Tun |
| 1857-81 | Michael | lab 8½ da @ $1 - $8.50. lay 2d track |
| 1855-88 | Flaghing, Frederick | cop'smith 24 da @ $1.60 - $38.40. Mach Dept |
| 1857-98 | Flaherty, Bernard | watch 30 da @ $1 - $30.00. NW Va RR, Rd Dept 3d s-div |
| 1855-28 | E. | prepar fuel 6 3/4 da @ $1 - $6.75. Trans Dept main stem |

140                                    B & O RR EMPLOYEES

| | | | |
|---|---|---|---|
| 1857-57 | Flaherty, Edw. | lab 25 da @ $1 - $25.00. Rd Dept main stem 11th s-div |
| 1855-47 | James | lab 22½ da @ $1 - $22.25. Rd Way Dept |
| 1855-69 | John | lab 22 3/4 da @ $1 - $22.75. Rd Way Dept |
| 1857-97 | " | lab 25 da @ $1 - $25.00. NW Va RR, Rd Dept 2d s-div |
| 1855-73 | M. | lab 23½ da @ $1 - $23.25. Rd Way Dept |
| 1855-57 | Matthew | lab 12 da @ $1 - $12.00. Rd Way Dept |
| 1857-71 | " | lab 18 da @ $1 - $18.00. Mt Clare, repair tracks in yd |
| 1857-85 | Michael | lab 10 da @ $1 - $10.00. grad, Board Tree Tun |
| 1855-59 | Mike | lab 24 da @ $1 - $24.00. Rd Way Dept |
| 1855-59 | Patrick | lab 10 da @ $1 - $10.00. Rd Way Dept |
| 1857-39 | " | attend stock 30 da @ $1.65 - $41.65. NW Va rd, Parkersburg sta |
| 1857-59 | " | fore 27 da @ $1.25 - $33.75. Rd Dept main stem 13th s-div |
| 1857-93 | " | smith help 20 da @$1 - $20.00. quarry & haul stone for Board Tree & Littleton Tun |
| 1857-97 | Peter | lab 26 da @ $1 - $26.00. NW Va RR, Rd Dept 2d s-div |
| 1857-93 | " | smith help 23½ da @ $1 - $23.50. quarry & haul stone for Board Tree & Littleton Tun |
| 1855-28 | Wm. | prepar fuel 8 3/4 da @ $1 - $8.75. Trans Dept main stem |
| 1857-91 | " | lab 24 da @ $1 - $24.00. grad, Littleton Tun |
| 1855-19 | Flahr, Wm. | ton eng'man 6 da @ $2.50 - $15.00. Trans Dept main stem |
| 1857-115 | Flake, George | boil mkr 19½ da @ $1.30 - $25.38. Mach Dept, Balto |
| 1855-52 | Flanagan, James | lab 10½ da @ $1 - $10.50. Rd Way Dept |
| 1857-85 | " | lab 1 da @ $.62½ - $.60. grad, Board Tree Tun |
| 1855-63 | Jos. | fire 19½ da @ $1.75 - $34.10. Rd Way Dept |
| 1855-69 | Laurance | lab 22 3/4 da @ $1 - $22.75. Rd Way Dept |
| 1855-46 | Pat. | lab 18½ da @ $1 - $18.50. Rd Way Dept |
| 1855-61 | Thomas | lab 23 da @ $1 - $23.00. Rd Dept main stem 1st s-div |
| 1857-135 | Flanegan, M. | lab 20 da @ $1 - $20.00. Rd Way Dept |
| 1857-70 | Flanery, Michael | clean eng 30 3/4 da @ $1 - $30.75. Mach Dept, Wheeling |
| 1857-136 | " | lab 20½ da @ $1 - $20.50. Mt Clare sta, Balto |
| 1857-87 | Thomas | fill tend @ $30 per mo - $30.00. Mach Dept, Wheeling |
| 1857-88 | Flanigan, Frank | lab 15 3/4 da @ $1.12 - $17.70. grad, Welling Tun |
| 1857-89 | James | oil boy 18½ da @ $.62 - $11.55. grad, Welling Tun |
| 1855-91 | Joseph | fore 23 da @ $1.75 - $40.25. grad, Welling Tun |
| 1857-130 | Luke | help 25 da @ $1 - $25.00. Mach Dept |
| 1857-69 | Martin | lab 19 3/4 da @ $1 - $19.75. Mach Dept, Piedmont |
| 1857-88 | Michael | hod carr 23½ da @ $1.37 - $32.30. Mt Clare sta, Balto |
| | | oil boy 27 da @ $.87 - $23.65. grad, Welling Tun |

| | | | |
|---|---|---|---|
| 1857-89 | Flanigan, Thomas | driv 26½ da @ $1 - $26.50. grad, Welling Tun |
| 1855-14 | Flannagan, John | conduc & brak 13½ da @ $40 per mo - $22.50. Trans Dept main stem |
| 1855-63 | " | lab 21½ da @ $1 - $21.50. Rd Way Dept |
| 1857-26 | " | ton brak 25½ da @ $40 per mo - $40.80. 3d & 4th div |
| 1857-80 | Flannegan, John | lab 19 3/4 da @$1 - $19.75. lay 2d track |
| 1855-48 | Flannery, D. | lab 19 da @ $1 - $19.00. Rd Way Dept |
| 1855-73 | Jas. | lab 22 3/4 da @ $1 - $22.75. Rd Way Dept |
| 1855-72 | M. | help 24 da @ $1 - $24.00. Rd Way Dept |
| 1855-26 | Michael | clean eng 29½ da @ $1 - $29.50. Trans Dept main stem |
| 1855-31 | T. | prepar fuel 28 da @ $1 - $28.00. Trans Dept main stem |
| 1855-69 | Thomas | lab 22 3/4 da @ $1 - $22.75. Rd Way Dept |
| 1855-66 | Flannigan, Francis | lab 21 da @ $1 - $21.00. Rd Way Dept |
| 1855-46 | M. | lab 6 da @ $1 - $6.00. Rd Way Dept |
| 1857-8 | Patrick | lab 24 da @ $30 per mo - $28.80. Camden sta |
| 1857-40 | Thomas | ton brak 5 da @ $40 per mo - $8.00. NW Va rd, Parkersburg sta |
| 1857-130 | Flarity, Edward | lab 20 da @ $1 - $20.00. Mach Dept, Piedmont |
| 1855-58 | Patrick | lab 18½ da @ $1 - $18.50. Rd Way Dept |
| 1855-58 | " | nail 16 da @ $1 - $16.00. Rd Way Dept |
| 1857-82 | Flattley, John | lab 21 da @ $1.12 - $23.60. grad, Board Tree Tun |
| 1857-47 | Flatty, Barnard | lab 27 da @ $1 - $27.00. Rd Dept main stem 1st s-div |
| 1857-59 | Flauty, John | lab 26 da @ $1 - $26.00. Rd Dept main stem 13th s-div |
| 1857-40 | Flaxcomb, Charles | ton eng'man 28½ da @ $3 - $85.50. NW Va rd, Parkersburg sta |
| 1855-4 | William | ton eng'man 8 da @ $2.50 - $20.00. Trans Dept, Wash br |
| 1857-38 | " | ton eng'man 21½ da @ $2.75 - $58.60. Wash br rd, Wash city sta |
| 1855-55 | Fleeming, John | lab 5½ da @ $1 - $5.50. Rd Way Dept |
| 1857-57 | Thomas | lab 25 da @ $1 - $25.00. Rd Dept main stem 11th s-div |
| 1855-58 | Flemans, Thomas | lab 19½ da @ $1 - $19.50. Rd Way Dept |
| 1855-59 | Fleming, George W. | fore 24 da @ $1.25 - $30.00. Rd Way Dept |
| 1857-62 | " " | fore 25 da @ $1.25 - $31.25. Rd Dept main stem 15th s-div |
| 1857-63 | James | lab 22 3/4 da @ $1 - $22.75. Rd Dept main stem 16th s-div |
| 1855-50 | Flemming, John | nail 30 da @ $1.06 - $31.80. Rd Dept main stem 11th s-div |
| 1857-63 | M. | watch cuts 28 da @ $1 - $28.00. Rd Way Dept |
| 1857-82 | Martin | watch 30 da @ $1 - $30.00. Rd Dept main stem 16th s-div |
| 1857-71 | Flemmings, Thos. | lab 12 da @ $1.12 - $13.50. grad, Board Tree Tun |
| 1857-59 | Flemmons, Thomas | gas man 19 da @ $1.50 - $28.50. Mt Clare, repair tracks in yd |
| | | lab 26½ da @ $1 - $26.50. Rd Dept main stem 13th s-div |

| | | | |
|---|---|---|---|
| 1855-14 | Fletcher, D. | conduc & brak 21¼ da @ $40 per mo - $35.40. Trans Dept main stem |
| 1857-26 | David A. | ton brak 11 da @ $40 per mo - $17.60. 3d & 4th div |
| 1855-10 | R. | conduc & brak 1 da @ $40 per mo - $1.65. Trans Dept main stem |
| 1855-14 | " | conduc & brak 10 3/4 da @ $40 per mo - $17.90. Trans Dept main stem |
| 1855-27 | Flinn, Edward | get out eng 13 da @ $1.40 - $18.20. Trans Dept main stem |
| 1857-21 | Michael | ton conduc 16 da @ $50 per mo - $32.00. 1st div |
| 1857-75 | Morris | lab 15½ da @ $.97 - $15.10. ballast train for 2d track |
| 1855-45 | Patrick | lab 16 da @ $1 - $16.00. Rd Way Dept |
| 1857-50 | William | lab 25½ da @ $1 - $25.50. Rd Dept main stem 4th s-div |
| 1857-77 | Flint, Morris | quarry 8 da @ $1 - $8.00. ballast train for 2d track |
| 1857-19 | Flohra, William | pass eng'man 21½ da @ $3 - $64.50. 2d div |
| 1855-94 | Flood, Francis | carp 30½ da @ $1.50 - $45.35. Mach Dept |
| 1857-135 | " | carp 19¾ da @ $1.60 - $31.20. Mach Dept, Wheeling |
| 1857-95 | James | lab 24 da @ $1 - $24.00. Wash br, Rd Dept |
| 1855-9 | Thomas | conduc 6 da @ $50 per mo - $12.50. Trans Dept main stem |
| 1857-122 | " | lab 30 da @ $1 - $30.00. Mach Dept, Balto |
| 1857-39 | " | pass brak 30 da @ $33.35 per mo - $33.35. NW Va rd, Parkersburg sta |
| 1855-75 | Flora, Archibald | lab 24½ da @ $1 - $24.50. Rd Way Dept |
| 1857-54 | William | lab 30 da @ $1 - $30.00. Rd Dept main stem 8th s-div |
| 1855-44 | Flory, S. | ton eng'man 10½ da @ $3 - $31.50. Board Tree Tun |
| 1857-86 | Flugal, Peter | lab 19 da @ $1 - $19.00. Rd Way Dept |
| 1857-125 | Flughing, Fredrick | cop'smith 27 3/4 da @ $1.70 - $47.15. Mach Dept, Martinsburg |
| 1855-33 | Flurchutz, George | port 25 da @ $35 per mo - $35.00. Cumb |
| 1855-65 | Flurscutz, G. | nt 28 da @ $1.15 - $32.20. Trans Dept main stem |
| 1857-72 | Flury, Henry | fore @ $50 per mo - $50.00. Rd Way Dept |
| " | " | supt @ $55 per mo - $55.00. Cumb depot |
| 1857-57 | Flyn, John | lab 28½ da @ $1 - $28.50. Rd Dept main stem 11th s-div |
| 1857-57 | Mike | lab 26½ da @ $1 - $26.50. Rd Dept main stem 11th s-div |
| 1857-82 | Flynn, Andrew | bricklay 18 3/4 da @ $2 - $37.50. grad, Board Tree Tun |
| 1855-46 | C. | lab 6½ da @ $1 - $6.50. Rd Way Dept |
| 1855-62 | Daniel | lab 18 da @ $1 - $18.00. Rd Way Dept |
| 1855-94 | Edward | lab 15 da @ $1 - $15.00. Mach Dept |
| 1857-123 | George | storekpr @ $35 per mo - $35.00. Mach Dept, Martinsburg |
| 1857-83 | John | lab 20¼ da @ $1.12 - $22.80. grad, Board Tree Tun |
| 1857-66 | Michael | lab 23 da @ $1 - $23.00. Rd Dept main stem 18th s-div |

| | | |
|---|---|---|
| 1855-61 | Flynn, Mike | lab 17 da @ $1 - $17.00. Rd Way Dept |
| 1857-83 | Patrick | lab 3½ da @ $1.12 - $3.65. grad, Board Tree Tun |
| 1857-79 | " | lab 26 3/4 da @ $1 - $36.75. lay 2d track |
| 1857-103 | " | lab 20¼ da @ $ 1.12 - $22.80. NW Va RR Tun |
| 1855-66 | Peter | lab 27¼ da @ $1 - $27.25. Rd Way Dept |
| 1857-67 | " | lab 23½ da @ $1 - $23.50. Rd Dept main stem 18th s-div |
| 1855-62 | Terence | lab 8¼ da @ $1 - $8.25. Rd Way Dept |
| 1857-46 | Thomas | lab 25 da @ $1 - $25.00. Rd Dept main stem 1st s-div |
| 1857-56 | Timothy | lab 16 da @ $1 - $16.00. Rd Dept main stem 10th s-div |
| 1855-80 | Foard, Samuel | carp 24 da @ $1.50 - $36.00. Mach Dept |
| 1857-119 | " | carp 17 da @ $1.55 - $26.35. Mach Dept, Balto |
| 1857-135 | Fogarty, John | lab 19 3/4 da @ $1 - $19.75. Mach Dept, Wheeling |
| 1855-57 | Fogelpoll, E. | lab 19½ da @ $1 - $19.50. Rd Way Dept |
| 1855-57 | R. | lab 19½ da @ $1 - $19.50. Rd Way Dept |
| 1857-136 | Fogler, Adam | clean pass cars @ #30 per mo - $30.00. Mach Dept, Wheeling |
| 1855-34 | Andrew | clean pass car 28 da @ $30 per mo - $30.00. Trans Dept main stem |
| 1855-65 | Folen, Patrick | lab 10 da @ $1 - $10.00. Rd Way Dept |
| 1857-92 | Foley, Bartlett | lab 22¼ da @ $1 - $22.25. grad, Littleton Tun |
| 1857-96 | Edward | lab 12½ da @ $1 - $12.50. NW Va RR, Rd Dept 1st s-div |
| 1857-35 | James | lab 9½ da @ $1 - $9.50. Edwards wd train 3d & 4th div |
| 1855-91 | John | help 24 da @ $1 - $24.00. Mach Dept |
| 1857-128 | " | blksmith help 16 da @ $1.15 - $18.40. Mach Dept, Piedmont |
| 1855-91 | Martin (No. 1) | help 26½ da @ $1 - $26.50. Mach Dept |
| 1855-91 | " (No. 2) | help 21¼ da @ $1 - $21.25. Mach Dept |
| 1855-49 | Michael | watch cuts 25½ da @ $1 - $25.50. Rd Way Dept |
| 1857-127 | " | mach help 26½ da @ $1 - $26.50. Mach Dept, Piedmont |
| 1855-91 | Mike | help 25 3/4 da @ $1 - $25.75. Mach Dept |
| 1855-53 | Patrick | lab 15 da @ $1 - $15.00. Rd Way Dept |
| 1857-129 | " | clean eng 31 da @ $1 - $31.00. Mach Dept, Piedmont |
| 1857-83 | Thomas | lab 10¼ da @ $1.12 - $11.55. grad, Board Tree Tun |
| 1857-90 | " | lab 12½ da @ $1.12 - $14.05. grad, Welling Tun |
| 1857-79 | " | lab 21 da @ $1 - $21.00. lay 2d track |
| 1857-57 | " | lab 25½ da @ $1 - $25.50. Rd Dept main stem 11th s-div |
| 1857-134 | Follingsbee, F. G. | mach 2¼ da @$1.50 - $3.35. Mach Dept, Wheeling |
| 1855-58 | Follon, M. | lab 13½ da @ $1 - $13.50. Rd Way Dept |
| 1855-60 | Fonfair, John | fore 11 da @ $1 - $11.00. Rd Way Dept |
| 1857-55 | Fopp, Lewis | lab 23¼ da @ $1 - $23.25. Rd Dept main stem 9th s-div |

144                     B & O RR EMPLOYEES

| | | |
|---|---|---|
| 1855-14 | Ford, F. M. | brak 16½ da @ $40 per mo - $27.10. Trans Dept main stem |
| 1857-34 | " M. | ton fire 40 da @ $1.75 - $70.00. Board Tree Tun |
| 1855-10 | " G. M. | conduc & brak 13¾ da @ $50 per mo - $27.60. Trans Dept main stem |
| 1857-18 | " " | pass train brak 30 da @ $33.35 per mo - $33.35. thr mail & exp |
| 1855-6 | " J. B. | agt 28 da @ $160.66 per mo - $166.66. Trans Dept main stem |
| 1857-17 | " " | lab 30 da @ $125 per mo - $125.00. Wheeling sta |
| 1857-49 | James | lab 25 da @ $1 - $25.00. Rd Dept main stem 3d s-div |
| 1857-81 | Martin | lab 21 da @ $1.12 - $23.60. grad, Board Tree Tun |
| 1855-60 | Patrick | lab 20 3/4 da @ $1 - $20.75. Rd Way Dept |
| 1857-99 | " | lab 25 da @ $1 - $25.00. NW Va R3, Rd Dept 4th s-div |
| 1857-66 | Thomas | lab 24 da @ $1.25 - $21.75. Rd Dept main stem 18th s-div |
| 1855-66 | Fordyce, Thomas | conduc & brak 6½ da @ $40 per mo - $11.85. Rd Way Dept |
| 1855-10 | Foreman, G. W. | ton conduc 18 3/4 da @ $50 per mo - $27.50. 2d div |
| 1857-22 | " George W. | lab 22½ da @ $1.12 - $25.30. repair bridges &c |
| 1857-74 | Forick, Ambrose | draught @ $50 per mo - $50.00. Mach Dept, Balto |
| 1857-108 | Forney, M. N. | help 24 da @ $1 - $24.00. Mach Dept |
| 1855-84 | Forrest, J. | blksmith 18 da @ $1.85 - $33.30. Mt Clare sta, Balto |
| 1857-70 | " Leonard | fire 9 da @ $1.75 - $15.75. Trans Dept main stem |
| 1855-22 | Zack | ton fire 16½ da @ $1.75 - $28.85. 1st div |
| 1857-31 | Forrester, John | paint 17 3/4 da @ $1.65 - $29.30. Mach Dept, Balto |
| 1857-121 | Forsith, Edward | paint 21 3/4 da @ $1.65 - $35.90. Mach Dept |
| 1855-80 | Forsyth, Edw. | pass train brak 25 da @ $33.35 per mo - $27.80. thr mail & exp |
| 1857-18 | " F. | clk 28 da @ $58.35 per mo - $58.35. Trans Dept main stem |
| 1855-7 | " Wm. | pass eng'man 18½ da @ $3 - $55.50. 4th div |
| 1857-19 | Fortling, George | conduc & brak 15½ da @ $40 per mo - $21.25. Trans Dept main stem |
| 1855-10 | Fost, A. T. | conduc & brak 23½ da @ $40 per mo - $11.65. Trans Dept main stem |
| 1855-10 | " T. J. | fore 26 da @ $1.75 - $45.50. grad, McGuire's Tun |
| 1857-86 | Foster, George G. | fire 10¾ da @ $1.75 - $17.95. Trans Dept main stem |
| 1855-22 | " Jacob | ton fire 1 da @ $33.33 per mo - $1.40. Trans Dept, Wash br |
| 1855-5 | " " | lab 19 da @ $1 - $19.00. Rd Dept main stem 2d s-div |
| 1857-48 | " " | app 23¾ da @ $.55 - $12.80. Mach Dept |
| 1855-82 | Wm. | swit tend 25 da @ $35 per mo - $35.00. Putney's swit |
| 1857-12 | Fountain, R. | clk 28 da @ $11.65 per mo - $11.65. Trans Dept main stem |
| 1855-6 | Fowler, A. G. | ton brak 11 da @ $40 per mo - $17.60. 1st div |
| 1857-24 | " Alfred | lab 24½ da @ $25 per mo - $25.25. Trans Dept main stem |
| 1855-36 | Daniel | |

## B & O RR EMPLOYEES 145

| ID | Name | Details |
|---|---|---|
| 1857-31 | Fowler, Henry | ton fire 23½ da @ $1.75 - $41.10. 1st div |
| 1855-10 | J. H. | conduc & brak 24½ da @ $30 per mo - $30.30. Trans Dept main stem |
| 1857-24 | Jerry | ton brak 26 3/4 da @@$30 per mo - $32.10. 1st div |
| 1855-84 | John | mach (includ boil mkr, work sht iron, &c) 24½ da @ $1.55 -$38.00. Mach Dept |
| 1857-115 | " | boil mkr 18 da @ $1.55 - $27.90. Mach Dept, Balto |
| 1855-39 | Joseph | lab 24 da @ $1 - $24.00. Rd Way Dept |
| 1855-10 | T. | conduc & brak 17½ da @ $50 per mo - $36.45. Trans Dept main stem |
| 1855-25 | Thomas | clean eng 26½ da @ $1.15 - $30.45. Trans Dept main stem |
| 1855-39 | " | lab 24 da @ $1.25 -$30.00. Rd Way Dept |
| 1857-122 | " | eng clean 10 3/4 da @$1.15 - $12.35. Mach Dept, Balto |
| 1857-32 | " | ton fire 16 da @ $1.75 - $28.00. 2d div |
| 1855-10 | William | conduc & brak 17 3/4 da @ $50 per mo - $36.95. Trans Dept main stem |
| 1857-21 | " | ton conduc 17½ da @ $50 per mo - $35.00. 1st div |
| 1857-40 | Fox, C. | pass fire 25½ da @ $40 per mo - $34.00. NW Va rd, Parkersburg sta |
| 1857-98 | James | fore 25 da @ $1.25 - $31.25. NW Va RR, Rd Dept 3d s-div |
| 1857-59 | Mark | lab 25 da @ $1 - $25.00. Rd Dept main stem 12th s-div |
| 1857-80 | Matthew | lab 19 3/4 da @ $1 - $19.75. lay 2d track |
| 1855-74 | Patrick | lab 15 da @ $1 - $15.00. Rd Way Dept |
| 1857-92 | " | lab 22½ da @ $1.12 - $25.30. grad, Littleton Tun |
| 1855-61 | Thomas | fore 22½ da @ $1.25 - $28.10. Rd Way Dept |
| 1857-66 | " | fore 25 da @ $1.25 - $31.25. Rd Dept main stem 18th s-div |
| 1857-40 | Foy, Benjamin | ton eng'man 2 da @ $3 -$6.00. NW Va rd, Parkersburg sta |
| 1857-52 | David | lab 24½ da @ $1 - $24.50. Rd Dept main stem 6th s-div |
| 1857-79 | John | lab 8½ da @ $1 - $8.50. lay 2d track |
| 1857-52 | " | lab 22 da @ $1 - $22.00. Rd Dept main stem 6th s-div |
| 1855-91 | Foye, Benjamin | help 27 da @ $1 -$27.00. Mach Dept |
| 1857-29 | " | ton eng'man 20½ da @ $3 - $61.50. 2d div |
| 1857-87 | Frail, Henry | lab 23½ da @ $1 - $23.50. grad, McGuire's Tun |
| 1857-139 | Frain, John | clean eng 30 da @ $1 - $30.00. NW Va RR, Mach Dept, Parkersburg |
| 1855-50 | Frainer, Owen | watch cuts 30 da @$1 - $30.00. Rd Way Dept |
| 1857-126 | France, Frederick | clean eng 24½ da @ $1.15 - $28.15. Mach Dept, Martinsburg |
| 1855-56 | Francis, Thomas | lab 8 da @ $1 - $8.00. Rd Way Dept |
| 1855-97 | " | lab 26 da @ $1 - $26.00. NW Va RR, Rd Dept 2d s-div |
| 1857-135 | Frank, Louis | carp 19 da @ $1.45 - $27.55. Mach Dept, Wheeling |
| 1857-19 | Franklin, William | pass eng'man 19 da @ $2.75 - $52.25. 1st div |
| 1857-28 | " | ton eng'man 18 da @ $3 - $54.00. 1st div |

# B & O RR EMPLOYEES

| Ref | Name | Description |
|---|---|---|
| 1857-97 | Frasier, Joseph | watch 30 da @$1 - $30.00. NW Va RR, Rd Dept 1st s-div |
| 1857-35 | Lat | lab 13 da @ $1 - $13.00. Edwards wd train 3d & 4th div |
| 1857-130 | William | clean eng 30 da @ $1 - $30.00. Mach Dept, Newburg |
| 1857-130 | William H. | clean eng 30 da @ $1 - $30.00. Mach Dept, Newburg |
| 1855-34 | Fray, Patrick | watch 28 da @$1.15 -$32.20. Trans Dept main stem |
| 1857-137 | Frays, Patrick | watch 30 da @$1.15 -$34.50. Mach Dept, Cumb |
| 1857-118 | Frazier, Elisha | blksmith help 17 da @ $1.25 -$21.25. Mach Dept, Balto |
| 1855-22 | G. W. | fire 24 da @$1.75 - $42.00. Trans Dept main stem |
| 1855-29 | J. T. | prepar fuel 9 da @ $1 - $9.00. Trans Dept main stem |
| 1855-29 | W. H. | prepar fuel 19 da @ $1 -$19.00. Trans Dept main stem |
| 1857-50 | Washington | lab 21 3/4 da @ $1 - $21.75. Rd Dept main stem 4th s-div |
| 1855-35 | William | watch 28 da @ $1 - $28.00. Trans Dept main stem |
| 1857 -114 | " | iron mould app 20 da @ $.75 - $15.00. Mach Dept, Balto |
| 1857-104 | Freasy, Michael | lab 23 da @ $1.12 - $25.90. NW Va RR Tun |
| 1855-85 | Frederick, C. | help 22½ da @ $1.15 - $25.85. Mach Dept |
| 1855-73 | " | tin 18¼ da @ $1.73 - $31.60. Rd Way Dept |
| 1857-69 | Charles | tin 25 da @$1.73 - $43.25. Mt Clare sta, Balto |
| 1857-117 | Christian | blksmith help 13¾ da @ $1.15 - $15.25. Mach Dept, Balto |
| 1857-69 | David | tin 25 da @ $1.25 - $31.25. Mt Clare sta, Balto |
| 1855-82 | Mike | lock 27 3/4 da @ $1.45 - $40.25. Mach Dept |
| 1855-76 | Thos. | mach 17¾ da @ $1.50 - $25.85. Mach Dept |
| 1855-82 | Wm. | app 26 da @ $.65 - $16.90. Mach Dept |
| 1857-113 | Fredrick, Michael | lock 18¼ da @ $1.55 - $28.30. Mach Dept, Balto |
| 1857-110 | Thomas | mach 22 da @ $1.60 - $35.20. Mach Dept, Balto |
| 1855-72 | Freeberger, A. | mach 18½ da @ $1.73 - $32.00. Rd Way Dept |
| 1857-123 | Isaac | mach 16 3/4 da @$1.50 - $25.10. Mach Dept, Martinsburg |
| 1857-69 | Freeburger, Andrew | mach 17 3/4 da @ $1.73 - $30.70. Mt Clare sta, Balto |
| 1855-41 | Freeman, David | lab 21 da @ $1 - $21.00. Rd Way Dept |
| 1655-10 | John | conduc & brak 15 da @ $50 per mo - $33.75. Trans Dept main stem |
| 1657-21 | " | ton conduc 28 3/4 da @$50 per mo - $57.50. 2d div |
| 1857-15 | William H. | agt 30 da @ $75 per mo - $75.00. Grafton sta |
| 1857-31 | Freize, John | ton fire 20½ da @ $1.75 - $35.85. 1st div |
| 1855-10 | French, A. | conduc & brak 19 da @ $40 per mo - $31.65. Trans Dept main stem |
| 1857-24 | Andrew | ton brak 21 da @ $30 per mo; 3 da @ $50 per mo - $89.25. 3d div |
| 1857-29 | George | ton eng'man 29 3/4 da @ $3 - $89.25. 3d div |
| 1857-81 | James | lab 20 3/4 da @ $1 - $20.75. lay 2d track |

| ID | Name | Details |
|---|---|---|
| 1855-41 | French, John | lab 16 da @ $1 - $16.00. Rd Way Dept |
| 1857-52 | " | lab 22 da @ $1 - $22.00. Rd Dept main stem 6th s-div |
| 1857-123 | " | mach ¼ da @ $1 - $.25. Mach Dept, Martinsburg |
| 1857-32 | John A. | ton fire 14 3/4 da @ $1.75 - $25.80. 2d div |
| 1855-41 | Joseph | lab 17½ da @ $1 -$17.50. Rd Way Dept |
| 1857-52 | " | lab 24½ da @ $1 - $24.50. Rd Dept main stem 6th s-div |
| 1857-90 | Martin | lab 11½ da @ $1.12 - $12.95. grad, Welling Tun |
| 1857-22 | Mason | ton conduc 29 da @ $50 per mo - $58.00. 3d & 4th div |
| 1857-19 | Robert | pass eng'man 42 da @ $3 - $126.00. 4th div |
| 1857-125 | Frengle, Andrew | lab 26 3/4 da @ $1 - $26.75. Mach Dept, Martinsburg |
| 1857-88 | Fresch, Frederick | eng'man 25¼ da @ $1.15 - $29.05. Mach Dept |
| 1857-124 | Fresh, Frederick | mach 26½ da @ $1.25 - $33.10. Mach Dept, Martinsburg |
| 1857-14 | Frethey, G. G. | watch 25 da @ $35 per mo - $35.00. Cumb |
| 1855-33 | Frethy, G. G. | St 28 da @ $1 - $28.00. Trans Dept main stem |
| 1855-27 | Fretwell, Charles | clean eng 18 da @ $1 - $18.00. Trans Dept main stem |
| 1855-87 | Freuzel, Andrew | help 22½ da @ $1 - $22.50. Mach Dept |
| 1857-31 | Frey, George | ton fire 17 da @ $1.75 - $29.75. 1st div |
| 1857-31 | Jacob | ton fire 19½ da @ $1.75 - $34.10. 1st div |
| 1857-97 | Thomas | lab 26 da @ $1 - $26.00. NW Va RR, Rd Dept 2d s-div |
| 1857-25 | William | ton brak ¼ da @ $40 per mo - $.40. 2d div |
| 1857-66 | Frian, W. H. | fore 24 da @$1.25 - $30.00. Rd Dept main stem 18th s-div |
| 1855-61 | Friar, W. H. | fore 15 da @ $1.25 - $18.71. Rd Way Dept |
| 1857-122 | Fridinger, David | fire 19¼ da @ $1.75 - $33.70. Trans Dept main stem |
| 1855-89 | Friend, Henry | boil mkr 20½ da @ $1.55 - $28.70. Mach Dept |
| 1855-28 | Frieze, John | reg eng 26½ da @ $1.50 - $39.75. Trans Dept main stem |
| 1857-98 | Frill, J. B. | supv @ $60 per mo - $60.00. NW Va RR, Rd Dept 3d s-div |
| 1857-103 | Fring, Martin | lab 21 da @ $1.12 - $23.60. NW Va RR Tun |
| 1857-98 | Frinnan, Dennis | lab 25 da @ $1 - $25.00. NW Va RR, Rd Dept 3d s-div |
| 1857-53 | Friskey, George | lab 21½ da @$1 - $21.50. Rd Dept main stem 7th s-div |
| 1855-43 | John | lab 14½ da @ $1 - $14.50. Rd Way Dept |
| 1857-53 | " | lab 22½ da @ $1 - $22.50. Rd Dept main stem 7th s-div |
| 1857-126 | Fritch, Richard H. | lab 9½ da @ $1 - $9.50. Mach Dept, Martinsburg |
| 1857-53 | Fronts, William | fore 24 da @ $1.25 - $30.00. Rd Dept main stem 7th s-div |
| 1857-71 | Frosi, H. | track lay 23½ da @ $1.50 - $23.50. Camden sta, repair tracks |
| 1857-21 | Frost, Thomas J. | ton conduc 14¼ da @ $50 per mo - $28.50. 2d div |
| 1855-74 | Frothingham, Andr. | fore 24 da @ $1.25 - $30.00. Rd Way Dept |

## B & O RR EMPLOYEES

| | | |
|---|---|---|
| 1855-75 | Fryatt, B. | fore 25 da @ $1.25 - $31.25. Rd Way Dept |
| 1855-32 | Fryer, James | tele oper 28 da @ $30 per mo - $30.00. Trans Dept main stem |
| 1855-10 | " Jesse | conduc & brak 21½ da @$50 per mo - $47.80. Trans Dept main stem |
| 1857-21 | " | ton conduc 30 3/4 da @ $50 per mo - $61.50. 2d div |
| 1855-14 | M. | conduc & brak 1 da @ $40 per mo - $1.65. Trans Dept main stem |
| 1855-22 | Fugett, John | fire 4 da @$1.75 - $7.00. Trans Dept main stem |
| 1857-132 | Fullen, James | iron mould 25 da @ $1.50 - $37.50. Mach Dept, Grafton |
| 1857-92 | Fuller, Frederick | driv 31 da @ $1 - $31.00. grad, Littleton Tun |
| 1855-82 | " Joseph | lab 25 da @ $1.15 - $28.75. Mach Dept |
| 1857-110 | " " | mach 18 da @ $1.25 - $22.50. Mach Dept, Balto |
| 1855-51 | Fullerton, John | lab 20 da @ $1 - $20.00. Rd Way Dept |
| 1857-34 | " " | ton fire 36 da @$1.75 -$63.00. Board Tree Tun |
| 1855-80 | | trim 23 3/4 da @ $1.50 - $35.60. Mach Dept |
| 1855-76 | Fullim, F. | help 26½ da @ $1 - $26.50. Mach Dept |
| 1855-96 | Fullin, James | app 24 da @ 3.65 - $15.60. Mach Dept |
| 1857-112 | Fullman, Francis | mach help 18 da @ $1 -$18.00. Mach Dept, Balto |
| 1855-79 | Fullum, Peter | cart boy @ $14 per mo - $14.00. Mach Dept |
| 1857-112 | " | mach app 16 da @ $.65 - $10.40. Mach Dept, Balto |
| 1855-94 | Fullwright, Wm. | lab 21½ da @ $1 - $21.50. Mach Dept |
| 1855-15 | Fulton, J. | pass eng'man 25 da @ $3 - $75.00. Trans Dept main stem |
| 1855-11 | " James | fore 24 da @ $1.25 - $30.00. Rd Way Dept |
| 1857-50 | " " | fore 24 da @ $1.25 - $30.00. Rd Dept main stem 4th s-div |
| 1857-19 | " Joseph | pass eng'man 39 da @ $3 - $117.00. 4th div |
| 1855-9 | Funk, Thomas | conduc 21½ da @ $50 per mo - $44.25. Trans Dept main stem |
| 1855-60 | Furbee, W. | lab 28 da @ $1 -$28.00. Rd Way Dept |
| 1857-119 | Furgeon, William | tin 24½ da @$1.55 - $37.60. Mach Dept, Balto |
| 1855-37 | Furguson, William | lab 28½ da @$1 - $28.50. Rd Way Dept |
| 1855-79 | " | tin 24 da @ $1.55 - $27.20. Mach Dept |
| 1857-16. | " | brak on incline 30 da @ $30 per mo - $30.00. Benwood sta |
| 1857-91 | Furlow, James | lab 16½ da @ $1 - $16.50. grad, Welling Tun |
| 1857-92 | Furman, Nailer | lab 24 3/4 da @ $1.12 - $27.80. grad, Littleton Tun |
| 1857-111 | Furney, James | greas cars 30 da @ $1 - $30.00. Mach Dept, Fetterman |
| 1857-98 | Furry, John | mach help 17½ da @ $1.15 - $20.10. Mach Dept, Balto |
| 1855-45 | Fuslow, James | fore 25⅝ da @ $1.25 -$31.85. NW Va RR, Rd Dept 3d s-div |
| 1855-27 | Fusner, Daniel | lab 19 da @ $1 - $19.00. Rd Way Dept |
| | | clean eng 24½ da @ $1 - $24.50. Trans Dept main stem |

B & O RR EMPLOYEES    149

| ID | Name | | Description |
|---|---|---|---|
| 1857-130 | Fusner, G. | | lab 25¼ da @ $1 - $25.25. Mach Dept, Piedmont |
| 1855-92 | " | Joseph | app 24 da @ $.45 -$10.80. Mach Dept |
| 1857-128 | " | Martin | blksmith 16¼ da @ $1.50 - $24.35. Mach Dept, Piedmont |
| 1857-98 | Gafney, James | | lab 23½ da @ $1 - $23.50. NW Va RR, Rd Dept 3d s-div |
| 1857-135 | Gahan, James | | boil mkr 31 da @ $1.75 - $54.25. Mach Dept, Wheeling |
| 1855-49 | " | M. | watch cuts 7 da @ $1 - $7.00. Rd Way Dept |
| 1855-85 | Gahler, Noah | | help 24 3/4 da @$1.10 - $27.25. Mach Dept |
| 1857-118 | Gahler, Noah | | blksmith help 18 3/4 da @ $1.10 - $20.65. Mach Dept, Balto |
| 1855-37 | Gailor, George | | lab 28 da @ $1 - $28.00. Rd Way Dept |
| 1855-16 | Gainer, P. | | pass fire 31 da @ $40 per mo - $44.30. Trans Dept main stem |
| 1857-93 | Gainor, William | | smith help 23 da @ $1 - $23.00. quarry & haul stone for Board Tree & Littleton Tun |
| 1855-88 | Gaither, R. C. | | paint 20¾ da @ $40 per mo - $31.40. Mach Dept |
| 1855-7 | " | S. C. | bag mast 13 da @ $40 per mo - $18.60. Trans Dept main stem |
| 1857-18 | " | Samuel | pass train conduc 8 da @ $62.50 per mo - $16.65. w end |
| 1855-42 | " | William | lab 14½ da @ $1 - $14.50. Rd Way Dept |
| 1857-19 | " | " | bag mast 7 da @ $45 per mo - $10.50. w end |
| 1857-53 | " | " | lab 18 da @ $1 - $18.00. Rd Dept main stem 7th s-div |
| 1857-97 | Gaitly, Michael | | watch 30 da @ $1 - $30.00. NW Va RR, Rd Dept 2d s-div |
| 1857-23 | Gaitner, William | | ton conduc 4 da @ $40 per mo; 6½ da @ $50 per mo - $19.40. 3d & 4th div |
| 1857-64 | Gaitz, Michael | | lab 8 3/4 da @ $1 - $8.75. Rd Dept main stem 17th s-div |
| 1857-91 | Galahai, Philip | | lab 20⅞ da @ $1 - $20.25. grad, Welling Tun |
| 1857-103 | Galbert, Joseph | | lab 6 da @ $1.12 -$6.75. NW Va RR Tun |
| 1855-6 | Gale, S. C. | | clk 28 da @ $50 per mo - $50.00. Trans Dept main stem |
| 1857-8 | " | " | rec clk 30 da @ $58.35 per mo - $58.35. Camden sta |
| 1855-49 | Galegher, Luke | | watch cuts 28 da @ $1 - $28.00. Rd Way Dept |
| 1857-59 | " | Michael | lab 26½ da @ $1 - $26.50. Rd Dept main stem 13th s-div |
| 1857-52 | Galesin, John | | lab 25 da @ $1 - $25.00. Rd Dept main stem 6th s-div |
| 1855-43 | Galiher, John | | lab 15 da @ $1 - $15.00. Rd Way Dept |
| 1857-53 | " | " | lab 24 da @ $1 - $24.00. Rd Dept main stem 7th s-div |
| 1855-36 | Gallagher, Edward | | lab 25 da @ $25 per mo - $26.05. Trans Dept main stem |
| 1857-122 | " | Francis | lab 22 @ $1.15 -$25.30. Mach Dept, Balto |
| 1857-66 | " | Patrick | lab 21½ da @ $1 - $21.25. Rd Way Dept |
| 1855-88 | " | " | lab 20¾ da @ $1.12 -$22.80. grad, Welling Tun |
| 1855-45 | Gallaher, D. | | lab 13½ da @ $1 -$13.50. Rd Way Dept |
| 1855-9 | " | J. D. | conduc 12 da @ $50 per mo - $25.00. Trans Dept main stem |
| 1857-92 | " | John | fore 23 da @ $1.25 - $28.75. grad, Littleton Tun |

| | | | |
|---|---|---|---|
| 1855-52 | Gallaher, Patrick | lab 16½ da @ $1 - $16.50. Rd Way Dept |
| 1855-39 | " William | lab 19 da @ $1 - $19.00. Rd Way Dept |
| 1855-80 | Galleger, F. | lao 26¼ da @ $1.10 - $28.85. Mach Dept |
| 1855-96 | " William | lab 26 3/4 da @ $1.10 - $1.10 - $29.45. Mach Dept |
| 1857-60 | Galleghar, Luke | watch 30 da @ $1 - $30.00. Rd Dept main stem 13th s-div |
| 1857-89 | Gallegher, Peter | lab 10½ da @ $1.12 - $11.80. grad, Welling Tun |
| 1857-54 | Galleher, Daniel | pump water @ $35 per mo - $35.00. Rd Dept main stem 8th s-div |
| 1857-65 | " Thomas | lab 24½ da @ $1 - $24.25. lay 2d track |
| 1857-79 | Galligan, Anthony | lab 25¼ da @ $1 - $25.25. lay 2d track |
| 1857-17 | Galliger, William | lab 25 da @ $1 - $25.00. frt transfer force at Bellaire, opp Benwood |
| 1857-50 | Galliher, John | lab 25½ da @ $1 - $25.50. Rd Dept main stem 5th s-div |
| 1855-75 | " Michael | lab 15 da @ $1 - $15.00. Rd Way Dept |
| 1857-51 | " " | lab 21½ da @ $1 - $21.50. Rd Dept main stem 5th s-div |
| 1855-75 | " Patk. | lab 22½ da @ $1 - $22.50. Rd Way Dept |
| 1855-5 | Galloway, A. | eng clean 24 da @ $32.20 per mo - $32.20. Trans Dept, Wash br |
| 1855-4 | " " | pass fire 3 da @ $40 per mo - $4.30. Trans Dept, Wash br |
| 1857-112 | " " | mach help 3½ da @ $1 - $3.50. Mach Dept, Balto |
| 1857-20 | " Aquilla | pass fire 2 da @ $40 per mo - $2.65. 1st div |
| 1857-38 | " " | pass fire 18 da @ $40 per mo - $24.00. Wash br rd, Wash city sta |
| 1855-80 | " G. | paint 7½ da @ $1.25 - $9.40. Mach Dept |
| 1855-82 | " Jesse | app 19 da @ $.55 - $14.25. Mach Dept |
| 1857-109 | " " | mach 17½ da @ $1.80 - $31.05. Mach Dept, Balto |
| 1857-35 | " John | lab 21 da @ $1 - $21.00. J. R. Shrodes wd train 4th div |
| 1855-89 | " Thomas | mach 10½ da @ $1.65 - $17.30. Mach Dept |
| 1855-17 | " " | ton eng'man 8 da @ $3 - $24.00. Trans Dept main stem |
| 1857-133 | " " | mach 24½ da @ $1.70 - $41.65. Mach Dept, Fetterman |
| 1857-70 | " Vincent | help 19 da @ $1.06 - $20.15. Mt Clare sta, Balto |
| 1857-111 | " W. | mach 5½ da @ $1.25 - $6.85. Mach Dept, Balto |
| 1855-4 | " William | eng'man 32 da @ $2.50 - $80.00. Trans Dept, Wash br |
| 1857-38 | " " | pass eng'man 15 da @ $3 - $45.00. Wash br rd, Wash city sta |
| 1857-56 | Galvin, John | horse & cart 24½ da @ $1.25 - $30.60. Rd Dept main stem 10th s-div |
| 1857-57 | " Patrick | nail 18½ da @ $1.06 - $19.60. Rd Dept main stem 11th s-div |
| 1857-48 | " Roderick | watch 30 da @ $1 - $30.00. Rd Dept main stem 2d s-div |
| 1857-56 | " Thomas | lab 24½ da @ $1 - $24.50. Rd Dept main stem 10th s-div |
| 1855-26 | Galway, Thomas | clean eng 26 da @ $1 - $26.00. Trans Dept main stem |
| 1855-11 | Gambrill, George | conduc & brak 11½ da @ $40 per mo - $19.15. Trans Dept main stem |

| | | |
|---|---|---|
| 1855-9 | Gandy, G. W. | conduc 14 da @ $50 per mo - $29.15. Trans Dept main stem |
| 1857-41 | Jehu | ton fire 20 da @ $1.75 - $35.00. NW Va rd, Parkersburg sta |
| 1857-92 | Ganey, John | lab 25 da @ $1 - $25.00. grad, Littleton Tun |
| 1857-91 | Martin | lab 24 da @ $1 - $24.00. grad, Littleton Tun |
| 1857-51 | Michael | lab 25 da @ $1 - $25.00. Rd Dept main stem 5th s-div |
| 1855-60 | Ganghan, P. | lab 20 da @ $1 - $20.00. Rd Way Dept |
| 1857-85 | Gannan, John | lab 8 da @ $1.12 - $9.00. grad, Board Tree Tun |
| 1855-80 | Gannell, W. | carp 24¼ da @ $1.45 - $35.15. Mach Dept |
| 1857-119 | W. W. | carp 18 da @ $1.60 - $28.80. Mach Dept, Balto |
| 1855-31 | Gannon, John | saw wd 53 cords @ $.35 - $18.55. Trans Dept main stem |
| 1857-88 | " | lab 18 3/4 da @ $1.12 - $21.10. grad, Welling Tun |
| 1855-50 | L. | watch cuts 30 da @ $1 - $30.00. Rd Way Dept |
| 1855-60 | M. | fore 23 da @ $1 - $23.00. Rd Way Dept |
| 1857-53 | Ganoe, Thornton | lab 22 da @ $1 - $22.00. Rd Dept main stem 7th s-div |
| 1855-42 | Gant, Danl. | lab 23¼ da @ $1 - $23.25. Rd Way Dept |
| 1855-42 | Jas. | lab 19¼ da @ $1 - $19.25. Rd Way Dept |
| 1855-42 | Jno. | fore 24 da @ $1.25 - $30.00. Rd Way Dept |
| 1857-93 | Garahety, Michael | smith help 23¼ da @ $1 - $23.25. quarry & haul stone for Board Tree & Littleton Tun |
| 1857-125 | Gard, David F. | put away eng &c 22 3/4 da @ $1.50 - $34.10. Mach Dept, Martinsburg |
| 1855-86 | William | mach 23½ da @ $1.72 - $40.55. Mach Dept |
| 1857-123 | " | mach 21 da @ $1.72½ - $36.20. Mach Dept, Martinsburg |
| 1855-87 | Gardener, Geo. | help 19¼ da @ $1 - $19.25. Mach Dept |
| 1855-87 | J. | help 23 da @ $1 - $23.00. Mach Dept |
| 1857-124 | Gardner, George | boil mkr help 18¼ da @ $1 - $18.25. Mach Dept, Martinsburg |
| 1857-128 | John | boil mkr 18½ da @ $1.70 - $31.45. Mach Dept, Piedmont |
| 1857-74 | Garey, Wm. | lab 21 da @ $1.12 - $23.65. repair bridges &c |
| 1857-112 | Garity, Charles | mach app 23¼ da @ $.45 - $10.45. Mach Dept, Balto |
| 1857-133 | John | clean eng 34 da @ $1 - $34.00. Mach Dept, Board Tree Tun |
| 1857-64 | Thomas | lab 23 da @ $1 - $23.00. Rd Dept main stem 17th s-div |
| 1857-14 | Garner, Joseph | lab 14 da @ $30 per mo - $16.80. Cumb |
| 1857-32 | " | ton fire 1 da @ $33.35 per mo - $1.35. 2d div |
| 1855-61 | Garr, T. O. | lab 22 da @ $1 - $22.00. Rd Way Dept |
| 1857-66 | Thomas O. | lab 15¼ da @ $1 - $15.25. Rd Dept main stem 18th s-div |
| 1855-63 | Garreson, L. | fire 3 da @ $1.75 - $5.25. Rd Way Dept |
| 1855-57 | Garrett, Michl. | lab 28½ da @ $1 - $18.50. Rd Way Dept |
| 1857-55 | William | lab 23½ da @ $1 - $23.50. Rd Dept main stem 9th s-div |

152  B & O RR EMPLOYEES

| | | | |
|---|---|---|---|
| 1857-66 | Garrey, James | lab 22½ da @ $1 - $22.50. Rd Dept main stem 18th s-div |
| 1855-48 | Pat. | train hand 20½ da @ $1 - $20.50. Rd Way Dept |
| 1855-20 | Garrison, Leonard | fire 15½ da @ $1.75 - $27.10. Trans Dept main stem |
| 1857-34 | " | ton fire 34¼ da @ $1.75 - $60.35. Board Tree Tun |
| 1857-84 | William | ton fire 1 da @ $1.75 - $1.75. 4th div |
| 1857-81 | Garrity, John | carp 11½ da @ $1.12 - $12.95. grad, Board Tree Tun |
| 1857-97 | Joseph | lab 12½ da @ $1 - $12.50. lay 2d track |
| 1857-65 | Thomas | lab 27 da @ $1 - $27.00. NW Va RR, Rd Dept 2d s-div |
| 1857-66 | Garry, Washington | watch 30 da @ $1 - $30.00. Rd Dept main stem 17th s-div |
| 1855-26 | Garvain, George | lab 22 3/4 da @ $1 - $22.75. Rd Dept main stem 18th s-div |
| 1857-83 | Garvey, C. | clean eng 2 da @ $1 - $2.00. Trans Dept main stem |
| 1857-82 | John | lab 5 da @ $1.12 - $5.60. grad, Board Tree Tun |
| 1857-86 | Patrick | lab 24 da @ $1.12 - $27.00. grad, Board Tree Tun |
| 1857-18 | William | lab 24½ da @ $1 - $24.50. grad, McGuire's Tun |
| 1855-64 | Gary, A. C. | pass train brak 10 da @ $33.35 per mo - $11.10. w end |
| 1855-64 | C. R. | mason 24 da @ $1.75 - $42.00. Rd Way Dept |
| 1855-66 | D. R. | supv @ $75 per mo - $75.00. Rd Way Dept |
| 1857-91 | " " | supt carp @ $20 per mo - $20.00. Rd Way Dept |
| 1857-92 | " " | horse hire 25 da @ $2 - $50.00. grad, Welling Tun |
| 1857-92 | " " | 2 horses hire 50 da @ $1 - $50.00. grad, Littleton Tun |
| 1857-91 | David R. | 3 horses hire 71 da @ $1 - $71.00. grad, Littleton Tun |
| 1857-85 | James | supt @ $75 per mo - $75.00. grad, Littleton Tun |
| 1857-94 | Michael | watch 25 da @ $1 - $25.00. grad, Board Tree Tun |
| 1857-74 | Owen | lab 20¼ da @ $1 - $20.25. quarry & haul stone for Board Tree & Littleton Tun |
| 1855-66 | Patrick | lab 23 da @ $1.12 - $25.85. repair bridges &c |
| 1857-25 | Gaskins, William | carp @ $50 per mo - $50.00. Rd Way Dept |
| 1857-109 | Gatch, Charles | ton brak 11½ da @ $40 per mo - $18.40. 2d div |
| 1855-54 | Gates, Wendel | mach 17 da @ $1.55 - $26.35. Mach Dept, Balto |
| 1855-45 | William | fore 25 da @ $1.25 - $31.25. Rd Dept main stem 8th s-div |
| 1857-89 | Gatewood, Jesse | fore 21 3/4 da @ $1.25 - $27.20. Rd Way Dept |
| 1855-84 | Gatzel, Thos. | brak 13 da @ $1 - $13.00. grad, Welling Tun |
| 1857-63 | Gaughan, Frank | mach (includ boil mkr, work sht iron, &c) 23½ da @ $1.65 - $38.35. Mach Dept |
| 1857-90 | John | lab 22 3/4 da @ $1 - $22.75. Rd Dept main stem 16th s-div |
| 1857-91 | Patrick | blast 23⅔ da @ $1.12 - $26.15. grad, Welling Tun |
| 1857-91 | " | lab 14 3/4 da @ $1 - $14.75. grad, Welling Tun |
| 1857-100 | Gauhen, Michael | lab 18½ da @ $1 - $18.50. NW Va RR, Rd Dept 5th s-div |

| ID | Name | Details |
|---|---|---|
| 1855-14 | Gaukey, John | brak 15¾ da @ $40 per mo - $25.40. Trans Dept main stem |
| 1857-89 | Gavin, John | lab 9 da @ $1.12 - $10.15. grad, Welling Tun |
| 1857-94 | " | lab 4½ da @ $1 - $4.50. quarry & haul stone for Board Tree & Littleton Tun |
| 1857-82 | Thomas | lab 22 da @ $1.12 - $24.75. grad, Board Tree Tun |
| 1855-34 | Gavner, David | lab 24 da @ $30 per mo - $30.00. Trans Dept main stem |
| 1855-34 | Gavrey, Joseph | lab 24 da @ $30 per mo - $30.00. Trans Dept main stem |
| 1857-51 | Gawire, John | lab 25 da @ $1 - $25.00. Rd Dept main stem 5th s-div |
| 1857-21 | Gawire, William | ton conduc 18½ da @ $50 per mo - $37.00. Rd Dept main stem 5th s-div |
| 1857-137 | Geahauf, John | carp 18¾ da @ $1.40 - $25.55. Mach Dept, Cumb |
| 1855-84 | Geddes, Richard | help 24½ da @ $1 - $24.25. Mach Dept |
| 1855-11 | Geltion, E. | conduc & brak 14½ da @ $40 per mo - $26.65. Trans Dept main stem |
| 1855-42 | " P. | lab 20½ da @ $1 - $20.50. Rd Way Dept |
| 1857-53 | Patrick | lab 21 3/4 da @ $1 - $21.75. Rd Dept main stem 7th s-div |
| 1857-124 | Gemwell, Matthew | fore boil mkr @ $55 per mo - $55.00. Mach Dept, Martinsburg |
| 1855-86 | General, N. | mach @ $55 per mo - $55.00. Mach Dept |
| 1857-70 | George, Ezekiel | help 20½ da @ $1.12 - $23.05. Mt Clare sta, Balto |
| 1855-33 | Gephart, O. C. | clk 28 da @ $40 per mo - $40.00. Trans Dept main stem |
| 1857-14 | " | clk 30 da @ $50 per mo - $50.00. Cumb |
| 1857-32 | Summerfield | ton fire 18 da @ $1.75 - $31.50. 2d div |
| 1857-100 | Geraughty, Patrick | lab 24 da @ $1. - $24.00. NW Va RR, Rd Dept 5th s-div |
| 1857-103 | " | lab 20 da @ $1 - $20.00. NW Va R? Tun |
| 1857-104 | " | miner 15 da @ $1 - $15.00. NW Va RR Tun |
| 1857-126 | Gerhling, Ferdinand | clean eng 29 da @ $1.15 - $33.35. Mach Dept, Martinsburg |
| 1855-59 | Gerkin, Frederick | fore 24 da @ $1.25 - $30.00. Rd Way Dept |
| 1855-53 | Gerling, Henry | fore 24 da @ $1.25 - $30.00. Rd Way Dept |
| 1855-87 | Germon, John | help 24 da @ $1 - $24.00. Mach Dept |
| 1857-75 | " | fire 6⅞ da @ $33 per mo - $7.95. ballast train for 2d track |
| 1857-31 | Gerrges, E. M. | ton fire 11½ da @ $1.75 - $20.10. 1st div |
| 1855-82 | Gershner, Charles | lab 26⅔ da @ $1.15 - $30.45. Mach Dept |
| 1857-11 | Gethart, August | lab 24 da @ $30 per mo - $28.80. Locust Pt |
| 1857-11 | Getteir, John | lab 23 3/4 da @ $1 - $23.75. Locust Pt |
| 1857-118 | Gettele, David | blksmith help 16½ da @ $1 - $16.50. Mach Dept, Balto |
| 1857-28 | Gettell, Louis | ton eng'man 17¼ da @ $3 - $51.75. 1st div |
| 1857-34 | Gettev, George | ton fire 24 da @ $1.75 - $42.00. 4th div |
| 1857-111 | Gettier, Geo. | mach help 13½ da @ $1.15 - $15.50. Mach Dept, Balto |
| 1855-76 | | help 24 da @ $1.15 - $27.60. Mach Dept |

| | | |
|---|---|---|
| 1855-95 | Gettings, Edward | mould 17 3/4 da @ $1.60 - $28.40. Mach Dept |
| 1855-22 | Gettle, David | fire 15 da @ $1.75 - $26.25. Trans Dept main stem |
| 1857-40 | " | ton eng'man 6¾ da @ $3 -$18.75. NW Va rd, Parkersburg sta |
| 1857-125 | " Henry | lab 19½ da @ $1 - $19.25. Mach Dept, Martinsburg |
| 1855-28 | " L. | reg eng 16½ da @ $1.50 - $24.75. Trans Dept main stem |
| 1855-33 | Getzandanner, C. | disp 28 da @ $50 per mo - $50.00. Trans Dept main stem |
| 1855-11 | Getzandauner, C. | conduc & brak 1 da @ $40 per mo - $1.65. Trans Dept main stem |
| 1857-121 | Getzendamer, Jacob | car trim help 17½ da @ $1.15 - $20.10. Mach Dept, Balto |
| 1855-80 | Getzendaner, L. | carp 5½ da @ $1.50 - $8.25. Mach Dept |
| 1857-65 | Gibbin, Michael | watch 29 da @ $1 - $29.00. Rd Dept main stem 17th s-div |
| 1855-60 | Gibbins, John | lab 25 da @ $1 - $25.00. Rd Way Dept |
| 1857-66 | Gibbons, John | lab 25½ da @ $1 - $25.50. Rd Dept main stem 18th s-div |
| 1857-110 | " | mach 15 3/4 da @ $1.50 - $23.60. Mach Dept, Balto |
| 1855-61 | " Mike | lab 20 3/4 da @ $1 - $20.75. Rd Way Dept |
| 1855-61 | " Patrick | lab 20 da @ $1 - $20.00. Rd Way Dept |
| 1857-66 | " " | fore 25 da @ $1.25 - $31.25. Rd Dept main stem 18th s-div |
| 1857-40 | Gibbs, W. | ton brak 29 da @ $40 per mo - $46.40. NW Va rd, Parkersburg sta |
| 1857-64 | Giblin, John | lab 19½ da @ $1 - $19.50. Rd Dept main stem 17th s-div |
| 1855-60 | " M. | lab 24 da @ $1 - $24.00. Rd Way Dept |
| 1857-101 | " Patrick | lab 21 da @ $1 - $21.00. NW Va RR ballast train |
| 1857-83 | Gibling, Patrick | lab 24½ da @ $1.12 - $27.55. grad, Board Tree Tun |
| 1857-72 | Gibson, James | carp 20¼ da @ $1.50 - $30.40. Cumb depot |
| 1855-17 | " Jeremiah | ton eng'man 8 da @ $3 - $24.00. Trans Dept main stem |
| 1855-14 | " John | brak 2 da @ $1.65 - $3.35. Trans Dept main stem |
| 1855-9 | " " | conduc 1 da @ $50 per mo - $2.10. Trans Dept main stem |
| 1857-123 | " John H. | mach 20 3/4 da @ $1.65 - $34.25. Mach Dept, Martinsburg |
| 1857-127 | " Joseph | mach 10 3/4 da @ $2 - $21.50. Mach Dept, Piedmont |
| 1857-24 | " Thomas H. | ton brak 20½ da @ $40 per mo - $32.80. 1st div |
| 1855-80 | Gidleman, Frederick | carp 21¾ da @ $1.60 - $38.80. Mach Dept |
| 1855-4 | Gilbert, E. E. | collec 28 da @ $41.65 per mo - $41.65. Trans Dept, Wash br |
| 1857-37 | " " | clk 30 da @ $41.65 per mo - $41.65. Wash br rd, Wash city sta |
| 1855-4 | " G. F. | clk 28 da @ $50 per mo - $50.00. Trans Dept, Wash br |
| 1857-37 | " " | clk 30 da @ $62.50 per mo - $62.50. Wash br rd, Wash city sta |
| 1855-14 | " James | brak 19¾ da @ $40 per mo - $32.10. Trans Dept main stem |
| 1857-21 | " Thomas | ton conduc 7¾ da @ $50 per mo - $14.50. 1st div |
| 1855-64 | Gilboy, Mart. | lab 23½ da @ $1 - $23.50. Rd Way Dept |

B & O RR EMPLOYEES    155

| Ref | Name | Details |
|---|---|---|
| 1857-24 | Gilder, L. L. | ton brak 19 da @ $40 per mo - $30.40. 1st div |
| 1857-11 | Giles, George W. | lab 24 da @ $30 per mo - $28.80. Locust Pt |
| 1857-11 | " | Sun watch 5 da @ $1.15 - $5.75. Locust Pt |
| 1857-98 | Gilfoy, Patrick | lab 23 3/4 da @ $1 - $23.75. NW Va RR, Rd Dept 3d s-div |
| 1857-101 | Gilgallin, Anthony | lab 23½ da @ $1 - $23.50. NW Va RR ballast train |
| 1857-20 | Gill, Lewis R. | pass fire 1½ da @ $40 per mo - $2.00. 4th div |
| 1857-34 | " | ton fire 1½ da @ $1.75 - $2.60. 4th div |
| 1857-18 | Samuel | pass train brak 30 da @ $33.35 per mo - $33.35. w end |
| 1857-48 | Shederick | lab 24¼ da @ $1 - $24.25. Rd Dept main stem 2d s-div |
| 1855-47 | Thomas | lab 19½ da @ $1 - $19.50. Rd Way Dept |
| 1857-63 | Gillbay, John | watch 30 da @ $1 - $30.00. Rd Dept main stem 16th s-div |
| 1855-50 | Gillboy, John | watch cuts 32 da @ $1 - $32.00. Rd Way Dept |
| 1855-55 | Gillegan, Patrick | lab 19 3/4 da @ $1 - $19.75. Rd Way Dept |
| 1857-15 | Gillegan, James | unload coal &c 26 da @ $1 - $26.00. Cameron sta |
| 1855-30 | Gillen, James | prepar fuel 28 da @ $30 per mo - $30.00. Trans Dept main stem |
| 1855-122 | " | tend fill @ $30 per mo - $30.00. Mach Dept, Balto |
| 1855-41 | Gillessen, Jno. | lab 20¼ da @ $1 - $20.25. Rd Way Dept |
| 1857-112 | Gillespe, F. A. | mach app 20 da @ $.65 - $13.00. Mach Dept, Balto |
| 1855-60 | Gillespie, Edward | lab 19¼ da @ $1 - $19.50. Rd Way Dept |
| 1855-68 | Robert | lab 22 3/4 da @ $1 - $22.75. Rd Way Dept |
| 1855-60 | Patrick | lab 18 3/4 da @ $1 - $18.75. Rd Way Dept |
| 1855-61 | Gilligan, James | lab 11½ da @ $1 - $11.50. Rd Way Dept |
| 1857-47 | Michael | lab 28 da @ $1 - $28.00. Rd Dept main stem 1st s-div |
| 1857-98 | Gillin, Thomas | watch 30 da @ $1 - $30.00. NW Va RR, Rd Dept 3d s-div |
| 1857-9 | Gillingham, Edw. | disp 30 da @ $50 per mo - $50.00. Mt Clare sta |
| 1855-24 | George | pass & bur driv 26 da @ $30 per mo - $32.50. Trans Dept main stem |
| 1857-112 | " | mach app 16½ da @ $.55 - $8.95. Mach Dept, Balto |
| 1857-21 | " | ton conduc 11½ da @ $50 per mo - $23.00. 1st div |
| 1857-110 | Henry | mach 16½ da @ $1.55 - $25.60. Mach Dept, Balto |
| 1855-58 | Gillmore, John | lab 24½ da @ $1 - $24.50. Rd Way Dept |
| 1857-60 | " | lab 31½ da @ $1 - $31.50. Rd Dept main stem 13th s-div |
| 1855-58 | M. | fore 24 da @ $1.25 - $30.00. Rd Way Dept |
| 1857-60 | Michael | fore 31 da @ $1 - $38.75. Rd Dept main stem 13th s-div |
| 1857-85 | Thomas | lab 10 3/4 da @ $1 - $10.75. grad, Board Tree Tun |
| 1857-134 | Gilmore, A. N. | mach 17⅞ da @ $1.75 - $30.20. Mach Dept, Wheeling |
| 1857-104 | Gilroy, Thomas | miner 23½ da @ $1.12 - $26.45. NW Va RR Tun |

## B & O RR EMPLOYEES

| | | |
|---|---|---|
| 1857-89 | Ginley, Michael | lab 14½ da @ $1.12 - $16.30. grad, Welling Tun |
| 1857-136 | Girkin, John | clean eng 29½ da @ $1 - $29.50. Mach Dept, Wheeling |
| 1857-50 | Gisebert, Cristian | lab 7 da @ $1 - $7.00. Rd Dept main stem 4th s-div |
| 1857-114 | Gittings, Edward | iron mould 17 3/4 da @ $1.60 - $28.40. Mach Dept, Balto |
| 1857-84 | Givins, Thomas | lab 23½ da @ $1.12 - $26.15. grad, Board Tree Tun |
| 1857-55 | Glancer, Henry | lab 24 da @ $1 - $24.00. Rd Dept main stem 9th s-div |
| 1855-58 | Glancey, John | lab 23 da @ $1 - $23.00. Rd Way Dept |
| 1857-96 | Glancey, Michael | lab 22½ da @ $1 - $22.50. NW Va RR, Rd Dept 1st s-div |
| 1857-133 | Glanman, Thomas | blksmith 24½ da @ $1.50 - $36.75. Mach Dept, Fetterman |
| 1857-104 | Glasby, Anthony | lab 23 da @ $1.12 - $25.90. NW Va RR Tun |
| 1857-104 | Glasby, Robert | lab 20½ da @ $1.12 - $23.05. NW Va RR Tun |
| 1855-74 | Glason, Jno. | lab 23 da @ $1 - $23.00. Rd Way Dept |
| 1855-74 | Glason, Michl. | lab 9 da @ $1 - $9.00. Rd Way Dept |
| 1857-9 | Glass, Emory | asst 30 da @ $35 per mo - $35.00. hp exp, Balto |
| 1857-136 | Glasser, Jacob | clean eng 20½ da @ $1 - $20.25. Mach Dept, Wheeling |
| 1857-33 | Gleason, James | ton fire 23 3/4 da @ $1.75 - $41.55. 3d div |
| 1857-75 | Gleeson, John | lab 17 da @ $1.15 - $19.40. ballast train for 2d track |
| 1857-89 | Glen, Patrick | lab 11 da @ $1.12 - $12.35. grad, Welling Tun |
| 1857-63 | Glenan, Edward | lab 14½ da @ $1 - $14.50. Rd Dept main stem 16th s-div |
| 1855-17 | Glenn, E. B. | ton eng'man 7 3/4 da @ $2.50 - $19.35. Trans Dept main stem |
| 1857-30 | Glenn, Elijah B. | ton eng'man 26 da @ $3 - $78.00. 3d div |
| 1857-92 | " Hugh | lab 25½ da @ $1 - $25.50. grad, Littleton Tun |
| 1857-68 | " John | lab 17¼ da @ $1 - $17.25. Rd Dept main stem 19th s-div |
| 1857-64 | " Michael | lab 26 da @ $1 - $26.00. Rd Dept main stem 17th s-div |
| 1857-127 | " Patrick | mach help 19¼ da @ $1 - $19.25. Mach Dept, Piedmont |
| 1855-80 | " W. R. | carp 24 da @ $1.60 - $38.40. Mach Dept |
| 1855-51 | Glennon, John | lab @ $31 per mo - $31.00. Rd Way Dept |
| 1857-52 | Gletner, David | lab 17½ da @ $1 - $17.50. Rd Dept main stem 6th s-div |
| 1857-104 | Glinn, John | miner 18 da @ $1 - $18.00. NW Va RR Tun |
| 1857-91 | Glispy, Patrick | lab 12 da @ $1 - $12.00. grad, Welling Tun |
| 1857-99 | Glispy, William | watch 30 da @ $1 - $30.00. NW Va RR, Rd Dept 4th s-div |
| 1855-46 | Gluck, John | blksmith 24 da @ $1.25 - $30.00. Rd Way Dept |
| 1855-70 | Goan, John | lab 16¼ da @ $1 - $16.25. Rd Way Dept |
| 1855-70 | " Patrick | lab 14 3/4 da @ $1 - $14.75. Rd Way Dept |
| 1857-121 | Gobright, J. | car trim 8½ da @ $1.65 - $14.00. Mach Dept, Balto |
| 1855-74 | Godman, Samuel | spik 28 da @ $1.05 - $29.40. Rd Way Dept |

B & O RR EMPLOYEES  157

| ID | Name | Description |
|---|---|---|
| 1857-95 | Godman, Samuel | nail 30 da @ $1.05 - $31.50. Wash br, Rd Dept |
| 1855-27 | Goff, James | clean eng 22 da @ $1 - $22.00. Trans Dept main stem |
| 1855-4 | " | eng'man 32 da @ $2.50 - $80.00. Trans Dept, Wash br |
| 1857-126 | Goheen, Michael | prepar fuel 10 da @ $1 - $10.00. Mach Dept, Martinsburg |
| 1855-41 | Gohein, M. | lab 19½ da @ $1 - $19.50. Rd Way Dept |
| 1855-59 | Golaher, John | lab 14 3/4 da @ $1 - $14.75. Rd Way Dept |
| 1857-39 | Gold, C. W. | pass conduc 30 da @ $50 per mo - $50.00. NW Va rd, Parkersburg sta |
| 1855-10 | " Charles | conduc & brak 19¼ da @ $50 per mo - $40.10. Trans Dept main stem |
| 1857-82 | Golden, Harman | bricklay 12 3/4 da @ $2 - $25.50. grad, Board Tree Tun |
| 1857-99 | " Michael | watch 30 da @ $1 - $30.00. NW Va RR, Rd Dept 4th s-div |
| 1855-11 | " Samuel | conduc & brak 7½ da @ $50 per mo - $16.60. Trans Dept main stem |
| 1855-22 | " William | fire ½ da @ $1.75 - $.85. Trans Dept main stem |
| 1855-29 | " | ton eng'man 19 3/4 da @ $3 - $59.25. 2d div |
| 1857-73 | Goldsborough, Thos. | lab 14½ da @ $1 - $14.25. repair bridges &c |
| 1857-139 | Gole, Luther | mach app 26½ da @ $.45 - $11.90. NW Va RR, Mach Dept, Parkersburg |
| 1857-54 | Golleher, James | lab 21½ da @ $1 - $21.50. Rd Dept main stem 8th s-div |
| 1855-15 | Goltry, C. | pass eng'man 2 da @ $2.50 - $5.00. Trans Dept main stem |
| 1855-22 | " Moore | fire 13½ da @ $1.75 - $23.60. Trans Dept main stem |
| 1855-24 | Good, Frederick | pass & bur driv 25 da @ $30 per mo - $31.25. Trans Dept main stem |
| 1855-77 | Goodman, J. | mach 25 3/4 da @ $1.60 - $41.20. Mach Dept |
| 1857-110 | " Jacob | mach 27½ da @ $1.60 - $44.00. Mach Dept, Balto |
| 1857-29 | Goodrich, Leroy | ton eng'man 20¼ da @ $3 - $60.75. 2d div |
| 1857-91 | Goodyard, C. | bricklay 15 da @ $2 - $30.00. grad, Littleton Tun |
| 1855-69 | Gordan, M. | lab 25 da @ $1 - $25.05. Rd Way Dept |
| 1857-127 | Gorden, Charles | mach 24 da @ $1.70 - $40.80. Mach Dept, Piedmont |
| 1857-91 | Gordon, A. B. | fore 26 da @ $2.25 - $58.50. grad, Littleton Tun |
| 1857-7 | " L. S. | gen frt agt @ $208.35 per mo. Gen Frt Agt Ofc |
| 1855-14 | " William | brak 19½ da @ $40 per mo - $32.50. Trans Dept main stem |
| 1855-27 | " | ton brak 17 da @ $40 per mo - $27.20. Board Tree Tun |
| 1857-26 | " William H. | ton brak 6 da @ $40 per mo - $9.60. 3d & 4th div |
| 1855-11 | Gore, C. F. | conduc & brak 16½ da @ $40 per mo - $27.10. Trans Dept main stem |
| 1857-134 | " Charles F. | mach 32 da @ $1.60 - $51.20. Mach Dept, Wheeling |
| 1857-118 | " Jacob | blksmith app 24 3/4 da @ $.55 - $13.60. Mach Dept, Balto |
| 1857-116 | " Phil. | blksmith 23 3/4 da @ $1.85 - $43.90. Mach Dept, Balto |
| 1855-60 | Gorety, Thomas | lab 22 da @ $1 - $22.00. Rd Way Dept |
| 1855-46 | Goring, C. | lab 24 da @ $1 - $24.00. Rd Way Dept |

| | | |
|---|---|---|
| 1855-85 | Gorman, Edw. | help 23 da @ $1.15 - $26.45. Mach Dept |
| 1857-117 | Henry | blksmith help 18 da @ $1 - $18.00. Mach Dept, Balto |
| 1855-11 | John | conduc & brak 14 da @ $40 per mo - $23.35. Trans Dept main stem |
| 1855-82 | " | lab 24 da @ $1.15 - $27.60. Mach Dept |
| 1857-68 | Martin | watch 30 da @ $1 - $30.00. Rd Dept main stem 19th s-div |
| 1857-80 | Michael | lab 4¼ da @ $1 - $4.25. lay 2d track |
| 1857-65 | " | lab 4½ da @ $1 - $4.50. Rd Dept main stem 17th s-div |
| 1855-68 | Patrick | lab 20 3/4 da @ $1 - $20.75. Rd Way Dept |
| 1855-74 | " | lab 15 da @ $1 - $15.00. Rd Way Dept |
| 1857-82 | " | lab 23¼ da @ $.75 - $17.45. grad, Board Tree Tun |
| 1857-83 | " | lab 20 da @ $1.12 - $22.50. grad, Board Tree Tun |
| 1857-84 | Tarry | lab 26¼ da @ $1.12 - $29.55. grad, Board Tree Tun |
| 1857-61 | Gormely, Edward | lab 23½ da @ $1 - $23.50. Rd Dept main stem 14th s-div |
| 1857-96 | Gormly, Philip | lab 24½ da @ $1 - $24.50. NW Va RR, Rd Dept 1st s-div |
| 1855-75 | Gorney, Jno. | lab 24 da @ $1 - $24.00. Rd Way Dept |
| 1855-7 | Gorsuch, W. P. | pass conduc 28 da @ $62.50 per mo - $62.50. Trans Dept main stem |
| 1857-18 | Wm. P. | pass train conduc 30 da @ $75 per mo - $75.00 thr mail & exp |
| 1857-127 | Gorton, A. M. G. | clk @ $50 per mo - $50.00. Mach Dept, Piedmont |
| 1855-7 | W. A. | timekpr 28 da @ $50 per mo - $50.00. Trans Dept main stem |
| 1857-9 | William A. | timekpr 30 da @ $50 per mo - $50.00. Mt Clare sta |
| 1857-112 | Gosnell, Charles | mach app 20½ da @ $.65 - $13.35. Mach Dept, Balto |
| 1855-39 | D. | fore 24 da @ $1.25 - $30.00. Rd Way Dept |
| 1857-48 | David | lab 26 da @ $1 -$26.00. Rd Dept main stem 2d s-div |
| 1857-119 | F. M. | carp 18½ da @ $1.50 - $27.75. Mach Dept, Balto |
| 1857-24 | Peter | ton brak 21½ da @ $40 per mo - $34.40. 1st div |
| 1855-86 | U. S. | app 29½ da @ $.55 - $16.20. Mach Dept |
| 1857-73 | W. | carp 23 3/4 da @ $1.50 - $35.60. repair bridges &c |
| 1857-116 | W. S. | blksmith 16 3/4 da @$1.55 - $25.95. Mach Dept, Balto |
| 1857-24 | Walter | ton brak 19½ da @ $40 per mo -$31.20. 1st div |
| 1855-53 | Washington | carp 21¼ da @ $1.37½ da @ $29.20. Rd Way Dept |
| 1857-112 | William T. | mach app 20 da @ $.55 - $11.00. Mach Dept, Balto |
| 1855-34 | Gosselin, E. W. | store & oil kpr 24 da @ $1 - $24.00. Trans Dept main stem |
| 1857-10 | Goston, Robert | blksmith 25 da @ $32.50 - $32.50. op exp, Balto |
| 1857-131 | Goty, Charles | mach 18¼ da @ $1.50 -$27.35. Mach Dept, Grafton |
| 1857-108 | Goudy, John | mach 18¼ da @ $1.65 - $30.10. Mach Dept, Balto |
| 1855-11 | Gould, C. W. | conduc & brak 2¾ da @ $50 per mo -$4.70. Trans Dept main stem |

| | | |
|---|---|---|
| 1857-55 | Goving, Charles | lab 25 da @ $1 -$25.00. Rd Dept main stem 9th s-div |
| 1857-93 | Gowens, Patrick | smith help 20¼ da @ $1 - $20.25. quarry & haul stone for Board Tree & Littleton Tun |
| 1857-61 | Gower, Isaac | lab 29 da @ $1 -$29.00. Rd Dept main stem 14th s-div |
| 1855-81 | Grace, Daniel | lab 24½ da @ $1 - $24.50. Mach Dept |
| 1857-47 | Edmond | lab 24 da @ $1 - $24.00. Rd Dept main stem 1st s-div |
| 1855-74 | Edwd. | lab 21 3/4 da @ $1 - $21.75. Rd Way Dept |
| 1855-37 | James | lab 25¼ da @ $1 - $25.25. Rd Way Dept |
| 1857-46 | " | lab 24 da @ $1 - $24.00. Rd Dept main stem 1st s-div |
| 1855-55 | Grade, Frank | lab 6¼ da @ $1 - $6.25. Rd Way Dept |
| 1857-66 | Gradey, Michael | lab 22½ da @ $1 -$22.50. Rd Dept main stem 18th s-div |
| 1855-56 | Grady, Mart. | lab 13¼ da @ $1 - $13.25. Rd Way Dept |
| 1855-61 | Mike | lab 18 da @ $1 - $18.00. Rd Way Dept |
| 1855-28 | Patrick | prepar fuel 9½ da @ $1 - $9.50. Trans Dept main stem |
| 1855-49 | " | watch cuts 26 da @ $1 - $26.00. Rd Way Dept |
| 1857-129 | " | inspec cars @ $32 per mo - $32.00. Mach Dept, Piedmont |
| 1857-74 | " | lab 23 3/4 da @ $.90 - $21.35. repair bridges &c |
| 1855-79 | Graham, John | tin 26 da @ $1.72 - $44.70. Mach Dept |
| 1857-63 | Martin | lab 26 da @ $1 - $26.00. Rd Dept main stem 16th s-div |
| 1855-85 | William | blksmith 22¼ da @ $1.45 - $32.25. Mach Dept |
| 1855-57 | " | conduc 11¼ da @ $50 per mo - $21.65. Rd Way Dept |
| 1855-9 | " | conduc 8½ da @ $50 per mo - $17.70. Trans Dept main stem |
| 1857-23 | " | ton conduc 2 da @ $50 per mo - $4.00. 3d & 4th div |
| 1857-136 | Graley, James | clean eng 9 3/4 da @ $1 - $9.75. Mach Dept, Wheeling |
| 1857-112 | Granan, Bernard | mach app 22 3/4 da @ $.45 - $10.25. Mach Dept, Balto |
| 1857-118 | Granes, Walter | blksmith help 17 3/4 da @ $1.25 - $22.20. Mach Dept,Balto |
| 1857-88 | Graney, John | driv 27 da @ $1 - $27.00. grad, Welling Tun |
| 1857-84 | William | lab 22 da @ $1.12 - $24.75. grad, Board Tree Tun |
| 1857-136 | Granman, P. G. | mach 13½ da @ $1.60 - $21.60. Mach Dept, Cumb |
| 1855-89 | Grannon, P. G. | mach 18½ da @ $1.55 - $28.70. Mach Dept |
| 1855-43 | Grant, James | lab 17 da @ $1 - $17.00. Rd Way Dept |
| 1855-38 | " | nail 23 da @ $1.05 - $29.40. Rd Way Dept |
| 1855-eratta | " | nail - instead of 23, 28 da |
| 1857-82 | John | lab 24¼ da @ $1.12 - $27.30. grad, Board Tree Tun |
| 1855-93 | M. | mach 18 da @ $1.65 - $29.70. Mach Dept |
| 1857-127 | Malcolm | mach 28½ da @ $2 - $57.00. Mach Dept, Piedmont |
| 1855-53 | Richard | lab 17 da @ $1 - $17.00. Rd Way Dept |

| | | |
|---|---|---|
| 1855-43 | Grant, Robert | lab 17½ da @ $1 - $17.50. Rd Way Dept |
| 1855-43 | Graves, William | lab 22 da @ $1 - $22.00. Rd Way Dept |
| 1855-87 | Graves, B. F. | help 22 da @ $1 - $22.00. Mach Dept |
| 1855-44 | " Solomon | supv @ $45 per mo - $45.00. Rd Way Dept |
| 1857-61 | Graw, John O. | lab 25 da @ $1 - $25.00. Rd Dept main stem 14th s-div |
| 1857-35 | Gray, Elias | lab 21½ da @ $1 - $21.50. J. R. Shrode's wd train 4th div |
| 1857-27 | Gray, John F. | ton brak 20 da @ $40 per mo - $32.00. Board Tree Tun |
| 1857-23 | " " | ton conduc 6 da @ $1 - $12.00. Board Tree Tun |
| 1855-85 | " W. H. | help 20 da @ $1 - $20.00. Mach Dept |
| 1857-24 | " William H. | ton brak 19¼ da @ $40 per mo - $30.80. 1st div |
| 1855-55 | Grayham, Mart. | lab 21 da @ $1 - $21.00. Rd Way Dept |
| 1855-75 | Gready, Michl. | lab 23 da @ $1 - $23.00. Rd Way Dept |
| 1857-50 | Greedy, Michael | lab 30 da @ $1 - $30.00. Rd Dept main stem 5th s-div |
| 1857-81 | Greeley, Michael | lab 18 da @ $1.12 - $20.25. grad, Board Tree Tun |
| 1855-10 | Green, G. A. | conduc & brak 11 da @ $40 per mo - $18.35. Trans Dept main stem |
| 1855-10 | " Henry | conduc & brak 26 da @ $40 per mo - $43.35. Trans Dept main stem |
| 1857-21 | " " | ton conduc 26¾ da @ $45 per mo - $47.25. Camden sta |
| 1855-43 | " John | lab 4½ da @ $1 - $4.50. Rd Way Dept |
| 1855-52 | " Mart. | lab 15 da @ $1 - $15.00. Rd Way Dept |
| 1857-61 | " Matthew | lab 28 da @ $1 - $28.00. Rd Dept main stem 14th s-div |
| 1857-25 | " Michael | clean eng 25½ da @ $1.15 - $29.05. Trans Dept main stem |
| 1857-122 | " Mike | eng clean 29 da @ $1.15 - $33.35. Mach Dept, Balto |
| 1857-133 | " Miner | clean eng 3 da @ $1 - $3.00. Mach Dept, Fetterman |
| 1857-41 | " Minor | ton fire 7½ da @ $1.75 - $13.10. NW Va rd, Parkersburg sta |
| 1857-33 | " " | ton fire 1½ da @ $1.75 - $2.60. 3d div |
| 1857-9 | " Noah | coup 27½ da @ $30 per mo - $33.00. Mt Clare sta |
| 1855-76 | " Patrick | help 24 da @ $1.15 - $27.60. Mach Dept |
| 1855-68 | " " | lab 22 3/4 da @ $1 - $22.75. Rd Way Dept |
| 1855-87 | " " | lab 23 da @ $1 - $23.00. grad, McGuire's Tun |
| 1857-122 | " " | lab 25 da @ $1.25 - $1.25. Mach Dept, Balto |
| 1857-104 | " " | lab 25¾ da @ $1.12 - $28.40. NW Va RR Tun |
| 1857-10 | " Richard | bur reg 25 da @ $40 per mo - $40.00. hp exp, Balto |
| 1857-37 | " Robert | brak 20 da @ $33.33 per mo - $22.20. Wash br rd, Wash city sta |
| 1857-10 | Greener, Joseph | bur reg 25 da @ $40 per mo - $40.00. hp exp, Balto |
| 1855-65 | Greerman, H. | lab 14 da @ $1 - $14.00. Rd Way Dept |
| 1857-56 | Greenslade, John | lab 25½ da @ $1 - $25.50. Rd Dept main stem 10th s-div |

| | | | |
|---|---|---|---|
| 1855-67 | Greenwood, John | mason 20½ da @ $2 - $41.00. Rd Way Dept | |
| 1857-94 | Greeny, Michael | lab 12 da @ $1 - $12.00. quarry & haul stone for Board Tree & Littleton Tun | |
| 1857-34 | Greer, Charles | ton fire 9 da @ $1.75 - $15.75. Board Tree Tun | |
| 1857-31 | " | ton fire 1½ da @ $1.75 - $2.60. 1st div | |
| 1857-36 | " M. | tele oper 30 da @ $10 per mo - $10.00. Wheeling | |
| 1855-43 | Gregary, John | lab 24 da @ $1 - $24.00. Rd Way Dept | |
| 1855-43 | " Thomas | lab 24 da @ $1 - $24.00. Rd Way Dept | |
| 1855-51 | Gregg, Samuel | lab @ $17.50 per mo - $17.50. Rd Way Dept | |
| 1857-60 | " | watch 17½ da @ $1 - $17.50. Rd Dept main stem 13th s-div | |
| 1855-76 | " Thomas | help 26 3/4 da @ $1.15 - $30.75. Mach Dept | |
| 1857-112 | " Thomas C. | mach app 24 da @ $.45 - $10.80. Mach Dept, Balto | |
| 1855-33 | " Wm. | watch 28 da @ $35 per mo - $35.00. Trans Dept main stem | |
| 1857-99 | Gregory, Thomas | watch 30 da @ $1 - $30.00. NW Va RR, Rd Dept 4th s-div | |
| 1857-78 | Grey, Henry | lab 16 3/4 da @ $1 - $16.75. lay 2d track | |
| 1857-84 | Grier, Charles | fire 1 da @ $1.75 - $1.75. grad, Board Tree Tun | |
| 1857-87 | Griffin, Andrew | stone mason 21 3/4 da @ $2 - $43.50. grad, McGuire's Tun | |
| 1857-46 | " Dennis | lab 25 da @ $1 - $25.00. Rd Dept main stem 1st s-div | |
| 1857-110 | " George | mach 23½ da @ $1.75 - $40.70. Mach Dept, Balto | |
| 1857-122 | " J. | carter 17 3/4 da @ $1 - $17.75. Mach Dept, Balto | |
| 1857-110 | " " | mach 19¾ da @ $1.35 - $26.00. Mach Dept, Balto | |
| 1857-64 | " James | lab 15 da @ $1 - $15.00. Rd Way Dept | |
| 1857-139 | " " | clean eng 26½ da @ $1 - $26.50. NW Va RR, Mach Dept, Parkersburg | |
| 1855-26 | " " | clean eng 25 3/4 da @ $1 - $25.75. Trans Dept main stem | |
| 1855-46 | " M. | lab 21½ da @ $1 - $21.50. Rd Way Dept | |
| 1855-61 | " " | lab 16½ da @ $1 - $16.50. Rd Way Dept | |
| 1857-100 | " Malichi | lab 22½ da @ $1 - $22.50. NW Va RR, Rd Dept 5th s-div | |
| 1855-57 | " Michael | lab 20½ da @ $1 - $20.50. Rd Way Dept | |
| 1857-59 | " " | nail 30 da @ $1.05 - $31.50. Rd Dept main stem 12th s-div | |
| 1855-76 | " Patrick | help 24 3/4 da @ $1 - $24.75. Mach Dept | |
| 1857-112 | " " | mach help 17 da @ $1 - $17.00. Mach Dept, Balto | |
| 1855-90 | " Thomas | mach 25½ da @ $1.75 - $44.50. Mach Dept | |
| 1857-87 | " William | stone mason 22 3/4 da @ $2 - $45.50. grad, McGuire's Tun | |
| 1857-132 | Griffith, Charles | clean eng 29¾ da @ $1 - $29.25. Mach Dept, Grafton | |
| 1855-35 | " M. R. | disp of trains 28 da @ $50 per mo - $50.00. Trans Dept main stem | |
| 1857-14 | " " " | disp 30 da @ $50 per mo - $50.00. Newburg sta | |
| 1857-41 | " W. | ton fire 25 da @ $33.35 per mo - $33.35. NW Va rd, Parkersburg sta | |

| | | | |
|---|---|---|---|
| 1855-5 | Griffith, W. F. | ton fire 5 da @ $33.33 per mo - $6.95. Trans Dept, Wash br |
| 1855-22 | " Wm. F. | fire 5½ da @ $1.75 - $9.60. Trans Dept main stem |
| 1855-37 | Grifford, John | lab 24½ da @ $1 - $24.50. Rd Way Dept |
| 1857-8 | Grigg, William | watch 30 da @ $35 per mo - $35.00. Camden sta |
| 1857-129 | Grim, Charles | carp 14 3/4 da @ $1.50 - $22.10. Mach Dept, Piedmont |
| 1857-20 | " Frank | pass fire 27 da @ $40 per mo - $36.00. 3d div |
| 1855-92 | " Frederick | carp 24½ da @ $34.10. Mach Dept |
| 1857-129 | " George M. | carp 18 da @ $1.50 - $27.00. Mach Dept, Piedmont |
| 1857-129 | " Matthias | carp 19¼ da @ $1.50 - $22.85. Mach Dept, Piedmont |
| 1857-30 | " " | ton eng'man 1 da @ $2.50 - $2.50. 3d div |
| 1855-14 | " N. | ton fire 25½ da @ $1.75 - $44.60. 3d div |
| 1857-50 | " Samuel | brak 7 da @ $40 per mo - $11.65. Trans Dept main stem |
| 1857-10 | Grimes, Jahiel | lab 30 da @ $1.05 - $31.50. Rd Dept main stem 4th s-div |
| 1855-65 | " M. | stab'man 25 da @ $1 - $25.00. hp exp, Balto |
| 1857-57 | " Martin | lab 6 da @ $1 - $6.00. Rd Way Dept |
| 1855-65 | " P. | lab 25½ da @ $1 - $25.50. Rd Dept main stem 11th s-div |
| 1857-89 | " Philip | watch 28 da @ $1 - $28.00. Rd Way Dept |
| 1855-40 | Grin, Samuel | nail 28 da @ $1 - $30.00. grad, Welling Tun |
| 1855-76 | Grindle, William | watch 30 da @ $1.05 - $29.40. Rd Way Dept |
| | " | help 23 da @ $1.25 - $28.75. Mach Dept |
| 1857-111 | " | mach help 17½ da @ $1.25 - $21.90. Mach Dept, Balto |
| 1857-61 | Grineman, Henry | lab 27 da @ $1 - $27.00. Rd Dept main stem 14th s-div |
| 1857-10 | Grinsketter, W. | bur reg 25 da @ $40 per mo - $40.00. hp exp, Balto |
| 1857-23 | Grinstaff, William | ton conduc 25 da @ $60 per mo - $60.00. 3d & 4th div |
| 1855-7 | Griswold, H. E. | mess 28 da @ $12.50 per mo - $12.50. Trans Dept main stem |
| 1857-40 | Grodes, Elias | ton brak 5½ da @ $40 per mo - $8.80. NW Va rd, Parkersburg sta |
| 1855-4 | Groff, Jacob | bag mast 28 da @ $35.00 per mo - $35.00. Trans Dept, Wash br |
| 1857-37 | " " | bag mast 30 da @ $35 per mo - $35.00. Wash br rd, Wash city sta |
| 1857-116 | Groshent, Edward | brass mould 17 3/4 da @$1.45 - $25.75. Mach Dept, Balto |
| 1857-40 | Gross, Dennis | ton brak 28 da @ $40 per mo - $44.80. NW Va rd, Parkersburg sta |
| 1855-44 | " James | lab 11½ da @ $1 - $11.50. Rd Way Dept |
| 1855-14 | " John | brak 6 3/4 da @ $40 per mo - $11.25. Trans Dept main stem |
| 1857-41 | " " | ton fire 7 da @ $1.75 - $12.25. NW Va rd, Parkersburg sta |
| 1855-33 | " Martin | ton fire 8½ da @ $1.75 - $14.85. 3d div |
| 1855-22 | " Thomas | fire 6¼ da @ $1.75 - $10.95. Trans Dept main stem |
| 1857-55 | " " | lab 19½ da @ $1 - $19.50. Rd Dept main stem 9th s-div |

B & O RR EMPLOYEES    163

| Years | Name | Description |
|---|---|---|
| 1857-85 | Gross, William | bricklay 7½ da @ $2.25 - $16.85. grad, Board Tree Tun |
| 1857-87 | " | bricklay 18¼ da @ $2.25 - $41.05. grad, Welling Tun |
| 1857-125 | Grove, David | put away eng &c 27½ da @ $1.50 - $41.25. Mach Dept, Martinsburg |
| 1857-26 | " | ton brak 3 da @ $40 per mo - $4.80. 3d & 4th div |
| 1857-34 | Groves, Elias | ton brak 16 da @ $40 per mo - $25.60. 3d & 4th div |
| 1857-34 | Groves, Philip | ton fire 21 da @ $1.75 -$36.75. Board Tree Tun |
| 1855-43 | " | ton fire 1 3/4 da @ $1.75 - $3.05. 4th div |
| 1857-54 | S. | lab 22 da @ $1 - $22.00. Rd Way Dept |
| 1855-31 | Solomon | horse hire 30 da @ $.90 - $27.00. Rd Dept main stem 8th s-div |
| 1857-139 | " | supv @ $45 per mo - $45.00. Rd Dept main stem 8th s-div |
| 1857-40 | Crow, George W. | saw wd 66¾ cords @ $.35 - $32.15. Trans Dept main stem |
| 1855-8 | Grubb, W. | mach 27½ da @ $1.35 -$36.80. NW Va RR, Mach Dept, Parkersburg |
| 1857-8 | W. A. A. J. | ton brak 2 da @$40 per mo - $3.20. NW Va rd, Parkersburg sta |
| 1857-26 | W. A. J. J. | brak 28 da @ $33.35 per mo - $33.35. Trans Dept main stem |
| 1855-84 | William | rec clk 30 da @ $58.35 per mo - $58.35. Camden sta |
| 1857-115 | Gruber, Jacob | ton brak 21½ da @ $40 per mo - $34.40. 3d & 4th div |
| 1857-72 | " | mach (includ boil mkr, work sht iron, &c) 23 da @ $1.90 - $43.70. Mach Dept |
| 1855-25 | Gruly, George | boil mkr 16 da @ $1.90 - $30.40. Mach Dept, Balto |
| 1857-126 | Gruner, Joseph | lab 30 da @ $1.50 - $45.00. repair tele line |
| 1857-125 | Guffin, Michael | bur driv 24 da @ $40 per mo - $40.00. Trans Dept main stem |
| 1855-38 | Morris | clean eng 23¾ da @ $1 - $23.25. Mach Dept, Martinsburg |
| 1857-129 | Guffon, Patrick | lab 22½ da @ $1 - $22.50. Mach Dept, Martinsburg |
| 1857-35 | Guhugan, Henry | lab 20 da @ $1 - $20.00. Rd Way Dept |
| 1857-35 | Gul, George | clean eng 31 da @ $1 - $31.00. Mach Dept, Piedmont |
| 1857-64 | Philip | lab 13 da @ $1 -$13?00. Edwards wd train 3d & 4th div |
| 1855-14 | Gulloher, John | lab 13 da @ $1 - $13.00. Edwards wd train 3d & 4th div |
| 1857-27 | Gump, Jack | lab 26 da @ $1 - $26.00. Rd Dept main stem 17th s-div |
| 1857-50 | Jackson | brak 1 da @ $40 per mo - $1.65. Trans Dept main stem |
| 1857-131 | Gundloch, Conrad | ton brak 31 da @ $40 per mo - $49.60. Board Tree Tup |
| 1855-49 | Gundy, Morgan | lab 24½ da @ $1 - $24.50. Rd Dept main stem 4th s-div |
| 1857-62 | Gunson, John | boil kpr 3 da @ $1 - $3.00. Mach Dept, Grafton |
| 1855-14 | Gurkin, Frederick | watch cuts 28 da @ $1 - $28.00. Rd Way Dept |
| 1857-120 | Guseman, J. | fore 25 da @ $1.25 - $31.25. Rd Dept main stem 15th s-div |
| 1855-83 | Guyer, D. | conduc & brak 22 3/4 da @ $40 per mo - $37.90. Trans Dept main stem |
| | | carp 18 da @ $1.50 - $27.00. Mach Dept, Balto |
| | Gwinn, Charles | help 22 da @ $1.10 - $24.20. Mach Dept |

| | | |
|---|---|---|
| 1857-117 | Gwyn, Charles H. | blksmith 18 da @ $1.50 - $27.00. Mach Dept, Balto |
| 1857-121 | Haake, Wm. | paint 17 3/4 da @ $1.25 - $22.20. Mach Dept, Balto |
| 1855-54 | Hack, Ben. | track lay 6 da @ $1.12½ - $6.75. Rd Way Dept |
| 1857-51 | Henry | lab 25 da @ $1 - $25.00. Rd Dept main stem 5th s-div |
| 1857-10 | Hackerty, Michael | blksmith 25 da @ $32.50 per mo - $32.50. hp exp, Balto |
| 1855-24 | Patrick | pass & bur driv 24 da @ $32.20 - $32.20. Trans Dept main stem |
| 1857-10 | " | blksmith 25 da @ $32.50 per mo - $32.50. hp exp, Balto |
| 1855-38 | Hackett, J. | lab 21½ da @ $1 - $21.50. Rd Way Dept |
| 1857-48 | Joshua | lab 26 da @ $1 - $26.00. Rd Dept main stem 2d s-div |
| 1855-38 | M. | lab 24 da @ $1 - $24.00. Rd Way Dept |
| 1857-28 | Zachariah | ton eng'man 12½ da @ $3 - $37.50. 1st div |
| 1857-110 | Hackman, Lewis | mach 24½ da @ $1.50 - $36.75. Mach Dept, Balto |
| 1855-53 | Hackner, Henry | lab 14½ da @ $1 - $14.50. Rd Way Dept |
| 1857-10 | Haden, Michael | pio'r to pass trains 25 da @ $30 per mo - $30.00. hp exp, Balto |
| 1855-56 | Wm. | lab 2½ da @ $1.75 - $4.40. Rd Way Dept |
| 1855-76 | Hadenott, H. | mach 22¼ da @ $1.40 - $31.15. Mach Dept |
| 1855-64 | Hafer, Jacob | watch 28 da @ $1 - $28.00. Rd Way Dept |
| 1855-64 | Samuel | carp 20 da @ $1.25 - $25.00. Rd Way Dept |
| 1857-84 | " | lab 17⅓ da @ $1.12 - $19.40. grad, Board Tree Tun |
| 1857-34 | W. B. | ton fire 10 da @ $1.75 - $17.50. 4th div |
| 1855-69 | William | attend gashouse 25 da @ $1.25 - $31.25. Rd Way Dept |
| 1857-26 | William B. | ton brak 25½ da @ $40 per mo - $40.80. 3d & 4th div |
| 1857-139 | Haffer, Hiram | boil mkr 28¼ da @ $1.44 - $40.70. NW Va RR, Mach Dept, Parkersburg |
| 1855-11 | Haffner, D. | conduc & brak 5 da @ $50 per mo - $10.40. Trans Dept main stem |
| 1857-125 | David T. | carp 18 3/4 da @ $1.25 - $23.45. Mach Dept, Martinsburg |
| 1855-35 | J. H. | coup 25-1 ex da @ $30 per mo - $31.25. Trans Dept main stem |
| 1855-89 | Joseph | blksmith 29¼ da @ $1.70 - $49.70. Mach Dept |
| 1857-136 | " | fore blksmith @ $48 per mo - $48.00. Mach Dept, Cumb |
| 1857-65 | Hagan, Martin | lab 3½ da @ $1 - $3.50. Rd Dept main stem 17th s-div |
| 1855-45 | Thomas | fore 18¼ da @ $1.25 - $22.80. Rd Way Dept |
| 1857-16 | " | watch 30 da @ $1 - $30.00. Moundsville sta |
| 1857-31 | Wm. E. | ton fire 9 3/4 da @$1.75 - $17.05. 1st div |
| 1857-91 | Hagans, Peter | lab 19 da @ $1 -$19.00. grad, Welling Tun |
| 1857-91 | Thomas | lab 22¼ da @ $1 - $22.25. grad, Welling Tun |
| 1857-65 | Hagen, James | lab 11½ da @ $1 - $11.50. Rd Dept main stem 17th s-div |
| 1857-65 | Michael | lab 23½ da @ $1 - $23.50. Rd Dept main stem 17th s-div |
| 1857-87 | Hager, Albert F. | carp 20 3/4 da @ $1.75 -$36.30. grad, McGuire's Tun |

# B & O RR EMPLOYEES 165

| |  | |  |
|---|---|---|---|
| 1857-86 | Hager, George | lab 23 da @ $.75 - $17.25. grad, McGuire's Tun |
| 1857-63 | Hagerty, Michael | lab 24 da @ $1 - $24.00. Rd Dept main stem 16th s-div |
| 1857-75 | " Patrick | dril 24½ da @ $1.04 - $24.60. ballast train for 2d track |
| 1855-61 | Haggans, P. | lab 20½ da @ $1 - $20.50. Rd Way Dept |
| 1855-61 | Haggerty, James | lab 21½ da @ $1 - $21.50. Rd Way Dept |
| 1855-55 | " Michael | lab 24 da @ $1 - $24.00. Rd Way Dept |
| 1855-82 | Hagner, Jno. | mach 14½ da @ $1.50 - $21.75. Mach Dept |
| 1855-76 | " William | help 28 da @ $1.45 - $40.60. Mach Dept |
| 1857-110 | " " | mach 26 da @ $1.45 - $37.70. Mach Dept, Balto |
| 1857-51 | Hagney, Thomas | lab 26 da @ $1 - $26.00. Rd Dept main stem 5th s-div |
| 1857-79 | Hailin, Daniel | lab 26 3/4 da @$1 -$26.75. lay 2d track |
| 1855-48 | Haily, John | dril 20 3/4 da @ $1.10 - $22.80. Rd Way Dept |
| 1857-94 | Haines, Elijah | carp 12½ da @ $1.65 - $20.60. repair bridges |
| 1855-65 | Hains, Jacob | carp 10 da @ $1.70 - $17.00. Rd Way Dept |
| 1857-113 | " James | iron mould 16 3/4 da @$1.65 - $27.65. Mach Dept, Balto |
| 1855-77 | " Wm. | app 19 3/4 da @ $.75 - $14.80. Mach Dept |
| 1855-48 | Halagan, J. | tool boy 24 da @ $.50 - $12.00. Rd Way Dept |
| 1855-48 | " Patrick | blksmith 21½ da @ $1.25 - $26.85. Rd Way Dept |
| 1855-11 | Halbergett, J. | conduc & brak 12½ da @ $2 -$41.50. grad, McGuire's Tun |
| 1857-86 | Hale, Casper | stone mason 20 3/4 da @ $30 per mo - $15.60. Trans Dept main stem |
| 1855-74 | Haley, Jno. | lab 24 da @ $1 - $24.00. Rd Way Dept |
| 1855-73 | " Richd. | lab 24½ da @ $1 - $24.50. Rd Way Dept |
| 1857-86 | " Thomas | lab 22¼ da @ $1 - $22.25. grad, McGuire's Tun |
| 1857-86 | " " | lab 20¼ da @ $1 - $20.25. grad, McGuire's Tun |
| 1857-125 | Halferstay, George | carp 16 da @ $1 - $16.00. Mach Dept, Martinsburg |
| 1657-15 | Halkner, Henry | bag mast 30 da @ $1 - $30.00. Grafton sta |
| 1857-104 | Hall, A. E. | fore @ $60 per mo - $60.00. NW Va RR, build sand & wd houses |
| 1857-23 | " Albert | ton conduc 26½ da @ $50 per mo - $53.00. 3d & 4th div |
| 1857-100 | " Bush | watch 30 da @ $1 - $30.00. NW Va RR, Rd Dept 5th s-div |
| 1857-82 | " Daniel | lab 25 da @ $1.12 - $28.10. grad, Board Tree Tun |
| 1855-12 | " David | conduc & brak 8 3/4 da @ $40 per mo - $16.10. Trans Dept main stem |
| 1855-29 | " " | haul & saw firewd 5½ da @ $1 - $5.50. Trans Dept main stem |
| 1857-131 | " Festus | mach 25 da @ $1.35 - $33.75. Mach Dept, Grafton |
| 1855-39 | " Jesse | nail 28 da @ $1.05 - $29.40. Rd Way Dept |
| 1857-49 | " " | nail 30 da @ $1.05 - $31.50. Rd Dept main stem 3d s-div |
| 1855-56 | " William | eng'man 11¼ da @ $3 - $33.75. Rd Way Dept |

166  B & O RR EMPLOYEES

| ID | Name | Details |
|---|---|---|
| 1855-17 | Hall, William | ton eng'man 11 da @ $3 - $33.00. Trans Dept main stem |
| 1857-115 | " | pat mkr 16 3/4 da @ $1.60 - $26.80. Mach Dept, Balto |
| 1857-30 | " | ton eng'man 2 da @ $3 - $6.00. 3d div |
| 1857-24 | Haller, Samuel | ton brak 19¾ da @ $40 per mo - $30.80. 1st div |
| 1857-58 | Halpenny, Thomas | watch 30 da @ $1 - $30.00. Rd Dept main stem 11th s-div |
| 1857-49 | Halpeny, M. | watch cuts 28 da @ $1 - $28.00. Rd Way Dept |
| 1855-49 | Halpins, James | fore 25 da @ $1.25 - $31.25. Rd Dept main stem 5th s-div |
| 1857-50 | Halstine, J. H. | dry sand 30 da @ $25 per mo - $25.00. Rowlesburg sta |
| 1857-44 | Halton, Owen | lab 20 3/4 da @ $1 - $20.75. lay 2d track |
| 1857-80 | Halvy, Martin | lab 14 da @ $1 - $14.00. Rd Dept main stem 11th s-div |
| 1857-57 | Hambaker, John | carp 24 da - $33.75. Mach Dept |
| 1855-92 | Hambleton, Wesley | blksmith 23 da @ $2.25 - $51.75. Mach Dept, Balto |
| 1857-117 | Hamblin, James | lab 22 da @ $1 - $22.00. Rd Way Dept |
| 1857-57 | Hamer, H. H. | lab 5 da @ $1 - $5.00. NW Va rd, Athey's wd train |
| 1857-41 | Hamill, James P. | help 24 3/4 da @ $1 - $24.75. Mach Dept |
| 1855-91 | Hamilton, C. M. | lab 20 da @ $1 - $20.00. Rd Way Dept |
| 1855-42 | Hamilton, Charles M. | lab 25 da @ $1 - $25.00. Rd Dept main stem 7th s-div |
| 1857-53 | Hugh | bricklay 11 3/4 da @ $2 - $23.50. Rd Way Dept |
| 1855-71 | John | bur driv 24 da @ $30 per mo - $30.00. Trans Dept main stem |
| 1855-25 | " | fore 18 da @ $1.25 - $18.00. Rd Way Dept |
| 1855-42 | " | fore 24 da @ $1.25 - $30.00. Rd Dept main stem 7th s-div |
| 1857-53 | Michael | lab 25 da @ $1.12 - $28.10. grad, Board Tree Tun |
| 1857-84 | R. | lab 20 da @ $1 - $20.00. Rd Way Dept |
| 1855-61 | S. | lab 24 da @ $30 per mo - $30.00. Trans Dept main stem |
| 1855-32 | Samuel | lab 24 da @ $28 per mo - $28.00. Benwood sta |
| 1857-16 | T. | lab 24 da @ $30 per mo - $30.00. Trans Dept main stem |
| 1855-32 | Thomas | watch 30 da @ $30 per mo - $30.00. frt transfer force at Bellaire, opp Benwood |
| 1857-17 | W. | mach 27¾ da @ $1.70 - $46.30. Mach Dept |
| 1855-86 | Washington | ton eng'man 18 da @ $2.50 - $45.00. Trans Dept main stem |
| 1855-19 | " | ton eng'man 24 da @ $3 - $72.00. Board Tree Tun |
| 1857-30 | " | ton eng'man 4 da @ $3 - $12.00. 4th div |
| 1857-30 | William L. | mach 26½ da @ $1.70 - $45.05. Mach Dept, Martinsburg |
| 1857-123 | Hammer, James | ton brak 15½ da @ $40 per mo - $24.80. 1st div |
| 1857-24 | Hammon, Conrad | lab 19 3/4 da @ $1 - $19.75. Rd Dept main stem 7th s-div |
| 1857-53 | George | iron mould 11 da @ $1.65 - $18.25. Mach Dept, Grafton |
| 1857-132 | Jacob | lab 24 da @ $1 - $24.00. Rd Dept main stem 7th s-div |
| 1857-53 | | |

| | | |
|---|---|---|
| 1857-36 | Hammond, C. A. | tele oper 30 da @ $40 per mo - $40.00. Grafton |
| 1855-90 | George | help 20 da @ $1 - $20.00. Mach Dept |
| 1857-20 | " | pass fire 10 da @ $40 per mo - $13.35. 2d div |
| 1857-33 | " | ton fire 1 da @ $1.75 - $1.75. 3d div |
| 1855-80 | Hammondtree, Wm. | paint 23 da @ $1.45 - $33.35. Mach Dept |
| 1857-121 | Hamontree, Wm. H. | paint 13¼ da @ $1.45 - $19.20. Mach Dept, Balto |
| 1857-27 | Hampton, Jesse | ton brak 24 da @ $40 per mo - $38.40. Board Tree Tun |
| 1857-26 | " | ton brak 1 da @ $40 per mo - $1.60. 3d & 4th div |
| 1857-23 | " | ton conduc 10½ da @ $50 per mo - $21.00. Board Tree Tun |
| 1857-91 | Hanahan, Anthony | lab 22½ da @ $1 - $22.50. grad, Welling Tun |
| 1855-61 | Hanaker, John | lab 19 da @ $1 - $19.00. Rd Way Dept |
| 1855-72 | Hand, Henry | help 11¼ da @ $1.12½ - $12.65. Rd Way Dept |
| 1855-70 | Thomas | lab 16¼ da @ $1 - $16.25. Rd Way Dept |
| 1857-85 | " | lab 7½ da @ $1.12 - $8.45. grad, Board Tree Tun |
| 1857-87 | " | lab 18¼ da @ $1.12 - $20.55. grad, Welling Tun |
| 1855-30 | William | prepar fuel 13½ da @ $1 - $13.50. Trans Dept main stem |
| 1857-82 | Handerham, John | bricklay 4 3/4 da @ $2 - $9.50. grad, Board Tree Tun |
| 1857-34 | Handley, Joseph | ton fire 10¼ da @ $1.75 - $17.95. 4th div |
| 1855-47 | Timothy | lab 18 da @ $1 - $18.00. Rd Way Dept |
| 1857-16 | Handly, James | fire 3½ da @ $33.35 per mo - $4.65. Benwood sta |
| 1857-28 | Hands, John N. | ton eng'man 21 da @ $3 - $63.00. 1st div |
| 1857-103 | Handy, Jefferson | carp 22 da @ $1.60 - $35.20. N W Va RR depot |
| 1857-101 | Hanefer, Dan. | fire 26 da @ $1.75 - $45.50. NW Va RR ballast train |
| 1857-122 | Hanegan, Cornelius | eng clean 20½ da @ $1.15 - $23.55. Mach Dept, Balto |
| 1855-44 | Hanen, D. | lab 27½ da @ $1 -$27.50. Rd Way Dept |
| 1855-44 | Hugh | lab 23½ da @ $1 - $23.50. Rd Way Dept |
| 1855-51 | Haney, Michael | lab @ $30 per mo - $30.00. Rd Way Dept |
| 1855-25 | Hanigan, Corn. | clean eng 28 da @ $1.15 - $32.75. Trans Dept main stem |
| 1855-68 | Hanlan, M. | tend to masons 8½ da @ $1 - $8.50. Rd Way Dept |
| 1857-122 | Hanley, Edward | tend fill @ $30 per mo - $30.00. Mach Dept, Balto |
| 1857-96 | James | lab 24 3/4 da @ $1 - $24.75. NW Va RR, Rd Dept 1st s-div |
| 1855-28 | John | reg eng 16½ da @ $1.15 - $18.95. Trans Dept main stem |
| 1857-126 | " | clean eng 24½ da @ $1 - $24.50. Mach Dept, Martinsburg |
| 1857-34 | " | ton fire 16½ da @ $1.75 - $28.85. 4th div |
| 1857-97 | Michael | watch 30 da @ $1 - $30.00. NW Va RR, Rd Dept 1st s-div |
| 1855-49 | Patrick | watch cuts 28 da @ $1 - $28.00. Rd Way Dept |

| | | | |
|---|---|---|---|
| 1857-57 | Hanley, Patrick | lab 23 da @ $1 - $23.00. Rd Dept main stem 11th s-div |
| 1857-58 | " | lab 26 da @ $1 - $26.00. Rd Dept main stem 12th s-div |
| 1857-122 | " | tend fill @ $30 per mo - $30.00. Trans Dept, Balto |
| 1855-27 | Thomas | get out eng 28 da @ $1 - $28.00. Trans Dept main stem |
| 1857-11 | Hanlin, Martin | lab 6 da @ $1 - $6.00. NW Va rd, Athey's wd train |
| 1855-14 | Hannagan, J. | brak 15 3/4 da @ $40 per mo - $26.25. Trans Dept main stem |
| 1857-49 | Hannison, William | lab 21 da @ $1 - $21.00. Rd Dept main stem 3d s-div |
| 1857-68 | Hannon, Francis | lab 18 da @ $1 - $18.00. Rd Dept main stem 19th s-div |
| 1857-128 | John | mach help 25 da @ $.50 - $12.50. Mach Dept, Piedmont |
| 1857-68 | Patrick | lab 22½ da @ $1 - $22.50. Rd Dept main stem 19th s-div |
| 1855-20 | Hannum, M. | fire 4½ da @ $1.75 - $7.85. Trans Dept main stem |
| 1857-41 | Hansford, D. W. | lab 24 da @ $1 - $24.00. NW Va rd, Athey's wd train |
| 1855-88 | Hanshew, Allen | app 20¼ da @ $.45 - $9.10. Mach Dept |
| 1857-31 | William | ton fire 24½ da @ $1.75 - $42.85. 1st div |
| 1855-22 | Hanson, Elias | fire 6 da @ $1.75 - $10.50. Trans Dept main stem |
| 1857-121 | J. | carp app 21 da @ $.65 - $13.65. Mach Dept, Balto |
| 1855-81 | Jno. | app 23 da @ $.45 - $10.35. Mach Dept |
| 1857-10 | Happy, Henry | bur reg 25 da @ $40 per mo - $40.00. hp exp, Balto |
| 1855-90 | Hardagan, John | mach 25⅜ da @ $1.50 - $37.85. Mach Dept |
| 1857-46 | Harden, Patrick | lab 25 da @ $1 - $25.00. Rd Dept main stem 1st s-div |
| 1857-66 | Harden, Michael | lab 25⅝ da @ $1.60 - $48.00. Rd Dept main stem 18th s-div |
| 1857-127 | Hardigan, Jno. | mach 30 da @ $1.60 - $48.00. Mach Dept, Piedmont |
| 1855-11 | Harding, Charles | conduc & brak 18½ da @ $50 per mo - $38.55. Trans Dept main stem |
| 1857-21 | " | ton conduc 17⅔ da @ $50 per mo - $34.50. 1st div |
| 1857-24 | Joseph | ton brak 25 da @ $30 per mo - $30.00. 1st div |
| 1857-38 | William | brak 25 da @ $30 per mo - $30.00. Wash br rd, Wash city sta |
| 1857-133 | Hardman, Conrad | clean eng 30 da @ $1 - $30.00. Mach Dept, Fetterman |
| 1857-133 | Moses | put away eng 30 da @ $1.50 - $45.00. Mach Dept, Fetterman |
| 1855-45 | Hardy, Abraham | nail 26 da @ $1 - $26.00. Rd Way Dept |
| 1857-55 | Alvaha | lab 24½ da @ $1 - $24.50. Rd Dept main stem 9th s-div |
| 1855-12 | Charles | conduc & brak 1 da @ $50 per mo - $2.10. Trans Dept main stem |
| 1855-67 | Francis | lab 22½ da @ $1 - $22.50. Rd Way Dept |
| 1857-76 | George | dril 11½ da @ $1 - $12.65. ballast train for 2d track |
| 1857-71 | Hugh | app 24 da @ $.60 - $14.40. Mt Clare sta, Balto |
| 1855-35 | James | lab 24 da @ $30 per mo - $30.00. Trans Dept main stem |
| 1857-122 | " | lab 20½ da @ $1 - $20.50. Mach Dept, Balto |

| ID | Name | | Description |
|---|---|---|---|
| 1855-79 | Hardy, John | | driv 24 da @ $1 - $24.00. Mach Dept |
| 1855-73 | " | | driv 24 da @ $.54 - $12.95. Rd Way Dept |
| 1857-70 | Samuel | | app 2½ da @ $.60 - $1.35. Mt Clare sta, Balto |
| 1857-112 | William | | mach app 20 3/4 da @ $.75 - $15.55. Mach Dept, Balto |
| 1855-66 | " | | lab 23½ da @ $1.50 - $35.25. Rd Way Dept |
| 1857-88 | " | | carp 17 da @ $1.75 - $29.75. grad, Welling Tun |
| 1857-112 | " | | mach app 21 da @ $.75 - $15.75. Mach Dept, Balto |
| 1857-26 | " | | ton brak 8½ da @ $40 per mo - $13.60. 3d & 4th div |
| 1857-47 | Hardyman, John | | lab 24 da @ $1 - $24.00. Rd Dept main stem 1st s-div |
| 1855-44 | Hare, H. | | lab 14 3/4 da @ $1 - $14.75. Rd Way Dept |
| 1855-80 | Harford, George R. | | coach mkr 19½ da @ $1.65 - $32.15. Mach Dept |
| 1857-120 | " " | | carp 20 da @ $1.90 - $38.00. Mach Dept, Balto |
| 1855-54 | Harken, Henry | | fore @ $60 per mo - $60.00. Rd Way Dept |
| 1857-8 | Harkness, A. J. | | lab 25 da @ $30 per mo - $30.00. Camden sta |
| 1857-23 | Harlan, Richard | | ton conduc 17¾ da @ $40 per mo; 9 da @ $50 per mo - $45.60. 3d & 4th div |
| 1855-52 | Harley, Conrad | | lab 14½ da @ $1. Rd Way Dept |
| 1855-49 | Daniel | | watch cuts 24 da @ $1 - $24.00. Rd Way Dept |
| 1855-56 | Thomas | | lab 14 3/4 da @ $1 - $14.75. Rd Way Dept |
| 1857-114 | " | | iron mould help 12 da @ $1 - $12.00. Mach Dept, Balto |
| 1857-75 | Harlow, Martin | | dril 25½ da @ $1.04 - $26.60. ballast train for 2d track |
| 1857-56 | Harman, Andrew | | lab 24½ da @ $1 - $24.50. Rd Dept main stem 10th s-div |
| 1857-74 | John M. | | supv @ $45 per mo - $45.00. Rd Way Dept |
| 1857-51 | " " | | horse & cart 25 da @ $1.25 - $31.25. Rd Dept main stem 5th s-div |
| 1857-50 | " " | | supv @ $45 per mo - $45.00. Rd Dept main stem 5th s-div |
| 1855-29 | William | | haul & saw firewd 11½ da @ $1 - $11.50. Trans Dept main stem |
| 1855-78 | " | | help 24 da @ $1.15 - $27.60. Mach Dept |
| 1855-54 | Harmes, Henry | | track lay 15 da @ $1.12½ - $16.90. Rd Way Dept |
| 1855-73 | Harney, John | | lab 22 da @ $1 - $22.00. Rd Way Dept |
| 1855-28 | Harper, R. | | reg eng 19 3/4 da @ $1.50 - $29.60. Trans Dept main stem |
| 1857-32 | Robert | | ton fire 21¾ da @ $1.75 - $37.20. 2d div |
| 1855-79 | W. W. | | carp 23¾ da @ $1.45 - $33.70. Mach Dept |
| 1857-121 | Wm. W. | | paint 17¾ da @ $1.50 - $25.85. Mach Dept, Balto |
| 1857-108 | Harr, James W. | | mach 18¼ da @ $1.45 -$26.45. Mach Dept, Balto |
| 1855-61 | John O. | | lab 9 da @ $1 - $9.00. Rd Way Dept |
| 1855-65 | Harrett, Charles | | plast 1 da @ $1.50 - $1.50. Rd Way Dept |
| 1855-30 | Harrigan, John | | prepar fuel 28 da @ $30 per mo - $30.00. Trans Dept main stem |

| | | |
|---|---|---|
| 1855-56 | Harrigan, Michl. | lab 16 da @ $1 - $16.00. Rd Way Dept |
| 1857-84 | Harrington, Luke | lab 24½ da @ $1.12 -$27.55. grad, Board Tree Tun |
| 1855-76 | R. | help 26 da @ $1.15 - $29.90. Mach Dept |
| 1857-111 | Robert | mach help 28½ da @ $1.15 - $32.75. Mach Dept, Balto |
| 1855-27 | Harriott, Joseph | clean eng 25½ da @ $1 - $25.50. Trans Dept main stem |
| 1857-127 | Harris, F. A. | mach help 19¼ da @ $1 -$19.25. Mach Dept, Piedmont |
| 1855-78 | George | help 24½ da @ $1.15 - $28.15. Mach Dept |
| 1857-118 | " | blksmith help 32¼ da @ $1.15 - $37.10. Mach Dept, Balto |
| 1855-16 | John | pass fire 12 da @ $40 per mo -$17.15. Trans Dept main stem |
| 1857-30 | " | ton eng'man 18 da @ $3 - $54.00. 4th div |
| 1855-73 | R. | driv 24 da @ $.75 - $18.00. Rd Way Dept |
| 1857-122 | Richard | carter 20¼ da @ $1 -$20.25. Mach Dept, Balto |
| 1857-71 | " | exp driv 28½ da @ $1 -$28.50. Mt Clare, repair tracks in yd |
| 1857-112 | William | mach help 14¼ da @ $1 -$14.25. Mach Dept, Balto |
| 1857-36 | Harrison, C. J. | tele oper 30 da @ $30 per mo - $30.00. Moundsville |
| 1857-64 | Dennis | lab 23 3/4 da @$1 - $23.75. Rd Dept main stem 17th s-div |
| 1857-17 | G. W. | clk 30 da @ $58.35 per mo - $58.35. Wheeling sta |
| 1855-84 | George | mach (includ boil mkr, work sht iron, &c) 22¼ da @ $1.35 - $30.05. Mach Dept |
| 1857-115 | " | boil mkr 12½ da @ $1.50 - $18.75. Mach Dept, Balto |
| 1857-25 | Jacob | ton brak 17½ da @ $40 per mo -$28.00. 2d div |
| 1855-89 | William | mach 18¼ da @ $1.75 - $31.95. Mach Dept |
| 1857-133 | " | fore mach @ $60 per mo - $60.00. Mach Dept, Fetterman |
| 1857-111 | " | mach help 18 da @ $1 -$18.00. Mach Dept, Balto |
| 1855-1 | William G. | pres $3000 per annum - $250. Ofc Hanover St |
| 1857-128 | Harrit, Andrew | mach help 23 3/4 da @ $.75 -$17.80. Mach Dept, Piedmont |
| 1857-128 | James | mach help 28½ da @ $.55 - $15.65. Mach Dept, Piedmont |
| 1855-92 | Harritt, A. J. | app 20 da @ $.55 - $11.00. Mach Dept |
| 1857-130 | James | lab 17¼ da @ $1 -$17.25. Mach Dept, Piedmont |
| 1857-100 | Harro, Patrick O. | lab 25 da @ $1 -$25.00. NW Va RR, Rd Dept 5th s-div |
| 1855-41 | Harah, B. | lab 20 da @ $1 - $20.00. Rd Way Dept |
| 1857-109 | Hart, Francis | mach 17¼ da @ $1.60 -$27.60. Mach Dept, Balto |
| 1855-54 | Geo. | lab 23¼ da @ $1.25 -$23.25. Rd Way Dept |
| 1857-78 | Hugh | lab 25 da @ $1 - $25.00. lay 2d track |
| 1855-11 | J. A. | conduc & brak 13¼ da @ $50 per mo -$27.60. Trans Dept main stem |
| 1855-57 | Owen | lab 28 da @ $1.05 - $29.40. Rd Way Dept |
| 1857-58 | " | fore 25 da @ $1.25 -$31.25. Rd Dept main stem 12th s-div |

## B & O RR EMPLOYEES

| | | | |
|---|---|---|---|
| 1855-44 | Hartee, James | lab 17 da @ $1 -$17.00. Rd Way Dept |
| 1855-25 | Hartigan, Moris | clean eng 27¾ da @ $1.15 - $31.35. Trans Dept main stem |
| 1857-122 | " | eng clean 19¾ da @ $1.15 -$22.15. Mach Dept, Balto |
| 1855-85 | Hartley, Edward | help 20½ da @ $1 - $20.50. Mach Dept |
| 1855-14 | Hartman, Samuel | brak 16½ da @ $40 per mo -$27.50. Trans Dept main stem |
| 1855-16 | Hartman, J. | pass fire 4 da @ $40 per mo - $5.70. Trans Dept main stem |
| 1857-29 | " John | ton eng'man 21½ da @ $2.50 - $53.75. 2d div |
| 1855-27 | " M. | clean eng 18 da @ $1 - $18.00. Trans Dept main stem |
| 1855-52 | " Matthias | lab 28 da @ $1 - $28.00. Rd Way Dept |
| 1855-9 | Hartsoc, Samuel | conduc 11½ da @ $50 per mo - $23.95. Trans Dept main stem |
| 1857-62 | Hartzog, Samuel | lab 6 3/4 da @ $1 - $6.75. Rd Dept main stem 15th s-div |
| 1855-78 | Harvey, A. J. | mach @ $45 per mo - $45.00. Mach Dept |
| 1855-11 | " C. W. | conduc & brak 19¾ da @ $50 per mo -$40.10. Trans Dept main stem |
| 1855-8 | " Charles | brak 3 da @ $33.35 per mo - $3.55. Trans Dept main stem |
| 1855-11 | " " | conduc & brak 3 da @ $40 per mo - $5.00. Trans Dept main stem |
| 1857-21 | " " | ton conduc 25 da @$50 per mo - $50.00. 1st div |
| 1857-126 | " Henry | clean eng 29¼ da @ $1 - $29.25. Mach Dept, Martinsburg |
| 1857-89 | " James | lab 22½ da @ $1.12 - $25.05. grad, Welling Tun |
| 1855-74 | " Levi | spik 28 da @ $1.05 - $29.40. Rd Way Dept |
| 1857-95 | " " | nail 29 da @ $1.05 - $30.45. Wash br, Rd Dept |
| 1857-83 | " Michael | lab 22 dá @ $1.12 - $24.75. grad, Board Tree Tun |
| 1857-80 | " Tim | lab 20 da @ $1 -$20.00. lay 2d track |
| 1855-85 | " W. | help 19½ da @ $1 - $19.50. Mach Dept |
| 1857-118 | " Washington | blksmith help 18 da @ $1 - $18.00. Mach Dept, Balto |
| 1857-111 | Hase, Jos. | mach help 17 3/4 da @ $1 - $17.75. Mach Dept, Balto |
| 1857-102 | Hashberger, Wm. | help 23 da @ $1.15 - $26.45. NW Va RR, rwy depot |
| 1855-55 | Hashon, John | lab 16½ da @ $1 - $16.50. Rd Way Dept |
| 1855-53 | Haskett, Thomas N. | supv @ $65 per mo - $65.00. Rd Way Dept |
| 1855-95 | Haskins, George | pat mkr 24 da @ $1.65 - $39.60. Mach Dept |
| 1855-95 | Haslup, John | help 25 3/4 da @ $1 - $25.75. Mach Dept |
| 1857-132 | " " | iron mould 25 da @ $1.66 - $41.90. Mach Dept, Grafton |
| 1855-26 | Hassen, James | clean eng 16 3/4 da @ $1 - $16.75. Trans Dept main stem |
| 1857-72 | Hast, George | lab 18 3/4 da @ $1 - $18.75. Cumb depot |
| 1855-5 | Hasten, J. | lab 24 da @ $30 per mo - $30.00. Trans Dept, Wash br |
| 1857-35 | Haston, Columbus | fire 7 da @ $1.75 - $12.25. Edwards' wd train 3d & 4th div |
| 1855-39 | Hatfield, Benjamin | lab 24 da @ $1 - $24.00. Rd Way Dept |

| | | | |
|---|---|---|---|
| 1855-39 | Hatfield, D. | lab 21 da @ $1 - $21.00. | Rd Way Dept |
| 1857-47 | " Daniel | lab 25½ da @ $1 - $25.50. | Rd Dept main stem 2d s-div |
| 1857-47 | " Elisha | lab 24½ da @ $1 - $24.50. | Rd Dept main stem 2d s-div |
| 1855-39 | " G. | lab 19 da @ $1 - $19.00. | Rd Way Dept |
| 1857-47 | " Gustavus J. | lab 25 da @ $1 - $25.00. | Rd Dept main stem 2d s-div |
| 1855-39 | " Thomas O. | lab 9 da @ $1 - $9.00. | Rd Way Dept |
| 1857-48 | " | lab 11 da @ $1 - $11.00. | Rd Dept main stem 2d s-div |
| 1855-78 | Hatry, Chas. | ton eng'man 3/4 da @ $2.50 - $1.85. | Trans Dept main stem |
| 1857-78 | Hatts, Benjamin | fire 25 da @ $1.35 - $33.75. | lay 2d track |
| 1857-65 | Haught, Marrion | lab 12¼ da @ $1 - $12.25. | Rd Dept main stem 17th s-div |
| 1857-64 | Haughton, Nicholas | lab 15½ da @ $1 - $15.50. | Rd Dept main stem 17th s-div |
| 1857-77 | Haul, James | fore 16 da @ $2 - $32.00. | lay 2d track |
| 1857-102 | Hauley, M. | carp 18 da @ $1.65 - $29.70. | NW Va RR bridges |
| 1855-48 | Havey, Brine | lab 13½ da @ $1 - $13.50. | Rd Way Dept |
| 1857-82 | Havy, John | lao 21½ da @ $1.12 - $24.20. | grad, Board Tree Tun |
| 1857-82 | Hawk, George | lab 21½ da @ $1.12 - $24.20. | grad, Board Tree Tun |
| 1855-88 | Hawkins, Frederick | work inspec @ $30 per mo - $30.00. | Mach Dept |
| 1857-125 | " | carp @ $30 per mo - $30.00. | Mach Dept, Martinsburg |
| 1855-65 | " Henry | supv @ $75 per mo - $70.00. | Rd Way Dept |
| 1857-73 | " John | supt @ $75 per mo - $75.00. | repair water sta, M.S. & P.B. |
| 1857-74 | Hawley, F. | fore @ $65 per mo - $65.00. | put swit on line of rd |
| 1855-70 | " | lab 14 da @ $1 - $14.00. | Rd Way Dept |
| 1855-90 | " Frank | mach 5 da @ $1.50 - $7.50. | Mach Dept |
| 1855-15 | " Thomas | pass eng'man 16 3/4 da @ $3 - $50.25. | Trans Dept main stem |
| 1857-30 | " | ton eng'man 25 3/4 da @ $3 - $77.25. | 3d div |
| 1855-53 | Hayden, Barney | lab 15½ da @ $1 - $15.50. | Rd Way Dept |
| 1857-61 | " Thurity | lab 27 da @ $1 - $27.00. | Rd Dept main stem 14th s-div |
| 1857-121 | " | paint help 5½ da @ $1.15 - $6.30. | Mach Dept, Balto |
| 1855-24 | " | pass & bur driv 24 da @ $30 per mo - $30.00. | Trans Dept main stem |
| 1857-9 | " George J. | pass driv 25 da @ $30 per mo - $30.00. | hp exp, Balto |
| 1855-72 | " " | draft @ $70 per mo - $70.00. | Rd Way Dept |
| 1857-45 | " Michael | pass & bur driv 24 da @ $30 per mo -$30.00. | Trans Dept main stem |
| 1855-24 | " S. C. | lab 14 da @ $1 - $14.00. | NW Va rd, Athey's wd train |
| 1857-41 | Hayes, Jacob | fire 13½ da @ $1.75 - $23.60. | Trans Dept main stem |
| 1855-20 | " James | prepar fuel 27 da @ $30 per mo - $28.90. | Trans Dept main stem |

# B & O RR EMPLOYEES 173

| ID | Name | Description |
|---|---|---|
| 1857-111 | Hayes, John | mach help 31 da @ $1.15 - $35.65. Mach Dept, Balto |
| 1855-1 | " S. J. | mast mach $2000 per annum - $166.66 |
| 1857-102 | Haymond, Lewis | horse & cart 7 da @ $1.50 - $10.50. NW Va RR, rwy depot |
| 1857-102 | " | lab 4 da @ $1.25 - $5.00. NW Va RR, rwy depot |
| 1857-131 | Hayner, Charles | mach 16 da @ $1.45 - $23.20. Mach Dept, Grafton |
| 1857-79 | Hays, John | watch 32 da @ $1.15 - $36.80. Mach Dept |
| 1857-116 | Hazard, Robert | boil mkr help 19 da @ $1 - $19.00. Mach Dept, Balto |
| 1857-110 | Hazell, William | mach 18½ da @ $1.72 - $31.80. Mach Dept, Balto |
| 1855-45 | Heacerote, L. | lab 13½ da @ $1 - $13.50. Rd Way Dept |
| 1855-17 | Head, Wm. T. | ton eng'man 14 da @ $3 - $42.00. Trans Dept main stem |
| 1855-53 | Headley, John | lab 13½ da @ $1 - $13.50. Rd Way Dept |
| 1857-66 | Heaffenor, Batty | lab 9½ da @ $1 - $9.50. Rd Dept main stem 18th s-div |
| 1857-57 | Healey, B. | fore 28½ da @ $1.25 - $35.65. Rd Dept main stem 11th s-div |
| 1855-56 | " Bryan | lab 12 3/4 da @ $1.50 - $12.75. Rd Way Dept |
| 1857-68 | " Charles | carp 25 da @ $1.50 - $37.50. Rd Dept main stem 19th s-div |
| 1855-36 | " James | lab 25 da @ $25 per mo - $26.05. Trans Dept main stem |
| 1857-126 | " John | clean eng 28 da @ $1.15 - $32.20. Mach Dept, Martinsburg |
| 1855-94 | " M. | app 29½ da @ $.75 - $22.15. Mach Dept |
| 1857-134 | " Michael | mach 20 da @$1.60 - $32.00. Mach Dept, Wheeling |
| 1855-36 | " Pat. | lab 6 da @ $25 per mo -$6.25. Trans Dept main stem |
| 1855-62 | Heally, William | fore 24 da @ $1.25 - $30.00. Rd Way Dept |
| 1857-16 | Healy, John | watch 30 da @ $30 per mo -$30.00. Benwood sta |
| 1857-16 | " William | swit tend 30 da @ $30 per mo - $30.00. Benwood sta |
| 1855-26 | Heap, Henry | clean eng 25 da @ $1 - $25.00. Trans Dept main stem |
| 1857-135 | " | put away eng &c 30 da @ $1.25 - $37.50. Mach Dept, Wheeling |
| 1857-52 | Hearsh, Bartley | lab 25 da @ $1 -$25.00. Rd Dept main stem 6th s-div |
| 1857-27 | Hebb, David | ton brak 31 da @ $40 per mo - $49.60. Board Tree Tun |
| 1857-26 | " | ton brak 1 da @ $40 per mo - $1.60. 3d & 4th div |
| 1855-51 | " T. F. | lab @ $30 per mo - $30.00. Rd Way Dept |
| 1857-26 | " T. F. | ton brak 20½ da @ $40 per mo - $32.80. 3d & 4th div |
| 1857-60 | " Thornton | brak 6½ da @ $1.53 - $9.95. Rd Dept main stem 13th s-div |
| 1857-26 | " | ton brak 3 da @ $40 per mo - $4.80. 3d & 4th div |
| 1857-48 | Heckathorne, William | lab 20 da @ $1 -$20.00. Rd Dept main stem 2d s-div |
| 1855-22 | Heckerthover, Wm. | fire 11 da @ $1.75 - $19.25. Trans Dept main stem |
| 1857-79 | Hefferin, Bartly | lab 6¾ da @ $1 -$6.25. lay 2d track |
| 1857-80 | " Patrick | lab 20 3/4 da @ $1.25 -$25.95. lay 2d track |

## B & O RR EMPLOYEES

| | | | |
|---|---|---|---|
| 1857-81 | Hefferone, John | lab 24 da @ $.65 - $15.60. lay 2d track |
| 1855-87 | Hefferstay, G. | help 21 3/4 da @ $1 - $21.75. Mach Dept |
| 1857-88 | Hefner, Bernhart | driv 25½ da @ $1 - $25.50. grad, Welling Tun |
| 1855-15 | Hefnere, C. | pass eng'man 21 da @ $3 - $63.00. Trans Dept main stem |
| 1855-71 | Heison, Jno. | smith 23 3/4 da @ $1.45 - $34.40. Rd Way Dept |
| 1855-71 | " Thos. Jr | smith 22 da @ $1.45 - $31.90. Rd Way Dept |
| 1855-71 | " Thos. Sr. | smith 24 da @ $1.73 - $41.50. Rd Way Dept |
| 1855-88 | Helan, John | app 27½ da @ $.50 - $13.75. Mach Dept |
| 1855-19 | Helfenstary, Jas. | ton eng'man 20 da @ $3 - $60.00. Trans Dept main stem |
| 1857-125 | Helfferstay, Harrison | carp @ $30 per mo - $30.00. Mach Dept, Martinsburg |
| 1855-23 | " Luther | fire 30 da @ $1.75 - $52.50. Trans Dept main stem |
| 1855-88 | " W. | carp 21¼ da @ $1.35 - $28.70. Mach Dept |
| 1857-29 | Hellferstey, James | ton eng'man 26 da @ $50 per mo - $50.00. 2d div |
| 1855-14 | Helms, C. M. | brak 12 da @ $40 per mo - $20.00. Trans Dept main stem |
| 1857-31 | " Charles | ton fire 34 da @ $1.75 - $59.50. 1st div |
| 1855-27 | " Thomas | ton brak 40 da @ $1.35 - $28.70. Mach Dept |
| 1857-60 | Helton, Thomas | clean eng 24 da @ $1 - $24.00. Board Tree Tun |
| 1857-60 | " | fore 26⅔ da @ $1.25 - $33.15. Rd Dept main stem 13th s-div |
| 1855-19 | Helty, Chas. | lab 23 da @ $1 - $23.00. Rd Dept main stem 13th s-div |
| 1857-124 | Helym, John | ton eng'man 12½ da @ $2.50 - $31.25. Trans Dept main stem |
| 1857-70 | Hemling, Wm. | mach app 16¾ da @ $.70 - $1.55. Mach Dept, Martinsburg |
| 1857-127 | Hemnich, Christopher | mach 16⅔ da @ $1.73 - $28.15. Mt Clare sta, Balto |
| 1857-8 | Hemphill, J. | mach help 24⅔ da @ $1 - $24.25. Mach Dept, Piedmont |
| 1855-28 | Hempter, Pins | lab 25 da @ $30 per mo - $30.00. Camden sta |
| 1857-54 | Hencerode, John | reg eng 24¼ da @ $1.15 - $28.15. Trans Dept main stem |
| 1857-54 | " Lawrence | lab 27½ da @ $1 - $27.50. Rd Dept main stem 8th s-div |
| 1857-54 | " Martin | watch 27⅔ da @ $1 - $27.50. Rd Dept main stem 8th s-div |
| 1855-49 | Hencerote, John | watch cuts 26 da @ $1 - $26.00. Rd Dept main stem 8th s-div |
| 1855-64 | Henchan, Jno. | watch 18 da @ $1 - $18.00. Rd Way Dept |
| 1855-76 | Henderson, A. | mach 24 3/4 da @ $1.72 - $42.60. Mach Dept |
| 1857-109 | " Andrew | mach 19½ da @ $1.72 - $33.55. Mach Dept, Balto |
| 1857-116 | " James | fore brass mould 18 da @ $2.50 - $45.00. Mach Dept, Balto |
| 1857-132 | " " | watch 19½ da @ $1.25 - $24.35. Mach Dept, Grafton |
| 1857-132 | " William | blksmith help 17½ da @ $1 - $17.50. Mach Dept, Grafton |
| 1857-116 | " " | brass mould help 15 da @ $1 - $15.00. Mach Dept, Balto |
| 1855-64 | Hendrick, M. | carp 21 da @ $1.25 - $26.25. Rd Way Dept |

| | | | |
|---|---|---|---|
| 1857-93 | Hendrick, Murray | carp 23 da @ $1.50 - $34.50. quarry & haul stone for Board Tree & Littleton Tun |
| 1855-46 | Henley, M. | lab 5 da @ $1 - $5.00. Rd Way Dept |
| 1857-123 | Henneberg, Gustav | mach 23 3/4 da @ $1.50 - $35.60. Mach Dept, Martinsburg |
| 1855-17 | Henniker, G. | ton eng'man 8 da @ $2.50 - $20.00. Trans Dept main stem |
| 1855-15 | Henning, John | pass eng'man 3 da @ $2.50 - $7.50. Trans Dept main stem |
| 1857-133 | " Matt. | clean eng 34 da @ $1 - $34.00. Mach Dept, Board Tree Tun |
| 1855-74 | " Matthias | lab 24 da @ $1 - $24.00. Rd Way Dept |
| 1857-95 | Hennington, Dennis | lab 22 da @ $1 - $22.00. Wash br, Rd Dept |
| 1857-125 | Hennixman, Henry | sht iron work help 24 da @ $1 - $24.00. Mach Dept, Martinsburg |
| 1855-19 | Henry, John | ton eng'man 13 da @ $3 - $39.00. Trans Dept main stem |
| 1857-111 | Henrick, Henry | mach help 26 3/4 da @ $1.15 - $30.75. Mach Dept, Balto |
| 1857-56 | Henry, G. W. | lab 22 da @ $1 - $22.00. Rd Dept main stem 10th s-div |
| 1855-80 | " J. B. | carp 23¼ da @ $1.50 - $34.85. Mach Dept |
| 1855-6 | " James | clk 14 da @ $50 per mo - $25.00. Trans Dept main stem |
| 1855-42 | " " | lab 15 da @ $1 - $15.00. Rd Way Dept |
| 1857-103 | " John | lab 23¼ da @ $1.12 - $26.15. NW Va RR Tun |
| 1855-25 | " " | clean eng 27¼ da @ $1.15 - $31.35. Trans Dept main stem |
| 1857-80 | " " | lab 20 3/4 da @ $1 - $20.75. lay 2d track |
| 1857-59 | " Samuel T. | lab 26¼ da @ $1 - $26.50. Rd Dept main stem 13th s-div |
| 1857-131 | " " | mach app 28 da @ $.45 - $12.60. Mach Dept, Grafton |
| 1855-80 | " Thomas W. | carp 26 3/4 da @ $1.45 - $38.80. Mach Dept |
| 1857-121 | " W. L. | lumber yd kpr 25 da @ $1.50 - $37.50. Mach Dept, Balto |
| 1857-119 | " " | carp 19 da @ $1.65 - $31.35. Mach Dept, Balto |
| 1855-79 | " William | carp 24 da @ $1.75 - $42.00. Mach Dept |
| 1857-120 | Hensee, Philip | carp 16 3/4 da @ $1.50 - $25.10. Mach Dept, Balto |
| 1857-116 | Hensell, Joseph | boil mkr help 24 da @ $1 - $24.00. Mach Dept, Balto |
| 1857-69 | Henshew, Dan. | carp 17¼ da @ $1.60 - $27.60. Mt Clare sta, Balto |
| 1857-126 | Henthorn, George | clean eng 25 da @ $1.15 - $28.75. Mach Dept, Martinsburg |
| 1857-12 | Hentze, John | lab 25 da @ $1 - $25.00. Fred sta |
| 1857-58 | Hepburn, C. | fore 26 da @ $1.25 - $32.50. Rd Dept main stem 12th s-div |
| 1857-97 | " " | watch 30 da @ $1 - $30.00. NW Va RR, Rd Dept 2d s-div |
| 1855-91 | Hepsley, J. | help 4 da @ $1 - $4.00. Mach Dept |
| 1855-16 | " Z. | pass fire 14 da @ $1.25 - $17.50. Trans Dept main stem |
| 1855-38 | Herbert, Jos. | lab 20 da @ $1 - $20.00. Rd Way Dept |
| 1855-38 | | lab 9 da @ $1 - $9.00. Rd Way Dept |
| 1857-117 | | blksmith 16 3/4 da @ $1.25 - $20.95. Mach Dept, Balto |

| Years | Name | Description |
|---|---|---|
| 1857-55 | Herbin, Lawrence | lab 21¼ da @ $1 - $21.25. Rd Dept main stem 9th s-div |
| 1857-80 | Herby, Michael | lab 20 3/4 da @ $1 - $20.75. lay 2d track |
| 1855-28 | Hern, Wm. O. | reg eng 24 3/4 da @ $1.15 - $28.45. Trans Dept main stem |
| 1857-83 | Hernes, Patrick | lab 21½ da @ $1.12 - $24.20. grad, Board Tree Tun |
| 1857-61 | Herr, J. F. | supv @ $50 per mo - $50.00. Rd Dept main stem 14th s-div |
| 1857-23 | Herr, James | ton conduc 14 3/4 da @ $1 - $29.50. 3d & 4th div |
| 1857-61 | Herr, John S. | watch 5 da @ $1 - $5.00. Rd Dept main stem 14th s-div |
| 1855-56 | Herr, Josh. F. | supv @ $50 per mo - $50.00. Rd Way Dept |
| 1857-26 | Herr, Thomas | ton brak 7 da @ $40 per mo - $11.20. 3d & 4th div |
| 1855-86 | Herrberg, G. | mach 23½ da @ $1.45 - $33.70. Mach Dept |
| 1857-56 | Herrick, Adam | lab 12½ da @ $1 - $12.50. Rd Dept main stem 10th s-div |
| 1857-91 | Herrigan, Rodger | lab 22½ da @ $1 - $22.50. grad, Welling Tun |
| 1857-73 | Herring, William | carp 25 da @ $1.65 - $41.25. repair water sta, M.S. & P.B. |
| 1855-59 | Herrington, John | fore 23 da @ $1.25 - $28.75. Rd Way Dept |
| 1857-64 | " | lab 24 3/4 da @ $1 - $24.75. Rd Dept main stem 17th s-div |
| 1857-99 | " Luke | watch 30 da @ $1 - $30.00. NW Va RR, Rd Dept 4th s-div |
| 1855-59 | " Wm. | lab 15½ da @ $1 - $15.50. Rd Way Dept |
| 1855-48 | Herron, John | train hand 9 3/4 da @ $1 - $9.75. Rd Way Dept |
| 1857-70 | Hershey, Sylvester | help 18 da @ $1 - $18.00. Mt Clare sta, Balto |
| 1855-56 | Hershey, David | fore 24 da @ $1.25 - $30.00. Rd Way Dept |
| 1857-134 | Heskett, J. A. | mach 28 da @ $1.75 - $49.00. Mach Dept, Wheeling |
| 1857-73 | Heskett, T. N. | carp 18 3/4 da @ $1.62 - $30.45. repair bridges &c |
| 1857-73 | " | fore @ $70 per mo - $70.00. repair bridges &c |
| 1857-119 | Hess, Emanual | carp 17⅞ da @ $1.50 - $25.85. Mach Dept, Balto |
| 1855-9 | " William | conduc 12 da @ $50 per mo - $1.50 - $32.25. Mach Dept |
| 1855-89 | Hessen, H. | blksmith 21½ da @ $1.50 - $32.25. Mach Dept |
| 1857-94 | Hesser, Newton | carp 24½ da @ $1.75 - $42.90. repair bridges |
| 1857-83 | Hester, Michael | lab 5½ da @ $1.12 - $6.20. grad, Board Tree Tun |
| 1857-83 | Hestin, Thomas | lab 5½ da @ $1.12 - $6.20. grad, Board Tree Tun |
| 1857-135 | Hestner, Conrad | lab 5½ da @ $1.12 - $6.20. grad, Board Tree Tun |
| 1857-47 | Heston, William | boil mkr help 23½ da @ $1 - $23.50. Mach Dept, Wheeling |
| 1857-125 | Hettle, Jacob | lab 25 da @ $1 - $25.00. Rd Dept main stem 1st s-div |
| 1857-131 | Hetzell, Frederick | sht iron work 22 da @ $1 - $22.00. Mach Dept, Martinsburg |
| 1857-23 | Heuran, John A. | boil kpr 21½ da @ $1 - $21.25. Mach Dept, Grafton |
| 1855-53 | Hevern, John | ton conduc 30 3/4 da @ $1 - $50 per mo - $61.50. 3d & 4th div |
| | Hewett, O. | carp 23¾ da @ $1.25 - $29.05. Rd Way Dept |

| ID | Name | Description |
|---|---|---|
| 1857-117 | Hewit, Barney | blksmith help 17½ da @ $1 - $17.50. Mach Dept, Balto |
| 1857-89 | Hewitt, Robert M. | brak 9 da @ $1 - $9.00. grad, Welling Tun |
| 1857-31 | Hewitt, J. C. | ton fire 19¾ da @ $1.75 - $33.70. 1st div |
| 1855-68 | Hewitt, Robert | brak 24 da @ $1.25 - $30.00. Rd Way Dept |
| 1857-21 | Hewling, Robert C. | ton conduc 20⅞ da @ $50 per mo - $40.50. 1st div |
| 1857-108 | Hewling, C. A. | mach 1½ da @ $1.50 - $2.25. Mach Dept, Balto |
| 1857-79 | Hews, John | lab 14½ da @ $1 - $14.50. lay 2d track |
| 1857-77 | Hews, Patrick | lab 15 da @ $1 - $15.00. lay 2d track |
| 1857-126 | Hibbard, Conrad | clean eng 27½ da @ $1.15 - $31.60. Mach Dept, Martinsburg |
| 1855-59 | Hickell, John T. | fore 24 da @ $1.25 - $30.00. Rd Way Dept |
| 1855-30 | Hicker, William | prepar fuel 24 da @ $30 per mo - $30.00. Trans Dept main stem |
| 1857-11 | " | team 25 da @ $30 per mo - $30.00. Locust Pt |
| 1855-50 | Hickey, James | watch cuts 28 da @ $1 - $28.00. Rd Way Dept |
| 1857-48 | " | lab 22½ da @ $1 - $22.50. Rd Dept main stem 2d s-div |
| 1857-65 | " | watch 30 da @ $1 - $30.00. Rd Dept main stem 17th s-div |
| 1855-29 | Jere | prepar fuel 24 da @ $30 per mo - $30.00. Trans Dept main stem |
| 1857-62 | Jeremiah | lab 24¼ da @ $1 - $24.25. Rd Dept main stem 15th s-div |
| 1855-27 | John | clean eng 23 da @ $1 - $23.00. Trans Dept main stem |
| 1857-130 | " | lab 18¾ da @ $1 - $18.75. Mach Dept, Piedmont |
| 1855-26 | Lawrence | clean eng 26½ da @ $1 - $26.50. Trans Dept main stem |
| 1857-129 | " | clean eng 31 3/4 da @ $1.15 - $36.50. Mach Dept, Piedmont |
| 1857-134 | " | mach app 20 da @ $.55 - $11.00. Mach Dept, Wheeling |
| 1855-31 | M. | prepar fuel 12 da @ $1 - $12.00. Trans Dept main stem |
| 1857-51 | Michael | lab 25 da @ $1 - $25.00. Rd Dept main stem 5th s-div |
| 1857-102 | Patrick | lab 20¼ da @ $1 - $20.25. NW Va RR, rwy depot |
| 1857-48 | " | lab 23 da @ $1 - $23.00. Rd Dept main stem 2d s-div |
| 1855-29 | T. | prepar fuel 24 da @ $30 per mo - $30.00. Trans Dept main stem |
| 1857-62 | Timothy | watch 30 da @ $1 - $30.00. Rd Dept main stem 15th s-div |
| 1855-16 | Hickman, E. | pass fire 24 da @ $33.35 per mo - $34.30. Trans Dept main stem |
| 1855-22 | Hickman, T. R. | fire 24 da @ $33.35 per mo - $33.35. Trans Dept main stem |
| 1855-85 | Hicks, Albert | help 22½ da @ $1 - $22.50. Mach Dept |
| 1857-117 | Hicks, Alfred | blksmith help 13 da @ $1 - $13.00. Mach Dept, Balto |
| 1857-104 | Hiffen, William | lab 21 3/4 da @ $1 - $21.75. NW Va RR Tun |
| 1857-10 | Higeston, John | stab'man 25 da @ $30 per mo - $30.00. hp exp, Balto |
| 1855-59 | Higgans, M. | lab 24 da @ $1 - $24.00. Rd Way Dept |
| 1855-59 | Higgans, P. | lab 15¼ da @ $1 - $15.25. Rd Way Dept |

## B & O RR EMPLOYEES

| | | | |
|---|---|---|---|
| 1855-24 | Higgeston, John | pass & bur driv 24 da @ $1 - $24.00. Trans Dept main stem |
| 1857-51 | Higgins, Edward | lab 24 da @ $1 - $24.00. Rd Dept main stem 5th s-div |
| 1855-75 | " Emanl. | lab 24 da @ $1 - $24.00. Rd Way Dept |
| 1855-47 | " H. | lab 9 da @ $1 - $9.00. Rd Way Dept |
| 1855-62 | " John | fore 22 da @ $1.25 - $27.50. Rd Way Dept |
| 1855-62 | " " | lab 24 da @ $1 - $24.00. Rd Way Dept |
| 1857-16 | " " | stab'man 25 da @ $1 - $25.00. Moundsville sta |
| 1857-97 | " Michael | lab 26 da @ $1 - $26.00. NW Va RR, Rd Dept 2d s-div |
| 1855-75 | " Patrick | lab 24 da @ $1 - $24.00. Rd Way Dept |
| 1857-80 | " " | lab 18 3/4 da @ $1 - $18.75. lay 2d track |
| 1857-51 | " Peter | lab 20½ da @ $1 - $20.50. Rd Dept main stem 5th s-div |
| 1857-60 | " Thomas | lab 26½ da @ $1 - $26.50. Rd Dept main stem 13th s-div |
| 1855-70 | " Valentine | lab 16¼ da @ $.75 - $12.20. Rd Way Dept |
| 1857-51 | Higgs, Henry | lab 25 da @ $1 - $25.00. Rd Dept main stem 5th s-div |
| 1857-86 | High, Francis | lab 13 3/4 da @ $1 - $13.75. grad, McGuire's Tun |
| 1855-12 | " Thomas | conduc & brak 21½ da @ $40 per mo - $38.85. Trans Dept main stem |
| 1857-113 | " " | iron mould 18 da @ $1.65 - $29.70. Mach Dept, Balto |
| 1855-83 | | help 20¼ da @ $1.10 - $22.25. Mach Dept |
| 1857-117 | | blksmith help 17½ da @ $1.15 - $20.10. Mach Dept, Balto |
| 1857-113 | | iron mould 18 da @ $1.65 - $29.70. Mach Dept, Balto |
| 1855-55 | Hiland, Patrick | lab 7½ da @ $1 - $7.50. Rd Way Dept |
| 1855-52 | Hilbert, Conrad | lab 4 3/4 da @ $1.25 - $5.95. Rd Way Dept |
| 1857-48 | Hilbridge, Thomas | lab 20 da @ $1 - $20.00. Rd Dept main stem 2d s-div |
| 1855-34 | Hildebrand, C. | emigrant agt 28 da @ $40 per mo - $40.00. Trans Dept main stem |
| 1855-34 | " H. K. | greas cars 25 da @ $1 - $25.00. Trans Dept main stem |
| 1855-90 | | mach 31 da @ $1.90 - $58.90. Mach Dept |
| 1857-7 | Hildebrandt, C. | emig agt @ $41.65 per mo. Gen Tick Agt Ofc |
| 1857-137 | " John H. | lab 20½ da @ $1 - $20.50. Mach Dept, Cumb |
| 1857-82 | Hilderbran, George | bricklay 14¼ da @ $2 - $28.50. grad, Board Tree Tun |
| 1857-55 | Hilderbrant, August | blksmith 25¼ da @ $1.25 - $31.55. Rd Dept main stem 9th s-div |
| 1855-85 | Hilery, John | help 21½ da @ $1.10 - $23.65. Mach Dept |
| 1857-61 | Hilgertnu, Baltzer | fore 27½ da @ $1.25 - $34.35. Rd Dept main stem 14th s-div |
| 1857-41 | Hill, A. R. | lab 28 da @ $1 - $28.00. Rd Dept main stem 14th s-div |
| 1855-29 | " James | ton fire 24½ da @ $1.75 - $42.85. NW Va rd, Parkersburg sta |
| 1857-124 | " Joseph | haul & saw firewd 7½ da @ $1 - $7.50. Trans Dept main stem |
| | | mach app 1 3/4 da @ $.45 - $.80. Mach Dept, Martinsburg |

B & O RR EMPLOYEES 179

| ID | Name | Entry |
|---|---|---|
| 1857-104 | Hill, Thomas | fore 25 da @ $1.50 - $37.50. NW Va RR fun |
| 1857-131 | " William | mach 25½ da @ $1.75 - $43.75. Mach Dept, Grafton |
| 1857-34 | Hilleary, Adam | ton fire 28 da @ $1.75 - $49.00. 4th div |
| 1855-27 | " Aug. | get out eng 28 da @ $1.50 - $42.00. Trans Dept main stem |
| 1855-39 | " H. J. | fore 21 da @ $1.25 - $26.25. Rd Way Dept |
| 1855-40 | " John | fore 24 da @ $1.25 - $30.00. Rd Way Dept |
| 1857-122 | Hillen, Charles | put away eng &c 28½ da @ $1.15 - $32.75. Mach Dept, Balto |
| 1855-84 | " " | mach (includ boil mkr, work sht iron, &c) 23 3/4 da @ $1.25 - $29.70. Mach Dept |
| 1857-115 | " Hiram | boil mkr 26½ da @ $1.40 - $37.10. Mach Dept, Balto |
| 1857-128 | Hiller, John | blksmith help 19½ da @ $1 - $19.75. Mach Dept, Piedmont |
| 1857-95 | Hillery, John A. | lab 24 da @ $1 - $24.00. Wash br, Rd Dept |
| 1857-17 | Hillman, William | coup 26½ da @ $30 per mo - $31.80. Mt Clare sta |
| 1857-24 | Hilton, Horace | watch 30 da @ $40 per mo - $40.00. Wheeling sta |
| 1857-108 | " John | ton brak 6 da @ $30 per mo; 18 da @ $18 per mo - $36.00. 1st div |
| 1855-11 | " William | mach 18 3/4 da @ $1.60 - $30.00. Mach Dept, Balto |
| 1857-69 | Himes, Alexander | conduc & brak 10½ da @ $40 per mo - $17.50. Trans Dept main stem |
| 1857-50 | " Samuel | carp 18 da @ $1.60 - $28.80. Mt Clare sta, Balto |
| 1857-73 | " Silas | lab 25 da @ $1 - $25.00. Rd Dept main stem 4th s-div |
| 1857-26 | Hinebaugh, John | carp 22½ da @ $1.50 - $33.35. repair bridges &c |
| 1855-66 | Hineman, David | ton brak 32 da @ $40 per mo - $51.20. 3d & 4th div |
| 1857-61 | " " | lab 19 da @ $1.62½ - $30.85. Rd Way Dept |
| 1857-31 | Hines, Benj. F. | fore 26 da @ $1.25 - $32.50. Rd Dept main stem 14th s-div |
| 1857-88 | " Patrick | ton fire 26 da @ $1.33.35 per mo - $34.65. 1st div |
| 1855-47 | Hinks, M. | lab 26 da @ $1.12 - $29.25. grad, Welling Tun |
| 1857-32 | Hinman, Walter | lab 6 da @ $1 - $6.00. Rd Way Dept |
| 1857-136 | Hinsey, Mary | ton fire 22½ da @ $1.75 - $38.90. 2d div |
| 1855-56 | Hinton, E. | clean pass cars @ $20 per mo - $20.00. Mach Dept, Wheeling |
| 1857-58 | " " | fore 20 da @ $1.25 - $25.00. Rd Way Dept |
| 1855-95 | " Selby | watch 30 da @ $1 - $30.00. Rd Dept main stem 11th s-div |
| 1855-38 | Hipsley, John | mould 21 da @ $1.55 - $32.55. Mach Dept |
| 1857-48 | " " | fore 27 da @ $1.25 - $33.75. Rd Dept main stem 2d s-div |
| 1855-11 | " N. S. | conduc & brak 24 da @ $1.25 - $30.30. Rd Dept main stem |
| 1857-21 | Hirons, Joshua | ton conduc 25 da @ $50 per mo - $50.00. Trans Dept main stem |
| 1857-73 | Hirst, Franklin | carp 25 da @ $1.65 - $41.25. repair water sta, M.S. & P.B. |
| 1857-91 | " " | lab 25 da @ $1 - $25.00. grad, Welling Tun |

180    B & O RR EMPLOYEES

| | | |
|---|---|---|
| 1855-65 | Hirst, Samuel N. | lab 26 da @ $1.25 - $32.50. Rd Way Dept |
| 1855-41 | Hiser, John | lab 15 da @ $1 - $15.00. Rd Way Dept |
| 1855-82 | Hiskey, John | app 23½ da @ $.55 - $12.90. Mach Dept |
| 1857-116 | Hiss, Benjamin | boil mkr help 19½ da @ $1.15 - $22.40. Mach Dept, Balto |
| 1855-96 | Hissey, A. | lab 19 da @ $1.05 - $19.95. Mach Dept |
| 1855-85 | " H. | lab 28 da @ $1.10 - $30.80. Mach Dept |
| 1857-18 | Hitchcock, A. W. | blksmith 22 3/4 da @ $1.45 - $33.00. Mach Dept |
| 1857-109 | Hitchew, J. H. | pass train brak 30 da @ $33.35 per mo - $33.35. thr mail & exp |
| 1857-26 | Hobbs, Armstead | mach 18 da @$1.72 - $30.95. Mach Dept, Balto |
| 1855-8 | " E. M. | ton brak 8½ da @ $40 per mo - $13.60. 3d & 4th div |
| 1855-19 | " Elias | brak 24 da @ $33.35 per mo - $28.55. Trans Dept main stem |
| 1857-48 | " Joseph | ton eng'man 12 da @ $3 - $36.00. Trans Dept main stem |
| 1855-35 | " Thomas | fore 25½ da @ $1.25 - $31.85. Rd Dept main stem 2d s-div |
| 1857-126 | " " | watch 28 da @ $1.25 - $35.00. Trans Dept main stem |
| 1857-9 | " " | clean eng 26½ da @ $1.15 - $30.45. Mach Dept, Martinsburg |
| 1857-9 | " " | watch 30 da @ $1.25 - $37.50. hp exp, Balto |
| 1855-78 | Hoblitzel, O. | watch 30 da @ $1.25 - $37.50. Mt Clare sta |
| 1857-107 | Hoblitzell, O. C. G. | clk @ $35 per mo - $35.00. Mach Dept |
| 1857-81 | Hodge, Isaac | chief clk $66.65 per mo. Mach Dept |
| 1857-75 | " J. M. | brak 1 da @ $1.50 - $1.50. lay 2d track |
| 1857-76 | " J. N. | conduc 18 da @ $1.92 - $34.65. ballast train for 2d track |
| 1857-108 | Hodgson, J. B. | conduc 8 da @ $2 - $16.00. ballast train for 2d track |
| 1855-82 | " James | mach 18 da @ $1.72 - $30.95. Mach Dept, Balto |
| 1857-19 | Hoenicka, George | mach 29 da @ $1.72 - $49.90. Mach Dept |
| 1857-30 | " " | pass eng'man 4 da @ $2.50 - $10.00. 3d div |
| 1857-54 | Hoferkamp, Henry | ton eng'man 16 da @ $3 - $48.00. 3d div |
| 1857-11 | Hoff, A. M. | track lay 19½ da @ $1.37½ - $26.80. Rd Way Dept |
| 1855-36 | Hoffler, J. | clk 30 da @ $11.65 per mo - $11.65. Locust Pt |
| 1857-17 | Hoffman, D. C. | lab 24½ da @ $25 per mo - $25.25. Trans Dept main stem |
| 1855-90 | " John | disp 30 da @ $60 per mo - $60.00. Wheeling sta |
| 1855-29 | " N. A. | help 30 da @ $1.15 - $34.50. Mach Dept |
| 1857-26 | " W. | haul & saw firewd 5½ da @ $1 - $5.50. Trans Dept main stem |
| 1855-79 | " William | ton brak 25 da @ $40 per mo - $40.00. 3d & 4th div |
| 1855-119 | " " | tin 24 da @ $1.72 - $41.30. Mach Dept |
| 1855-59 | Hoffmeyer, F. | tin 24 da @ $1.75 - $42.00. Mach Dept, Balto |
| | | lab 24 da @ $1 - $24.00. Rd Way Dept |

| | | |
|---|---|---|
| 1857-108 | Hofselter, Joseph | mach 18 da @ $1.65 - $29.70. Mach Dept, Balto |
| 1855-24 | Hogan, Cornelius | pass & bur driv 24 da @ $1 - $24.00. Trans Dept main stem |
| 1857-10 | " | stab'man 25 da @ $1 - $25.00. hp exp, Balto |
| 1857-46 | Daniel | lab 16 da @ $1 - $16.00. Rd Dept main stem 1st s-div |
| 1855-62 | Edward | lab 6 da @ $1 - $6.00. Rd Way Dept |
| 1857-39 | James | lab 28½ da @ $1 - $28.50. NW Va rd, Parkersburg sta |
| 1857-114 | John | iron mould help 18 da @ $1.10 - $19.80. Mach Dept, Balto |
| 1855-68 | Michael | lab 19½ da @ $1 - $19.50. Rd Way Dept |
| 1857-130 | " | lab 27½ da @ $1 - $27.50. Mach Dept, Piedmont |
| 1857-114 | Patrick | iron mould help 19 da @ $1.10 - $20.90. Mach Dept, Balto |
| 1855-88 | Hogelin, J. C. | carp 22 da @ $1.25 - $27.50. Mach Dept |
| 1857-122 | Hogett, James | eng clean 17½ da @ $1. - $17.50. Mach Dept, Balto |
| 1855-25 | Hoggett, James | clean eng 24 da @ $1.15 - $27.60. Trans Dept main stem |
| 1857-53 | Holbert, John | lab 24½ da @ $1 - $24.50. Rd Dept main stem 7th s-div |
| 1857-52 | Riley | lab 25 da @ $1 - $25.00. Rd Dept main stem 6th s-div |
| 1855-42 | William | lab 11 da @ $1 - $11.00. Rd Way Dept |
| 1857-53 | " | lab 23 da @ $1 - $23.00. Rd Dept main stem 7th s-div |
| 1857-7 | Holden, E. P. | clk @ $40 per mo. Clk of Errors Ofc |
| 1857-83 | Michael | lab 7½ da @ $1.12 - $8.45. grad, Board Tree Tun |
| 1855-75 | Holin, Pat. | lab 23 da @ $1 -$23.00. Rd Way Dept |
| 1857-97 | Holion, Martin | lab 26½ da @ $1 - $26.50. NW Va RR, Rd Dept 2d s-div |
| 1857-92 | Holland, Stephen | lab 20⅚ da @ $1.12 - $22.75. grad, Littleton Tun |
| 1857-84 | Holliday, William | fire 17⅞ da @ $1.75 - $30.20. grad, Board Tree Tun |
| 1857-32 | " | ton fire 11½ da @ $1.75 - $19.70. 2d div |
| 1857-8 | Hollingshead, G. R. | rec clk 30 da @ $58.35 per mo - $58.35. Camden sta |
| 1857-23 | Hollis, James | ton conduc 26½ da @ $50 per mo - $53.00. 3d & 4th div |
| 1857-19 | Holly, Frank | pass eng'man 4 da @ $2.50 - $10.00. 3d div |
| 1855-67 | Holmes, George B. | mason 24 da @ $2 - $48.00. Rd Way Dept |
| 1857-33 | J. | ton fire 24 da @ $1.75 - $42.00. 3d div |
| 1855-36 | John | lab 24½ da @ $25 per mo - $25.25. Trans Dept main stem |
| 1855-32 | " | saw wd 13 7/8 cords @ $.50 - $6.95. Trans Dept main stem |
| 1857-86 | M. S. | lab 23 3/4 da @ $1 - $23.25. grad, McGuire's Tun |
| 1855-35 | " | disp of trains 28 da @ $50 per mo - $50.00. Trans Dept main stem |
| 1857-23 | Holpins, Jas. | ton conduc 25 da @ $60 per mo - $60.00. 3d & 4th div |
| 1855-75 | Holstead, Sam'l. | fore 25 da @ $1.25 - $31.25. Rd Way Dept |
| 1855-20 | | fire 14 3/4 da @ $1.75 - $25.80. Trans Dept main stem |

| | | |
|---|---|---|
| 1857-30 | Holsted, Samuel | ton eng'man 27 da @ $2.50 - $67.50. 3d div |
| 1855-14 | Holstein, H. | brak 9½ da @ $40 per mo - $15.85. Trans Dept main stem |
| 1855-57 | Holstine, Jno. H. | brak 11¼ da @ $40 per mo - $17.30. Rd Way Dept |
| 1857-135 | Holt, John | lab 20 3/4 da @ $1 - $20.75. Mach Dept,Wheeling |
| 1857-48 | Thomas | lab 22½ da @ $1 - $22.50. Rd Dept main stem 2d s-div |
| 1857-48 | William | lab 24¼ da @ $1 - $24.25. Rd Dept main stem 2d s-div |
| 1857-118 | Holtraver, Lewis | blksmith help 17¼ da @ $1 - $17.25. Mach Dept, Balto |
| 1857-74 | Holts, John | track lay 22 3/4 da @ $1 - $22.75. put swit on line of rd |
| 1857-107 | Holtz, David | mess $13 per mo. Mach Dept |
| 1857-131 | John | iron mould 12 da @ $1.50 - $18.00. Mach Dept, Grafton |
| 1857-115 | " | stat'ry eng'man 26 da @ $1.50 - $39.00. Mach Dept, Balto |
| 1855-73 | Holtzgrabe, Wm. | track lay 22 da @ $1.12½ - $24.75. Rd Way Dept |
| 1857-71 | Holtzgrebe, Wm. | track lay 23 da @ $1.12 - $25.85. Camden sta, repair tracks |
| 1857-24 | Holtzman, A. J. | ton brak 16 da @ $40 per mo - $25.60. 1st div |
| 1855-90 | John | carp 23¼ da @ $1.45 - $33.70. Mach Dept |
| 1855-77 | " | help 34 da @ $1.15 - $39.10. Mach Dept |
| 1857-129 | " | carp 14½ da @ $1.50 - $21.75. Mach Dept, Piedmont |
| 1857-9 | Holtzon, A. J. | lab 7½ da @ $30 per mo - $9.00. Mt Clare sta |
| 1855-77 | Holzte, Jno. | help 26¼ da @ $1.25 -$32.80. Mach Dept |
| 1857-123 | Homerick, John | mach 18 3/4 da @ $1.50 - $28.10. Mach Dept, Martinsburg |
| 1857-31 | Honcke, Simon | ton fire 19¼ da @ $1.75 - $33.70. 1st div |
| 1857-31 | Hood, George W. | ton fire 5¼ da @ $1.75 - $9.20. 1st div |
| 1857-31 | " " | ton fire 16½ da @ $1.75 - $28.85. 1st div |
| 1857-24 | John W. | ton brak 25 da @ $30 per mo; 1 da @ $50 per mo - $32.00. 1st div |
| 1855-22 | Lewis | fire 12¼ da @ $1.75 - $21.45. Trans Dept main stem |
| 1857-137 | Hoofman, Henry | lab 23¼ da @ $1.15 - $26.75. Mach Dept, Cumb |
| 1855-95 | Hoofnagle, A. | mould 26 3/4 da @ $1.72 - $46.00. Mach Dept |
| 1855-96 | James | app 17 da @ $.75 - $12.75. Mach Dept |
| 1855-96 | John | app 24 da @ $.45 - $10.80. Mach Dept |
| 1855-95 | William | fore @ $83.35 per mo - $83.35. Mach Dept |
| 1855-88 | Hooge, Frederick | carp @ $45 per mo - $45.00. Mach Dept |
| 1857-125 | " | fore carp @ $48.75 per mo - $48.75. Mach Dept, Martinsburg |
| 1855-88 | Henry | app 27 3/4 da @ $.60 - $16.65. Mach Dept |
| 1855-77 | Hook, Jas. | mach 23 da @ $1.50 - $34.50. Mach Dept |
| 1855-53 | Robert | carp 24 da @ $1.60 - $38.40. Rd Way Dept |
| 1857-69 | " | carp 11 3/4 da @ $1.60 - $18.80. Mt Clare sta, Balto |

B & O RR EMPLOYEES  183

| ID | Name | Description |
|---|---|---|
| 1855-48 | Hooleham, Pat. | train hand 11 da @ $1 - $11.00. Rd Way Dept |
| 1857-123 | Hooper, Nelson | mach 16 da @ $1.50 - $24.00. Mach Dept, Martinsburg |
| 1857-19 | Hooper, W. H. | bag mast 9 da @ $45 per mo - $13.50. thr mail & exp |
| 1857-18 | Wm. H. | pass train brak 21 da @ $33.35 per mo - $23.35. thr mail & exp |
| 1855-90 | Hoopman, C. A. | help 16 3/4 da @ $1 - $16.75. Mach Dept |
| 1857-129 | Hoopper, James | carp 15 3/4 da @ $1.50 - $23.60. Mach Dept, Piedmont |
| 1857-111 | Hoops, F. B. | mach help 15½ da @ $1.15 - $17.80. Mach Dept, Balto |
| 1855-76 | Frank | help 22 da @ $1.15 - $25.30. Mach Dept |
| 1855-7 | Hoover, G. W. | pass conduc 28 da @ $62.50 per mo - $62.50. Trans Dept main stem |
| 1857-37 | Geo. W. | pass train conduc 30 da @ $75 per mo - $75.00. Wash br rd, Wash city sta |
| 1855-45 | John | lab 20 3/4 da @ $1 - $20.75. Rd Way Dept |
| 1855-92 | Lewis | carp @ $32 per mo - $32.00. Mach Dept |
| 1857-129 | " | inspec cars @ $32 per mo - $32.00. Mach Dept, Piedmont |
| 1857-129 | S. | inspec cars @ $32 per mo - $32.00. Mach Dept, Piedmont |
| 1855-5 | Hopkins, F. | ton fire 6 da @ $33.33 per mo - $8.35. Trans Dept, Wash br |
| 1857-36 | J. F. | tele oper 30 da @ $30 per mo - $30.00. Benwood |
| 1855-55 | John | lab 23 da @ $1 - $23.00. Rd Way Dept |
| 1855-89 | " | mach 18½ da @ $1.60 - $29.20. Mach Dept |
| 1857-103 | " | horse & cart 2 da @ $1.50 - $3.00. NW Va RR depot |
| 1857-97 | " | lab 26 da @ $1 - $26.00. NW Va RR, Rd Dept 2d s-div |
| 1857-73 | " | lab 8 da @ $1.12 - $9.00. repair water sta, M.S. & P.B. |
| 1857-63 | " | lab 23 3/4 da @ $1 - $23.75. Rd Dept main stem 16th s-div |
| 1855-55 | Patrick | lab 24 da @ $1 - $24.00. Rd Way Dept |
| 1855-75 | " | lab 21 da @ $1 - $21.00. Rd Way Dept |
| 1857-51 | " | lab 25 da @ $1 - $25.00. Rd Dept main stem 5th s-div |
| 1857-63 | " | lab 23 da @ $1 - $23.00. Rd Dept main stem 16th s-div |
| 1855-6 | Hopper, George | clk 28 da @ $62.50 per mo -$62.50. Trans Dept main stem |
| 1857-9 | " | clk 30 da @ $62.50 per mo - $62.50. Mt Clare sta |
| 1855-73 | Hopps, Geo. | lab 13 3/4 da @ $1 - $13.75. Rd Way Dept |
| 1857-100 | Horan, Bartly | lab 25 3/4 da @ $1 -$25.75. NW Va RR, Rd Dept 5th s-div |
| 1857-104 | Dennis | miner 23 da @ $1 - $23.00. NW Va RR Tun |
| 1855-59 | James | lab 20¼ da @ $1 - $20.25. Rd Way Dept |
| 1857-62 | " | lab 24½ da @ $1 - $24.50. Rd Dept main stem 15th s-div |
| 1855-59 | Kearons L. | lab 10 da @ $1 - $10.00. Rd Way Dept |
| 1857-62 | Laurence | lab 19½ da @ $1 - $19.50. Rd Dept main stem 15th s-div |

# B & O RR EMPLOYEES

| Date | Name | Description |
|---|---|---|
| 1857-104 | Horan, Maley | miner 21¼ da @ $1 - $21.25. NW Va RR Tun |
| 1857-62 | " Michael | lab 24 da @ $1 - $24.00. Rd Dept main stem 15th s-div |
| 1857-104 | " " | miner 23 3/4 da @ $1 - $23.75. NW Va RR Tun |
| 1855-59 | " Patrick | lab 15¼ da @ $1 - $15.25. Rd Way Dept |
| 1857-62 | " " | lab 24¼ da @ $1 - $24.25. Rd Dept main stem 15th s-div |
| 1857-62 | " Peter | lab 26 da @ $.87 - $22.75. Rd Dept main stem 15th s-div |
| 1857-62 | " Thomas | lab 18½ da @ $1 - $18.50. Rd Dept main stem 15th s-div |
| 1857-61 | Horchlee, William | lab 8½ da @ $1 - $8.50. Rd Dept main stem 14th s-div |
| 1855-62 | Hore, John | help 3 da @ $1 - $3.00. Rd Way Dept |
| 1857-67 | " " | lab 21 da @ $1 - $21.00. Rd Dept main stem 19th s-div |
| 1857-51 | Horgan, Cristian | lab 25 da @ $1 - $25.00. Rd Dept main stem 5th s-div |
| 1857-76 | Horine, Martin | dril 24 da @ $1.10 - $26.40. ballast train for 2d track |
| 1855-48 | Horley, Chas. | train hand 20¼ da @ $1 - $20.25. Rd Way Dept |
| 1855-48 | " John | train hand 12 3/4 da @ $1 - $12.75. Rd Way Dept |
| 1857-135 | Horne, Michael | lab 19 3/4 da @ $1 - $19.75. Mach Dept, Wheeling |
| 1857-124 | Horner, Thomas | blksmith 17 3/4 da @ $1.45 - $25.75. Mach Dept, Martinsburg |
| 1857-51 | Hosier, James | lab 25 da @ $1 - $25.00. Rd Dept main stem 5th s-div |
| 1857-17 | Hosimer, James | clk 30 da @ $50 per mo - $50.00. frt transfer force at Bellaire, opp Benwood |
| 1857-115 | Hoskins, George | pat mkr 18½ da @$1.65 - $30.50. Mach Dept, Balto |
| 1855-16 | Houck, C. | pass fire 10 da @$40 per mo - $14.30. Trans Dept main stem |
| 1857-40 | " " | pass fire 17 da @ $40 per mo - $22.65. NW Va rd, Parkersburg sta |
| 1855-20 | " Charles | fire 8½ da @ $1.75 - $14.85. Trans Dept main stem |
| 1855-22 | " " | fire 7½ da @$1.75 - $13.10. Mach Dept, Grafton |
| 1857-132 | " " | lab 3 da @ $1 - $3.00. Mach Dept, Grafton |
| 1857-30 | " " | ton eng'man 22 3/4 da @$2.50 - $56.85. 4th div |
| 1855-26 | " Frederick | clean eng 18 da @ $1 - $18.00. Trans Dept main stem |
| 1857-137 | " " | pass car clean @ $30 per mo - $30.00. Mach Dept, Cumb |
| 1855-23 | Hough, Robert | fire 26 da @ $1.75 - $45.50. Trans Dept main stem |
| 1857-35 | " James | lab 19 da @ $1 - $19.00. Edwards' wd train 3d & 4th div |
| 1855-11 | " Sol. | conduc & brak 27 da @ $50 per mo - $56.25. Trans Dept main stem |
| 1857-91 | Houke, Charles | help 2 da @ $1 - $2.00. Mach Dept |
| 1855-64 | Houran, Thos. | lab 23½ da @ $1 - $23.50. Rd Way Dept |
| 1855-63 | House, Jno. | fore 20 da @ $1.25 - $25.00. Rd Way Dept |
| 1855-40 | " L. | nail 25 da @ $1.05 - $26.25. Rd Way Dept |
| 1857-50 | " Lawson | nail 30 da @$1.05 - $31.50. Rd Dept main stem 4th s-div |
| 1855-44 | " Samuel | lab 20½ da @ $1 - $20.50. Rd Way Dept |

B & O RR EMPLOYEES 185

| | | |
|---|---|---|
| 1857-54 | House, Samuel | lab 12 da @ $1 - $12.00. Rd Dept main stem 8th s-div |
| 1855-51 | " William | lab @ $30 per mo - $30.00. Rd Way Dept |
| 1857-54 | " " | pump water 30 da @ $1 - $30.00. Rd Dept main stem 8th s-div |
| 1857-52 | Householder, Samuel | lab 21½ da @ $1 - $21.50. Rd Dept main stem 6th s-div |
| 1855-22 | " William | lab 20 da @ $1 - $20.00. Rd Dept main stem 6th s-div |
| 1857-13 | Houser, Dennis | fire 11 da @ $1.75 - $19.25. Trans Dept main stem |
| 1857-108 | Houseworth, J. W. | load cars 30 da @ $35 per mo - $35.00. Martinsburg |
| 1855-22 | Housh, C. | mach 17½ da @ $1.65 - $28.85. Mach Dept, Balto |
| 1855-27 | Houston, C. C. | clean eng 16 da @ $1 - $16.00. Trans Dept main stem |
| 1857-133 | " " | clean eng 18 da @ $1 - $18.00. Mach Dept, Fetterman |
| 1855-30 | " John | prepar fuel 28 da @ $30 per mo - $30.00. Trans Dept main stem |
| 1857-108 | " " | asst mast mech @ $60 per mo - $60.00. Mach Dept, Balto |
| 1857-131 | " Samuel | mast mech @ $83.35 per mo - $83.35. Mach Dept, Grafton |
| 1857-131 | " William | mach 17¾ da @ $1.60 - $27.60. Mach Dept, Grafton |
| 1855-49 | Hoverscamp, C. | watch cuts 28 da @ $1 - $28.00. Rd Way Dept |
| 1857-58 | " " | watch 29 da @ $1 - $29.00. Rd Dept main stem 11th s-div |
| 1855-27 | Howard, James | clean eng 19½ da @ $1 - $19.50. Trans Dept main stem |
| 1855-9 | " John | conduc 9½ da @ $50 per mo - $19.80. Trans Dept main stem |
| 1857-128 | " " | blksmith help 17 3/4 da @ $1 - $17.75. Mach Dept, Piedmont |
| 1857-82 | " " | lab 24 da @ $1.12 - $27.00. grad, Board Tree Tun |
| 1857-33 | " " | ton fire 11 3/4 da @ $1.75 - $20.55. 3d div |
| 1855-89 | Howe, J. | boil mkr 20½ da @ $1.70 - $34.85. Mach Dept |
| 1857-128 | " Thomas | boil mkr 19¼ da @ $1.50 - $28.85. Mach Dept, Piedmont |
| 1857-94 | Howley, Michael | lab 14 da @ $1 - $14.00. quarry & haul stone for Board Tree & Littleton Tun |
| 1855-88 | Howrich, John | app 22¼ da @ $.60 - $13.35. Mach Dept |
| 1855-5 | Howser, Dennis | ton fire 1 da @ $33.33 per mo - $1.40. Trans Dept, Wash br |
| 1857-22 | " Israel | ton conduc 24 da @ $50 per mo - $48.00. 2d div |
| 1855-94 | Hubbard, H. | lab 9 da @ $1 - $9.00. Mach Dept |
| 1857-116 | " Thomas | blksmith 15½ da @ $1.65 - $25.55. Mach Dept, Balto |
| 1857-48 | Huberson, James | lab 26½ da @ $1 - $26.50. Rd Dept main stem 2d s-div |
| 1855-90 | Huddle, John | help 21½ da @ $1 - $21.25. Mach Dept |
| 1857-136 | " " | blksmith help 19 da @ $1 - $19.00. Mach Dept, Cumb |
| 1855-90 | " Joseph | help 21½ da @ $1 - $21.25. Mach Dept |
| 1857-35 | Hudson, James | eng'man 7 da @ $2.50 - $17.50. Edwards' wd train 3d & 4th div |
| 1857-132 | " " | lab 3 da @ $1.25 - $3.75. Mach Dept, Grafton |
| 1857-40 | " " | ton eng'man 9 da @ $2.50 - $22.50. NW Va rd, Parkersburg sta |

186                B & O RR EMPLOYEES

| | | | |
|---|---|---|---|
| 1855-17 | Hudson, T. | ton eng'man 20 3/4 da @ $2.50 - $51.85. Trans Dept main stem |
| 1855-91 | " William | help 25 da @ $1 - $25.00. Mach Dept |
| 1857-127 | " | mach 18½ da @ $1.25 - $23.10. Mach Dept, Piedmont |
| 1855-38 | Hues, Patrick | lab 25½ da @ $1 - $25.50. Rd Way Dept |
| 1855-89 | Huggins, A. L. | mach 6½ da @ $1.50 - $9.00. Mach Dept |
| 1855-6 | " A. L. | agt 28 da @ $83.35 per mo - $83.35. Trans Dept main stem |
| 1857-14 | " " | agt 30 da @ $100 per mo - $100.00. Cumb |
| 1857-130 | " Albert Jr. | blksmith help ½ da @ $1 - $.50. Mach Dept, Newburg |
| 1855-27 | " Ben. | clean eng 25 da @ $1 - $25.00. Trans Dept main stem |
| 1857-14 | " " | watch 30 da @$30 per mo - $30.00. Newburg sta |
| 1857-101 | Hughes, Anthony | lab 7½ da @ $1 - $7.50. NW Va RR ballast train |
| 1855-11 | " C. E. | conduc & brak 3½ da @ $.40 per mo - $5.85. Trans Dept main stem |
| 1855-96 | " Charles | app 24 da @ $.65 - $15.60. Mach Dept |
| 1857-9 | " Charles E. | watch 22 da @$1.25 - $27.50. Mt Clare sta |
| 1855-8 | " E. C. | brak 3 da @$33.35 per mo - $3.55. Trans Dept main stem |
| 1857-47 | " Edward | lab 27 da @ $1 - $27.00. Rd Dept main stem 1st s-div |
| 1857-61 | " Felix | fore 28 da @ $1.25 - $35.00. Rd Dept main stem 14th s-div |
| 1855-68 | " Francis | mason 7½ da @ $2 - $15.00. Rd Way Dept |
| 1855-53 | " " | swit lay 24 da @ $1.50 - $36.00. Rd Way Dept |
| 1857-61 | " Frank | fore 28 da @ $1.50 - $42.00. Rd Dept main stem 14th s-div |
| 1857-82 | " Geo. | bricklay 1½ da @$2 - $28.50. grad, Board Tree Tun |
| 1857-73 | " Henry | carp 4 da @$1.25 - $5.00. repair bridges &c |
| 1855-56 | " " | lab 23 3/4 da @ $1 - $23.75. Rd Way Dept |
| 1857-58 | " James | watch 24 da @ $1 - $24.00. Rd Dept main stem 11th s-div |
| 1857-48 | " John | lab 24½ da @ $1 - $24.50. Rd Dept main stem 2d s-div |
| 1857-102 | " Joseph | stone mason 13½ da @ $2 - $27.00. NW Va RR, rwy depot |
| 1857-82 | " M. | bricklay 20 3/4 da @ $2 - $41.50. grad, Board Tree Tun |
| 1855-80 | " " | carp 24 da @ $1.45 - $34.80. Mach Dept |
| 1855-48 | " Martin | lab 22½ da @ $1 - $22.25. Rd Way Dept |
| 1857-139 | " " | blksmith help 25 3/4 da @ $.90 - $23.15. NW Va RR, Mach Dept, Parkersburg |
| 1857-59 | " Michael | lab 25 da @ $1 - $25.00. Rd Dept main stem 12th s-div |
| 1857-85 | " " | lab 6½ da @ $1.12 - $7.30. grad, Board Tree Tun |
| 1857-88 | " " | lab 18 da @ $1.12 - $20.25. grad, Welling Tun |
| 1857-130 | " " | lab 19¾ da @ $1 - $19.25. Mach Dept, Piedmont |
| 1857-101 | " " | lab 22 da @ $.75 - $16.50. NW Va RR ballast train |
| 1855-48 | " Mike | fire 24 da @ $1.33 - $32.00. Rd Way Dept |

| ID | Name | Details |
|---|---|---|
| 1857-120 | Hughes, Mike | carp 18 3/4 da @ $1.65 - $30.95. Mach Dept, Balto |
| 1857-104 | " Thomas | miner 23½ da @ $1.12 - $26.45. NW Va RR Tun |
| 1855-80 | " W. H. | supt pass cars @ $62.50 per mo - $62.50. Mach Dept |
| 1855-77 | " Wm. | help 25¼ da @ $1.15 - $29.05. Mach Dept |
| 1855-7 | " Wm. H. | 28 da @ $15 per mo - $15.00. Trans Dept main stem |
| 1857-121 | " " | pass car supt @ $62.50 per mo - $62.50. Mach Dept, Balto |
| 1855-8 | Hull, E. J. | brak 23 da @ $5.90 - $22.50. Rd Dept main stem 6th s-div |
| 1857-52 | Hume, Franklin | lab 25 da @ $.90 - $22.50. Rd Dept main stem 6th s-div |
| 1855-4 | Humphreys, O. T. | conduc 28 da @ $62.50 per mo - $62.50. Trans Dept, Wash br |
| 1857-24 | Hungerford, Thomas | ton brak 18½ da @ $40 per mo - $29.60. 1st div |
| 1855-61 | Hunt, George | lab 13 da @ $1 - $13.00. Rd Way Dept |
| 1857-67 | " H. L. | fore 23 3/4 da @ $1.25 - $28.45. Rd Dept main stem 18th s-div |
| 1855-60 | " " | supv @ $50 per mo - $50.00. Rd Way Dept |
| 1857-64 | " " | horse hire 27 da @ $1 - $27.00. Rd Dept main stem 17th s-div |
| 1857-65 | " " | horses & carts 50 da @ $1.12 - $56.25. Rd Dept main stem 17th s-div |
| 1857-64 | " " | supv @ $50 per mo - $50.00. Rd Dept main stem 17th s-div |
| 1855-48 | " James | fore 28 da @ $1.25 - $30.00. Rd Way Dept |
| 1855-85 | " Stephen | blksmith 24 da @ $1.50 - $36.00. Mach Dept |
| 1857-116 | " " | blksmith 18 da @ $1.50 - $27.00. Mach Dept, Balto |
| 1857-98 | Hunter, Alexander | lab 23 3/4 da @ $1 - $23.75. NW Va RR, Rd Dept 3d s-div |
| 1857-8 | " H. | lab 25 da @ $30 per mo - $30.00. Camden sta |
| 1855-34 | " James | lab 4 da @ $1 - $4.00. Trans Dept main stem |
| 1857-75 | " John M. | lab 25¼ da @ $1 - $25.50. ballast train for 2d track |
| 1855-80 | " " | carp 23 da @ $1.55 - $35.65. Mach Dept |
| 1857-120 | " " | carp 17¼ da @ $1.55 - $26.75. Mach Dept, Balto |
| 1855-32 | " O. B. | tele oper 28 da @ $30 per mo - $30.00. Trans Dept main stem |
| 1857-18 | " " | pass train brak 1 da @ $33.35 per mo - $1.10. w end |
| 1855-34 | " R. B. | lab 24 da @ $1 - $24.00. Trans Dept main stem |
| 1857-16 | " " | stock yd 15 da @ $1 - $15.00. Moundsville sta |
| 1857-117 | Hupton, Michael | ton fire 19½ da @ $1.75 - $34.10. 3d div |
| 1855-19 | Hurbut, Thomas E. | blksmith help 17 3/4 da @ $1 - $17.75. Mach Dept, Balto |
| 1855-77 | Hurd, E. A. | ton eng'man 2½ da @ $2.50 - $6.25. Trans Dept main stem |
| 1857-28 | Hurdle, W. W. | mach 14½ da @ $1.72 - $24.50. Mach Dept |
| 1855-34 | Hurley, J. | ton eng'man 27 da @ $2.50 - $67.50. 1st div |
| 1855-34 | " " | clean pass car 28 da @ $30 per mo - $30.00. Trans Dept main stem |
| 1857-136 | " James | clean pass cars @ $30 per mo - $30.00. Mach Dept, Wheeling |

B & O RR EMPLOYEES

| ID | Name | Description |
|---|---|---|
| 1855-12 | Hurley, M. | conduc & brak 14 da @ $50 per mo - $31.15. Trans Dept main stem |
| 1855-73 | " | lab 27 da @ $1 - $27.00. Rd Way Dept |
| 1857-71 | Hushin, Michael | help 18 da @ $1 - $18.00. Mt Clare sta, Balto |
| 1857-90 | Hushin, Thomas | lab 10½ da @ $1.12 - $11.80. grad, Welling Tun |
| 1857-89 | Huskin, Michael | lab 12½ da @$1.12 - $14.05. grad, Welling Tun |
| 1855-15 | Hussell, C. | pass eng'man 21 da @ $3 - $63.00. Trans Dept main stem |
| 1857-19 | " G. | pass eng'man 21 da @ $3 - $63.00. 1st div |
| 1855-16 | Hussey, Chris. | pass fire 8 da @ $40 per mo; 9 da @ $1 - $20.45. Trans Dept main stem |
| 1857-93 | Hussy, Cristy | driv 26 da @ $1.50 - $26.00. quarry & haul stone for Board Tree & Littleton Tun |
| 1855-63 | Huston, Columbus | flag 17 3/4 da @ $1 - $17.75. Rd Way Dept |
| 1857-32 | " | ton fire 2 da @ $1.75 - $3.50. 2d div |
| 1855-82 | James T. | lab 22 da @ $1 - $22.00. Mach Dept |
| 1857-111 | John | mach help 18 da @ $1.15 - $20.70. Mach Dept, Balto |
| 1855-77 | " | mach 23¾ da @ $1.60 -$37.20. Mach Dept |
| 1857-122 | " | tend fill @ $30 per mo - $30.00. Mach Dept, Balto |
| 1855-78 | Samuel | asst fore @ $60 per mo - $60.00. Mach Dept |
| 1857-78 | William | help 24 da @ $1 - $24.00. Mach Dept |
| 1855-88 | Hutchinson, W. | carp 21½ da @ $1.25 - $26.90. Mach Dept |
| 1855-11 | Huzza, Jacob | conduc & brak 3 3/4 da @ $40 per mo - $6.25. Trans Dept main stem |
| 1857-49 | Hyatt, Eli | lab 25 da @ $1 - $25.00. Rd Dept main stem 3d s-div |
| 1855-40 | Henry | lab 23 da @ $1 - $23.00. Rd Way Dept |
| 1857-49 | " | lab 23¾ da @ $1 - $23.25. Rd Dept main stem 3d s-div |
| 1857-21 | Robert P. | ton conduc 19 da @ $50 per mo - $38.00. 1st div |
| 1857-49 | Thomas | lab 25 da @ $1 - $25.00. Rd Dept main stem 3d s-div |
| 1857-133 | Hyde, R. | mach 29¾ da @ $1.75 - $51.20. Mach Dept, Cameron |
| 1857-124 | Hynes, John | mach app 21 da @ $.45 - $9.45. Mach Dept, Martinsburg |
| 1857-78 | Robert | lab 26 da @ $.70 - $18.20. lay 2d track |
| 1855-40 | Samuel | lab 24 da @ $1 - $24.00. Rd Way Dept |
| 1857-93 | Hynn, Daniel | watch 23 da @ $1.50 - $23.00. quarry & haul stone for Board Tree & Littleton Tun |
| 1857-46 | Ichaelhart, Larkin | lab 22 da @ $1 - $22.00. Rd Dept main stem 1st s-div |
| 1855-89 | Iglehart, R. | mach 27 3/4 da @ $1.80 - $49.95. Mach Dept |
| 1857-130 | Igner, Richard | mach 30 da @ $1.80 - $54.00. Mach Dept, Newburg |
| 1857-137 | Igo, William | lab @ $30 per mo - $30.00. Mach Dept, Cumb |
| 1857-96 | Ijams, John | lab 24½ da @ $1 - $24.50. NW Va RR, Rd Dept 1st s-div |
| 1855-1 | William H. | carp 17 da @ $1.60 - $27.20. Mt Clare sta, Balto |
| | | transfer clk $750 per annum - $62.50. Ofc Hanover St |

## B & O RR EMPLOYEES

| | | |
|---|---|---|
| 1857-3 | Ijams, William H. | transfer clk @ $100 per mo. Gen Ofc |
| 1857-7 | Ilgenfritz, M. S. | clk @ $41.65 per mo. Mast of Trans Ofc |
| 1855-1 | Ing, William | bkkpr @ $750 per annum - $62.50. Ofc Hanover St |
| 1857-3 | " | bkkpr @ $83.33 per mo. Gen Ofc |
| 1855-35 | Ingham, Rand | lab 24 da @ $30 per mo - $30.00. Trans Dept main stem |
| 1857-20 | Ingle, Abraham | pass fire 9 da @ $40 per mo - $12.00. 1st div |
| 1857-38 | " | pass fire 14 da @ $40 per mo - $18.65. Wash br rd, Wash city sta |
| 1857-133 | Inglehart, Conrad | put away eng 2 da @ $1.50 - $3.00. Mach Dept, Fetterman |
| 1855-91 | " William | help 2½ da @ $1 - $2.50. Mach Dept |
| 1857-134 | Ingler, Hiram T. | mach 19 3/4 da @ $1.75 - $34.55. Mach Dept, Wheeling |
| 1857-40 | Irving, Loyd | ton brak 4 da @ $40 per mo - $6.40. NW Va rd, Parkersburg sta |
| 1857-26 | Iser, John | ton brak 9 da @ $40 per mo - $14.40. 3d & 4th div |
| 1855-51 | Ivory, Thomas | lab 28 da @ $1 - $28.00. Rd Way Dept |
| 1857-52 | Jack, James | lab 23 da @ $1 - $23.00. Rd Dept main stem 6th s-div |
| 1857-25 | Jack, Mathias | ton brak 20½ da @ $40 per mo - $32.80. 2d div |
| 1855-58 | Jackey, M. | lab 21 da @ $1 - $21.00. Rd Way Dept |
| 1855-12 | Jackson, G. W. | conduc & brak 9½ da @ $50 per mo - $20.80. Trans Dept main stem |
| 1857-122 | George W. | lab 18 da @ $1 - $18.00. Mach Dept, Balto |
| 1857-32 | " | ton fire 16 da @ $1.75 - $28.00. 2d div |
| 1855-90 | James | mach 23½ da @ $1.67½ - $39.35. Mach Dept |
| 1855-78 | John | help 15 da @ $1.15 - $17.25. Mach Dept |
| 1857-128 | " | blksmith 9 da @ $2 - $18.00. Mach Dept, Piedmont |
| 1855-36 | Joseph | lab 25 da @ $25 per mo - $26.05. Trans Dept main stem |
| 1855-84 | Thomas | help 24 3/4 da @ $1.15 - $28.45. Mach Dept |
| 1855-1 | " | watch $360 per annum - $30.00. Ofc Hanover St |
| 1857-111 | " | mach help 18 da @ $1.15 - $20.70. Mach Dept, Balto |
| 1857-3 | " | port @ $40 per mo. Gen Ofc |
| 1855-6 | Jacobs, B. L. | agt 28 da @ $75 per mo - $75.00. Trans Dept main stem |
| 1857-7 | " " | asst supv trains (w. end & NW Va RR) @ $41.65 per mo. Supv Trains on Rd |
| 1855-7 | J. C. | supt of eng 28 da @ $3.50 - $98.00. Trans Dept main stem |
| 1857-112 | James, Charles | mach app 24 da @ $.45 - $10.80. Mach Dept, Balto |
| 1855-42 | Elisha | lab 17 da @ $1 - $17.00. Rd Way Dept |
| 1857-53 | " | lab 21 da @ $1 - $21.00. Rd Dept main stem 7th s-div |
| 1855-82 | G. W. | mach 26¼ da @ $1.72 - $45.60. Mach Dept |
| 1857-109 | G. W. | mach 17 3/4 da @ $1.80 - $31.95. Mach Dept, Balto |
| 1855-23 | Isaac | fire 11 da @ $1.75 - $19.25. Trans Dept main stem |

## B & O RR EMPLOYEES

| ID | Name | Details |
|---|---|---|
| 1857-28 | James, Isaac | ton eng'man 16⅔ da @ $2.50 - $40.60. 1st div |
| 1855-33 | John | lab 7 da @ $1 - $7.00. Trans Dept main stem |
| 1855-41 | Tobin | lab 15 da @ $1 - $15.00. Rd Way Dept |
| 1855-82 | William | lab 20½ da @ $1.10 - $22.55. Mach Dept |
| 1857-133 | Jamison, J. | mach 30 3/4 da @ $1.75 - $53.80. Mach Dept, Cameron |
| 1857-8 | Thomas | lab 25 da @ $30 per mo - $30.00. Camden sta |
| 1855-90 | Janer, C. | help 24 da @ $1 - $24.00. Mach Dept |
| 1857-128 | Jarboe, Wm. | mach help 24 da @ $.40 - $9.60. Mach Dept, Piedmont |
| 1855-20 | Jarrett, Jackson | fire 2½ da @ $1.75 - $4.35. Trans Dept main stem |
| 1857-77 | Jeff, William | quarry 23⅜ da @ $1 - $23.25. ballast train for 2d track |
| 1857-92 | Jefferis, Joseph | lab 16 3/4 da @ $1 - $16.75. grad, Littleton Tun |
| 1855-77 | Jeffers, A. | mach 23½ da @ $1.25 - $29.40. Mach Dept |
| 1855-95 | T. | core mkr 24 da @ $1.35 - $32.40. Mach Dept |
| 1855-77 | Wm. | mach 12½ da @ $1.50 - $18.75. Mach Dept |
| 1857-88 | Jeffries, Philip | carp 26 da @ $2 - $52.00. grad, Welling Tun |
| 1857-114 | Tim | core mkr 23 3/4 da @ $1.50 - $35.60. Mach Dept, Balto |
| 1855-9 | Jenkins, F. | conduc 18⅜ da @ $50 per mo - $38.00. Trans Dept main stem |
| 1857-132 | Franklin | blksmith 21 da @ $1.69 - $33.60. Mach Dept, Grafton |
| 1855-40 | G. | lab 22½ da @ $1 - $22.50. Rd Way Dept |
| 1857-123 | George | mach 17½ da @ $1.25 - $21.85. Mach Dept, Martinsburg |
| 1855-4 | J. H. | pass fire 28 da @ $40 per mo - $40.00. Trans Dept, Wash br |
| 1855-50 | James | watch cuts 30 da @ $1 - $30.00. Rd Way Dept |
| 1857-62 | " | fore 25 da @ $1.25 - $31.25. Rd Dept main stem 15th s-div |
| 1857-31 | " | ton fire 29½ da @ $33.35 per mo - $39.35. 1st div |
| 1855-40 | Joseph | lab 22 da @ $1 - $22.00. Rd Way Dept |
| 1857-13 | " | swit'man at Duffield's 30 da @ $35 per mo - $35.00. Martinsburg |
| 1855-9 | R. | conduc 24 da @ $55 per mo - $55.00. Trans Dept main stem |
| 1855-56 | Thos. J. | lab 9 da @ $1.50 - $13.50. Rd Way Dept |
| 1857-26 | W. H. | ton brak 20½ da @ $40 per mo - $32.80. 3d & 4th div |
| 1855-26 | William | ton brak 33½ da @ $40 per mo - $53.60. 3d & 4th div |
| 1857-127 | Jenks, G. W. | mach 22 da @ $1.65 - $36.30. Mach Dept, Piedmont |
| 1857-127 | Thomas | mach help 18 da @ $1 - $18.00. Mach Dept, Piedmont |
| 1857-67 | Jenning, Henry | lab 19 3/4 da @ $1 - $19.75. Rd Dept main stem 19th s-div |
| 1857-79 | Jennings, Edward | lab 26½ da @ $1 - $26.50. lay 2d track |
| 1855-77 | J. | help 24 3/4 da @ $1.15 - $28.45. Mach Dept |
| 1855-68 | John | lab 25 da @ $1 - $25.00. Rd Way Dept |

B & O RR EMPLOYEES 191

| ID | Name | Details |
|---|---|---|
| 1857-83 | Jennings, John | lab 25 da @ $1.12 - $28.10. grad, Board Tree Tun |
| 1857-111 | " Joshua | mach help 19 3/4 da @ $1.25 - $24.70. Mach Dept, Balto |
| 1857-97 | " Michael | watch 30 da @ $1 - $30.00. NW Va RR, Rd Dept 1st s-div |
| 1857-83 | " Patrick | lab 24½ da @ $1.12 - $27.55. grad, Board Tree Tun |
| 1857-131 | " Thomas | mach help 10 3/4 da @ $1 - $10.75. Mach Dept, Grafton |
| 1857-83 | " " | lab 17 da @ $1.12 - $10.10. grad, Board Tree Tun |
| 1857-41 | Jessup, Wm. | lab 5 da @ $1 - $5.00. NW Va rd, Athey's wd train |
| 1857-31 | " Wm. W. | ton fire 26 3/4 da @ $33.35 per mo - $35.65. 1st div |
| 1857-111 | Jett, Daniel | mach help 1 da @ $1.25 - $1.25. Mach Dept, Balto |
| 1855-19 | " " | ton eng'man 24 da @ $50 per mo - $50.00. Trans Dept main stem |
| 1857-10 | Joachim, J. | bur brak 20 da @ $1.15 - $23.00. hp exp, Balto |
| 1855-5 | Joachlin, J. | watch 28 da @ $30 per mo - $30.00. Trans Dept, Wash br |
| 1857-37 | Johns, G. | watch 30 da @ $30 per mo - $30.00. Wash br rd, Wash city sta |
| 1855-75 | Johnson, A. L. | lab 24 da @ $1 - $24.00. Rd Way Dept |
| 1857-50 | " Arthur | lab 25½ da @ $1 - $25.50. Rd Dept main stem 5th s-div |
| 1857-112 | " Bend | mach app 19 da @ $1 - $19.00. Mach Dept, Balto |
| 1857-35 | " Benj. | lab 10 da @ $1 - $10.00. J. R. Shrode's wd train 4th div |
| 1855-19 | " David | ton eng'man 6½ da @ $3 - $19.50. Trans Dept main stem |
| 1855-83 | " " | help 23 da @ $1.10 - $25.30. Mach Dept |
| 1857-129 | " " | clean eng 30 da @ $1 - $30.00. Mach Dept, Piedmont |
| 1857-91 | " " | lab 20 da @ $1 - $20.00. grad, Littleton Tun |
| 1857-127 | " George | mach 17 3/4 da @ $1.50 - $26.60. Mach Dept, Piedmont |
| 1857-115 | " H. T. | boil mkr 12½ da @ $1.35 - $16.90. Mach Dept, Balto |
| 1855-80 | " Henry A. | carp 23 3/4 da @ $1.55 - $36.80. Mach Dept |
| 1857-119 | " J. | carp 18½ da @ $1.50 - $27.75. Mach Dept, Balto |
| 1855-29 | " " | prepar fuel 13 da @ $1 - $13.00. Trans Dept main stem |
| 1857-26 | " J. R. M. | ton brak 24 da @ $40 per mo - $38.40. 3d & 4th div |
| 1857-104 | " John | carp 25 da @ $1.25 - $31.25. NW Va RR Tun |
| 1855-47 | " " | lab 10½ da @ $1 - $10.50. Rd Way Dept |
| 1855-28 | " " | reg eng 24 3/4 da @ $1.50 - $37.10. Trans Dept main stem |
| 1857-116 | " " | blksmith 18 da @ $1.50 - $27.00. Mach Dept, Balto |
| 1857-60 | " " | brak 7 da @ $1.53 - $10.70. Rd Dept main stem 13th s-div |
| 1857-79 | " " | lab 21 3/4 da @ $1 - $21.75. lay 2d track |
| 1857-125 | " " | put away eng &c 27 da @ $1.50 - $40.50. Mach Dept, Martinsburg |
| 1857-69 | " Joseph | carp 18 da @ $1.73 - $31.15. Mt Clare sta, Balto |
| 1857-127 | " " | mach 18 da @ $1.70 - $30.60. Mach Dept, Piedmont |

# B & O RR EMPLOYEES

| ID | Name | Description |
|---|---|---|
| 1855-30 | Johnson, Park | prepar fuel 22 da @ $1.15 - $25.30. Trans Dept main stem |
| 1855-33 | " R. | lab 24 da @ $30 per mo - $30.00. Trans Dept main stem |
| 1857-26 | " R. M. | ton brak 26 da @ $40 per mo - $41.60. 3d & 4th div |
| 1857-12 | " R. R. | conduc & brak 24 da @ $40 per mo - $40.00. Trans Dept main stem |
| 1855-7 | " Samuel | ton brak 5 da @ $40 per mo - $8.00. 3d & 4th div |
| 1855-88 | " | asst supv 28 da @ $35 per mo - $35.00. Trans Dept main stem |
| 1855-35 | " | boil clean 23 3/4 da @ $1.25 - $29.70. Mach Dept |
| 1857-9 | " | port 28 da @ $15 per mo - $15.00. Trans Dept main stem |
| 1857-26 | " | St supv 30 da @ $50 per mo - $50.00. hp exp, Balto |
| 1855-33 | " T. | ton brak 19 da @ $40 per mo - $30.40. 3d & 4th div |
| 1857-8 | " Thomas | lab 2 da @ $30 per mo - $2.50. Trans Dept main stem |
| 1855-82 | " William | lab 25 da @ $30 per mo - $30.00. Camden sta |
| 1855-8 | " | app 23 3/4 da @ $.65 - $15.45. Mach Dept |
| 1857-125 | " | bag mast 28 da @ $35 per mo - $35.00. Trans Dept main stem |
| 1857-131 | " | app 20½ da @ $.45 - $9.20. Mach Dept, Martinsburg |
| 1857-11 | " | mach 15½ da @ $1.55 - $24.05. Mach Dept, Grafton |
| 1857-17 | " William F. | swit tend 30 da @ $35 per mo - $35.00. Ellicott's Mills |
| 1857-17 | " William Jr | rec 30 da @ $60 per mo - $60.00. Wheeling sta |
| 1855-90 | " William Y. | lab 29 da @ $25 per mo - $29.00. Wheeling sta |
| 1857-104 | Johnston, George | mach 13 3/4 da @ $1.50 - $20.65. Mach Dept |
| 1855-67 | " Henry | carp 16¼ da @ $1.25 - $20.30. NW Va RR Tun |
| 1857-139 | Joice, John | tend to masons 7 da @ $1 - $7.00. Rd Way Dept |
| 1857-84 | " | fill tend 14½ da @ $1 - $14.50. NW Va RR, Mach Dept, Parkersburg |
| 1857-67 | " | lab 7½ da @ $1.12 - $8.45. grad, Board Tree Tun |
| 1857-49 | " Michael | lab 16 da @ $1 - $16.00. Rd Dept main stem 19th s-div |
| 1857-78 | " | watch cuts 28 da @ $1 - $28.00. Rd Way Dept |
| 1857-83 | " Thomas | lab 13 3/4 da @ $1 - $13.75. lay 2d track |
| 1855-69 | " William | lab 26 3/4 da @ $1.12 - $30.10. grad, Board Tree Tun |
| 1857-92 | Joint, Patrick | lab 21 3/4 da @ $1 - $21.75. Rd Way Dept |
| 1855-24 | Jollans, Benj. | lab 26 da @ $1.12 - $29.25. grad, Littleton Tun |
| 1855-14 | Jolly, E. | pass & bur driv 24 da @ $46 per mo - $46.00. Trans Dept main stem |
| 1855-12 | " Henry | brak 15 3/4 da @ $40 per mo - $26.25. Trans Dept main stem |
| 1857-12 | " John | conduc & brak 8 da @ $40 per mo - $13.35. Mach Dept, Balto |
| 1857-118 | Jones, A. | blksmith help 17 3/4 da @ $1 - $17.75. Mach Dept, Balto |
| 1855-73 | " | fore 24½ da @ $1.50 - $36.75. Rd Way Dept |
| 1857-121 | " Benjamin | car trim help 18 3/4 da @ $1 - $18.75. Mach Dept, Balto |

# B & O RR EMPLOYEES

| ID | Name | Details |
|---|---|---|
| 1857-120 | Jones, Benjamin B. | carp 22 da @ $1.50 - $33.00. Mach Dept, Balto |
| 1855-85 | " C. P. | help 22 da @ $1.15 - $25.30. Mach Dept |
| 1857-10 | " Clement | stab'man 25 da @ $1 - $25.00. hp exp, Balto |
| 1855-16 | " Geo. | pass fire 24 da @ $40 per mo - $34.30. Trans Dept main stem |
| 1857-108 | " Geo. W. | mach 15 3/4 da @ $1.60 - $25.20. Mach Dept, Balto |
| 1855-17 | " Isaac | ton eng'man 17½ da @ $3 - $52.50. Trans Dept main stem |
| 1857-17 | " J. C. | clk 30 da @ $58.35 per mo - $58.35. Wheeling sta |
| 1855-91 | " J. D. | help 22 da @ $1 - $22.00. Mach Dept |
| 1857-104 | " James | lab 2½ da @ $1 - $2.50. NW Va RR Tun |
| 1857-16 | " John | eng'man 26 da @ $2.50 - $65.00. Benwood sta |
| 1855-19 | " John O. | ton eng'man 15 da @ $2.50 - $37.50. Trans Dept main stem |
| 1855-20 | " L. D. | fire 19 da @ $1.75 - $33.25. Trans Dept main stem |
| 1855-72 | " Richard | help 23 3/4 da @ $1.12½ - $26.70. Rd Way Dept |
| 1857-70 | " " | bolt cut 19 da @ $1.12 - $21.35. Mt Clare sta, Balto |
| 1855-93 | " Samuel | mach 4 da @ $1.72 - $6.85. Mach Dept |
| 1857-134 | " Samuel T. | mach 22½ da @ $1.75 - $39.35. Mach Dept, Wheeling |
| 1855-5 | " Thomas | ton fire 20 da @ $1.33 per mo - $27.80. Trans Dept, Wash br |
| 1857-10 | " Wm. | bur brak 24½ da @ $1.15 - $28.15. hp exp, Balto |
| 1857-45 | Jordan, J. B. | pur @ $83.35 per mo. Rd Dept |
| 1857-110 | " J. R. B. | mach 17½ da @ $1.50 - $26.25. Mach Dept, Balto |
| 1855-72 | " James R. | fore @ $83.35 per mo - $83.35. Rd Way Dept |
| 1855-9 | " John | conduc 15½ da @ $60 per mo - $32.95. Trans Dept main stem |
| 1857-102 | " " | blksmith 23 da @ $2 - $46.00. NW Va RR, rwy depot |
| 1857-65 | " Joseph | brak 23 da @ $1.50 - $34.50. Rd Dept main stem 17th s-div |
| 1855-69 | " Martin | lab 23½ da @ $1 - $23.50. Rd Way Dept |
| 1857-87 | " " | stone mason 25 da @ $1.50 - $37.50. grad, McGuire's Tun |
| 1857-86 | " Patrick | lab 22 da @ $1 - $22.00. grad, McGuire's Tun |
| 1855-16 | " W. | pass fire 33 da @ $40 per mo - $47.15. Trans Dept main stem |
| 1855-72 | " W. H. | timekpr @ $33 per mo - $33.00. Rd Way Dept |
| 1857-35 | " William | eng'man 2 da @ $2.50 - $5.00. J. R. Shrode's wd train 4th div |
| 1857-30 | " " | ton eng'man 24½ da @ $2.50 - $61.25. 4th div |
| 1857-84 | " William H. | timekpr @ $41.65 per mo - $41.65. grad, Board Tree Tun |
| 1857-112 | Jorden, Joseph | mach app 21 da @ 3.55 - $11.55. Mach Dept, Balto |
| 1855-54 | Jordon, Alex. | stonecut 4¼ da @ $2 - $8.50. Rd Way Dept |
| 1855-19 | Josleyn, Amasa | pass eng'man 24 da @ $2.50 - $60.00. 3d div |
| 1855-17 | Joslin, Amasa | ton eng'man 6¼ da @ $3 - $18.75. Trans Dept main stem |

193

# B & O RR EMPLOYEES

| ID | Name | Details |
|---|---|---|
| 1855-91 | Joslin, Amsey | mach 7½ da @ $1.62 - $12.20. Mach Dept |
| 1855-92 | Joslin, Charles | app 23¾ da @ $.55 - $12.90. Mach Dept |
| 1855-15 | Joslin, R. | pass eng'man 12 da @ $2.50 - $30.00. Trans Dept main stem |
| 1857-30 | Joslyn, Amasa | ton eng'man 1 da @ $3 - $3.00. 3d div |
| 1857-128 | Joslyn, Charles | mach help 22 da @ $.75 - $16.50. Mach Dept, Piedmont |
| 1855-28 | Joy, T. H. | reg eng 8 da @ $1.15 - $9.20. Trans Dept main stem |
| 1857-59 | Joyce, Edward | lab 26 da @ $1 - $26.00. Rd Dept main stem 13th s-div |
| 1855-61 | Joyce, M. | lab 18 da @ $1 - $18.00. Rd Way Dept |
| 1855-68 | Joyce, Martin | lab 26 da @ $1.50 - $39.00. Rd Way Dept |
| 1857-83 | " | fore @ $50 per mo - $50.00. grad, Board Tree Tun |
| 1857-97 | " | lab 26 da @ $1 - $26.00. NW Va RR, Rd Dept 2d s-div |
| 1857-65 | " Michael | lab 18½ da @ $1 - $18.50. Rd Dept main stem 17th s-div |
| 1855-66 | " | lab 21½ da @ $1 - $21.50. Rd Way Dept |
| 1855-66 | " | lab 23 da @ $1 - $23.00. Rd Way Dept |
| 1855-67 | " | tend to masons 21 da @ $1 - $21.00. Rd Way Dept |
| 1857-86 | " | lab 23 3/4 da @ $1 - $23.75. grad, McGuire's Tun |
| 1857-98 | " | lab 22½ da @ $1 - $22.50. NW Va RR, Rd Dept 3d s-div |
| 1857-97 | " Patrick | watch 30 da @ $1 - $30.00. NW Va RR, Rd Dept 2d s-div |
| 1855-68 | " | lab 23½ da @ $1 - $23.50. Rd Way Dept |
| 1855-68 | " | lab 24 da @ $1 - $24.00. Rd Way Dept |
| 1857-86 | " Thomas | lab 26¾ da @ $1.12 - $29.50. grad, McGuire's Tun |
| 1857-86 | " | lab 26¼ da @ $1.12 - $29.50. grad, McGuire's Tun |
| 1857-65 | " Tobias | lab 24 da @ $1 - $24.00. Rd Dept main stem 17th s-div |
| 1855-59 | " William | lab 13½ da @ $1 - $13.50. Rd Way Dept |
| 1857-67 | Judge, Thomas | lab 24 3/4 da @ $1 - $23.25. Rd Dept main stem 18th s-div |
| 1857-64 | Judkins, William | watch 19 da @ $1 - $19.00. Trans Dept main stem |
| 1855-35 | Judy, T. L. | blksmith 23½ da @ $1.25 - $24.75. Rd Dept main stem 17th s-div |
| 1855-89 | Judys, T. L. | blksmith 20½ da @ $1.25 - $25.60. Mach Dept, Cumb |
| 1857-136 | Kadin, Michael | pass & bur driv 26½ da @ $30 per mo - $33.10. Trans Dept main stem |
| 1855-24 | Kaihler, Charles | carp 24 da @ $1.40 - $33.60. Mach Dept |
| 1355-90 | Kailey, John | clean eng 24 da @ $1 - $24.00. Trans Dept main stem |
| 1355-27 | Kain, William | mach 16 da @ $1.85 - $29.60. Mach Dept, Wheeling |
| 1357-134 | Kalahan, C. | lab 12 da @ $30 per mo - $15.00. Trans Dept main stem |
| 1355-33 | Kalbaugh, Jno. D. | lab 17 3/4 da @ $1 - $17.75. Mach Dept, Piedmont |
| 1357-130 | Kalbfleish, C. | tin 16½ da @ $1.73 - $28.55. Rd Way Dept |
| 1855-73 | | |

| | | |
|---|---|---|
| 1857-135 | Kall, Jacob | boil mkr help 14¼ da @ $1.70 - $24.20. Mach Dept, Wheeling |
| 1857-131 | Jacob A. | boil mkr 6¼ da @ $1.70 - $10.60. Mach Dept, Grafton |
| 1857-69 | Kallfleish, Caleb | tin 13 da @ $1.73 - $22.50. Mt Clare sta, Balto |
| 1855-32 | Kane, M. | lab 24 da @$30 per mo - $30.00. Trans Dept main stem |
| 1855-67 | Patrick | tend to masons 21 da @ $1 - $21.00. Rd Way Dept |
| 1855-68 | " | tend to masons 19½ da @ $1 - $19.50. Rd Way Dept |
| 1857-85 | " | lab 5 3/4 da @ $1.12 - $5.45. grad, Board Tree Tun |
| 1857-39 | " | lab 25 da @ $30 per mo - $30.00. NW Va rd, Parkersburg sta |
| 1857-89 | Patrick 1st | lab 8¼ da @ $1.12 - $9.30. grad, Welling Tun |
| 1857-89 | " 2d | lab 15¼ da @ $1.12 - $17.15. grad, Welling Tun |
| 1857-83 | Thomas | lab 22½ da @ $1.12 - $25.30. grad, Board Tree Tun |
| 1857-117 | William | blksmith help 18 da @ $1 - $18.00. Mach Dept, Balto |
| 1857-102 | Kanney, Tim | lab 11 3/4 da @ $1 - $11.75. NW Va RR, rwy depot |
| 1857-114 | Karby, Mike | iron mould help 13¼ da @ $1.10 - $14.55. Mach Dept, Balto |
| 1857-129 | Karles, James | inspec cars @ $32 per mo - $32.00. Mach Dept, Piedmont |
| 1857-134 | Karney, H. J. | mach 18 3/4 da @ $1.75 - $32.80. Mach Dept, Wheeling |
| 1857-134 | John | mach app 23 da @ $.55 - $12.65. Mach Dept,Wheeling |
| 1857-82 | Karr, William | bricklay 3 da @ $2 -$6.00. grad, Board Tree Tun |
| 1857-118 | Kaufield, H. | blksmith help 18 da @ $1 - $18.00. Mach Dept, Balto |
| 1855-57 | Kavaner, Pat. | lab 19½ da @ $1 - $19.50. Rd Way Dept |
| 1857-88 | Kavannaugh, Patrick | lab 28 da @ $1.12 - $31.50. grad, Welling Tun |
| 1857-41 | Kaykendall, Nimrod | lab 23 da @ $1 - $23.00. NW Va rd, Athey's wd train |
| 1855-36 | Kayle, Robert | police watch 28 da @ $40 per mo - $40.00. Trans Dept main stem |
| 1857-59 | Keaden, John | lab 26½ da @ $1 - $26.50. Rd Dept main stem 13th s-div |
| 1857-60 | Patrick | lab 25½ da @ $1 - $25.50. Rd Dept main stem 13th s-div |
| 1857-59 | Keady, John | lab 26½ da @ $1 - $26.50. Rd Dept main stem 13th s-div |
| 1857-68 | Keaher, John | lab 22 da @ $1 - $22.00. Rd Dept main stem 19th s-div |
| 1855-62 | Owen | fore 24 da @ $1.25 - $30.00. Rd Way Dept |
| 1857-80 | Kealy, James | lab 13¼ da @ $1 - $13.25. lay 2d track |
| 1857-109 | Kean, R. R. | mach 18½ da @ $1.60 - $29.60. Mach Dept, Balto |
| 1857-93 | Kearnan, Michael | lab 21 da @ $1 - $21.00. quarry & haul stone for Board Tree & Littleton Tun |
| 1855-43 | Kearnes, D. | lab 20 da @ $1 - $20.00. Rd Way Dept |
| 1855-9 | J. | conduc 3½ da @ $50 per mo - $7.30. Trans Dept main stem |
| 1855-62 | Kearney, L. | lab 21 3/4 da @$1 - $21.75. Rd Way Dept |
| 1855-57 | Michael | lab 12 da @ $1 - $12.00. Rd Way Dept |
| 1855-36 | " | lab 24 da @ $30 per mo - $30.00. Trans Dept main stem |

B & O RR EMPLOYEES

| | | | |
|---|---|---|---|
| 1857-130 | Kearney, Michael | lab 19 3/4 da @ $1 - $19.75. Mach Dept, Piedmont |
| 1855-62 | " Patrick | lab 23 3/4 da @ $1 - $23.75. Rd Way Dept |
| 1855-62 | " Thomas | lab 20 da @ $1 - $20.00. Rd Way Dept |
| 1857-55 | Kearns, Dennis | fore 23¼ da @ $1.25 -$29.05. Rd Dept main stem 9th s-div |
| 1857-55 | " Frederick | lab 24½ da @ $1 - $24.50. Rd Dept main stem 9th s-div |
| 1855-44 | " Isaiah | lab 16 da @ $1 - $16.00. Rd Way Dept |
| 1857-130 | " Jacob | lab 21½ da @ $1 - $21.50. Mach Dept, Piedmont |
| 1857-93 | " Thomas | lab 23 da @ $1 - $23.00. quarry & haul stone for Board Tree & Littleton Tun |
| 1855-48 | Keating, M. | train hand 20½ da @ $1 - $20.50. Rd Way Dept |
| 1857-51 | " Michael | lab 25 da @ $1 - $25.00. Rd Dept main stem 5th s-div |
| 1855-48 | " P. | dril 14¼ da @ $1.10 -$15.65. Rd Way Dept |
| 1855-48 | " Thomas | dril 12 3/4 da @ $1.10 - $15.10. Rd Way Dept |
| 1857-51 | " " | lab 25 da @ $1 - $25.00. Rd Dept main stem 5th s-div |
| 1857-126 | Keedy, Jacob | clean eng 15 da @ $1.15 - $17.25. Mach Dept, Martinsburg |
| 1857-22 | Keef, John W. | ton conduc 25½ da @ $50 per mo - $50.00. 2d div |
| 1855-51 | Keefe, Michael | watch cuts 28 da @ $1 - $28.00. Rd Way Dept |
| 1857-67 | " | lab 19½ da @ $1 - $19.25. Rd Dept main stem 19th s-div |
| 1857-119 | Keek (Keck?), Alfred | blksmith app 28 da @ $.55 - $15.40. Mach Dept, Balto |
| 1857-119 | " Gilbert | blksmith app 15 da @ $.45 - $6.75. Mach Dept, Balto |
| 1857-116 | " Samuel | blksmith 17 3/4 da @ $1.40 - $24.85. Mach Dept, Balto |
| 1855-92 | Keen, Charles | carp @ $32 per mo - $32.00. Mach Dept |
| 1857-35 | " " | fire 15 da @ $1.75 - $26.25. Edwards' wd train 3d & 4th div |
| 1857-33 | " " | ton fire 1 da @ $1.75 - $1.75. 3d div |
| 1857-17 | Keenan, James | lab 7 da @ $1 - $7.00. frt transfer force at Bellaire, opp Benwood |
| 1857-68 | " " | lab 16 da @ $1 - $16.00. Rd Dept main stem 19th s-div |
| 1857-82 | " Thomas | lab 23 da @ $1.12 - $25.90. grad, Board Tree Tun |
| 1857-92 | Keener, Frank | lab 23 da @ $1.12 - $25.85. grad, Littleton Tun |
| 1855-29 | " George | prepar fuel 28 da @ $1 - $28.00. Trans Dept main stem |
| 1857-35 | " Louis | lab 2 da @ $1 - $7.00. Edwards' wd train 3d & 4th div |
| 1855-23 | " Peter | fire 13 3/4 da @ $1.75 - $24.05. Trans Dept main stem |
| 1857-34 | " " | ton fire 29 da @ $1.75 - $50.75. 4th div |
| 1855-32 | Keerle, J. W. | tele oper 28 da @ $35 per mo - $35.00. Trans Dept main stem |
| 1855-29 | Keffer, D. | prepar fuel 28 da @ $1 - $28.00. Trans Dept main stem |
| 1855-65 | Kefler(?), Joel | lab 17½ da @ $1 - $17.50. Rd Way Dept |
| 1857-104 | Keifer, L. | carp 20½ da @ $1.60 - $32.80. NW Va RR, build sand & wd houses |
| 1855-12 | Keiff, J. W. | conduc & brak 18 3/4 da @ $50 per mo - $43.50. Trans Dept main stem |

| | | | |
|---|---|---|---|
| 1855-94 | Keiffer, George | lab 24½ da @ $1 - $24.25. Mach Dept |
| 1857-63 | Keine, Timothy | lab 17 3/4 da @ $1 - $17.75. Rd Dept main stem 16th s-div |
| 1857-36 | Keirle, J. W. | tele oper 30 da @ $35 per mo - $35.00. Mt Clare |
| 1855-82 | Keis, Fdk. | mach 21½ da @ $1.72 - $37.00. Mach Dept |
| 1857-30 | Keith, Ed. H. | ton eng'man 29½ da @ $3 - $87.75. 3d div |
| 1855-42 | Keiting, M. | lab 9 da @ $1 - $9.00. Rd Way Dept |
| 1857-58 | Kelgallan, Thomas | lab 26 da @ $1 - $26.00. Rd Dept main stem 12th s-div |
| 1855-45 | Kellar, John | lab 12½ da @ $1 - $12.50. Rd Way Dept |
| 1855-47 | Kellegan, Thomas | lab 22½ da @ $1 - $22.50. Rd Way Dept |
| 1857-124 | Keller, Reaman | mach app 9 3/4 da @ $.50 - $4.85. Mach Dept, Martinsburg |
| 1855-12 | Keller, T. C. | conduc & brak 14 3/4 da @ $40 per mo - $24.60. Trans Dept main stem |
| 1857-116 | Kelley, Charles | boil mkr help 18 3/4 da @ $1 - $18.75. Mach Dept, Balto |
| 1857-101 | Kelley, James | lab 21 da @ $1 - $21.00. NW Va RR ballast train |
| 1857-129 | Kelley, Josiah | carp 12½ da @ $1.50 - $18.75. Mach Dept, Piedmont |
| 1855-61 | Kelley, M. | lab 18 da @ $1 - $18.00. Rd Way Dept |
| 1857-136 | Kelley, Martin | carter 20 da @ $1 - $20.00. Mach Dept, Wheeling |
| 1857-129 | Kelley, Michael | clean eng 15 da @ $1 - $15.00. Mach Dept, Piedmont |
| 1857-86 | " | lab 19½ da @ $1.12 - $21.90. grad, McGuire's Tun |
| 1857-114 | Kelley, Patrick | cupalo tend 18 da @ $1.45 - $26.10. Mach Dept, Balto |
| 1857-76 | Kelley, Richard | lab 15 da @ $.97 - $14.60. ballast train for 2d track |
| 1857-120 | Kelley, S. W. | carp 21 da @ $1.50 - $31.50. Mach Dept, Balto |
| 1857-81 | Kelley, Thomas | lab 20½ da @ $1.12 - $23.05. grad, Board Tree Tun |
| 1857-88 | " | lab 27 da @ $1.12 - $30.35. grad, Welling Tun |
| 1855-89 | " Tim | lab 14 3/4 da @ $1 - $14.75. NW Va RR, Rd Dept 1st s-div |
| 1857-96 | Kellman, A. | mach 20½ da @ $1.45 - $29.35. Mach Dept |
| 1857-68 | Kellon, Mark | lab 16 3/4 da @ $1 - $16.75. Rd Dept main stem 19th s-div |
| 1857-57 | Kellow, Thomas | lab 27½ da @ $1 - $27.50. Rd Dept main stem 11th s-div |
| 1857-135 | Kells, Ross | lab 17 3/4 da @ $.75 - $13.30. Mach Dept, Wheeling |
| 1857-75 | Kelly, A. | fore @ $60 per mo - $60.00. ballast train for 2d track |
| 1857-75 | " | horse hire 20 da @ $1 - $20.00. ballast train for 2d track |
| 1857-26 | " A. J. | ton brak 21 da @ $40 per mo - $33.60. 3d & 4th div |
| 1857-89 | " Andey | lab 24 3/4 da @ $1.12 - $27.85. grad, Welling Tun |
| 1857-109 | " C. | mach 18 da @ $1.55 - $27.90. Mach Dept, Balto |
| 1857-48 | " Francis | lab 21¼ da @ $1 - $21.25. Rd Dept main stem 18th s-div |
| 1857-67 | " | watch 30 da @ $1 - $30.00. Mt Clare sta, Balto |
| 1857-70 | " Henry | app 23½ da @ $.50 - $11.75. Mt Clare sta, Balto |

B & O RR EMPLOYEES

| | | | |
|---|---|---|---|
| 1855-71 | Kelly, Isaac | | smith 24 da @ $1.90 - $45.60. Rd Way Dept |
| 1857-70 | " | " | blksmith 18 da @ $1.90 - $34.20. Mt Clare sta, Balto |
| 1857-16 | " | Isaiah | mate 16 da @ $30 per mo - $16.00. transfer steam Brown Dick--Ohio Riv, bet Benwood & Bellaire |
| 1855-12 | " | J. H. | conduc & brak 15¾ da @ $40 per mo - $27.40. Trans Dept main stem |
| 1855-47 | " | James | lab 22 da @ $1 - $22.00. Rd Way Dept |
| 1855-61 | " | " | lab 19 3/4 da @ $1 - $19.75. Rd Way Dept |
| 1857-84 | " | " | lab 27 7/12 da @ $1.12 - $30.65. grad, Board Tree Tun |
| 1857-99 | " | " | watch 30 da @ $1 - $30.00. NW Va RR, Rd Dept 4th s-div |
| 1855-55 | " | John | lab 7¼ da @ $1 - $7.25. Rd Way Dept |
| 1855-62 | " | " | lab 19½ da @ $1 - $19.50. Rd Way Dept |
| 1855-86 | " | " | mach 23½ da @ $1.25 - $29.40. Mach Dept |
| 1857-118 | " | " | blksmith help 18 da @ $1 - $18.00. Mach Dept, Balto |
| 1857-57 | " | " | fore 26 da @$1.25 - $32.50. Rd Dept main stem 11th s-div |
| 1855-62 | " | L. | lab 24 da @ $1 - $24.00. Rd Way Dept |
| 1857-16 | " | Larry | lab 25 da @$25 per mo - $25.00. Benwood sta |
| 1855-96 | " | Luke | lab 23 da @ $1.10 - $25.30. Mach Dept |
| 1857-114 | " | " | iron mould help 17½ da @ $1.10 - $19.25. Mach Dept, Balto |
| 1855-59 | " | M. | lab 20 da @ $1 - $20.00. Rd Way Dept |
| 1857-120 | " | M. J. | carp 18 da @ $1.72 - $30.95. Mach Dept, Balto |
| 1855-75 | " | Mart. | lab 20 da @ $1 - $20.00. Rd Way Dept |
| 1855-69 | " | Michael | lab 19 3/4 da @ $1 - $19.75. NW Va RR ballast train |
| 1857-82 | " | " | bricklay 9½ da @ $1.12 - $19.00. grad, Board Tree Tun |
| 1857-41 | " | " | lab 4 da @ $1 - $4.00. NW Va rd, Athey's wd train |
| 1857-101 | " | " | lab 13 da @ $1 - $13.00. NW Va RR ballast train |
| 1855-47 | " | Mike | lab 16½ da @ $1 - $16.50. Rd Way Dept |
| 1855-34 | " | Patrick | car greas 24 da @ $35 per mo - $35.00. Trans Dept main stem |
| 1855-95 | " | " | cupola 21 da @$1.45 -$30.45. Mach Dept |
| 1855-44 | " | " | lab 10 da @ $1 - $10.00. Rd Way Dept |
| 1857-76 | " | " | lab 10 da @ $.97 - $9.75. ballast train for 2d track |
| 1857-35 | " | " | lab 26½ da @ $1 - $26.50. J. R. Shrode's wd train 4th div |
| 1857-80 | " | " | lab 18 3/4 da @ $1 - $18.75. lay 2d track |
| 1857-77 | " | " | quarry 8 da @ $1 - $8.00. ballast train for 2d track |
| 1855-96 | " | Patrick Jr | lab 18 da @ $1.10 - $19.80. Mach Dept |
| 1857-114 | " | " | iron mould help 17 3/4 da @ $1.10 - $19.55. Mach Dept, Balto |
| 1857-92 | " | Peter | lab 24 3/4 da @ $1 - $24.75. grad, Littleton Tun |

## B & O RR EMPLOYEES

| | | |
|---|---|---|
| 1857-76 | Kelly, Richard | dril 6¾ da @ $1.10 - $6.85. ballast train for 2d track |
| 1857-57 | Samuel | lab 16 da @ $1 - $16.00. Rd Dept main stem 11th s-div |
| 1855-56 | Thomas | lab 7 3/4 da @ $1 - $7.75. Rd Way Dept lay 2d track |
| 1857-80 | " | lab 12½ da @ $1 - $12.50. lay 2d track |
| 1857-57 | W. J. | lab 25 da @ $1 - $25.00. Rd Dept main stem 11th s-div |
| 1855-80 | W. W. | carp 23 3/4 da @ $1.60 - $38.00. Mach Dept |
| 1857-121 | William | carp app 25 da @ $.45 - $11.25. Mach Dept, Balto |
| 1855-84 | " | help 24 da @ $1.10 - $26.40. Mach Dept |
| 1857-80 | | lab 20 3/4 da @ $1 - $20.75. lay 2d track |
| 1855-30 | Kelso, William | prepar fuel 24 da @ $40 per mo - $40.00. Trans Dept main stem |
| 1857-11 | " | watch 25 da @ $40 per mo - $40.00. Locust Pt |
| 1855-47 | Keltey, P. H. | lab 8 da @ $1 - $8.00. Rd Way Dept |
| 1855-58 | Kelton, Thomas | fore 24 da @ $1.25 - $30.00. Rd Way Dept |
| 1855-47 | Kelty, Pat. | lab 8 da @ $1 - $8.00. Rd Way Dept |
| 1857-26 | Kemp, H. | ton brak 5 da @ $40 per mo - $8.00. 3d & 4th div |
| 1855-72 | Joseph F. | draft @ $62.50 per mo - $62.50. Rd Way Dept |
| 1857-45 | " | arch & draught @ $75 per mo. Rd Dept |
| 1857-73 | Milton | carp 23 da @ $1.30 - $29.90. repair bridges &c |
| 1857-73 | Oliver | carp 19½ da @ $1.30 - $25.35. repair bridges &c |
| 1855-72 | Thomas E. | app @ $15 per mo - $15.00. Rd Way Dept |
| 1855-16 | W. | pass fire 2 da @ $1.75; 10 3/4 da @ $1.25 - $21.95. Trans Dept main stem |
| 1857-57 | Ken, David M. | lab 22½ da @ $1 - $22.50. Rd Way Dept |
| 1855-49 | Kenady, M. S. | watch cuts 25½ da @ $1 - $25.50. Rd Way Dept |
| 1857-112 | Kenard, S. E. | mach app 22⅔ da @ $.45 - $10.10. Mach Dept, Balto |
| 1855-95 | Thomas | mould 19 da @ $1.55 - $29.45. Mach Dept |
| 1857-113 | " | iron mould 17 da @ $1.65 - $28.05. Mach Dept, Balto |
| 1857-139 | Kenarry, John | clean eng 30 da @ $.45 - $13.50. NW Va RR, Mach Dept, Parkersburg |
| 1855-38 | Kendels, William | lab 23 da @ $1 - $23.00. Rd Way Dept |
| 1857-63 | Kenedy, David | lab 22 3/4 da @ $1 - $22.75. Rd Dept main stem 16th s-div |
| 1855-79 | Henry | watch 24 da @ $1.15 - $27.60. Mach Dept |
| 1857-109 | M. J. | mach 18 da @ $1.60 - $28.80. Mach Dept, Balto |
| 1857-47 | Michael | nail 28 da @ $1 - $28.00. Rd Dept main stem 1st s-div |
| 1857-99 | Patrick | watch 30 da @ $1 - $30.00. NW Va RR, Rd Dept 4th s-div |
| 1855-70 | Kenhart, John | swit lay 19 da @ $1.22 - $23.20. Rd Way Dept |
| 1857-79 | Kennady, Michael | lab 25 3/4 da @ $1 - $25.75. lay 2d track |
| 1855-71 | Pat. | help 24 da @ $1.15 - $27.60. Rd Way Dept |

| | | | |
|---|---|---|---|
| 1857-70 | Kenneday, Pat. | help 18 da @ $1.15 - $20.70. Mt Clare sta, Balto |
| 1855-69 | Kennedy, Coleman | lab 22½ da @ $1 - $22.50. Rd Way Dept |
| 1855-55 | David | lab 24 da @ $1 - $24.00. Rd Way Dept |
| 1857-115 | Henry | watch 30 da @ $1 - $30.00. Mach Dept, Balto |
| 1855-24 | John | pass & bur driv 25 da @ $30 per mo - $31.25. Trans Dept main stem |
| 1857-71 | " | cart driv 24 da @ $.54 - $12.95. Mt Clare, repair tracks in yd |
| 1855-67 | Patrick | mason 15½ da @ $2 - $31.00. Rd Way Dept |
| 1857-35 | " | lab 12 da @ $1 - $12.00. J. R. Shrode's wd train 4th div |
| 1857-87 | " | stone mason 22 3/4 da @ $2 - $45.50. grad, McGuire's Tun |
| 1855-46 | Thomas | lab 22 da @ $1 - $22.00. Rd Way Dept |
| 1855-69 | " | lab 17 3/4 da @ $.50 - $8.90. Rd Way Dept |
| 1855-70 | William | lab 17 3/4 da @ $1 - $17.75. Rd Way Dept |
| 1857-87 | " | lab 18½ da @ $1 - $18.50. grad, McGuire's Tun |
| 1855-68 | Kennen, John | lab 22 3/4 da @ $1 - $22.75. Rd Way Dept |
| 1855-36 | Kenney, Edward | lab 25 da @ $25 per mo - $26.05. Trans Dept main stem |
| 1855-48 | James | help 24 da @ $.80 - $19.20. Rd Way Dept |
| 1857-84 | John | lab 26 da @ $1.12 - $29.25. grad, Board Tree Tun |
| 1855-62 | " | lab 20½ da @ $1 - $20.50. Rd Way Dept |
| 1857-96 | " | lab 22½ da @ $1 - $22.50. NW Va RR, Rd Dept 1st s-div |
| 1857-104 | Martin | lab 17 da @ $1 - $17.00. NW Va RR Tun |
| 1857-79 | Patrick | lab 25 3/4 da @ $1 - $25.75. lay 2d track |
| 1855-57 | " | lab 24 da @ $1 - $24.00. Rd Way Dept |
| 1855-50 | Thomas | watch cuts 28 da @ $1 - $28.00. Rd Way Dept |
| 1855-74 | " | lab 24 da @ $1 - $24.00. Rd Way Dept |
| 1855-24 | " | pass & bur driv 27 da @ $30 per mo - $33.75. Trans Dept main stem |
| 1855-5 | Kenny, Geo. | ton conduc 22 da @ $40 per mo - $36.65. Trans Dept, Wash br |
| 1857-10 | Jno. | bur reg 25 da @ $40 per mo - $40.00. hp exp, Balto |
| 1857-34 | P. | watch at Burton 10 da @ $1 - $10.00. Board Tree Tun |
| 1855-19 | Patrick | ton eng'man 7½ da @ $2.50 - $18.75. Trans Dept main stem |
| 1857-40 | " | ton conduc 11 da @ $50 per mo - $22.00. NW Va rd, Parkersburg sta |
| 1857-63 | T. | watch 30 da @ $1 - $30.00. Rd Dept main stem 16th s-div |
| 1857-46 | Thomas | ton brak 8½ da @ $40 per mo - $13.20. N W Va rd, Parkersburg sta |
| 1857-47 | " | lab 12 da @ $1 - $12.00. Rd Dept main stem 1st s-div |
| 1857-38 | " | lab 13 da @ $1 - $13.00. Rd Dept main stem 1st s-div |
| 1857-116 | Kenshaw, Bartlett | ton conduc 25 da @ $40 per mo - $40.00. Wash br rd, Wash city sta |
| | | boil mkr help 18¼ da @ $1 - $18.25. Mach Dept, Balto |

| | | |
|---|---|---|
| 1855-48 | Kerby, C. | train hand 5½ da @ $1 - $5.50. Rd Way Dept |
| 1855-29 | Kerfoot, James | haul & saw firewd 2 3/4 da @ $1.50 - $4.10. Trans Dept main stem |
| 1855-28 | Kerfott, Andrew | reg eng 22 da @ $1.50 - $33.00. Trans Dept main stem |
| 1855-28 | James | reg eng 4½ da @ $1.15 - $5.15. Trans Dept main stem |
| 1857-67 | Kerigan, Patrick | lab 20 3/4 da @ $1 - $20.75. Rd Dept main stem 18th s-div |
| 1857-59 | Kern, Michael | lab 25 da @ $1 - $25.00. Rd Dept main stem 12th s-div |
| 1855-68 | Kernamy, John | lab 24½ da @ $1 - $24.50. Rd Way Dept |
| 1855-69 | Kernan, M. | lab 16½ da @ $1 - $16.50. Rd Way Dept |
| 1857-46 | Samuel | lab 7 da @ $1 - $7.00. Rd Dept main stem 1st s-div |
| 1855-65 | Kernarney, M. | lab 25¼ da @ $1 - $25.25. Rd Way Dept |
| 1857-36 | Kerner, Marion | tele oper 30 da @ $30 per mo - $30.00. Camden sta |
| 1857-88 | Kernerney, John | lab 19¼ da @ $1.12 - $21.65. grad, Welling Tun |
| 1857-89 | William | lab 26½ da @ $1.12 - $29.80. grad, Welling Tun |
| 1855-31 | Kernes, Henry | saw wd 33½ da @ $.35 - $11.70. Trans Dept main stem |
| 1857-54 | Isiah | lab 21½ da @ $1 - $21.50. Rd Dept main stem 8th s-div |
| 1855-56 | Kerney, John | lab 14¼ da @ $1 - $14.25. Rd Way Dept |
| 1855-66 | " | lab 20 da @ $1 - $20.00. Rd Way Dept |
| 1857-118 | " | blksmith help 18 da @ $1 - $18.00. Mach Dept, Balto |
| 1857-59 | Michael | lab 25 da @ $1 - $25.00. Rd Dept main stem 12th s-div |
| 1857-132 | Kerns, Benjamin F. | iron mould app 27¼ da @ $.45 - $12.25. Mach Dept, Grafton |
| 1855-12 | Henry | conduc & brak 18 3/4 da @ $50 per mo - $41.05. Trans Dept main stem |
| 1857-22 | " | ton conduc 27 da @ $50 per mo - $54.00. 2d div |
| 1857-86 | Hugh | lab 21½ da @ $1 - $21.50. grad, McGuire's Tun |
| 1857-34 | Jacob | ton fire 23½ da @ $1.75 - $41.10. Board Tree Tun |
| 1857-33 | Jacob W. | ton fire 5½ da @ $1.75 - $9.60. 2d div |
| 1857-100 | James | lab 24 da @ $1 - $24.00. NW Va RR, Rd Dept 5th s-div |
| 1855-33 | Joseph | lab 28 da @ $30 per mo - $30.00. Trans Dept main stem |
| 1857-22 | " | ton conduc 27 da @ $45 per mo - $48.60. 2d div |
| 1857-54 | Zenos | lab 3½ da @ $1 - $3.50. Rd Dept main stem 8th s-div |
| 1857-10 | Kernsey, John | bur driv 16½ da @ $1.15 - $18.95. hp exp, Balto |
| 1855-71 | Kerr, James | carp 24 da @ $1.73 - $41.50. Rd Way Dept |
| 1857-69 | " | carp 24¼ da @ $1.87 - $45.45. Mt Clare sta, Balto |
| 1855-58 | Kershner, David | eng'man 24 da @ $2.50 - $60.00. Rd Way Dept |
| 1857-30 | * " | ton eng'man 24¼ da @ $3 - $73.50. 4th div |
| 1855-87 | Kesell, Theodore | blksmith 23 da @ $1.65 - $37.95. Mach Dept |
| 1857-54 | Keslar, Absolom | fore 25½ da @ $1.25 - $31.85. Rd Dept main stem 8th s-div |

| Name | ID | Description |
|---|---|---|
| Kesler, A. | 1855-48 | fore 24 da @ $1.25 - $30.00. Rd Way Dept |
| Kesler, Andrew | 1857-112 | mach app 23 da @ $.65 - $14.95. Mach Dept, Balto |
| Kesler, John | 1855-47 | lab 22 da @ $1 - $22.00. Rd Way Dept |
| Keslering, Philip | 1857-51 | watch 30 da @ $1 - $30.00. Rd Dept main stem 5th s-div |
| Keslering, John | 1857-124 | blksmith 20¼ da @ $1.45 - $29.35. Mach Dept, Martinsburg |
| Kessler, Frank | 1855-87 | help 5¼ da @ $1 - $5.25. Mach Dept |
| Kessler, F. P. | 1855-65 | driv 24 da @ $1 - $24.00. Rd Way Dept |
| Kessler, William | 1857-24 | ton brak 17½ da @ $40 per mo - $28.00. 1st div |
| Kesslering, John | 1855-87 | blksmith 15 da @ $1.25 - $18.75. Mach Dept |
| Kevins, Robert | 1855-29 | haul & saw firewd 12 da @ $1.25 - $15.00. Trans Dept main stem |
| Key, Gabriel P. | 1857-121 | paint 16½ da @ $1.65 - $27.20. Mach Dept, Balto |
| Keyho, Patrick | 1855-38 | lab 21 da @ $1 - $21.00. Rd Way Dept |
| Keys, G. P. | 1855-81 | paint 23 da @ $1.65 - $37.95. Mach Dept |
| Keys, Horace | 1855-38 | supv @ $45 per mo - $45.00. Rd Way Dept |
| " James | 1855-9 | conduc 3½ da @ $50 per mo - $7.30. Trans Dept main stem |
| " " | 1855-94 | lab 23¼ da @ $1 - $23.25. Mach Dept |
| " " | 1857-78 | blksmith 25 da @ $1.37 - $34.35. lay 2d track |
| Keyser, John A. | 1855-81 | lab 24 da @ $1.15 - $27.60. Mach Dept |
| Keyser, Harvey | 1857-33 | ton fire 12½ da @ $1.75 - $21.45. 2d div |
| " Samuel | 1855-30 | prepar fuel 21½ da @ $1 - $21.50. Trans Dept main stem |
| " " | 1857-11 | saw 22 3/4 da @ $1.15 - $27.30. Locust Pt |
| " Wm. | 1857-32 | ton fire 28¾ da @ $1.75 - $49.45. 2d div |
| Kidd, Robert | 1855-12 | conduc & brak 20½ da - $38.35. Trans Dept main stem |
| Kidwell, J. H. | 1855-9 | conduc 24 da @ $55 per mo - $55.00. Trans Dept main stem |
| " " | 1857-40 | ton conduc 25 da @ $55 per mo - $55.00. NW Va rd, Parkersburg sta |
| Kiener, Wash. | 1855-23 | fire 1½ da @ $1.75 - $2.60. Trans Dept main stem |
| Kietly, William | 1857-98 | lab 25 da @ $1 - $25.00. NW Va RR, Rd Dept 3d s-div |
| Kiger, John | 1857-134 | mach help 19½ da @ $1 - $19.50. Mach Dept, Wheeling |
| Kight, Enoch | 1857-129 | carp 17 da @ $1.50 - $25.50. Mach Dept, Piedmont |
| Kilfoil, John | 1855-68 | lab 23 da @ $1 - $23.00. Rd Way Dept |
| " M. | 1855-68 | lab 24 da @ $1 - $24.00. Rd Way Dept |
| Kilfoy, John | 1855-72 | help 3 da @ $1 - $3.00. Rd Way Dept |
| Kilkenny, James | 1857-68 | lab 22¼ da @ $1 - $22.25. Rd Dept main stem 19th s-div |
| Killdow, Michael | 1857-94 | carp 24 da @ $1.75 - $42.00. repair bridges |
| Killey, William | 1855-89 | mach 28 da @ $1.75 - $49.00. Mach Dept |
| Killfoil, Michael | 1857-82 | lab 24 3/4 da @ $1.12 - $27.85. grad, Board Tree Tun |
| " Patrick | 1857-84 | lab 25 da @ $.75 - $18.75. grad, Board Tree Tun |

# B & O RR EMPLOYEES

| ID | Name | Description |
|---|---|---|
| 1855-55 | Killrow, Thomas | lab 4 da @ $1 - $4.00. Rd Way Dept |
| 1857-82 | Killroy, Michael | lab 21 3/4 da @ $1.12 - $24.45. grad, Board Tree Tun |
| 1857-111 | Kilpatrick, John | mach help 28½ da @ $1.15 - $32.75. Mach Dept, Balto |
| 1857-128 | Kilroy, James | blksmith help 9¼ da @ $1 - $9.25. Mach Dept, Piedmont |
| 1857-18 | Kimball, John | pass train brak 10 da @ $33.35 per mo - $11.10. w end |
| 1857-26 | " William | ton brak 11 da @ $40 per mo - $17.60. 3d & 4th div |
| 1855-63 | Kine, Thos. | lab 17½ da @ $1 - $17.50. Rd Way Dept |
| 1857-126 | Kimmel, Frederick | clean eng 26 da @ $1.50 - $39.00. Mach Dept, Martinsburg |
| 1857-76 | Kimmell, James | dril 18 da @ $1.10 - $19.80. ballast train for 2d track |
| 1857-108 | Kimmell, Charles | mach 17⅞ da @ $1.50 - $25.85. Mach Dept, Balto |
| 1855-28 | " F. | reg eng 25 da @ $1.50 - $37.50. Trans Dept main stem |
| 1857-26 | " William | ton brak 17 da @ $40 per mo - $27.20. 3d & 4th div |
| 1857-23 | " " | ton conduc 2½ da @ $50 per mo - $5.00. 3d & 4th div |
| 1857-87 | Kincaid, James | bricklay 17½ da @ $70 per mo - $46.65. grad, Welling Tun |
| 1857-85 | Kincaide, James | fore 1/3 mo @ $70 per mo - $23.35. grad, Board Tree Tun |
| 1857-46 | Kindle, William | lab 24¼ da @ $1 - $24.50. Rd Dept main stem 1st s-div |
| 1857-90 | Kine, Barney | lab 12 da @ $1.12 - $13.50. grad, Welling Tun |
| 1855-58 | " M. | lab 22½ da @ $1 - $22.50. Rd Way Dept |
| 1857-59 | " Michael | lab 25½ da @ $1 - $25.50. Rd Dept main stem 13th s-div |
| 1857-97 | King, Bartley | lab 26½ da @ $1 - $26.50. NW Va RR, Rd Dept 2d s-div |
| 1857-98 | " Bernard | lab 25 da @ $1 - $25.00. NW Va RR, Rd Dept 3d s-div |
| 1857-97 | " Edward | watch 30 da @ $1 - $30.00. NW Va RR, Rd Dept 2d s-div |
| 1857-57 | " F. | lab 23 da @ $1 - $23.00. Rd Dept main stem 11th s-div |
| 1855-63 | " Farrel | lab 22 da @ $1 - $22.00. Rd Way Dept |
| 1857-97 | " Festus | fore 16½ da @$1.25 - $33.10. NW Va RR, Rd Dept 2d s-div |
| 1857-39 | " George | lab 19 da @ $1 - $19.00. NW Va rd, Parkersburg sta |
| 1855-72 | " George R. | mach 24 da @ $1.73 - $41.50. Rd Way Dept |
| 1857-69 | " " | mach 18 da @ $1.73 - $31.15. Mt Clare sta, Balto |
| 1857-136 | " H. | boil mkr 12 da @ $1.60 - $19.20. Mach Dept, Cumb |
| 1857-117 | " Henry | blksmith 18½ da @ $1.55 - $28.70. Mach Dept. Balto |
| 1855-89 | " Hilly | boil mkr 10 3/4 da @ $1.50 - $16.10. Mach Dept |
| 1855-95 | " Hugh | blksmith 26 da @ $1.45 - $37.70. Mach Dept |
| 1855-15 | " J. | pass eng'man 28 da @ $3 - $84.00. Trans Dept main stem |
| 1855-91 | " John | help 23 3/4 da @ $1 - $23.75. Mach Dept |
| 1857-128 | " " | blksmith help 18⅔ da @ $1 - $18.25. Mach Dept, Piedmont |
| 1857-94 | " " | carp 22 da @ $1.75 - $38.50. repair bridges |

| | | | |
|---|---|---|---|
| 1857-73 | King, John | lab 25 da @ $1.12 - $28.10. repair water sta, M.S. & P.B. |
| 1855-6 | John Jr | tick agt 28 da @ $62.50 per mo - $62.50. Trans Dept main stem |
| 1857-3 | " " | audit @ $125 per mo. Gen Ofc |
| 1857-119 | Jos. R. | carp 19¾ da @ $1.50 - $28.85. Mach Dept, Balto |
| 1857-38 | Joshua | pass eng'man 29½ da @ $3 - $88.50. Wash br rd, Wash city sta |
| 1855-81 | L. | mech 24 da @ $1.72 - $41.30. Mach Dept |
| 1857-119 | Livingston | carp 17⅞ da @ $1.50 - $25.85. Mach Dept, Balto |
| 1857-59 | Michael | fore 26 da @ $1.25 - $32.50. NW Va RR, Rd Dept 2d s-div |
| 1857-97 | " | lab 27 da @ $1 - $27.00. Rd Dept main stem 13th s-div |
| 1857-97 | Michael Jr | lab 26 da @ $1 - $26.00. NW Va RR, Rd Dept 2d s-div |
| 1857-97 | Miles | lab 26 da @ $1 - $26.00. NW Va RR, Rd Dept 2d s-div |
| 1857-123 | Oliver | mach 24½ da @ $1 - $24.25. Mach Dept, Martinsburg |
| 1857-97 | Patrick | lab 25 da @ $1 - $25.00. NW Va RR, Rd Dept 2d s-div |
| 1857-97 | " | lab 27 da @ $1 - $27.10. NW Va RR, Rd Dept 2d s-div |
| 1857-46 | " | lab 10 da @ $1 - $10.00. Rd Dept main stem 1st s-div |
| 1857-84 | Taddy | lab 24½ da @ $1.12 - $27.55. grad, Board Tree Tun |
| 1857-129 | Thomas | clean eng 14 da @ $1 - $14.00. Mach Dept, Piedmont |
| 1857-35 | " | lab 7½ da @ $1 - $7.50. Edwards' wd train 3d & 4th div |
| 1857-83 | " | lab 32¼ da @ $1.12 - $36.30. grad, Board Tree Tun |
| 1855-74 | Wm. | spik 28 da @ $1.05 - $29.40. Rd Way Dept |
| 1857-111 | Kingsland, Wm. | mach help 20¼ da @ $1.15 - $23.30. Mach Dept, Balto |
| 1855-82 | Kingsmore, F. | lab 20 da @ $1.15 - $23.00. Mach Dept |
| 1855-37 | Kinker, Henry | fore 24¼ da @ $1.37½ - $33.35. Rd Way Dept |
| 1857-89 | Kinney, James | lab 21 3/4 da @$1.12 - $24.45. grad, Welling Tun |
| 1857-104 | " | lab 4½ da @ $1.12 - $5.05. NW Va RR Tun |
| 1855-52 | John | lab 19 da @ $1 - $19.00. Rd Way Dept |
| 1855-19 | " | ton eng'man ½ da @ $2.50 - $1.25. Trans Dept main stem |
| 1857-61 | " | fore 28 da @ $1.25 - $35.00. Rd Dept main stem 14th s-div |
| 1857-56 | K. | lab 24 da @ $1 - $24.00. Rd Dept main stem 10th s-div |
| 1855-59 | Kearons | fore 24 da @ $1.25 - $30.00. Rd Way Dept |
| 1855-59 | Luke | fore 25 da @ $1.25 - $31.25. Rd Dept main stem 15th s-div |
| 1857-62 | " | lab 9 da @ $1 - $9.00. Rd Way Dept |
| 1857-88 | Michael | watch 29½ da @ $1 - $29.50. Rd Dept main stem 15th s-div |
| 1857-61 | Patrick | lab 25 3/4 da @ $1.12 - $28.95. grad, Welling Tun |
| 1857-62 | " | lab 27 da @ $1 - $27.00. Rd Dept main stem 14th s-div |
| 1857-62 | " | lab 25 da @ $1 - $25.00. Rd Dept main stem 15th s-div |

# B & O RR EMPLOYEES

| | | |
|---|---|---|
| 1855-49 | Kinney, Thomas | watch cuts 28 da @ $1 - $28.00. Rd Way Dept |
| 1857-61 | " | lab 26 da @ $1 - $26.00. Rd Dept main stem 14th s-div |
| 1857-25 | " | ton brak 9½ da @ $1.40 per mo - $15.20. 2d div |
| 1855-58 | Kinns, Hugh | nail 28 da @ $1 - $28.00. Rd Way Dept |
| 1857-39 | Kinny, Edward | lab 25 da @ $30 per mo - $30.00. NW Va rd, Parkersburg sta |
| 1857-52 | Kinsel, Joseph | lab 24 da @ $1 - $24.00. Rd Dept main stem 6th s-div |
| 1855-81 | Kinsey, Albert | fore @ $60 per mo - $60.00. Mach Dept |
| 1857-108 | " | fore mach @ $65 per mo - $65.00. Mach Dept, Balto |
| 1855-46 | Kiralhom, M. | lab 6 da @ $1 - $6.00. Rd Way Dept |
| 1855-50 | Kirbey, M. | watch cuts 30 da @ $1 - $30.00. Rd Way Dept |
| 1857-70 | Kirby, Hiram | blksmith 18 da @$1.45 - $26.10. Mt Clare sta, Balto |
| 1857-37 | " John | fire 25 da @ $35 per mo - $35.00. Wash br rd, Wash city sta |
| 1857-70 | " John T. | blksmith 18 da @ $2 - $36.00. Mt Clare sta, Balto |
| 1857-80 | " Michael | lab 26 da @$1.25 - $32.50. lay 2d track |
| 1857-62 | " " | watch 28 da @ $1 - $30.00. Rd Dept main stem 15th s-div |
| 1855-24 | Kircher, Frederick | pass & bur driv 24 da @ $40 per mo - $40.00. Trans Dept main stem |
| 1857-9 | " | watch 30 da @ $1.25 - $37.50. Mt Clare sta |
| 1855-55 | Kirk, John | lab 20 3/4 da @ $1 - $20.75. Rd Way Dept |
| 1857-120 | Kirkland, E. P. | carp 17 3/4 da @ $1.65 - $29.30. Mach Dept, Balto |
| 1857-8 | Kirkpatrick, S. | lab 25 da @ $30 per mo - $30.00. Camden sta |
| 1857-77 | Kirrmel, John | quarry 22 da @ $1 - $22.00. ballast train for 2d track |
| 1857-59 | Kirns, Hugh | lab 30 da @ $1 - $30.00. Rd Dept main stem 13th s-div |
| 1857-52 | Kiser, David | lab 21½ da @ $1 - $21.25. Rd Dept main stem 6th s-div |
| 1855-70 | Kisner, William | lab 26 da @ $1 - $26.00. Rd Way Dept |
| 1857-87 | " | conduc & brak 16 da @$1 - $26.00. grad, McGuire's Tun |
| 1855-12 | Kissinger, O. | conduc & brak 16 da @ $50 per mo - $33.35. Trans Dept main stem |
| 1855-19 | " Otho | ton eng'man 2 3/4 da @ $2.50 - $6.85. Trans Dept main stem |
| 1855-12 | Kizer, Thomas | conduc & brak 6⅔ da @ $40 per mo - $11.40. Trans Dept main stem |
| 1855-12 | " William | conduc & brak 15 da @ $24.15. Trans Dept main stem |
| 1857-60 | Kleennshallow, Otto | lab 26½ da @ $1 - $26.50. Rd Dept main stem 13th s-div |
| 1855-57 | Kline, Lary | lab 20½ da @ $1 - $20.50. Rd Way Dept |
| 1857-102 | Klunk, Charles | carp 26 da @ $1.70 - $44.20. NW Va RR, rwy depot |
| 1855-70 | " John B. | fore @ $60 per mo - $60.00. Rd Way Dept |
| 1857-102 | " " | fore @ $65 per mo - $65.00. NW Va RR, rwy depot |
| 1855-49 | Knaph, Henry | watch cuts 28 da @ $1 - $28.00. Rd Way Dept |
| 1855-12 | Knauff, L. | conduc & brak 4 da @ $40 per mo - $6.65. Trans Dept main stem |

# B & O RR EMPLOYEES

| | | | |
|---|---|---|---|
| 1857-48 | Knee, John | lab 24 3/4 da @ $1 - $24.75. Rd Dept main stem 2d s-div |
| 1857-48 | Knee, Martin | lab 26 da @ $1 - $26.00. Rd Dept main stem 2d s-div |
| 1855-23 | Knight, G. H. | fire 15¼ da @ $1.75 - $26.70. Trans Dept main stem |
| 1855-25 | Knight, John T. | bur driv 26½ da @ $30 per mo - $33.10. Trans Dept main stem |
| 1857-119 | " M. | blksmith app 25 da @ $.45 - $11.25. Mach Dept, Balto |
| 1855-77 | " Mike | help 24 da @ $1.15 - $27.60. Mach Dept |
| 1857-111 | " W. H. | mach help 15 3/4 da @ $1.15 - $18.10. Mach Dept, Balto |
| 1855-85 | " " | blksmith 24 da @ $1.40 - $33.60. Mach Dept |
| 1857-116 | " " | blksmith 17 3/4 da @ $1.45 -$25.75. Mach Dept, Balto |
| 1855-77 | " William | app 23 da @ $.55 - $12.65. Mach Dept |
| 1855-92 | " " | carp 22 da - $30.75. Mach Dept |
| 1857-129 | " " | inspec cars @ $40 per mo -$40.00. Mach Dept, Piedmont |
| 1857-10 | Knill, Frank | bur driv 27 da @ $1.15 - $31.05. hp exp, Balto |
| 1855-45 | Knirley, Eli | lab 11 da @ $1 -$11.00. Rd Way Dept |
| 1857-12 | Knootz, John | lab 25 da @ $30 per mo - $30.00. Fred sta |
| 1855-94 | Knott, Stephen | fore @ $50 per mo - $50.00. Mach Dept |
| 1855-9 | Knotts, William | conduc 15½ da @ $50 per mo - $32.30. Trans Dept main stem |
| 1857-10 | Knotz, Joseph | bur driv 27½ da @ $1.15 - $31.60. hp exp, Balto |
| 1855-80 | Knox, Adam | carp 28 da @ $1.55 - $43.40. Mach Dept |
| 1857-120 | " " | carp 30 da @ $1.65 -$49.50. Mach Dept, Balto |
| 1857-75 | " Richard | lab 18 da @ $1.15 - $20.50. ballast train for 2d track |
| 1855-87 | Kohl, Hewes | help 17⅝ da @ $1 - $17.50. Mach Dept |
| 1857-72 | Kolbaugh, Michael | carp 18 3/4 da @ $1.62 - $30.45. Piedmont depot |
| 1655-33 | Koniskey, Thomas | lab 28 da @ $30 per mo - $30.00. Trans Dept main stem |
| 1855-7 | Koonce, David | pass conduc 28 da @ $62.50 per mo - $62.50. Trans Dept main stem |
| 1855-19 | Koontz, Chas. | ton eng'man 16 3/4 da @ $2.50 - $40.60. Trans Dept main stem |
| 1857-18 | " David | pass train conduc 30 da @$75 per mo - $75.00. w end |
| 1855-7 | " G. S. | clk 28 da @ $75 per mo - $75.00. Trans Dept main stem |
| 1855-errata | " " | clk -- instead of $75, $50 per mo |
| 1857-11 | " George S. | agt 30 da @ $50 per mo - $50.00. Ellicott's Mills |
| 1855-19 | " Henry | ton eng'man 24 da @$2.25 - $54.00. Trans Dept main stem |
| 1855-43 | " Jacob | lab 4 3/4 da @ $1 -$4.75. Rd Way Dept |
| 1857-128 | " James H. | mach help 24 da @ $.65 -$15.60. Mach Dept, Piedmont |
| 1855-23 | " John | fire 9 3/4 da @ $1.75 - $17.05. Trans Dept main stem |
| 1855-91 | " " | help 5¼ da @ $1 - $5.25. Mach Dept |
| 1855-57 | " " | lab 15 da @ $1 -$15.00. Rd Way Dept |

B & O RR EMPLOYEES 207

| |  |  |
|---|---|---|
| 1855-33 | Koontz, John | watch 24 da @ $30 per mo -$30.00. Trans Dept main stem |
| 1857-32 | " | ton fire 18 3/4 da @ $1.75 - $32.80. 1st div |
| 1855-65 | N. | mill wright 24 da @$1.62½ - $39.00. Rd Way Dept |
| 1855-51 | Kooser, Jacob | lab 18 3/4 da @ $1 - $18.75. Rd Way Dept |
| 1855-25 | Kootz, George | clean eng 4 3/4 da @ $1.15 - $5.45. Trans Dept main stem |
| 1855-78 | Koster, Albert | mach 26½ da @$1.65 - $43.70. Mach Dept |
| 1857-110 | " | mach 27 3/4 da @ $1.72 - $48.60. Mach Dept, Balto |
| 1857-32 | Krafft, George | ton fire 15¾ da @$1.75 - $26.70. 1st div |
| 1855-82 | Kraft, Frederick | app 22 da @ $.55 - $12.10. Mach Dept |
| 1857-40 | Theodore | ton brak 7 da @ $40 per mo - $11.20. NW Va rd, Parkersburg sta |
| 1857-135 | Krager, Christian | boil mkr help 27 da @ $1.25 - $33.75. Mach Dept, Wheeling |
| 1857-23 | Kragler, George | ton conduc 6½ da @ $50 per mo - $13.00. 3d & 4th div |
| 1857-122 | Kramer, William | lab 16 3/4 da @ $1 - $16.75. Mach Dept, Balto |
| 1855-94 | Krate, Adam | mach 27 3/4 da @ $1.72 - $48.60. Mach Dept |
| 1857-116 | Kreager, Henry | carp 21½ da @ $1.45 - $31.15. Mach Dept |
| 1855-12 | Krebs, George C. | blksmith 17 3/4 da @ $1.40 - $24.85. Mach Dept, Balto |
| 1857-119 | William J. | conduc & brak 6½ da @ $40 per mo - $10.85. Trans Dept main stem |
| 1855-43 | | carp 18 da @ $1.50 - $27.00. Mach Dept, Balto |
| 1855-1 | Kretuck, H. | lab 13½ da @ $1 - $13.50. Rd Way Dept |
| 1855-53 | Kretzer, F. | clk $600 per annum - $50.00. Ofc Hanover St |
| 1855-82 | Kries, Henry | carp 19 da @$1.60 - $30.40. Rd Way Dept |
| 1857-135 | Kronder, J. | mach 29½ da @ $1.72 - $50.30. Mach Dept |
| 1857-109 | Krotz, Adam | carp 21½ da @ $1.45 - $31.15. Mach Dept, Wheeling |
| 1855-72 | Krowder, Jackson | mach 11 3/4 da @ $1.72 - $20.20. Mach Dept, Balto |
| 1857-132 | Kruzen, Edw. | mach 24 da @ $1.65 - $39.60. Rd Way Dept |
| 1857-132 | Kuh, George | stat'ry eng'man @ $30 per mo - $30.00. Mach Dept, Grafton |
| 1855-80 | Kuhn, John | clean eng 32 da @ $1 - $32.00. Mach Dept, Grafton |
| 1857-119 | G. W. | carp 23 da @ $1.50 - $34.50. Mach Dept, Balto |
| 1857-112 | " | carp 18 da @ $1.50 - $27.00. Mach Dept, Balto |
| 1857-114 | John | mach app 20 da @ $.45 - $9.00. Mach Dept, Balto |
| 1855-95 | R. M. | pat mkr 18¾ da @ $1.90 - $34.70. Mach Dept, Balto |
| 1855-91 | Robert | pat mkr 24 da @ $1.80 - $43.20. Mach Dept |
| 1855-86 | Kuise, Henry | help 16½ da @ $1 - $16.50. Mach Dept |
| 1855-39 | Kull, Jacob | mach 22 3/4 da @ $1.50 - $34.10. Mach Dept |
| 1857-68 | Kunkle, Joseph | lab 15 3/4 da @ $1 - $15.75. Rd Way Dept |
| 1857-70 | " | lab 19¼ da @ $1 - $19.25. Rd Dept main stem 19th s-div |
| | Kurtz, Samuel | blksmith 16½ da @ $1.85 - $30.50. Mt Clare sta, Balto |

## B & O RR EMPLOYEES

| ID | Name | Description |
|---|---|---|
| 1857-17 | Kyle, Robert | collec & doorkpr 30 da @ $50 per mo - $50.00. Wheeling sta |
| 1857-131 | " | mach 21 da @ $1.60 - $33.60. Mach Dept, Grafton |
| 1855-32 | " William | lab 24 da @ $30 per mo - $30.00. Trans Dept main stem |
| 1657-92 | Kyne, Anthony | lab 26 3/4 da @ $1.12 - $30.10. grad, Littleton Tun |
| 1657-97 | Patrick | lab 26 da @ $1 - $26.00. NW Va RR, Rd Dept 2d s-div |
| 1855-74 | Timy. | lab 24 da @ $1 - $24.00. NW Va RR ballast train |
| 1657-101 | Lacey, Bartlett | lab 23 da @ $1 - $23.00. Rd Way Dept |
| 1657-135 | John | lab 20 da @ $1 - $20.00. Mach Dept, Wheeling |
| 1655-20 | Lackey, James | fire 16½ da @ $1.75 - $28.45. Trans Dept main stem |
| 1857-30 | James W. | ton eng'man 28½ da @ $2.50 - $70.60. 3d div |
| 1855-52 | John | carp 23½ da @ $1.50 - $35.25. Rd Way Dept |
| 1657-93 | Lacy, Edw. | smith help 13 da @ $1 - $13.00. quarry & haul stone for Board Tree & Littleton Tun |
| 1657-86 | Laffee, Patrick | lab 21 da @ $1 - $21.00. grad, McGuire's Tun |
| 1855-74 | Lafferty, Dan. | lab 23 da @ $1 - $23.00. Rd Way Dept |
| 1655-89 | Laffey, Andrew | lab 20¾ da @ $1.12 - $22.80. grad, Welling Tun |
| 1657-71 | Lahey, Jno. | cart driv 7½ da @ $1 - $7.50. Mt Clare, repair tracks in yd |
| 1655-31 | Lain, Joshua | saw wd 15 cords @ $.44 - $6.60. Trans Dept main stem |
| 1655-41 | Lainey, R. | lab 17 da @ $1 - $17.00. Rd Way Dept |
| 1657-128 | Laird, Abraham | boil mkr 19¼ da @ $1.60 - $30.80. Mach Dept, Piedmont |
| 1855-44 | Lallery, Patrick | lab 23½ da @ $1 - $23.50. Rd Way Dept |
| 1855-69 | Lalless, John | lab 22¼ da @ $1 - $22.25. Rd Way Dept |
| 1857-88 | Lally, Michael | lab 27¼ da @ $1.12 - $30.65. grad, Welling Tun |
| 1855-66 | Richard | watch cuts 28 da @ $.62½ - $15.00. Rd Way Dept |
| 1655-50 | William | watch 30 da @ $1 - $30.00. Rd Dept main stem 18th s-div |
| 1857-67 | " | train inspec @ $34.50 per mo - $34.50. Mach Dept |
| 1855-86 | Lamar, Richard | lab 16 da @ $1 - $16.00. Rd Way Dept |
| 1657-103 | Lamb, Alexander | lab 18½ da @ $1.12 - $20.80. NW Va RR Tun |
| 1855-77 | Lambert, Geo. | mach 18½ da @ $1.72 - $31.80. Mach Dept |
| 1657-30 | John | lab 20 da @ $1 - $20.00. Trans Dept main stem |
| 1657-81 | Lamey, Michael | lab 20 3/4 da @ $1.25 - $20.75. lay 2d track |
| 1857-60 | Lammon, Hans | fore 30 da @ $1.25 - $37.50. Rd Dept main stem 13th s-div |
| 1855-82 | Lamphier, Jno. | mach 25½ da @ $1.60 - $40.80. Mach Dept |
| 1855-44 | Lanagan, James | lab 24½ da @ $1 - $24.50. Rd Way Dept |
| 1857-54 | " | lab 24 da @ $1 - $24.00. Rd Dept main stem 8th s-div |
| 1857-136 | Thomas | mach 21¼ da @ $1.75 - $37.20. Mach Dept, Cumb |

B & O RR EMPLOYEES

| | | |
|---|---|---|
| 1855-27 | Lanan, John | clean eng 26 da @ $1 - $26.00. Trans Dept main stem |
| 1855-67 | " Michael | mason 22½ da @ $2 - $45.00. Rd Way Dept |
| 1857-117 | Lance, David | blksmith help 16¼ da @ $1 - $16.25. Mach Dept, Balto |
| 1857-125 | " John | put away eng &c 26 da @ $1.50 - $39.00. Mach Dept, Martinsburg |
| 1857-124 | " Joseph | mach app 21¼ da @ $.55 - $11.70. Mach Dept, Martinsburg |
| 1857-130 | Land, Robert | lab 19¼ da @ $1 - $19.25. Mach Dept, Piedmont |
| 1857-35 | Landolf, John | lab 8¼ da @ $1 - $8.25. Edwards' wd train 3d & 4th div |
| 1857-55 | Landwer, Casper | fore 23 3/4 da @ $1.25 - $29.70. Rd Dept main stem 9th s-div |
| 1855-96 | Lane, H. C. | app 23 da @ $.45 - $10.35. Mach Dept |
| 1857-114 | " Henry C. | iron brak 6 da @ $.75 - $17.25. Mach Dept, Balto |
| 1857-27 | " James | ton brak 6 da @ $40 per mo - $9.60. Board Tree Tun |
| 1855-42 | " " | ton brak 26 da @ $40 per mo - $41.60. 3d & 4th div |
| 1855-39 | " John | lab 13 da @ $1 - $13.00. Rd Way Dept |
| 1855-32 | " William | lab 24 da @ $1 - $24.00. Rd Way Dept |
| 1857-49 | Lanehart, Henry | saw wd 30 cords @ $.35 - $10.50. Trans Dept main stem |
| 1855-36 | Lang, Thomas | lab 25 da @ $1 - $25.00. Rd Dept main stem 3d s-div |
| 1855-47 | Langan, Patrick | lab 25 da @ $25 per mo - $26.05. Trans Dept main stem |
| 1855-52 | " " | lab 19½ da @ $1 - $19.50. Rd Way Dept |
| 1855-55 | Langherry, Patrick | lab 28 da @ $1 - $28.00. Rd Way Dept |
| 1857-18 | Langley, Charles | fore 24 da @ $1.25 - $30.00. Rd Way Dept |
| 1857-121 | " George | pass train brak 10 da @ $3.35 per mo - $11.10. thr mail & exp |
| 1857-20 | " J. C. | carp help 20 da @ $1.15 - $23.00. Mach Dept, Balto |
| 1855-80 | " James | pass fire 37 da @ $40 per mo - $49.35. 2d div |
| 1857-119 | " " | carp 28¼ da @ $1.65 - $47.00. Mach Dept |
| 1857-64 | Lanhead, Jos. | carp 24¼ da @ $1.65 - $40.00. Mach Dept, Balto |
| 1857-108 | Lannan, J. | mason 17 da @ $1.50 - $35.50. Rd Way Dept |
| 1855-30 | " Patrick | storekpr @ $55 per mo - $55.00. Mach Dept, Balto |
| 1855-30 | " Peter | fill tend 28 da @ $1 - $28.00. Trans Dept main stem |
| 1857-125 | " Richard | fill tend 28 da @ $1 - $28.00. Trans Dept main stem |
| 1855-75 | Lanning, Thomas | inspec cars 25 da @ $1.33 - $33.25. Mach Dept, Martinsburg |
| 1857-61 | " " | lab 17½ da @ $1 - $17.50. Rd Way Dept |
| 1857-130 | Lannon, James | lab 27 da @ $1 - $27.00. Rd Dept main stem 14th s-div |
| 1857-130 | " John | lab 9 da @ $1 - $9.00. Mach Dept, Piedmont |
| 1857-57 | " " | lab 19 da @ $1 - $19.00. Mach Dept, Piedmont |
| 1857-33 | " " | lab 25½ da @ $1 - $25.50. Rd Dept main stem 11th s-div |
| | " " | ton fire 3 da @ $1.75 - $5.25. 3d div |

## 210 — B & O RR EMPLOYEES

| Ref | Name | Details |
|---|---|---|
| 1857-129 | Lannon, John Sr | clean eng 25 da @ $1 - $25.00. Mach Dept, Piedmont |
| 1857-129 | Patrick | clean eng 31 1/7 da @ $1 - $31.15. Mach Dept, Piedmont |
| 1857-129 | Peter | clean eng 16 da @ $1 - $16.00. Mach Dept, Piedmont |
| 1855-82 | Peter W. | clean eng 14 da @ $1 - $14.00. Mach Dept, Piedmont |
| 1855-78 | Lanon, John | mach 23 da @ $1.60 - $36.80. Mach Dept |
| 1857-35 | " | storekpr 27½ da @ $2 - $55.00. Mach Dept |
| 1855-82 | Robert | lab 22 3/4 da @ $.65 - $13.65. Mach Dept |
| 1857-38 | William | app 21 da @ $1 - $22.75. Edwards' wd train 3d & 4th div |
| 1855-30 | Lansbury, Richard | ton fire 24 da @ $33.33 per mo - $32.00. Wash br rd, Wash city sta |
| 1857-136 | Lantridge, Robert | prepar fuel 28 da @ $30 per mo - $30.00. Trans Dept main stem |
| 1857-122 | Lantz, Charles | mach 17 3/4 da @ $1.40 - $24.85. Mach Dept, Cumb |
| 1855-58 | Lantze, Jacob | eng clean 22 3/4 da @ $1 - $22.75. Mach Dept, Balto |
| 1855-94 | Larale, A. | lab 19½ da @ $1 - $19.50. Rd Way Dept |
| 1855-47 | Largert, John | app 26 da @ $.80 - $20.80. Mach Dept |
| 1855-39 | Lark, Henry | lab 13½ da @ $1 - $13.50. Rd Way Dept |
| 1857-49 | " | lab 24 da @ $1 - $24.00. Rd Way Dept |
| 1857-54 | Larkin, Michael | lab 24 da @ $1 - $24.00. Rd Dept main stem 3d s-div |
| 1857-126 | Larkins, James | fore 25 da @ $1.25 - $31.25. Rd Dept main stem 8th s-div |
| 1855-49 | John | clean eng 21½ da @ $1.15 - $24.70. Mach Dept, Martinsburg |
| 1855-44 | M. | watch 24 da @ $1 - $24.00. Rd Way Dept |
| 1855-67 | Patrick | fore 25½ da @ $1.25 - $25.50. Rd Way Dept |
| 1855-95 | Thomas | lab 21 3/4 da @ $1 - $21.75. Rd Way Dept |
| 1857-82 | Larner, Martin | lab 25¼ da @ $1 - $25.25. Mach Dept |
| 1855-67 | William | brickLay 6½ da @ $2 - $13.00. grad, Board Tree Tun |
| 1857-82 | " | mason 24 da @ $2 - $48.00. Rd Way Dept |
| 1857-26 | Larue, James | brickLay 9 da @ $2 - $18.00. grad, Board Tree Tun |
| 1855-5 | Lash, Ely | ton brak 2 da @ $40 per mo - $3.20. 3d & 4th div |
| 1857-78 | Lassia, August | eng clean 32 da @ $1.15 - $36.80. Trans Dept, Wash br |
| 1855-1 | Latrobe, B. H. | lab 16 3/4 da @ $1 - $16.75. lay 2d track |
| 1855-1 | ", J. H. B. | chief engr $1000 per annum - $83.33. Ofc Hanover St |
| 1855-90 | Laub, Charles | counsel $1000 per annum - $83.33. Ofc Hanover St |
| 1855-90 | John | app 24 da @ $.55 - $13.20. Mach Dept |
| 1855-64 | Lauet, Thos. | app 24 da @ $.65 - $15.60. Mach Dept |
| 1857-97 | Laughney, John | carp 22½ da @ $1 - $22.50. Rd Way Dept |
| 1857-104 | Lavell, Patrick | watch 30 da @ $1 - $30.00. NW Va RR, Rd Dept 2d s-div |
| | | lab 16½ da @ $1 - $16.50. NW Va RR Tun |

| Name | Years | Description |
|---|---|---|
| Lavelle, Thomas | 1857-93 | lab 15½ da @ $1 - $15.50. quarry & haul stone for Board Tree & Littleton Tun |
| Laven, Tim. | 1857-79 | lab 24¼ da @ $1 - $24.25. lay 2d track |
| Laville, Anthony | 1857-65 | watch 30 da @ $1 - $30.00. Rd Dept main stem 17th s-div |
| " Owen | 1857-62 | lab 26 da @ $1 - $26.00. Rd Dept main stem 15th s-div |
| " P. | 1855-60 | lab 21 da @ $1 - $21.00. Rd Way Dept |
| Lawden, B. M. | 1855-12 | conduc & brak 25 da @ $40 per mo - $41.65. Trans Dept main stem |
| Lawless, Patrick | 1857-78 | lab 25½ da @ $1 - $25.50. lay 2d track |
| Lawrence, Henry | 1857-117 | blksmith 24 da @ $1.25 - $30.00. Mach Dept, Balto |
| " Jno. | 1855-64 | lab 23½ da @ $1.62½ - $38.15. Rd Way Dept |
| Lawson, John T. | 1857-45 | storekpr @ $40 per mo. Rd Dept |
| Lawther, William | 1855-90 | fore @ $83.35 per mo - $83.35. Mach Dept |
| Lawton, C. H. | 1857-119 | blksmith app 25 da @ $.65 - $16.25. Mach Dept, Balto |
| " Carlos | 1857-30 | ton eng'man 6 da @ $3 - $18.00. 4th div |
| " Charles | 1857-31 | ton eng'man 7 da @ $3 - $21.00. Board Tree Tun |
| Layden, Thomas | 1857-11 | lab 16 da @ $1 - $16.00. NW Va rd, Athey's wd train |
| Layfield, Sanford | 1857-99 | watch 30 da @ $1 - $30.00. NW Va RR, Rd Dept 4th s-div |
| Layman, Andrew | 1857-139 | lab 35 da @ $1.10 - $38.50. NW Va RR, Mach Dept, Parkersburg |
| " Jacob | 1857-28 | ton eng'man 17½ da @ $3 - $51.75. 1st div |
| " James | 1857-40 | pass eng'man 6 da @ $3 - $18.00. NW Va rd, Parkersburg sta |
| " " | 1857-40 | ton eng'man 14 da @ $2.50 - $35.00. NW Va rd, Parkersburg sta |
| Laymey, M. | 1855-46 | lab 5 3/4 da @ $1 - $5.75. Rd Way Dept |
| Laymyer, William | 1855-52 | fore 24 da @ $1.25 - $30.00. Rd Way Dept |
| " " | 1857-61 | fore 29 da @ $1.25 - $36.25. Rd Dept main stem 14th s-div |
| Laypole, Henry | 1855-40 | lab 24 da @ $1 - $24.00. Rd Way Dept |
| " John | 1855-40 | lab 25 da @ $1 - $25.00. Rd Way Dept |
| " " | 1857-50 | lab 20½ da @ $1 - $20.50. Rd Dept main stem 4th s-div |
| " T. | 1855-40 | lab 24 da @ $1 - $24.00. Rd Way Dept |
| Leahman, Jacob | 1857-71 | watch 30 da @ $1.25 - $37.50. Mt Clare, repair tracks in yd |
| Leaman, J. | 1855-73 | watch 28 da @ $1.25 - $35.00. Rd Way Dept |
| Leaney, Nic. | 1855-75 | lab 16 da @ $1 - $16.00. Rd Way Dept |
| Lear, D. W. | 1857-120 | carp 17½ da @ $1.50 - $26.25. Mach Dept, Balto |
| " Edward | 1855-85 | blksmith 24 3/4 da @ $1.45 - $35.90. Mach Dept |
| " " | 1857-117 | blksmith 13¼ da @ $1.55 - $20.55. Mach Dept, Balto |
| " John | 1855-77 | mach 21 3/4 da @ $1.72 - $37.40. Mach Dept |
| " " | 1857-117 | blksmith 18 da @ $1.40 - $25.20. Mach Dept, Balto |
| Learey, Thomas | 1855-62 | lab 22 3/4 da @ $1 - $22.75. Rd Way Dept |

B & O RR EMPLOYEES

| ID | Name | Description |
|---|---|---|
| 1857-52 | Leary, Thomas | lab 25 da @ $1 - $25.00. Rd Dept main stem 6th s-div |
| 1855-35 | Leathers, D. | reg 24 da @ $30 per mo - $30.00. Trans Dept main stem |
| 1857-51 | Leavy, Nicholas | lab 23 da @ $1 - $23.00. Rd Dept main stem 5th s-div |
| 1857-26 | Lechmere, Henry E. | ton brak 5 da @ $40 per mo - $8.00. 3d & 4th div |
| 1857-121 | Ledley, Jacob | carp help 20 da @ $1.15 - $23.00. Mach Dept, Balto |
| 1857-121 | " Jacob C. | carp help 20 da @ $1.15 - $23.00. Mach Dept, Balto |
| 1857-10 | Ledlow, Thomas | stab'man 25 da @ $35 per mo - $35.00. hp exp, Balto |
| 1857-87 | Lee, Albert | lab 26 da @ $1.25 - $32.50. grad, McGuire's Tun. |
| 1857-10 | " | lab 9 3/4 da @ $1.25 - $12.20. grad, McGuire's Tun |
| 1855-23 | Beall | stab'man 27 da @ $1 - $27.00. hp exp, Balto |
| 1857-103 | Daniel | fire 17⅞ da @ $33.35 per mo - $23.95. Trans Dept main stem |
| 1857-77 | E. C. | carp 22 da @ $1.60 - $35.20. NW Va RR depot |
| 1855-42 | Edward | quarry 16 da @ $1 - $16.00. ballast train for 2d track |
| 1857-9 | John | lab 24 da @ $1 - $24.00. Rd Way Dept |
| 1857-103 | " | coup 25 da @ $30 per mo - $30.00. Mt Clare sta |
| 1855-6 | Patrick | lab 22 3/4 da @ $1.12 - $25.60. NW Va RR Tun |
| 1857-9 | Samuel | St supv 28 da @ $50 per mo - $50.00. Trans Dept main stem |
| 1857-121 | Leeds, Ed. | St supv 30 da @ $50 per mo - $50.00. hp exp, Balto |
| 1855-80 | Lefener, Chs. | paint 18 da @ $2.62 - $47.15. Mach Dept, Balto |
| 1857-119 | Lefner, Charles | carp 22 da @ $1.55 - $34.10. Mach Dept |
| 1857-41 | Leggett, Daniel | carp 16 da @ $1.50 - $24.00. Mach Dept, Balto |
| 1857-89 | LeGourde, L. | lab 20 da @ $1 - $20.00. NW Va rd, Athey's wd train |
| 1855-90 | Leherman, H. | timekpr @ $40 per mo - $40.00. grad, Welling Tun |
| 1855-73 | Lehey, Jno. | help 23½ da @ $1 - $23.50. Mach Dept |
| 1855-67 | Leitka, H. | lab 22⅞ da @ $1 - $22.25. Rd Way Dept |
| 1857-98 | Leman, Henry | mason 20½ da @ $2 - $40.50. Rd Way Dept |
| 1855-20 | Lemmon, George | lab 25½ da @ $1 - $25.50. NW Va RR, Rd Dept 3d s-div |
| 1857-35 | " | fire 18½ da @ $1.75 - $32.35. Trans Dept main stem |
| 1857-30 | " | eng'man 19¼ da @ $2.50 -$48.75. J. R. Shrode's wd train 4th div |
| 1857-21 | J. S. | ton eng'man 9 da @ $3 -$27.00. 4th div |
| 1857-83 | James | ton conduc 18½ da @ $50 per mo - $37.00. 1st div |
| 1857-82 | Robert | lab 1 da @ $1.12 - $1.10. grad, Board Tree Tun |
| 1855-15 | W. | bricklay 2¼ da @ $2 - $4.50. grad, Board Tree Tun |
| 1855-17 | William | pass eng'man 11½ da @ $2.50 - $28.75. Trans Dept main stem |
| 1857-30 | " | ton eng'man 28 da @ $3 - $84.00. 4th div |

# B & O RR EMPLOYEES

| | | |
|---|---|---|
| 1855-58 | Lemon, H. | fore 26 da @ $1.25 - $32.50. Rd Way Dept |
| 1857-92 | Lemorick, H. Francis | driv 30 da @ $1 - $30.00. grad, Littleton Tun |
| 1857-125 | Lempes, Theodore | carp 19 da @ $1.15 - $21.85. Mach Dept, Martinsburg |
| 1857-97 | Lenahan, Michael | lab 26 da @ $1 - $26.00. NW Va RR, Rd Dept 2d s-div |
| 1857-120 | Lenard, Jacob H. | carp 17 3/4 da @ $1.50 - $26.60. Mach Dept, Balto |
| 1857-119 | William H. | blksmith app 27 3/4 da @$.65 - $18.05. Mach Dept, Balto |
| 1855-93 | Lenior, Thomas | eng'man 25¾ da - $36.25. Mach Dept |
| 1857-53 | Lenis, Samuel | lab 23¼ da @ $1 - $23.25. Rd Dept main stem 7th s-div |
| 1857-89 | Lennen, Michael | mason 1 da @ $2 - $2.00. grad, Welling Tun |
| 1857-90 | Lenner, Michael | stone mason 7 da @ $2 - $14.00. grad, Welling Tun |
| 1857-104 | Lennon, Martin | miner 22½ da @ $1 - $22.50. NW Va RR Tun |
| 1857-91 | Lenon, Michael | bricklay 11½ da @ $2 - $23.00. grad, Littleton Tun |
| 1855-35 | Lentz, H. | clean cars 28 da @ $30 per mo - $30.00. Trans Dept main stem |
| 1855-35 | P. | clean cars 28 da @ $30 per mo - $30.00. Trans Dept main stem |
| 1857-37 | Peter | wd cars 30 da @ $25 per mo - $25.00. Wash br rd, Wash city sta |
| 1857-120 | Lenvard, George | carp 21½ da @ $1.80 - $44.10. Mach Dept, Balto |
| 1857-36 | Leonard, Allison | lab 21 da @ $1 - $21.00. J. R. Shrode's wd train 4th div |
| 1855-79 | George | carp 24 da @ $1.80 - $43.20. Mach Dept |
| 1855-50 | James | watch cuts 28 da @ $1 - $28.00. Rd Way Dept |
| 1857-63 | " | watch 30 da @ $1 - $30.00. Rd Dept main stem 16th s-div |
| 1857-69 | John M. | app 24 da @ $.50 - $12.00. Mt Clare sta, Balto |
| 1857-36 | Porter | lab 17½ da @ $1 - $17.50. J. R. Shrode's wd train 4th div |
| 1855-71 | William | carp 24 da @ $1.73 - $41.50. Rd Way Dept |
| 1857-69 | " | carp 17¼ da @ $1.73 -$29.85. Mt Clare sta, Balto |
| 1855-6 | Lepper, G. A. | clk 16 da @ $66.65 per mo - $38.10. Trans Dept main stem |
| 1855-71 | Lepson, Daniel | fore @ $50 per mo - $50.00. Rd Way Dept |
| 1855-71 | William H. | 24 da @ $1.25 - $30.00. Rd Way Dept |
| 1857-92 | Lerew, James | lab 13 da @ $1.12 - $14.60. grad, Littleton Tun |
| 1857-134 | Lery, Charles | mach help 1¼ da @ $1 - $1.25. Mach Dept, Wheeling |
| 1857-134 | Lesourd, Joseph | mach 4 da @ $1.50 - $6.00. Mach Dept, Wheeling |
| 1855-96 | Lester, Mike | lab 27¼ da @ $1.10 - $29.95. Mach Dept |
| 1857-114 | " | iron mould help 18 3/4 da @ $1.10 - $20.65. Mach Dept, Balto |
| 1855-70 | William | lab 13 3/4 da @ $1.50 - $20.65. Rd Way Dept |
| 1857-86 | Levo, Goshart | stone mason 20 3/4 da @ $2 - $41.50. grad, McGuire's Tun |
| 1855-29 | Levy, Charles | haul & saw firewd 6½ da @ $1 - $6.50. Trans Dept main stem |
| 1857-20 | " | pass fire 27½ da @ $40 per mo - $36.65. 4th div |

| | | |
|---|---|---|
| 1855-88 | Levy, John | carp 20½ da @ $1.25 - $25.60. Mach Dept |
| 1857-124 | Lewing, George | mach app 29½ da @ $.60 - $17.70. Mach Dept, Martinsburg |
| 1855-81 | Lewis, H. B. | mech 13 da @ $1.25 - $16.25. Mach Dept |
| 1857-119 | " " | carp 19¼ da @ $1.35 - $26.30. Mach Dept, Balto |
| 1857-132 | " John | blksmith 21½ da @ $1.80 - $38.70. Mach Dept, Grafton |
| 1857-95 | " " | lab 24 da @ $1 - $24.00. Wash br, Rd Dept |
| 1855-19 | " Joshua | ton eng'man 9 da @ $3; 6 da @ $2.35; 3 da @ $2 - $46.00. Trans Dept main stem |
| 1857-29 | " " | ton eng'man 20¾ da @ $2.25 - $45.55. 2d div |
| 1855-42 | " McLeod | tele oper 30 da @ $30 per mo - $30.00. Camden sta |
| 1857-36 | " Samuel | lab 18 da @ $1 - $18.00. Rd Way Dept |
| 1855-93 | " Wm. | mach 3 da @ $1.60 - $4.80. Mach Dept |
| 1857-89 | Liason, Joshua | driv 21½ da @ $1 - $21.50. grad, Welling Tun |
| 1857-22 | Lichtenberger, E. M. | ton conduc 11½ da @ $50 per mo - $23.00. 2d div |
| 1857-26 | Liddard, B. H. | ton brak 18 da @ $40 per mo - $28.80. 3d & 4th div |
| 1857-88 | Liden, John | lab 18 3/4 da @ $1.12 - $21.10. grad, Welling Tun |
| 1857-90 | " Patrick | lab 11 da @ $1.12 - $12.35. grad, Welling Tun |
| 1855-15 | Lidon, John | lab 17¾ da @ $1 - $17.25. lay 2d track |
| 1857-123 | Light, J. W. | pass eng'man 10 da @ $3 - $30.00. Trans Dept main stem |
| 1857-29 | " Jacob | mach 1¼ da @ $1.25 - $1.55. Mach Dept, Martinsburg |
| 1855-42 | " Jacob W. | ton eng'man 27 3/4 da @ $3 - $83.25. 2d div |
| 1857-28 | " John | lab 18 da @ $1 - $18.00. Rd Way Dept |
| 1855-42 | " W. H. | ton eng'man 18 da @ $3 - $54.00. 1st div |
| 1857-33 | " Wm. F. | ton fire 2 da @ $1.75 - $3.50. 2d div |
| 1857-29 | " William H. | lab 15½ da @ $1 - $15.50. Rd Way Dept |
| 1855-26 | Lightner, Henry | ton eng'man 18 da @ $3 - $54.00. 2d div |
| 1857-115 | " " | clean eng 22 da @ $1 - $22.00. Trans Dept main stem |
| 1857-131 | " John | boil mkr 17½ da @ $1.50 - $26.25. Mach Dept, Balto |
| 1855-9 | Lillen, William | boil mkr 2½ da @ $1.60 - $4.00. Mach Dept, Grafton |
| 1855-38 | Lilley, William | conduc 18¼ da @ $50 per mo - $38.55. Trans Dept main stem |
| 1855-51 | " " | lab 24 da @ $1 - $24.00. Rd Way Dept |
| 1857-55 | " " | lab @ $31 per mo - $31.00. Rd Way Dept |
| 1855-50 | Limerick, F. | watch 31 da @ $1 - $31.00. Rd Dept main stem 9th s-div |
| 1855-23 | Linch, James | watch cuts 28 da @ $1 - $28.00. Rd Way Dept |
| 1855-38 | " M. | fire 2 da @ $1.75 - $3.50. Trans Dept main stem |
| | | lab 24 da @ $1 - $24.00. Rd Way Dept |

| | | |
|---|---|---|
| 1855-58 | Linch, M. | lab 23½ da @ $1 - $23.50. Rd Way Dept |
| 1857-99 | Michael | lab 25 da @ $1 - $25.00. NW Va RR, Rd Dept 4th s-div |
| 1857-55 | Lindamin, Adam | lab 24 da @ $1 - $24.00. Rd Dept main stem 9th s-div |
| 1857-41 | Lindsay, B. F. | ton fire 16¼ da @$1.75 -$28.45. NW Va rd, Parkersburg sta |
| 1855-32 | J. M. | tele oper 28 da @ $50 per mo - $50.00. Trans Dept main stem |
| 1855-70 | Link, Frederick | track lay 9 da @$1.12½ - $10.10. Rd Way Dept |
| 1855-63 | Linskly, M. | lab 18¼ da @ $1 - $18.25. Rd Way Dept |
| 1855-19 | Linsley, Andrew | ton eng'man 13 da @ $2.50 -$32.50. Trans Dept main stem |
| 1857-17 | Linsroy, Patrick | lab 2½ da @ $1 - $2.50. frt transfer force at Bellaire, opp Benwood |
| 1855-16 | Linthicum, I. | pass fire 7 da @ $40 per mo - $10.00. Trans Dept main stem |
| 1857-75 | John | eng'man 12 da @ $60 per mo - $27.60. ballast train for 2d track |
| 1857-29 | " | ton eng'man 12¼ da @ $3 - $36.75. 2d div |
| 1857-48 | Thomas | lab 21 da @ $1 - $21.00. Rd Dept main stem 2d s-div |
| 1855-92 | Lintze, Bernard | carp 23 3/4 da @ $32.00. Mach Dept |
| 1857-116 | Lipard, Frederick | blksmith 16 3/4 da @ $1.45 - $24.30. Mach Dept, Balto |
| 1857-127 | Lippincott, Edward | mach 26¼ da @ $2 - $52.50. Mach Dept, Piedmont |
| 1857-128 | Lirours, James | boil mkr 25 da @ $1.80 - $45.00. Mach Dept, Piedmont |
| 1855-86 | List, Frederick | mach 20 3/4 da @$1.25 -$25.95. Mach Dept |
| 1857-123 | " | mach 20 da @ $1.50 - $30.00. Mach Dept, Martinsburg |
| 1857-109 | Litchfield, S. A. | mach 17 3/4 da @ $2 - $35.50. Mach Dept, Balto |
| 1855-89 | Litley, R. J. | mach 21¼ da @ $1.70 - $36.10. Mach Dept |
| 1857-115 | Litsinger, Richard | pat mkr 18½ da @ $1.75 - $32.40. Mach Dept, Balto |
| 1855-78 | Little, Joseph | mach 28 3/4 da @ $1.35 -$38.80. Mach Dept |
| 1857-131 | " | boil mkr 1½ da @ $1 - $1.50. Mach Dept, Grafton |
| 1857-110 | " | mach 27 da @ $1.50 - $40.50. Mach Dept, Balto |
| 1857-38 | " | pass eng'man 1½ da @$3 - $4.50. Wash br rd, Wash city sta |
| 1855-93 | Livers, James | boil mkr 20½ da - $34.30. Mach Dept |
| 1855-87 | Living, Frank. | mach 11¼ da @ $1.55 - $17.45. Mach Dept |
| 1855-89 | George | app 32 da @ $.45 - $14.40. Mach Dept |
| 1855-91 | Llewellyn, T. J. | mach 22 3/4 da @$1.62 - $35.00. Mach Dept |
| 1855-82 | Lloyd, Henry | app 23¼ da @ $.75 - $17.45. Mach Dept |
| 1857-128 | Loar, George W. | carp 14 3/4 da @ $1.45 - $21.40. Mach Dept, Piedmont |
| 1855-63 | Locker, Pat. | lab 18 da @ $1 - $18.00. Rd Way Dept |
| 1857-9 | Lockey, J. M. | mess 25 da @ $35 per mo - $35.00. Mt Clare sta |
| 1855-35 | Joseph M. | mess 24 da @$30 per mo; 4 da @ $1.25 -$35.00. Trans Dept main stem |
| 1857-102 | Lockhart, Moses | carp 16½ da @ $1.60 - $26.40. NW Va RR, rwy depot |

## B & O RR EMPLOYEES

| | | |
|---|---|---|
| 1855-25 | Loffren, C. | bur driv 24 da @$40 per mo - $40.00. Trans Dept main stem |
| 1855-55 | Loftip, Daniel | lab 21 da @ $1 - $21.00. Rd Way Dept |
| 1857-63 | Loftis, David | lab 26 da @ $1 - $26.00. Rd Dept main stem 16th s-div |
| 1857-98 | Loftis, Michael | watch 30 da @ $1 - $30.00. NW Va RR, Rd Dept 3d s-div |
| 1857-94 | Loftus, John 1st | lab 7½ da @ $1 - $7.50. quarry & haul stone for Board Tree & Littleton Tun |
| 1857-88 | " 2d | lab 26 da @ $1.12 - $29.25. grad, Welling Tun |
| 1857-89 | " Patrick | lab 9½ da @ $1.12 - $10.70. grad, Welling Tun |
| 1857-90 | " | mason 1 da @$2 - $2.00. grad, Welling Tun |
| 1855-58 | " | stone mason 7⅞ da @ $1 - $2 -$14.50. grad, Welling Tun |
| 1855-88 | " Thomas | watch 30 da @ $1 - $30.00. Rd Dept main stem 11th s-div |
| 1857-102 | " William | carp 28 da @ $1.35 - $37.80. Mach Dept |
| 1857-36 | Logston, Frank | lab 20 da @ $1 - $20.00. NW Va RR, rwy depot |
| 1855-51 | Lohen, John | lab 22 da @ $1 - $22.00. J. R. Shrode's wd train 4th div |
| 1857-30 | Lohr, David | watch cuts 28 da @ $1 -$28.00. Rd Way Dept |
| 1857-33 | " | ton eng'man 1 da @$2.50 - $2.50. 3d div |
| 1855-87 | " Geo. | ton fire 26 3/4 da @ $1.75 - $46.80. 3d div |
| 1855-88 | " J. | help 18 da @$1.15 - $20.70. Mach Dept |
| 1857-123 | " Jeremiah | app 25 3/4 da @$.50 - $12.85. Mach Dept |
| 1855-90 | Loiso, Lewis | mach 19 3/4 da @$1.60 - $31.60. Mach Dept, Martinsburg |
| 1857-136 | Loleman, Joseph | help 28 da @ $1 - $28.00. Mach Dept |
| 1855-59 | Lollus, John | blksmith help 22 da @ $1 - $22.00. Mach Dept, Cumb |
| 1857-62 | " | lab 8 3/4 da @ $1 - $8.75. Rd Way Dept |
| 1855-60 | Londan, Daniel | lab 24 da @ $1 - $24.00. Rd Dept main stem 15th s-div |
| 1855-96 | Londy, David | supv @ $50 per mo - $50.00. Rd Way Dept |
| 1855-73 | Long, Adam | app 22 da @ $.50 - $11.00. Mach Dept |
| 1855-12 | " Daniel | tin 17 3/4 da @ $1.73 - $30.70. Rd Way Dept |
| 1857-24 | " " | conduc & brak 11 da @ $30 per mo - $13.75. Trans Dept main stem |
| 1857-104 | " E. | ton brak 28 da @$40 per mo - $44.80. 1st div |
| 1857-110 | " F. | carp 23 da @ $1.60 - $36.80. NW Va RR, build sand & wd houses |
| 1855-14 | " H. | mach 21 3/4 da @ $1.50 - $32.60. Mach Dept, Balto |
| 1855-33 | " James | brak 5 da @$40 per mo - $8.35. Trans Dept main stem |
| 1857-134 | Longbottom, Abner | coup 28 da @ $28 per mo - $28.00. Trans Dept main stem |
| 1855-24 | Longbridge, John | mach help 20 3/4 da @ $1 - $20.75. Mach Dept, Wheeling |
| 1857-123 | Longhamer, Lewis | pass & bur driv 25 da @$30 per mo - $31.25. Trans Dept main stem |
| 1855-86 | Longhammer, L. | mach 20⅜ da @ $1.60 -$32.40. Mach Dept, Martinsburg |
| | | mach 29½ da @ $1.60 - $47.20. Mach Dept |

| | | |
|---|---|---|
| 1857-26 | Lorhorn, Robert | ton brak 29 3/4 da @$40 per mo -$47.60. 3d & 4th div |
| 1857-129 | Lormie, William | lab 12¼ da @ $1 - $12.25. Mach Dept, Piedmont |
| 1857-27 | Loshmer, Henry E. | ton brak 26 da @ $40 per mo -$41.60. Board Tree Tun |
| 1857-62 | Louden, Daniel | horses & carts 50 da @ $1 - $50.00. Rd Dept main stem 15th s-div |
| 1857-62 | " | supv @ $45 per mo - $45.00. Rd Dept main stem 15th s-div |
| 1855-95 | Loughlin, Wm. | mould 24 da @$1.45 -$34.80. Mach Dept |
| 1855-26 | Louise, Lewis | clean eng 18 da @ $1 - $18.00. Trans Dept main stem |
| 1855-27 | Lourerey, Thomas | reg eng 28 da @ $50 per mo - $50.00. Trans Dept main stem |
| 1857-124 | Loury, Harrison | mach app 19¼ da @ $.50 - $9.60. Mach Dept, Martinsburg |
| 1855-80 | Love, George | carp 21 da @ $1.50 - $31.50. Mach Dept |
| 1855-71 | James | fore @ $65 per mo -$65.00. Rd Way Dept |
| 1857-69 | " | fore @ $65 per mo - $65.00. Mt Clare sta, Balto |
| 1855-74 | Lovejoy, Jno. | lab 24 da @ $1 - $24.00. Rd Way Dept |
| 1857-37 | Loveless, John | mail driv 30 da @$30 per mo -$30.00. Wash br rd, Wash city sta |
| 1857-36 | Lovenstein, D. | tele oper 30 da @ $30 per mo - $30.00. Fairmount |
| 1855-34 | Lowe, Alexander | lab 24 da @ $1 - $24.00. Trans Dept main stem |
| 1857-91 | " | lab 10½ da @$1 - $10.50. grad, Welling Tun |
| 1857-91 | " | lab 17¼ da @ $1 - $17.25. grad, Welling Tun |
| 1857-25 | David | ton brak 28½ da @ $40 per mo - $45.60. 2d div |
| 1855-69 | Edward | fore 22 da @ $1.50 - $33.00. Rd Way Dept |
| 1857-89 | " | fore 1½ da @$2.25 -$3.35. grad, Welling Tun |
| 1857-90 | " | fore 8 da @$2.25 -$18.00. grad, Welling Tun |
| 1857-90 | Edward L. | yoke oxen 8 da @ $1.75 - $14.00. grad, Welling Tun |
| 1855-6 | J. M. | agt 28 da @ $33.35 per mo - $33.35. Trans Dept main stem |
| 1857-11 | " " | agt 30 da @$50 per mo - $50.00. Wash junc |
| 1857-22 | " " | ton conduc 13 3/4 da @ $50 per mo -$27.50. 2d div |
| 1855-12 | John | conduc & brak 19¼ da @ $50 per mo - $42.60. Trans Dept main stem |
| 1857-85 | Joshua | carp 26 da @ $1.50 - $39.00. grad, Board Tree Tun |
| 1855-66 | Patrick | lab 18 3/4 da @ $1 - $18.75. Rd Way Dept |
| 1857-18 | R. H. | pass train conduc 30 da @$40 per mo - $40.00. Ellicott's Mills |
| 1855-67 | Thomas | lab 20 da @ $1 - $20.00. Rd Way Dept |
| 1857-32 | William | ton fire 22½ da @ $1.75 - $39.40. 1st div |
| 1855-82 | Lowery, Geo. N. | mach 29¼ da @$1.65 -$48.25. Mach Dept |
| 1855-57 | Lowlas, Jno. | lab 18 3/4 da @ $1 - $18.75. Rd Way Dept |
| 1855-77 | Lowman, B. E. | help 28½ da @ $1.15 - $32.75. Mach Dept |
| 1855-93 | C. | boil mkr 24¼ da - $39.10. Mach Dept |

| | | | |
|---|---|---|---|
| 1857-108 | Lowry, George | mach 18 da @$1.80 - $32.40. Mach Dept, Balto |
| 1857-112 | James J. | mach app 21½ da @ $.45 - $9.65. Mach Dept, Balto |
| 1857-126 | Thomas | clean eng @ $50 per mo - $50.00. Mach Dept, Martinsburg |
| 1857-8 | William | clean eng 27 3/4 da @ $1 - $27.75. Mach Dept, Martinsburg |
| 1857-113 | Lowthers, James | watch, Ridgely St. 31 da @ $1.25 - $37.50. Camden sta |
| 1857-109 | Loyd, William | lock 18 da @ $1.72 - $30.95. Mach Dept, Balto |
| 1857-134 | William H. | mach 17¼ da @ $1.72 - $29.65. Mach Dept, Balto |
| 1855-82 | Loydd, John | mach 19½ da @$1.65 - $32.15. Mach Dept, Wheeling |
| 1855-12 | Lucas, Edward | lab 25 da @ $1.15 - $28.75. Mach Dept |
| 1855-49 | " | mach help 17¼ da @ $1.15 - $19.85. Mach Dept, Balto |
| 1857-61 | John | conduc & brak 20 da @ $26.25. Trans Dept main stem |
| 1855-83 | Joseph | watch cuts 28 da @ $1 - $28.00. Rd Way Dept |
| 1857-112 | " | lab 27 da @ $1 - $27.00. Rd Dept main stem 14th s-div |
| | Osborn | lab 24 da @ $1 - $24.00. Mach Dept |
| 1857-118 | Luckey, Wm. | mach help 17 da @ $1 - $17.00. Mach Dept, Balto |
| 1855-25 | Ludlow, Thomas | blksmith help 18 da @ $1 - $18.00. Mach Dept, Balto |
| 1857-49 | Luegay, Perry | bur driv 24 da @ $1 - $30 per mo - $30.00. Trans Dept main stem |
| 1857-86 | Luitka, Henry | lab 18 da @ $1 - $18.00. Rd Dept main stem 3d s-div |
| 1857-121 | Luke, Francis | stone mason 25 da @ $2 - $50.00. grad, McGuire's Tun |
| 1857-72 | Lumyer, William | paint 17¼ da @ $1.65 - $28.45. Mach Dept, Balto |
| 1857-87 | Lunch, Hugh | lab 5½ da @ $1 - $5.50. Piedmont depot |
| 1855-17 | Lurch, Wm. C. | stone mason 23 da @$2 -$46.00. grad, McGuire's Tun |
| 1857-132 | Lusio, Lewis | ton eng'man 17 3/4 da @$2.50 - $44.35. Trans Dept main stem |
| 1855-17 | Lusney, Wm. | carp 18¾ da @ $1.50 - $27.35. Mach Dept, Grafton |
| 1857-10 | Lut, Isaac | ton eng'man 16 da @$2.50 - $40.00. Trans Dept main stem |
| 1857-55 | Luteman, Henry | bur brak 26 da @ $1.15 - $29.90. hp exp, Balto |
| 1855-92 | Luttrell, F. B. | lab 25½ da @ $1 - $25.50. Rd Dept main stem 9th s-div |
| 1855-53 | Lutz, Frederick | help 17 3/4 da @ $1 - $17.75. Mach Dept |
| 1857-56 | " | blksmith 21 da @$1.25 - $26.25. Rd Way Dept |
| 1857-58 | Lyans, Barney | blksmith 24½ da @$1.25 - $30.60. Rd Dept main stem 10th s-div |
| 1857-78 | Lyden, Patrick | lab 26 da @$1 - $26.00. Rd Dept main stem 12th s-div |
| 1857-46 | " | lab 22 da @ $1 - $22.00. lay 2d track |
| 1857-34 | Lyder, Joseph | lab 27 da @ $1 - $27.00. Rd Dept main stem 1st s-div |
| 1857-91 | Lydick, Levi | ton fire 23 3/4 da @$1.75 - $41.55. 4th div |
| 1857-96 | Lydon, Bartley | blksmith 21 3/4 da @$1.25 -$27.20. grad, Welling Tun |
| | | lab 4 da @$1 - $4.00. NW Va RR, Rd Dept 1st s-div |

B & O RR EMPLOYEES 219

| ID | Name | | Entry |
|---|---|---|---|
| 1857-100 | Lyman, | Peter | lab 25 da @ $1 - $25.00. NW Va RR, Rd Dept 5th s-div |
| 1855-93 | Lynch, | C. | mach 29¾ da @ $1.75 - $51.20. Mach Dept |
| 1855-72 | " | D. | help 3 da @ $1 - $3.00. Rd Way Dept |
| 1855-61 | " | Daniel | lab 16¼ da @ $1 - $16.25. Mt Clare sta, Balto |
| 1857-70 | " | Dennis | help 31 da @ $1.12 - $34.85. Rd Way Dept |
| 1855-44 | " | E. | lab 21 da @ $1 - $21.00. Rd Way Dept |
| 1857-80 | " | Edward | help 22 da @ $1 - $22.00. Mach Dept |
| 1855-92 | " | James | lab 17 3/4 da @ $1 - $17.75. lay 2d track |
| 1857-18 | " | " | pass train brak 2 da @ $33.35 per mo - $2.20. thr mail & exp |
| 1857-82 | " | John | bricklay 16 3/4 da @ $2 - $33.50. grad, Board Tree Tun |
| 1855-65 | " | M. | watch 19½ da @ $1 - $19.50. Rd Way Dept |
| 1857-81 | " | Michael | lab 27 da @$1 - $27.00. lay 2d track |
| 1857-59 | " | " | lab 24 da @$1 - $24.00. Rd Dept main stem 13th s-div |
| 1857-27 | " | Peter | ton brak 11½ da @ $40 per mo - $18.40. Board Tree Tun |
| 1857-26 | " | " | ton brak 4½ da @ $40 per mo - $7.20. 3d & 4th div |
| 1855-94 | " | Philip | app 35½ da @ $.45 - $15.85. Mach Dept |
| 1855-46 | " | " | lab 20½ da @ $1.12½ - $23.05. Rd Way Dept |
| 1857-81 | " | " | lab 23 da @$1 - $23.00. lay 2d track |
| 1857-28 | " | Thomas | ton eng'man 16 da @$3 - $48.00. 1st div |
| 1857-64 | Lynit, | Patrick | lab 25 da @ $1 - $25.00. Rd Dept main stem 17th s-div |
| 1857-92 | Lynott, | Antony | lab 23¾ da @ $1 - $23.25. grad, Littleton Tun |
| 1855-24 | Lyon, | John | pass & bur driv 24 da @ $1 - $24.00. Trans Dept main stem |
| 1855-80 | " | R. H. | carp 22⅔ da @ $1.60 - $35.60. Mach Dept |
| 1857-119 | " | " | carp 6½ da @ $1.60 - $10.40. Mach Dept, Balto |
| 1855-77 | " | Theo. | mach 23 da @$1.50 - $34.50. Mach Dept |
| 1857-79 | Lyons, | Andrew | lab 26 3/4 da @$1 - $26.75. lay 2d track |
| 1855-57 | " | Barney | lab 18½ da @ $1 - $18.50. Rd Way Dept |
| 1855-35 | " | E. C. | kpr wareh 28 da @ $30 per mo - $30.00. Trans Dept main stem |
| 1857-14 | " | E. C. | wareh kpr 30 da @ $35 per mo - $35.00. Piedmont sta |
| 1857-78 | " | James | fire 25 da @$1.50 - $37.50. lay 2d track |
| 1857-10 | " | John | cart driv 25 da @$30 per mo - $30.00. hp exp, Balto |
| 1857-96 | " | Michael | lab 24½ da @$1 - $24.50. NW Va RR, Rd Dept 1st s-div |
| 1857-74 | " | " | lab 23 da @ $1.12 - $25.85. repair bridges &c |
| 1857-30 | " | Robert | ton eng'man 22 da @ $2.50 - $55.00. 4th div |
| 1857-90 | " | Simon | lab 12 da @ $1.12 - $13.50. grad, Welling Tun |
| 1857-81 | " | Thomas | lab 20¼ da @ $1 - $20.25. lay 2d track |

| | | | |
|---|---|---|---|
| 1855-69 | Lypot, John | lab 22 da @ $1 - $22.00. Rd Way Dept |
| 1855-82 | Lyturn, Geo. | mach 22 da @ $1.50 - $33.00. Mach Dept |
| 1855-80 | McAbee, John H. | carp 28 da @ $1.75 - $49.00. Mach Dept |
| 1855-44 | McAbee, John | lab 13½ da @ $1 - $13.50. Rd Way Dept |
| 1855-74 | Wm. | fore 24 da @ $1.50 - $36.00. Rd Way Dept |
| 1855-17 | " | ton eng'man 12½ da @ $3 - $37.50. Trans Dept main stem |
| 1857-11 | McAdow, James | lab 23¼ da @ $1 - $23.25. Locust Pt |
| 1857-93 | McAleer, Charles | driv 7 da @ $1 - $7.00. quarry & haul stone for Board Tree & Littleton Tun |
| 1855-91 | Charles F. | mach 21½ da @ $1.62 - $28.30. Mach Dept |
| 1857-127 | " " | mach 13¼ da @ $1.60 - $21.20. Mach Dept, Piedmont |
| 1855-58 | George W. | supv @ $55 per mo - $55.00. Rd Way Dept |
| 1857-94 | " | 6 horses hire 110 da @ $1 - $110.00. quarry & haul stone for Board Tree & Littleton Tun |
| 1855-75 | Henry | lab 19 da @ $1 - $19.00. Rd Way Dept |
| 1857-75 | Patrick | fore 17 da @ $35 per mo - $22.90. ballast train for 2d track |
| 1857-92 | McAleer, Charles | driv 3 da @ $1 - $3.00. grad, Littleton Tun |
| 1857-93 | G. W. | supt @ $55 per mo - $55.00. quarry & haul stone for Board Tree & Littleton Tun |
| 1857-90 | McAllester, Allen | lab 9 da @ $1.12 - $10.10. grad, Welling Tun |
| 1855-78 | McAllister, Daniel | carp 24 da @ $1.65 - $39.60. Mach Dept |
| 1855-12 | H. C. | conduc & brak 24 da @ $50 per mo - $58.50. 2d div |
| 1857-22 | McAnally, Henry | ton conduc 29⅞ da @ $50 per mo - $50.00. Trans Dept main stem |
| 1857-98 | McAndey, John | lab 25½ da @ $1 - $25.50. NW Va RR, Rd Dept 3d s-div |
| 1857-96 | McAnnelly, Patrick | lab 25 da @ $1 - $25.00. NW Va RR, Rd Dept 1st s-div |
| 1857-57 | McAnter, Patrick | lab 25 da @ $1 - $25.00. Rd Dept main stem 11th s-div |
| 1855-25 | McArdle, T. C. | clean eng 30⅞ da @ $1.15 - $34.80. Trans Dept main stem |
| 1857-22 | McAtee, John | ton conduc 22 da @ $50 per mo - $44.00. 2d div |
| 1857-54 | Patrick | lab 19½ da @ $1 - $19.50. Rd Dept main stem 8th s-div |
| 1857-111 | Walter | mach help 29 3/4 da @ $1.15 - $34.20. Mach Dept, Balto |
| 1857-25 | McAttee, George | ton brak 19¾ da @ $40 per mo - $30.80. 2d div |
| 1857-20 | McAvey, John | pass fire 32½ da @ $40 per mo - $43.35. 3d div |
| 1857-90 | McAvoy, Barney | lab 10 da @ $1.12 - $11.25. grad, Welling Tun |
| 1857-136 | John | fill tend @ $30 per mo - $30.00. Mach Dept, Wheeling |
| 1857-89 | Michael | lab 7½ da @ $1.12 - $8.45. grad, Welling Tun |
| 1855-36 | McBee, F. | lab 25 da @ $25 per mo - $26.05. Trans Dept main stem |
| 1855-43 | Zachariah | lab 9 da @ $1 - $9.00. Rd Way Dept |
| 1857-76 | | eng'man 25 da @ $3 - $75.00. ballast train for 2d track |

## B & O RR EMPLOYEES

| ID | Name | Description |
|---|---|---|
| 1857-134 | McBride, Henry | mach 20 da @ $1.65 - $33.00. Mach Dept, Wheeling |
| 1855-36 | James | lab 25 da @ $25 per mo - $26.05. Trans Dept main stem |
| 1857-128 | " | blksmith help 19½ da @ $1.15 -$22.40. Mach Dept, Piedmont |
| 1857-39 | Richard | lab 25 da @ $30 per mo - $30.00. NW Va rd, Parkersburg sta |
| 1855-36 | McBue, Thomas | lab 25 da @ $25 per mo - $26.05. Trans Dept main stem |
| 1857-104 | McCabe, Edward | fore 25 3/4 da @ $1.75 - $45.05. NW Va RR Tun |
| 1857-77 | James | quarry 21½ da @ $1 - $21.50. ballast train for 2d track |
| 1855-50 | John | watch cuts 28 da @ $1 - $28.00. Rd Way Dept |
| 1857-81 | Patrick | eng'man 13 da @ $2.25 - $29.25. lay 2d track |
| 1855-55 | " | fore 20 da @ $1.25 - $25.00. Rd Way Dept |
| 1857-99 | William | watch 30 da @ $1 - $30.00. NW Va RR, Rd Dept 4th s-div |
| 1857-99 | McCaffrey, F. J. | fore 25 da @ $1.25 - $31.25. NW Va RR, Rd Dept 4th s-div |
| 1855-86 | " | mach 15 da @ $1.65 - $24.75. Mach Dept |
| 1857-16 | McCahan, Patrick | agt 30 da @ $75 per mo - $75.00. Benwood sta |
| 1855-89 | " | help 24 da @ $1 - $24.00. Mach Dept |
| 1857-137 | McCall, James | lab 21¼ da @ $1 - $21.25. Mach Dept, Cumb |
| 1857-84 | McCalls, George | lab 17 da @ $1.12 - $19.10. grad, Board Tree Tun |
| 1857-125 | McCallys, David | clean eng 27½ da @ $1.15 - $31.60. Mach Dept, Martinsburg |
| 1857-136 | McCan, John | stat'ry eng'man @ $34.50 per mo - $34.50. Mach Dept, Cumb |
| 1857-36 | Owen | lab 21½ da @ $1 - $21.50. J. R. Shrode's wd train 4th div |
| 1857-76 | McCandles, H. | dril 23 da @ $1.10 - $25.30. ballast train for 2d track |
| 1855-43 | McCann, James | fore 24 da @ $1.25 - $30.00. Rd Way Dept |
| 1855-35 | Patrick | watch 28 da @ $1.25 - $35.00. Trans Dept main stem |
| 1855-34 | " | car greas 28 da @ $32 per mo - $32.00. Trans Dept main stem |
| 1857-129 | Thomas | greas cars @ $32 per mo - $32.00. Mach Dept, Piedmont |
| 1857-77 | McCarman, Patrick | quarry 8 da @ $1 - $8.00. ballast train for 2d track |
| 1855-31 | T. | prepar fuel 28 da @ $1 - $28.00. Trans Dept main stem |
| 1855-31 | " | prepar fuel 28 da @ $1 - $28.00. Trans Dept main stem |
| 1857-98 | McCarrole, John | lab 24 3/4 da @ $1 - $24.75. NW Va RR, Rd Dept 3d s-div |
| 1855-63 | McCarthy, Michl. | lab 23½ da @ $1 - $23.50. Rd Way Dept |
| 1857-75 | McCarty, Daniel | lab 13¼ da @ $1.06 - $14.10. ballast train for 2d track |
| 1855-37 | John | lab 24½ da @ $1 - $24.50. Rd Way Dept |
| 1857-46 | Michael | lab 25 da @ $1 - $25.00. Rd Dept main stem 1st s-div |
| 1857-82 | " | lab 17 da @ $1.12 - $19.10. grad, Board Tree Tun |
| 1857-93 | " | lab 21½ da @ $1 - $21.50. quarry & haul stone for Board Tree & Littleton Tun |
| 1857-46 | " | lab 25 da @ $1 - $25.00. Rd Dept main stem 1st s-div |

| | | | |
|---|---|---|---|
| 1857-47 | McCarty, Michael | lab 24 da @ $1 - $24.00. Rd Dept main stem 1st s-div |
| 1857-81 | Patrick | lab 18 3/4 da @ $1 - $18.75. lay 2d track |
| 1855-53 | William | lab 20½ da @ $1 - $20.50. Rd Way Dept |
| 1855-34 | McCaughn, H. | oil distrib 28 da @ $35 per mo - $35.00. Trans Dept main stem |
| 1857-92 | McCauley, John | lab 26¼ da @ $1 - $26.25. grad, Littleton Tun |
| 1855-48 | Patrick | lab 22 da @ $1 - $22.00. Rd Way Dept |
| 1857-10 | McClaney, James | blksmith 25 da @ $34.50 per mo - $34.50. hp exp, Balto |
| 1855-13 | McClay, John | conduc & brak 7½ da @ $40 per mo - $14.00. Trans Dept main stem |
| 1857-135 | McCleish, Jos. | blksmith 17¼ da @ $1.50 - $25.85. Mach Dept, Wheeling |
| 1855-54 | McClelland, Wm. | carp 23½ da @ $1.50 - $35.25. Rd Way Dept |
| 1857-134 | McClelland, J. | mach app 15 da @ $.45 - $6.75. Mach Dept, Wheeling |
| 1855-8 | " | brak 28 da @ $33.35 per mo - $33.35. Trans Dept main stem |
| 1857-8 | | watch 30 da @ $35 per mo - $35.00. Camden sta |
| 1857-128 | McClenehan, James | boil mkr 18½ da @$1.70 - $31.45. Mach Dept, Piedmont |
| 1855-24 | McClerrion, James | pass & bur driv 24 da @ $32.20 per mo - $32.20. Trans Dept main stem |
| 1855-36 | McClouskey, James | lab 25 da @ $25 per mo - $26.05. Trans Dept main stem |
| 1857-14 | McClung, A. | watch 30 da @$35 per mo - $35.00. Piedmont sta |
| 1855-92 | Alex. | help 34 da @$1 - $34.00. Mach Dept |
| 1855-28 | McClure, Wm. | reg eng 21½ da @ $1.50 - $32.25. Trans Dept main stem |
| 1857-117 | McCluvely, John | blksmith help 18 da @$1 - $18.00. Mach Dept, Balto |
| 1857-121 | McColgan, M. | carp help 24¼ da @ $1.15 - $27.90. Mach Dept, Balto |
| 1857-139 | McComas, Neal | put away eng &c 29 da @ $1.40 - $40.60. NW Va RR, Mach Dept, Parkersburg |
| 1855-54 | W. K. | carp @ $40 per mo - $40.00. Rd Way Dept |
| 1855-27 | McCombs, Neal | get out eng 15 da @ $1.40 - $21.00. Trans Dept main stem |
| 1857-64 | McCormick, John | lab 26 da @ $1 - $26.00. Rd Dept main stem 17th s-div |
| 1857-99 | McConder, Martin | lab 27 da @ $1 - $27.00. NW Va RR, Rd Dept 4th s-div |
| 1857-39 | McConnell, James | barge capt 30 da @ $50 per mo - $50.00. NW Va rd, Parkersburg sta |
| 1855-79 | McConnough, Owen | lab 13½ da @ $1 - $13.50. lay 2d track |
| 1855-56 | McConwek, Mart. | lab 10 da @ $1 - $10.00. Rd Way Dept |
| 1855-37 | McCoort, John | nail 2½ da @ $1 - $2.50. Rd Way Dept |
| 1855-47 | McCormac, M. | lab 17 da @ $1 - $17.00. Rd Way Dept |
| 1857-48 | McCormach, James | lab 22 da @ $1 - $22.00. Rd Dept main stem 2d s-div |
| 1857-103 | McCormack, Martin | lab 23 da @ $1.12 - $25.90. NW Va RR Tun |
| 1855-61 | T. | lab 9 da @ $1 - $9.00. Rd Way Dept |
| 1857-66 | Thomas | lab 25½ da @ $1 - $25.50. Rd Dept main stem 18th s-div |
| 1857-84 | McCormick, Cornelius | lab 21½ da @ $1.12 - $24.20. grad, Board Tree Tun |

| | | |
|---|---|---|
| 1857-92 | McCormick, Dennis | lab 22 3/4 da @ $1 - $22.75. grad, Littleton Tun |
| 1857-51 | Jeremiah | lab 23 da @ $1 -$23.00. Rd Dept main stem 5th s-div |
| 1857-76 | John | dril 21 3/4 da @ $1.10 - $23.95. ballast train for 2d track |
| 1857-92 | " | lab 23 1/4 da @ $1.12 - $26.15. grad, Littleton Tun |
| 1857-58 | Martin | watch 30 da @ $1 - $30.00. Rd Dept main stem 11th s-div |
| 1857-76 | Phil. | dril 18 1/2 da @ $1.10 - $20.35. ballast train for 2d track |
| 1855-52 | William | carp 14 1/2 da @ $1.50 - $21.75. Rd Way Dept |
| 1855-75 | McCorram, O. | lab 21 da @ $1 - $21.00. Rd Way Dept |
| 1857-100 | McCoy, Milo | fore 12 da @$1.25 -$15.00. NW Va RR, Rd Dept 5th s-div |
| 1855-59 | Roger | lab 15 1/2 da @ $1 - $15.50. Rd Way Dept |
| 1857-62 | M'Coy, Rodger | lab 25 da @ $1 - $25.00. Rd Dept main stem 15th s-div |
| 1855-32 | McCracken, William | lab 24 da @ $30 per mo - $30.00. Trans Dept main stem |
| 1857-63 | McCrae, Alpheus | pump water @ $35 per mo - $35.00. Rd Dept main stem 16th s-div |
| 1855-50 | S. | watch cuts 28 da @ $1 - $28.00. Rd Way Dept |
| 1855-62 | McCrone, A. | lab 24 da @ $1 - $24.00. Rd Way Dept |
| 1855-36 | McCullough, A. | lab 24 1/4 da @$25 per mo - $25.25. Trans Dept main stem |
| 1857-17 | " | lab 25 1/2 da @ $25 per mo - $25.50. Wheeling sta |
| 1857-8 | McCullum, J. | lab 24 da @$30 per mo -$28.80. Camden sta |
| 1855-89 | McCully, David | eng'man @ $34.50 per mo - $34.50. Mach Dept |
| 1855-57 | McCurdy, Alexander | lab 20 1/4 da @$1.25 -$25.30. Rd Way Dept |
| 1857-66 | " | fore 23 1/2 da @ $1.25 - $29.35. Rd Dept main stem 18th s-div |
| 1855-19 | James | ton eng'man 14 1/2 da @$3 -$43.50. Trans Dept main stem |
| 1857-29 | " | ton eng'man 17 1/2 da @ $3 - $52.50. 2d div |
| 1857-38 | " | ton eng'man 1 1/4 da @ $2.50 - $3.10. Wash br rd, Wash city sta |
| 1857-70 | John H. | app 25 1/2 da @ $.50 - $12.75. Mt Clare sta, Balto |
| 1857-112 | McCurley, Ed. | mach app 22 3/4 da @$.45 - $10.25. Mach Dept, Balto |
| 1857-79 | McCurrins, Bartly | lab 26 3/4 da @$1 - $26.75. lay 2d track |
| 1855-79 | McDade, Samuel | driv 24 da @$1.15 - $27.60. Mach Dept |
| 1857-104 | McDaniel, M. | carp 20 1/2 da @$1.60 - $32.80. NW Va RR, Build sand & wd houses |
| 1857-65 | McDeffet, Peter | lab 8 1/2 da @ $1 - $8.50. Rd Dept main stem 17th s-div |
| 1857-65 | McDeffett, James | lab 12 da @$1 - $12.00. Rd Dept main stem 17th s-div |
| 1857-51 | McDermit, Owen | watch 30 da @ $1 - $30.00. Rd Dept main stem 5th s-div |
| 1857-81 | McDermitt, Patrick | lab 24 da @ $1.12 - $27.00. grad, Board Tree Tun |
| 1857-8 | McDermot, Charles | lab 25 da @$30 per mo - $30.00. Camden sta |
| 1857-56 | James | lab 21 da @ $1 - $21.00. Rd Dept main stem 10th s-div |
| 1857-39 | R. | brak 29 1/4 da @$1.25 - $36.55. NW Va rd, Parkersburg sta |

224                B & O RR EMPLOYEES

| | | | |
|---|---|---|---|
| 1857-132 | McDermot, Thomas | lab @ $30 per mo - $30.00. Mach Dept, Grafton |
| 1855-47 | McDermott, Edward | lab 20 da @ $1 - $20.00. Rd Way Dept |
| 1855-67 | " | mason 24 da @ $2 - $8.00. Rd Way Dept |
| 1857-82 | " | fore 30¾ da @ $2.25 - $68.05. grad, Board Tree Tun |
| 1857-63 | James | lab 23 da @ $1 - $23.00. Rd Dept main stem 16th s-div |
| 1855-47 | Peter | lab 22½ da @ $1 - $22.50. Rd Way Dept |
| 1857-63 | " | lab 24 da @ $1 - $24.00. Rd Dept main stem 16th s-div |
| 1855-51 | Thomas | watch cuts 28 da @ $1 - $28.00. Rd Way Dept |
| 1857-68 | " | watch 30 da @ $1 - $30.00. Rd Dept main stem 19th s-div |
| 1855-29 | McDerrald, Larra | haul & saw firewd 28 da @ $1 - $28.00. Trans Dept main stem |
| 1857-23 | McDiffet, James | ton conduc 2 da @ $50 per mo - $4.00. Board Tree Tun |
| 1857-23 | McDiffitt, James | ton conduc 22¾ da @ $60 per mo - $44.50. 3d & 4th div |
| 1855-55 | McDonagh, Michael | fore 20 3/4 da @ $1.12½ - $23.35. Rd Way Dept |
| 1855-19 | McDonald, A. | ton eng'man 17 3/4 da @ $2.50 - $44.35. Trans Dept main stem |
| 1857-19 | Alexander | pass eng'man 34 da @ $3 - $102.00. 2d div |
| 1855-40 | B. | fore 25 da @ $1.37½ - $34.35. Rd Way Dept |
| 1857-73 | Barney | lab 18 da @ $1.12 - $20.25. repair bridges &c |
| 1855-28 | E. | reg eng 23 da @ $1.15 - $26.45. Trans Dept main stem |
| 1857-125 | Enos | put away eng &c 27 da @ $1.50 - $40.50. Mach Dept, Martinsburg |
| 1855-40 | F. | lab 25 da @ $1 - $25.00. Rd Way Dept |
| 1857-124 | Hugh | boil mkr 27 3/4 da @ $1.30 - $36.05. Mach Dept, Martinsburg |
| 1855-48 | James | lab 22 3/4 da @ $1 - $22.75. Rd Way Dept |
| 1857-129 | " | clean eng 30 da @ $1 - $30.00. Mach Dept, Piedmont |
| 1855-86 | M. | mach 27 da @ $1.50 - $40.50. Mach Dept |
| 1855-23 | Michael | fire 15 3/4 da @ $1.75 - $27.55. Trans Dept main stem |
| 1857-69 | " | hod carr 23 3/4 da @ $1.37 - $32.65. Mt Clare sta, Balto |
| 1857-56 | " | lab 21 da @ $1 - $21.00. Rd Dept main stem 10th s-div |
| 1857-66 | " | lab 24¼ da @ $1 - $24.25. Rd Dept main stem 18th s-div |
| 1857-56 | Owen | lab 24 da @ $1 - $24.00. Rd Dept main stem 10th s-div |
| 1855-43 | P. | lab 8½ da @ $1 - $8.50. Rd Way Dept |
| 1855-42 | Patrick | lab 21 da @ $1 - $21.00. Rd Way Dept |
| 1857-63 | " | lab 23 da @ $1 - $23.00. Rd Dept main stem 16th s-div |
| 1855-91 | R. A. | mach 23 3/4 da @ $1.62- $39.35. Mach Dept |
| 1857-85 | Thomas | lab 12 3/4 da @ $51 - $12.75. grad, Board Tree Tun |
| 1857-104 | McDonnell, Daniel | carp 13¼ da @ $1.50 - $19.85. NW Va RR Tun |

B & O RR EMPLOYEES    225

| ID | Name | | Entry |
|---|---|---|---|
| 1857-50 | McDonnell, Frank | | lab 7 da @ $1 - $7.00. Rd Dept main stem 4th s-div |
| 1855-28 | | J. | prepar fuel 8½ da @ $1 - $8.50. Trans Dept main stem |
| 1855-62 | | James | lab 8¼ da @ $1 - $8.25. Rd Way Dept |
| 1857-97 | | " | fore 25 da @ $1.25 - $31.25. NW Va RR, Rd Dept 2d s-div |
| 1857-80 | | John | lab 8½ da @ $1 - $8.50. lay 2d track |
| 1857-101 | | Michael | engr 16 da @ $3 - $48.00. NW Va RR ballast train |
| 1857-97 | | " | lab 25 da @ $1 - $25.00. NW Va RR, Rd Dept 2d s-div |
| 1855-60 | | P. | fore 24 da @ $1.25 - $30.00. Rd Way Dept |
| 1855-63 | | " | lab 22¼ da @ $1 - $22.25. Rd Way Dept |
| 1857-91 | | Thomas | lab 23¼ da @ $1 - $23.25. grad, Welling Tun |
| 1855-68 | McDonnogh, D. | | lab 23 da @ $1 - $23.00. Rd Way Dept |
| 1857-96 | McDonnough, Patrick | | lab 24½ da @ $1 - $24.50. NW Va RR, Rd Dept 1st s-div |
| 1857-67 | McDonough, Darby | | fore 25½ da @ $1.25 - $31.85. Rd Dept main stem 19th s-div |
| 1855-67 | | John | lab 21 da @ $1 - $21.00. Rd Way Dept |
| 1857-91 | | " | lab 20¼ da @ $1 - $20.25. grad, Welling Tun |
| 1857-99 | | Martin | lab 28 da @ $1 - $28.00. N W Va RR, Rd Dept 4th s-div |
| 1857-63 | | Michael | fore 25 da @ $1.25 - $31.25. Rd Dept main stem 16th s-div |
| 1857-79 | | Patrick | lab 15½ da @ $1 - $15.50. lay 2d track |
| 1857-104 | | " | lab 16½ da @ $1.12 - $18.55. NW Va RR Tun |
| 1857-67 | | " | lab 22½ da @ $1 - $22.50. Rd Dept main stem 19th s-div |
| 1857-88 | | William | lab 22½ da @ $1.12 - $25.30. grad, Welling Tun |
| 1855-12 | McDougall, Wm. | | conduc & brak 19½ da @ $50 per mo - $43.60. Trans Dept main stem |
| 1857-16 | McDowell, William | | lab 25 da @ $25 per mo - $25.00. Benwood sta |
| 1857-81 | McDugal, Alexander | | lab 20 3/4 da @ $1 - $20.75. lay 2d track |
| 1857-118 | McElemer, Duncan | | blksmith help 17¼ da @ $1 - $17.25. Mach Dept, Balto |
| 1857-85 | McElhaney, John | | brickley 7½ da @ $2.25 - $16.85. grad, Board Tree Tun |
| 1857-87 | McElhary, John | | brickley 18¼ da @ $2.25 - $41.05. grad, Welling Tun |
| 1857-131 | McElroy, Bartlet | | boil mkr 7 3/4 da @ $1.25 - $9.70. Mach Dept, Grafton |
| 1855-87 | | Charles | help 22¼ da @ $1 - $22.25. Mach Dept |
| 1857-70 | | Joseph | help 18 da @ $1.15 - $20.70. Mt Clare sta, Balto |
| 1855-64 | | Thomas | watch 22½ da @ $1 - $22.50. Rd Way Dept |
| 1857-93 | | " | smith help 24 da @ $1 - $24.00. quarry & haul stone for Board Tree & Littleton Tun |
| 1855-17 | McElvany, Jno. | | ton eng'man 14½ da @ $3 - $43.50. Trans Dept main stem |
| 1857-111 | McElwee, Robert | | mach help 18 3/4 da @ $1 - $18.25. Mach Dept, Balto |
| 1857-46 | McEnany, Owen | | fore 25½ da @ $1.25 - $31.85. Rd Dept main stem 1st s-div |
| 1857-78 | McEovy, Patrick | | lab 26½ da @ $1 - $26.50. lay 2d track |

# B & O RR EMPLOYEES

| | | |
|---|---|---|
| 1857-93 | McEvee, Patrick | smith help 23 da @ $23.00 - quarry & haul stone for Board Tree & Littleton Tun |
| 1857-80 | McEvoy, James | lab 20 3/4 da @ $1 - $20.75. lay 2d track |
| 1857-83 | McFadden, D. | lab 7½ da @ $1.12 - $8.45. grad, Board Tree Tun |
| 1855-78 | McFall, John | help 23½ da @ $1 - $23.50. Mach Dept |
| 1855-38 | McFarland, A. B. | lab 20 da @ $1 - $20.00. Rd Way Dept |
| 1855-15 | McFarlin, William | pass eng'man 23 da @ $3 - $69.00. Trans Dept main stem |
| 1857-84 | McFarren, D. | lab 12½ da @ $1.12 - $14.05. grad, Board Tree Tun |
| 1855-45 | | lab 13½ da @ $1 - $13.50. Rd Way Dept |
| 1855-45 | John | lab 20 da @ $1 - $20.00. Rd Way Dept |
| 1857-87 | McFrederick, James | lab 24½ da @ $.80 - $19.60. grad, McGuire's Tun |
| 1857-136 | McGahan, Patrick | clean pass cars @ $30 per mo - $30.00. Mach Dept, Wheeling |
| 1857-64 | McGarity, Peter | lab 23 3/4 da @ $1 - $23.75. Rd Dept main stem 17th s-div |
| 1857-15 | McGary, Patrick | swit tend 14 da @ $25 per mo - $11.65. Grafton sta |
| 1857-103 | McGaw, James | carp 21 3/4 da @ $1.25 - $27.20. NW Va RR Tun |
| 1857-90 | McGawah, Mark | lab 11½ da @ $1.12 - $12.95. grad, Welling Tun |
| 1857-26 | McGee, Charles | ton brak 36 da @ $40 per mo - $57.60. 3d & 4th div |
| 1857-67 | Edw. | lab 20½ da @ $1 - $20.50. Rd Dept main stem 19th s-div |
| 1855-29 | James | prepar fuel 28 da @ $1 - $28.00. Trans Dept main stem |
| 1857-130 | " | clean eng 30 da @ $1.10 - $26.40. Mach Dept, Newburg |
| 1855-96 | John | lab 24 da @ $1 - $24.00. Rd Way Dept |
| 1855-37 | McGeorge, James | lab 29½ da @ $1.12 - $33.20. grad, Board Tree Tun |
| 1857-82 | McGierney, James | ton brak 25 da @ $40 per mo - $40.00. 3d & 4th div |
| 1857-26 | McGill, George | fore 26 da @ $1.25 - $32.50. NW Va RR, Rd Dept 5th s-div |
| 1857-100 | John | carp 24 da @ $1.75 - $42.00. repair bridges |
| 1857-94 | Wm. | watch cuts 28 da @ $1 - $28.00. Rd Way Dept |
| 1855-49 | McGinnis, D. | watch 30 da @ $1 - $30.00. Rd Dept main stem 7th s-div |
| 1857-53 | Daniel | lab 28 da @ $1 - $28.00. NW Va RR, Rd Dept 4th s-div |
| 1857-99 | Patrick | lab 10 da @ $1.12 - $11.25. grad, Welling Tun |
| 1857-90 | McGinniss, Michael | tend to masons 24 da @ $1 - $24.00. Rd Way Dept |
| 1855-67 | McGivney, James | fore 25½ da @ $1 - $25.50. Rd Way Dept |
| 1855-37 | McGlaucklin, H. | blksmith 18½ da @ $1.30 - $24.05. Mach Dept, Piedmont |
| 1857-128 | McGlennan, Michael | clean eng 28 da @ $1 - $28.00. Trans Dept main stem |
| 1855-27 | McGliner, John | lab 24½ da @ $1.10 - $26.95. Mach Dept |
| 1855-96 | McGlover, John | iron mould help 19 da @ $1.10 - $20.90. Mach Dept, Balto |
| 1857-114 | McGovern, John | lab 25 da @ $25 per mo - $25.00. Benwood sta |
| 1857-16 | McGowan, John | |

| | | | |
|---|---|---|---|
| 1857-30 | McGowan, John | ton eng'man 25 da @ $3 - $75.00. 3d div |
| 1857-76 | " Thomas | dril 23 da @ $1.10 - $25.30. ballast train for 2d track |
| 1857-56 | McGown, James | lab 16 da @ $1 - $16.00. Rd Dept main stem 10th s-div |
| 1857-104 | McGrab, Patrick | lab 25 da @ $1.12 - $28.10. NW Va RR Tun |
| 1857-104 | " " | lab 24½ da @ $.62 - $15.30. NW Va RR Tun |
| 1857-86 | McGrade, Austin | lab 23 da @ $1 - $23.00. grad, McGuire's Tun |
| 1857-56 | " Francis | watch 30 da @ $1 - $30.00. Rd Dept main stem 10th s-div |
| 1857-133 | McGrann, John | lab 30 da @ $1 - $30.00. Mach Dept, Fetterman |
| 1857-104 | McGrate, Thomas | lab 19½ da @ $1.12 - $21.95. NW Va RR Tun |
| 1857-98 | McGraw, James | lab 4 da @ $1 - $4.00. NW Va RR, Rd Dept 3d s-div |
| 1855-56 | " John | lab 18 da @ $1 - $18.00. Rd Way Dept |
| 1857-76 | " " | quarry 24 da @ $1 - $24.00. ballast train for 2d track |
| 1857-39 | " M. | yd fire 19¾ da @ $1.27 - $24.45. NW Va rd, Parkersburg sta |
| 1855-63 | " Michael | fire 24 da @ $1.33½ - $32.00. Rd Way Dept |
| 1857-135 | " " | blksmith help 20⅞ da @ $1 - $20.25. Mach Dept, Wheeling |
| 1855-69 | " Patrick | lab 21 3/4 da @ $1 - $21.25. Rd Way Dept |
| 1857-76 | " " | quarry 22½ da @ $1 - $22.50. ballast train for 2d track |
| 1857-93 | " Thomas | lab 24 da @ $1 - $24.00. quarry & haul stone for Board Tree & Littleton Tun |
| 1855-46 | McGrovern, John | lab 21½ da @ $1 - $21.50. Rd Way Dept |
| 1857-62 | McGue, Michael | lab 23 da @ $1 - $23.00. Rd Dept main stem 15th s-div |
| 1857-75 | McGuick, John | lab 23 da @ $1 - $23.00. ballast train for 2d track |
| 1857-93 | McGuire, James Jr | smith help 23½ da @ $1 - $23.50. quarry & haul stone for Board Tree & Littleton Tun |
| 1857-93 | " James Sr | smith help 23½ da @ $1 - $23.50. quarry & haul stone for Board Tree & Littleton Tun |
| 1855-30 | " John | fill tend 28 da @ $1 -$28.00. Trans Dept main stem |
| 1855-46 | " " | lab 23 da @ $1.12½ - $25.85. Rd Way Dept |
| 1855-68 | " " | lab 19 da @ $1 - $19.00. Rd Way Dept |
| 1857-78 | " " | lab 30 da @ $1 - $30.00. lay 2d track |
| 1857-79 | " Owen | help 24 da @ $1 - $24.00. lay 2d track |
| 1855-60 | " Thomas | lab 24 da @ $1 - $24.00. Rd Way Dept |
| 1857-101 | " " | lab 24 da @ $1 - $24.00. NW Va RR ballast train |
| 1855-68 | " William | lab 22 3/4 da @ $1 - $22.75. Rd Way Dept |
| 1857-97 | " " | lab 26 da @ $1 - $26.00. NW Va RR, Rd Dept 2d s-div |
| 1855-81 | Machin, Jno. | paint 23 3/4 da @ $1.50 - $35.60. Mach Dept |
| 1855-80 | " Thomas | carp 3 da @ $1.60 - $4.80. Mach Dept |
| 1857-119 | " " | carp 18 da @ $1.60 - $28.80. Mach Dept, Balto |
| 1857-122 | McIntire, Daniel | lab 18 3/4 da @ $1 - $18.75. Mach Dept, Balto |

228          B & O RR EMPLOYEES

| | | | |
|---|---|---|---|
| 1857-73 | McIntire, Patrick | | stonecut 22 3/4 da @ $1.37 - $31.25. repair bridges &c |
| 1857-122 | McIntyre, Thomas | | lab 19¾ da @ $1.15 - $22.15. Mach Dept, Balto |
| 1857-124 | " | John F. | boil mkr help 21½ da @ $1 - $21.50. Mach Dept, Martinsburg |
| 1855-78 | " | T. | help 24 da @ $1 - $24.00. Mach Dept |
| 1855-95 | Mack, John | | lab 22½ da @ $1 - $22.50. Mach Dept |
| 1857-135 | " | | lab 30 da @ $1 - $30.00. Mach Dept, Wheeling |
| 1855-87 | McKaig, Andrew | | blksmith 23½ da @ $1.60 - $37.60. Mach Dept |
| 1857-135 | " | | fore blksmith 20 da @ $2 - $40.00. Mach Dept, Wheeling |
| 1855-32 | " | D. | lab 24 da @ $30 per mo - $30.00. Trans Dept main stem |
| 1855-96 | " | Robert | lab 23 da @ $1.10 - $25.30. Mach Dept |
| 1855-86 | " | " | mach 27½ da @ $1.25 - $34.40. Mach Dept |
| 1857-114 | " | " | iron mould help 18 da @ $1.10 - $19.80. Mach Dept, Balto |
| 1857-86 | McKandrew, Thomas | | lab 19 da @ $1 - $19.00. grad, McGuire's Tun |
| 1857-136 | McKarman, Thomas | | fill tend @ $30 per mo - $30.00. Mach Dept, Wheeling |
| 1857-17 | McKay, David | | lab 24 da @ $1 - $24.00. frt transfer force at Bellaire, opp Benwood |
| 1857-77 | McKean, Hugh | | lab 25 da @ $1.25 - $31.25. lay 2d track |
| 1857-11 | " | J. D. | agt 30 da @ $4-5 per da; $83.33 per mo - $66.70. Locust Pt |
| 1857-11 | " | John | swit tend 30 da @$1.25 - $37.50. Wash Junc |
| 1855-37 | McKee, Arthur | | fore 27 da @ $1.25 - $33.75. Rd Way Dept |
| 1857-46 | " | " | fore 27 da @ $1.25 - $33.75. Rd Dept main stem 1st s-div |
| 1855-32 | " | B. | mail contrac 14 da @ $115.00 per mo - $57.50. Trans Dept main stem |
| 1855-5 | " | Bernard | mail contrac 14 da @ $115.00 per mo - $57.50. Trans Dept, Wash br (furnishes his own horses and wagons) |
| 1855-58 | " | David | lab 22 da @ $1 - $22.00. Rd Way Dept |
| 1855-44 | " | James | lab 22 da @ $1 - $22.00. Rd Way Dept |
| 1855-24 | " | " | pass & bur driv 24 da @ $1 - $24.00. Trans Dept main stem |
| 1857-9 | " | " | pass brak 25 da @ $30 per mo - $30.00. hp exp, Balto |
| 1855-44 | " | John | lab 23 da @ $1 - $23.00. Rd Way Dept |
| 1855-8 | " | Patrick | bag mast 28 da @ $45 per mo - $45.00. Trans Dept main stem |
| 1857-19 | " | " | bag mast 30 da @ $45 per mo - $45.00. thr mail & exp |
| 1857-131 | " | Terrence | mach 16¼ da @ $1.50 - $24.35. Mach Dept, Grafton |
| 1857-75 | McKeever, James | | lab 13½ da @ $.97 - $13.15. ballast train for 2d track |
| 1855-73 | McKelby, John W. | | driv 24 da @ $.54 - $12.95. Rd Way Dept |
| 1857-70 | McKelvey, John | | app 24 da @ $.75 - $18.00. Mt Clare sta, Balto |
| 1857-120 | McKelvy, James | | carp 19 3/4 da @ $1.65 - $32.60. Mach Dept, Balto |
| 1855-88 | Macken, James | | app 27¼ da @ $.60 - $16.35. Mach Dept |

| ID | Name | Description |
|---|---|---|
| 1857-100 | Macken, Michael | lab 23 da @ $1 - $23.00. NW Va RR, Rd Dept 5th s-div |
| 1857-77 | McKenen, James | quarry 7 da @ $1 - $7.00. ballast train for 2d track |
| 1857-54 | McKeney, John | lab 17 da @ $1 - $17.00. Rd Dept main stem 8th s-div |
| 1855-64 | McKenna, Jas. | lab 20 da @ $1 - $20.00. Rd Way Dept |
| 1857-114 | McKenzie, David | iron mould help 17 3/4 da @ $1 - $17.75. Mach Dept, Balto |
| 1855-25 | McKeon, Illehad | clean eng 28 3/4 da @ $1.15 - $33.05. Trans Dept main stem |
| 1857-67 | | lab 15 3/4 da @ $1 - $15.75. Rd Dept main stem 18th s-div |
| 1857-67 | James | lab 15 3/4 da @ $1 - $15.75. Rd Dept main stem 18th s-div |
| 1857-75 | McKernan, James | lab 17 da @ $.97 - $16.55. ballast train for 2d track |
| 1857-86 | McKew, Andrew | lab 26 da @ $1.12 - $29.25. grad, McGuire's Tun |
| 1857-79 | Arthur | lab 21¼ da @ $1 - $24.25. lay 2d track |
| 1855-66 | John | lab 20 da @ $1 - $20.00. Rd Way Dept |
| 1857-86 | " | lab 26¼ da @ $1.12 - $29.50. grad, McGuire's Tun |
| 1855-67 | Mart. | tend to masons 23¼ da @ $1 - $23.25. Rd Way Dept |
| 1857-36 | Mackey, Elias | lab 13½ da @ $1 - $13.50. J. R. Shrode's wd train 4th div |
| 1855-37 | McKidrich, Thomas | lab 23½ da @ $1 - $23.50. Rd Way Dept |
| 1855-60 | Mackin, James | fore 23 da @ $1.25 - $28.75. Rd Way Dept |
| 1857-64 | " | fore 26 da @ $1.25 - $32.50. Rd Dept main stem 17th s-div |
| 1857-102 | William | carp 22 da @ $1.60 - $35.20. NW Va RR, rwy depot |
| 1857-30 | McKinley, Thomas | ton eng'man 1 3/4 da @ $2.50 - $4.35. 3d div |
| 1855-51 | Mackley, George | lab 19 da @ $1 - $19.00. Rd Way Dept |
| 1857-56 | " | lab 25 da @ $1 - $25.00. Rd Dept main stem 10th s-div |
| 1855-5 | McKnew, Charles | brak 19 da - $24.15. Trans Dept, Wash br |
| 1855-73 | Thos. | watch 14 da @ $1.15 - $16.10. Rd Way Dept |
| 1857-71 | " | watch 15 da @ $1.15 - $17.25. Mt Clare, repair tracks in yd |
| 1857-75 | McKniff, Thomas | lab 4 da @ $.97 - $3.90. ballast train for 2d track |
| 1855-13 | McKnight, E. | conduc & brak 2 da @ $40 per mo - $3.85, Trans Dept main stem |
| 1857-23 | Edw. | ton conduc 10 3/4 da @ $40 per mo; 7 da @ $50 per mo - $34.20. 3d & 4th div |
| 1855-90 | S. | carp 21 3/4 da @ $1.40 - $30.45. Mach Dept |
| 1857-77 | Macks, Patrick | quarry 8 da @ $1 - $8.00. ballast train for 2d track |
| 1857-77 | Macky, Lawrence | lab 1 da @ $1 - $1.00. lay 2d track |
| 1855-96 | McLain, Alexander | lab 20 da @ $1.10 - $22.00. Mach Dept |
| 1857-114 | " | iron mould help 18 da @ $1.10 - $19.80. Mach Dept, Balto |
| 1857-121 | Arthur | carp app 22 da @ $.75 - $16.50. Mach Dept, Balto |
| 1855-84 | John | help 24 da @ $1 - $24.00. Mach Dept |
| 1855-84 | Levin | mach 23 3/4 da @ $1.72 - $40.85. Mach Dept |
| 1857-115 | | boil mkr 18½ da @ $1.72 - $31.80. Mach Dept, Balto |

## B & O RR EMPLOYEES

| ID | Name | Description |
|---|---|---|
| 1357-134 | McLain, Thomas | mach app 27 3/4 da @ $.45 - $12.50. Mach Dept, Wheeling |
| 1355-16 | McLanahan, J. | pass fire 20 da @ $40 per mo - $28.55. Trans Dept main stem |
| 1355-19 | McLane, John | ton eng'man 24 da @ $2 - $48.00. 1st div |
| 1357-28 | " | ton eng'man 24 da @ $2 - $48.00. Trans Dept main stem |
| 1357-114 | Wm. | iron mould 21½ da @ $.55 - $32.95. Mach Dept, Balto |
| 1357-13 | McLarnie, John | haul wd 6 da @ $1 - $6.00. Martinsburg |
| 1855-69 | McLaughlin, D. | lab 13 da @ $1 - $13.00. Rd Way Dept |
| 1857-88 | Daniel | lab 19½ da @ $1.12 - $21.95. grad, Welling Tun |
| 1857-79 | Jas. | lab 5 3/4 da @ $1 - $5.75. lay 2d track |
| 1857-73 | John | carp 23¾ da @ $1.50 - $34.85. repair bridges &c |
| 1857-103 | " | lab 22 3/4 da @ $1.12 - $25.60. NW Va RR Tun |
| 1857-100 | Michael | fore 28 da @ $1.25 - $35.00. NW Va RR, Rd Dept 5th s-div |
| 1857-97 | " | watch 30 da @ $1 - $30.00. NW Va RR, Rd Dept 1st s-div |
| 1855-56 | Mike | lab 3 da @ $1 - $3.00. Rd Way Dept |
| 1855-92 | P. | carp 23¾ da @ $33.45. Mach Dept |
| 1857-132 | Peter | carp 18 3/4 da @ $1.50 - $28.10. Mach Dept, Grafton |
| 1857-92 | McLeig, James | lab 23¼ da @ $1 - $23.25. grad, Littleton Tun |
| 1857-82 | McLennan, James | bricklay 21½ da @ $2 - $43.00. grad, Board Tree Tun |
| 1855-42 | McLockin, F. | lab 19 da @ $1 - $19.00. Rd Way Dept |
| 1855-70 | McLoughlin, Michael | 21 da @ $1.12½ - $23.60. Rd Way Dept |
| 1857-99 | Thomas | lab 26 da @ $1 - $26.00. NW Va RR, Rd Dept 4th s-div |
| 1857-125 | McLure, James | put away eng &c 27 da @ $1.50 - $40.50. Mach Dept, Martinsburg |
| 1857-114 | McMachen, Thos. G. | pat mkr 18¼ da @ $2 - $36.50. Mach Dept, Balto |
| 1857-61 | McMahan, James | brak 5 da @ $1.54 - $7.70. Rd Dept main stem 14th s-div |
| 1855-37 | M. | fore 25½ da @ $1 - $25.50. Rd Way Dept |
| 1855-59 | " | lab 24 da @ $1 - $24.00. Rd Way Dept |
| 1857-84 | Patrick | lab 25 da @ $1.12 - $28.10. grad, Board Tree Tun |
| 1857-57 | McMahen, James | lab 24 3/4 da @ $1 - $24.75. Rd Dept main stem 11th s-div |
| 1857-26 | John | ton brak 26 da @ $40 per mo - $41.60. 3d & 4th div |
| 1857-26 | James | ton brak 2 da @ $40 per mo - $3.20. 3d & 4th div |
| 1855-53 | McMahon, James | lab 18 da @ $1 - $18.00. Rd Way Dept |
| 1855-55 | " | lab 13½ da @ $1 - $13.50. Rd Way Dept |
| 1857-62 | Martin | lab 24½ da @ $1 - $24.50. Rd Dept main stem 15th s-div |
| 1857-126 | Michael | prepar fuel 10 da @ $1 - $10.00. Mach Dept, Martinsburg |
| 1855-95 | McMakin, Thomas | pat mkr 21 3/4 da @ $1.90 - $41.35. Mach Dept |
| 1855-31 | McMan, John | prepar fuel 17 3/4 da @ $1 - $17.75. Trans Dept main stem |

B & O  RR EMPLOYEES   231

| ID | Name | Description |
|---|---|---|
| 1857-101 | McManus, Hugh | lab 11 3/4 da @ $1 - $11.75. NW Va RR ballast train |
| 1857-100 | " | lab 4 da @ $1 - $4.00. NW Va RR, Rd Dept 5th s-div |
| 1855-23 | James | fire ½ da @ $1.75 - $.85. Trans Dept main stem |
| 1855-23 | John | fire 14½ da @ $1.75 - $25.35. Trans Dept main stem |
| 1857-67 | Michael | fire 21 da @ $1 - $21.00. Rd Dept main stem 19th s-div |
| 1857-75 | Robert | fire 14 3/4 da @ $1.75 - $25.80. Trans Dept main stem |
| 1857-28 | " | eng'man 6¾ da @ $60 per mo - $14.40. ballast train for 2d track |
| 1855-56 | Thos. | ton eng'man 13¾ da @ $2.50 - $33.10. 1st div |
| 1857-89 | McMasters, Mat. | lab 2½ da @ $1.75 - $4.40. Rd Way Dept |
| 1857-29 | McMichael, Hugh | swit tend 17 da @ $1.12 - $19.15. grad, Welling Tun |
| 1855-72 | McMillan, James | ton eng'man 28½ da @ $2.50 - $71.25. 2d div |
| 1857-69 | " | mach 24 da @ $2 - $48.00. Rd Way Dept |
| 1857-70 | John | mach 23½ da @ $2 - $47.00. Mt Clare sta, Balto |
| 1857-17 | McMullan, William | lab 20 da @ $1 - $20.00. Mt Clare sta, Balto |
| 1855-54 | McMurphy, J. D. | lab 30 da @ $50 per mo - $50.00. frt transfer force at Bellaire, opp Benwood |
| 1857-16 | Silas D. | supv @ $100 per mo - $100.00. Rd Way Dept |
|  |  | capt 30 da @ $125 per mo - $125.00. transfer steam Brown Dick--Ohio Riv, bet Benwood & Bellaire |
| 1855-36 | McMurry, James | lab 25 da @ $25 per mo - $26.05. Trans Dept main stem |
| 1855-66 | McNally, James | lab 20½ da @ $1 -$20.50. Rd Way Dept |
| 1855-91 | John | mach 30½ da @ $1.62 - $39.90. Mach Dept |
| 1857-111 | " | mach help 30 3/4 da @ $1 - $30.75. Mach Dept, Balto |
| 1857-100 | Michael | lab 22½ da @ $1 - $22.50. NW Va RR, Rd Dept 5th s-div |
| 1857-92 | Miles | lab 24 da @ $1 - $24.00. grad, Littleton Tun |
| 1857-66 | William | lab 25½ da @ $1 - $25.50. Rd Dept main stem 18th s-div |
| 1857-54 | McNamara, Daniel | watch 27½ da @ $1 - $27.50. Rd Dept main stem 8th s-div |
| 1857-54 | John | lab 24 da @ $1 - $24.00. Rd Dept main stem 8th s-div |
| 1857-51 | McNamanow, Michael | lab 25 da @ $1 - $25.00. Rd Dept main stem 5th s-div |
| 1857-54 | McNamara, John | lab 23 da @ $1 - $23.00. Rd Dept main stem 8th s-div |
| 1857-100 | McNamarra, Patrick | lab 23½ da @ $1 - $23.50. NW Va RR, Rd Dept 5th s-div |
| 1855-37 | McNaney, Owen | fore 24 da @ $1 - $24.00. Rd Way Dept |
| 1857-77 | McNeal, Owen | quarry 23½ da @ $1 - $23.50. ballast train for 2d track |
| 1857-112 | McNearney, Michael | mach app 22 da @ $.75 - $16.50. Mach Dept, Balto |
| 1857-77 | McNeff, Michael | quarry 6½ da @ $1 - $6.50. ballast train for 2d track |
| 1857-76 | Thomas | dril 8 da @ $1.10 - $8.80. ballast train for 2d track |
| 1855-66 | McNerney, M. | lab 25 da @ $1 - $25.00. Rd Way Dept |

232  B & O RR EMPLOYEES

| ID | Name | Description |
|---|---|---|
| 1857-115 | McNew, T. | watch 30 da @ $.50 - $15.00. Mach Dept, Balto |
| 1855-79 | Thomas | watch 14 da @ $1.15 - $16.10. Mach Dept |
| 1857-10 | W. | bur driv 27½ da @ $1.15 - $31.60. hp exp, Balto |
| 1857-88 | McNicholas, James | lab 19 da @ $1.12 - $21.35. grad, Welling Tun |
| 1857-64 | Michael | lab 27 da @ $1 - $27.00. Rd Dept main stem 17th s-div |
| 1857-64 | Thomas | lab 26 da @ $1 - $26.00. Rd Dept main stem 17th s-div |
| 1855-60 | McNicholess, A. | lab 22 3/4 da @ $1 - $22.75. Rd Way Dept |
| 1855-26 | McNicholls, Alex. | clean eng 19½ da @ $1 - $19.50. Trans Dept main stem |
| 1857-68 | McNichols, Anthony | lab 16½ da @ $1 - $16.50. Rd Dept main stem 19th s-div |
| 1857-85 | James | lab 6¼ da @ $1.12 - $7.05. grad, Board Tree Tun |
| 1857-135 | John | boil mkr help 21¼ da @ $1 - $21.25. Mach Dept, Wheeling |
| 1857-39 | McNulty, H. | bag mast 30 da @ $1 - $30.00. N W Va rd, Parkersburg sta |
| 1857-88 | James | lab 20½ da @ $1.25 - $25.65. grad, Welling Tun |
| 1857-10 | John | stab'man 12 da @ $30 per mo - $14.40. hp exp, Balto |
| 1855-66 | M. | lab 27 da @ $1 - $27.00. Rd Way Dept |
| 1855-61 | Owen | lab 16 da @ $1 - $16.00. Rd Way Dept |
| 1857-17 | McPeck, Sam'l. | ton eng'man 13 da @ $3 - $39.00. Trans Dept main stem |
| 1857-103 | McQue, Thomas | lab 24 da @ $1.12 - $27.60. NW Va RR Run |
| 1857-126 | McSherry, James | lab 30 da @ $1 - $30.00. Mach Dept, Martinsburg |
| 1857-34 | McTauney, Peter | ton fire 22 da @ $1.75 - $38.50. Board Tree Tun |
| 1857-34 | " | ton fire 1 da @ $1.75 - $1.75. 4th div |
| 1857-98 | McTIge, Patrick | lab 24 3/4 da @ $1 - $24.75. NW Va RR, Rd Dept 3d s-div |
| 1855-60 | McTigne, James | lab 22 da @ $1 - $22.00. Rd Way Dept |
| 1857-134 | McVay, Samuel | mach help 35¼ da @ $1 - $35.25. Mach Dept, Wheeling |
| 1857-93 | McVeeney, William | lab 23 da @ $1 - $23.00. quarry & haul stone for Board Tree & Littleton Tun |
| 1855-66 | McVerney, William | lab 27½ da @ $1 - $27.50. Rd Way Dept |
| 1657-39 | McVertney, M. | watch, Wharf Boat 30 da @ $30 per mo - $30.00. NW Va rd, Parkersburg sta |
| 1657-17 | McVey, James | watch 30 da @ $1 - $30.00. frt transfer force at Bellaire, opp Benwood |
| 1855-92 | McVicker, John | help 22½ da - $24.45. Mach Dept |
| 1655-79 | McWard, Mike | ofc boy 24 da @ $.45 - $10.80. Mach Dept |
| 1857-27 | McWilliams, A. | ton brak 7 da @ $40 per mo - $11.20. Board Tree Tun |
| 1857-23 | " | ton conduc 17 da @ $50 per mo - $34.00. Board Tree Tun |
| 1857-23 | Adam | ton conduc 3 da @ $40 per mo; 3½ da @ $50 per mo - $11.80. 3d & 4th div |
| 1857-26 | B. | ton brak 27 da @ $40 per mo - $43.20. 3d & 4th div |
| 1857-61 | Benj. | brak 5 da @ $1.54 - $7.70. Rd Dept main stem 14th s-div |
| 1855-30 | James | prepar fuel 22 da @ $1 - $22.00. Trans Dept main stem |

B & O RR EMPLOYEES 233

| ID | Name | Description |
|---|---|---|
| 1855-14 | McWilliams, R. | brak 2 da @ $40 per mo - $3.35. Trans Dept main stem |
| 1855-29 | " | prepar fuel 28 da @ $1 - $28.00. Trans Dept main stem |
| 1857-33 | " Robert | ton fire 16¼ da @ $1.75 - $28.45. 3d div |
| 1857-60 | " | fire 6½ da @ $1.75 - $11.40. Rd Dept main stem 13th s-div |
| 1857-11 | " | lab 2 da @ $1 - $2.00. Locust Pt |
| 1857-99 | Madden, James | fore 26 da @ $1.25 - $32.50. NW Va RR, Rd Dept 4th s-div |
| 1857-68 | L. | tend to masons 21 da @ $1 - $21.00. Rd Way Dept |
| 1855-85 | Laurence | lab 21¼ da @ $1 - $21.25. grad, Board Tree Tun |
| 1857-16 | Michael | lab 14 da @ $1 - $14.00. Benwood sta |
| 1857-35 | Patrick | lab 7 3/4 da @ $1 - $7.75. Edwards' wd train 3d & 4th div |
| 1855-64 | S. | lab 23½ da @ $1 - $23.50. Rd Way Dept |
| 1857-63 | Simon | lab 22 da @ $1 - $22.00. Rd Dept main stem 16th s-div |
| 1855-61 | T. | lab 22 da @ $1 - $22.00. Rd Way Dept |
| 1857-66 | Timothy | lab 24 3/4 da @ $1 - $24.75. Rd Dept main stem 18th s-div |
| 1857-115 | Maddox, George | boil mkr 18 da @ $1.65 - $29.70. Mach Dept, Balto |
| 1857-114 | Maderson, John | iron mould app 22 da @ $.65 - $14.30. Mach Dept, Balto |
| 1857-112 | Magee, Edward | mach help 18½ da @ $1 - $18.50. Mach Dept, Balto |
| 1857-114 | " | iron mould help 17 3/4 da @ $1.10 - $19.55. Mach Dept main stem |
| 1855-29 | Maggs, John | haul & saw firewd 17½ da @ $1 - $17.50. Trans Dept main stem |
| 1857-110 | Magill, John | mach 16 3/4 da @ $1.50 - $25.10. Mach Dept, Balto |
| 1857-48 | Magorrian, John | lab 27 da @ $1 - $27.00. Rd Dept main stem 2d s-div |
| 1855-95 | Magrah, M. | lab 24 da @ $1.10 - $26.40. Mach Dept |
| 1855-41 | Magraw, John | lab 13 da @ $1 - $13.00. NW Va rd, Athey's wd train |
| 1855-77 | L. | help 9½ da @ $1 - $9.50. Mach Dept |
| 1857-139 | Martin | lab 12½ da @ $.90 - $11.25. NW Va RR, Mach Dept, Parkersburg |
| 1855-14 | T. | brak 4 3/4 da @ $40 per mo - $7.90. Trans Dept main stem |
| 1855-64 | Thos. | lab 11½ da @ $1 - $11.50. Rd Way Dept |
| 1857-136 | William | clean eng 25½ da @ $1 - $25.50. Mach Dept, Wheeling |
| 1855-12 | Magruder, John | conduc & brak 2 da @ $50 per mo - $4.15. Trans Dept main stem |
| 1857-32 | " | ton fire 25 3/4 da @ $1.75 - $45.05. 1st div |
| 1855-55 | Maguire, Charles | lab 23 da @ $1 - $23.00. NW Va RR, Rd Dept 3d s-div |
| 1857-98 | John | lab 23 da @ $58.35 per mo - $58.35. NW Va rd, Parkersburg sta |
| 1857-39 | John C. | clk 30 da @ $58.35 per mo - $58.35. NW Va RR, Rd Dept 1st s-div |
| 1857-96 | Thomas | fore 24 da @ $1.25 - $30.00. NW Va RR, Rd Dept 1st s-div |
| 1855-92 | Mahaffey, William | help 30 da @ $1 - $30.00. Mach Dept |
| 1857-99 | Mahan, Bryan | lab 25½ da @ $1 - $25.50. NW Va RR, Rd Dept 4th s-div |

| | | |
|---|---|---|
| 1855-54 | Mahaney, Thomas | carp 24 da @ $1.50 - $36.00. Rd Way Dept |
| 1857-48 | Mahar, John | lab 22 3/4 da @ $1 - $22.75. Rd Dept main stem 2d s-div |
| 1857-117 | Maher, Jos. | blksmith help 16 3/4 da @ $1 - $16.75. Mach Dept, Balto |
| 1855-51 | Mahoney, George | lab @ $17.50 per mo - $17.50. Rd Way Dept |
| 1857-72 | Mahoney, Thomas | carp 20¼ da @ $1.50 - $30.40. Cumb depot |
| 1855-51 | Mahony, George | lab @ $17.50 per mo - $17.50. Rd Way Dept |
| 1855-84 | Major, Martin | mach 22½ da @ $1.65 - $37.10. Mach Dept |
| 1857-115 | " | boil mkr 20 3/4 da @ $1.65 - $34.25. Mach Dept, Balto |
| 1857-111 | Makenzie, Alexander | mach help 16¼ da @ $1 - $16.25. Mach Dept, Balto |
| 1857-122 | David | eng clean 21½ da @ $1 - $21.50. Mach Dept, Balto |
| 1857-110 | M. | mach 19½ da @ $1.50 - $29.25. Mach Dept, Balto |
| 1855-31 | Malarkey, James | prepar fuel 24 da @ $1.25 - $30.00. Trans Dept main stem |
| 1857-127 | Malcolmson, John | mach help 12½ da @ $1 - $12.50. Mach Dept, Piedmont |
| 1857-55 | Malcomb, Kenner | lab 23 da @ $1 - $23.00. Rd Dept main stem 9th s-div |
| 1857-61 | Maley, James | lab 25½ da @ $1 - $25.50. Rd Dept main stem 14th s-div |
| 1857-101 | Valentine | lab 23 da @ $1 - $23.00. NW Va RR ballast train |
| 1855-61 | William | lab 21 da @ $1 - $21.00. Rd Way Dept |
| 1855-47 | Malice, James | lab 21½ da @ $1 - $21.50. Rd Way Dept |
| 1855-63 | Mallan, Michl. | lab 23½ da @ $1 - $23.50. Rd Way Dept |
| 1857-84 | Maller, Martin | lab 23½ da @ $1.12 - $26.45. grad, Board Tree Tun |
| 1857-101 | Malley, Patrick | lab 24 da @ $1 - $24.00. NW Va RR ballast train |
| 1857-93 | Mallin, Michael | smith help 22 da @ $1 - $22.00. quarry & haul stone for Board Tree & Littleton Tun |
| 1855-63 | Malloy, Edward | lab 19½ da @ $1 - $19.50. Rd Way Dept |
| 1857-101 | " | lab 26 da @ $1 - $26.00. NW Va RR ballast train |
| 1855-48 | George | train hand 7 da @$1 - $7.00. Rd Way Dept |
| 1855-71 | Thos. | help 24 da @ $1.15 -$27.60. Rd Way Dept |
| 1857-139 | " | chair mkr 18 3/4 da @ $1.15 - $21.55. Mt Clare sta, Balto |
| 1855-70 | Mally, Sarah | clean pass cars 30 da @ $.50 - $15.00. NW Va RR, Mach Dept, Parkersburg |
| 1857-103 | Malolly, John | lab 12¼ da @ $1 - $12.25. Rd Way Dept |
| 1855-42 | Malona, William | carp 23¼ da @ $1.25 - $29.05. NW Va RR Tun |
| 1855-30 | Malone, Jas. | lab 19 da @ $1 - $19.00. Rd Way Dept |
| 1857-128 | John | fill tend 28 da @ $1 - $28.00. Trans Dept main stem |
| 1855-65 | " | boil mkr 16 3/4 da @ $1.25 - $20.95. Mach Dept, Piedmont |
| 1855-81 | Patrick | lab 10½ da @ $1 - $10.50. Rd Way Dept |
| 1857-67 | W. D. | lab 27 da @ $1.15 - $31.05. Mach Dept |
| 1857-67 | Maloney, Daniel | lab 22 3/4 da @ $1 - $22.75. Rd Dept main stem 18th s-div |

| | | | |
|---|---|---|---|
| 1857-97 | Maloney, Edward | lab 26 da @ $1 - $26.00. NW Va RR, Rd Dept 2d s-div |
| 1857-60 | " | lab 32 da @ $1 - $32.00. Rd Dept main stem 13th s-div |
| 1857-84 | James | lab 4½ da @ $1.12 - $5.05. grad, Board Tree Tun |
| 1857-96 | John | lab 24 3/4 da @ $1 - $24.75. NW Va RR, Rd Dept 1st s-div |
| 1855-50 | Thomas | watch cuts 28 da @ $1 - $28.00. Rd Way Dept |
| 1857-67 | " | watch 30 da @ $1 - $30.00. Rd Dept main stem 18th s-div |
| 1857-66 | Maloy, B. | lab 25 da @ $1 - $25.00. Rd Dept main stem 18th s-div |
| 1855-42 | George | lab 6 da @ $1 - $6.00. Rd Way Dept |
| 1857-63 | " | lab 20 da @ $1 - $20.00. Rd Dept main stem 16th s-div |
| 1855-48 | Hugh | lab 21 3/4 da @ $1 - $21.75. Rd Way Dept |
| 1855-17 | James | ton eng'man 14½ da @ $3 - $43.50. Trans Dept main stem |
| 1857-93 | " | smith help 11⅜ da @ $1 - $11.25. quarry & haul stone for Board Tree & Littleton Tun |
| 1855-92 | John | help 24½ da @ $1 - $24.50. Mach Dept |
| 1857-104 | " | lab 21 3/4 da @ $1 - $21.75. NW Va RR Tun |
| 1857-92 | Martin | lab 24½ da @ $1 - $24.50. grad, Littleton Tun |
| 1857-66 | " | lab 22 3/4 da @ $1 - $22.75. Rd Dept main stem 18th s-div |
| 1855-50 | Thomas | watch cuts 28 da @ $1 - $28.00. Rd Way Dept |
| 1857-100 | " | lab 27¼ da @ $1 - $27.25. NW Va RR, Rd Dept 5th s-div |
| 1857-63 | " | watch 30 da @ $1 - $30.00. Rd Dept main stem 16th s-div |
| 1857-95 | Malthar, Herman | fore 23 da @ $1.25 - $28.75. Wash br, Rd Dept |
| 1857-66 | Maly, Martin | lab 24 da @ $1 - $24.00. Rd Dept main stem 18th s-div |
| 1857-67 | William | watch 30 da @ $1 - $30.00. Rd Dept main stem 18th s-div |
| 1855-39 | Manard, R. | lab 21½ da @ $1 - $21.50. Rd Way Dept |
| 1855-25 | Manden, Edward | clean eng 28¾ da @ $1.15 - $32.50. Trans Dept main stem |
| 1855-23 | Manford, J. M. | fire 18 da @ $1.75 - $31.50. $2.50 -$58.75. 2d div |
| 1857-29 | James | ton eng'man 23½ da @ $1 - $19.50. quarry & haul stone for Board Tree & Littleton Tun |
| 1857-94 | Mangan, Michael | lab 19½ da @ $1 - $19.50. quarry & haul stone for Board Tree & Littleton Tun |
| 1857-124 | Mangold, Endle | blksmith 18 3/4 da @ $1.35 - $25.30. Mach Dept, Martinsburg |
| 1855-74 | Mangum, James | lab 19 da @ $1 - $19.00. Rd Way Dept |
| 1857-95 | " | pump water 30 da @ $1 - $30.00. Wash br, Rd Dept |
| 1857-93 | Manion, Patrick | smith help 17⅜ da @ $1 -$17.25. quarry & haul stone for Board Tree & Littleton Tun |
| 1855-60 | Mankey, Peter | lab 21 da @ $1 - $21.00. Rd Way Dept |
| 1857-92 | Manley, Brine | lab 24½ da @ $1.12 - $27.25. grad, Littleton Tun |
| 1857-65 | Edw. | watch 29 da @ $1 - $29.00. Rd Dept main stem 17th s-div |
| 1857-92 | Frank | lab 23 da @ $1 -$23.00. grad, Littleton Tun |
| 1857-86 | James | lab 22 da @ $1 -$22.00. grad, McGuire's Tun |
| 1857-65 | " | watch 30 da @ $1 - $30.00. Rd Dept main stem 17th s-div |

## B & O RR EMPLOYEES

| | | | |
|---|---|---|---|
| 1857-95 | Manley, John | lab 24 da @ $1 - $24.00. Wash br, Rd Dept |
| 1857-65 | Peter | watch 30 da @ $1 - $30.00. Rd Dept main stem 17th s-div |
| 1855-50 | William | watch cuts 28 da @ $1 - $28.00. Rd Way Dept |
| 1855-60 | Manly, Edward | lab 23½ da @ $1 - $23.50. Rd Way Dept |
| 1855-70 | James | lab 16 da @ $1 - $16.00. Rd Way Dept |
| 1857-91 | John | lab 25 da @ $1 - $25.00. grad, Littleton Tun |
| 1857-93 | " | smith help 21 da @ $1 - $21.00. quarry & haul stone for Board Tree & Littleton Tun |
| 1857-108 | Mann, John | mach 18¼ da @ $1.60 - $29.20. Mach Dept, Balto |
| 1855-17 | Manning, Hugh | ton eng'man 14 da @ $2.50 - $35.00. Trans Dept main stem |
| 1857-85 | James | fire 7 da @ $1.75 - $12.25. grad, Board Tree Tun |
| 1857-27 | " | ton brak 36 da @ $40 per mo - $57.60. Board Tree Tun |
| 1857-23 | John | ton conduc 3½ da @ $50 per mo - $7.00. Board Tree Tun |
| 1855-47 | P. | lab 15 da @ $1 - $15.00. Rd Dept main stem 19th s-div |
| 1855-21 | Patrick | lab 22 3/4 da @ $1 - $22.75. Rd Way Dept |
| 1855-1 | S. | fire 12¾ da @ $1.75 - $21.45. Trans Dept main stem |
| 1857-111 | Mannion, Michael | audit $1500 per annum - $125.00. Ofc Hanover St |
| 1857-59 | Patrick | mach help 20¼ da @ $1 - $20.25. Mach Dept, Balto |
| 1857-60 | Thomas | nail 30 da @ $1.05 - $31.50. Rd Dept main stem 12th s-div |
| 1857-60 | | lab 27 da @ $1 - $27.00. Rd Dept main stem 13th s-div |
| 1857-112 | Mansfield, B. W. | lab 23 da @ $1 - $23.00. Rd Dept main stem 13th s-div |
| 1857-85 | James | mach app 19 da @ $.45 - $8.55. Mach Dept, Balto |
| 1857-87 | " | bricklay 7½ da @$2.25 - $16.85. grad, Board Tree Tun |
| 1857-116 | Levi | bricklay 17 3/4 da @ $2.25 - $39.95. grad, Welling Tun |
| 1855-85 | N. | blksmith 16 da @ $1.80 - $28.80. Mach Dept, Balto |
| 1857-118 | Nathan | help 20½ da @ $1.10 - $22.55. Mach Dept |
| 1857-123 | Mansford, James | blksmith help 18 da @$1.10 - $19.80. Mach Dept, Balto |
| 1855-35 | Mantz, Francis | mach 1 3/4 da @$1.25 - $2.20. Mach Dept, Martinsburg |
| 1855-51 | " | disp 24 da @ $20 per mo - $20.00. Trans Dept main stem |
| 1857-12 | " | lab 28 da @ $1 - $28.00. Rd Way Dept |
| 1857-49 | Jacob | swit tend 30 da @ $20 per mo - $20.00. Monocacy |
| 1855-32 | " | watch 30 da @ $1 - $30.00. Rd Dept main stem 3d s-div |
| 1857-55 | " | saw wd 45 cords @ $.35 - $15.75. Trans Dept main stem |
| 1855-29 | Peter | watch 31 da @ $1 - $31.00. Rd Dept main stem 9th s-div |
| 1855-40 | " | haul & saw firewd 28 da @$27.50 per mo -$27.50. Trans Dept main stem |
| 1857-50 | " | supv @ $45 per mo - $45.00. Rd Way Dept |
| | | horse hire 30 da @ $.90 - $27.00. Rd Dept main stem 4th s-div |

| | | |
|---|---|---|
| 1857-56 | Mantz, Peter | pump water 17½ da @ $1 - $17.50. Rd Dept main stem 10th s-div |
| 1857-50 | " | supv @ $45 per mo - $45.00. Rd Dept main stem 4th s-div |
| 1857-32 | " | ton fire 9 da @ $1.75 - $15.75. 1st div |
| 1857-56 | " | watch 17½ da @ $1 - $17.50. Rd Dept main stem 10th s-div |
| 1857-90 | Marahahn, Nicholas | lab 23 da @ $1 -$23.00. grad, Welling Tun |
| 1857-58 | Marion, Patrick | lab 25 da @ $1 - $25.00. Rd Dept main stem 11th s-div |
| 1855-83 | Marks, Albert | lab 24¼ da @ $1.15 - $27.90. Mach Dept |
| 1855-19 | Lemuel | ton eng'man 14 da @ $2.50 - $35.00. Trans Dept main stem |
| 1857-28 | " | ton eng'man 24 da @ $2 - $48.00. 1st div |
| 1857-76 | Patrick | lab 17 da @ $.97 - $16.55. ballast train for 2d track |
| 1857-78 | Marley, John | lab 24½ da @ $1 - $24.50. lay 2d track |
| 1855-14 | Marlow, D. | brak 2 da @ $40 per mo - $3.35. Trans Dept main stem |
| 1857-112 | Marman, Charles | mach help 18 da @ $1 - $18.00. Mach Dept, Balto |
| 1855-95 | Marriott, Edward | mould 14 da @ $1.60 - $22.40. Mach Dept |
| 1855-77 | Marrow, Danl. | help 27 da @ $1 - $27.00. Mach Dept |
| 1857-135 | Marsh, Norman | carp 19½ da @ $1.50 - $39.25. Mach Dept, Wheeling |
| 1855-16 | R. | pass fire 2 da @ $40 per mo - $2.85. Trans Dept main stem |
| 1855-19 | William | ton eng'man 9½ da @ $2.50 - $23.10. Trans Dept main stem |
| 1857-28 | " | ton eng'man 23¾ da @ $3 -$69.75. 1st div |
| 1855-25 | Marshall, Charles | bur driv 27 da @$30 per mo - $33.75. Trans Dept main stem |
| 1855-16 | J. | pass fire 30½ da @$1.25 - $28.10. Trans Dept main stem |
| 1855-79 | John | blksmith 24 da @$1.55 - $37.20. Mach Dept |
| 1857-117 | " | blksmith 18½ da @ $1.55 - $28.70. Mach Dept, Balto |
| 1857-129 | " | lab 21 da @ $1 - $21.00. Mach Dept, Piedmont |
| 1855-25 | Luke | clean eng 30¼ da @ $1.15 - $34.80. Trans Dept main stem |
| 1857-117 | Marson, Thomas | blksmith 18½ da @ $1.60 - $29.60. Mach Dept, Balto |
| 1857-84 | Marston, William | fire 6 da @ $1.75 - $10.50. grad, Board Tree Tun |
| 1857-34 | " | ton fire 4½ da @ $1.75 - $7.85. 4th div |
| 1857-79 | Marten, Patrick | lab 1½ da @ $1 - $1.50. lay 2d track |
| 1855-95 | Martin, C. M. | pat mkr 21 3/4 da @$1.65 - $35.90. Mach Dept |
| 1857-114 | Charles | pat mkr 18¾ da @ $1.75 - $31.95. Mach Dept, Balto |
| 1855-27 | George | clean eng 7 da @ $1 - $7.00. Trans Dept main stem |
| 1857-99 | George G. | watch 30 da @ $1 - $30.00. NW Va RR, Rd Dept 4th s-div |
| 1857-133 | George F. | put away eng 16 da @ $1.50 - $24.00. Mach Dept, Fetterman |
| 1855-76 | James | lab 20 da @ $1 - $20.00. Rd Way Dept |
| 1855-36 | " | lab 24 da @ $25 per mo - $25.00. Trans Dept main stem |
| 1857-120 | " | carp 20 da @ $1.50 - $30.00. Mach Dept, Balto |

| | | |
|---|---|---|
| 1857-74 | Martin, James | lab 10½ da @ $.90 - $9.45. repair bridges &c |
| 1855-95 | " John | lab 17 da @ $1 - $17.00. Mach Dept |
| 1855-66 | " " | lab 23 da @ $1.25 - $28.75. Rd Way Dept |
| 1857-51 | " " | watch cuts 24 da @$1 - $24.00. Rd Way Dept |
| 1857-126 | " " | clean eng 26½ da @ $1.15 - $30.45. Mach Dept, Martinsburg |
| 1857-79 | " " | lab 2 da @ $1 - $2.00. lay 2d track |
| 1857-73 | " " | stone mason 2½ da @ $2 - $5.00. repair bridges &c |
| 1857-98 | " Michael | lab 22½ da @ $1 - $22.25. N W Va RR, Rd Dept 3d s-div |
| 1855-46 | " P. | lab 24 da @$1 - $24.00. Rd Way Dept |
| 1855-66 | " Patrick | lab 24 da @ $1 - $24.00. Rd Way Dept |
| 1857-115 | " " | boil mkr help 20 3/4 da @$1.10 - $22.85. Mach Dept, Balto |
| 1857-71 | " Paul | lab 24 da @ $1 - $24.00. Mt Clare, repair tracks in yd |
| 1855-51 | " Thomas | lab 28 da @ $1 - $28.00. Rd Way Dept |
| 1857-51 | " " | watch 30 da @ $1 - $30.00. Rd Dept main stem 5th s-div |
| 1855-6 | " W. P. | clk 28 da @ $25 per mo - $25.00. Trans Dept main stem |
| 1855-70 | " Walter | lab 14 3/4 da @ $1 - $14.75. Rd Way Dept |
| 1855-58 | " William | fore 24 da @ $1.25 - $30.00. Rd Way Dept |
| 1855-57 | " " | lab 13½ da @ $1 - $13.50. Rd Way Dept |
| 1857-18 | " " | pass train brak 30 da @$33.35 per mo - $3.35. w end |
| 1857-135 | " William H. | boil mkr help 31 da @ $1 - $31.00. Mach Dept, Wheeling |
| 1855-55 | Mary, Charles | lab 24 da @$1 - $24.00. Rd Way Dept |
| 1855-53 | Mason, John | stonecut 30 ston @ $2 - $60.00. Rd Way Dept |
| 1855-40 | " B. | lab 16 3/4 da @ $1 - $16.75. Rd Way Dept |
| 1855-31 | " Charles | lab 24 da @ $1 - $24.00. Rd Way Dept |
| 1857-49 | " George | saw wd 50½ da @$.35 - $17.65. Trans Dept main stem |
| 1855-40 | " John | lab 25 da @ $1 - $25.00. Rd Dept main stem 3d s-div |
| 1857-49 | " William | lab 24 da @ $1 - $24.00. Rd Way Dept |
| 1857-15 | " " | lab 22½ da @ $1 - $22.50. Rd Dept main stem 3d s-div |
| 1855-34 | " William D. | watch 30 da @ $1 - $30.00. Fetterman sta |
| 1857-20 | " William P. | watch 28 da @ $1 - $28.00. Trans Dept main stem |
| 1857-36 | Mass, Frank | tele oper 30 da @ $30 per mo - $30.00. Newburg |
| 1857-20 | " Van Buren | pass fire 27½ da @ $40 per mo - $36.65. 1st div |
| 1857-116 | Massey, James | blksmith 16¼ da @ $1.50 - $24.35. Mach Dept, Balto |
| 1857-83 | Masters, Jesse | lab 9 da @ $1.12 - $10.10. grad, Board Tree Tun |
| 1857-65 | Mastron, William | fire 18 da @$1.75 - $31.50. Rd Dept main stem 17th s-div |
| 1855-61 | Mastus, Jesse | lab 22 da @ $1 - $22.00. Rd Way Dept |

# B & O RR EMPLOYEES 239

| ID | Name | Description |
|---|---|---|
| 1857-132 | Matchen, John | paint 18½ da @ $1.85 - $34.20. Mach Dept, Grafton |
| 1855-74 | Mathar, Herm. | lab 24 da @ $1 - $24.00. Rd Way Dept |
| 1857-112 | Mathews, Edward | mach app 22¼ da @ $.45 - $10.00. Mach Dept, Balto |
| 1855-58 | " Henry | haul wd 2 da @ $1 - $2.00. Martinsburg |
| 1857-131 | " Patrick | carp 23 da @ $1.25 - $28.75. Rd Way Dept |
| 1855-57 | Mathis, William | mach 19½ da @ $1.50 - $29.25. Mach Dept, Grafton |
| 1857-85 | Matthew, David | lab 21 da @ $1 - $21.00. Rd Way Dept |
| 1855-44 | " | stone mason 15 da @ $1.50 - $22.50. grad, Board Tree Tun |
| 1855-55 | Matthews, O. C. H. | lab 22 da @ $1 - $22.00. Rd Way Dept |
| 1857-63 | " " " | supv @ $45 per mo - $45.00. Rd Way Dept |
| 1857-63 | " " " | horses & carts 50 da @ $1 - $50.00. Rd Dept main stem 16th s-div |
| 1855-67 | " " " | supv @ $45 per mo - $45.00. Rd Dept main stem 16th s-div |
| 1855-70 | " Frederick | mason 23½ da @ $2 - $47.00. Rd Way Dept |
| 1857-69 | " George H. | supv @ $50 per mo - $50.00. Rd Way Dept |
| 1857-65 | " " | fore @ $50 per mo - $50.00. Mt Clare sta, Balto |
| 1857-93 | " John | lab 8¼ da @ $1 - $8.25. Rd Dept main stem 17th s-div |
| 1855-67 | " Patrick | fore 26 da @ $1.25 - $32.50. quarry & haul stone for Board Tree & Littleton Tun |
| 1855-24 | " Philip | mason 20 da @ $2 - $40.00. Rd Way Dept |
| 1855-28 | Mattingly, John | pass & bur driv 26½ da @ $30 per mo - $33.10. Trans Dept main stem |
| 1857-74 | Maulon, Pat. | prepar fuel 8 3/4 da @ $1 - $8.75. Trans Dept main stem |
| 1857-111 | Maurey, Charles | lab 23 da @ $1.12 - $25.85. repair bridges &c |
| 1857-112 | Maxwell, F. | mach help 24½ da @ $1 - $24.25. Mach Dept, Balto |
| 1857-36 | " George | mach app 22 3/4 da @ $.55 - $12.50. Mach Dept, Martinsburg |
| 1857-119 | " H. | tele oper 30 da @ $30 per mo - $30.00. Martinsburg |
| 1857-108 | " Henry | carp 17 3/4 da @ $1.50 - $26.60. Mach Dept, Balto |
| 1855-82 | " R. | fore mach 19 3/4 da @ $2 - $39.50. Mach Dept, Balto |
| 1855-77 | " Robert | mach 29 da @ $1.85 - $53.65. Mach Dept |
| 1855-82 | " W. J. | mach 24¼ da @ $1.50 - $36.35. Mach Dept |
| 1857-108 | May, Frederick | mach 27 3/4 da @ $1.75 - $48.60. Mach Dept, Balto |
| 1857-73 | " | mach 18 da @ $1.85 - $33.30. Mach Dept, Balto |
| 1855-54 | " Geo. | stonecut 22 3/4 da @ $1.75 - $39.80. repair bridges &c |
| 1857-73 | " Jno. | stone mason 4½ da @ $2.25 - $10.00. Rd Way Dept |
| 1855-66 | " " | fore @ $75 per mo - $75.00. repair bridges &c |
| 1857-103 | Mayer, Lewis | lab 21½ da @ $1.62½ - $34.95. Rd Way Dept |
| 1857-94 | Mayers, Alexander | carp 17 3/4 da @ $1.50 - $26.60. NW Va RR depot |
| | George | fore @ $50 per mo - $50.00. repair bridges |

| |  |  |
|---|---|---|
| 1855-65 | Mayers, S. | bridge repair 24 da @ $50 per mo - $50.00. Rd Way Dept |
| 1857-46 | " S. H. | horse hire 25 da @ $.90 - $22.50. Rd Dept main stem 1st s-div |
| 1857-46 | " " | supv @ $55 per mo - $55.00. Rd Dept main stem 1st s-div |
| 1857-33 | Meadows, Michael | ton fire 23 da @ $1.75 - $40.25. 2d div |
| 1857-38 | Meagher, D. | lab 21 da @ $1 - $21.00. Rd Way Dept |
| 1855-38 | " John | lab 24 da @ $1 - $24.00. Rd Way Dept |
| 1857-76 | Meahan, John | dril 21½ da @ $1.10 - $23.65. ballast train for 2d track |
| 1855-49 | Mealey, John | watch cuts 20 da @ $1 - $20.00. Rd Way Dept |
| 1857-58 | " " | watch 30 da @ $1 - $30.00. Rd Dept main stem 11th s-div |
| 1857-68 | " Thomas | lab 23 da @ $1 - $23.00. Rd Dept main stem 19th s-div |
| 1857-94 | Meally, Charles | lab 18½ da @ $1 - $18.50. quarry & haul stone for Board Tree & Littleton Tun |
| 1857-57 | Mealy, Thomas | lab 25 da @ $1 - $25.00. Rd Dept main stem 11th s-div |
| 1855-14 | Meare, Frank | brak 3 da @ $40 per mo - $5.00. Trans Dept main stem |
| 1855-75 | Mechan, Jno. | lab 21 da @ $1 - $21.00. Rd Way Dept |
| 1855-91 | Medcalf, George W. | mach 21 3/4 da @ $1.62 - $32.45. Mach Dept |
| 1857-134 | " James | mach help 21½ da @ $.80 - $17.20. Mach Dept, Wheeling |
| 1855-94 | " R. | app 31½ da @ $.60 - $18.75. Mach Dept |
| 1857-134 | " Richard | mach 7 3/4 da @ $1.60 - $12.40. Mach Dept, Wheeling |
| 1855-4 | " Thomas | eng'man 28½ da @ $2.50 - $71.25. Trans Dept, Wash br |
| 1857-19 | " " | pass eng'man 12 da @ $3 - $36.00. 1st div |
| 1857-38 | " " | pass eng'man 20 da @$3 - $60.00. Wash br rd, Wash city sta |
| 1855-43 | Meddel, Jas. | lab 21½ da @ $1 - $21.50. Rd Way Dept |
| 1857-124 | Meddle, Daniel | sht iron work 22½ da @ $1.25 - $27.80. Mach Dept, Martinsburg |
| 1855-49 | Medler, P. | watch cuts 30 da @ $1 - $30.00. Rd Way Dept |
| 1857-62 | Medley, Adam | watch 30 da @ $1 - $30.00. Rd Dept main stem 15th s-div |
| 1855-63 | " " | eng'man 20½ da @ $2.50 - $51.25. Rd Way Dept |
| 1857-35 | " " | eng'man 1½ da @ $2.50 - $3.75. J. R. Shrode's wd train 4th div |
| 1857-28 | Meehan, James | ton eng'man 10 da @ $2.50 - $25.00. 1st div |
| 1857-59 | Meekins, Arch. | lab 25½ da @ $1 - $25.50. Rd Dept main stem 13th s-div |
| 1857-55 | " Joseph | pump water 30 da @ $1 - $30.00. Rd Dept main stem 9th s-div |
| 1857-109 | Meeks, John W. | lab 14 3/4 da @ $1 - $14.75. Rd Way Dept |
| 1855-48 | Meenehan, P. | mach 18 da @ $1.80 - $32.40. Mach Dept, Balto |
| 1857-23 | Meese, William | train hand 20 3/4 da @ $1 - $20.75. Rd Way Dept |
| 1857-75 | Megran, Thomas | ton conduc 38 da @ $50 per mo - $76.00. 3d & 4th div |
| 1855-73 | Mehan, Mike | lab 1 da @ $.97 - $.95. ballast train for 2d track |
| | | lab 3 da @ $1 - $3.00. Rd Way Dept |

| ID | Name | Details |
|---|---|---|
| 1857-102 | Meiser, Joseph | carp 25¾ da @ $1.60 - $40.40. NW Va RR, rwy depot |
| 1857-78 | Mellan, Patrick | lab 21½ da @ $1 - $21.50. lay 2d track |
| 1855-83 | Mellen, John | lab 24 da @ $1 - $24.00. Mach Dept |
| 1857-93 | Mellet, Patrick | lab 21½ da @ $1 - $21.50. quarry & haul stone for Board Tree & Littleton Tun |
| 1855-91 | Mellon, James | mach 24 3/4 da @ $1.62 - $41.00. Mach Dept |
| 1855-80 | Melolgan, M. | lab 25 da @ $1.15 - $28.75. Mach Dept |
| 1857-60 | Melvin, John | lab 28 da @ $1 - $28.00. Rd Dept main stem 13th s-div |
| 1855-42 | Mendenhall, U. | supv @ $45 per mo - $45.00. Rd Way Dept |
| 1857-53 | " | horse hire 30 da @ $.90 - $27.00. Rd Dept main stem 7th s-div |
| 1857-53 | " | supv @ $45 per mo - $45.00. Rd Dept main stem 7th s-div |
| 1857-115 | Meneker, George | boil mkr help 18¾ da @ $1.15 - $21.00. Mach Dept, Balto |
| 1855-56 | Menley, Thomas | splk 21 da @ $1.06 - $22.25. Rd Way Dept |
| 1857-133 | Menser, William | put away eng 13 da @ $1.50 - $19.50. Mach Dept, Fetterman |
| 1855-34 | Menter, James | lab 24 da @$30 per mo - $30.00. Trans Dept main stem |
| 1857-58 | Menton, Michael | lab 29½ da @ $1 - $29.50. Rd Dept main stem 12th s-div |
| 1855-1 | Mentzel, H. | clk @$600 per annum - $50.00. Ofc Hanover St |
| 1855-erratta | " | clk -- instead of $600, $500 per yr |
| 1855-1 | Wm. | collec $1000 per annum - $83.33. Ofc Hanover St |
| 1857-3 | Mentzell, Henry | asst collec @ $50 per mo. Gen Ofc |
| 1857-3 | " | collec @ $83.33 per mo. Gen Ofc |
| 1855-20 | Mentzer, William | fire 20½ da @ $1.75 - $35.85. Trans Dept main stem |
| 1857-30 | " | ton eng'man 2½ da @ $2.50 - $6.25. 3d div |
| 1855-6 | Menzies, James | clk 28 da @ $83.35 per mo - $83.35. Trans Dept main stem |
| 1857-113 | Thomas | mach app 24 da @ $.45 - $10.80. Mach Dept, Balto |
| 1857-8 | Mercer, C. H. | carry mail 30 da @$57.50 per mo - $57.50. Camden sta |
| 1857-37 | Charles H. | mail carr 30 da @ $57.50 per mo - $57.50. Wash br rd, Wash city sta |
| 1857-97 | Cornelius | supv @ $60 per mo - $60.00. N W Va RR, Rd Dept 2d s-div |
| 1857-89 | Elisha | lab 22½ da @ $1.12 - $25.30. grad, Welling Tun |
| 1857-67 | Merchant, B. F. | lab 20 3/4 da @ $1 - $20.75. Rd Dept main stem 18th s-div |
| 1855-61 | G. W. | supv @ $50 per mo - $50.00. Rd Way Dept |
| 1857-67 | " | horse & carts 41½ da @ $1.12 - $46.70. Rd Dept main stem 18th s-div |
| 1857-66 | " | horse hire 23 3/4 da @ $1.12 - $26.70. Rd Dept main stem 18th s-div |
| 1857-66 | " | supv @ $45 per mo - $45.00. Rd Dept main stem 18th s-div |
| 1857-104 | J. R. | lab 20 da @ $.65 - $16.25. NW Va RR Tun |
| 1857-103 | James | fore @ $75 per mo - $75.00. NW Va RR Tun |
| 1855-29 | W. P. | haul & saw firewd 7½ da @ $1 - $7.50. Trans Dept main stem |

## B & O RR EMPLOYEES

| | | | |
|---|---|---|---|
| 1857-26 | Meredith, A. | ton brak 21½ da @ $40 per mo - $34.40. 3d & 4th div |
| 1857-115 | Merley, George | boil mkr help 18 da @ $1 - $18.00. Mach Dept, Balto |
| 1857-99 | Merritt, Valentine | watch 29½ da @ $1 - $29.50. NW Va RR, Rd Dept 4th s-div |
| 1857-103 | Merryfield, A. S. | carp 2 da @ $1.25 - $2.50. NW Va RR Tun |
| 1857-78 | Mersen, George | fire 25 da @ $1.50 - $37.50. lay 2d track |
| 1857-70 | Merson, John | blksmith 18¼ da @ $1.50 - $27.35. Mt Clare sta, Balto |
| 1855-85 | " William | help 24 da @ $1 - $24.00. Mach Dept |
| 1857-118 | " William G. | blksmith help 18 da @ $1 - $18.00. Mach Dept, Balto |
| 1857-117 | " " | blksmith 19¼ da @ $1.65 - $31.75. Mach Dept, Balto |
| 1857-23 | Messe, Frank | ton conduc 25 da @ $60 per mo - $60.00. 3d & 4th div |
| 1857-79 | Messett, Richard | lab 26 3/4 da @ $1 - $26.75. lay 2d track |
| 1855-70 | Messey, Peter | track lay 17 da @ $1.12½ - $19.10. Rd Way Dept |
| 1857-65 | Metze, Matthias | lab 8 da @ $1 - $8.00. Rd Dept main stem 17th s-div |
| 1857-109 | Metzerman, Lewis | mach 11¼ da @ $1.25 - $14.05. Mach Dept, Balto |
| 1857-136 | Metzger, Jacob | blksmith help 20½ da @ $1 - $20.50. Mach Dept, Cumb |
| 1857-71 | Meyer, A. | track lay 23 da @ $1 - $23.00. Camden sta, repair tracks |
| 1857-137 | Miceler, John | lab 22 3/4 da @ $1.25 - $28.45. Mach Dept, Cumb |
| 1857-131 | Michael, Abraham | mach help 18½ da @ $1 - $18.50. Mach Dept, Grafton |
| 1855-40 | " Henry | lab 25 da @ $1 - $25.00. Rd Way Dept |
| 1857-132 | " Isaac | clean eng 32 3/4 da @ $1 - $32.75. Mach Dept, Grafton |
| 1857-8 | " J. | lab 25 da @ $30 per mo - $30.00. Camden sta |
| 1857-25 | " James | ton brak 23½ da @ $40 per mo - $37.60. 2d div |
| 1855-40 | " Thomas | fore 25 da @ $1.25 - $31.25. Rd Way Dept |
| 1857-50 | " " | fore 25 da @ $1.25 - $31.25. Rd Dept main stem 4th s-div |
| 1857-121 | Michel, Peter | paint help 18 da @ $1.15 - $20.70. Mach Dept, Balto |
| 1857-129 | Michulbeck, Lewis | inspec cars @ $32 per mo - $32.00. Mach Dept, Piedmont |
| 1857-115 | Mideman, John | boil mkr help 21 3/4 da @ $1.25 - $27.20. Mach Dept, Balto |
| 1857-88 | Miers, James | blksmith 27 da @ $1.50 - $40.50. grad, Welling Tun |
| 1857-60 | Miland, Michael | lab 27½ da @ $1 - $27.50. Rd Dept main stem 13th s-div |
| 1855-35 | Milbert, M. | car greas 28 da @ $32 per mo - $32.00. Trans Dept main stem |
| 1857-129 | " Martin | greas cars 24½ da @ $1.25 - $30.60. Mach Dept, Piedmont |
| 1855-84 | Miles, John | mach 24½ da @ $1.25 - $30.60. Mach Dept |
| 1855-49 | " " | watch cuts 28 da @ $1 - $28.00. Rd Way Dept |
| 1857-115 | " " | boil mkr help 19½ da @ $1.25 - $24.40. Mach Dept, Balto |
| 1857-61 | " Richard | watch 30 da @ $1 - $30.00. Rd Dept main stem 14th s-div |
| 1857-95 | | lab 22½ da @ $1 - $22.50. Wash br, Rd Dept |

| | | |
|---|---|---|
| 1855-77 | Miles, Samuel | mach 24¼ da @ $1.72 - $41.70. Mach Dept |
| 1857-109 | " | mach 16 da @ $1.72 - $27.50. Mach Dept, Balto |
| 1855-12 | Thomas | conduc & brak 9½ da @ $50 per mo - $19.80. Trans Dept main stem |
| 1855-94 | Miley, Thomas | blksmith 12¼ da @ $1.65 - $20.20. Mach Dept |
| 1857-10 | Milisen, Charles | bur brak 26 da @ $1.15 - $29.90. hp exp, Balto |
| 1855-81 | Millar, D. A. | lab 27 da @ $1.15 - $31.05. Mach Dept |
| 1855-80 | James H. | carp 24 da @ $1.72 - $41.30. Mach Dept |
| 1857-30 | John W. | ton eng'man 1 da @ $3 - $3.00. 4th div |
| 1857-114 | Joseph | iron mould 22 3/4 da @ $1.50 - $34.10. Mach Dept, Balto |
| 1855-80 | O. M. | carp 26½ da @ $1.90 - $50.35. Mach Dept |
| 1855-26 | Miller, August | clean eng 14 da @ $1 - $14.00. Trans Dept main stem |
| 1855-95 | " | lab 13¼ da @ $1 - $13.25. Mach Dept |
| 1857-36 | B. | tele oper 30 da @ $30 per mo - $30.00. Cumb |
| 1855-15 | C. | pass eng'man 21 da @ $3 - $63.00. Trans Dept main stem |
| 1857-21 | Charles | ton conduc 14¼ da @ $50 per mo - $28.50. 1st div |
| 1855-19 | Conrad | ton eng'man 3¼ da @ $3 - $9.75. Trans Dept main stem |
| 1857-121 | D. A. | carp help 20 da @ $1.15 - $23.00. Mach Dept, Balto |
| 1857-72 | Daniel | watch @ $5 per mo - $5.00. Locust Pt, load mat |
| 1855-41 | David | lab 9¼ da @ $1 - $9.25. Rd Way Dept |
| 1855-87 | E. | help 10 da @ $1 - $10.00. Mach Dept |
| 1857-14 | E. D. | clk 30 da @ $50 per mo - $50.00. Piedmont sta |
| 1857-104 | Edward | lab 15½ da @ $1 - $15.50. NW Va RR Tun |
| 1855-14 | F. | brak 14 da @ $40 per mo - $23.35. Trans Dept main stem |
| 1855-16 | G. W. | pass fire 30 da @ $40 per mo - $42.85. Trans Dept main stem |
| 1855-12 | George | conduc & brak 17¼ da @ $50 per mo - $35.95. Trans Dept main stem |
| 1857-131 | " | oil house kpr @ $30 per mo - $30.00. Mach Dept, Grafton |
| 1857-20 | " | pass fire 24 da @ $40 per mo - $32.00. 1st div |
| 1857-22 | " | ton conduc 1 da @ $50 per mo - $2.00. 2d div |
| 1857-22 | George W. | ton conduc 25¼ da @ $50 per mo - $50.50. 2d div |
| 1855-88 | H. | mach 30¼ da @ $1.50 - $45.35. Mach Dept |
| 1855-12 | H. F. | 16¼ da @ $50 per mo - $35.85. Trans Dept main stem |
| 1855-17 | Henry | ton eng'man 10 da @ $2.50 - $25.00. Trans Dept main stem |
| 1857-66 | " | lab 23½ da @ $1 - $23.50. Rd Dept main stem 18th s-div |
| 1855-69 | Hezekiah | lab 16½ da @ $1.12½ - $18.50. Rd Way Dept |
| 1855-15 | J. | pass eng'man 1 da @ $2.50 - $2.50. Trans Dept main stem |
| 1855-9 | J. A. | conduc 4½ da @ $50 per mo - $8.85. Trans Dept main stem |

## B & O RR EMPLOYEES

| | | |
|---|---|---|
| 1855-6 | Miller, J. B. | supt of stock 28 da @ $66.65/per mo - $66.65. Trans Dept main stem |
| 1857-17 | " " | agt 30 da @ $25 per mo - $25.00. Wheeling sta |
| 1857-36 | " " | tele oper 30 da @ $25 per mo - $25.00. Wheeling sta |
| 1855-21 | J. C. | fire 12 da @ $1.75 - $21.00. Trans Dept main stem |
| 1857-19 | J. J. H. | bag mast 30 da @ $45 per mo - $45.00. thr mail & exp |
| 1857-117 | Jacob | blksmith help 23¾ da @ $1.25 - $29.05. Mach Dept, Balto |
| 1855-77 | James | mach 24 da @ $1.45 - $34.80. Mach Dept |
| 1857-127 | James E. | mach 25 3/4 da @ $1.85 - $47.65. Mach Dept, Piedmont |
| 1857-119 | James H. | fore carp @ $55 per mo - $55.00. Mach Dept, Balto |
| 1857-15 | Jesse F. | carry mail 30 da @ $10 per mo -$10.00. Fairmont sta |
| 1855-27 | John | clean eng 18 da @ $1 - $18.00. Trans Dept main stem |
| 1855-69 | " | lab 16½ da @ $1.50 - $24.75. Rd Way Dept |
| 1855-17 | " | ton eng'man 16 da @ $3 - $48.00. Trans Dept main stem |
| 1857-61 | " | lab 28½ da @ $1 - $28.50. Rd Dept main stem 14th s-div |
| 1857-36 | " | tele oper 30 da @ $10 per mo - $10.00. Cumb |
| 1857-31 | John C. | ton eng'man 23 da @ $3 - $69.00. Board Tree Tun |
| 1857-31 | John W. | ton eng'man 32 da @ $3 - $96.00. Board Tree Tun |
| 1857-72 | Jonathan | carp 21 da @ $1.37 - $28.90. Martinsburg depot |
| 1857-132 | Joseph | blksmith app 16½ da @ $.75 - $12.35. Mach Dept, Grafton |
| 1857-113 | " | iron mould 17 3/4 da @ $1.72 - $30.55. Mach Dept, Balto |
| 1857-26 | " | track lay 22½ da @ $1 - $44.40. 3d & 4th div |
| 1857-74 | Lewis | ton brak 17¾ da @ $40 per mo - $22.25. put swit on line of rd |
| 1857-25 | Martin | ton brak 17¾ da @ $40 per mo; 2 da @ $50 per mo - $31.60. 2d div |
| 1857-119 | Oliver M. | carp 22¼ da @ $1.90 - $42.30. Mach Dept, Balto |
| 1855-38 | Peter | lab 8 da @ $1 - $8.00. Rd Way Dept |
| 1857-48 | " | lab 27 da @ $1 - $27.00. Rd Dept main stem 2d s-div |
| 1855-35 | R. | coup 24 da @ $30 per mo - $30.00. Trans Dept main stem |
| 1857-9 | Robert | coup 29½ da @ $30 per mo - $35.40. Mt Clare sta |
| 1855-14 | William | brak 2 da @ $40 per mo - $3.35. Trans Dept main stem |
| 1855-9 | " | conduc 4½ da @ $50 per mo - $9.35. Trans Dept main stem |
| 1855-93 | " | mach 25 da @ $1.60 - $40.00. Mach Dept |
| 1857-137 | " | carp 21 3/4 da @ $1.40 - $30.45. Mach Dept, Cumb |
| 1855-33 | William J. | ton fire 25¾ da @ $1.75 - $44.20. 2d div |
| 1855-91 | Millett, William B. | mach 24¼ da @ $1.62 - $40.45. Mach Dept |
| 1857-26 | | ton brak 33½ da @ $40 per mo - $53.60. 3d & 4th div |
| 1855-64 | Millot, Patk. | lab 16½ da @ $1 - $16.50. Rd Way Dept |

B & O RR EMPLOYEES 245

| | | | |
|---|---|---|---|
| 1857-90 | Mills, James | lab 22 da @ $1 - $22.00. grad, Welling Tun |
| 1857-33 | Samuel | ton fire 25 3/4 da @ $1.75 - $45.05. 3d div |
| 1855-77 | Zack. | mach 19 3/4 da @ $1.55 - $30.60. Mach Dept |
| 1857-109 | " | mach 15 3/4 da @ $1.55 - $24.40. Mach Dept, Balto |
| 1855-17 | Millsbugle, Jno. | ton eng'man 16 da @ $3 - $48.00. Trans Dept main stem |
| 1855-30 | Millscagle, John | ton eng'man 16 da @ $3 - $48.00. 3d div |
| 1855-60 | Miltong, Jacob | fore 24 da @ $1.25 - $30.00. Rd Way Dept |
| 1857-78 | Minegan, Patrick | lab 23 da @ $1 - $23.00. lay 2d track |
| 1855-88 | Mingle, John | carp 17 da @ $1.25 - $21.25. Mach Dept |
| 1857-104 | Mink, Frederick | blksmith 16 da @ $1.35 - $21.60. NW Va RR Tun |
| 1857-117 | Minkhouse, Henry | blksmith 18 da @ $1.50 - $27.00. Mach Dept, Balto |
| 1857-78 | Minnegan, Martin | lab 25 da @ $1 - $25.00. lay 2d track |
| 1855-17 | Minor, Albert | ton eng'man 16½ da @ $2.50 - $41.25. Trans Dept main stem |
| 1855-63 | Henry | lab 15¼ da @ $1 - $15.25. Rd Way Dept |
| 1857-68 | " | lab 21 da @ $1 - $21.00. Rd Dept main stem 19th s-div |
| 1857-77 | Mirely, Frederick | quarry 20 da @ $1 - $20.00. ballast train for 2d track |
| 1857-50 | Missberg, Henry | lab 25 da @ $1 - $25.00. Rd Dept main stem 4th s-div |
| 1857-75 | Misslen, Jno. | lab 17 3/4 da @$1.15 - $20.20. ballast train for 2d track |
| 1857-36 | Mitchell, A. J. | lab 5 da @ $1 - $5.00. J. R. Shrode's wd train 4th div |
| 1857-58 | Daniel | watch 30 da @ $1 - $30.00. Rd Dept main stem 11th s-div |
| 1855-74 | George | lab 20 da @ $1 - $20.00. Rd Way Dept |
| 1857-37 | " | brak 29½ da @ $33.33 per mo - $32.80. Wash br rd, Wash city sta |
| 1857-117 | James | blksmith help 24 3/4 da @ $1 - $24.75. Mach Dept, Balto |
| 1857-95 | John | lab 15 da @ $1 - $15.00. Wash br, Rd Dept |
| 1855-59 | L. | lab 14½ da @ $1 - $14.50. Rd Way Dept |
| 1855-23 | Lewis | fire 15 da @ $1.75 - $26.25. Trans Dept main stem |
| 1857-28 | " | ton eng'man 4¼ da @ $3 - $12.75. 1st div |
| 1855-59 | M. | lab 10½ da @ $1 - $10.50. Rd Way Dept |
| 1855-59 | Mike | lab 10 da @ $1 - $10.00. Rd Way Dept |
| 1855-37 | P. G. | supv @ $55 per mo - $55.00. Rd Way Dept |
| 1855-27 | Pat. | clean eng 28 da @ $1 - $28.00. Trans Dept main stem |
| 1855-31 | Robert | prepar fuel 18 da @ $1 - $18.00. Trans Dept main stem |
| 1855-59 | Thomas | lab 13½ da @ $1 - $13.50. Rd Way Dept |
| 1857-114 | Uriah | iron mould 8 3/4 da @ $1.55 - $13.55. Mach Dept, Balto |
| 1855-56 | William | lab 23 3/4 da @ $1 - $23.75. Rd Way Dept |
| 1857-87 | " | blksmith 22½ da @$1.50 - $33.35. grad, McGuire's Tun |

## B & O RR EMPLOYEES

| |  |  |
|---|---|---|
| 1857-129 | Mitchell, William | clean eng 15 da @ $1 - $15.00. Mach Dept, Piedmont |
| 1857-64 | Mittong, J. M. | fore 30 da @ $1.50 - $45.00. Rd Dept main stem 17th s-div |
| 1855-14 | Mix, John E. | brak 30 da @ $40 per mo - $50.00. Trans Dept main stem |
| 1857-23 | " " | ton conduc 19½ da @ $50 per mo - $39.00. Board Tree Tun |
| 1857-23 | " " | ton conduc 7 da @ $50 per mo - $14.00. 3d & 4th div |
| 1857-35 | Moats, Martin | lab 6 3/4 da @ $1 - $6.75. Edwards' wd train 3d & 4th div |
| 1857-41 | Mobley, H. | eng'man 19½ da @ $2.50 - $48.75. NW Va rd, Athey's wd train |
| 1857-40 | " Horace | ton eng'man 5 da @ $2.50 - $12.50. N W Va rd, Parkersburg sta |
| 1857-19 | " William | pass eng'man 13 da @ $3 - $39.00. 1st div |
| 1857-38 | | pass eng'man 10½ da @ $3 - $31.50. Wash br rd, Wash city sta |
| 1855-15 | Mobly, W. | pass eng'man 7 da @ $3 - $21.00. Trans Dept main stem |
| 1855-19 | Modue, Henry | ton eng'man 14½ da @ $2.50 - $36.25. Trans Dept main stem |
| 1857-41 | Moffatt, James | lab 24 da @ $1 - $24.00. NW Va rd, Athey's wd train |
| 1857-41 | Joseph T. | lab 21 da @ $1 - $21.00. NW Va rd, Athey's wd train |
| 1855-49 | Moffitt, Thomas | watch cuts 28 da @ $1 - $28.00. Rd Way Dept |
| 1857-93 | Mogan, Francis | smith help 13 da @ $1 - $13.00. quarry & haul stone for Board Tree & Littleton Tun |
| 1857-83 | | lab 8½ da @ $1.12 - $9.55. grad, Board Tree Tun |
| 1857-82 | Moister, Charles | bricklay 22 3/4 da @ $2 - $45.50. grad, Board Tree Tun |
| 1857-77 | Molligan, John | lab 22 3/4 da @ $1 - $22.75. lay 2d track |
| 1855-95 | Mollin, N. | lab 24 da @ $1 - $24.00. Mach Dept |
| 1857-129 | Molloy, John | clean eng 31 1/7 da @ $1 - $31.15. Mach Dept, Piedmont |
| 1857-98 | Patrick | watch 30 da @ $1 - $30.00. NW Va RR, Rd Dept 3d s-div |
| 1857-19 | Mome, Henry | pass eng'man 33½ da @ $2.50 - $83.75. 4th div |
| 1855-60 | Monahan, P. | lab 21 da @ $1 - $21.00. Rd Way Dept |
| 1857-88 | Monahon, Anthony | lab 19½ da @ $1.12 - $21.95. grad, Welling Tun |
| 1857-132 | Monchan, Dennis | carp 26 da @ $1.50 - $39.00. Mach Dept, Grafton |
| 1855-82 | Moncreft, Jas. | app 18 da @ $.45 - $8.10. Mach Dept |
| 1855-92 | Monday, Frank | carp 22 3/4 da - $31.90. Mach Dept |
| 1857-62 | Mondell, Wm. | lab 23½ da @ $1 - $23.50. Rd Dept main stem 15th s-div |
| 1857-16 | Monihan, William | deck hand 30 da @ $20 per mo - $20.00. transfer steam Brown Dick--Ohio Riv, bet Benwood & Bellaire |
| 1857-104 | Monnahon, James | miner 23½ da @ $1.12 - $26.45. NW Va RR Tun |
| 1855-45 | Monnett, John | lab 17½ da @ $1 - $17.50. Rd Way Dept |
| 1855-39 | Monngrote, J. | lab 24 da @ $1 - $24.00. Rd Way Dept |
| 1855-97 | Monon, W. T. | fore 26 da @ $1.25 - $32.50. NW Va RR, Rd Dept 2d s-div |
| 1855-35 | Monroe, James | port 28 da @ $10 per mo - $10.00. Trans Dept main stem |

| | | |
|---|---|---|
| 1855-43 | Monroe, John | lab 15 da @ $1 - $15.00. Rd Way Dept |
| 1855-53 | Montage, Christian | stonecut 3¼ da @ $2 - $6.50. Rd Way Dept |
| 1857-74 | Montague, Chris. | stonecut 24 da @$2 - $48.00. repair bridges &c |
| 1857-124 | Joseph | mach app 29¼ da @ $.45 - $13.15. Mach Dept, Martinsburg |
| 1855-33 | Montgomery, G. | lab 24 da @ $30 per mo - $30.00. Trans Dept main stem |
| 1857-8 | George | lab 24 da @ $30 per mo - $28.80. Camden sta |
| 1855-9 | H. | conduc 29 da @ $60 per mo - $60.00. Trans Dept main stem |
| 1855-14 | J. | brak 23 da @ $40 per mo - $38.35. Trans Dept main stem |
| 1857-139 | James | mast mach @ $70 per mo - $70.00. NW Va RR, Mach Dept, Parkersburg |
| 1857-23 | Joseph | ton conduc 29½ da @ $50 per mo - $59.00. Board Tree Tun |
| 1857-23 | " | ton conduc 6 da @ $50 per mo - $12.00. 3d & 4th div |
| 1855-12 | Moody, J. P. | conduc & brak 20 da @ $50 per mo - $43.15. Trans Dept main stem |
| 1857-77 | Moon, Daniel | lab 25 3/4 da @$1 - $25.75. lay 2d track |
| 1857-30 | Schuyler | ton eng'man 4 da @ $2.50 - $10.00. 3d div |
| 1857-33 | " | ton fire 22 da @ $1.75 - $38.50. 3d div |
| 1855-58 | Mooney, John | lab 19½ da @ $1 - $19.50. Rd Way Dept |
| 1855-82 | " | mach 22¼ da @ $1.55 - $31.50. Mach Dept |
| 1855-49 | " | watch cuts 28 da @ $1 - $28.00. Rd Way Dept |
| 1857-87 | " | lab 23 da @$1 - $23.00. grad, McGuire's Tun |
| 1857-108 | " | mach 19¼ da @ $1.60 - $30.80. Mach Dept, Balto |
| 1857-60 | " | watch 30 da @ $1 - $30.00. Rd Dept main stem 13th s-div |
| 1855-62 | M. | lab 10 da @ $1 - $10.00. Rd Way Dept |
| 1857-67 | Michael | lab 21¼ da @ $1 - $21.25. Rd Dept main stem 19th s-div |
| 1855-60 | P. | lab 19 da @ $1 - $19.00. Rd Way Dept |
| 1855-95 | Thomas | lab 7 da @ $1 - $7.00. Mach Dept |
| 1857-135 | " | blksmith help 20¼ da @ $1 - $20.25. Mach Dept, Wheeling |
| 1857-88 | " | lab 21½ da @ $1.12 - $24.00. grad, Welling Tun |
| 1857-11 | " | lab 20 da @ $1.15 - $23.00. Locust Pt |
| 1855-93 | Wm. | mach 29 da @ $1.70 - $49.30. Mach Dept |
| 1857-90 | Moor, George | lab 9 da @ $1.25 - $11.25. grad, Welling Tun |
| 1855-12 | S. | conduc & brak 6 3/4 da @ $50 per mo -$14.05. Trans Dept main stem |
| 1857-48 | William | lab 24½ da @ $1 - $24.50. Rd Dept main stem 2d s-div |
| 1857-82 | Mooran, Martin | lab 22 da @ $1.12 - $24.75. grad, Board Tree Tun |
| 1857-139 | Moore, Barney | clean eng 29½ da @ $1 - $29.50. NW Va RR, Mach Dept, Parkersburg |
| 1855-87 | Edward | help 18½ da @ $1 - $18.50. Mach Dept |
| 1855-66 | George | lab 15½ da @ $1.12½ - $17.40. Rd Way Dept |

# B & O RR EMPLOYEES

| | | | | |
|---|---|---|---|---|
| 1855-19 | Moore, George | ton eng'man 21 da @ $2.25 - $47.25. Trans Dept main stem |
| 1855-27 | " " | ton brak 13½ da @ $40 per mo - $21.60. Board Tree Tun |
| 1855-66 | " Henry | lab 10 3/4 da @ $1.62½ - $17.45. Rd Way Dept |
| 1857-94 | " " | carp 26 da @ $1.65 - $42.90. repair bridges |
| 1857-20 | " James | pass fire 31½ da @ $40 per mo - $42.00. 4th div |
| 1855-43 | " John | lab 11 da @ $1 - $11.00. Rd Way Dept |
| 1857-69 | " " | fore @ $50 per mo - $50.00. Mt Clare sta, Balto |
| 1855-69 | " John R. | attend gashouse 25 da @ $1.25 - $31.25. Rd Way Dept |
| 1857-102 | " " " | gas mkr 30 da @ $1.50 - $45.00. NW Va RR, rwy depot |
| 1855-32 | " John T. | tele oper 28 da @ $33.35 per mo - $33.35. Trans Dept main stem |
| 1857-124 | " Joseph | mach app 27½ da @ $.45 - $12.35. Mach Dept, Martinsburg |
| 1855-57 | " Michael | lab 25 da @ $1.05 - $26.25. Rd Way Dept |
| 1857-91 | " " | stone mason 20 da @ $2 - $40.00. grad, Littleton Tun |
| 1857-133 | " O. | clean eng 12 da @ $1 - $12.00. Mach Dept, Board Tree Tun |
| 1855-32 | " P. | lab 24 da @ $30 per mo - $30.00. Trans Dept main stem |
| 1857-8 | " Patrick | seal 25 da @ $1.50 - $39.00. lay 2d track |
| 1857-79 | " Richard | fore 26 da @ $1.50 - $39.00. lay 2d track |
| 1855-21 | " Schuyler | fire 24 da @ $1.50 - $36.00. Trans Dept main stem |
| 1855-93 | " Walter | clk @ $45 per mo - $45.00. Mach Dept |
| 1855-43 | " William | lab 19 da @ $1 - $19.00. Rd Way Dept |
| 1855-29 | " " | prepar fuel 28 da @ $1 - $28.00. Trans Dept main stem |
| 1857-127 | " William B. | mach help 24 da @ $1 - $24.00. Mach Dept, Piedmont |
| 1857-128 | Moot, John | mach help 25 da @ $.45 - $11.25. Mach Dept, Piedmont |
| 1857-126 | Moran, Anthony | lab 9½ da @ $1 - $9.50. Mach Dept, Martinsburg |
| 1857-65 | " Charles | lab 21½ da @ $1 - $21.50. Rd Dept main stem 17th s-div |
| 1857-62 | " Daniel | watch 30 da @ $1 - $30.00. Rd Dept main stem 15th s-div |
| 1855-48 | " E. | supv @ $50 per mo - $50.00. Rd Way Dept |
| 1855-56 | " Edward | lab 6 da @ $1 - $6.00. Rd Way Dept |
| 1855-60 | " " | fore 16¼ da @ $1 - $16.25. Rd Way Dept |
| 1855-30 | " " | prepar fuel 28 da @ $1 - $28.00. Trans Dept main stem |
| 1857-129 | " " | fill tend 29½ da @ $1 - $29.50. Mach Dept, Piedmont |
| 1857-57 | " F. | lab 25 3/4 da @ $1 - $25.75. Rd Dept main stem 11th s-div |
| 1855-34 | " Frank | swit tend 28 da @ $30 per mo - $30.00. Trans Dept main stem |
| 1855-21 | " James | fire 17⅞ da @ $1.75 - $30.20. Rd Dept main stem |
| 1857-74 | " John | lab 24 da @ $1.12 - $27.00. repair bridges &c |
| 1855-56 | " " | lab 16 da @ $1 - $16.00. Rd Way Dept |

B & O RR EMPLOYEES    249

| | | |
|---|---|---|
| 1855-64 | Moran, John | lab 23 da @ $1 - $23.00. Rd Way Dept |
| 1855-68 | " | lab 22¾ da @ $1 - $22.25. Rd Way Dept |
| 1857-35 | " | lab 14½ da @ $1 - $14.50. Edwards' wd train 3d & 4th div |
| 1857-83 | " | lab 3½ da @ $1.22 - $3.95. grad, Board Tree Tun |
| 1857-97 | " | lab 26 da @ $1 - $26.00. NW Va RR, Rd Dept 2d s-div |
| 1857-103 | " | lab 24 da @ $1.12 - $27.00. NW Va RR Tun |
| 1857-26 | Joseph | ton brak 9 3/4 da @ $40 per mo - $15.60. 3d & 4th div |
| 1857-133 | M. | clean eng 28½ da @ $1 - $28.50. Mach Dept, Fetterman |
| 1855-50 | Michael | watch cuts 29 da @ $1 - $29.00. Rd Way Dept |
| 1855-51 | " | lab 28 da @ $1 - $28.00. Rd Way Dept |
| 1857-132 | " | blksmith help 13¼ da @ $1 - $13.25. Mach Dept, Grafton |
| 1857-92 | " | lab 16½ da @ $1 - $16.50. grad, Littleton Tun |
| 1857-96 | " | lab 20 da @ $1 - $20.00. NW Va RR, Rd Dept 1st s-div |
| 1857-103 | " | lab 12½ da @ $1 - $12.50. NW Va RR Tun |
| 1857-126 | " | prepar fuel 30 da @ $1 - $30.00. Mach Dept, Martinsburg |
| 1857-98 | " | watch 27 da @ $1 - $27.00. NW Va RR, Rd Dept 3d s-div |
| 1855-65 | Mike | lab 8¼ da @ $1 - $8.25. Rd Way Dept |
| 1855-16 | P. | pass fire 1 da @ $40 per mo - $1.45. Trans Dept main stem |
| 1855-56 | Patrick | lab 15 3/4 da @ $1 - $15.75. Rd Way Dept |
| 1857-85 | " | lab 13¼ da @ $1 - $13.25. grad, Board Tree Tun |
| 1857-78 | " | lab 25 da @ $1.25 - $31.25. lay 2d track |
| 1857-81 | " | lab 17 3/4 da @ $1 - $17.75. lay 2d track |
| 1857-98 | " | lab 24½ da @ $1 - $24.50. NW Va RR, Rd Dept 3d s-div |
| 1857-30 | Peter | ton eng'man 17 3/4 da @ $2.50 - $44.35. 4th div |
| 1857-121 | R. H. | paint 18 da @ $1.65 - $29.70. Mach Dept, Balto |
| 1857-112 | R. T. | mach app 21 da @ $.45 - $9.45. Mach Dept, Balto |
| 1857-15 | Robert | watch 30 da @ $1 - $30.00. Fetterman sta |
| 1855-45 | Moraty, Daniel | lab 18½ da @ $1 - $18.50. Rd Way Dept |
| 1857-112 | Morecraft, James | mach app 11 da @ $.75 - $8.25. Mach Dept, Balto |
| 1857-49 | Morely, Rueben | lab 25 da @ $1 - $25.00. Rd Dept main stem 3d s-div |
| 1855-70 | Moren, Edward | 19 da @ $1.22 - $23.20. Rd Way Dept |
| 1855-70 | Michael | track lay 19 da @ $1.12½ - $21.35. Rd Way Dept |
| 1857-33 | Morgan, Frank | ton fire 22 3/4 da @ $1.75 - $39.80. 2d div |
| 1857-69 | James | lab 18 da @ $1.12 - $20.25. Mt Clare sta, Balto |
| 1855-35 | Jeremiah | reg 24 da @ $30 per mo - $30.00. Trans Dept main stem |
| 1857-21 | Jerry | ton conduc 16½ da @ $50 per mo - $33.00. 1st div |

| | | | |
|---|---|---|---|
| 1855-67 | Morgan, Mart. | lab 22 da @ $1 - $22.00. Rd Way Dept |
| 1857-104 | Michael | lab 24 3/4 da @ $1 - $24.75. NW Va RR Tun |
| 1857-17 | Patrick | lab 30 da @ $1 - $30.00. frt transfer force at Bellaire, opp Benwood |
| 1857-101 | " | lab 23½ da @ $1 - $23.50. NW Va RR ballast train |
| 1857-77 | Samuel | quarry 6 da @ $1 - $6.00. ballast train for 2d track |
| 1857-33 | " | ton fire 4 da @ $1.75 - $7.00. 2d div |
| 1857-60 | Thomas | lab 31 da @ $1 - $31.00. Rd Dept main stem 13th s-div |
| 1857-48 | William | lab 23½ da @ $1 - $23.50. Rd Dept main stem 2d s-div |
| 1857-123 | Moriarty, Dennis | rig 20¼ da @ $1.45 - $29.35. Mach Dept, Martinsburg |
| 1855-48 | John | fore 24 da @ $1.25 - $30.00. Rd Way Dept |
| 1855-35 | Morningstar, Susan | clean cars 28 da @ $.89 per mo - $25.00. Trans Dept main stem |
| 1857-90 | Moron, John | lab 11 da @ $1.12 - $12.35. grad, Welling Tun |
| 1855-38 | Moroney, Edward | lab 24 da @ $1 - $24.00. Rd Way Dept |
| 1857-21 | Morrell, Washington | ton conduc 16 3/4 da @ $50 per mo - $33.50. 1st div |
| 1857-22 | William | ton conduc 1½ da @ $50 per mo - $3.00. 2d div |
| 1857-99 | Morrer, Michael C. | watch 30 da @ $1 - $30.00. NW Va RR, Rd Dept 4th s-div |
| 1857-75 | Morris, Edward | lab 25½ da @ $1 - $25.50. ballast train for 2d track |
| 1857-25 | John | ton brak 26 da @ $40 per mo - $41.60. 2d div |
| 1857-136 | Peggy | clean pass cars @ $15 per mo - $15.00. Mach Dept, Wheeling |
| 1857-35 | Richard | lab 23¼ da @ $1 - $23.25. Edwards' wd train 3d & 4th div |
| 1855-1 | Robert | pres secy $1000 per annum - $83.33. Ofc Hanover St |
| 1857-19 | " | pass eng'man 30 da @ $3 - $90.00. 2d div |
| 1857-30 | Morrison, Andy | ton eng'man 1 da @ $2.50 - $2.50. 3d div |
| 1857-87 | James H. | bricklay 16¼ da @ $2.25 - $36.55. grad, Welling Tun |
| 1857-112 | John | mach app 19 da @ $.75 - $14.25. Mach Dept, Balto |
| 1857-132 | Robt. | carp 21 da @ $1.50 - $31.50. Mach Dept, Grafton |
| 1855-74 | Morriss. Andrew | lab 12 da @ $1 - $12.00. Rd Way Dept |
| 1857-85 | Barney | bricklay 2 da @ $2.25 - $4.50. grad, Board Tree Tun |
| 1857-96 | Morrow, R. | lab 28 da @ $1 - $28.00. NW Va RR, Rd Dept 1st s-div |
| 1855-36 | Morton, Frederick | lab 25 da @ $1 - $25 per mo - $26.05. Trans Dept main stem |
| 1857-86 | Mosley, Samuel | fore @ $75 per mo - $75.00. grad, McGuire's Tun |
| 1855-23 | Moss, Philip | fire 11 3/4 da @ $1.75 - $20.55. Trans Dept main stem |
| 1857-71 | Mossberg, Henry | lab 24¼ da @ $1 - $24.25. Mt Clare, repair tracks in yd |
| 1855-11 | Mossburg, Edw. | lab 25 da @ $1 - $25.00. Rd Way Dept |
| 1857-21 | Mott, John | ton conduc 19½ da @ $50 per mo - $39.00. 1st div |
| 1855-12 | | conduc & brak 9¾ da @ $50 per mo - $19.25. Trans Dept main stem |

# B & O RR EMPLOYEES 251

| | | |
|---|---|---|
| 1857-137 | Motter, Amelia | pass car clean @ $20 per mo - $20.00. Mach Dept, Cumb |
| 1857-63 | Jerome | fore 25 da @ $1.25 - $1.25. Rd Dept main stem 16th s-div |
| 1857-24 | Moulsworth, Asbury | ton brak 18½ da @ $40 per mo - $29.60. 1st div |
| 1857-26 | Mountz, John | ton brak 5 da @ $40 per mo; 15 da @ $50 per mo - $38.00. 3d & 4th div |
| 1857-49 | Mounyrote, Jacob | nail 30 da @ $1.05 - $31.50. Rd Dept main stem 3d s-div |
| 1857-49 | Mounystar, Michael | lab 25 da @ $1 - $25.00. Rd Dept main stem 3d s-div |
| 1855-89 | Mowradt, V. | blksmith 24½ da @ $1.25 - $30.60. Mach Dept |
| 1855-39 | Moxley, John | lab 18½ da @ $1 - $18.50. Rd Way Dept |
| 1855-12 | P. | conduc & brak 4½ da @ $10 per mo - $7.50. Trans Dept main stem |
| 1857-32 | Perry | ton fire 24 da @ $33.35 per mo - $32.00. 1st div |
| 1855-12 | R. | conduc & brak 7½ da @ $10 per mo - $3.50. Trans Dept main stem |
| 1857-139 | Muchum, John | carp 3 3/4 da @ $1.67 - $6.25. N W Va RR, Mach Dept, Parkersburg |
| 1855-90 | Mucler, John | help 23 da @ $1.15 - $26.45. Mach Dept |
| 1855-53 | Mudge, William R. | supv @ $45 per mo - $45.00. Rd Way Dept |
| 1857-56 | " | horse hire 25 da @ $1 - $25.00. Rd Dept main stem 10th s-div |
| 1857-56 | " | supv @ $45 per mo - $45.00. Rd Dept main stem 10th s-div |
| 1855-33 | Mulcahry, James | swit 33 da @ $1.25 - $41.25. Trans Dept main stem |
| 1857-123 | Mulcahy, Timothy | mach 13 3/4 da @ $1.75 - $24.05. Mach Dept, Martinsburg |
| 1855-74 | Mulcare, M. | lab 11 3/4 da @ $1 - $11.75. Rd Way Dept |
| 1855-85 | Mules, Thomas | help 22 da @ $1 - $22.00. Mach Dept |
| 1857-96 | Mulheren, John | lab 25 da @ $1 - $25.00. N W Va RR, Rd Dept 1st s-div |
| 1857-104 | Mulherron, Thomas | carp 20½ da @ $1.25 - $25.60. NW Va RR Tun |
| 1857-77 | Mulhoning, John | quarry 8 da @ $1 - $8.00. ballast train for 2d track |
| 1857-63 | Mull, John | lab 14 3/4 da @ $1 - $11.75. Rd Dept main stem 16th s-div |
| 1857-80 | Mullaby, James | lab 21¼ da @ $1 - $21.25. lay 2d track |
| 1857-80 | Michael | lab 20 3/4 da @ $1 - $20.75. lay 2d track |
| 1857-56 | Mulleary, Daniel | lab 24 da @ $1 - $24.00. Rd Dept main stem 10th s-div |
| 1857-129 | Mullen, Edward | fill tend 29½ da @ $1 - $29.50. Mach Dept, Piedmont |
| 1855-28 | James | prepar fuel 28 da @ $1 - $28.00. Trans Dept main stem |
| 1857-37 | Lawrence | brak 7 da @ $33.33 per mo - $7.80. Wash br rd, Wash city sta |
| 1857-129 | P. | lab 19 3/4 da @ $1 - $19.75. Mach Dept, Piedmont |
| 1855-37 | Patrick | lab 25 da @ $1 - $25.00. Rd Way Dept |
| 1857-46 | Muller, Geo. | lab 25 da @ $1 - $25.00. Rd Dept main stem 1st s-div |
| 1855-73 | Mullet, Jno. | tin 19 da @ $1.73 - $32.85. Rd Way Dept |
| 1857-73 | Mullhaear, John | lab 14 3/4 da @ $1 - $14.75. repair bridges &c |
| 1857-76 | Mullican, James | lab 17½ da @ $.97 - $17.05. ballast train for 2d track |
| 1857-108 | mach 18 3/4 da @ $1.55 - $29.05. Mach Dept, Balto |

| | | | |
|---|---|---|---|
| 1857-82 | Mulligan, Andrew | lab 8 da @ $1.12 - $9.00. grad, Board Tree Tun |
| 1857-85 | " Andy | lab 7½ da @ $1.12 - $8.45. grad, Board Tree Tun |
| 1857-88 | " Henry | lab 17½ da @ $1.12 - $19.70. grad, Welling Tun |
| 1857-103 | " James | fore 24 da @ $1.25 - $30.00. NW Va RR Tun |
| 1855-82 | " " | mach 21 da @ $1.45 - $30.45. Mach Dept |
| 1855-67 | " " | mason 24 da @ $2 - $48.00. Rd Way Dept |
| 1857-74 | " Michael | stonecut 22 da @ $2 - $44.00. repair bridges &c |
| 1855-75 | " " | lab 24 da @ $1 - $24.00. Rd Way Dept |
| 1857-50 | " " | lab 25½ da @ $1 - $25.50. Rd Dept main stem 5th s-div |
| 1857-104 | " Thomas | lab. NW Va RR Tun |
| 1857-102 | Mullikin, John | carp 9 3/4 da @ $1.60 - $15.60. NW Va RR, rwy depot |
| 1855-31 | Mullin, M. | prepar fuel 15½ da @ $1 - $15.50. Trans Dept main stem |
| 1857-82 | " Martin | lab 12½ da @ $1.12 - $14.05. grad, Board Tree Tun |
| 1857-129 | " Matthew | lab 14½ da @ $1 - $14.50. Mach Dept, Piedmont |
| 1857-49 | Mulliner, Chartlin | lab 25 da @ $1 - $25.00. Rd Dept main stem 3d s-div |
| 1855-12 | Mullinix, B. A. | conduc & brak 23½ da @ $40 per mo - $39.15. Trans Dept main stem |
| 1857-25 | " Basil A. | ton brak 26 da @$40 per mo - $41.60. 2d div |
| 1855-40 | " C. | lab 24 da @ $1 - $24.00. Rd Way Dept |
| 1855-12 | " John | conduc & brak 24 da @ $50 per mo - $50.00. Trans Dept main stem |
| 1857-77 | Mullone, Thomas | lab 30 da @ $1 - $30.00. lay 2d track |
| 1855-48 | Mulloney, M. | train hand 13½ da @ $1 - $13.50. Rd Way Dept |
| 1857-63 | Mulohill, John | fore 25 da @ $1.25 - $31.25. Rd Dept main stem 16th s-div |
| 1857-96 | " Peter | lab 22 da @ $1 - $22.00. Rd Dept main stem 16th s-div |
| 1855-26 | Mulrenan, John | lab 24 3/4 da @ $1 - $24.75. NW Va RR, Rd Dept 1st s-div |
| 1855-65 | Mulrey, Charles | clean eng 28 da @ $1 - $28.00. Trans Dept main stem |
| 1857-66 | Mulroney, P. | lab 13½ da @ $1 - $13.50. Rd Way Dept |
| 1855-66 | Mulroy, James | lab 25½ da @ $1 - $25.50. Rd Dept main stem 18th s-div |
| 1855-70 | Mulsey, Patrick | lab 20½ da @ $1 - $20.50. Rd Way Dept |
| 1857-92 | Mulvaney, M. | lab 10 3/4 da @ $1 - $10.75. Rd Way Dept |
| 1855-55 | Mulvay, Michael | lab 23 da @ $1 - $23.00. grad, Littleton Tun |
| 1855-55 | Mulvehill, John | lab 24 da @ $1 - $24.00. Rd Way Dept |
| 1857-80 | " Peter | lab 20 da @ $1 - $20.00. Rd Way Dept |
| 1857-129 | Mulvey, Bernard | lab 19½ da @ $1 - $19.75. lay 2d track |
| 1857-88 | " Charles | fill tend 29½ da @ $1 - $29.50. Mach Dept, Piedmont |
| 1857-103 | " Patrick | lab 25¾ da @ $1.12 - $28.40. grad, Welling Tun |
| | Mulvy, Michael | lab 19 da @ $1 - $19.00. NW Va RR depot |

## B & O RR EMPLOYEES 253

| | | | |
|---|---|---|---|
| 1855-6 | Muncks, John | clk 28 da @ $62.50 per mo - $62.50. Trans Dept main stem |
| 1857-8 | " | rec clk 30 da @ $58.35 per mo - $58.35. Camden sta |
| 1857-22 | Munday, Peter | ton conduc 16 3/4 da @$50 per mo - $33.50. 2d div |
| 1855-29 | Mundell, B. | prepar fuel 24 da @ $30 per mo - $30.00. Trans Dept main stem |
| 1857-108 | Murdoch, Charles N. | draught @ $35 per mo - $35.00. Mach Dept, Balto |
| 1855-36 | J. | Lab 24¼ da @ $25 per mo - $25.25. Trans Dept main stem |
| 1855-25 | Murdock, Robert | bur driv 28 da @$30 per mo - $32.50. Trans Dept main stem |
| 1857-129 | Murphy, Daniel | clean eng 31 1/7 da @ $1 - $31.15. Mach Dept, Piedmont |
| 1857-64 | " | lab 5 da @ $1 - $5.00. Rd Dept main stem 17th s-div |
| 1855-50 | Darby | watch cuts 28 da @ $1 - $28.00. Rd Way Dept |
| 1857-63 | " | watch 30 da @ $1 - $30.00. Rd Dept main stem 16th s-div |
| 1857-47 | Dennis | lab 24 da @ $1 - $24.00. Rd Dept main stem 1st s-div |
| 1855-71 | Edw. | help 24 da @ $1.15 - $27.60. Rd Way Dept |
| 1857-70 | " | help 18⅞ da @ $1.06 - $19.35. Mt Clare sta, Balto |
| 1855-62 | G. | lab 23 da @ $1 - $23.00. Rd Way Dept |
| 1857-67 | Garret | lab 14½ da @ $1 - $14.50. Rd Dept main stem 19th s-div |
| 1855-92 | Henry | help 32¼ da @ $1 - $32.25. Mach Dept |
| 1855-59 | Hugh | lab 24 da @ $1 - $24.00. Rd Way Dept |
| 1857-62 | " | watch 30 da @ $1 - $23.00. Rd Dept main stem 15th s-div |
| 1855-29 | James | haul & saw firewd 16½ da @ $1 - $16.50. Trans Dept main stem |
| 1855-50 | " | watch cuts 28 da @$1 - $28.00. Rd Way Dept |
| 1857-126 | " | dry sand 30 da @ $1 - $30.00. Mach Dept, Martinsburg |
| 1857-102 | " | lab 20½ da @ $1 - $20.50. NW Va RR, rwy depot. |
| 1857-127 | " | mach help @ $15.75 per mo - $15.75. Mach Dept, Piedmont |
| 1857-63 | " | watch 30 da @ $1 - $30.00. Rd Dept main stem 16th s-div |
| 1857-84 | Jeremiah | carp 22 da @ $1.12 - $24.75. grad, Board Tree Tun |
| 1857-133 | John | clean eng 23 da @ $1 - $23.00. Mach Dept, Fetterman |
| 1857-136 | " | fill tend @ $30 per mo - $30.00. Mach Dept, Wheeling |
| 1857-35 | " | fire 2 da @ $1.75 - $3.50. Edwards' wd train 3d & 4th div |
| 1857-85 | " | fire 5 da @ $1.75 - $8.75. grad, Board Tree Tun |
| 1857-90 | " | lab 12 da @ $1.12 - $13.50. grad, Welling Tun |
| 1855-94 | Joseph | app 35¾ da @ $.45 - $15.85. Mach Dept |
| 1855-31 | L. B. | prepar fuel 28 da @ $1 - $28.00. Trans Dept main stem |
| 1855-92 | L. B. | help 24½ da @ $1 - $24.25. Mach Dept |
| 1857-68 | Larry | pump water @ $35 per mo - $35.00. Rd Dept main stem 19th s-div |
| 1855-38 | M. | lab 25 da @ $1 - $25.00. Rd Way Dept |

## B & O RR EMPLOYEES

| ID | Name | Entry |
|---|---|---|
| 1855-65 | Murphy, M. | lab 12½ da @ $1 - $12.50. Rd Way Dept |
| 1855-31 | " | prepar fuel 28 da @ $1 - $28.00. Trans Dept main stem |
| 1855-52 | " | lab 22½ da @ $1. Rd Way Dept |
| 1857-136 | Michael | fill tend @ $30 per mo - $30.00. Mach Dept, Wheeling |
| 1857-59 | " | lab 26¼ da @ $1 - $26.50. Rd Dept main stem 13th s-div |
| 1855-96 | Mike | lab 21 da @ $1.10 - $23.10. Mach Dept |
| 1857-114 | " | iron mould help 18 da @ $1.10 - $19.80. Mach Dept, Balto |
| 1857-63 | Nicholas | lab 20¼ da @ $1 - $20.25. Rd Dept main stem 16th s-div |
| 1855-33 | P. | lab 2½ da @ $30 per mo - $3.10. Trans Dept main stem |
| 1855-47 | Patrick | lab 23 da @ $1 - $23.00. Rd Way Dept |
| 1855-57 | " | lab 18 da @ $1 - $18.00. Rd Way Dept |
| 1855-73 | " | lab 24½ da @ $1 - $24.50. Rd Way Dept |
| 1855-75 | " | lab 19 da @ $1 - $19.00. Rd Way Dept |
| 1855-33 | " | port 28 da @ $30 per mo - $30.00. Trans Dept main stem |
| 1857-76 | " | dril 24 da @ $1.10 - $26.40. ballast train for 2d track |
| 1857-71 | " | lab 24 da @ $1 - $24.00. Mt Clare, repair tracks in yd |
| 1857-98 | " | lab 23½ da @ $1 - $23.50. NW Va RR, Rd Dept 3d s-div |
| 1857-94 | " | lab 9½ da @ $1 - $9.50. quarry & haul stone for Board Tree & Littleton Tun |
| 1857-51 | " | lab 21½ da @ $1 - $21.50. Rd Dept main stem 5th s-div |
| 1857-59 | " | lab 25½ da @ $1 - $25.50. Rd Dept main stem 12th s-div |
| 1857-18 | " | pass train brak 30 da @ $30 per mo - $30.00. thr mail & exp |
| 1857-11 | Peter | lab 25 da @ $30 per mo - $30.00. Locust Pt |
| 1855-60 | Thomas | lab 24 da @ $1 - $24.00. Rd Way Dept |
| 1855-58 | " | nail 28 da @ $1 - $28.00. Rd Way Dept |
| 1857-41 | " | fire 5 da @ $1.75 - $8.75. NW Va rd, Athey's wd train |
| 1857-83 | " | lab 7 da @ $1.12 - $7.85. grad, Board Tree Tun |
| 1857-91 | " | lab 17½ da @ $1 - $17.50. grad, Welling Tun |
| 1857-96 | " | lab 24½ da @ $1 - $24.50. NW Va RR, Rd Dept 1st s-div |
| 1857-59 | " | lab 30 da @ $1 - $30.00. Rd Dept main stem 13th s-div |
| 1857-41 | Tim. | ton fire 19 da @ $1.75 - $33.25. NW Va rd, Parkersburg sta |
| 1855-71 | William | lab 4 da @ $1 - $4.00. Mt Clare, repair tracks in yd |
| 1855-12 | " | conduc & brak 22½ da @ $40 per mo - $40.50. Trans Dept main stem |
| 1857-64 | " | lab 25½ da @ $1 - $25.50. Rd Dept main stem 17th s-div |
| 1857-131 | Murr, Jacob | mach 22 3/4 da @ $1.50 - $31.10. Mach Dept, Grafton |
| 1857-108 | Murray, Albert | mach 16 3/4 da @ $1.60 - $26.80. Mach Dept, Balto |
| 1857-109 | " | mach 14 da @ $1.80 - $25.20. Mach Dept, Balto |

# B & O RR EMPLOYEES 255

| | | | |
|---|---|---|---|
| 1855-57 | Murray, Charles | | lab 28 da @ $1.05 - $29.40. Rd Way Dept |
| 1857-59 | " | | watch 30 da @ $1 - $30.00. Rd Dept main stem 12th s-div |
| 1855-63 | | Hugh | lab 21 da @ $1 - $21.00. Rd Way Dept |
| 1857-77 | | " | lab 26 da @ $1 - $26.00. lay 2d track |
| 1855-59 | | James | lab 15 da @ $1 - $15.00. Rd Way Dept |
| 1857-34 | | " | dry sand 30 da @ $1 - $30.00. Board Tree Tun |
| 1857-71 | | " | track lay 27 da @ $1 - $27.00. Camden sta, repair tracks |
| 1855-49 | | John | watch cuts 14 da @ $1 - $14.00. Rd Way Dept |
| 1857-67 | | " | fore 25 da @ $1.25 - $31.25. Rd Dept main stem 18th s-div |
| 1857-96 | | " | lab 24 3/4 da @ $1 - $24.75. NW Va RR, Rd Dept 1st s-div |
| 1857-54 | | " | lab 25 da @ $1 - $25.00. Rd Dept main stem 8th s-div |
| 1855-62 | | Joseph | lab 13 da @ $1 - $13.00. Rd Way Dept |
| 1857-68 | | " | fore 24½ da @ $1.25 - $30.60. Rd Dept main stem 19th s-div |
| 1855-47 | | M. | lab 19½ da @ $1 - $19.50. Rd Way Dept |
| 1855-58 | | " | lab 27 da @ $1 - $27.00. Rd Way Dept |
| 1855-62 | | " | lab 20 da @ $1 - $20.00. Rd Way Dept |
| 1857-85 | | Matthew Jr | tele oper @ $30 per mo - $30.00. grad, Board Tree Tun |
| 1857-68 | | Michael | fore 25½ da @ $1.25 - $31.85. Rd Dept main stem 19th s-div |
| 1857-86 | | " | lab 20¼ da @ $1 - $20.25. grad, McGuire's Tun |
| 1857-86 | | " | lab 21½ da @ $1 - $21.50. grad, McGuire's Tun |
| 1857-59 | | " | lab 27 da @ $1 - $27.00. Rd Dept main stem 13th s-div |
| 1857-34 | | " | ton fire 8 da @ $1.75 - $13.95. 4th div |
| 1855-41 | | P. | help 16¼ da @ $1 - $16.25. Rd Way Dept |
| 1855-87 | | Patrick | help 24¼ da @ $1.15 - $27.90. Mach Dept |
| 1855-28 | | " | prepar fuel 12½ da @ $1 - $12.50. Trans Dept main stem |
| 1857-83 | | " | lab 25½ da @ $1.12 - $28.70. grad, Board Tree Tun |
| 1857-123 | | " | mach 20 da @ $1.15 - $23.00. Mach Dept, Martinsburg |
| 1857-46 | | Peter | lab 22 da @ $1 - $22.00. Rd Dept main stem 1st s-div |
| 1857-33 | | Richard | ton fire 5 da @ $1.75 - $8.75. 3d div |
| 1855-67 | | Robert | supt masonry @ $75 per mo - $75.00. Rd Way Dept |
| 1857-84 | | " | 6 horses hire 150 da @ $1 - $150.00. grad, Board Tree Tun |
| 1857-81 | | " | supt @ $75 per mo - $75.00. grad, Board Tree Tun |
| 1857-71 | | Thomas | help 21 da @ $1 - $21.00. Mt Clare sta, Balto |
| 1857-76 | Murrey, Patrick | | dril 14½ da @ $1.02 - $14.85. ballast train for 2d track |
| 1857-111 | Murrow, Daniel | | mach help 18 da @ $1 - $18.00. Mach Dept, Balto |
| 1855-79 | Murry, Albert | | app 22¼ da @ $.55 - $12.25. Mach Dept |

B & O RR EMPLOYEES

| Year-Page | Name | Description |
|---|---|---|
| 1855-37 | Murry, James | lab 20 3/4 da @ $1 - $20.75. Rd Way Dept |
| 1855-89 | " | mach @ $75 per mo - $75.00. Mach Dept |
| 1855-61 | John | fore 26 da @ $1.25 - $32.50. Rd Way Dept |
| 1855-61 | M. | fore 26 da @ $1.25 - $32.50. Rd Way Dept |
| 1857-101 | Patrick | lab 21½ da @ $1 - $21.50. NW Va RR ballast train |
| 1857-96 | " | lab 24 da @ $1 - $24.00. NW Va RR, Rd Dept 1st s-div |
| 1857-77 | " | quarry 8 da @ $1 - $8.00. ballast train for 2d track |
| 1857-122 | Murson, Charles | eng clean 22½ da @ $1 - $22.50. Mach Dept, Balto |
| 1857-80 | Murtaugh, John | fire 11 da @ $2 - $22.00. lay 2d track |
| 1857-80 | " | lab 15 da @ $1.25 - $18.75. lay 2d track |
| 1857-66 | Murther, Henry | lab 25½ da @ $1 - $25.50. Rd Dept main stem 18th s-div |
| 1855-46 | Murtrugh, John | fore 24½ da @ $1.25 - $30.60. Rd Way Dept |
| 1855-25 | Musgrave, Stephen | clean eng 29 da @ $1.15 - $33.35. Trans Dept main stem |
| 1857-122 | Musgrove, John | eng clean 8 3/4 da @ $1 - $8.75. Mach Dept, Balto |
| 1855-40 | S. | put away eng &c 28½ da @ $1.15 - $32.75. Mach Dept, Balto |
| 1855-23 | Musseter, John | lab 24 da @ $1 - $24.00. Rd Way Dept |
| 1857-32 | Mussetter, Charles | fire 16¼ da @ $1.75 - $28.45. Trans Dept main stem |
| 1857-18 | Lewis | ton fire 21½ da @ $1.75 - $42.45. 1st div |
| 1857-73 | Musson, James | pass train brak 5 da @ $33.35 per mo - $5.55. thr mail & exp |
| 1857-62 | Muth, John | mason 25 da @ $2 - $50.00. repair water sta, M.S. & P.B. |
| 1857-133 | Muzum, Benj. | pump water @ $35 per mo - $35.00. Rd Dept main stem 15th s-div |
| 1855-12 | Myers, Jesse | clean eng 30 da @ $1 - $30.00. Mach Dept, Fetterman |
| 1857-112 | Charles | conduc & brak 10 da @ $50 per mo - $23.85. Trans Dept main stem |
| 1855-89 | Christ. | mach app 23 da @ $.55 - $12.65. Mach Dept, Balto |
| 1857-137 | D. B. | yd supt @ $45 per mo - $45.00. Mach Dept |
| 1857-108 | " | carp @ $45 per mo - $45.00. Mach Dept, Cumb |
| 1655-23 | Frederick | storekpr clk @ $30 per mo - $30.00. Mach Dept, Balto |
| 1855-69 | George | fire 15 da @ $1.75 - $26.25. Trans Dept main stem |
| 1855-69 | " | lab 19½ da @ $1 - $19.50. Rd Way Dept |
| 1857-85 | " | lab 10 da @ $1 - $10.00. grad, Board Tree Tun |
| 1857-117 | H. | blksmith 17¼ da @ $1.45 - $25.00. Mach Dept, Balto |
| 1857-55 | Henry | lab 24 da @ $1 - $24.00. Rd Dept main stem 9th s-div |
| 1855-85 | Herman | help 22 da @ $1 - $22.00. Mach Dept |
| 1855-12 | J. O. | conduc & brak 16 da @ $50 per mo - $33.35. Trans Dept main stem |
| 1857-15 | Jacob M. | lab 25 da @ $30 per mo - $30.00. Grafton sta |
| 1855-69 | James | driv 22 da @ $1.37½ - $30.25. Rd Way Dept |

B & O RR EMPLOYEES 257

| | | | |
|---|---|---|---|
| 1855-96 | Myers, John | lab 29 3/4 da @ $1.10 - $32.75. Mach Dept |
| 1855-73 | " | lab 24 da @ $1 - $24.00. Rd Way Dept |
| 1857-114 | " | iron mould help 17 3/4 da @ $1.10 - $19.55. Mach Dept, Balto |
| 1857-71 | Samuel | load mat 24 da @ $1 - $24.00. Mt Clare, repair tracks in yd |
| 1855-23 | Thomas | fire 24 da @ $33.35 per mo - $33.35. Trans Dept main stem |
| 1857-15 | Naff, Charles | swit tend 30 da @ $1 - $30.00. Grafton sta |
| 1855-13 | " | conduc & brak 24½ da @ $30 per mo - $30.30. Trans Dept main stem |
| 1857-24 | Nagle, Michael | ton brak 26 3/4 da @ $30 per mo - $32.10. 1st div |
| 1857-90 | Naill, D. | stone mason 1¼ da @ $2 - $2.50. grad, Welling Tun |
| 1855-14 | Nalgal, Michael | brak 18 3/4 da @ $40 per mo - $31.25. Trans Dept main stem |
| 1857-82 | Nalley, Henry | bricklay 6 da @ $2 - $12.00. grad, Board Tree Tun |
| 1855-74 | Levi | lab 23½ da @ $1 - $23.50. Rd Way Dept |
| 1855-74 | " | lab 24 da @ $1 - $24.00. Rd Way Dept |
| 1857-95 | Nally, Henry | nail 30 da @ $1.05 - $31.50. Wash br, Rd Dept |
| 1857-95 | Richard | lab 20 da @ $1 - $20.00. Wash br, Rd Dept |
| 1857-103 | Narry, John | lab 19½ da @ $1.12 - $21.95. NW Va RR Tun |
| 1857-66 | Nash, Ephraim | lab 22½ da @ $1 - $22.50. Rd Dept main stem 18th s-div |
| 1857-88 | Naughton, John | lab 27 da @ $1 - $27.00. Rd Dept main stem 1st s-div |
| 1855-27 | M. | lab 14½ da @ $1.12 - $16.30. grad, Welling Tun |
| 1855-47 | " | clean eng 28 da @ $1 - $28.00. Trans Dept main stem |
| 1857-129 | Michael | lab 22 da @ $1 - $22.00. Rd Way Dept |
| 1857-87 | " | clean eng 31 3/4 da @ $1 - $1.15 - $26.50. Mach Dept, Piedmont |
| 1857-91 | Peter | lab 23 3/4 da @ $1 - $23.75. grad, Mc Guire's Tun |
| 1857-104 | " | lab 23½ da @ $1 - $23.25. grad, Welling Tun |
| 1857-81 | Naval, John | lab 22 3/4 da @ $1.12 - $25.60. NW Va RR Tun |
| 1857-81 | Navey, Peter | lab 18 da @ $1.12 - $20.25. grad, Board Tree Tun |
| 1857-93 | Nay, Edw. | lab 23½ da @ $1.12 - $26.45. grad, Board Tree Tun |
| 1855-85 | Naydenire, W. | fore 26 da @ $1.50 - $39.00. quarry & haul stone for Board Tree & Littleton Tun |
| 1857-74 | Nayler, Jacob | help 23½ da @ $1 - $23.50. Mach Dept |
| 1857-120 | Naylor, Nelson | blksmith 24½ da @ $1.50 - $36.75. repair bridges &c |
| 1855-81 | " | carp 18 da @ $1.75 - $31.50. Mach Dept, Balto |
| 1857-103 | Neagel, Thomas | carp 24 da @ $1.65 - $39.60. Mach Dept |
| 1855-28 | Neale, Robert | lab 23 da @ $1 - $23.00. NW Va RR Tun |
| 1857-125 | " | reg eng 16 3/4 da @ $1.15 - $19.25. Trans Dept main stem |
| 1857-76 | Neartney, Michael | put away eng &c 24 da @ $1.50 - $36.00. Mach Dept, Martinsburg |
| | | blast 23 da @ $1.25 - $28.75. ballast train for 2d track |

258  B & O RR EMPLOYEES

| | | |
|---|---|---|
| 1857-77 | Neartney, Patrick | quarry 8 da @ $1 - $8.00. ballast train for 2d track |
| 1857-63 | Neary, Charles | lab 25 da @ $1 - $25.00. Rd Dept main stem 16th s-div |
| 1855-38 | Nee, John | lab 21 da @ $1 - $21.00. Rd Way Dept |
| 1855-38 | Nee, Martin | lab 19½ da @ $1 - $19.50. Rd Way Dept |
| 1855-69 | Needham, Thomas | help 24¼ da @ $1 - $24.25. Mach Dept |
| 1855-17 | " | lab 8½ da @ $1 - $8.50. Rd Way Dept |
| 1857-87 | " | ton eng'man 1 da @ $2 - $2.00. Trans Dept main stem |
| 1857-86 | Neel, Samuel | lab 23 3/4 da @ $1 - $23.75. grad, McGuire's Tun |
| 1855-15 | Neer, J. | bricklay 20¼ da @ $2.25 - $45.55. grad, McGuire's Tun |
| 1855-4 | J. W. | pass eng'man 4 da @$2.50 - $10.00. Trans Dept main stem |
| 1855-19 | Jno. W. | ton eng'man 2 da @ $2.50 - $5.00. Trans Dept, Wash br |
| 1857-121 | Neetze, Oliver T. | ton eng'man 9⅖ da @ $2.50 - $23.10. Trans Dept main stem |
| 1857-132 | Neff, Henry | paint 18 da @ $1.65 - $29.70. Mach Dept, Balto |
| 1857-54 | Neheley, Patrick | carp 19 3/4 da @ $1.25 - $24.70. Mach Dept, Grafton |
| 1857-13 | Neil, John | lab 19 da @ $1 - $19.00. Rd Dept main stem 8th s-div |
| 1855-71 | Neilson, A. J. | swit'man at Opequon 30 da @ $35¢ per mo - $35.00. Martinsburg |
| 1857-69 | " | paint 24 da @ $1.75 - $42.00. Rd Way Dept |
| 1857-86 | James | fore @ $50 per mo - $50.00. Mt Clare sta, Balto |
| 1855-58 | Neling, Patrick | bricklay 9 3/4 da @ $2.25 - $21.90. grad, McGuire's Tun |
| 1857-51 | Nelligan, Jerry | lab 24 da @ $1 - $24.00. Rd Way Dept |
| 1855-75 | Nelligon, Jerry | lab 24 da @ $1 - $24.00. Rd Dept main stem 5th s-div |
| 1855-86 | Nelson, James | lab 17 da @ $1 - $17.00. Rd Way Dept |
| 1857-108 | " | mach 23 da @ $1.72 - $39.60. Mach Dept |
| 1857-120 | Joseph P. | mach 18 da @ $1.60 - $28.80. Mach Dept, Balto |
| 1855-81 | Wm. | carp 17 da @ $1.50 - $25.50. Mach Dept, Balto |
| 1857-15 | Neptune, A. | carp 15 3/4 da @ $1.55 - $24.40. Mach Dept |
| 1857-18 | Amos | carry mail 30 da @ $5 per mo - $5.00. Farmington sta |
| 1857-75 | Nerheney, James | pass train brak 30 da @ $33.35 per mo - $33.35. w end |
| 1857-76 | Patrick | fire 8 da @ $1.28 - $10.25. ballast train for 2d track |
| 1855-32 | Nesbit, J. | lab 14 3/4 da @ $.97 - $14.35. ballast train for 2d track |
| 1857-36 | J. G. | tele oper 28 da @ $30 per mo - $30.00. Trans Dept main stem |
| 1855-25 | Ness, William | tele oper 30 da @ $30 per mo - $30.00. Oakland |
| 1857-122 | " | clean eng 27½ da @ $1.15 -$31.60. Trans Dept main stem |
| 1857-82 | Neston, Michael | eng clean 26½ da @ $1.15 -$18.95. Mach Dept, Balto |
| 1857-101 | Neswanger, R. P. | lab 7 da @ $1.12 - $7.85. grad, Board Tree Tun |
| | | fore @ $60 per mo - $60.00. NW Va RR ballast train |

B & O RR EMPLOYEES 259

| Ref | Name | Details |
|---|---|---|
| 1855-86 | Neumier, Max. | mach 27½ da @ $1.35 - $37.15. Mach Dept |
| 1855-28 | Neville, M. | reg eng 16½ da @ $1.15 - $18.95. Trans Dept main stem |
| 1857-120 | " Wm. J. | carp 16½ da @ $1.50 - $24.75. Mach Dept, Balto |
| 1857-101 | Nevils, Jerome | lab 22 da @ $.75 - $16.50. NW Va RR ballast train |
| 1855-30 | Nevins, James | fill tend 28 da @ $1 - $28.00. Trans Dept main stem |
| 1857-62 | Newbrough, Joshua | fore 25 da @ $1.25 - $31.25. Rd Dept main stem 15th s-div |
| 1857-89 | Newel, Mark | lab 13 da @ $1.12 - $14.60. grad, Welling Tun |
| 1855-13 | Newell, James | conduc & brak 16 3/4 da @ $40 per mo - $28.75. Trans Dept main stem |
| 1857-122 | Newhouse, John | lab 18 da @ $1 - $18.00. Mach Dept, Balto |
| 1857-64 | Newland, Patrick | lab 25½ da @ $1 - $25.50. Rd Dept main stem 17th s-div |
| 1855-13 | Newman, Charles | conduc & brak 18 3/4 da @ $40 per mo - $31.25. Trans Dept main stem |
| 1855-19 | " David | ton eng'man 9½ da @ $3 - $27.75. Trans Dept main stem |
| 1857-31 | " | ton eng'man 17 da @ $3 - $51.00. Board Tree Tun |
| 1857-29 | " | ton eng'man 2 da @ $3 - $6.00. 2d div |
| 1857-123 | Newmyer, Max | mach 23 da @ $1.50 - $34.50. Mach Dept, Martinsburg |
| 1857-120 | Newton, Isaac | carp 17½ da @ $1.50 - $26.25. Mach Dept, Balto |
| 1855-77 | " Thomas | mach 22 3/4 da @ $1.50 - $34.10. Mach Dept |
| 1857-110 | " " | mach 18 3/4 da @ $1.50 - $28.10. Mach Dept, Balto |
| 1855-81 | " W. T. | lab 28 da @ $1.15 - $32.20. Mach Dept |
| 1855-82 | " Wm. | mach 21 da @ $1.65 - $34.65. Mach Dept |
| 1857-108 | " Wm. S. | mach 18 da @ $1.65 - $29.70. Mach Dept, Balto |
| 1857-92 | Nicholas, John | lab 25¼ da @ $1 - $25.25. grad, Littleton Tun |
| 1857-66 | " Thomas | lab 22½ da @ $1 - $22.50. Rd Dept main stem 18th s-div |
| 1857-98 | Nicholson, John | lab 11¼ da @ $1 - $11.25. NW Va RR, Rd Dept 3d s-div |
| 1855-19 | " Joseph | ton eng'man 15½ da @ $3 - $46.50. Trans Dept main stem |
| 1855-93 | " M. | tin 22 3/4 da - $35.20. Mach Dept |
| 1857-41 | " Martin | lab 17 da - $17.00. NW Va rd, Athey's wd train |
| 1857-128 | " Michael | cop'smith & tin 26¾ da @ $1.75 - $45.95. Mach Dept, Piedmont |
| 1855-61 | Niclous, Thomas | lab 21 da @ $1 - $21.00. Rd Way Dept |
| 1857-26 | Nicodemus, A. | ton brak 30¼ da @ $40 per mo - $48.40. 3d & 4th div |
| 1857-22 | Nigh, Daniel R. | ton conduc 1 da @ $50 per mo - $2.00. 2d div |
| 1857-61 | Nightengale, Daniel | lab 28½ da @ $1 - $28.50. Rd Dept main stem 14th s-div |
| 1857-122 | Nihoff, James | carter 18 da @ $1 - $18.00. Mach Dept, Balto |
| 1855-28 | Niland, Patrick | prepar fuel 15 da @ $1 - $15.00. Trans Dept main stem |
| 1857-60 | " | lab 32 da @ $1 - $32.00. Rd Dept main stem 13th s-div |
| 1857-115 | Niles, George | boil mkr 17 da @ $1.35 - $22.95. Mach Dept, Balto |

260                       B & O RR EMPLOYEES

| | | | |
|---|---|---|---|
| 1857-81 | Nilon, Michael | lab 20½ da @ $1.12 - $23.05. grad, Board Tree Tun |
| 1857-81 | " | lab 21 da @ $1.12 - $23.60. grad, Board Tree Tun |
| 1857-50 | Nisnanger, Stephen | lab 23 3/4 da @ $1 - $23.75. Rd Dept main stem 4th s-div |
| 1855-23 | Niswaner, S. J. | fire 12 3/4 da @ $1.75 - $22.30. Trans Dept main stem |
| 1857-78 | Nockton, Michael | lab 24 3/4 da @ $1 - $24.75. lay 2d track |
| 1857-59 | Nocton, James | lab 26 da @ $1 - $26.00. Rd Dept main stem 13th s-div |
| 1857-85 | John | lab 6½ da @ $1.12 - $7.30. grad, Board Tree Tun |
| 1857-55 | Noel, Robert | lab 23 3/4 da @ $1 - $23.75. Rd Dept main stem 9th s-div |
| 1857-62 | Noland, Thomas | fore 25 da @ $1.25 - $31.25. Rd Dept main stem 15th s-div |
| 1857-58 | Noland, Henry | lab 19 3/4 da @ $1 - $19.75. lay 2d track |
| 1857-56 | William | fore 25½ da @ $1.25 - $31.55. Rd Dept main stem 12th s-div |
| 1855-59 | Nolen, Michael | lab 22½ da @ $1 - $22.50. Rd Dept main stem 10th s-div |
| 1857-61 | Noon, Thomas | fore 24 da @ $1.25 - $30.00. Rd Way Dept |
| 1855-67 | Noon, James | lab 25 da @ $1 - $25.00. Rd Dept main stem 14th s-div |
| 1857-78 | " | tend to masons 16½ da @ $1 - $16.50. Rd Way Dept |
| 1857-79 | " | lab 25 3/4 da @ $1 - $25.75. lay 2d track |
| 1857-39 | " | lab 9 3/4 da @ $1 - $9.75. lay 2d track |
| 1855-67 | Michael | lab 25 da @ $30 per mo - $30.00. NW Va rd, Parkersburg sta |
| 1857-86 | " | tend to masons 22 da @ $1 - $22.00. Rd Way Dept |
| 1857-93 | Patrick | lab 22½ da @ $1.12 - $25.30. grad, McGuire's Tun |
| 1855-60 | " | smith help 23½ da @ $1 - $23.25. quarry & haul stone for Board Tree & Littleton Tun |
| 1857-83 | Thomas | lab 22 3/4 da @ $1 - $22.75. Rd Way Dept |
| 1855-67 | " | lab 25 da @ $1.12 - $28.10. grad, Board Tree Tun |
| 1857-39 | " | lab 22 da @ $1 - $22.00. Rd Way Dept |
| 1857-56 | Noonan, Michael | lab 25 da @ $30 per mo - $30.00. NW Va rd, Parkersburg sta |
| 1855-58 | Noone, Owen | lab 24 da @ $1 - $24.00. Rd Dept main stem 10th s-div |
| 1857-60 | " | lab 24 da @ $1 - $24.00. Rd Way Dept |
| 1855-48 | Norman, D. | lab 29½ da @ $1 - $29.50. Rd Dept main stem 13th s-div |
| 1857-113 | Richard | train hand 19 3/4 da @ $.45 - $19.75. Rd Way Dept |
| 1855-81 | Norris, Geo. | mach app 23 da @$.45 - $10.35. Mach Dept, Balto |
| 1855-53 | Norris, George | mech 27½ da @ $1.15 - $31.60. Mach Dept |
| 1855-53 | John | lab 23½ da @ $1 - $23.50. Rd Dept main stem 7th s-div |
| 1857-74 | " | carp 23 da @ $1.25 - $28.75. Rd Way Dept |
| 1855-53 | William | carp 23½ da @ $1.50 - $35.25. repair bridges &c |
| 1857-73 | " | carp 24 da @ $1.75 - $42.00. Rd Way Dept |
| | " | carp 25 da @ $1.75 - $43.75. repair bridges &c |

# B & O RR EMPLOYEES

| | | | |
|---|---|---|---|
| 1857-81 | Nortney, James | fire 13 da @ $1.35 - $16.20. lay 2d track | |
| 1857-67 | Norton, James | lab 17¼ da @ $1 - $17.25. Rd Dept main stem 18th s-div | |
| 1855-70 | Norton, Michael | lab 6 da @ $1 - $6.00. Rd Way Dept | |
| 1855-47 | Norton, Thomas | lab 19¼ da @ $1 - $19.25. Rd Way Dept | |
| 1855-40 | Norwood, William | lab 24 da @ $1 - $24.00. Rd Way Dept | |
| 1857-49 | " | lab 22 3/4 da @ $1 - $22.75. Rd Dept main stem 3d s-div | |
| 1855-31 | Nott, Chris. | prepar fuel 15½ da @ $1 - $15.50. Trans Dept main stem | |
| 1855-49 | Noughten, Timothy | watch cuts 28 da @ $1 - $28.00. Rd Way Dept | |
| 1857-99 | Noughton, John | watch 30 da @ $1 - $30.00. NW Va RR, Rd Dept 4th s-div | |
| 1857-94 | " Michael | lab 22 da @ $1 - $22.00. quarry & haul stone for Board Tree & Littleton Tun | |
| 1857-80 | " Patrick | lab 20 3/4 da @ $1 - $20.75. lay 2d track | |
| 1857-54 | " Timothy | watch 30 da @ $1 - $30.00. Rd Dept main stem 8th s-div | |
| 1857-57 | Now, Conrad | lab 25 3/4 da @ $1 - $25.75. Rd Dept main stem 11th s-div | |
| 1855-46 | Nowland, Wm. | lab 20 da @ $1.12½ - $22.50. Rd Way Dept | |
| 1857-118 | Nudemire, William | blksmith help 18 da @ $1.10 - $19.80. Mach Dept, Balto | |
| 1855-69 | Null, David | lab 18½ da @ $1 - $18.50. Rd Way Dept | |
| 1857-124 | Nulty, Anthony | boil mkr help 23 3/4 da @ $1 - $23.75. Mach Dept, Martinsburg | |
| 1855-87 | Nultz, Anthony | help 24 3/4 da @ $1 - $24.75. Mach Dept | |
| 1857-113 | Nunn, Stephen | mach app 10 da @ $.75 - $7.50. Mach Dept, Balto | |
| 1855-46 | Nyland, B. | lab 24 da @ $1.12½ - $27.00. Rd Way Dept | |
| 1855-79 | " Bartly | lab 25 da @ $1.37 - $34.35. lay 2d track | |
| 1855-46 | " D. | lab 6½ da @ $1 - $6.50. Rd Way Dept | |
| 1857-79 | " Dennis | lab 25 da @ $1.25 - $31.35. lay 2d track | |
| 1855-46 | " M. | lab 20½ da @ $1 - $20.50. Rd Way Dept | |
| 1857-78 | " Matthew | lab 24 da @ $1 - $24.00. lay 2d track | |
| 1857-78 | " Patrick | lab 25½ da @ $1 - $25.50. lay 2d track | |
| 1857-78 | " Wash. | lab 1 da @ $1 - $1.00. lay 2d track | |
| 1857-95 | Oakes, James | fore 24 da @ $1.25 - $30.00. Wash br, Rd Dept | |
| 1855-74 | Oaks, Jos. | fore 24 da @ $1.25 - $30.00. Rd Way Dept | |
| 1855-64 | Oats, William | mason 21½ da @ $1.75 - $37.60. Rd Way Dept | |
| 1857-34 | " | ton fire 11 da @ $1.75 - $19.25. Board Tree Tun | |
| 1855-57 | O'Brian, John | watch 20½ da @ $1 - $20.50. Rd Way Dept | |
| 1857-56 | " | watch 30 da @ $1 - $30.00. Rd Dept main stem 10th s-div | |
| 1857-88 | " Michael | lab 18 3/4 da @ $1.12 - $21.10. grad, Welling Tun | |
| 1857-80 | " Patrick | lab 17 3/4 da @ $1 - $17.75. lay 2d track | |
| 1857-122 | " | lab 18 da @ $1 - $18.00. Mach Dept, Balto | |

261

## B & O RR EMPLOYEES

| | | |
|---|---|---|
| 1857-91 | O'Brian, Thomas | lab 21 da @ $1 - $21.00. grad, Welling Tun |
| 1857-74 | " | lab 23 da @ $1.12 - $25.85. repair bridges &c |
| 1855-60 | O'Brien, A. | fore 25¼ da @ $1 - $25.25. Rd Way Dept |
| 1855-81 | " C. | lab 29 da @ $1.15 - $33.35. Mach Dept |
| 1857-121 | " " | carp help 16½ da @ $1.15 - $18.95. Mach Dept, Balto |
| 1855-70 | " D. | lab 22 3/4 da @ $1 - $22.75. Rd Way Dept |
| 1855-68 | " Daniel | lab 9 3/4 da @ $1 - $9.75. Rd Way Dept |
| 1855-49 | " Hughey | lab 19¼ da @ $1 - $19.25. Rd Way Dept |
| 1857-84 | " John | watch cuts 28 da @ $1 - $28.00. Rd Way Dept |
| 1857-95 | " " | lab 25 da @ $1.12 - $28.10. grad, Board Tree Tun |
| 1855-48 | " Patrick | lab 22 da @ $1 - $22.00. Wash br, Rd Dept |
| 1857-80 | " Richard | lab 20¼ da @ $1 - $20.25. Rd Way Dept |
| 1855-7 | " Thos. | train hand 20¼ da @ $1 - $20.25. lay 2d track |
| 1855-73 | " Wm. | clk 28 da @ $40 per mo - $40.00. Trans Dept main stem |
| 1857-63 | Obrion, John | lab 24½ da @ $1 - $24.50. Rd Way Dept |
| 1857-85 | O'Brion, Michael | watch 30 da @ $1 - $30.00. Rd Dept main stem 16th s-div |
| 1857-82 | " Thomas | lab 6 da @ $1.12 - $6.75. grad, Board Tree Tun |
| 1855-22 | O'Bryan, John | lab 27 3/4 da @ $1.12 - $31.20. grad, Board Tree Tun |
| 1855-50 | " P. | fire 5 da @ $53.35 per mo - $6.95. Trans Dept main stem |
| 1857-80 | O'Connell, Pat. | watch cuts 28 da @ $1 - $28.00. Rd Way Dept |
| 1855-34 | O'Connor, Hugh | lab 20¼ da @ $1 - $20.25. lay 2d track |
| 1855-76 | " Jno. | distrib bills 28 da @ $10 - $10.00. Trans Dept main stem |
| 1855-72 | " Mike | lab 6 da @ $1 - $6.00. Rd Way Dept |
| 1855-87 | " Pat. | help 20½ da @ $.50 - $10.25. Rd Way Dept |
| 1857-61 | O'Day, Michael | help 28 da @ $1.15 - $32.20. Mach Dept |
| 1857-58 | " Rodey | fore 25 da @ $1.25 - $1.25. Rd Dept main stem 14th s-div |
| 1855-69 | " Thomas | lab 25½ da @ $1 - $25.50. Rd Way Dept |
| **1857-136** | O'Donald, Barney | lab 22½ da @$1 - $22.50. Rd Way Dept |
| 1857-64 | O'Donley, John | blksmith 19 3/4 da @ $1.40 - $27.65. Mach Dept, Cumb |
| 1855-70 | O'Donnal, C. | lab 24½ da @ $1 - $24.50. Rd Dept main stem 12th s-div |
| 1855-58 | O'Donnel, Edward | lab 6½ da @ $1 - $6.50. Rd Way Dept |
| 1855-58 | " James | lab 21 da @ $1 - $21.00. Rd Way Dept |
| 1855-58 | " Patrick | lab 24 da @ $1 - $24.00. Rd Way Dept |
| 1857-103 | O'Donnell, Arthur | lab 23½ da @ $1.12 - $26.15. NW Va RR Tun |
| 1857-60 | " Austen | lab 26½ da @ $1 - $26.50. Rd Dept main stem 13th s-div |

B & O RR EMPLOYEES 263

| ID | Name | Description |
|---|---|---|
| 1857-103 | O'Donnell, Barry | lab 4 3/4 da @ $1 - $4.75. NW Va RR Tun |
| 1857-39 | E. H. | pass conduc 30 da @ $50 per mo - $50.00. N W Va rd, Parkersburg sta |
| 1857-86 | Edward | lab 18 3/4 da @$1 - $18.75. grad, McGuire's Tun |
| 1857-87 | James | watch 13 da @ $1 - $13.00. grad, McGuire's Tun |
| 1855-68 | John | lab 15 da @$1 - $15.00. grad, Mc Guire's Tun |
| 1855-28 | M. | lab 23½ da @ $1 - $23.50. Rd Way Dept |
| 1857-60 | Martin | prepar fuel 24 da @ $25 per mo - $25.00. Trans Dept main stem |
| 1857-58 | " | lab 24 da @ $1 - $24.00. Rd Dept main stem 13th s-div |
| 1857-61 | Michael | watch 26 da @ $.50 - $13.00. Rd Dept main stem 11th s-div |
| 1857-59 | Patrick | watch 30 da @$1 - $30.00. Rd Dept main stem 14th s-div |
| 1855-77 | T. E. | lab 21½ da @ $1 - $21.50. Rd Dept main stem 13th s-div |
| 1857-127 | Thos. E. | mach 14 da @ $1.25 - $17.50. Mach Dept |
| 1857-129 | O'Driskell, Timothy | storekpr @ $35 per mo - $35.00. Mach Dept, Piedmont |
| 1857-28 | Ogden, Ambrose | fill tend 29½ da @ $1 - $29.50. Mach Dept, Piedmont |
| 1857-139 | Ogden, Henry C. | ton eng'man 3 da @ $3 - $9.00. 1st div |
| 1855-30 | Ogh, Jacob | carp 26¼ da @ $1.35 - $35.45. NW Va RR, Mach Dept, Parkersburg |
| 1857-11 | Ogle, Jacob | prepar fuel 23½ da @ $1 - $23.50. Trans Dept main stem |
| 1857-80 | O'Hare, Martin | lab 23 3/4 da @ $1 - $23.75. Locust Pt |
| 1857-104 | O'Harra, John | lab 20 3/4 da @ $1 - $20.75. lay 2d track |
| 1855-60 | " P. | blksmith 20 da @ $1.25 - $25.00. NW Va RR Tun |
| 1857-64 | O'Harrah, Patrick Jr | lab 21 da @ $1 - $21.00. Rd Way Dept |
| 1857-67 | Ohawer, Daniel | lab 23 da @ $1 - $23.00. Rd Dept main stem 17th s-div |
| 1857-67 | James | lab 11½ da @ $1 - $11.50. Rd Dept main stem 18th s-div |
| 1855-26 | O'Hern, Patrick | lab 19 da @ $1 - $19.00. Rd Dept main stem 18th s-div |
| 1857-126 | " | clean eng 26 da @ $1 - $26.00. Trans Dept main stem |
| 1857-126 | William | clean eng 24 3/4 da @ $1 - $24.75. Mach Dept, Martinsburg |
| 1857-101 | O'Hore, Patrick | clean eng 20 da @ $1 - $20.00. Mach Dept, Martinsburg |
| 1857-64 | O'Horrow, Patrick | lab 22 da @ $1 - $22.00. NW Va RR ballast train |
| 1857-136 | O'Keefe, Ann | lab 25 da @ $1 - $25.00. Rd Dept main stem 17th s-div |
| 1857-132 | O'Leary, Henry | clean pass cars @ $20 per mo - $20.00. Mach Dept, Wheeling |
| 1857-131 | Richard | blksmith 14½ da @ $1.60 - $23.20. Mach Dept, Grafton |
| 1855-92 | Oliver, G. | mach app 25 da @ $.75 - $18.75. Mach Dept, Grafton |
| 1855-17 | Greenbury | help 7½ da @ $3 - $7.50. Mach Dept |
| 1857-30 | " | ton eng'man 11½ da @ $3 - $34.50. Trans Dept main stem |
| 1855-50 | John | ton eng'man 20 da @ $3 - $60.00. 3d div |
| | | watch cuts 28 da @ $1 - $28.00. Rd Way Dept |

B & O RR EMPLOYEES

| | | | |
|---|---|---|---|
| 1857-84 | Oliver, Martin | lab 7 da @ $1.12 - $7.85. grad, Board Tree Tun |
| 1855-52 | O'Marra, Timothy | lab 28 da @ $1 - $28.00. Rd Way Dept |
| 1857-65 | " | watch 30 da @ $1 - $30.00. Rd Dept main stem 17th s-div |
| 1857-87 | Ommercost, James | bricklay 18¼ da @ $2.25 - $41.05. grad, Welling Tun |
| 1855-63 | O'Neal, Danl. | lab 21¼ da @ $1 - $21.25. Rd Way Dept |
| 1857-102 | Henry | pump water 30 da @ $1 - $30.00. NW Va RR |
| 1857-56 | James | watch 30 da @ $1 - $30.00. Rd Dept main stem 10th s-div |
| 1857-122 | John | eng clean 23¼ da @ $1 - $23.25. Mach Dept, Balto |
| 1857-88 | " | lab 26 3/4 da @ $1.12 - $30.10. grad, Welling Tun |
| 1857-73 | John R. | lab 21¼ da @ $1.12 - $23.90. repair water sta, M.S. & P.B. |
| 1855-87 | Luke | help 16 da @ $1 - $16.00. Mach Dept |
| 1855-69 | Michael | lab 18 3/4 da @ $1 - $18.75. Rd Way Dept |
| 1855-70 | " | lab 19 3/4 da @ $1 - $19.75. Rd Way Dept |
| 1857-47 | Thomas | lab 27 da @ $1 - $27.00. Rd Dept main stem 1st s-div |
| 1857-80 | William | lab 20 3/4 da @ $1 - $20.75. lay 2d track |
| 1857-96 | O'Neil, Michael | lab 24 da @ $1 - $24.00. NW Va RR, Rd Dept 1st s-div |
| 1857-84 | Owen | lab 24 da @ $1.12 - $27.00. grad, Board Tree Tun |
| 1857-81 | O'Neill, Daniel | lab 23¼ da @ $1.12 - $26.15. grad, Board Tree Tun |
| 1857-68 | James | lab 13 3/4 da @ $1 - $13.75. Rd Dept main stem 19th s-div |
| 1855-53 | " | carp 24 da @ $1.37½ - $33.00. Rd Way Dept |
| 1857-74 | Patrick | carp 25 da @ $1.37 - $34.35. repair bridges &c |
| 1857-92 | O'Proke, A. | lab 18½ da @ $1 - $18.25. grad, Littleton Tun |
| 1855-46 | Oran, T. E. | lab 22½ da @ $1 - $22.50. Rd Way Dept |
| 1855-23 | Orman, Nathan | fire 31 da @ $33.35 per mo - $43.05. Trans Dept main stem |
| 1857-86 | O'Roak, John | lab 17½ da @ $1 - $17.50. grad, McGuire's Tun |
| 1857-90 | Orr, David | lab 23½ da @ $1 - $23.50. grad, Welling Tun |
| 1855-91 | John | mach 12 da @ $1.50 - $18.00. Mach Dept |
| 1857-78 | Lawrence | lab 23 da @ $1 - $23.00. lay 2d track |
| 1857-78 | Orrick, C. | lab 14½ da @ $1 - $14.50. lay 2d track |
| 1855-32 | Osborn, Jos. | saw wd 23½ cords @ $.35 - $8.20. Trans Dept main stem |
| 1855-54 | Osbourne, William | blksmith 4½ da @ $1.25 - $5.65. Rd Way Dept |
| 1857-114 | Oscler, Edward | core mkr 4 da @ $1.50 - $6.00. Mach Dept, Balto |
| 1857-131 | O'Sulivan, John | fore iron mould 25 da @ $2.25 - $56.25. Mach Dept, Grafton |
| 1855-71 | Ott, John | carp 22 da @ $1.60 - $35.20. Rd Way Dept |
| 1857-118 | | blksmith help 18 da @ $1 - $19.80. Mach Dept, Balto |
| 1857-58 | | lab 28½ da @ $1 - $28.50. Rd Dept main stem 12th s-div |

| ID | Name | Details |
|---|---|---|
| 1857-91 | Ott, Martin | stone mason 24¼ da @ $2 - $48.50. grad, Littleton Tun |
| 1855-53 | Otta, Christian | lab 15 da @ $1 - $15.00. Rd Way Dept |
| 1855-29 | Ours, Simon | prepar fuel 28 da @ $1 - $28.00. Trans Dept main stem |
| 1857-135 | Outt, Valentine | sht iron work help 27½ da @ $1 - $27.50. Mach Dept, Wheeling |
| 1857-77 | Outten, James | mach 14 da @ $1.65 - $23.10. Mach Dept |
| 1857-109 | " John | mach 16 da @ $1.72 - $27.50. Mach Dept, Balto |
| 1857-37 | Owen, R. | mail driv 30 da @ $30 per mo - $30.00. Wash br rd, Wash city sta |
| 1857-112 | " Samuel | mach help 18 da @ $1.10 - $19.80. Mach Dept, Balto |
| 1855-74 | Owens, Chas. | lab 23 da @ $1 - $23.00. Rd Way Dept |
| 1855-58 | " James | lab 24 da @ $1 - $24.00. Rd Way Dept |
| 1857-118 | " " | blksmith help 18 da @ $1 - $18.00. Mach Dept, Balto |
| 1857-60 | " " | watch 30 da @ $1 - $30.00. Rd Dept main stem 13th s-div |
| 1857-70 | " John | lab 19 da @ $1 - $19.00. Rd Dept main stem 13th s-div |
| 1857-96 | " Levi | blksmith 17⅞ da @ $1.45 - $25.00. Mt Clare sta, Balto |
| 1857-96 | " Patrick | lab 24 da @ $1 - $24.00. NW Va RR, Rd Dept 1st s-div |
| 1855-78 | " " | lab 24 3/4 da @ $1 - $24.75. NW Va RR, Rd Dept 1st s-div |
| 1855-58 | " Thomas | help 24½ da @ $1 - $24.50. Mach Dept |
| 1857-60 | " " | supv @ $50 per mo - $50.00. Rd Way Dept |
| 1857-59 | " " | horse hire (3 horses) 75 da @ $1 - $75.00. Rd Dept main stem 13th s-div |
| 1857-70 | " " | supv @ $50 per mo - $50.00. Rd Dept main stem 13th s-div |
| 1855-4 | " Washington | help 9 3/4 da @ $1 - $9.75. Mt Clare sta, Balto |
| 1857-133 | " Wm. | conduc 28 da @ $62.50 per mo - $62.50. Trans Dept, Wash br |
| 1857-77 | Owerts, Simon | fill tend 30 da @ $1 - $30.00. Mach Dept, Fetterman |
| 1855-77 | Owings, Samuel | help 24½ da @ $1.10 - $26.95. Mach Dept |
| 1857-103 | Packett, J. G. | fore 23½ da @ $1.50 - $35.25. NW Va RR Tun |
| 1857-66 | Padden, Michael | lab 24 da @ $1 - $24.00. Rd Dept main stem 18th s-div |
| 1855-55 | " Patrick | lab 24 da @ $1 - $24.00. Rd Way Dept |
| 1857-63 | " " | lab 24 da @ $1 - $21.00. Rd Dept main stem 16th s-div |
| 1855-21 | Padget, J. W. | fire 21 da @ $33.35 per mo - $29.15. Trans Dept main stem |
| 1855-14 | Padgett, D. | brak 12 da @$40 per mo - $20.00. Trans Dept main stem |
| 1857-116 | Page, Lewis | brass mould 3½ da @ $1.85 - $6.45. Mach Dept, Balto |
| 1855-50 | Pain, Martin | watch cuts 30 da @ $1 - $30.00. Rd Way Dept |
| 1857-88 | Palmer, Benjamin | carp 15 da @ $1.30 - $19.50. Mach Dept |
| 1855-13 | " James | conduc & brak 13¼ da @ $40 per mo - $22.10. Trans Dept main stem |
| 1857-28 | " Samuel | ton eng'man 15 da @ $3 - $45.00. 1st div |
| 1857-81 | Pampele, Jerome | fire 13 da @ $1.35 - $17.50. lay 2d track |

266                                   B & O RR EMPLOYEES

| | | | |
|---|---|---|---|
| 1855-33 | Pamphilion, N. | watch 28 da @ $35 per mo - $35.00. Trans Dept main stem |
| 1857-103 | Pane, William M. | fore @ $50 per mo - $50.00. NW Va RR depot |
| 1855-83 | Panks, M. | mach 24¾ da @ $1.72 - $41.70. Mach Dept |
| 1857-74 | Pardon, John | fore 23 da @ $1.50 - $34.50. repair bridges &c |
| 1857-26 | Parker, Archibald | ton brak ½ da @ $40 per mo - $26.40. 3d & 4th div |
| 1857-15 | " B. | watch 30 da @ $1 - $30.00. Cameron sta |
| 1855-9 | " C. J. | conduc 24 da @ $55 per mo - $55.00. Trans Dept main stem |
| 1857-15 | " Frank | train disp 30 da @ $60 per mo - $60.00. Cameron sta |
| 1857-36 | " Henry | tele oper 30 da @ $30 per mo - $30.00. Board Tree Tun |
| 1857-35 | " " | fire 11 da @ $1.75 - $19.25. J. R. Shrode's wd train 4th div |
| 1857-34 | " " | ton fire 1 da @ $1.75 - $1.75. 4th div |
| 1857-122 | " Jacob | lab 18½ da @ $1 - $18.50. Mach Dept, Balto |
| 1857-72 | " James T. | carp 16½ da @ $1.40 - $22.40. Piedmont depot |
| 1857-34 | " Milton | ton fire 5 da @ $1.75 - $8.75. Board Tree Tun |
| 1857-34 | " " | ton fire 11 da @ $1.75 - $19.25. 4th div |
| 1855-34 | " " | watch 10 da @ $1 - $10.00. Board Tree Tun |
| 1855-34 | " P. H. | watch 17 da @ $1 - $17.00. Trans Dept main stem |
| 1857-67 | " Patrick | lab 22 da @ $1 - $22.00. Rd Dept main stem 19th s-div |
| 1855-92 | " Richard | help 23½ da @ $1.75 - $41.15. 4th div |
| 1855-9 | " S. | conduc 7 da @ $50 per mo - $11.60. Mach Dept |
| 1857-23 | " Sample | ton conduc 26½ da @ $50 per mo - $44.60. Trans Dept main stem |
| 1857-27 | " William | ton brak 27 da @ $40 per mo - $43.20. 3d & 4th div |
| 1857-130 | Parkinson, William F. | mach 17½ da @ $1.75 - $30.60. Mach Dept, Newburg |
| 1857-102 | Parks, Solomon | carp 25¼ da @ $1.60 - $40.40. NW Va RR, rwy depot |
| 1857-108 | " Wm. | mach 19½ da @ $1.72 - $33.55. Mach Dept, Balto |
| 1857-136 | Parrington, Richard | pass fire 19½ da @ $1.25 - $8.75. Mach Dept, Cumb |
| 1857-20 | " " | pass fire 19½ da @ $40 per mo - $26.0C. 3d div |
| 1855-92 | Parsons, Edward | carp 22 da - $31.05. Mach Dept |
| 1857-37 | " T. H. | agt 30 da @ $100 per mo - $100.00. Wash br rd, Wash city sta |
| 1855-4 | " Thos. H. | agt 28 da @ $83.35 per mo - $83.35. Trans Dept, Wash br |
| 1857-120 | Pascall, M. | carp 19 da @ $1.50 - $28.50. Mach Dept, Balto |
| 1857-22 | Paschal, M. H. | ton conduc 2⁹⁄₃₀ da @ $50 per mo - $59.00. 2d div |
| 1855-13 | Pasliff, Wm. | conduc & brak 17 3/4 da @ $50 per mo - $36.95. Trans Dept main stem |
| 1855-41 | Patengale, John | lab 24 da @ $1 - $24.00. Rd Way Dept |
| 1857-50 | " " | lab 21½ da @ $1 - $21.50. Rd Dept main stem 4th s-div |
| 1855-41 | Patrick, Jno. | lab 17 da @ $1 - $17.00. Rd Way Dept |

| ID | Name | Description |
|---|---|---|
| 1857-113 | Pattent, James | mach app 22 3/4 da @ $.45 - $10.25. Mach Dept, Balto |
| 1855-48 | Patterson, John | supv @ $50 per mo - $50.00. Rd Way Dept |
| 1857-128 | " John S. | mach help 23½ da @ $.55 - $12.90. Mach Dept, Piedmont |
| 1857-20 | " W. T. | pass fire 6 da @ $40 per mo - $8.00. 3d div |
| 1855-92 | " W. T. | help 24 3/4 da @ $1 - $24.75. Mach Dept |
| 1855-42 | Patton, Jno. | lab 26 da @ $1 - $26.00. Rd Way Dept |
| 1855-70 | Paul, Joseph | carp 14 3/4 da @ $1.60 - $23.60. Rd Way Dept |
| 1855-16 | Paxton, H. | pass fire 24 da @ $1.75 - $42.00. Trans Dept main stem |
| 1857-128 | " Henry | carp 9½ da @ $1.50 - $14.25. Mach Dept, Piedmont |
| 1857-132 | " Joseph | carp 18½ da @ $1.50 - $27.75. Mach Dept, Grafton |
| 1855-71 | Payne, John | carp 21½ da @ $1.60 - $34.40. Rd Way Dept |
| 1857-69 | " | carp 29 da @ $1.60 - $46.40. Mt Clare sta, Balto |
| 1855-93 | " | mach 20 da @ $1.72 - $34.40. Mach Dept |
| 1857-74 | Peacock, John D. | lab 20 da @$1.25 - $25.00. repair bridges &c |
| 1855-93 | " Robert | mach 20 3/4 da @ $1.70 - $35.25. Mach Dept |
| 1857-134 | Pearce, Enoch | mach 17 3/4 da @ $2 - $35.50. Mach Dept, Wheeling |
| 1857-134 | " J. F. G. | mast mech @ $63.35 per mo - $83.35. Mach Dept, Wheeling |
| 1855-40 | " John | lab 24 da @ $1 - $24.00. Rd Way Dept |
| 1855-93 | " " | mach 27 3/4 da @ $1.75 - $48.60. Mach Dept |
| 1857-49 | " S. W. | lab 25 da @ $1 - $25.00. Rd Dept main stem 3d s-div |
| 1855-11 | " Wesley | brak 11 da @ $40 per mo - $18.35. Trans Dept main stem |
| 1855-26 | " Wm. | ton brak 17½ da @ $40 per mo - $28.00. 3d & 4th div |
| 1857-20 | Pearl, Edw. | pass fire 30 da @$1.25 - $37.50. 4th div |
| 1857-89 | " Samuel | water carr 25 da @ $1 - $25.00. grad, Welling Tun |
| 1857-28 | " T. J. | ton eng'man 18½ da @ $3 - $54.75. 1st div |
| 1857-26 | " Thomas E. | ton brak 1 da @ $40 per mo - $1.60. 3d & 4th div |
| 1857-27 | Pease, James | ton brak 26 da @ $40 per mo - $41.60. Board Tree Tun |
| 1855-27 | Peaster, William | get out eng 28 da @ $1.50 - $42.00. Trans Dept main stem |
| 1855-23 | " | fire 29½ da @ $33.35 per mo - $40.95. Trans Dept main stem |
| 1857-111 | " | mach help 23 da @ $1 - $23.00. Mach Dept, Balto |
| 1855-41 | Peck, Isaac | lab 16 da @ $1 - $16.00. Rd Way Dept |
| 1857-52 | " | watch 31 da @ $1 - $31.00. Rd Dept main stem 6th s-div |
| 1857-19 | " J. D. | bag mast 30 da @ $45 per mo - $45.00. thr mail & exp |
| 1855-8 | " John D. | bag mast 26 da @ $45 per mo - $36.80. Trans Dept main stem |
| 1857-34 | " Stephen | rec @ $35 per mo - $35.00. Trans Dept main stem |
| 1857-3 | " " | clk to paymast @ $50 per mo. Gen Ofc |

## B & O RR EMPLOYEES

| |  | |  |
|---|---|---|---|
| 1857-19 | Peddicord, Frank | | bag mast 7 da @ $45 per mo - $10.50. w end |
| 1857-18 | " | | pass train brak 23 da @ $33.35 per mo - $25.55. w end |
| 1857-86 | Peddington, Patrick | | lab 22½ da @ $1 - $22.50. grad, McGuire's Tun |
| 1855-26 | Pedrick, John | | clean eng 20 da @ $1.15 - $23.00. Trans Dept main stem |
| 1855-25 | Pender, Josh. | | clean eng 30½ da @ $1.15 - $35.05. Trans Dept main stem |
| 1855-24 | Pender, John | | pass & bur driv 26½ da @ $30 per mo - $33.10. Trans Dept main stem |
| 1857-98 | Pendergast, Charles | | lab 25 da @ $1 - $25.00. NW Va RR, Rd Dept 3d s-div |
| 1855-49 | Pendergrass, M. | | watch cuts 28 da @ $1 - $28.00. Rd Way Dept |
| 1857-59 | | Michael | watch 30 da @ $1 - $30.00. Rd Dept main stem 12th s-div |
| 1857-59 | | Stephen | lab 24 da @ $1 - $24.00. Rd Dept main stem 12th s-div |
| 1855-49 | | T. | watch cuts 28 da @ $1 - $28.00. Rd Way Dept |
| 1857-59 | | Thos. | watch 30 da @ $1 - $30.00. Rd Dept main stem 12th s-div |
| 1855-50 | Pendergrast, P. | | watch cuts 28 da @ $1 - $28.00. Rd Way Dept |
| 1857-64 | Pendergrist, Michael | | lab 26 da @ $1 - $26.00. Rd Dept main stem 17th s-div |
| 1857-65 | | Patrick | watch 29 da @ $1 - $29.00. Rd Dept main stem 17th s-div |
| 1857-16 | Penderville, G. | | lab 25 da @ $1 - $25.00. Moundsville sta |
| 1855-40 | Penn, James | | lab 24 da @ $1 - $24.00. Rd Way Dept |
| 1857-116 | | Thomas | brass mould help 18 3/4 da @ $1.25 - $23.45. Mach Dept, Balto |
| 1855-16 | | William | pass fire 23 da @ $40 per mo - $32.85. Trans Dept main stem |
| 1855-4 | " | | pass fire 2½ da @ $40 per mo - $3.55. Trans Dept, Wash br |
| 1857-20 | " | | pass fire 29 da @ $40 per mo - $38.65. 1st div |
| 1855-29 | Pennernan, Fred. | | haul & saw firewd 8 da @ $1 - $8.00. Trans Dept main stem |
| 1855-1 | Pentz, A. J. P. | | clk $600 per annum - $50.00. Ofc Hanover St |
| 1855-26 | Percell, Thomas | | clean eng 13 da @ $1 - $13.00. Trans Dept main stem |
| 1857-112 | " | | mach help 37⅞ da @ $33.35 per mo - $37.25. Mach Dept, Balto |
| 1855-7 | | W. B. | clk 28 da @ $33.35 per mo - $33.35. Trans Dept main stem |
| 1857-25 | Peregoy, C. E. | | ton brak 18⅞ da @ $40 per mo - $36.50. 2d div |
| 1857-40 | " | | ton conduc 6¼ da @ $50 per mo - $12.50. NW Va rd, Parkersburg sta |
| 1857-24 | Perine, Wesley | | ton brak 18 da @ $40 per mo - $28.80. 1st div |
| 1857-25 | Perkins, William E. | | ton brak ½ da @ $40 per mo - $.80. 2d div |
| 1855-40 | | John | lab 24 da @ $1 - $24.00. Rd Way Dept |
| 1855-25 | | William | clean eng 17 3/4 da @ $1.15 - $19.85. Trans Dept main stem |
| 1855-31 | Perry, Israel | | saw wd 58 3/4 cords @ $.35 - $20.55. Trans Dept main stem |
| 1857-122 | | J. C. | put away eng &c 22¾ da @ $1.50 - $33.35. Mach Dept, Balto |
| 1857-117 | | J. Jr | blksmith 18 da @ $1.65 - $29.70. Mach Dept, Balto |
| 1855-83 | | | app 21⅜ da @ $.75 - $15.95. Mach Dept |

| | | | |
|---|---|---|---|
| 1855-25 | Perry, Jerret | clean eng 28 3/4 da @ $1.50 - $43.10. Trans Dept main stem |
| 1855-8 | M. C. | brak 28 da @ $33.35 per mo - $33.35. Trans Dept main stem |
| 1857-19 | M. H. C. | bag mast 30 da @ $45 per mo - $45.00. thr mail & exp |
| 1857-53 | Milton | lab 23½ da @ $1 - $23.50. Rd Dept main stem 7th s-div |
| 1857-28 | Perryman, Edward | reg eng 20 da @ $1.15 - $23.00. Trans Dept main stem |
| 1855-75 | John | lab 28 da @ $1 - $28.00. Rd Way Dept |
| 1857-51 | " | lab 30 da @ $1 - $30.00. Rd Dept main stem 5th s-div |
| 1857-26 | Pertt, B. F. | ton brak 62 da @ $40 per mo - $10.40. 3d & 4th div |
| 1855-33 | Peterman, John | lab 28 da @ $35 per mo - $35.00. Trans Dept main stem |
| 1857-123 | " | oil house clk @ $35 per mo - $35.00. Mach Dept, Martinsburg |
| 1857-13 | " | oil house kpr @ $35 per mo. Martinsburg |
| 1857-41 | Peters, Andrew | lab 23 da @ $1 - $23.00. NW Va rd, Athey's wd train |
| 1857-110 | Charles | mach 15½ da @ $1.50 - $23.25. Mach Dept, Balto |
| 1857-102 | Joseph | lab 11 3/4 da @ $.75 - $8.80. NW Va RR, rwy depot |
| 1855-32 | William | saw wd 14 3/4 cords @ $.50 - $7.35. Trans Dept main stem |
| 1857-109 | Pethman, Herman | mach 16 da @ $1.72 - $27.50. Mach Dept, Balto |
| 1855-85 | Peticord, George | help 23¾ da @ $1 - $23.25. Mach Dept |
| 1855-45 | Pettet, Charles | lab 16 da @ $1 - $16.00. Rd Way Dept |
| 1855-8 | Petticord, C. | brak 23 da @ $33.35 per mo - $27.40. Trans Dept main stem |
| 1855-50 | Pettit, William | watch cuts 28 da @ $1 - $28.00. Rd Way Dept |
| 1855-46 | Pezen, C. | lab 22 3/4 da @ $1 - $22.75. Rd Way Dept |
| 1855-39 | Phebus, Peter | nail 28 da @ $1.05 - $29.40. Rd Way Dept |
| 1857-110 | Phelan, William | mach 18 da @ $1.50 - $27.00. Mach Dept, Balto |
| 1857-49 | Phelius, Peter | nail 30 da @ $1.05 - $31.50. Rd Dept main stem 3d s-div |
| 1857-18 | Phelps, A. Jackson | pass train conduc 30 da @$75 per mo - $75.00. thr mail & exp |
| 1857-132 | Francis | carp 30 da @ $1.35 - $40.50. Mach Dept, Grafton |
| 1857-95 | Frank | fore 21½ da @ $1.25 - $26.85. Wash br, Rd Dept |
| 1857-95 | Henry | lab 24 da @ $1 - $24.00. Wash br, Rd Dept |
| 1855-7 | John | pass conduc 28 da @ $2.50 per mo - $62.50. Trans Dept main stem |
| 1857-139 | Lewis W. | carp 24 da @ $1.35 - $32.40. NW Va RR, Mach Dept, Parkersburg |
| 1857-132 | Walter W. | pat mkr 26½ da @ $1.75 - $45.95. Mach Dept, Grafton |
| 1855-84 | Phifer, F. | mach 21½ da @ $1.25 - $26.90. Mach Dept |
| 1857-102 | Phillips, James | carp 20 3/4 da @ $1.60 - $33.20. NW Va RR, rwy depot |
| 1855-91 | Phillips, Edward | mach 21 3/4 da @ $40.00. Mach Dept |
| 1857-20 | Isaac | pass fire 18 da @ $40 per mo - $24.00. 3d div |
| 1855-29 | J. | prepar fuel 28 da @ $1 - $28.00. Trans Dept main stem |

B & O RR EMPLOYEES

| ID | Name | Description |
|---|---|---|
| 1857-100 | Phillips, James | lab 25¾ da @ $1 - $25.25. NW Va RR, Rd Dept 5th s-div |
| 1855-29 | Levi | prepar fuel 28 da @ $1 - $28.00. Trans Dept main stem |
| 1857-71 | Michael | lab 23 da @ $1 - $23.00. Mt Clare, repair tracks in yd |
| 1857-89 | Patrick | lab 12½ da @ $1.12 - $14.05. grad, Welling Tun |
| 1855-85 | Samuel | blksmith 22¼ da @ $1.65 - $36.70. Mach Dept |
| 1857-116 | " | blksmith 17¾ da @ $1.85 - $31.90. Mach Dept, Balto |
| 1857-120 | Wm. | carp 20¼ da @ $1.65 - $33.40. Mach Dept, Balto |
| 1857-37 | Picken, Alex. | clk 30 da @ $30 per mo - $30.00. Wash br rd, Wash city sta |
| 1855-5 | T. | nail 28 da @ $40 per mo - $40.00. Trans Dept, Wash br |
| 1857-37 | Thomas | mail carr 30 da @ $40 per mo - $40.00. Wash br rd, Wash city sta |
| 1857-35 | Pickering, John | lab 15 da @ $1 - $15.00. Edwards' wd train 3d & 4th div |
| 1855-81 | Picket, O. H. | carp 24 da @ $1.55 - $37.20. Mach Dept |
| 1855-39 | Pickett, C. W. | lab 19½ da @ $1 - $19.50. Rd Way Dept |
| 1857-35 | Edman | lab 4½ da @ $1 - $4.50. Edwards' wd train 3d & 4th div |
| 1857-102 | Edward | lab 9 3/4 da @ $1 - $9.75. NW Va RR, rwy depot |
| 1857-132 | John | fill tend @ $30 per mo - $30.00. Mach Dept, Grafton |
| 1857-119 | O. H. | carp 18 da @ $1.55 - $27.90. Mach Dept, Balto |
| 1857-74 | Patrick | track lay 21 3/4 da @ $1 - $21.75. put swit on line of rd |
| 1857-30 | Silas E. | tend to masons 20½ da @ $2.50 - $20.50. Rd Way Dept |
| 1855-68 | Thomas | ton brak 24 3/4 da @ $10 per mo - $39.60. 3d div |
| 1857-25 | Pickings, Adam | Ton conduc 23½ da @ $50 per mo - $47.00. 2d div |
| 1857-22 | John T. | lab 10 da @ $1 - $10.00. Rd Way Dept |
| 1855-42 | Pickins, Adam | lab 6½ da @ $1 - $6.50. Rd Way Dept |
| 1855-42 | C. | lab 15 da @ $1 - $15.00. Rd Way Dept |
| 1855-75 | Pierce, Jno. | lab 22 da @ $1 - $22.00. Rd Way Dept |
| 1855-63 | Pige, James | ton fire 27½ da @ $33.35 per mo - $36.65. 1st div |
| 1857-32 | Pilcher, James | eng'man 4 da @ $2.50 - $10.00. Trans Dept, Wash br |
| 1855-4 | Pilson, John | pass fire 17½ da @ $40 per mo - $25.00. Trans Dept, Wash br |
| 1855-4 | " | lab 31 da @ $1 - $31.00. Mt Clare sta, Balto |
| 1857-70 | Pimenetzkye, A. | ton fire 20½ da @ $33.35 per mo - $27.35. 1st div |
| 1857-32 | Pimm, John | yd eng'man 33 3/4 da @ $1.92 - $68.65. NW Va rd, Parkersburg sta |
| 1857-39 | Thomas | help 14 da @ $1 - $14.00. Mach Dept |
| 1855-87 | Pinim, John | mach 25 da @ $1.15 - $28.75. Mach Dept, Martinsburg |
| 1857-125 | Pins, Hemler | clean eng 25 da @ $2 - $50.00. Mach Dept, Balto |
| 1857-108 | Piper, H. H. | fire 3¼ da @ $1.75 - $5.70. Trans Dept main stem |
| 1855-21 | J. H. | |

# B & O RR EMPLOYEES

| ID | Name | Description |
|---|---|---|
| 1857-23 | Piper, Jacob | ton conduc 16 da @ $50 per mo - $32.00. 3d & 4th div |
| 1855-29 | " John | haul & saw firewd 11 da @ $1.25 - $13.75. Trans Dept main stem |
| 1855-13 | " S. L. | conduc & brak 13 3/4 da @ $50 per mo - $31.15. Trans Dept main stem |
| 1857-23 | " Samuel | ton conduc 12½ da @ $50 per mo - $25.00. Board Tree Tun |
| 1857-23 | " Samuel L. | ton conduc 3 da @ $50 per mo - $6.00. 3d & 4th div |
| 1855-1 | " Washington | clk $400 per annum - $33.33. Ofc Hanover St |
| 1855-46 | Pirby, Owen | lab 20 da @ $1 - $20.00. Rd Way Dept |
| 1857-28 | Pitcher, Samuel | ton eng'man 27 da @ $2.25 - $60.75. 1st div |
| 1855-83 | Pitt, W. | mach 29¼ da @ $1.72 - $50.30. Mach Dept |
| 1855-13 | Pleasants, A. W. | conduc & brak 7½ da @ $1.72 - $13.30. Trans Dept main stem |
| 1857-77 | Pleuty, Hugh | quarry 8 da @ $1 - $8.00. ballast train for 2d track |
| 1857-90 | Plotts, Janatius | stone mason 7¼ da @ $2 - $14.50. grad, Welling Tun |
| 1855-81 | Ploughman, James | lab 21 da @ $1.15 - $24.15. Mach Dept |
| 1857-121 | " | car trim help 18 da @ $1.15 - $20.70. Mach Dept, Balto |
| 1855-56 | Plumb, Wm. | lab 3 da @ $1 - $3.00. Rd Way Dept |
| 1855-39 | Plummer, Jesse | supv @ $45 per mo - $45.00. Rd Way Dept |
| 1857-49 | " | horse hire 50 da @ $.90 - $45.00. Rd Dept main stem 3d s-div |
| 1857-49 | " | supv @ $45 per mo - $45.00. Rd Dept main stem 3d s-div |
| 1857-40 | " John | ton conduc 23 da @ $50 per mo - $46.00. NW Va rd, Parkersburg sta |
| 1855-17 | " Patrick | ton eng'man 16½ da @ $3 - $49.50. Trans Dept main stem |
| 1857-31 | " | ton eng'man 34 da @ $3 - $102.00. Board Tree Tun |
| 1855-73 | " W. W. | supv @ $50 per mo - $50.00. Rd Way Dept |
| 1857-95 | " " " | supv @ $75 per mo - $75.00. Wash br, Rd Dept |
| 1857-95 | " " " | 3 horses hire 73 da @ $1 - $73.00. Wash br, Rd Dept |
| 1857-101 | Plunket, James | lab 13¼ da @ $1 - $13.25. NW Va RR ballast train |
| 1855-83 | Plunkett, Mike | app 23 da @ $.75 - $17.25. Mach Dept |
| 1855-90 | Poggenpohl, H. | help 5½ da @ $1.15 - $6.30. Mach Dept |
| 1855-66 | Poisal, Jacob | lab 20 da @ $1 - $20.00. Rd Way Dept |
| 1855-66 | " Samuel | lab 14½ da @ $2 - $29.00. Rd Way Dept |
| 1857-88 | " | carp 16 da @ $2 - $32.00. grad, Welling Tun |
| 1855-72 | Poist, Charles | app 23¼ da @ $.60 - $13.95. Rd Way Dept |
| 1857-109 | " Charles D. | mach 15½ da @ $1.50 - $23.25. Mach Dept, Balto |
| 1855-84 | " J. | help 21½ da @ $1.10 - $23.65. Mach Dept |
| 1855-85 | " William | help 22¼ da @ $1.10 - $24.15. Mach Dept |
| 1857-111 | Polegon, Minkey | mach help 18 da @ $1 - $18.00. Mach Dept, Balto |
| 1855-43 | Polen, Dennis | lab 19½ da @ $1 - $19.50. Rd Way Dept |

## B & O RR EMPLOYEES

| | | | |
|---|---|---|---|
| 1855-29 | Pomeroy, T. | prepar fuel 2¼ da @$35 per mo - $35.00. Trans Dept main stem |
| 1857-41 | Pool, Cornelius | lab 13 da @ $1 - $13.00. NW Va rd, Athey's wd train |
| 1857-9 | Poole, E. R. | clk 30 da @ $25 per mo - $25.00. Mt Clare sta |
| 1855-21 | George | fire 22 da @ $33.35 per mo - $30.55. Trans Dept main stem |
| 1857-12 | " | lab 25 da @ $1.20 - $30.00. Monocacy |
| 1855-40 | Hanson | lab 25 da @ $1 - $25.00. Rd Way Dept |
| 1857-50 | " | lab 19¾ da @ $1 - $19.25. Rd Dept main stem 4th s-div |
| 1855-65 | Samuel | carp 18 3/4 da @ $1.50 - $28.10. Rd Way Dept |
| 1857-71 | Pope, Henry | track lay 30 da @ $1 - $30.00. Camden sta, repair tracks |
| 1855-29 | Porsall, John | haul & saw firewd 1 da @ $1 - $1.00. Trans Dept main stem |
| 1855-40 | Portenfield, A. | lab 23 da @ $1 - $23.00. Rd Way Dept |
| 1855-21 | Porter, Alexander | fire 19½ da @ $1.75 - $34.10. Trans Dept main stem |
| 1857-30 | " | ton eng'man 22¼ da @ $2.50 - $55.60. 3d div |
| 1857-48 | Charles | watch 26 da @ $1 - $26.00. Rd Dept main stem 2d s-div |
| 1857-47 | James | lab 24½ da @ $1 - $24.50. Rd Dept main stem 1st s-div |
| 1857-134 | John | mach 18 da @ $1.70 - $30.60. Mach Dept, Wheeling |
| 1855-36 | Richard | police watch 28 da @ $40 per mo - $40.00. Trans Dept main stem |
| 1855-91 | Robert | blksmith 23½ da - $36.55. Mach Dept |
| 1857-72 | " | blksmith 5 da @ $1.50 - $7.50. Piedmont depot |
| 1855-58 | W. E. | blksmith 21 da @ $1.50 - $31.50. Rd Dept main stem 11th s-div |
| 1855-55 | " | supv @ $50 per mo - $50.00. Rd Way Dept |
| 1857-58 | " | horse & cart 25 da @ $1.12 - $28.10. Rd Dept main stem 11th s-div |
| 1857-57 | " | horse hire 25 da @ $1 - $25.00. Rd Dept main stem 11th s-div |
| 1857-58 | William E. | horse & cart 25 da @ $1.12 - $28.10. Rd Dept main stem 11th s-div |
| 1855-6 | " | supv @ $50 per mo - $50.00. Rd Dept main stem 11th s-div |
| 1855-6 | Posey, H. C. | clk 28 da @ $25 per mo - $25.00. Trans Dept main stem |
| 1855-68 | Post, Eugene | clk 28 da @ $50 per mo - $50.00. Trans Dept main stem |
| 1855-13 | Poston, John | fire 12 da @ $1.75 - $21.00. Rd Way Dept |
| 1857-24 | Potter, John | conduc & brak 15½ da @ $50 per mo - $34.30. Trans Dept main stem |
| 1857-52 | " | ton brak 18½ da @ $40 per mo - $37.00. 1st div |
| 1857-55 | Levi | lab 25 da @ $1 - $25.00. Rd Dept main stem 6th s-div |
| 1855-78 | Poulas, Francis | watch @ $35 per mo - $35.00. Rd Dept main stem 9th s-div |
| 1855-83 | Poulton, Alexander | help 29¾ da @$1.15 - $33.65. Mach Dept |
| 1857-109 | George | mach 22½ da @$1.60 - $36.00. Mach Dept |
| 1857-40 | Pounall, J. A. | mach 18¾ da @ $1.65 - $30.10. Mach Dept, Balto |
| | " | ton eng'man 12 da @ $2.50 - $30.00. NW Va rd, Parkersburg sta |

| Year-# | Name | Details |
|---|---|---|
| 1857-34 | Pourvall, J. | disp w.s. 22 da @$50 per mo - $44.00. Board Tree Tun |
| 1855-79 | Powell, Benjamin | driv 24 da @$1 - $24.00. Mach Dept |
| 1855-63 | Powers, John | lab 9 da @ $1 - $9.00. Rd Way Dept |
| 1855-37 | " | fore 26 da @ $1.25 - $32.50. Rd Way Dept |
| 1857-16 | " | greas cars 28 da @$30 per mo - $30.00. Trans Dept main stem |
| 1857-46 | " | fire 17½ da @ $33.35 per mo - $23.35. Benwood sta |
| 1857-79 | " | fore 24 da @$1.25 - $30.00. Rd Dept main stem 1st s-div |
| 1857-135 | " | lab 24½ da @ $1 - $24.50. lay 2d track |
| 1857-135 | Michael | lab 5¼ da @$1 - $5.25. Mach Dept, Wheeling |
| 1857-78 | Patrick | lab 26 3/4 da @$1 - $26.75. Mach Dept, Wheeling |
| 1857-46 | Richard | lab 26½ da @ $1 - $26.50. lay 2d track |
| 1857-76 | Thomas | lab 24 da @ $1 - $24.00. Rd Dept main stem 1st s-div |
| 1855-51 | Powlas, Francis | quarry 18½ da @ $1 - $18.50. ballast train for 2d track |
| 1855-21 | Pownall, J. A. | lab @ $35 per mo - $35.00. Rd Way Dept |
| 1857-23 | Jonathan | fire 3½ da @ $1.75 - $6.10. Trans Dept main stem |
| 1855-13 | Joseph | ton brak 8½ da @ $50 per mo - $17.00. Board Tree Tun |
| 1857-27 | Pratt, Abram | conduc & brak 24 da @ $55 per mo - $55.00. Trans Dept main stem |
| 1857-26 | Ephraim | ton brak 10½ da @ $40 per mo - $16.80. 3d & 4th div |
| 1857-23 | Ezeriah | ton brak 17 da @ $40 per mo - $27.40. 3d & 4th div |
| 1857-133 | William | ton conduc 8 da @ $50 per mo - $16.00. 3d & 4th div |
| 1855-41 | Presler, F. | lab 7 da @ $1 - $7.00. Mach Dept, Fetterman |
| 1857-52 | Frank | lab 20 da @ $1 - $20.00. Rd Way Dept |
| 1855-24 | Preston, John | lab 25 da @ $1 - $25.00. Rd Dept main stem 6th s-div |
| 1857-49 | Thomas | pass & bur driv 24 da @$32.20 - $32.20. Trans Dept main stem |
| 1857-7 | Price, F. S. | lab 23¾ da @ $1 - $23.25. Rd Dept main stem 3d s-div |
| 1855-77 | George | clk @ $41.65 per mo. Gen Tick Agt Ofc |
| 1857-132 | " | mach 22½ da @ $1.50 - $33.35. Mach Dept |
| 1855-66 | Jacob | lock 21 da @ $1.50 - $31.50. Mach Dept, Grafton |
| 1857-96 | James | lab 28 da @ $1 - $28.00. Rd Way Dept |
| 1855-14 | John | lab 21 3/4 da @ $1 - $21.75. NW Va RR, Rd Dept 1st s-div |
| 1857-131 | " | brak 23 da @ $40 per mo - $38.35. Trans Dept main stem |
| 1857-28 | Nathan | boil mkr 11 3/4 da @ $1.75 - $20.55. Mach Dept, Grafton |
| 1857-25 | Thomas | ton eng'man 11¼ da @ $3 - $33.75. 1st div |
| 1857-23 | William | ton brak 24 da @ $40 per mo - $38.40. 2d div |
| 1857-23 | " | ton conduc 11½ da @ $50 per mo - $23.00. Board Tree Tun |
| 1857-23 | " | ton conduc 21¼ da @ $50 per mo - $42.50. 3d & 4th div |

## B & O RR EMPLOYEES

| | | | |
|---|---|---|---|
| 1857-97 | Prichard, John | watch 30 da @ $1 - $30.00. NW Va RR, Rd Dept 2d s-div |
| 1857-62 | Prickett, Sanford | lab 25 da @ $1 - $25.00. Rd Dept main stem 15th s-div |
| 1855-72 | Primrose, John | mach 17 3/4 da @ $1.73 - $30.70. Rd Way Dept |
| 1857-69 | " | mach 14½ da @ $1.73 - $25.05. Mt Clare sta, Balto |
| 1855-8 | S. T. | brak 9 da @ $33.35 per mo - $10.70. Trans Dept main stem |
| 1857-69 | William G. | fore @ $75 per mo - $75.00. Mt Clare sta, Balto |
| 1855-8 | Prince, Thomas C. | fdk conduc 28 da @ $40 per mo - $40.00. Trans Dept main stem |
| 1857-18 | " | pass train conduc 30 da @ $50 per mo - $50.00. Fred accom |
| 1855-90 | Prior, Benjamin | carp 24½ da @ $1.50 - $36.75. Mach Dept |
| 1855-34 | Proby, James | mail carr 28 da @ $1.25 - $35.00. Trans Dept main stem |
| 1857-14 | " | mail carr 30 da @ $1.15 - $34.50. Cumb |
| 1857-112 | Prunty, P. | mach help 17½ da @ $1 - $17.50. Mach Dept, Balto |
| 1855-30 | Patrick | prepar fuel 28 da @ $30 per mo - $30.00. Trans Dept main stem |
| 1855-88 | Pryer, Thomas | app 31 3/4 da @ $.50 - $15.85. Mach Dept |
| 1857-132 | Pryor, Benjamin | carp 7¾ da @ $45 per mo - $45.00. Mach Dept, Grafton |
| 1857-83 | Patrick | lab 7¾ da @ $1.12 - $8.15. grad, Board Tree Tun |
| 1857-124 | Thomas | mach app 25¾ da @ $.70 - $17.65. Mach Dept, Martinsburg |
| 1857-133 | Purcell, James | clean eng 34 da @ $1 - $34.00. Mach Dept, Board Tree Tun |
| 1857-28 | Purday, John | ton eng'man 26½ da @ $2 - $53.00. 1st div |
| 1857-36 | Purdy, George | lab 18½ da @ $1 - $18.50. J. R. Shrode's wd train 4th div |
| 1855-83 | John | mach 28 da @ $1.85 - $51.80. Mach Dept |
| 1855-19 | " | ton eng'man 25¾ da @ $2 - $50.50. Trans Dept main stem |
| 1857-109 | John H. | mach 18 da @ $1.80 - $32.40. Mach Dept, Balto |
| 1855-78 | William | mach 12 da @ $1.60 - $19.20. Mach Dept |
| 1857-48 | Purkins, John | fore 24½ da @ $1.25 - $30.00. Rd Dept main stem 2d s-div |
| 1857-48 | William | lab 22½ da @ $1 - $22.25. Rd Dept main stem 2d s-div |
| 1855-55 | Purp, George | lab 16¼ da @ $1 - $16.25. Rd Way Dept |
| 1855-5 | " | lab 6 3/4 da @ $1 - $6.75. Trans Dept, Wash br |
| 1855-84 | Pursh, L. | help 23 3/4 da @ $1.15 - $27.30. Mach Dept |
| 1857-11 | Purse, George | saw 22 3/4 da @ $1.15 - $27.30. Locust Pt |
| 1855-40 | Pustin, Thomas | fore 24 da @ $1.25 - $30.00. Rd Way Dept |
| 1857-27 | Putt, Daniel | ton brak 27 da @ $40 per mo - $43.20. Board Tree Tun |
| 1857-7 | Pyfer, Wm. | mess @ $12.50 per mo. Gen Tick Agt Ofc |
| 1855-14 | Quaid, R. | brak 18½ da @ $40 per mo - $30.85. Trans Dept main stem |
| 1855-56 | Quannon, John | lab 24 3/4 da @ $1 - $24.75. Rd Way Dept |
| 1857-134 | Quig, John | mach app 3½ da @ $.45 - $1.55. Mach Dept, Wheeling |

| | | | |
|---|---|---|---|
| 1855-62 | Quigg, James | supv @ $50 per mo - $50.00. Rd Way Dept |
| 1857-68 | " | horse & cart 26 da @ $1.12 - $29.25. Rd Dept main stem 19th s-div |
| 1857-68 | " | horses & cart 79 da @ $1.12 - $88.85. Rd Dept main stem 19th s-div |
| 1857-67 | Quigley, Pat. | supv @ $50 per mo - $50.00. Rd Dept main stem 19th s-div |
| 1857-75 | Quill, Daniel | fore 19 da @ $35 per mo - $25.60. grad, Board Tree Tun |
| 1857-82 | Quinline, James | bricklay 21 da @ $2 - $42.00. grad, Board Tree Tun |
| 1857-80 | Quinn, Charles | lab 20 3/4 da @ $1 - $20.75. lay 2d track |
| 1857-84 | Edward | lab 20½ da @ $1.12 - $23.05. grad, Board Tree Tun |
| 1855-58 | | lab 21 da @ $1 - $21.00. Rd Way Dept |
| 1857-60 | Henry | watch 30 da @ $1 - $30.00. Rd Dept main stem 13th s-div |
| 1855-27 | | get out eng 28 da @ $1.50 - $42.00. Trans Dept main stem |
| 1857-129 | James | clean eng 31 3/4 da @ $1.15 - $36.50. Mach Dept, Piedmont |
| 1855-37 | " | lab 26½ da @ $1 - $25.50. Rd Way Dept |
| 1855-erratta | " | lab -- instead of $25.50, $26.50 rec'd |
| 1857-46 | John | lab 27 da @ $1 - $27.00. Rd Dept main stem 1st s-div |
| 1857-88 | " | driv 23 da @ $1 - $23.00. grad, Welling Tun |
| 1857-75 | " | fore 25½ da @ $1.25 - $31.85. ballast train for 2d track |
| 1857-56 | " | lab 10 da @ $1 - $10.00. Rd Dept main stem 10th s-div |
| 1857-80 | Luke | lab 20¼ da @ $1 - $20.25. lay 2d track |
| 1857-64 | Mark | lab 29 da @ $1 - $29.00. Rd Dept main stem 17th s-div |
| 1855-67 | Michael | tend to masons 22 da @ $1 - $22.00. Rd Way Dept |
| 1857-83 | " | lab 6½ da @ $1.12 - $7.30. grad, Board Tree Tun |
| 1857-86 | | lab 8¼ da @ $1 - $8.25. grad, McGuire's Tun |
| 1855-70 | Owen | lab 20½ da @ $1 - $20.50. Rd Dept main stem 19th s-div |
| 1857-67 | Patrick | lab 21 3/4 da @ $1 - $21.74. Rd Way Dept |
| 1857-84 | " | lab 26½ da @ $1.12 - $29.80. grad, Board Tree Tun |
| 1857-87 | | lab 24 da @ $1 - $24.00. grad, McGuire's Tun |
| 1857-86 | Thomas | lab 23 da @ $1 - $23.00. grad, McGuire's Tun |
| 1857-55 | Quinz, Augustus | lab 22 3/4 da @ $1 - $22.75. Rd Dept main stem 9th s-div |
| 1855-56 | Quoftos, Patrick | lab 4 3/4 da @ $1 - $4.75. Rd Way Dept |
| 1857-129 | Quynn, J. C. | clean eng 25 3/4 da @ $.75 - $19.30. Mach Dept, Piedmont |
| 1857-12 | John T. | agt 30 da @ $58.35 per mo - $58.35. Fred sta |
| 1855-6 | Rabee, Wm. | agt 28 da @ $58.35 per mo - $58.35. Trans Dept main stem |
| 1857-70 | Rabitt, Patrick | help 17¾ da @ $1.06 - $18.30. Mt Clare sta, Balto |
| 1855-68 | Radcliff, Richard | tend to masons 20 da @ $1 - $20.00. Rd Way Dept |
| 1857-131 | | boil mkr 6¼ da @ $1.75 - $7.80. Mach Dept, Grafton |

| ID | Name | Details |
|---|---|---|
| 1857-135 | Radcliff, Richard H. | boil mkr help 13 3/4 da @ $1.25 -$17.20. Mach Dept, Wheeling |
| 1857-11 | Raddin, Michael | lab 2 da @ $1 - $2.00. Locust Pt |
| 1857-99 | Raferty, John | lab 25 da @ $1 - $25.00. NW Va RR, Rd Dept 4th s-div |
| 1855-56 | Rafferdy, Mart. | lab 13¼ da @ $1 - $13.25. Rd Way Dept |
| 1855-9 | Rafferty, John | conduc 17¾ da @ $50 per mo - $35.95. Trans Dept main stem |
| 1857-133 | " | clean eng 22 da @ $1 - $22.00. Mach Dept, Board Tree Tun |
| 1857-18 | " | pass train brak 8 da @ $33.35 per mo - $8.00. W end |
| 1857-90 | Ragan, Richard | lab 4 da @ $1.12 - $4.50. grad, Welling Tun |
| 1855-50 | Raiden, John | watch cuts 28 da @ $1 - $28.00. Rd Way Dept |
| 1855-25 | Rairden, John | bur driv 24 da @ $30 per mo - $30.00. Trans Dept main stem |
| 1857-9 | Randall, George | pass brak 25 da @ $30 per mo - $30.00. hp exp, Balto |
| 1857-34 | " | ton fire 17 da @ $1.75 - $29.75. 4th div |
| 1857-41 | " L. E. | ton fire 3 da @ $1.75 - $5.25. NW Va rd, Parkersburg sta |
| 1855-7 | " | pass conduc 28 da @ $62.50 per mo - $62.50. Trans Dept main stem |
| 1857-13 | Ranely, Thomas | agt 30 da @ $75 per mo - $75.00. Martinsburg |
| 1857-31 | Raneman, Charles | ton eng'man 22½ da @ $3 - $67.50. Board Tree Tun |
| 1857-102 | Ranford, A. | lab 20 da @ $1 - $20.00. NW Va RR, rwy depot |
| 1855-29 | Ranking, Aaron | unload coal 9 da @ $1 - $9.00. Trans Dept main stem |
| 1857-52 | Rankins, John | fore 25 da @ $1.25 -$31.25. Rd Dept main stem 6th s-div |
| 1857-84 | Raphels, Stephen | carp 12 da @ $1.65 - $19.80. grad, Board Tree Tun |
| 1857-131 | Ratagan, M. | draught @ $41.70 per mo - $41.70. Mach Dept, Grafton |
| 1855-48 | Ratigan, Michael | lab 6 da @ $1 - $6.00. Rd Way Dept |
| 1855-54 | Ravenscraft, J. H. | lab 21½ da @ $1 - $21.50. Rd Way Dept |
| 1857-33 | " James | ton fire 26 3/4 da @ $1.75 - $56.75. 3d div |
| 1857-130 | " S. | lab 22 da @ $1 - $22.00. Mach Dept, Piedmont |
| 1855-16 | " Sam'l. | pass fire 27 da @ $1.25 -$33.75. Trans Dept main stem |
| 1857-33 | " W. P. | ton fire 20 da @ $1.75 - $35.00. 3d div |
| 1857-15 | " " | pass eng'man 31½ da @ $3 -$94.50. Trans Dept main stem |
| 1857-19 | " " | pass eng'man 2 da @ $2.50 - $5.00. 3d div |
| 1857-30 | " " | ton eng'man 14 da @ $3 - $42.00. 3d div |
| 1857-27 | Ravenscroft, James | ton brak 18 da @ $40 per mo - $28.80. 3d & 4th div |
| 1855-35 | " R. | mail carr 28 da @ $15 per mo - $15.00. Trans Dept main stem |
| 1857-8 | Rawlings, Benjamin | rec clk 30 da @ $50 per mo - $50.00. Camden sta |
| 1855-6 | " C. A. | ex conduc &c 28 da @ $75 per mo -$75.00. Trans Dept main stem |
| 1857-18 | " George A. | pass train conduc 30 da @ $75 per mo - $75.00. thr mail & exp |
| 1857-34 | Ray, A. | ton fire 19½ da 3 $1.75 - $34.10. Board Tree Tun |

# B & O RR EMPLOYEES 277

| Date | Name | Description |
|---|---|---|
| 1857-35 | Ray, Abraham | fire 5½ da @ $1.75 - $9.60. J. R. Shrode's wd train 4th div |
| 1857-33 | " | ton fire 6 da @ $1.75 - $10.50. 3d div |
| 1857-20 | Abram | pass fire 1 da @ $40 per mo - $1.35. 4th div |
| 1857-133 | Holster, William D. | clean eng 26 da @ $1 - $26.00. Mach Dept, Fetterman |
| 1857-25 | Raysinger, J. | ton brak 21 da @ $30 per mo -$42.00. 2d div |
| 1855-13 | " John | conduc & brak 18½ da @ $50 per mo -$38.55. Trans Dept main stem |
| 1857-21 | " M. | ton conduc 20¼ da @ $50 per mo - $40.50. 1st div |
| 1855-19 | " " | ton eng'man 4 da @ $2.50 - $10.00. Trans Dept main stem |
| 1855-4 | " " | ton eng'man 14 da @ $2.50 - $35.00. Trans Dept, Wash br |
| 1857-28 | " Martin | ton eng'man 18½ da @ $3 - $55.50. 1st div |
| 1855-17 | Rea, Jno. C. | ton eng'man 5 3/4 da @ $3 - $17.25. Trans Dept main stem |
| 1857-118 | Read, Flavs. | blksmith help 18½ da @ $1 - $18.50. Mach Dept, Balto |
| 1857-66 | Readington, William | lab 22 da @ $1 - $22.00. Rd Dept main stem 18th s-div |
| 1855-44 | Ready, Jere | lab 23 da @ $1 - $23.00. Rd Way Dept |
| 1855-47 | Patrick | lab 19½ da @ $1 - $19.50. Rd Way Dept |
| 1855-62 | Reaher, John | lab 9 3/4 da @ $1 - $9.75. Rd Way Dept |
| 1855-58 | Reaidey, John | lab 17½ da @ $1 - $17.50. Rd Way Dept |
| 1855-81 | Reanes, Jas. | paint 24 da @ $2 - $48.00. Mach Dept |
| 1855-85 | William | blksmith 19 da @ $1.60 - $30.40. Mach Dept |
| 1857-25 | Reather, Charles | ton brak 22 da @ $40 per mo - $35.20. 2d div |
| 1857-71 | Rebber, C. | track lay 24 da @ $1.37 -$33.00. Camden sta, repair tracks |
| 1857-76 | Reck, John | dril 24½ da @ $1.10 - $26.95. ballast train for 2d track |
| 1855-46 | Reckelman, John | lab 19 da @ $1 - $19.00. Rd Way Dept |
| 1857-55 | " | fore 25 da @ $1.12 - $28.10. Rd Dept main stem 9th s-div |
| 1857-17 | Rector, Andrew | coop 25 da @ $1.25 -$31.25. frt transfer force at Bellaire, opp Benwood |
| 1855-28 | Wm. | prepar fuel 24 da @ $40 per mo -$40.00. Trans Dept main stem |
| 1855-43 | Redden, John | lab 21½ da @ $1 - $21.50. Rd Way Dept |
| 1857-129 | Reddington, John | clean eng 30 5/8 da @ $1 - $30.60. Mach Dept, Piedmont |
| 1855-26 | Redington, John | clean eng 28 da @ $1 - $28.00. Trans Dept main stem |
| 1857-90 | Michael | lab 9 da @ $1.12 - $10.15. grad, Welling Tun |
| 1855-61 | W. | lab 19 da @ $1 - $19.00. Rd Way Dept |
| 1855-36 | Redman, E. | conduc & brak 22 3/4 da @ $30 per mo - $28.45. Trans Dept main stem |
| 1855-36 | " | lab 2 da @ $25 per mo - $2.10. Trans Dept main stem |
| 1857-32 | Elijah | ton fire 13 da @ $1.75 - $22.75. 1st div |
| 1855-19 | Jesse | ton eng'man 18 3/4 da @ $2.50 - $42.20. Trans Dept main stem |
| 1857-118 | W. H. | blksmith help 18¼ da @ $1 - $18.25. Mach Dept, Balto |

## B & O RR EMPLOYEES

| | | | |
|---|---|---|---|
| 1855-16 | Reed, A. | pass fire 3 da @ $40 per mo - $4.30. Trans Dept main stem |
| 1857-28 | Alexander | ton eng'man 19½ da @ $3 - $58.50. 1st div |
| 1855-21 | Amos | fire 3 da @ $1.75 - $5.25. Trans Dept main stem |
| 1857-28 | " | ton eng'man 16 3/4 da @ $3 - $50.25. 1st div |
| 1855-24 | Jacob | pass & bur driv 24 da @ $30 per mo - $30.00. Trans Dept main stem |
| 1855-49 | James | watch cuts 28 da @ $1 - $28.00. Rd Way Dept |
| 1857-124 | John | mach app 29 da @ $.45 - $13.05. Mach Dept, Martinsburg |
| 1857-13 | Joseph | watch 30 da @ $40 per mo - $40.00. Martinsburg |
| 1857-95 | Thomas | lab 27 da @ $1 - $27.00. Wash br, Rd Dept |
| 1857-33 | Reeder, Alexander | ton fire 18½ da @ $1.75 - $31.95. 2d div |
| 1855-46 | Reedy, John | lab 4½ da @ $1 - $4.50. Rd Way Dept |
| 1857-46 | Michael | lab 17 da @ $1 - $17.00. Rd Dept main stem 1st s-div |
| 1855-19 | Reel, Otho | ton eng'man 12 da @ $2.50 - $30.00. Trans Dept main stem |
| 1855-80 | Rees, Peter | carp 24 da @ $1.60 - $38.40. Mach Dept |
| 1855-90 | Reese, Jacob | help 15 da @ $1 - $15.00. Mach Dept |
| 1855-51 | " | lab 15 da @ $1 - $15.00. Rd Way Dept |
| 1857-137 | " | lab @ $15 per mo - $15.00. Mach Dept, Cumb |
| 1857-55 | Reeside, John | pump water 15 da @ $1 - $15.00. Rd Dept main stem 9th s-div |
| 1857-121 | Wm. | carp app 31 da @ $.65 - $20.15. Mach Dept, Balto |
| 1855-24 | " | pass & bur driv 24 da @ $30 per mo - $30.00. Trans Dept main stem |
| 1857-10 | " | pass reg 25 da @ $40 per mo - $40.00. hp exp, Balto |
| 1857-121 | Reeves, James | fore paint 18 da @ $2 - $36.00. Mach Dept, Balto |
| 1857-117 | William | blksmith 18 da @ $1.60 - $28.80. Mach Dept, Balto |
| 1855-26 | Regan, Patrick | clean eng 26 da @ $1 - $26.00. Trans Dept main stem |
| 1857-93 | " | smith help 25 da @ $1 - $25.00. quarry & haul stone for Board Tree & Littleton Tun |
| 1855-13 | Reidenour, C. | conduc & brak 6¼ da @ $40 per mo - $10.85. Trans Dept main stem |
| 1855-8 | Reilley, James | brak 8 da @ $33.35 per mo - $9.50. Trans Dept main stem |
| 1855-34 | Mart. | lab 28 da @ $1 - $28.00. Trans Dept main stem |
| 1855-27 | Reilly, Eugene | clean eng 28½ da @ $1 - $28.50. Trans Dept main stem |
| 1857-24 | George | ton brak 23½ da @ $30 per mo - $28.20. 1st div |
| 1855-13 | James | conduc & brak 8 da @ $40 per mo - $13.35. Trans Dept main stem |
| 1855-36 | " | lab 24½ da @ $25 per mo - $25.25. Trans Dept main stem |
| 1855-36 | O. | lab 24½ da @ $25 per mo - $25.25. Trans Dept main stem |
| 1857-24 | Stephen | ton brak 2 da @ $30 per mo - $4.00. 1st div |
| 1857-101 | Reily, Edward | fore 24 da @ $1.25 - $30.00. NW Va RR ballast train |
| 1857-101 | Michael | lab 24 da @ $1 - $24.00. NW Va RR ballast train |

## B & O RR EMPLOYEES 279

| | | |
|---|---|---|
| 1857-101 | Reily, Patrick | lab 12 3/4 da @ $1 - $12.75. NW Va RR ballast train |
| 1857-103 | Phil. | lab 23 da @ $1.12 - $25.90. NW Va RR Tun |
| 1855-26 | Reister, Hazes | clean eng 26 da @ $1 - $26.00. Trans Dept main stem |
| 1857-20 | Reiter, Abram | pass fire 19 da @ $40 per mo - $25.35. 1st div |
| 1855-93 | Reitzel, J. B. | pack 23½ da - $33.15. Mach Dept |
| 1855-92 | Reitzell, J. H. | app 24 da @ $.25 - $6.00. Mach Dept |
| 1857-128 | Jacob | mach help 24 3/4 da @ $.65 - $16.10. Mach Dept, Piedmont |
| 1855-40 | Rench, John | lab 19 da @ $1 - $19.00. Rd Way Dept |
| 1855-27 | Rendle, George | clean eng 17 da @ $1 - $17.00. Trans Dept main stem |
| 1857-123 | Renebde, Agusta | mach 23 3/4 da @ $1.50 - $35.60. Mach Dept, Martinsburg |
| 1855-53 | Reneman, Charles | lab 15½ da @ $1 - $15.50. Rd Way Dept |
| 1857-100 | Rennals, Patrick | lab 25¼ da @ $1 - $25.25. NW Va RR, Rd Dept 5th s-div |
| 1855-37 | Rennels, John | nail 30 da @ $1 - $30.00. Rd Way Dept |
| 1857-73 | Renner, Henry | carp 23¼ da @ $1.30 - $30.20. repair bridges &c |
| 1855-26 | Renney, John | clean eng 22½ da @ $1 - $22.50. Trans Dept main stem |
| 1857-91 | Rennick, Edward | lab 22½ da @ $1 - $22.50. grad, Welling Tun |
| 1855-1 | Rennie, D. P. | asst mast mach $1200 per annum - $100.00 |
| " | " | asst mast of mach @ $100 per mo. Mach Dept, Ofc, Grafton sta |
| 1857-107 | Reoder, John | lab 23 da @ $1 - $23.00. Rd Dept main stem 9th s-div |
| 1857-55 | Rerden, Dennis | dril 8 da @ $1.10 - $8.80. ballast train for 2d track |
| 1857-76 | Reter, Abraham | fill tend 28 da @ $1 - $28.00. Trans Dept main stem |
| 1855-30 | Rethman, H. | mach 25 da @ $1.72 - $43.00. Mach Dept |
| 1855-83 | Retz, John | help 28 da @ $1 - $28.00. Mach Dept |
| 1855-87 | " | sht iron work 21 3/4 da @ $1.25 - $27.20. Mach Dept, Martinsburg |
| 1857-124 | Reuter, Abram | ton fire 18 da @ $1.75 - $31.50. 1st div |
| 1857-32 | Rewark, Richard | lab 21 da @ $1 - $21.00. Rd Way Dept |
| 1855-58 | Reyan, A. | lab 15 da @ $1 - $15.00. ballast train for 2d track |
| 1857-76 | Reynolds, Allen | clean eng 11¼ da @ $1.15 - $12.95. Trans Dept main stem |
| 1855-25 | Barnard | lab 25½ da @ $1 - $25.50. Rd Dept main stem 12th s-div |
| 1857-58 | Briant | lab 22 3/4 da @ $1.12 - $25.60. NW Va RR Tun |
| 1857-103 | C. | conduc & brak 12½ da @ $50 per mo - $26.05. Trans Dept main stem |
| 1855-13 | Charles | ton conduc 14 da @ $50 per mo - $28.00. 1st div |
| 1857-21 | Columbus | blksmith help 14¼ da @ $1 - $14.25. Mach Dept, Balto |
| 1857-118 | Howard | ton fire 15 da @ $1.75 - $26.25. 1st div |
| 1857-32 | Hugh | lab 30½ da @ $25 per mo - $30.50. Wheeling sta |
| 1857-17 | James | lab 23 da @ $1 - $23.00. Rd Dept main stem 10th s-div |
| 1857-56 | John | lab 30 da @ $1 - $30.00. Rd Dept main stem 1st s-div |
| 1857-47 | | |

## B & O RR EMPLOYEES

| | | | |
|---|---|---|---|
| 1857-117 | Reynolds, Jos. | blksmith help 16 3/4 da @ $1.15 - $19.25. Mach Dept, Balto |
| 1855-18 | L. S. | ton eng'man 24 da @ $2.50 - $60.00. Trans Dept main stem |
| 1857-88 | Martin | lab 16 da @ $1.12 - $18.00. grad, Welling Tun |
| 1857-103 | Thomas | lab 23¼ da @ $.87 - $20.35. NW Va RR Tun |
| 1855-19 | William | ton eng'man 23 da @ $2.50 -$57.50. Trans Dept main stem |
| 1857-28 | " | ton eng'man 24 da @ $2.50 - $60.00. 1st div |
| 1857-49 | Rheam, Henry | lab 24 da @ $1 - $24.00. Rd Dept main stem 3d s-div |
| 1857-124 | Rhoda, Haman | boil mkr 10 da @ $1.65 - $16.50. Mach Dept, Martinsburg |
| 1855-83 | Rhodes, John | mach 26 3/4 da @@$1.72 - $46.00. Mach Dept |
| 1855-73 | Z. | iron inspec @ $58.35 per mo - $58.35. Rd Way Dept |
| 1857-45 | Zachariah | iron inspec @ $53.35 per mo. Rd Dept |
| 1857-52 | Rhoe, Jacob | lab 26½ da @ $1 - $26.50. Rd Dept main stem 6th s-div |
| 1857-18 | Rice, Amos | pass train brak 5 da @ $33.35 per mo - $5.55. thr mail & exp |
| 1855-94 | Calvin | paint 17 3/4 da @ $1.50 - $26.60. Mach Dept |
| 1857-65 | David | lab 10¼ da @ $1 - $10.25. Rd Dept main stem 17th s-div |
| 1857-65 | Henry | lab 14½ da @ $1 - $14.50. Rd Dept main stem 17th s-div |
| 1857-32 | James | ton fire 24½ da @ $1.35 per mo - $32.00. 1st div |
| 1855-34 | John | mak fires 24½ da @ $1 - $24.50. Trans Dept main stem |
| 1857-65 | Marmaduke | lab 14½ da @ $1 - $14.50. Rd Dept main stem 17th s-div |
| 1857-65 | Richard | lab 14½ da @ $1 - $14.50. Rd Dept main stem 17th s-div |
| 1857-8 | Ricely, D. | watch 30 da @ $25 per mo - $25.00. Camden sta |
| 1855-5 | Daniel | car clean 28 da @ $30 per mo - $30.00. Trans Dept, Wash br |
| 1857-93 | Rich, Anthony | smith help 12½ da @ $1 - $12.25. quarry & haul stone for Board Tree & Littleton Tun |
| 1857-28 | August | ton eng'man 13 3/4 da @ $2.50 - $34.35. 1st div |
| 1857-132 | John | blksmith help 20¼ da @ $1 - $20.25. Mach Dept, Grafton |
| 1855-38 | Richards, Joseph | lab 20 da @ $1 - $20.00. Rd Way Dept |
| 1857-48 | " | lab 14½ da @ $1 - $14.50. Rd Dept main stem 2d s-div |
| 1855-83 | " | lab 11 3/4 da @ $1.15 - $13.50. Mach Dept |
| 1857-25 | Richardson, George W. | ton brak 13¼ da @ $40 per mo - $21.60. 2d div |
| 1855-72 | M. | mach 23 da @ $1.50 - $34.50. Rd Way Dept |
| 1857-69 | Morris | mach 16 3/4 da @ $1.65 - $27.65. Mt Clare sta, Balto |
| 1857-119 | Robert | carp 18 da @ $1.50 - $27.00. Mach Dept, Balto |
| 1855-83 | T. | mach (includ boil mkr, work sht iron, &c) 25½ da @ $2.50 - $63.75. Mach Dept |
| 1857-115 | Thomas | fore boil mkr @ $65 per mo - $65.00. Mach Dept, Balto |
| 1857-24 | William | ton brak 17½ da @ $40 per mo - $28.00. 1st div |
| 1857-94 | Riche, Ferede | lab 22 da @ $1 - $22.00. quarry & haul stone for Board Tree & Littleton Tun |

| | | | |
|---|---|---|---|
| 1857-28 | Richie, William | ton eng'man 23½ da @ $2.50 - $58.75. 1st div |
| 1855-89 | Richmond, D. | app 28 da @ $.50 - $14.00. Mach Dept |
| 1857-123 | Daniel | mach 5 da @ $1.25 - $6.25. Mach Dept, Martinsburg |
| 1857-20 | John | pass fire 2 da @ $40 per mo - $2.65. 1st div |
| 1857-47 | Rick, Daniel | lab 15 3/4 da @ $1 - $15.75. Rd Way Dept |
| 1855-38 | Rickey, James | lab 20 da @ $1 - $20.00. Rd Way Dept |
| 1857-97 | Ricter, Henry | watch 30 da @ $1 - $30.00. NW Va RR, Rd Dept 2d s-div |
| 1857-28 | Riddle, Adam | ton eng'man 19 da @ $3 - $57.00. 1st div |
| 1855-95 | Beal | mould 18¼ da @ $1.72 - $31.40. Mach Dept |
| 1857-131 | James | mach 26⅔ da @ $1.60 - $42.00. Mach Dept, Grafton |
| 1855-13 | Rider, H. | conduc & brak 18 da @ $40 per mo - $32.00. Trans Dept main stem |
| 1857-83 | J. | lab 5⅖ da @ $1.12 - $6.20. grad, Board Tree Tun |
| 1857-91 | John | bricklay 12 3/4 da @ $2 - $25.50. grad, Littleton Tun |
| 1857-63 | Luke | lab 25½ da @ $1 - $25.50. Rd Dept main stem 16th s-div |
| 1857-113 | Ridgeway, Thomas | mach app 23 da @ $.45 - $10.35. Mach Dept, Balto |
| 1857-98 | Ridge, Thos. | watch 30 da @ $1 - $30.00. NW Va RR, Rd Dept 2d s-div |
| 1857-134 | Ridgely, Frederick | mach 21 3/4 da @ $1.75 - $38.05. Mach Dept, Wheeling |
| 1857-18 | R. H. L. | pass train brak 17 da @ $33.35 per mo - $18.90. thr mail & exp |
| 1857-93 | Rielly, Thomas | lab 22 da @ $1 - $22.00. quarry & haul stone for Board Tree & Littleton Tun |
| 1857-23 | Riely, Stephen | ton conduc 26½ da @ $50 per mo - $53.00. Board Tree Tun |
| 1857-15 | Rieman, George S. | clk 30 da @ $35 per mo - $35.00. Grafton sta |
| 1857-75 | Rierdon, Dennis | lab 3 da @ $.97 - $2.90. ballast train for 2d track |
| 1855-66 | Rige, Patrick | lab 23 da @ $1 - $23.00. Rd Way Dept |
| 1857-16 | Riggens, John | lab 25 da @ $25 per mo - $25.00. Benwood sta |
| 1855-21 | Riggs, James | fire 19 da @ $1.75 - $33.25. Trans Dept main stem |
| 1855-39 | Joel | lab 24 da @ $1 - $24.00. Rd Way Dept |
| 1855-39 | Joseph | lab 23 da @ $1.25 - $28.75. Rd Way Dept |
| 1855-7 | Rigney, E. T. | bag mast 28 da @ $58.35 per mo - $45.00. Trans Dept main stem |
| 1857-8 | J. H. | rec clk 30 da @ $58.35 per mo - $58.35. Camden sta |
| 1855-6 | J. T. | agt 28 da @ $100 per mo - $100.00. Trans Dept main stem |
| 1855-6 | John H. | clk deliv 28 da @ $25 per mo - $25.00. Trans Dept main stem |
| 1857-9 | John T. | agt 30 da @ $100 per mo - $100.00. Mt Clare sta |
| 1855-6 | W. H. | clk 28 da @ $62.50 per mo - $62.50. Trans Dept main stem |
| 1857-123 | Rigsby, Samuel | mach 21½ da @ $1.10 - $23.65. Mach Dept, Martinsburg |
| 1855-52 | Riley, James | lab 28 da @ $1 - $28.00. Rd Way Dept |
| 1855-21 | Riley, Benjamin | fire 14 da @ $1.75 - $24.50. Trans Dept main stem |

# B & O RR EMPLOYEES

| ID | Name | Description |
|---|---|---|
| 1857-114 | Riley, George | iron mould help 18 3/4 da @ $1 – $18.75. Mach Dept, Balto |
| 1857-115 | " Henry | boil mkr 20 da @ $1.50 – $30.00. Mach Dept, Balto |
| 1857-121 | " J. | lumber yd help 7 da @ $1.15 – $8.05. Mach Dept, Balto |
| 1857-36 | " J. J. G. | tele oper 30 da @ $50 per mo – $50.00. Camden sta |
| 1855-21 | " J. W. | fire 17 da @ $1.75 – $29.75. Trans Dept main stem |
| 1855-46 | " James | lab 22 da @ $1 – $22.00. Rd Way Dept |
| 1857-118 | " | blksmith help 17¾ da @ $1 – $17.25. Mach Dept, Balto |
| 1857-36 | " | tele oper 30 da @ $30 per mo – $30.00. # 12 w sta |
| 1857-87 | " | watch 10 da @ $1 – $10.00. grad, McGuire's Tun |
| 1855-30 | " John | fill tend 14 da @ $1 – $14.00. Trans Dept main stem |
| 1855-59 | " | lab 13 3/4 da @ $1 – $13.75. Rd Way Dept |
| 1857-53 | " | lab 23½ da @ $1 – $23.50. Rd Dept main stem 7th s-div |
| 1855-31 | " John C. | ton eng'man 8½ da @ $3 – $25.50. Board Tree Tun |
| 1855-32 | " John W. | tele oper 28 da @ $30 per mo – $30.00. Trans Dept main stem |
| 1857-30 | " | ton eng'man 20 da @ $3 – $60.00. 4th div |
| 1855-33 | " M. | greas cars 14 da @ $30 per mo – $15.00. Trans Dept main stem |
| 1857-139 | " Michael | clean eng 27½ da @ $1.15 – $27.50. NW Va RR, Mach Dept, Parkersburg |
| 1857-75 | " | lab 15 da @ $1 – $17.20. ballast train for 2d track |
| 1857-60 | " | lab 30½ da @ $1 – $30.50. Rd Dept main stem 13th s-div |
| 1857-32 | " Michael J. | ton fire 20¼ da @ $1.75 – $35.45. 1st div |
| 1855-81 | " Mike | lab 24 da @ $1.15 – $27.60. Mach Dept |
| 1857-121 | " | carp help 16 da @ $1.15 – $18.40. Mach Dept, Balto |
| 1857-78 | " Owen | lab 22 3/4 da @ $1 – $22.75. lay 2d track |
| 1855-44 | " Patrick | lab 6 da @ $1 – $6.00. Rd Way Dept |
| 1857-85 | " | watch 29 da @ $1.25 – $36.25. Mach Dept |
| 1857-95 | " | lab 11½ da @ $1 – $11.50. grad, Board Tree Tun |
| 1857-99 | " | lab 24½ da @ $.75 – $18.20. NW Va RR, Rd Dept 4th s-div |
| 1857-115 | " | watch 30 da @ $1.25 – $37.50. Mach Dept, Balto |
| 1855-85 | " Peter | blksmith 24 da @ $1.72 – $41.30. Mach Dept |
| 1855-60 | " | fore 24 da @ $1.25 – $30.00. Rd Way Dept |
| 1857-64 | " | fore 25 da @ $1.25 – $32.50. Rd Dept main stem 17th s-div |
| 1855-46 | " Phillip | lab 12½ da @ $1 – $12.50. Rd Way Dept |
| 1855-28 | " R. | reg eng 21 da @ $1.50 – $31.50. Trans Dept main stem |
| 1857-74 | " Richard | lab 25 da @ £.12 – $28.15. repair bridges &c |
| 1857-27 | " Stephen | ton brak 3 da @ $40 per mo –$4.80. Board Tree Tun |
| 1857-130 | " William | mach 23¾ da @ $1.75 – $40.70. Mach Dept, Newburg |

| ID | Name | Description |
|---|---|---|
| 1857-121 | Riley, William L. | paint 17¾ da @ $1.65 - $28.45. Mach Dept, Balto |
| 1857-114 | Rimby, Reuben | iron mould 19¼ da @ $1.65 - $31.75. Mach Dept, Balto |
| 1857-83 | Rine, Patrick | lab 27 da @ $1.12 - $30.35. grad, Board Tree Tun |
| 1857-128 | Rinercomb, Oliver | carp 15½ da @ $1.50 - $23.25. Mach Dept, Piedmont |
| 1857-98 | Ringer, Samuel | watch 30 da @ $1 - $30.00. NW Va RR, Rd Dept 2d s-div |
| 1855-87 | Ringgold, E. | blksmith 22½ da @ $1.25 - $28.15. Mach Dept |
| 1855-78 | Ringland, William | help 24 da @ $1.15 - $27.60. NW Va RR bridges |
| 1857-102 | Ringler, Franklin | carp 18 da @ $1.65 - $29.70. NW Va RR bridges |
| 1855-29 | Rinker, A. | prepar fuel 28 da @ $1 - $28.00. Trans Dept main stem |
| 1857-15 | " | dry sand 30 da @ $1 - $30.00. Fetterman sta |
| 1855-38 | Rion, James | lab 21 da @ $1 - $21.00. Rd Way Dept |
| 1857-8 | Ripley, James | watch 30 da @ $35 per mo - $35.00. Camden sta |
| 1857-47 | Ripple, Samuel | lab 10½ da @ $1 - $10.50. Rd Dept main stem 2d s-div |
| 1857-120 | Rireiman, Henry | carp 21 da @ $1.50 - $31.50. Mach Dept, Balto |
| 1857-52 | Riser, Benjamin | lab 6 da @ $.90 - $5.40. Rd Dept main stem 6th s-div |
| 1855-41 | " Geo. | lab 18 da @ $1 - $18.00. Rd Way Dept |
| 1857-52 | " John | watch 30 da @ $1 - $30.00. Rd Dept main stem 6th s-div |
| 1855-41 | " Saml. | lab 17 da @ $1 - $17.00. Rd Way Dept |
| 1855-92 | Risher, Henry | help 3 da @$1 -$3.00. Mach Dept |
| 1857-67 | Rist, George | lab 20 3/4 da @ $1 - $20.75. Rd Dept main stem 19th s-div |
| 1855-19 | Ritchie, Wm. | ton eng'man 31¼ da @ $2.50 -$78.10. Trans Dept main stem |
| 1857-13 | Ritter, G. M. | conduc & brak 1¼ da - $25.40. Trans Dept main stem |
| 1857-36 | Rizer, George W. | tele oper 30 da @$40 per mo - $40.00. Piedmont |
| 1857-25 | " Hamilton | ton brak 25 da @$40 per mo - $40.00. 2d div |
| 1855-42 | Roach, Edward | lab 18½ da @ $1 - $18.50. Rd Way Dept |
| 1855-32 | " | saw wd 55 cords @ $.35 - $19.25. Trans Dept main stem |
| 1857-52 | " | lab 27½ da @ $1 - $27.50. Rd Dept main stem 6th s-div |
| 1855-78 | " James | help 23 da @ $1.15 - $26.45. Mach Dept |
| 1857-76 | " | drill 11½ da @ $1.02 - $11.75. ballast train for 2d track |
| 1857-111 | " | mach help 18 da @$1.15 - $20.70. Mach Dept, Balto |
| 1857-77 | " Jeremiah | quarry 8 da @ $1 - $8.00. ballast train for 2d track |
| 1857-27 | " John | ton brak 32 3/4 da @ $40 per mo -$52.40. 3d & 4th div |
| 1857-53 | " Michael | lab 4 da @ $1 - $4.00. Rd Dept main stem 7th s-div |
| 1857-74 | " Patrick | lab 23 da @ $1.12 - $25.85. repair bridges &c |
| 1855-42 | " | lab 19 da @ $1 - $19.00. Rd Way Dept |
| 1855-50 | " | watch cuts 28 da @ $1 - $28.00. Rd Way Dept |

| | | |
|---|---|---|
| 1857-80 | Roach, Patrick | lab 20 3/4 da @ $1 - $20.75. lay 2d track |
| 1857-63 | " | watch 30 da @ $1 - $30.00. Rd Dept main stem 16th s-div |
| 1855-87 | Richard | help 24¼ da @ $1 - $24.25. Mach Dept |
| 1857-79 | Thos. | lab 23 3/4 da @ $1 - $23.75. lay 2d track |
| 1855-93 | Robbins, Harvey | paint 25½ da - $42.40. Mach Dept |
| 1857-129 | " | paint 18¼ da @ $1.75 - $31.95. Mach Dept, Piedmont |
| 1857-36 | Roberson, Thomas | lab 22½ da @ $1 - $22.50. J. R. Shrode's wd train 4th div |
| 1855-28 | Roberts, G. W. | reg eng 10 da @ $1.15 - $11.50. Trans Dept main stem |
| 1855-91 | L. J. | mach 15 da @ $1.50 - $22.50. Mach Dept |
| 1857-24 | Luther | ton brak 18 3/4 da @ $30 per mo - $22.50. 1st div |
| 1855-24 | Will | pass & bur driv 24 da @ $30 per mo - $30.00. Trans Dept main stem |
| 1855-39 | William | lab 24 da @ $1 - $24.00. Rd Way Dept |
| 1855-50 | Robertson, James | watch cuts 22 da @ $1 - $22.00. Rd Way Dept |
| 1855-32 | Robinson, A. | weigh mast 24 da @ $41.65 per mo - $41.65. Trans Dept main stem |
| 1857-8 | " | weigh mast 25 da @ $50 per mo -$50.00. Camden sta |
| 1855-29 | Andrew | haul & saw firewd 13½ da @ $1 - $13.50. Trans Dept main stem |
| 1857-124 | " | blksmith help 18 da @ $1 - $18.00. Mach Dept, Martinsburg |
| 1855-13 | B. L. | conduc & brak 16 3/4 da @ $40 per mo - $27.90. Trans Dept main stem |
| 1855-77 | D. | mach 23½ da @ $1.50 - $35.25. Mach Dept |
| 1855-19 | Edward | ton eng'man 3 da @ $2.50 - $7.50. Trans Dept main stem |
| 1857-28 | " | ton eng'man 19 3/4 da @ $3 - $59.25. 1st div |
| 1857-23 | F. H. | ton conduc 6½ da @ $50 per mo - $13.00. Board Tree Tun |
| 1857-84 | Francis H. | conduc 26¼ da @ $1.90 - $49.85. grad, Board Tree Tun |
| 1855-29 | Israel | haul & saw firewd 12 da @ $1 - $12.00. Trans Dept main stem |
| 1857-124 | " | blksmith help 18 da @ $1 - $18.00. Mach Dept, Martinsburg |
| 1855-84 | Jesse | mach 19½ da @ $1.35 - $26.30. Mach Dept |
| 1855-33 | John | greas cars 28 da @ $30 per mo - $30.00. Trans Dept main stem |
| 1857-126 | " | dry sand 30 da @ $1 - $30.00. Mach Dept, Martinsburg |
| 1857-55 | Moses | lab 18¼ da @ $1 - $18.25. Rd Dept main stem 9th s-div |
| 1855-21 | Samuel | fire 18¼ da @ $1.75 - $31.95. Trans Dept main stem |
| 1857-118 | " | blksmith help 17 3/4 da @ $1 - $17.75. Mach Dept, Balto |
| 1857-120 | W. T. | carp 18¼ da @ $1.65 - $30.10. Mach Dept, Balto |
| 1855-29 | William | haul & saw firewd 10 da @ $1 - $10.00. Trans Dept main stem |
| 1857-45 | William R. | asst clk @ $15 per mo. Rd Dept |
| 1857-17 | Robison, William | lab 25 da @ $1 - $25.00. frt transfer force at Bellaire, opp Benwood |
| 1855-34 | Robson, Joseph | greas cars 18 da @ $1 - $18.00. Trans Dept main stem |

# B & O RR EMPLOYEES 285

| ID | Name | Details |
|---|---|---|
| 1855-86 | Robson, Wm. | mach 23 da @ $1.90 - $43.70. Mach Dept |
| 1855-92 | Rochelle, James | help 28 3/4 da @ $1 - $28.75. Mach Dept |
| 1857-130 | Rochelle, James | lab 24 3/4 da @ $1 - $24.75. Mach Dept, Piedmont |
| 1857-22 | Rock, J. J. | ton conduc 6 da @ $40 per mo; 12 da @ $50 per mo - $33.60. 2d div |
| 1855-41 | Rock, Patrick | lab 25 da @ $1 - $25.00. Rd Way Dept |
| 1857-50 | " | nail 30 da @ $1.05 - $31.50. Rd Dept main stem 4th s-div |
| 1855-13 | Rockwell, Charles | conduc & brak 16½ da @ $50 per mo - $36.85. Trans Dept main stem |
| 1857-52 | Elias | lab 23 da @ $1 - $23.00. Rd Dept main stem 6th s-div |
| 1857-34 | Samuel | watch 22 da @ $1 - $22.00. Board Tree Tun |
| 1855-13 | T. | conduc & brak 12 da @ $50 per mo - $26.00. Trans Dept main stem |
| 1857-25 | Thomas | ton brak 3¾ da @ $30 per mo - $6.50. 2d div |
| 1857-23 | " | ton conduc 28 da @ $50 per mo - $56.00. Board Tree Tun |
| 1855-43 | Rockwill, W. | lab 18 da @ $1 - $18.00. Rd Way Dept |
| 1855-42 | E. | lab 24 da @ $1 - $24.00. Rd Way Dept |
| 1855-42 | P. | lab 23¾ da @ $1 - $23.25. Rd Way Dept |
| 1857-36 | Roderick, J. | tele oper 30 da @ $30 per mo - $30.00. Rowlesburg |
| 1855-40 | Rodes, Elisha | lab 26 da @ $1 - $26.00. Rd Way Dept |
| 1855-40 | Rodgers, William | lab 24½ da @ $1 - $24.50. Rd Way Dept |
| 1857-87 | Rodgers, Ashbal | lab 22½ da @ $1 - $22.50. grad, McGuire's Tun |
| 1857-119 | J. C. | carp 15¼ da @ $1.50 - $23.25. Mach Dept, Balto |
| 1857-111 | James | mach help 18 3/4 da @ $1.15 - $21.55. Mach Dept, Balto |
| 1857-71 | John | chair mkr 18 da @ $1 - $18.00. Mt Clare sta, Balto |
| 1857-70 | John W. | chair mkr 17½ da @ $1.25 - $21.85. Mt Clare sta, Balto |
| 1855-61 | Patrick | lab 21 da @ $1 - $21.00. Rd Way Dept |
| 1857-66 | " | lab 21½ da @ $1 - $21.50. Rd Dept main stem 18th s-div |
| 1857-115 | Thomas | boil mkr help 18 da @ $1.15 - $20.70. Mach Dept, Balto |
| 1857-113 | W. H. | mach app 23 da @ $.45 - $10.35. Mach Dept, Balto |
| 1857-135 | Rodman, Robert | blksmith help 6 3/4 da @ $1 - $6.75. Mach Dept, Wheeling |
| 1855-46 | Rodon, Henry | help 20½ da @ $1 - $20.50. Rd Way Dept |
| 1855-75 | Roeder, E. | lab 21 da @ $1 - $21.00. Rd Way Dept |
| 1857-50 | Earnest | lab 24½ da @ $1 - $24.50. Rd Dept main stem 5th s-div |
| 1857-51 | William | lab 9 da @ $1 - $9.00. Rd Dept main stem 5th s-div |
| 1855-1 | Rogan, Tim. | lab 30 da @ $1 - $30.00. lay 2d track |
| 1857-3 | Rogers, H. W. | asst collec $700 per annum - $58.33. Ofc Hanover St |
| 1855-21 | J. W. | asst collec @ $66.66 per mo. Gen Ofc |
| 1855-21 | Henry W. | fire 13½ da @ $1.75 - $23.60. Trans Dept main stem |

## B & O RR EMPLOYEES

| | | |
|---|---|---|
| 1855-71 | Rogers, John W. | help 22½ da @ $1.15 - $25.85. Rd Way Dept |
| 1857-32 | " " | ton fire 19 da @ $1.75 - $33.25. 1st div |
| 1855-93 | " Joseph | mach 23 da @ $1.75 - $40.25. Mach Dept |
| 1855-69 | " " | mach 23 da @ $1.75 - $40.25. Mach Dept |
| 1857-87 | " L. J. | lab 3¼ da @ $1.75 - $5.70. Rd Way Dept |
| 1857-24 | " Laban J. | stone mason 19 3/4 da @ $2 - $39.50. grad, McGuire's Tun |
| 1857-95 | " Patrick | ton brak 20 3/4 da @ $2 - $41.50. 1st div |
| 1855-46 | " Peter | lab 22½ da @ $1 - $22.50. Wash br, Rd Dept |
| 1855-41 | " Tim. | lab 22½ da @ $1 - $22.50. Rd Way Dept |
| 1855-31 | Rohl, Jacob | lab 20 3/4 da @ $1 - $20.75. Rd Way Dept |
| 1857-55 | Rohn, Charles | prepar fuel 10½ da @ $1 - $10.50. Trans Dept main stem |
| 1855-13 | Rohr, Charles | lab 22 da @ $1 - $22.00. Rd Dept main stem 9th s-div |
| 1857-22 | " James | conduc & brak 4 3/4 da @ $50 per mo - $10.40. Trans Dept main stem |
| 1857-40 | Rohrer, Joseph | ton conduc 13 da @ $50 per mo - $26.00. 2d div |
| 1855-16 | Roland, George W. | pass fire 24 da @ $40 per mo - $32.00. NW Va rd, Parkersburg sta |
| 1855-53 | " M. | pass fire 20 da @ $40 per mo - $28.55. Trans Dept main stem |
| 1857-119 | Roleman, John | lab 16½ da @ $1 - $16.50. Rd Way Dept |
| 1857-133 | Rollins, Edward | tin 22½ da @ $1.65 - $36.70. Mach Dept, Balto |
| 1857-55 | " Henry M. | mach help 24½ da @ $1 - $24.50. Mach Dept, Petterman |
| 1857-139 | Rollman, John | lab 23 3/4 da @ $1 - $23.75. Rd Dept main stem 9th s-div |
| 1855-16 | Rolls, Daniel | boll mkr help 26¼ da @ $.90 - $23.60. NW Va RR, Mach Dept, Parkersburg |
| 1857-39 | Roloson, H. | bag mast 25 da @ $35 per mo - $29.15. NW Va rd, Parkersburg sta |
| 1857-139 | " Richard | mach app 25 da @ $.45 - $11.25. NW Va RR, Mach Dept, Parkersburg |
| 1855-73 | Roman, Frank | lab 24½ da @ $1.06 - $25.95. Rd Way Dept |
| 1857-71 | " " | lab 24 da @ $1.06 - $25.45. Mt Clare, repair tracks in yd |
| 1857-17 | " Michael | lab 25 da @ $1 - $25.00. frt transfer force at Bellaire, opp Benwood |
| 1857-100 | Ronan, Michael | lab 27½ da @ $1 - $27.50. NW Va RR, Rd Dept 5th s-div |
| 1855-81 | Roner, Peter | lab 28¼ da @ $1.15 - $32.50. Mach Dept |
| 1857-52 | Roney, James | lab 23¼ da @ $1 - $23.50. Rd Dept main stem 6th s-div |
| 1857-78 | " John | lab 25½ da @ $1 - $25.50. lay 2d track |
| 1857-25 | Rooney, Albert | ton brak 25 da @ $40 per mo - $40.00. 2d div |
| 1857-98 | " James | watch 30 da @ $1 - $30.00. NW Va RR, Rd Dept 3d s-div |
| 1857-57 | " John | lab 25½ da @ $1 - $25.50. Rd Dept main stem 11th s-div |
| 1857-96 | " Larry | lab 25 da @ $1 - $25.00. NW Va RR, Rd Dept 1st s-div |
| 1857-84 | " Patrick | lab 24 da @ $1.12 - $27.00. grad, Board Tree Tun |
| 1855-5 | Roscum, Henry | lab 23 da @ $1 - $23.00. Trans Dept, Wash br |
| 1855-71 | Rose, John | carp 22 da @ $1.25 - $27.50. Rd Way Dept |

B & O RR EMPLOYEES  287

| | | | |
|---|---|---|---|
| 1857-68 | Rosemburg, Godlip | carp 24 da @ $1.50 - $36.00. Rd Dept main stem 19th s-div |
| 1855-95 | Rosey, Frederick | lab 28½ da @ $1 - $28.50. Mach Dept |
| 1857-134 | Friend | mach help 37 3/4 da @ $1.25 - $47.20. Mach Dept, Wheeling |
| 1857-131 | Ross, Charles | boil mkr 20 da @$1.60 - $32.00. Mach Dept, Grafton |
| 1857-117 | Henry | blksmith 3 da @ $1.50 - $4.50. Mach Dept, Balto |
| 1857-128 | William | boil mkr 11¼ da @ $1.25 - $14.05. Mach Dept, Piedmont |
| 1857-130 | Roten, William | lab 19½ da @ $1 - $19.50. Mach Dept, Piedmont |
| 1855-86 | Roth, Adam | mach 26 da @ $1.40 - $36.40. Mach Dept |
| 1857-123 | " | mach 24 3/4 da @ $1.50 - $37.10. Mach Dept, Martinsburg |
| 1857-119 | Roundtree, William | carp 18 da @ $1.50 - $27.00. Mach Dept, Balto |
| 1855-62 | Rourk, B. | lab 10 da @ $1 - $10.00. Rd Way Dept |
| 1857-67 | Bernard | lab 20½ da @ $1 - $20.50. Rd Dept main stem 19th s-div |
| 1855-63 | Jno. | lab 21¼ da @ $1 - $21.25. Rd Way Dept |
| 1857-127 | Rourke, Patrick | rig 22¼ da @ $1.25 - $27.80. Mach Dept, Piedmont |
| 1855-90 | Rouse, John | help 23 da @ $1 - $23.00. Mach Dept |
| 1855-83 | William | lab 24 da @ $1 - $24.00. Mach Dept |
| 1857-112 | " | mach help 18 da @ $1 - $18.00. Mach Dept, Balto |
| 1857-101 | Rowan, Darby | lab 22½ da @ $1 - $22.50. NW Va RR ballast train |
| 1855-67 | John | lab 17 da @ $1 - $17.00. Rd Way Dept |
| 1857-98 | " | lab 18 da @ $1 - $18.00. NW Va RR, Rd Dept 3d s-div |
| 1857-100 | " | lab 23½ da @ $1 - $23.50. NW Va RR, Rd Dept 5th s-div |
| 1857-101 | Michael | lab 20 da @ $1 - $20.00. NW Va RR ballast train |
| 1855-9 | Rowland, George | conduc 15½ da @ $50 per mo - $32.30. Trans Dept main stem |
| 1857-65 | Rowns, George | watch 28 da @ $1 - $28.00. Rd Dept main stem 17th s-div |
| 1857-17 | Roy, Deacon | lab 23½ da @ $1 - $23.50. frt transfer force at Bellaire, opp Benwood |
| 1857-83 | Royall, Patrick | lab 3½ da @ $1.12 - $3.95. grad, Board Tree Tun |
| 1857-57 | Ruan, John | lab 26 3/4 da @ $1 - $26.75. Rd Dept main stem 11th s-div |
| 1857-90 | Michael | lab 22 3/4 da @ $1 - $22.75. grad, Welling Tun |
| 1857-59 | Ruberry, John | lab 17 da @ $1 - $17.00. Rd Dept main stem 12th s-div |
| 1857-58 | Patrick | lab 25 da @ $1 - $25.00. Rd Dept main stem 12th s-div |
| 1857-59 | Thomas | lab 24½ da @ $1 - $24.50. Rd Dept main stem 12th s-div |
| 1855-77 | Rugg, Charles | mach 26 da @ $1.65 - $42.90. Mach Dept |
| 1855-96 | Rullman, A. | app 18¼ da @ $.45 - $8.20. Mach Dept |
| 1857-65 | Rumble, Joseph | lab 14 da @ $1 - $14.00. Rd Dept main stem 17th s-div |
| 1857-112 | Rumney, Robert | mach help 27 3/4 da @$1.35 -$37.45. Mach Dept, Balto |
| 1857-99 | Runey, John | lab 23½ da @ $1 - $23.50. NW Va RR, Rd Dept 4th s-div |
| 1855-65 | Runk, M. | lab 13 3/4 da @ $1 - $13.75. Rd Way Dept |

| | | |
|---|---|---|
| 1857-72 | Runk, Martin | carp 20½ da @ $1.12 - $23.05. Cumb depot |
| 1855-55 | Runn, John | lab 11 da @ $1 - $11.00. Rd Way Dept |
| 1855-95 | Runnells, Thomas | lab 24½ da @ $1 - $24.50. Mach Dept |
| 1857-135 | Runnels, Thomas | lab 28½ da @ $1 - $28.50. Mach Dept, Wheeling |
| 1855-78 | Runney, Robert | help 26½ da @ $1.15 - $30.45. Mach Dept |
| 1857-114 | Ruork, Owen | iron mould help 17 3/4 da @ $1.10 -$19.55. Mach Dept, Balto |
| 1857-56 | Rurk, Frederick | lab 25 da @ $1 - $25.00. Rd Dept main stem 10th s-div |
| 1857-89 | Rush, John | lab 22½ da @ $1.12 - $25.30. grad, Welling Tun |
| 1855-57 | Rusha, Henry | blksmith 17 3/4 da @ $1.25 - $22.20. Rd Way Dept |
| 1855-65 | " | blksmith 4 da @ $1.25 - $5.00. Rd Way Dept |
| 1857-139 | " | blksmith 28 3/4 da @ $1.57 - $45.15. NW Va RR, Mach Dept, Parkersburg |
| 1857-125 | Rusk, William | lab 22¼ da @ $1 - $22.25. Mach Dept, Martinsburg |
| 1857-22 | Rusler, Thomas | ton conduc 22¼ da @ $50 per mo - $44.50. 2d div |
| 1855-70 | Russel, James | lab 4 da @ $1 - $4.00. Rd Way Dept |
| 1855-32 | Russell, James | lab 24 da @ $30 per mo - $30.00. Trans Dept main stem |
| 1855-4 | John | pass fire 32 da @ $40 per mo - $45.70. Trans Dept, Wash br |
| 1855-81 | R. B. | carp 19½ da @ $1.55 - $30.25. Mach Dept |
| 1857-119 | " " | carp 18½ da @ $1.45 - $26.85. Mach Dept, Balto |
| 1855-81 | Thomas | lab 22 3/4 da @ $1.15 - $26.15. Mach Dept |
| 1857-17 | " | lab 25 da @ $1 - $25.00. frt transfer force at Bellaire, opp Benwood |
| 1855-13 | W. H. | conduc & brak 12¾ da @ $50 per mo - $25.50. Trans Dept main stem |
| 1857-21 | William H. | ton conduc 23¼ da @ $50 per mo - $46.50. 1st div |
| 1855-29 | Rust, William | haul & saw firewd 3 da @ $1 -$3.00. Trans Dept main stem |
| 1855-78 | Rutherford, A. | help 19½ da @ $1 - $19.50. Mach Dept |
| 1857-112 | Alexander | mach help 20 3/4 da @ $1.25 - $25.95. Mach Dept, Balto |
| 1855-21 | Ruthersdale, Robert | fire 9½ da @ $1.75 - $16.60. Trans Dept main stem |
| 1855-57 | Ruwan, Darby | lab 19 3/4 da @ $1 - $19.75. Rd Way Dept |
| 1855-69 | Ryan, Anthony | lab 20½ da @ $1 - $20.50. Rd Way Dept |
| 1855-68 | James | tend to masons 24 da @ $1 - $24.00. Rd Way Dept |
| 1857-89 | " | lab 25 3/4 da @ $1.12 - $28.95. grad, Welling Tun |
| 1855-94 | John | carp 25¼ da @ $1.45 - $36.60. Mach Dept |
| 1855-60 | " | fore 24 da @ $1.25 - $30.00. Rd Way Dept |
| 1855-68 | " | tend to masons 23 da @ $1 - $23.00. Rd Way Dept |
| 1857-135 | " | carp 30½ da @ $1.50 - $45.75. Mach Dept, Wheeling |
| 1857-64 | " | fore 27½ da @ $1.25 - $34.35. Rd Dept main stem 17th s-div |
| 1857-46 | " | lab 24 da @ $1 - $24.00. Rd Dept main stem 1st s-div |

B & O RR EMPLOYEES 289

| Year-Page | Name | Entry |
|---|---|---|
| 1855-48 | Ryan, M. | train hand 11½ da @ $1 - $14.50. Rd Way Dept |
| 1855-54 | " Michael | lab 16 3/4 da @ $1 - $16.75. Rd Way Dept |
| 1857-78 | " " | lab 25 3/4 da @ $1 - $25.75. lay 2d track |
| 1857-71 | " " | lab 10½ da @ $1 - $10.50. Mt Clare, repair tracks in yd |
| 1857-98 | " " | lab 25 da @ $1 - $25.00. N W Va RR, Rd Dept 3d s-div |
| 1857-73 | " " | lab 23 3/4 da @ $1.12 - $26.55. repair bridges &c |
| 1857-65 | " " | lab 24½ da @ $1 - $24.50. Rd Dept main stem 17th s-div |
| 1857-77 | Patrick | quarry 18½ da @ $1 - $18.50. ballast train for 2d track |
| 1857-81 | Peter | lab 19 3/4 da @ $1 - $19.75. lay 2d track |
| 1857-66 | Philip | lab 24½ da @ $1 - $24.50. Rd Dept main stem 18th s-div |
| 1855-34 | " | car greas 24 da @ $38.35 per mo - $38.00. Trans Dept main stem |
| 1857-137 | " | car greas @ $38.25 per mo - $38.25. Mach Dept, Cumb |
| 1855-64 | Robert, Jr. | lab 23½ da @ $1 - $23.50. Rd Way Dept |
| 1855-64 | Robert, Sr. | lab 10½ da @ $1 - $10.50. Rd Way Dept |
| 1857-88 | Robert, 1st | lab 27 da @ $1.12 - $30.35. grad, Welling Tun |
| 1857-88 | Robert, 2d | lab 26 3/4 da @ $1.12 - $30.10. grad, Welling Tun |
| 1857-75 | Thomas | lab 21 3/4 da @ $1 - $21.75. ballast train for 2d track |
| 1857-80 | " | lab 19 3/4 da @ $1 - $19.75. lay 2d track |
| 1857-101 | " | lab 2 da @ $1 - $2.00. NW Va RR ballast train |
| 1857-98 | " | lab 5 da @ $1 - $5.00. NW Va RR, Rd Dept 3d s-div |
| 1857-122 | Thomas D. | lab 25 da @ $1 - $25.00. Mach Dept, Balto |
| 1857-74 | Tim | lab 12 da @ $.90 - $10.80. repair bridges &c |
| 1855-75 | Timy. | lab 7 da @ $1 - $7.00. Rd Way Dept |
| 1857-39 | Ryland, John | pass brak 21 da @ $33.35 per mo - $23.35. NW Va rd, Parkersburg sta |
| 1857-40 | " | ton brak 6 da @ $40 per mo - $9.60. NW Va rd, Parkersburg sta |
| 1855-83 | Rylon, John | lab 24 da @ $1 - $24.00. Mach Dept |
| 1857-129 | Rymes, Thomas | fill tend 29 da @ $1 - $29.00. Mach Dept, Piedmont |
| 1857-125 | Ryneal, Fredrick | carp 20 3/4 da @ $1.40 - $20.95. Mach Dept, Martinsburg |
| 1855-5 | Ryon, D. | eng clean 24 da @ $32.20 per mo - $32.20. Trans Dept, Wash br |
| 1857-112 | " John | mach help 18½ da @ $1 - $18.50. Mach Dept, Balto |
| 1855-84 | Sackman, F. | mach 23½ da @ $1.25 - $29.40. Mach Dept |
| 1857-115 | " Frederick | boil mkr 23 da @ $1.50 - $34.50. Mach Dept, Balto |
| 1857-116 | " George | boil mkr help 20½ da @ $1.25 - $25.60. Mach Dept, Balto |
| 1855-83 | Saddler, Wm. | lab 25½ da @ $1.15 - $29.30. Mach Dept |
| 1857-115 | Sadler, W. | stat'ry eng'man 20⅞ da @ $1.25 - $25.30. Mach Dept, Balto |
| 1857-28 | " William | ton eng'man 19½ da @ $3 - $58.50. 1st div |

290  B & O RR EMPLOYEES

| | | | |
|---|---|---|---|
| 1857-50 | Saffel, James | lab 23 3/4 da @ $1 - $23.75. Rd Dept main stem 4th s-div |
| 1855-40 | Saffell, James | lab 25 da @ $1 - $25.00. Rd Way Dept |
| 1857-10 | Saffron, Conrad | bur reg 25 da @ $40 per mo -$40.00. hp exp, Balto |
| 1857-55 | Sager, Charles | lab 23½ da @ $1 - $23.50. Rd Dept main stem 9th s-div |
| 1855-19 | Sagle, Charles | ton eng'man 16 da @ $2.50 - $40.00. Trans Dept main stem |
| 1857-28 | " | ton eng'man 13¼ da @ $3 - $40.50. 1st div |
| 1857-21 | James | fire 16 da @ $28.00. Trans Dept main stem |
| 1857-28 | Joseph | ton eng'man 18 3/4 da @ $3 - $56.25. 1st div |
| 1857-32 | Thomas | ton fire 25½ da @ $1 - $24.50. Rd Dept main stem 13th s-div |
| 1857-60 | Salmon, Michael | lab 24½ da @ $1 - $24.50. Rd Dept main stem 13th s-div |
| 1857-68 | Salsburry, Joseph | carp 23 3/4 da @ $1.62 - $38.60. Rd Dept main stem 19th s-div |
| 1857-95 | Sampson, Thomas | fore 21 da @ $1.25 - $26.25. Wash br, Rd Dept |
| 1857-23 | Sanburn, Supil | ton conduc 25 da @ $50 per mo -$50.00. 3d & 4th div |
| 1857-126 | Sanders, Michael | clean eng 24½ da @ $1 - $24.50. Mach Dept, Martinsburg |
| 1855-85 | Sands, John | blksmith 24 da @$1.55 -$37.20. Mach Dept |
| 1855-83 | " | mach 24 da @$1.45 -$34.80. Mach Dept |
| 1857-117 | " | blksmith 18 3/4 da @ $1.65 - $30.95. Mach Dept, Balto |
| 1857-109 | Thomas | mach 18 da @ $1.15 - $20.70. Mach Dept, Balto |
| 1857-119 | " | blksmith app 27¾ da @ $.45 - $12.25. Mach Dept, Balto |
| 1855-13 | Sandsbury, R. | conduc & brak 11¼ da @ $50 per mo - $23.45. Trans Dept main stem |
| 1857-40 | Sanfern, S. | ton conduc 2 da @ $50 per mo - $4.00. NW Va rd, Parkersburg sta |
| 1855-78 | Sank, Abner | carp 26¼ da @ $1.60 - $42.00. Mach Dept |
| 1857-120 | " | carp 18 3/4 da @ $1.60 - $29.20. Mach Dept, Balto |
| 1857-23 | Sannsbury, Isaac | ton conduc 5½ da @ $40 per mo; 2½ da @ $50 per mo - $57.80. 3d & 4th div |
| 1855-21 | Sansbury, Edward | fire 21 da @ $33.35 per mo - $32.50. Trans Dept main stem |
| 1855-66 | S. | lab 21½ da @ $1.25 - $26.85. Rd Way Dept |
| 1857-128 | Sansom, Richard | mach help 22½ da @ $.55 - $12.35. Mach Dept, Piedmont |
| 1857-65 | Santee, Samuel | lab 12½ da @ $1 - $12.25. Rd Dept main stem 17th s-div |
| 1855-36 | Santos, J. | lab 24½ da @ $25 per mo - $25.25. Trans Dept main stem |
| 1855-5 | Sapp, Robert | eng clean 24 da @ $1.15 - $27.60. Trans Dept, Wash br |
| 1855-4 | " | pass fire 5 da @ $40 per mo -$7.15. Trans Dept, Wash br |
| 1857-111 | " | mach help 18 da @ $1.15 - $20.70. Mach Dept, Balto |
| 1855-85 | Sarburg, Jacob | blksmith 24 da @$1.60 -$38.40. Mach Dept, Balto |
| 1857-24 | Sarsfield, J. J. | ton brak 17½ da @ $40 per mo - $28.00. 1st div |
| 1857-78 | Lawrence | lab 26½ da @ $1 - $26.50. lay 2d track |
| 1855-44 | Sates, W. | fore 19 da @$1.25 - $23.75. Rd Way Dept |

| | | |
|---|---|---|
| 1857-62 | Satterfield, Benjamin | lab 19½ da @ $1 - $19.50. Rd Dept main stem 15th s-div |
| 1855-69 | Saucer, C. | lab 11½ da @ $1 - $11.50. Rd Way Dept |
| 1857-50 | Sauerwine, Christian | pump water 22¼ da @ $1 - $22.25. Rd Dept main stem 4th s-div |
| 1855-54 | Saulsberry, Jas. | carp 3 da @ $1.90 - $5.70. Rd Way Dept |
| 1855-54 | Jos. | carp 2 da @ $1.90 - $3.80. Rd Way Dept |
| 1855-41 | Saunders, S. | fore 9 da @ $1.25 - $11.25. Rd Way Dept |
| 1857-139 | Saville, Anthony | lab 27½ da @ $.90 - $24.75. NW Va RR, Mach Dept, Parkersburg |
| 1855-83 | John | mach 24½ da @ $1.65 - $40.40. Mach Dept |
| 1857-109 | " | mach 17½ da @$1.80 -$31.50. Mach Dept, Balto |
| 1857-64 | Patrick | lab 22½ da @ $1 - $22.50. Rd Dept main stem 17th s-div |
| 1857-139 | Peter | fill tend 28 da @ $1 - $28.00. NW Va RR, Mach Dept, Parkersburg |
| 1857-113 | W. O. | mach app 23 da @ $.65 - $14.95. Mach Dept, Balto |
| 1857-124 | William | mach app 19½ da @ $.50 - $9.75. Mach Dept, Martinsburg |
| 1857-130 | Saxon, Martin | lab 30¼ da @ $1 - $30.25. Mach Dept, Piedmont |
| 1855-8 | Saxton, Owen | bag mast 28 da @ $45 per mo - $42.90. Trans Dept main stem |
| 1857-19 | " | bag mast 30 da @ $45 per mo - $45.00. thr mail & exp |
| 1857-103 | Sayers, James | carp 22½ da @ $1.60 - $36.00. NW Va RR depot |
| 1855-61 | Sayhawk, Samuel | lab 9 da @ $1 - $9.00. Rd Way Dept |
| 1855-19 | Sayster, Lewis | ton eng'man 7½ da @ $2.50 - $18.75. Trans Dept main stem |
| 1857-134 | Scaggs, Charles | mach 3¼ da @ $1.50 - $4.85. Mach Dept, Wheeling |
| 1857-30 | " | ton eng'man 5 da @ $2.50 - $12.50. 4th div |
| 1857-93 | Scally, Andrew | smith help 22½ da @ $1 - $22.50. quarry & haul stone for Board Tree & Littleton Tun |
| 1857-82 | Martin | lab 25¼ da @ $1.12 - $28.40. grad, Board Tree Tun |
| 1857-47 | Scanlin, Michael | lab 27 da @ $1 - $27.00. Rd Dept main stem 2d s-div |
| 1855-49 | Scarey, Patrick | watch cuts 25 da @ $1 - $25.00. Rd Way Dept |
| 1857-50 | Scarff, Jacob | lab 25 da @$1 - $25.00. Rd Dept main stem 4th s-div |
| 1855-41 | James | lab 24 da @ $1 - $24.00. Rd Way Dept |
| 1857-50 | " | lab 19 da @ $1 - $19.00. Rd Dept main stem 4th s-div |
| 1857-60 | Scarry, Patrick | watch 29 da @ $1 - $29.00. Rd Dept main stem 13th s-div |
| 1855-79 | Scars, George | cart boy @ $14 per mo - $14.00. Mach Dept |
| 1855-65 | Scater, John | carp 16½ da @ $1.62½ - $26.80. Rd Way Dept |
| 1855-87 | Schad, William | mach 29 da @ $1.55 - $44.95. Mach Dept |
| 1855-72 | Schaeffer, Adam | help 24 da @$.75 - $18.00. Rd Way Dept |
| 1857-70 | " | blksmith 18 da @ $1.50 - $27.00. Mt Clare sta, Balto |
| 1857-132 | Schaffer, A. | lab 10 3/4 da @ $1.25 - $13.45. Mach Dept, Grafton |
| 1857-123 | Henry | mach 22 da @ $1.40 - $30.80. Mach Dept, Martinsburg |

| | | |
|---|---|---|
| 1857-123 | Schaffer, Jacob | mach 22 da @ $1 - $22.00. Mach Dept, Martinsburg |
| 1855-9 | John | conduc 24 da @ $55 per mo - $55.00. Trans Dept main stem |
| 1857-128 | " | blksmith 19½ da @ $1.65 - $32.15. Mach Dept, Piedmont |
| 1857-124 | Joseph | mach 19¼ da @$1 - $19.25. Mach Dept, Martinsburg |
| 1857-81 | Schahel, John | lab 18½ da @ $1.12 - $20.80. grad, Board Tree Tun |
| 1857-11 | Schank, J. W. | deliv clk 30 da @ $58.35 per mo - $58.35. Locust Pt |
| 1857-118 | Scharf, William | blksmith app 25 da @ $.45 - $11.25. Mach Dept, Balto |
| 1855-89 | Scheeke, William | app 27 da @ $.45 - $12.15. Mach Dept |
| 1857-137 | Scheiber, Conrad | car greas @ $35 per mo - $35.00. Mach Dept, Cumb |
| 1855-28 | Schiber, Peter | prepar fuel 24 da @$1 - $24.00. Trans Dept main stem |
| 1857-70 | Schier, Henry | app 24 da @ $.50 - $12.00. Mt Clare sta, Balto |
| 1855-34 | Schiller, C. | lab 24 da @ $30 per mo - $30.00. Trans Dept main stem |
| 1857-137 | Schilling, John | lab 21 da @ $1 - $21.00. Mach Dept, Cumb |
| 1855-91 | Schmidt, Adam | mach 26½ da @ $1.50 - $39.75. Mach Dept |
| 1857-110 | Schnaff, R. | mach 20¼ da @ $1.35 -$27.35. Mach Dept, Balto |
| 1857-123 | Schodd, William | mach 20 da @$1.65 - $33.00. Mach Dept, Martinsburg |
| 1857-132 | Schooley, Henry | clean eng 29 da @ $1 - $29.00. Mach Dept, Grafton |
| 1857-123 | Schoppert, Wm. | mach 28¼ da @ $1.50 - $42.35. Mach Dept, Martinsburg |
| 1855-54 | Schroeder, Frantz | track lay 15 da @ $1.12½ - $16.90. Rd Way Dept |
| 1855-81 | Schryack, J. S. | coach mkr 23½ da @ $2.10 - $49.35. Mach Dept |
| 1855-86 | Schulke, Henry | mach 23 da @ $1.72 - $39.65. Mach Dept |
| 1855-90 | Schultz, Henry | help 23 da @ $1 - $23.00. Mach Dept |
| 1855-34 | Schwertferger, C. | clean pass car 28 da @$30 per mo - $30.00. Trans Dept main stem |
| 1857-123 | Scoles, Walter | mach 19½ da @ $1.70 - $33.15. Mach Dept, Martinsburg |
| 1855-13 | Scolly, John | conduc & brak 24 da @ $50 per mo - $50.00. Trans Dept main stem |
| 1857-63 | Scott, Charles | lab 26 da @ $1 - $26.00. Rd Dept main stem 16th s-div |
| 1857-31 | E. | ton eng'man ½ da @ $2.50 - $1.25. Board Tree Tun |
| 1857-40 | " | ton eng'man 8½ da @$2.50 - $21.25. NW Va rd, Parkersburg sta |
| 1855-63 | Edw. | ballman 18½ da @ $1 - $18.50. Rd Way Dept |
| 1855-21 | Ephraim | fire 1¼ da @ $1.75 - $2.20. Trans Dept main stem |
| 1855-23 | " | fire 11¼ da @ $1.75 - $19.70. Trans Dept main stem |
| 1857-30 | " | ton eng'man 13¼ da @ $3 - $39.75. 3d div |
| 1855-37 | Erin | fore 27½ da @ $1.25 -$34.35. Rd Way Dept |
| 1857-23 | J. D. | ton conduc 10 da @ $50 per mo - $20.00. 3d & 4th div |
| 1857-39 | J. H. | pass conduc 30 da @ $50 per mo - $50.00. NW Va rd, Parkersburg sta |
| 1855-4 | J. S. | brak 28 da @ $33.35 per mo - $33.35. Trans Dept, Wash br |

# B & O RR EMPLOYEES 293

| ID | Name | Details |
|---|---|---|
| 1857-95 | Scott, Joshua | lab 15 da @ $1 - $15.00. Wash br, Rd Dept |
| 1857-136 | " William | mach 7½ da @ $1.60 - $11.60. Mach Dept, Cumb |
| 1855-8 | Scrivener, S. C. | brak 28 da @ $33.35 per mo - $33.35. Trans Dept main stem |
| 1857-15 | Scroggin, James | clk 30 da @ $50 per mo - $50.00. Petterman sta |
| 1855-90 | Scuff, Charles | carp @ $45 per mo - $45.00. Mach Dept |
| 1857-136 | " | fore carp @ $45 per mo - $45.00. Mach Dept, Cumb |
| 1857-86 | Sculley, Peter | lab 21 da @ $1.12 - $23.60. grad, McGuire's Tun |
| 1855-50 | Sqymes, Joseph | watch cuts 28 da @ $1 - $28.00. Rd Way Dept |
| 1855-84 | Seabright, William | help 23 da @ $1 - $23.00. Mach Dept |
| 1855-54 | Seabrooks, Wm. | stonecut 2 3/4 da @ $2 - $5.50. Rd Way Dept |
| 1857-73 | " | stonecut 21¼ da @ $2.25 - $47.80. repair bridges &c |
| 1855-78 | Seaman, Lewis | help 24 3/4 da @$1.15 - $28.45. Mach Dept |
| 1855-17 | Seamar, D. C. | ton eng'man 19 da @ $3 - $57.00. Trans Dept main stem |
| 1855-30 | Seamore, John | prepar fuel 15 da @$1 - $15.00. Trans Dept main stem |
| 1857-81 | Searey, Patrick | lab 25⅜ da @ $1.12 - $28.40. grad, Board Tree Tun |
| 1857-67 | " Thomas | fore 20½ da @ $1.12 - $23.05. Rd Dept main stem 19th s-div |
| 1855-62 | " William | lab 18 da @ $1 - $18.00. Rd Way Dept |
| 1857-27 | Sears, Emanuel | ton brak 2½ da @ $40 per mo - $4.00. 3d & 4th div |
| 1855-84 | " Thomas | mach 24 da @ $1.50 -$36.00. Mach Dept |
| 1857-115 | " William | boil mkr 20 da @ $1.50 - $30.00. Mach Dept, Balto |
| 1855-95 | " | mould 23 da @ $1.55 - $35.65. Mach Dept |
| 1857-114 | Seary, John | iron mould 17 3/4 da @$1.65 - $29.30. Mach Dept, Balto |
| 1855-62 | " | lab 19½ da @ $1 - $19.50. Rd Way Dept |
| 1857-68 | Seayers, George | lab 19 da @ $1 - $19.00. Rd Dept main stem 19th s-div |
| 1857-111 | Sebert, Adam | mach help 18 3/4 da @$1.15 - $21.55. Mach Dept, Balto |
| 1855-45 | Secafoose, H. | lab 21 da @ $1 - $21.00. Rd Way Dept |
| 1855-40 | Seeger, Henry | lab 21 da @ $1 - $21.00. Rd Way Dept |
| 1857-134 | Selby, R. M. | mach 23 3/4 da @$1.75 - $40.70. Mach Dept, Wheeling |
| 1855-86 | " | help 21½ da @ $1.15 -$24.75. Mach Dept |
| 1857-117 | " | blksmith 16 da @ $1.45 - $23.20. Mach Dept, Balto |
| 1857-56 | Seller, Joseph | lab 25 da @ $1 - $25.00. Rd Dept main stem 10th s-div |
| 1855-93 | Sellers, Morgan | help 13 da @ $1 - $13.00. Mach Dept |
| 1857-49 | Sellman, Rufus | fore 25 da @ $1.25 - $31.25. Rd Dept main stem 3d s-div |
| 1855-38 | Selman, Charles | lab 18 da @ $1 - $18.00. Rd Way Dept |
| 1857-48 | Selmon, Charles | lab 25 da @ $1 - $25.00. Rd Dept main stem 2d s-div |
| 1857-85 | Selvage, William | bricklay 7½ da @ $2.25 - $16.85. grad, Board Tree Tun |

## B & O RR EMPLOYEES

| | | |
|---|---|---|
| 1855-81 | Sembleman, A. | lab 28 da @ $1 - $28.00. Mach Dept |
| 1855-52 | Senseney, William | lab @ $35 per mo - $35.00. Rd Way Dept |
| 1857-102 | " | pump water @ $45 per mo - $45.00. NW Va RR |
| 1855-83 | Sensnor, Geo. | app 23 3/4 da @$.65 - $15.45. Mach Dept |
| 1855-71 | Sewell, Daniel | smith 16½ da @ $1.85 - $30.50. Rd Way Dept |
| 1857-117 | " | blksmith 17 3/4 da @ $1.80 - $31.95. Mach Dept, Balto |
| 1857-113 | George W. | mach app 23 3/4 da @ $.55 - $13.05. Mach Dept, Balto |
| 1855-79 | James | blksmith 30 da @ $1.65 -$49.50. Mach Dept |
| 1857-117 | " | blksmith 31½ da @ $1.75 - $55.15. Mach Dept, Balto |
| 1857-109 | Richard | mach 17½ da @ $1.65 - $28.85. Mach Dept, Balto |
| 1855-85 | W. R. | blksmith 23½ da @ $1.90 - $44.65. Mach Dept |
| 1857-116 | " | blksmith 18¾ da @ $2 - $36.50. Mach Dept, Balto |
| 1855-64 | Sexton, A. | lab 20 3/4 da @ $1 - $20.75. Rd Way Dept |
| 1857-92 | Armstead | lab 9 3/4 da @ $1 - $9.75. grad, Littleton Tun |
| 1857-47 | John | lab 24 da @ $1 - $24.00. Rd Dept main stem 1st s-div |
| 1857-66 | Seymes, Josiah | fore 23 da @ $1.25 - $28.75. Rd Dept main stem 18th s-div |
| 1857-111 | Seymore, David | mach help 17 3/4 da @ $1 - $17.75. Mach Dept, Balto |
| 1855-81 | Shade, David | help 23 da @ $1.15 - $26.45. Mach Dept |
| 1857-121 | Shades, David | paint 21¼ da @ $1.25 - $26.55. Mach Dept, Balto |
| 1857-64 | Shae, James | lab 25 da @ $1 - $25.00. Rd Dept main stem 17th s-div |
| 1857-64 | Shafer, Ely | lab 25 da @ $1 - $25.00. Rd Dept main stem 17th s-div |
| 1855-31 | Henry | saw wd 5¼ cords @ $.35 - $18.90. Trans Dept main stem |
| 1857-13 | John | haul wd 2 da @ $1 - $2.00. Martinsburg |
| 1855-93 | John B. | help 20 da @ $1 - $20.00. Mach Dept |
| 1857-23 | Shaferman, H. | ton conduc 25 da @ $60 per mo - $60.00. Board Tree Tun |
| 1855-53 | Shaffer, Abram | lab 14½ da @ $1 - $14.50. Rd Way Dept |
| 1857-61 | Henry | fore 25 da @ $1.25 - $31.25. Rd Dept main stem 14th s-div |
| 1857-28 | George | ton eng'man 21¼ da @ $3 - $63.75. 1st div |
| 1855-14 | " | brak 11 da @ $40 per mo - $18.35. Trans Dept main stem |
| 1855-23 | " | fire 7 3/4 da @ $1.75 - $13.55. Trans Dept main stem |
| 1857-60 | " | fire 1½ da @ $1.75 - $2.65. Rd Dept main stem 13th s-div |
| 1857-33 | Henry | ton fire 15 da @ $1.75 -$26.25. 3d div |
| 1855-18 | " | ton eng'man 23 da @ $2.25 - $51.75. Trans Dept main stem |
| 1857-28 | Jacob | ton eng'man 14 da @ $2.25 - $31.50. 1st div |
| 1855-88 | John | earp 17½ da @ $1.25 - $21.90. Mach Dept |
| 1857-19 | | pass eng'man 21 da @ $3 - $63.00. 2d div |

| ID | Name | Description |
|---|---|---|
| 1855-39 | Shaffer, Peter | lab 17 da @ $1 - $17.00. Rd Way Dept |
| 1857-32 | Simon P. | ton fire 20¾ da @ $1.75 - $35.45. 1st div |
| 1857-114 | William | iron mould 17 3/4 da @ $1.65 - $29.30. Mach Dept, Balto |
| 1857-133 | Shahan, Joseph M. | oil house clk &c @ $30 per mo - $30.00. Mach Dept, Fetterman |
| 1857-69 | Shaley, William | lab 19 da @ $1 - $19.00. Mt Clare sta, Balto |
| 1857-101 | Shalley, Michael | lab 21 da @ $1 - $21.00. NW Va RR ballast train |
| 1857-54 | Shambaugh, Elijah | lab 22¾ da @ $1 - $22.25. Rd Dept main stem 8th s-div |
| 1855-95 | Shane, Joseph | mould 23 da @ $1.55 - $35.65. Mach Dept |
| 1857-13 | Shanen, Grafton | watch 30 da @ $1 - $30.00. Harpers Ferry |
| 1857-116 | Shaney, Thomas | boil mkr help 18 da @ $1 - $18.00. Mach Dept, Balto |
| 1857-64 | Shanghancy, John | lab 24 da @ $1 - $24.00. Rd Dept main stem 17th s-div |
| 1857-64 | Martin | lab 24 da @ $1 - $24.00. Rd Dept main stem 17th s-div |
| 1855-37 | Shanks, G. | fore 26 da @ $1.25 - $32.50. Rd Way Dept |
| 1857-46 | Shanley, Gilbert | lab 26 da @ $1 - $26.00. Rd Dept main stem 1st s-div |
| 1855-27 | Shanley, Barney | get out eng 27 da @ $1.25 - $33.75. Trans Dept main stem |
| 1857-135 | " | put away eng &c 30½ da @ $1.25 - $38.10. Mach Dept, Wheeling |
| 1855-31 | Patrick | prepar fuel 28 da @ $1 - $28.00. Trans Dept main stem |
| 1855-47 | Shannasey, B. | lab 19½ da @ $1 - $19.50. Rd Way Dept |
| 1857-73 | Shanner, Martin | lab 23 3/4 da @ $1.12 - $26.65. repair bridges &c |
| 1857-39 | Shannon, G. N. | yd conduc 34½ da @ $40 per mo - $45.65. NW Va rd, Parkersburg sta |
| 1855-54 | Michl. | lab 15 3/4 da @ $1 - $15.75. Rd Way Dept |
| 1857-118 | Mike | blksmith help 18½ da @ $1 - $18.50. Mach Dept, Balto |
| 1855-17 | Sam'l. | ton eng'man 5 3/4 da @ $2.50 - $14.35. Trans Dept main stem |
| 1857-73 | Wm. | lab 23 3/4 da @ $1.12 - $26.65. repair bridges &c |
| 1857-54 | Sharan, Edward | lab 27 da @ $1 - $27.00. Rd Dept main stem 8th s-div |
| 1857-114 | Share, Joseph | iron mould 17 3/4 da @ $1.55 - $27.50. Mach Dept, Balto |
| 1855-85 | Sharen, William | blksmith 24 3/4 da @ $1.90 - $47.05. Mach Dept |
| 1857-22 | Sharff, Henry | ton conduc 28 da @ $50 per mo - $56.00. 2d div |
| 1857-22 | John | ton conduc 24 da @ $50 per mo - $48.00. 2d div |
| 1855-11 | John A. | conduc & brak 14½ da @ $40 per mo - $26.15. Trans Dept main stem |
| 1855-21 | Shark, John H. | fire 20 da @ $1.75 - $35.00. Trans Dept main stem |
| 1857-81 | Sharkey, Michael | lab 22 da @ $.87 - $19.25. lay 2d track |
| 1857-35 | Sharman, Patrick | lab 23¾ da @ $1 - $23.25. Edwards' wd train 3d & 4th div |
| 1857-133 | Shaughnessy, Patrick | clean eng 34 da @ $1 - $34.00. Mach Dept, Board Tree Tun |
| 1857-89 | Shaugnassay, Tim. | lab 27 da @ $1.12 - $30.35. grad, Welling Tun |
| 1857-117 | Shaven, William | blksmith 18½ da @ $1.90 - $35.15. Mach Dept, Balto |

| | | |
|---|---|---|
| 1855-32 | Shaw, Alexander | saw wd 28½ cords @ $.50 - $14.20. Trans Dept main stem |
| 1855-26 | J. | clean eng 4½ da @ $1 - $4.50. Trans Dept main stem |
| 1855-43 | James | lab 18 da @ $1 - $18.00. Rd Way Dept |
| 1857-27 | John | ton brak 3½ da @ $40 per mo - $5.60. 3d & 4th div |
| 1855-26 | Joseph | clean eng 24 da @ $1 - $24.00. Trans Dept main stem |
| 1855-93 | Shawan, Geo. | help 10 da @ $1.20 - $12.00. Mach Dept |
| 1857-101 | Shawancy, John | lab 18 da @ $1 - $18.00. NW Va RR ballast train |
| 1855-60 | Shaween, W. M. | lab 24 da @ $1 - $24.00. Rd Way Dept |
| 1855-56 | Shawen, D. | fore 20 da @ $1.50 -$30.00. Rd Way Dept |
| 1855-57 | G. | fore 26½ da @ $1.25 - $33.15. Rd Dept main stem 11th s-div |
| 1855-33 | W. M. | watch 28 da @ $1 - $28.00. Trans Dept main stem |
| 1857-48 | " " | horse hire 45 da @ $1.12 - $55.10. Rd Dept main stem 2d s-div |
| 1857-47 | " " | supv @ $45 per mo - $45.00. Rd Dept main stem 2d s-div |
| 1857-65 | Shay, Darby | watch 30 da @ $1 - $30.00. Rd Dept main stem 17th s-div |
| 1857-126 | Shea, John | clean eng 24½ da @ $1 -$24.50. Mach Dept, Martinsburg |
| 1857-131 | " | fore boil mkr 22½ da @ $2 - $45.00. Mach Dept, Grafton |
| 1857-131 | Patrick | mach app 25 da @ $.50 - $12.50. Mach Dept, Grafton |
| 1857-80 | Shear, Daniel | lab 8 da @ $1 - $8.00. lay 2d track |
| 1857-104 | Shearon, John | miner 24½ da @ $1.12 -$27.55. NW Va RR Tun |
| 1857-21 | Sheckles, Cephas | ton conduc 16 da @ $50 per mo - $32.00. 1st div |
| 1855-26 | Shed, John | clean eng 22½ da @ $1 - $22.50. Trans Dept main stem |
| 1855-89 | Sheehan, William | app 21½ da @ $.45 - $9.65. Mach Dept |
| 1857-124 | Sheelk, William | mach app 20½ da @ $.80 - $12.30. Mach Dept, Martinsburg |
| 1857-101 | Sheeran, Martin | lab 7 da @ $1 - $7.00. NW Va RR ballast train |
| 1857-68 | Sheets, John | pump water @ $45 per mo - $45.00. Rd Dept main stem 19th s-div |
| 1855-65 | John H. | mill wright 24 da @ $1.62½ - $39.00. Rd Way Dept |
| 1855-75 | William | lab 22 da @ $1 - $22.00. Rd Way Dept |
| 1857-51 | " | lab 24 da @ $1 - $24.00. Rd Dept main stem 5th s-div |
| 1855-81 | Shelley, M. | lab 27½ da @ $1 - $27.50. Mach Dept |
| 1855-47 | Mike | lab 24 da @ $1 - $24.00. Rd Way Dept |
| 1857-63 | Shellum, James | lab 22½ da @ $1 - $22.50. Rd Dept main stem 16th s-div |
| 1857-16 | Shelly, James | recheck bag 30 da @ $25 per mo - $25.00. Benwood sta |
| 1857-97 | Shepard, Wm. | lab 26 da @ $1 - $26.00. NW Va RR, Rd Dept 2d s-div |
| 1855-33 | Shepherd, H. | lab 24 da @ $27.50 per mo - $27.50. Trans Dept main stem |
| 1855-41 | Jacob | supv @ $45 per mo - $45.00. Rd Way Dept |
| 1855-70 | Morgan | lab 15 3/4 da @ $1 - $15.75. Rd Way Dept |

| | | | |
|---|---|---|---|
| 1855-41 | Shepherd, Wm. | fore 23 da @ $1.25 - $31.05. Rd Way Dept |
| 1857-95 | Sheppard, Abraham | lab 24 da @ $1 - $24.00. Wash br, Rd Dept |
| 1857-33 | Edward T. | ton fire 14 da @ $33.33 per mo - $18.65. 2d div |
| 1857-13 | John H. | lab 25 da @ $27.50 per mo - $27.50. Harpers Ferry |
| 1855-6 | John N. A. | ton eng'man 17¾ da @ $3 - $51.75. 1st div |
| 1857-8 | " " | clk 28 da @ $58.65 per mo - $58.65. Trans Dept main stem |
| 1855-19 | Shepperd, Jno. | rec clk 30 da @ $58.35 - $58.35. Camden sta |
| 1855-47 | Sherdon, John | ton eng'man 12½ da @ $2.50 - $31.25. Trans Dept main stem |
| 1857-99 | " | lab 19½ da @ $1 - $19.50. Rd Way Dept |
| 1855-86 | Sherdy, Henry | lab 23¼ da @ $1 - $23.25. NW Va RR, Rd Dept 4th s-div |
| 1857-88 | Sherelock, John | help 23½ da @ $1.10 - $25.85. Mach Dept |
| 1857-17 | Sherick, Martin | lab 11 da @ $1.12 - $12.35. grad, Welling Tun |
| 1857-79 | Sheridan, Henry | emig agt 30 da @ $30 per mo - $30.00. Wheeling sta |
| 1855-69 | James | blksmith 24 da @ $1.50 - $36.00. lay 2d track |
| 1855-71 | Luther | lab 21¼ da @ $1 - $21.25. Rd Way Dept |
| 1857-70 | " | fore @ $65 per mo - $65.00. Rd Way Dept |
| 1855-72 | William | fore @ $65 per mo - $65.00. Mt Clare sta, Balto |
| 1857-69 | Sheridon, John | mach 24 da @ $1.73 - $41.50. Rd Way Dept |
| 1855-54 | Sheriff, Jno. R. | fore 25 da @ $1.25 - $31.60. Mt Clare sta, Balto |
| 1855-81 | Sherlin, Peter | fore 25 da @ $1.25 - $31.25. Rd Dept main stem 8th s-div |
| 1855-48 | Sherlock, John | mech 24 da @ $1.25 - $30.00. Mach Dept |
| 1857-80 | " | train hand 15¼ da @ $1 - $15.25. Rd Way Dept |
| 1857-90 | Michael | fire 25 da @ $2 - $50.00. lay 2d track |
| 1855-78 | Sherman, George | miner 11 3/4 da @ $1.12 - $13.20. grad, Welling Tun |
| 1855-86 | " | lab 22½ da @ $1 - $22.25. lay 2d track |
| 1857-118 | John | help 23 3/4 da @ $1.10 - $26.15. Mach Dept |
| 1857-54 | Sherwood, Daniel | blksmith help 18 da @ $1 - $19.80. Mach Dept, Balto |
| 1855-51 | William | lab 24 da @ $1 - $24.00. Rd Dept main stem 8th s-div |
| 1857-16 | Shickells, John | lab 6¼ da @ $1 - $6.25. Rd Way Dept |
| 1855-4 | Shidon, Edward | recheck bag 30 da @ $45 per mo - $45.00. Benwood sta |
| 1857-104 | Shield, Patrick | ton eng'man 21 da @ $2.25 - $47.25. Trans Dept, Wash br |
| 1855-68 | Shields, James | miner 16 da @ $.55 - $8.80. NW Va RR Tun |
| 1855-51 | Martin | lab 21 3/4 da @ $1 - $21.75. Rd Way Dept |
| 1857-100 | " | lab 31 da @ $1 - $31.00. Rd Way Dept |
| 1857-17 | Michael | fore 26½ da @ $1.25 - $33.10. NW Va RR, Rd Dept 5th s-div |
| | | watch 30 da @ $30 per mo - $30.00. Wheeling sta |

| | | |
|---|---|---|
| 1857-100 | Shields, Patrick | lab 25½ da @ $1 - $25.50. NW Va RR, Rd Dept 5th s-div |
| 1857-131 | Shiffler, George | mach 21 da @ $1.70 - $35.70. Mach Dept, Grafton |
| 1857-51 | Shilcum, Theodore | lab 25½ da @ $1 - $25.50. Rd Dept main stem 5th s-div |
| 1855-90 | Shilling, J. M. | help 25⅜ da @ $1 - $25.25. Mach Dept |
| 1855-92 | Shimp, T. | help 33 da @ $37.00. Mach Dept |
| 1857-130 | " Thompson | lab 25 3/4 da @ $1.25 - $32.20. Mach Dept, Piedmont |
| 1857-85 | Shin, William | brickley 7½ da @ $2.25 - $16.85. grad, Board Tree Tun |
| 1855-31 | Shipley, A. H. | saw wd 30 cords @ $.35 - $10.50. Trans Dept main stem |
| 1855-61 | " B. | lab 10 da @ $1 - $10.00. Rd Way Dept |
| 1855-9 | " C. | conduc 13 da @ $50 per mo - $27.10. Trans Dept main stem |
| 1857-40 | " " | pass eng'man 28 da @ $3 - $84.00. NW Va rd, Parkersburg sta |
| 1857-36 | " Calvin | lab 8 da @ $1 - $8.00. J. R. Shrode's wd train 4th div |
| 1857-19 | " Columbus | pass eng'man 1½ da @ $3 - $4.50. 4th div |
| 1855-18 | " George | ton eng'man 12 3/4 da @ $3 - $38.25. Trans Dept main stem |
| 1857-41 | " " | eng'man 5 da @ $3 - $15.00. NW Va rd, Athey's wd train |
| 1857-40 | " " | ton eng'man 12 3/4 da @ $3 - $38.25. N W Va rd, Parkersburg sta |
| 1855-85 | " H. | blksmith 24 da @ $2.15 - $51.60. Mach Dept |
| 1855-11 | " " | conduc & brak 11½ da @ $40 per mo - $26.15. Trans Dept main stem |
| 1855-86 | " Henry | app 30½ da @ $.65 - $19.85. Mach Dept |
| 1857-116 | " " | blksmith 16 3/4 da @ $1.65 - $27.65. Mach Dept, Balto |
| 1855-13 | " J. | conduc & brak 14½ da @ $40 per mo - $7.50. Trans Dept main stem |
| 1855-81 | " Jesse | app 23½ da @ $.55 - $12.90. Mach Dept |
| 1855-14 | " John | brak 11 da @ $40 per mo - $18.35. Trans Dept main stem |
| 1857-40 | " Joseph | pass eng'man 22 da @ $2.50 - $55.00. NW Va rd, Parkersburg sta |
| 1855-26 | " Joshua B. | clean eng 22 da @ $1.15 - $25.30. Trans Dept main stem |
| 1857-122 | " Lewis | eng clean 21 da @ $1.15 - $24.15. Mach Dept, Balto |
| 1855-25 | " " | clean eng 26 3/4 da @ $1.15 - $30.75. Trans Dept main stem |
| 1857-122 | " P. W. | eng clean 19 da @ $1.15 - $21.85. Mach Dept, Balto |
| 1855-11 | " " | conduc & brak 23½ da @ $30 per mo - $29.35. Trans Dept main stem |
| 1857-40 | " Perry | pass fire 21 da @ $40 per mo - $28.00. NW Va rd, Parkersburg sta |
| 1855-11 | " Peter | conduc & brak 19½ da @ $40 per mo - $36.00. Trans Dept main stem |
| 1855-71 | " Plummer | carp 20 3/4 da @ $1.73 - $35.90. Rd Way Dept |
| 1857-41 | " T. B. | ton fire 6½ da @ $1.75 - $11.35. NW Va rd, Parkersburg sta |
| 1855-16 | " " | pass fire 30 da @ $40 per mo - $42.85. Trans Dept main stem |
| 1855-38 | " Thomas | lab 15 da @ $1 - $15.00. Rd Way Dept |
| 1855-83 | " W. | app 23 da @ $.65 - $14.95. Mach Dept |
| 1855-79 | | carp 18 da @ $1.50 - $27.00. Mach Dept |

| Name | Dates | Description |
|---|---|---|
| Shipley, W. H. | 1855-84 | fore 24 3/4 da @ $2.50 - $61.85. Mach Dept |
| W. W. | 1857-117 | blksmith 25 da @ $2.50 - $62.50. Mach Dept, Balto |
| Wesley | 1857-120 | carp 18½ da @ $1.50 - $27.75. Mach Dept, Balto |
| William | 1855-83 | app 23½ da @ $.75 - $17.65. Mach Dept |
| " | 1855-11 | conduc & brak 3 da @ $40 per mo - $5.00. Trans Dept main stem |
| " | 1855-79 | watch 28 da @ $1.25 - $35.00. Mach Dept |
| " | 1857-115 | watch 30 da @ $1 - $30.00. Mach Dept, Balto |
| William B. | 1857-109 | mach 18½ da @ $1.60 - $29.60. Mach Dept, Balto |
| William H. | 1857-116 | fore blksmith 25½ da @ $2.50 - $63.75. Mach Dept, Balto |
| William H. Jr. | 1857-118 | blksmith app 24½ da @ $.75 - $18.40. Mach Dept, Balto |
| Shippley, P. | 1855-11 | conduc & brak 3/4 da @ $40 per mo - $1.25. Trans Dept main stem |
| Shirkey, P. | 1855-30 | prepar fuel 17 3/4 da @ $1 - $17.75. Trans Dept main stem |
| Shirley, Catharine | 1855-35 | clean cars 28 da @ $25 per mo - $25.00. Trans Dept main stem |
| Shoemaker, Wm. | 1857-92 | lab 6½ da @ $1 - $6.50. grad, Littleton Tun |
| Shoff, Isaac | 1857-32 | ton fire 14½ da @ $1.75 - $25.35. 1st div |
| Shoffer, Charles | 1855-57 | lab 23 da @ $1 - $23.00. Rd Way Dept |
| Shommell, John | 1857-61 | lab 28½ da @ $1 - $28.50. Rd Dept main stem 14th s-div |
| Shonaman, H. | 1855-53 | lab 15 da @ $1 - $15.00. Rd Way Dept |
| Shope, M. | 1857-12 | lab 24 da @ $1 - $24.00. Fred sta |
| Shoper, John | 1857-136 | blksmith help 18 3/4 da @ $1 - $18.75. Mach Dept, Cumb |
| Short, Otho | 1855-45 | lab 16 3/4 da @ $1 - $16.75. Rd Way Dept |
| Owen | 1855-45 | lab 16 da @ $1 - $16.00. Rd Way Dept |
| " | 1857-99 | lab 25 da @ $1 - $25.00. NW Va RR, Rd Dept 4th s-div |
| Patrick | 1855-45 | lab 26 da @ $1 - $26.00. Rd Way Dept |
| " | 1857-99 | lab 24½ da @ $1 - $24.50. NW Va RR, Rd Dept 4th s-div |
| Shoves, W. L. | 1855-14 | brak 13 da @ $40 per mo - $21.65. Trans Dept main stem |
| Showacre, J. W. | 1857-7 | pass conduc 28 da @ $62.50 per mo - $62.50. Trans Dept main stem |
| John W. | 1857-37 | pass train conduc 30 da @ $75 per mo - $75.00. Wash br rd, Wash city sta |
| W. H. H. | 1857-36 | tele oper 40 da @ $40 per mo - $40.00. Cameron |
| Showers, John | 1855-52 | carp 24 da @ $1.50 - $36.00. Rd Way Dept |
| Shreck, Jacob S. | 1857-120 | fore carp 18 da @ $2.10 - $37.80. Mach Dept, Balto |
| Shrigley, Mintz | 1857-73 | lab 20 da @ $1.12 - $22.50. repair water sta, M.S. & P.B. |
| Shroden, William | 1857-58 | lab 6 da @ $1 - $6.00. Rd Dept main stem 12th s-div |
| Shrodes, J. R. | 1855-9 | conduc 24 da @ $55 per mo - $55.00. Trans Dept main stem |
| " | 1855-35 | conduc 25 da @ $60 per mo - $60.00. J. R. Shrode's wd train 4th div |
| J. W. | 1855-9 | conduc 4⅔ da @$50 per mo - $8.85. Trans Dept main stem |
| John S. | 1857-36 | lab 3 da @ $1 - $3.00. J. R. Shrode's wd train 4th div |

| | | |
|---|---|---|
| 1857-104 | Shuber, L. | carp 23 da @ $1.50 - $34.50. NW Va RR, build sand & wd houses |
| 1855-35 | Shubrick, W. H. | watch 28 da @ $1.25 - $35.00. Trans Dept main stem |
| 1857-27 | Shuck, Joseph | ton brak 10 da @ $40 per mo - $16.00. 3d & 4th div |
| 1855-87 | Shue, William | bricklay 13 da @ $2.25 - $29.25. grad, Welling Tun |
| 1855-31 | Shultz, Joseph | prepar fuel 15½ da @ $1 - $15.50. Trans Dept main stem |
| 1857-27 | " W. D. | ton brak 26 da @ $40 per mo - $41.60. 3d & 4th div |
| 1857-51 | Shurley, John | lab 17½ da @ $1 - $17.50. Rd Dept main stem 5th s-div |
| 1855-7 | Shutt, A. P. | pass conduc 28 da @ $62.50 per mo - $62.50. Trans Dept main stem |
| 1857-18 | " " " | pass train conduc 30 da @ $75 per mo - $75.00. thr mail & exp |
| 1855-27 | Shuttleworth, C. L. | clean eng 14 da @ $1 - $14.00. Trans Dept main stem |
| 1857-17 | Shwin, William | lab 25 da @ $25 per mo - $25.00. Wheeling sta |
| 1855-47 | Siball, J. | lab 24 da @ $1 - $24.00. Rd Way Dept |
| 1855-70 | Siber, David | 19 da @ $1.22 - $23.20. Rd Way Dept |
| 1857-136 | Sibley, R. J. | mach 20 3/4 da @ $1.75 - $36.30. Mach Dept, Cumb |
| 1857-54 | Sibole, Jerome | lab 25 da @ $1 - $25.00. Rd Dept main stem 8th s-div |
| 1855-63 | Sicener, Wm. | eng'man 3 da @ $2.50 - $7.50. Rd Way Dept |
| 1857-50 | Sigafoose, Henry | lab 24 da @ $1 - $24.00. Rd Dept main stem 4th s-div |
| 1855-70 | Siggs, Frederick | lab 18 da @ $1 - $18.00. Rd Way Dept |
| 1855-11 | Siler, David | conduc & brak 18 3/4 da @ $40 per mo - $35.75. Trans Dept main stem |
| 1857-25 | " | ton brak 17 da @ $40 per mo - $27.20. 2d div |
| 1857-56 | Silk, John | lab 26½ da @ $1 - $26.50. Rd Dept main stem 10th s-div |
| 1855-29 | Silligan, James | prepar fuel 10 da @ $1 - $10.00. Trans Dept main stem |
| 1855-39 | Sillman, R. | nail 24 da @ $1.05 - $25.20. Rd Way Dept |
| 1855-17 | Silvens, Jos. | ton eng'man 19 da @ $3 - $57.00. Trans Dept main stem |
| 1855-94 | Silver, Amos | blksmith 25½ da @ $2 - $51.00. Mach Dept |
| 1855-91 | " S. | mach @ $60 per mo - $60.00. Mach Dept |
| 1857-127 | " Sylvester A. | asst mast mech @ $60 per mo - $60.00. Mach Dept, Piedmont |
| 1857-134 | Silverwright, Wm. | boil mkr 21¼ da @ $1.75 - $37.20. Mach Dept, Wheeling |
| 1855-14 | Simms, G. F. | brak 14¾ da @ $40 per mo - $23.75. Trans Dept main stem |
| 1857-80 | " Wm. | lab 19 3/4 da @ $1 - $19.75. lay 2d track |
| 1857-121 | Simonson, Joseph | paint 18 da @ $1.50 - $27.00. Mach Dept, Balto |
| 1857-27 | Simpson, John | ton brak 31 da @ $40 per mo - $49.60. 3d & 4th div |
| 1857-19 | " L. R. | bag mast 30 da @ $45 per mo - $45.00. thr mail & exp |
| 1855-21 | " Samuel | fire 3 da @ $1.75 - $5.25. Trans Dept main stem |
| 1855-5 | " " | ton fire 12 da @ $33.33 per mo - $16.65. Trans Dept, Wash br |
| 1855-51 | " Thomas | lab @ $30 per mo - $30.00. Rd Way Dept |

B & O RR EMPLOYEES 301

| Year-Page | Name | Details |
|---|---|---|
| 1855-74 | Simpson, Thomas | lab 23 da @ $1 - $23.00. Rd Way Dept |
| 1857-134 | " | mach app 24½ da @ $.55 - $13.45. Mach Dept, Wheeling |
| 1857-61 | " | pump water @ $35 per mo - $35.00. Rd Dept main stem 14th s-div |
| 1857-81 | Sinclair, Alexander | blksmith 21 da @ $1.50 - $31.50. lay 2d track |
| 1857-27 | S. | ton brak 3 da @ $40 per mo - $4.80. 3d & 4th div |
| 1855-13 | Sincle, Adr. | conduc & brak 11¼ da @ $50 per mo - $23.45. Trans Dept main stem |
| 1855-78 | Sindall, S. | clk @ $66.70 per mo - $66.70. Mach Dept |
| 1857-108 | Samuel | clk @ $66.70 per mo - $66.70. Mach Dept, Balto |
| 1857-54 | Sinevan, David | lab 21 da @ $1 - $21.00. Rd Dept main stem 8th s-div |
| 1857-54 | John | lab 22 da @ $1 - $22.00. Rd Dept main stem 8th s-div |
| 1857-112 | Sintard, D. | mach app 22 3/4 da @ $.45 - $10.25. Mach Dept, Balto |
| 1857-84 | Sipole, Clark | carp 25 da @ $1.25 - $31.25. grad, Board Tree Tun |
| 1857-83 | Wm. | lab 18½ da @ $1.12 - $20.80. grad, Board Tree Tun |
| 1857-125 | Sisco, John | app 32¼ da @ $.45 - $14.50. Mach Dept, Martinsburg |
| 1855-87 | Peter | mach 29 da @ $1.90 - $55.10. Mach Dept |
| 1857-123 | " | mach 32½ da @ $1.65 - $53.20. Mach Dept, Martinsburg |
| 1855-55 | Skellion, James | lab 21½ da @ $1 - $21.50. Rd Way Dept |
| 1857-47 | Sketien, Thomas | lab 23 da @ $1 - $23.00. Rd Dept main stem 1st s-div |
| 1857-64 | Skully, Patrick | lab 25 3/4 da @ $1 - $25.75. Rd Dept main stem 17th s-div |
| 1857-139 | Slack, Joseph | mach 29 da @ $1.65 - $47.85. NW Va RR, Mach Dept, Parkersburg |
| 1857-54 | Slase, John | lab 23 da @ $1 - $23.00. Rd Dept main stem 8th s-div |
| 1857-109 | Slater, Rebeun | mach 14½ da @ $1.60 - $22.80. Mach Dept, Balto |
| 1857-96 | William | lab 24 3/4 da @ $1 - $24.75. NW Va RR, Rd Dept 1st s-div |
| 1857-109 | Slaughter, Wm. | mach 13¾ da @ $1.72 - $22.80. Mach Dept, Balto |
| 1857-20 | " | pass fire 8 da @ $40 per mo - $10.65. 1st div |
| 1857-38 | Slaven, John | pass fire 9½ da @ $40 per mo - $12.65. Wash br rd, Wash city sta |
| 1857-116 | Sloan, Charles | boil mkr help 19½ da @ $1 - $19.50. Mach Dept, Balto |
| 1857-9 | Small, Eli | clk 30 da @ $33.35 per mo - $33.35. Mt Clare sta |
| 1855-19 | " | ton eng'man 1 da @ $2 - $2.00. Trans Dept main stem |
| 1857-55 | William | eng'man 11 da @ $2.25 - $24.75. Rd Dept main stem 9th s-div |
| 1857-125 | Smallwood, George | wheel 13½ da @ $1.35 - $17.90. Mach Dept, Martinsburg |
| 1855-78 | " | help 25½ da @ $1.15 - $29.30. Mach Dept |
| 1857-121 | Joseph | lumber yd help 19¼ da @ $1.15 - $22.40. Mach Dept, Balto |
| 1855-9 | " | conduc 1 da @ $50 per mo - $2.10. Trans Dept main stem |
| 1857-46 | W. | lab 27 da @ $1 - $27.00. Rd Dept main stem 1st s-div |
| 1855-93 | | help 14 3/4 da @ $1.20 - $17.70. Mach Dept |

302                                    B & O RR EMPLOYEES

| | | | |
|---|---|---|---|
| 1857-132 | Smallwood, William | put away eng 30 da @ $1.50 - $45.00. Mach Dept, Grafton |
| 1855-11 | Smith, A. D. | conduc & brak 8½ da @ $50 per mo - $18.20. Trans Dept main stem |
| 1857-19 | " | bag mast 30 da @ $45 per mo - $45.00. w end |
| 1855-44 | Adw. | lab 23 da @ $1 - $23.00. Rd Way Dept |
| 1857-90 | August | lab 7 da @ $1.12 - $7.85. grad, Welling Tun |
| 1857-100 | Barney | lab 26½ da @ $1 - $26.50. NW Va RR, Rd Dept 5th s-div |
| 1855-45 | C. | lab 21 da @ $1.25 - $26.25. Rd Way Dept |
| 1857-39 | " | pass brak 7 da @ $33.35 per mo - $7.75. NW Va rd, Parkersburg sta |
| 1857-107 | C. C. | supv of mach on rd 2d div @ $83.35 per mo. Mach Dept |
| 1855-81 | Calvin | coach mkr 20 da @ $1.55 - $31.00. Mach Dept |
| 1855-16 | " | pilot 20 da @ $50 per mo - $33.35. transfer steam Brown Dick--Ohio Riv, bet Benwood & Bellaire |
| 1855-54 | Charles | lab 23 3/4 da @ $1.25 - $29.70. Rd Way Dept |
| 1857-79 | " | lab 26 3/4 da @ $1 - $26.75. lay 2d track |
| 1857-44 | " | pilot pass trains 16 da @ $1 - $16.00. Cumb |
| 1855-18 | Christian | ton eng'man 28 da @ $83.35 per mo - $83.35. Trans Dept main stem |
| 1857-55 | " | fore 24 da @ $1.25 - $30.00. Rd Dept main stem 9th s-div |
| 1857-123 | " | supv of mach @ $83.35 per mo - $83.35. Mach Dept, Martinsburg |
| 1857-111 | Cyrus E. | mach help 18 da @ $1.15 - $20.70. Mach Dept, Balto |
| 1857-3 | Daniel | watch @ $30 per mo. Gen Ofc |
| 1855-46 | F. | lab 23 3/4 da @ $1 - $23.75. Rd Way Dept |
| 1855-15 | " | pass eng'man 10 da @ $3 - $30.00. Trans Dept main stem |
| 1857-55 | Frieth | fore 25 da @ $1.25 - $31.25. Rd Dept main stem 9th s-div |
| 1855-5 | George | eng clean 29 da @ $1.15 - $33.35. Trans Dept, Wash br |
| 1855-75 | " | lab 17½ da @ $1 - $17.50. Rd Way Dept |
| 1855-4 | " | pass fire 1½ da @ $40 per mo - $2.15 - Trans Dept, Wash br |
| 1857-20 | " | pass fire 1 da @ $40 per mo - $1.35. 1st div |
| 1857-38 | " | pass fire 3 da @ $40 per mo - $4.00. Wash br rd, Wash city sta |
| 1857-35 | George H. | lab 13½ da @ $1 - $13.50. Edwards' wd train 3d & 4th div |
| 1857-14 | George W. | asst disp 30 da @ $45 per mo - $45.00. Piedmont sta |
| 1857-27 | " | ton brak 1 da @ $40 per mo - $1.60. 3d & 4th div |
| 1855-36 | H. C. | lab 22 da @ $25 per mo - $26.05. Trans Dept main stem |
| 1855-13 | H. J. | conduc & brak 15½ da @ $50 per mo - $32.30. Trans Dept main stem |
| 1857-27 | H. T. | ton brak 5½ da @ $40 per mo - $8.80. 3d & 4th div |
| 1857-52 | Harrison | lab 19 da @ $1 - $19.00. Rd Dept main stem 6th s-div |
| 1855-40 | Henry | lab 24 da @ $1 - $24.00. Rd Way Dept |
| 1855-61 | " | lab 12 da @ $1 - $12.00. Rd Way Dept |

B & O RR EMPLOYEES                303

| | | | |
|---|---|---|---|
| 1855-35 | Smith, Henry | lab 25 da @ $35 per mo - $36.45. Trans Dept main stem |
| 1857-49 | " | lab 25 da @ $1 - $25.00. Rd Dept main stem 3d s-div |
| 1857-67 | " | lab 19½ da @ $1 - $19.50. Rd Dept main stem 18th s-div |
| 1857-17 | " | load stock 30 da @ $35 per mo - $35.00. Wheeling sta |
| 1857-112 | " | mach help 18½ da @ $1.15 - $21.25. Mach Dept, Balto |
| 1857-34 | " | ton fire 29 da @ $1.75 - $50.75. 4th div |
| 1857-17 | Henry C. | load stock 30 da @ $25 per mo - $25.00. Wheeling sta |
| 1857-33 | Henry J. | ton fire 22½ da @ $1.75 - $39.35. 2d div |
| 1855-83 | Hugh | lab 21 3/4 da @ $1.15 - $25.00. Mach Dept |
| 1855-42 | " | lab 9½ da @ $1 - $9.50. Rd Way Dept |
| 1855-44 | J. | lab 25 da @ $1 - $25.00. Rd Way Dept |
| 1855-16 | " | pass fire 16 da @ $40 per mo - $22.55. Trans Dept main stem |
| 1857-27 | J. F. | ton brak 14 da @ $40 per mo - $22.40. 3d & 4th div |
| 1857-107 | J. R. | supv of mach on rd 1st div & Wash br @ $83.35 per mo. Mach Dept |
| 1857-27 | J. W. | ton brak 20 da @ $40 per mo - $32.00. 3d & 4th div |
| 1855-5 | Jacob | car clean 28 da @ $30 per mo - $30.00. Trans Dept, Wash br |
| 1857-83 | James | blksmith 19¾ da @ $1.55 - $30.25. Mach Dept |
| 1857-117 | " | blksmith 18 da @ $1.55 - $27.90. Mach Dept, Balto |
| 1857-79 | " | lab 22¼ da @ $1 - $22.25. lay 2d track |
| 1857-17 | " | lab 25 da @ $25 per mo - $25.00. Wheeling sta |
| 1855-11 | Jere. | conduc & brak 24 da @ $55 per mo -$55.00. Trans Dept main stem |
| 1855-71 | Joel | bricklay 11 3/4 da @ $2 - $23.50. Rd Way Dept |
| 1855-25 | John | bur driv 24 da @ $40 per mo - $40.00. Trans Dept main stem |
| 1855-94 | " | carp 22 3/4 da @ $1.45 - $33.00. Mach Dept |
| 1855-26 | " | clean eng 3¼ da @ $1 - $3.25. Trans Dept main stem |
| 1855-9 | " | conduc 22½ da @ $50 per mo - $46.85. Trans Dept main stem |
| 1855-68 | " | eng'nman 17 da @ $2.50 - $42.50. Rd Way Dept |
| 1855-87 | " | help 22 3/4 da @ $1 - $22.75. Mach Dept |
| 1855-44 | " | lab 19½ da @ $1 - $19.50. Rd Way Dept |
| 1855-53 | " | lab 19 da @ $1 - $19.00. Rd Way Dept |
| 1855-77 | " | mach 23¾ da @ $1.35 - $31.75. Mach Dept |
| 1855-84 | " | mach 24½ da @ $1.50 - $36.75. Mach Dept |
| 1855-54 | " | track lay 15 da @ $1.12½ - $16.90. Rd Way Dept |
| 1857-128 | " | blksmith help 17½ da @ $1 - $17.50. Mach Dept, Piedmont |
| 1857-115 | " | boil mkr 27 3/4 da @ $1.60 - $44.40. Mach Dept, Balto |
| 1857-135 | " | carp 26¼ da @ $1.45 - $38.40. Mach Dept, Wheeling |

| | | |
|---|---|---|
| 1857-89 | Smith, John | eng'man @ $75 per mo -$75.00. grad, Welling Tun |
| 1857-41 | " | lab 6 da @ $1 - $6.00. NW Va rd, Athey's wd train |
| 1857-10 | " | pass reg 25 da @ $40 per mo - $40.00. hp exp, Balto |
| 1857-23 | " | ton conduc 20 da @ $50 per mo - $40.00. 3d & 4th div |
| 1857-34 | " | ton fire 22½ da @ $1.75 -$39.35. 4th div |
| 1857-110 | John F. | mach 17 da @ $1.50 - $25.50. Mach Dept, Balto |
| 1857-30 | John H. | ton eng'man 3½ da @ $3 -$10.50. 4th div |
| 1855-53 | John K | carp 22½ da @ $1.62½ - $36.55. Rd Way Dept |
| 1857-73 | " " | carp 24½ da @ $1.62 - $39.80. repair bridges &c |
| 1857-33 | John Q. | ton fire 25 da @ $33.33 per mo - $33.75. 2d div |
| 1855-18 | John R. | ton eng'man 28 da @ $83.35 per mo - $83.35. Trans Dept main stem |
| 1857-34 | John S. | ton fire 7 da @ $1.75 - $12.25. Board Tree Tun |
| 1857-109 | John T. | mach 18¼ da @ $1.40 - $25.55. Mach Dept, Balto |
| 1857-123 | John W. | mach 24 da @ $1 - $24.00. Mach Dept, Martinsburg |
| 1857-36 | Joseph | lab 19½ da @ $1 - $19.50. J. R. Shrode's wd train 4th div |
| 1857-10 | Lawrence | bur reg 25 da @ $40 per mo - $40.00. hp exp, Balto |
| 1857-101 | Morandy | fire 27 da @ $1.75 - $47.25. NW Va RR ballast train |
| 1857-16 | N. | engr 30 da @ $75 per mo - $75.00. transfer steam Brown Dick--Ohio Riv, bet Benwood & Bellaire |
| 1855-72 | N. O. | help 22½ da @ $1.06 - $23.85. Rd Way Dept |
| 1857-70 | " " | chair mkr 17¼ da @ $1.25 - $21.55. Mt Clare sta, Balto |
| 1857-102 | Neilson R. | pump water @ $45 per mo - $45.00. NW Va RR |
| 1855-81 | Oliver | carp 22 da @ $1.50 - $33.00. Mach Dept |
| 1855-16 | P. | pass fire 29¼ da @ $1.75 - $51.20. Trans Dept main stem |
| 1857-41 | " | ton fire 2 da @ $1.75 - $3.50. NW Va rd, Parkersburg sta |
| 1855-96 | Patrick | lab 23½ da @ $1.15 - $27.00. Mach Dept |
| 1857-58 | " | horse & cart 26 da @ $1.12 - $29.25. Rd Dept main stem 11th s-div |
| 1857-114 | " | iron mould help 18¼ da @ $1.15 -$21.00. Mach Dept, Balto |
| 1857-79 | " | lab 25 3/4 da @ $1 - $25.75. lay 2d track |
| 1855-92 | Peter | carp 24 da - $33.75. Mach Dept |
| 1857-128 | " | carp 18¼ da @ $1.50 - $27.35. Mach Dept, Piedmont |
| 1855-83 | Philip | blksmith 18 da @ $1.55 - $27.90. Mach Dept |
| 1857-117 | " | blksmith 15 3/4 da @ $1.55 -$24.40. Mach Dept, Balto |
| 1857-126 | " | clean eng 28 da @ $1.15 - $32.20. Mach Dept, Martinsburg |
| 1857-20 | " | pass fire 10½ da @ $1.75 -$18.35. 3d div |
| 1857-33 | " | ton fire 5½ da @ $1.75 -$9.60. 3d div |

B & O RR EMPLOYEES 305

| ID | Name | Details |
|---|---|---|
| 1857-49 | Smith, Randolph | lab 25 da @ $1 - $25.00. Rd Dept main stem 3d s-div |
| 1857-119 | Samuel A. | carp 23 3/4 da @ $1.50 - $28.10. Mach Dept, Balto |
| 1857-64 | Thomas | lab 23½ da @ $1 - $23.25. Rd Dept main stem 17th s-div |
| 1855-83 | Thomas A. | fore 24 da @ $2 - $48.00. Mach Dept |
| 1857-117 | " | blksmith 18 da @ $2 - $36.00. Mach Dept, Balto |
| 1855-19 | W. P. | ton eng'man 15¼ da @ $2.50 - $38.10. Trans Dept main stem |
| 1857-7 | W. P. | asst mast trans @ $125 per mo. Mast of Trans Ofc |
| 1855-83 | William | app 19¼ da @ $.65 - $12.50. Mach Dept |
| 1855-65 | " | carp 11 da @ $1.62½ - $17.85. Rd Way Dept |
| 1855-21 | " | fire 16½ da @ $1.75 - $28.85. Trans Dept main stem |
| 1855-46 | " | gather iron 2 da @ $1.75 - $3.50. Rd Way Dept |
| 1855-27 | " | get out eng 18 da @ $1.15 - $20.70. Trans Dept main stem |
| 1857-13 | " | haul wd 6½ da @ $1 - $6.50. Martinsburg |
| 1857-86 | " | lab 20⅞ da @ $1 - $20.25. grad, McGuire's Tun |
| 1857-33 | " | ton fire 14 da @ $1.75 - $24.50. 3d div |
| 1855-42 | William H. | lab 19 da @ $1 - $19.00. Rd Way Dept |
| 1855-1 | William P. | asst mast of trans $1200 per annum - $100.00 |
| 1855-87 | Smithlutz, John | mach 26½ da @ $1.30 - $31.45. Mach Dept |
| 1855-86 | M. | mach 24 3/4 da @ $1 - $32.20. Mach Dept |
| 1855-77 | Smothers, Thomas | quarry 21½ da @ $1 - $21.25. ballast train for 2d track |
| 1857-76 | Wm. | blksmith 24 da @ $1.25 - $30.00. ballast train for 2d track |
| 1855-14 | Smouse, G. D. | brak 18 3/4 da @ $1.60 per mo - $31.25. Trans Dept main stem |
| 1857-123 | Smuer, William | mach 21 da @ $1.60 - $33.60. Mach Dept, Martinsburg |
| 1855-63 | Snider, Abner | fore @ $45 per mo - $45.00. Rd Way Dept |
| 1857-68 | " | fore @ $50 per mo - $50.00. Rd Dept main stem 19th s-div |
| 1855-21 | Frank | fire 8 da @ $1.75 - $14.00. Trans Dept main stem |
| 1857-10 | " | stab'man 25 da @ $1 - $25.00. hp exp, Balto |
| 1855-76 | Henry | lab 21 da @ $1 - $21.00. Rd Way Dept |
| 1857-51 | " | lab 24 da @ $1 - $24.00. Rd Dept main stem 5th s-div |
| 1855-65 | John | mason 15 da @ $2 - $30.00. Rd Way Dept |
| 1857-87 | Snively, Henry | stone mason 23 3/4 da @ $2 - $47.50. grad, McGuire's Tun |
| 1855-38 | Snoden, Samuel | lab 24 da @ $1 - $24.00. Rd Way Dept |
| 1857-99 | Snodgrass, John | watch 30 da @ $1 - $30.00. NW Va RR. Rd Dept 4th s-div |
| 1855-88 | Snook, Samuel | carp 23¼ da @ $1.35 - $31.70. Mach Dept |
| 1855-87 | Snowdeal, John | help 20 da @ $1.15 - $23.00. Mach Dept |
| 1857-48 | Snowden, Samuel | lab 13½ da @ $1 - $13.50. Rd Dept main stem 2d s-div |

| |  | |  |
|---|---|---|---|
| 1857-47 | Snowden, William | lab 25 3/4 da @ $1 - $25.75. Rd Dept main stem 2d s-div |
| 1857-95 | Snyder, Adam | lab 21 da @ $1 - $21.00. Wash br, Rd Dept |
| 1855-33 | " B. B. | sta bag mast 28 da @ $40 per mo - $40.00. Trans Dept main stem |
| 1855-73 | " F. | track lay 19 da @ $1.45 - $27.55. Rd Way Dept |
| 1857-47 | " Francis | fire 24 da @ $1.28 - $30.70. Rd Dept main stem 1st s-div |
| 1855-7 | " John | bag mast 28 da @ $45 per mo - $45.00. Trans Dept main stem |
| 1855-71 | " " | carp 23 da @ $1.60 - $36.80. Rd Way Dept |
| 1857-69 | " " | carp 18 da @ $1.60 - $28.80. Mt Clare sta, Balto |
| 1857-102 | " " | pass train conduc 30 da @ $66.65 per mo - $66.65. thr mail & exp |
| 1855-8 | " Justus | stone mason 19 3/4 da @ $2 - $39.50. NW Va RR, rwy depot |
| 1857-18 | " " | bag mast 28 da @ $45 per mo - $45.00. Trans Dept main stem |
| 1857-110 | " Nicholas | pass train conduc 30 da @ $62.50 per mo - $62.50. thr mail & exp |
| 1857-9 | " R. B. | mach 23½ da @ $1.40 - $32.55. Mach Dept, Balto |
| 1855-27 | " Sim. | weigh mast 30 da @ $11.65 per mo - $11.65. Mt Clare sta |
| 1857-34 | " Simeon | clean eng 8 da @ $1 - $8.00. Trans Dept main stem |
| 1857-30 | " Simon | ton fire 22½ da @ $1.75 - $39.35. Board Tree Tun |
| 1857-32 | " " | ton eng'man 1 da @ $2.50 - $2.50. 4th div |
| 1855-31 | " T. | ton fire 4½ da @ $1.75 - $7.85. 1st div |
| 1857-54 | " William | saw wd 181 cords @ $.35 - $63.35. Trans Dept main stem |
| 1857-73 | Soakely, Wm. | lab 24 da @ $1 - $24.00. Rd Dept main stem 8th s-div |
| 1857-117 | Sockdale, Samuel | carp 25 da @ $1.62 - $40.60. repair bridges &c |
| 1857-27 | Sollers, Benjamin | blksmith 17 3/4 da @ $1.25 - $22.20. Mach Dept, Balto |
| 1855-31 | Sonders, P. W. | ton brak 22 da @ $40 per mo - $35.20. 3d & 4th div |
| 1855-71 | Sorter, Daniel | saw wd 9¾ cords @ $.35 - $3.30. Trans Dept main stem |
| 1857-114 | Southord, Joseph | carp 23 da @ $1.60 - $36.80. Rd Way Dept |
| 1855-53 | Soutkey, William | iron mould help 17 3/4 da @ $1 - $17.75. Mach Dept, Balto |
| 1855-67 | Sowerman, John | carp 24 da @ $1.50 - $36.00. Rd Way Dept |
| 1857-75 | Spairman, Francis | mason 16 da @ $2 - $32.00. Rd Way Dept |
| 1857-37 | Spakes, N. | dril 22½ da @ $1.04 - $23.50. ballast train for 2d track |
| 1855-11 | Spalding, Joseph | ofcr 30 da @ $35 per mo - $35.00. Wash br rd, Wash city sta |
| 1857-76 | Spariman, Martin | conduc & brak 10¼ da @ $40 per mo - $18.60. Trans Dept main stem |
| 1855-44 | Sparran, Edward | lab 12 da @ $.97 - $11.70. ballast train for 2d track |
| 1857-11 | Sparrow, Henry | lab 23½ da @ $1 - $23.50. Rd Way Dept |
| 1857-96 | Spates, T. S. | supv @ $50 per mo - $60.00. NW Va RR, Rd Dept 1st s-div |
| 1855-11 | Spauier, B. | conduc & brak 27 da @ $40 per mo - $45.00. Trans Dept main stem |

| | | | |
|---|---|---|---|
| 1855-11 | Spauler, William | conduc & brak 23½ da @ $50 per mo - $48.95. Trans Dept main stem |
| 1855-87 | Spea, John | mach 21 3/4 da @ $1.60 - $34.80. Mach Dept |
| 1857-119 | Speaks, John W. | carp 16 3/4 da @ $1.50 - $25.10. Mach Dept, Balto |
| 1855-5 | N. | car clean 28 da @ $30 per mo - $30.00. Trans Dept, Wash br |
| 1855-92 | Spedden, John | help 29 da @ $1 - $29.00. Mach Dept |
| 1855-92 | John A. | app 23 3/4 da @ $.45 - $10.70. Mach Dept |
| 1857-128 | John A., Jr. | mach help 23½ da @ $.75 - $17.60. Mach Dept, Piedmont |
| 1857-127 | John Sr. | mach help 25½ da @ $1.25 - $31.85. Mach Dept, Piedmont |
| 1857-29 | Speelman, Frederick | ton eng'man 17 da @ $3 - $51.00. 2d div |
| 1857-101 | Spellman, Frank | lab 26 da @ $1 - $26.00. NW Va RR ballast train |
| 1857-87 | Thomas | lab 23½ da @ $1 - $23.50. grad, McGuire's Tun |
| 1857-25 | Spero, Jacob | ton brak 24½ da @ $40 per mo - $39.20. 2d div |
| 1857-37 | Spicer, George | brak 7 da @ $33.33 per mo - $7.80. Wash br rd, Wash city sta |
| 1857-18 | " | pass train brak 8 da @ $33.35 per mo - $8.90. thr mail & exp |
| 1857-116 | Thomas | brass mould app 16½ da @ $.45 - $7.30. Mach Dept, Balto |
| 1857-65 | Spindle, George | lab 12 da @ $1 - $12.00. Rd Dept main stem 17th s-div |
| 1857-32 | Spinks, Thomas | ton fire 1¼ da @ $1.75 - $2.95. 1st div |
| 1855-21 | Spotts, G. W. | fire 16¼ da @ $1.75 - $28.45. Trans Dept main stem |
| 1857-40 | " " | ton eng'man 24½ da @ $3 - $73.50. NW Va rd, Parkersburg sta |
| 1855-21 | J. A. | fire 11 3/4 da @ $1.75 - $20.55. Trans Dept main stem |
| 1857-36 | Sprange, Stephen | lab 17 da @ $1.60 - $27.20. J. R. Shrode's wd train 4th div |
| 1857-113 | Spreight, James J. | mach app 20½ da @ $.45 - $9.20. Mach Dept, Balto |
| 1857-114 | Thomas | iron mould app 22 da @ $.45 - $9.90. Mach Dept, Balto |
| 1855-89 | Sprigg, John | tin 24½ da @ $1.50 - $36.35. Mach Dept |
| 1857-125 | " | tin 20½ da @ $1.50 - $30.75. Mach Dept, Martinsburg |
| 1855-13 | Samuel | conduc & brak 2 da @ $50 per mo - $4.15. Trans Dept main stem |
| 1857-21 | " | ton conduc 20 3/4 da @ $50 per mo - $41.50. 1st div |
| 1857-23 | Stephen | ton conduc 2 da @ $50 per mo - $4.00. 3d & 4th div |
| 1855-87 | William | help 27 da @ $1 - $27.00. Mach Dept |
| 1857-124 | " | sht iron work 15 da @ $1.25 - $18.75. Mach Dept, Martinsburg |
| 1857-127 | Springle, Jacob | mach help 21½ da @ $1 - $21.25. Mach Dept, Piedmont |
| 1855-68 | Sprucebank, James | fire 10 da @ $1.75 - $17.50. Rd Way Dept |
| 1855-23 | " | fire 6 da @ $1.75 - $10.50. Trans Dept main stem |
| 1855-89 | Sprucebanks, A. | mach 17½ da @ $1.75 - $30.65. Mach Dept |
| 1855-19 | Spurier, T. B. | ton eng'man 23½ da @ $2.50 - $58.75. Trans Dept main stem |
| 1855-19 | Thos. | ton eng'man 30 da @ $2.50 - $75.00. Trans Dept main stem |

## B & O RR EMPLOYEES

| ID | Name | Description |
|---|---|---|
| 1857-27 | Spurrier, Beal | ton brak 25 da @ $40 per mo - $40.00. 3d & 4th div |
| 1857-32 | Beale | ton fire 3/4 da @ $1.75 - $1.30. 1st div |
| 1857-28 | Benedict | ton fire 22½ da @ $1.75 -$39.35. 1st div |
| 1857-28 | Thomas Jr | ton eng'man 18 da @ $2.25 - $40.50. 1st div |
| 1855-35 | Thomas Sr | ton eng'man 25 da @ $75 per mo - $75.00. 1st div |
| 1857-121 | William | watch 28 da @ $1.25 - $35.00. Trans Dept main stem |
| 1857-22 | " | carp app 22½ da @ $.55 - $12.25. Mach Dept, Balto |
| 1857-9 | " | ton conduc 26 da @ $50 per mo - $52.00. 2d div |
| 1855-7 | Stabler, A. G. | watch 30 da @ $1.25 - $37.50. Mt Clare sta |
| 1857-8 | " " | pass conduc 28 da @ $62.50 per mo - $62.50. Trans Dept main stem |
| 1855-32 | S. | tick sell 30 da @ $75 per mo - $75.00. Camden sta |
| 1857-80 | Stack, James | tele oper 28 da @ $30 per mo - $30.00. Trans Dept main stem |
| 1857-80 | Stacks, John | lab 20 3/4 da @ $1 - $20.75. lay 2d track |
| 1857-100 | Stafford, Michael | lab 24 da @ $.65 - $15.60. lay 2d track |
| 1857-21 | Stailman, George | lab 27 da @ $1 - $27.00. NW Va RR, Rd Dept 5th s-div |
| 1855-30 | Stallions, William | ton conduc 22 da @ $50 per mo - $44.00. 1st div |
| 1855-41 | Staly, Lewis | lab 18 da @ $1 - $18.00. Trans Dept main stem |
| 1855-87 | Stane, Henry | lab 22 da @ $1 - $22.00. Rd Way Dept |
| 1855-77 | Stanger, John | blksmith 22 da @ $1.50 - $33.00. Mach Dept |
| 1857-70 | Stanley, Oliver | mach 24½ da @ $1.25 - $30.60. Mt Clare sta, Balto |
| 1855-21 | Stansbury, --- | help 18 da @ $1 - $18.00. Mt Clare sta, Balto |
| 1855-7 | D. R. | fire ¼ da @ $1.75 - $.45. Trans Dept main stem |
| 1857-41 | J. | pass conduc 28 da @ $62.50 per mo - $62.50. Trans Dept main stem |
| 1857-115 | Stanton, D. L. | ton fire 12 da @ $1.75 - $21.00. NW Va rd, Parkersburg sta |
| 1855-49 | George | pat mkr app 24 da @ $.45 - $10.80. Mach Dept, Balto |
| 1857-56 | " | watch cuts 28 da @ $1 - $28.00. Rd Way Dept |
| 1855-53 | James | watch 30 da @ $1 - $30.00. Rd Dept main stem 10th s-div |
| 1857-56 | " | fore 24 da @ $1.25 - $30.00. Rd Way Dept |
| 1857-81 | Joseph | fore 25 da @ $1.25 - $41.25. Rd Dept main stem 10th s-div |
| 1857-77 | " | lab 20 3/4 da @ $1 - $20.75. lay 2d track |
| 1857-58 | Laurence | quarry 7½ da @ $1 - $7.50. ballast train for 2d track |
| 1857-36 | Martin | lab 26 da @ $1 - $26.00. Rd Dept main stem 12th s-div |
| 1857-135 | " | lab 25 da @ $25 per mo - $26.05. Trans Dept main stem |
| 1855-54 | Patrick | lab 23½ da @ $1 - $23.50. Mach Dept, Wheeling |
| 1857-89 | " | watch 30 da @ $1 - $19.75. Rd Way Dept |
| | | lab 19 3/4 da @ $1 - $30.00. grad, Welling Tun |

# B & O RR EMPLOYEES 309

| ID | Name | Details |
|---|---|---|
| 1855-5 | Starks, C. | port 28 da @ $25 per mo - $25.00. Trans Dept, Wash br |
| 1857-37 | " Charles | port 30 da @ $25 per mo. Ten Ofc - $25.00. Wash br rd, Wash city sta |
| 1857-3 | Starr, Samuel W. | clk @ $50 per mo. Ten Ofc |
| 1855-65 | Startzman, John | carp 5 da @ $1.50 - $7.50. Rd Way Dept |
| 1855-54 | Starzman, Jno. | carp 16½ da @ $1.50 - $24.65. Rd Way Dept |
| 1857-109 | Stater, John T. | mach 18 da @ $1.72 - $30.95. Mach Dept, Balto |
| 1857-33 | Staub, Daniel | ton fire 23 da @ $1.75 - $40.25. 2d div |
| 1857-124 | Staul, Henry | blksmith 20 da @ $1.80 - $36.00. Mach Dept, Martinsburg |
| 1855-65 | Staunton, P. | lab 18½ da @ $1 - $18.50. Rd Way Dept |
| 1855-75 | Staven, Christ. | lab 23 da @ $1 - $23.00. Rd Way Dept |
| 1857-121 | Steal, Robert | lab @ $35 per mo - $35.00. Mach Dept, Balto |
| 1855-18 | Stearns, Wm. | ton eng'man 6½ da @ $3 - $19.50. Trans Dept main stem |
| 1855-16 | Steavens, R. | pass fire ½ da @ $40 per mo - $.70. Trans Dept main stem |
| 1857-77 | Steel, Washington | quarry 22 da @ $1 - $22.00. ballast train for 2d track |
| 1857-133 | " William | clean eng 30 da @ $1 - $30.00. Mach Dept, Board Tree Tun |
| 1855-33 | Steele, D. | watch 28 da @ $1 - $28.00. Trans Dept main stem |
| 1855-7 | " John T. | bag mast 28 da @ $45 per mo - $45.00. Trans Dept main stem |
| 1857-18 | " " | pass train conduc 30 da @ $62.50 per mo - $62.50. thr mail & exp |
| 1857-27 | " Joseph | ton brak 20½ da @ $40 per mo - $32.80. 3d & 4th div |
| 1855-48 | " Robt. | mach @ $35 per mo - $35.00. Mach Dept |
| 1855-32 | " W. | eng'man 24 da @ $2.25 - $54.00. Rd Way Dept |
| 1855-92 | " William J. | saw wd 67 1/8 cords @ $.50 - $33.55. Trans Dept main stem |
| 1857-8 | Stein, David | app 27 da @ $.45 - $12.15. Mach Dept |
| 1857-50 | " John | lab 25 da @ $30 per mo - $30.00. Camden sta |
| 1855-65 | Steiner, Joshua | lab 25 da @ $1 - $25.00. Rd Dept main stem 5th s-div |
| 1857-72 | " " | fore 17⅞ da @ $45 per mo - $45.00. Rd Way Dept |
| 1855-33 | Steirman, U. | carp 20½ da @ $1.50 - $30.40. Cumb depot |
| 1857-127 | Stemner, A. K. | tak nos 28 da @ $40 per mo - $40.00. Trans Dept main stem |
| 1855-85 | Stepens, Henry | mach 14 3/4 da @ $1.60 - $23.60. Mach Dept, Piedmont |
| 1857-63 | Stephen, Finnan | help 21½ da @ $1 - $24.25. Mach Dept |
| 1857-134 | " John | fore boil mkr 14⅓ da @ $2 - $48.50. Mach Dept, Wheeling |
| 1857-63 | " Lewis | fore 25 da @ $1.25 - $31.25. Rd Dept main stem 16th s-div |
| 1855-4 | Stephenson, J. A. | clk 28 da @ $50 per mo - $50.00. Wash br rd, Wash city sta |
| 1857-37 | " " | clk 30 da @ $62.50 per mo - $62.50. Wash br rd, Wash city sta |
| 1855-29 | Sterick, Joseph | haul & saw firewd 28 da @ $27.50 per mo - $27.50. Trans Dept main stem |

| ID | Surname, Given | Description |
|---|---|---|
| 1857-12 | Sterick, Joseph | lab 25 da @ $1.20 - $30.00. Monocacy |
| 1857-110 | Sterling, Wm. H. | mach 22½ da @ $1.55 - $34.50. Mach Dept, Balto |
| 1855-29 | Stern, James | prepar fuel 28 da @ $1 - $28.00. Trans Dept main stem |
| 1857-83 | Steuart, John | app 23¼ da @ $.65 - $15.10. Mach Dept |
| 1857-118 | " Joseph | ton brak 25 da @ $40 per mo - $40.00. 2d div |
| 1857-37 | Stevens, Henry | blksmith help 18 da @ $1 - $18.00. Mach Dept, Balto |
| 1855-94 | " James W. | orak 30 da @ $33.33 per mo - $33.35. Wash br rd, Wash city sta |
| 1857-11 | " John | boil mkr 21 3/4 da @ $1.85 - $40.20. Mach Dept |
| 1855-21 | " Michael | lab 2 da @ $1 - $2.00. Locust Pt |
| 1857-32 | " Richard | fire 11½ da @ $1.75 - $19.70. Trans Dept main stem |
| 1855-71 | " " | ton fire 26½ da @ $33.35 per mo - $35.00. 1st div |
| 1855-58 | " William | paint 18 da @ $1.75 - $31.50. Rd Way Dept |
| 1855-7 | Steward, James | lab 19½ da @ $1 - $19.50. Rd Way Dept |
| 1857-125 | Stewart, A. | supt of trains 28 da @ $75 per mo - $75.00. Trans Dept main stem |
| 1857-36 | " Bururet | lab @ $35 per mo - $35.00. Mach Dept, Martinsburg |
| 1855-14 | " Charles | tele oper 30 da @ $30 per mo - $30.00. Ellicotts Mills |
| 1855-9 | " E. F. | brak 1 da @ $40 per mo - $1.65. Trans Dept main stem |
| 1857-18 | " " " | conduc 1 da @ $50 per mo - $2.10. Trans Dept main stem |
| 1857-27 | " E. R. | pass train brak 10 da @ $33.35 per mo - $11.10. w end |
| 1857-130 | " Edwin R. | ton brak 4 da @ $40 per mo - $6.40. 3d & 4th div |
| 1855-125 | " Hamilton | lab 19½ da @ $1 - $19.25. Mach Dept, Piedmont |
| 1855-37 | " Jacob | lab @ $35 per mo - $35.00. Mach Dept, Martinsburg |
| 1855-19 | " James | lab 28 da @ $1 - $28.00. Rd Way Dept |
| 1857-109 | " " | ton eng'man 5 da @ $2.50 - $12.50. Trans Dept main stem |
| 1855-21 | " John | mach 18 da @ $1.65 - $29.70. Mach Dept, Balto |
| 1855-26 | Stewellyn, Thomas | fire 19 da @ $33.35 per mo - $26.40. Trans Dept main stem |
| 1857-71 | Stigers, Jno. | clean eng 28¼ da @ $1 - $28.25. Mt Clare sta, Balto |
| 1355-72 | Stiges, Jno. | help 21 da @ $1.06 - $22.25. Rd Way Dept |
| 1855-72 | " Jos. | help 24 da @ $1.06 - $25.45. Rd Way Dept |
| 1857-47 | Stimax, George | help 24 da @ $1.06 - $25.45. Rd Way Dept |
| 1857-47 | " Isaac | lab 22½ da @ $1 - $22.50. Rd Dept main stem 2d s-div |
| 1857-47 | " William | lab 26½ da @ $.75 - $19.90. Rd Dept main stem 2d s-div |
| 1855-85 | Stinchcomb, J. | lab 27 da @ $1.12 - $30.35. Rd Dept main stem 2d s-div |
| 1857-111 | Stine, Frederick | blksmith 24 da @ $1.40 - $33.60. Mach Dept |
| 1855-87 | " J. | mach help 22 da @ $1.15 - $25.30. Mach Dept, Balto |
| | | help 19½ da @ $1 - $19.50. Mach Dept |

| | | |
|---|---|---|
| 1855-28 | Stinebaugh, Jacob | reg eng 27½ da @ $1.15 - $31.60. Trans Dept main stem |
| 1857-54 | " | lab 24½ da @ $1 - $24.50. Rd Dept main stem 8th s-div |
| 1855-14 | Stinecamp, H. | brak 17 da @ $40 per mo - $28.35. Trans Dept main stem |
| 1855-14 | Stineman, W. | tak nos 25 da @ $40 per mo - $40.00. Cumb |
| 1857-118 | Stiners, Jos. | blksmith app 25 da @ $.45 - $11.25. Mach Dept, Balto |
| 1855-52 | Stipes, G. | lab 14 da @ $1. Rd Way Dept |
| 1855-32 | " | tele oper 28 da @ $30 per mo - $30.00. Trans Dept main stem |
| 1855-13 | " William | conduc & brak 25 3/4 da @ $30 per mo - $32.20. Trans Dept main stem |
| 1857-21 | " | ton conduc 18½ da @ $50 per mo - $37.00. 1st div |
| 1857-117 | Stivers, Henry | blksmith 16 3/4 da @ $1.85 - $30.95. Mach Dept, Balto |
| 1857-122 | " Thomas | lab 22½ da @ $1 - $22.50. Mach Dept, Balto |
| 1855-85 | Stockdale, Samuel | blksmith 24 da @ $1.25 - $30.00. Mach Dept |
| 1855-19 | Stoddard, George | bag mast 30 da @ $1.45 per mo - $45.00. W end |
| 1857-27 | " J. J. | ton brak 23 da @ $40 per mo - $36.80. 3d & 4th div |
| 1857-27 | " Thomas | ton brak 3 da @ $40 per mo - $4.80. 3d & 4th div |
| 1855-11 | Stoddart, George W. | conduc & brak 15 3/4 da - $31.75. Trans Dept main stem |
| 1855-9 | " T. | conduc 14½ da @ $50 per mo - $29.70. Trans Dept main stem |
| 1857-55 | Stogens, Martin | lab 21 da @ $1 - $21.00. Rd Dept main stem 9th s-div |
| 1857-11 | Stokes, William | nt watch 30 da @ $35 per mo - $35.00. Locust Pt |
| 1857-135 | Stone, M. S. | fore carp @ $50 per mo - $50.00. Mach Dept, Wheeling |
| 1855-94 | " Melvain | carp 25½ da @ $1.45 - $37.00. Mach Dept |
| 1857-119 | Storer, George W. | carp 17 3/4 da @ $1.65 - $29.30. Mach Dept, Balto |
| 1857-109 | Storey, George | mach 17 da @ $1.65 - $28.05. Mach Dept, Balto |
| 1857-115 | Stork, John | pat mkr 17¼ da @ $1.55 - $26.75. Mach Dept, Balto |
| 1857-77 | Storm, George | quarry 24 da @ $1 - $24.00. ballast train for 2d track |
| 1857-56 | Stormer, Henry | lab 18 3/4 da @ $1 - $18.50. Rd Dept main stem 10th s-div |
| 1855-77 | Storry, George | mach 25 3/4 da @ $1.65 - $42.50. Mach Dept |
| 1855-95 | " John | mould 23 da @ $1.55 - $35.65. Mach Dept |
| 1857-114 | " | iron mould 15 3/4 da @ $1.55 - $24.40. Mach Dept, Balto |
| 1855-15 | Story, W. | pass eng'man 27 da @ $3 - $81.00. Trans Dept main stem |
| 1857-107 | " | supv of mach on rd 4th div @ $83.35 per mo. Mach Dept |
| 1857-61 | Stotlu, Harman | lab 28½ da @ $1 - $28.50. Rd Dept main stem 14th s-div |
| 1855-89 | Stott, John | blksmith 22½ da @ $1.50 - $33.35. Mach Dept |
| 1857-23 | " R. R. | ton conduc 31 3/4 da @ $50 per mo - $63.50. 3d & 4th div |
| 1857-53 | " William | lab 24½ da @ $1 - $24.50. Rd Dept main stem 7th s-div |
| 1855-77 | Stout, Joseph | mach 15 da @ $1.30 - $19.50. Mach Dept |

B & O RR EMPLOYEES

| ID | Name | Details |
|---|---|---|
| 1857-63 | Straight, Peter | watch 30 da @ $1 - $30.00. Rd Dept main stem 16th s-div |
| 1855-13 | Strailman, G. | conduc & brak 15 3/4 da @ $50 per mo - $32.80. Trans Dept main stem |
| 1855-92 | Strain, George | carp 22 3/4 da - $32.00. Mach Dept |
| 1857-104 | " John | carp 19¼ da @ $1.25 - $24.05. NW Va RR Tun |
| 1857-129 | " William | carp app 25 da @ $.50 - $12.50. Mach Dept, Piedmont |
| 1855-93 | Strainer, Peter | boil mkr 15 3/4 da - $25.55. Mach Dept |
| 1855-93 | Straney, Edward | boil mkr 26½ da - $43.95. Mach Dept |
| 1857-123 | " John | mach 18 da @ $1.60 - $28.80. Mach Dept, Martinsburg |
| 1855-84 | " " | mach 24 3/4 da @ $1.30 - $32.20. Mach Dept |
| 1857-115 | Stratton, Isaac | boil mkr 18½ da @ $1.30 - $24.05. Mach Dept, Balto |
| 1857-128 | Straw, Joseph | boil mkr 16 3/4 da @ $1.70 - $28.45. Mach Dept, Piedmont |
| 1855-21 | Strawbridge, I. S. | fire 7 da @ $1.75 - $12.25. Trans Dept main stem |
| 1855-6 | Stray, Lewis | agt 28 da @ $35 per mo - $35.00. Trans Dept main stem |
| 1855-83 | Street, James | app 24 da @ $.65 - $15.60. Mach Dept |
| 1857-127 | Stribling, F. J. | mach 17 da @ $1.70 - $28.90. Mach Dept, Piedmont |
| 1855-34 | " " | disp of trains 28 da @ $60 per mo - $60.00. Trans Dept main stem |
| 1857-15 | Stricklin, John | train disp 30 da @ $40 per mo - $58.40. Fetterman sta |
| 1857-27 | Strider, C. | ton brak 36½ da @ $40 per mo - $58.40. Board Tree Tun |
| 1855-13 | " " | conduc & brak 12 da @ $50 per mo - $26.00. Trans Dept main stem |
| 1855-75 | " Howard | lab 20 da @ $1 - $20.00. Rd Way Dept |
| 1857-51 | " " | lab 24½ da @ $1 - $24.50. Rd Dept main stem 5th s-div |
| 1857-77 | " John | quarry 15 da @ $1 - $15.00. ballast train for 2d track |
| 1855-52 | Stroads, Daniel | carp 9 da @ $1.50 - $13.50. Rd Way Dept |
| 1855-53 | Stromenger, Michael | lab 18½ da @ $1 - $18.50. Rd Way Dept |
| 1855-55 | Strouse, Isaiah | fore 25 da @ $1.25 - $31.25. Rd Way Dept |
| 1855-56 | Stuart, H. | spiker 5½ da @ $1.06 - $5.85. Rd Way Dept |
| 1857-99 | Stuck, L. D. | lab 25 da @ $1 - $25.00. NW Va RR, Rd Dept 4th s-div |
| 1857-99 | " Samuel | fore 25 da @ $1.25 - $31.25. NW Va RR, Rd Dept 4th s-div |
| 1855-58 | Stuckey, M. | nail 11 da @ $1 - $11.00. Rd Way Dept |
| 1857-73 | Stuff, Hezekiah | carp 2½ da @ $1.30 - $3.25. repair bridges &c |
| 1855-92 | Stump, Cass | help 14½ da - $17.55. Mach Dept |
| 1857-127 | " " | mach help 19¼ da @ $1.25 - $24.05. Mach Dept, Piedmont |
| 1855-72 | " Henry | app 22 3/4 da @ $.60 - $13.65. Rd Way Dept |
| 1857-109 | " " | mach 20¼ da @ $1.60 - $32.40. Mach Dept, Balto |
| 1855-45 | " James | fore 16½ da @ $1.25 - $20.60. Rd Way Dept |
| 1855-26 | " John | clean eng 15 da @ $1 - $15.00. Trans Dept main stem |

B & O RR EMPLOYEES 313

| ID | Name | Description |
|---|---|---|
| 1857-55 | Stump, Joseph | fore 24½ da @ $1.25 - $30.60. Rd Dept main stem 9th s-div |
| 1855-1 | Wm. | tell $750 per annum - $62.50. Ofc Hanover St |
| 1855-40 | Stunkle, F. | lab 25 da @ $1 - $25.00. Rd Way Dept |
| 1857-50 | Stunkle, Frederick | lab 24 da @ $1 - $24.00. Rd Dept main stem 4th s-div |
| 1857-125 | Stuttions, William | clean eng 28 3/4 da @ $1.15 - $33.05. Mach Dept, Martinsburg |
| 1855-5 | Stymax, George | brak 1 da @ $30 per mo - $1.25. Trans Dept, Wash br |
| 1855-11 | " | conduc & brak 8 da @ $40 per mo - $13.35. Trans Dept main stem |
| 1855-27 | Suffran, Robert | get out eng 28 da @ $1.25 - $35.00. Trans Dept main stem |
| 1857-54 | Suitley, George | lab 25 da @ $1 - $25.00. Rd Dept main stem 8th s-div |
| 1857-79 | Sullivan, Cornelius | lab 14¼ da @ $1 - $14.25. lay 2d track |
| 1855-37 | D. | lab 23 3/4 da @ $1 - $23.75. Rd Way Dept |
| 1857-78 | Daniel | lab 11 da @ $1 - $11.00. lay 2d track |
| 1857-79 | Dennis | lab 26 da @ $.65 - $16.90. lay 2d track |
| 1855-28 | Edward | reg eng 21 3/4 da @ $1.15 - $25.00. Trans Dept main stem |
| 1857-80 | " | lab 19 3/4 da - $19.75. lay 2d track |
| 1857-125 | " | put away eng &c 26 3/4 da @ $1.50 - $40.10. Mach Dept, Martinsburg |
| 1855-28 | J. | prepar fuel 5 da @ $1 - $5.00. Trans Dept main stem |
| 1857-130 | James | lab 1½ da @ $1 - $1.50. Mach Dept, Piedmont |
| 1857-57 | " | lab 24 da @ $1 - $24.00. Rd Dept main stem 11th s-div |
| 1857-64 | " | lab 23 3/4 da @ $1 - $23.75. Rd Dept main stem 17th s-div |
| 1857-27 | " | ton brak 8½ da @ $40 per mo - $13.60. 3d & 4th div |
| 1857-33 | " | ton fire 1¼½ da @ $1.75 - $25.35. 3d div |
| 1857-51 | Jerry | lab 25 da @ $1 - $25.00. Rd Dept main stem 5th s-div |
| 1855-38 | John | lab 19 da @ $1 - $19.00. Rd Way Dept |
| 1855-30 | " | unload coal 6½ da @ $30 per mo - $6.95. Trans Dept main stem |
| 1857-118 | " | blksmith help 16½ da @ $1 - $16.50. Mach Dept, Balto |
| 1857-78 | " | fire 25 da @ $1.35 - $33.75. lay 2d track |
| 1857-80 | " | lab 24 da @ $.65 - $15.60. lay 2d track |
| 1857-51 | " | lab 25¾ da @ $1 - $25.50. Rd Dept main stem 5th s-div |
| 1857-126 | " | prepar fuel 30 da @ $1 - $30.00. Mach Dept, Martinsburg |
| 1857-78 | Michael | lab 22¼ da @ $1 - $22.25. lay 2d track |
| 1857-74 | Owen | lab 12 da @ $.90 - $10.80. repair bridges &c |
| 1855-44 | P. | lab 19¼ da @ $1 - $19.25. Rd Way Dept |
| 1857-47 | Patrick | lab 23½ da @ $1 - $23.50. Rd Dept main stem 1st s-div |
| 1857-52 | Paul | lab 21 da @ $1 - $21.00. Rd Dept main stem 6th s-div |
| 1855-48 | R. | fire 24 da @ $1.28 - $30.70. Rd Way Dept |

314  B & O RR EMPLOYEES

| Name | Year-No. | Details |
|---|---|---|
| Sullivan, Richard | 1855-88 | help 4 3/4 da @ $1 - $4.75. Mach Dept |
| " | 1857-81 | eng'man 7 da @ $2.25 -$15.75. lay 2d track |
| " | 1857-28 | ton eng'man 1 da @ $2.50 - $2.50. 1st div |
| Thomas | 1857-126 | clean eng 26 da @ $1.15 - $29.90. Mach Dept, Martinsburg |
| " | 1857-75 | lab 17 da @ $1.15 - $19.40. ballast train for 2d track |
| Timothy | 1855-26 | clean eng 18½ da @ $1 - $18.50. Trans Dept main stem |
| " | 1857-126 | lab 23 3/4 da @ $1 - $23.75. Mach Dept, Martinsburg |
| Summers, John | 1855-81 | lab 24½ da @ $1.15 - $28.15. Mach Dept |
| " | 1857-113 | carp help 22 da @ $1.15 - $25.30. Mach Dept, Balto |
| Sumwalt, A. J. | 1857-111 | mach app 23 da @ $.65 - $14.95. Mach Dept, Balto |
| Alexander | 1855-81 | mach help 18½ da @ $1 - $18.50. Mach Dept, Balto |
| " | 1857-119 | carp 19½ da @ $1.60 - $31.20. Mach Dept |
| Surghner, V. H. | 1857-39 | carp 18 da @ $1.60 - $28.80. Mach Dept, Balto |
| Surtis, John Sr. | 1857-82 | bag mast 30 da @ $35 per mo - $35.00. NW Va rd, Parkersburg sta |
| Sustring, Caspar | 1857-121 | brickaly 10½ da @ $2 - $21.00. Board Tree Tun |
| Suter, Frederick | 1857-70 | carp help 20½ da @ $1.15 - $23.55. Mach Dept, Balto |
| George | 1857-72 | app 24 da @ $.60 - $14.40. Mt Clare sta, Balto |
| Samuel | 1855-11 | fore @ $60 per mo - $60.00. repair tele line |
| " | 1857-69 | conduc & brak 26 da @ $1.60 - $28.80. Trans Dept main stem |
| " | 1857-22 | carp 18 da @ $1.60 - $28.80. Mt Clare sta, Balto |
| Suters, Samuel | 1855-53 | ton conduc 29 da @ $50 per mo - $58.00. 2d div |
| Suthers, James | 1857-52 | carp 22 3/4 da @ $1.50 -$34.10. Rd Way Dept |
| Sutter, Thomas | 1857-53 | lab 24½ da @ $1 - $24.50. Rd Dept main stem 6th s-div |
| Sutton, Daniel | 1855-21 | lab 25 da @ $1 - $25.00. Rd Dept main stem 7th s-div |
| " | 1857-125 | fire 18¾ da @ $1.75 - $31.95. Trans Dept main stem |
| Swaalberg, F. | 1857-71 | wheel 21¼ da @ $1.15 - $24.45. Mach Dept, Martinsburg |
| Swain, J. K. | 1855-7 | track lay 23 da @ $1 - $23.00. Camden sta, repair track |
| John | 1855-94 | clk 28 da @ $58.35 per mo - $58.35. Trans Dept main stem |
| William | 1855-8 | app 16 da @ $.45 - $7.20. Mach Dept |
| " | 1857-85 | brak 28 da @ $33.35 per mo - $33.35. Trans Dept main stem |
| Swainscott, John | 1857-23 | conduc 4 da @ $1.94 -$7.75. grad, Board Tree Tun |
| Swaitze, Conrad | 1857-119 | ton conduc 16½ da @ $50 per mo -$32.50. 3d & 4th div |
| Swanberger, Harman | 1857-118 | carp 18 da @ $1.50 -$27.00. Mach Dept, Balto |
| Swann, John | 1857-46 | blksmith help 18 da @ $1.15 - $20.70. Mach Dept, Balto |
| " | 1857-24 | lab 26 da @ $1 - $26.00. Rd Dept main stem 1st s-div |
| " | 1857-24 | ton brak 15 da @ $40 per mo - $24.00. 1st div |

B & O RR EMPLOYEES 315

| ID | Name | Description |
|---|---|---|
| 1857-13 | Swartz, George W. | disp 30 da @ $1.45 per mo - $45.00. Martinsburg |
| 1857-131 | Swatzweller, Levi | mach 19½ da @ $1.60 - $31.20. Mach Dept, Grafton |
| 1857-76 | Sweaney, Thomas | quarry 25 da @ $1 - $25.00. ballast train for 2d track |
| 1855-23 | Swearingen, James | fire 15 da @ $1.75 - $26.25. Trans Dept main stem |
| 1857-30 | " | ton eng'man 26 da @ $3 - $78.00. 3d div |
| 1857-99 | Swearinger, William E. | fore 25 da @ $1.25 - $31.25. NW Va RR, Rd Dept 4th s-div |
| 1857-87 | Sweeden, Benjamin | bricklay 9 3/4 da @ $2.25 - $21.95. grad, Welling Tun |
| 1855-71 | Sweeney, Alfred | carp 24 da @ $1.60 - $38.40. Rd Way Dept |
| 1857-75 | " Daniel | train hand 8 3/4 da @ $1 - $8.75. Rd Way Dept |
| 1857-136 | " | lab 16 da @ $1.05 - $16.85. ballast train for 2d track |
| 1857-91 | " James | clean eng 30½ da @ $1 - $30.50. Mach Dept, Wheeling |
| 1857-91 | " John | lab 13 3/4 da @ $1 - $13.75. grad, Welling Tun |
| 1857-66 | " " | lab 18 da @ $1 - $18.00. grad, Welling Tun |
| 1855-68 | " " | lab 25½ da @ $1 - $25.50. Rd Dept main stem 18th s-div |
| 1857-66 | " Michael | lab 23 3/4 da @ $1 - $23.75. Rd Way Dept |
| 1857-89 | " Patrick | lab 23½ da @ $1 - $23.50. Rd Dept main stem 18th s-div |
| 1857-91 | " " | lab 11 da @ $1.12 - $12.35. grad, Welling Tun |
| 1857-66 | " " | lab 19 3/4 da @ $1 - $19.75. grad, Welling Tun |
| 1855-28 | " Peter | lab 24 da @ $1 - $24.00. Rd Dept main stem 18th s-div |
| 1855-59 | " Thomas | prepar fuel 11½ da @ $1 - $11.50. Trans Dept main stem |
| 1857-139 | " | lab 23 da @ $1 - $23.00. Rd Way Dept |
| 1855-93 | Sweeny, John | saw wd 26½ da @ $1 - $26.50. NW Va RR, Mach Dept, Parkersburg |
| 1855-63 | " | mach 24 3/4 da @ $1.60 - $39.60. Mach Dept |
| 1857-94 | " | watch 28 da @ $1 - $28.00. Rd Way Dept |
| 1857-77 | " | lab 8¼ da @ $1 - $8.25. quarry & haul stone for Board Tree & Littleton Tun |
| 1857-86 | " | quarry 24 3/4 da @ $1 - $24.75. ballast train for 2d track |
| 1855-93 | " Michael | lab 24½ da @ $1.60 - $24.50. grad, McGuire's Tun |
| 1857-48 | " Thomas | mach 15¼ da @ $1.60 - $24.40. Mach Dept |
| 1857-66 | Sweet, William | lab 24 da @ $1 - $24.00. Rd Dept main stem 2d s-div |
| 1857-118 | Sweney, Peter | lab 23½ da @ $1 - $23.50. Rd Dept main stem 18th s-div |
| 1855-61 | Swift, Henry | blksmith help 18 da @ $1 - $18.00. Mach Dept, Balto |
| 1857-68 | " L. | lab 18¼ da @ $1 - $18.25. Rd Way Dept |
| 1855-11 | " Lawrence | lab 21 da @ $1 - $21.00. Rd Dept main stem 19th s-div |
| 1857-124 | Swigart, Henry | conduc & brak 20 da @ $50 per mo - $44.15. Trans Dept main stem |
| 1855-93 | Switzer, Charles M. | mach app 19 da @ $.55 - $10.45. Mach Dept, Martinsburg |
| | Syck, G. | help 28 da @ $1 - $28.00. Mach Dept |

| | | |
|---|---|---|
| 1855-14 | Syholt, C. | brak 17¾ da @ $40 per mo - $28.75. Trans Dept main stem |
| 1855-54 | Sympson, Robt. | storecut 6½ da @ $2 - $13.00. Rd Way Dept |
| 1855-74 | Synder, Adam | lab 23 da @ $1 - $23.00. Rd Way Dept |
| 1857-82 | Syons, Simon | lab 8 da @ $1.12 - $9.00. grad, Board Tree Tun |
| 1857-53 | Syphers, Derias | lab 24½ da @ $1 - $24.50. Rd Dept main stem 7th s-div |
| 1857-53 | " Joseph | lab 22½ da @ $1 - $2.50. Rd Dept main stem 7th s-div |
| 1857-88 | Sypold, John | lab 2 da @ $1.12 - $2.25. grad, Welling Tun |
| 1857-90 | " William | oil boy 7½ da @ $.87 - $6.35. grad, Welling Tun |
| 1855-41 | Tabler, Adam | fore 24 da @ $1.25 - $30.00. Rd Way Dept |
| 1857-52 | Tables, Adam | fore 25 da @ $1.25 - $31.25. Rd Dept main stem 6th s-div |
| 1855-5 | Taff, J. | reg 24 da @ $30 per mo - $30.00. Trans Dept, Wash br |
| 1857-19 | Taft, J. H. | pass eng'man 26 da @ $2.25 - $58.50. 1st div |
| 1855-15 | " J. K. | pass eng'man 24 da @ $2.25 - $54.00. Trans Dept main stem |
| 1857-132 | Taggart, Charles W. | lab 25 @ $30 per mo - $30.00. Grafton sta |
| 1855-51 | Taggert, Charles | blksmith help 19 3/4 da @ $1 - $19.75. Mach Dept, Grafton |
| 1857-15 | Tall, Jones | lab 28 da @ $1 - $28.00. Rd Way Dept |
| 1857-84 | Tallant, Patrick | boil mkr 20½ da @ $1.35 - $27.65. Mach Dept, Balto |
| 1857-21 | Taney, Joseph | lab 25 da @ $1.12 - $28.10. grad, Board Tree Tun |
| 1855-58 | Tanner, William | ton conduc 20 da @ $50 per mo - $40.00. 1st div |
| 1857-52 | Tarpy, Mart. | lab 17½ da @ $1 - $17.50. Rd Way Dept |
| 1857-20 | Tate, Robert J. | lab 28 da @ $1 - $28.00. Rd Way Dept |
| 1857-33 | " " | pass fire 3 da @ $40 per mo - $4.00. 2d div |
| 1857-79 | Tauge, John | ton fire 2 da @ $1.75 - $3.50. 2d div |
| 1857-60 | Taylar, John | lab 15 da @ $1 - $15.00. lay 2d track |
| 1857-117 | Taylor, Charles | lab 24½ da @ $1 - $24.50. Rd Dept main stem 13th s-div |
| 1855-78 | " Henry | blksmith 18 3/4 da @ $1.72 - $32.25. Mach Dept, Balto |
| 1857-72 | " " | mach 17 3/4 da @ $1.45 - $25.75. Mach Dept |
| 1855-78 | " " | lab 30 da @ $1.50 - $45.00. repair tele line |
| 1857-8 | " Hezekiah | mach 23 da @ $1.90 - $43.70. Mach Dept |
| 1857-25 | " J. D. | deliv clk 30 da @ $15 per mo - $15.00. Camden sta |
| 1855-40 | " J. W. | ton brak 7 da @ $30 per mo - $8.40. 2d div |
| 1855-77 | " James | lab 24 da @ $1 - $24.00. Rd Way Dept |
| 1857-73 | " " | mach 18 da @ $1.15 - $20.70. Mach Dept |
| 1855-40 | " Jesse | lab 6 da @ $1 - $6.00. repair bridges &c |
| 1857-49 | " " | lab 20 da @ $1 - $20.00. Rd Way Dept |
| | | lab 21 da @ $1 - $21.00. Rd Dept main stem 3d s-div |

B & O RR EMPLOYEES 317

| | | | |
|---|---|---|---|
| 1855-78 | Taylor, S. | help 24 da @ $1 - $24.00. Mach Dept |
| 1857-27 | Thomas | ton brak 31 da @ $40 per mo; 3 3/4 da @ $50 per mo - $57.10. 3d & 4th div |
| 1857-8 | W. H. | deliv clk 30 da @ $1 - $11.65 per mo - $41.65. Camden sta |
| 1857-135 | William | lab 12 da @ $1 - $12.00. Mach Dept, Wheeling |
| 1857-110 | Tayman, Robert | mach 17 3/4 da @ $1.72 - $30.55. Mach Dept, Balto |
| 1855-21 | William | fire 14 3/4 da @ $1.75 - $25.80. Trans Dept main stem |
| 1855-19 | " | ton eng'man 4 3/4 da @ $2.50 - $11.85. Trans Dept main stem |
| 1857-29 | | ton eng'man 19½ da @ $3 - $58.50. 2d div |
| 1855-84 | Teagler, Charles | help 25½ da @ $1.15 - $29.30. Mach Dept |
| 1855-83 | Teal, James | mach 24 da @ $1.40 - $33.60. Mach Dept |
| 1857-109 | " | mach 17¾ da @ $1.40 - $24.15. Mach Dept, Balto |
| 1857-123 | James R. | mach 22¼ da @ $1.60 - $35.60. Mach Dept, Martinsburg |
| 1857-78 | Tearney, John | lab 26½ da @ $1 - $26.50. lay 2d track |
| 1857-87 | Tearry, Michael | lab 23¼ da @ $1 - $23.25. grad, McGuire's Tun |
| 1857-87 | Thomas | lab 23½ da @ $1 - $23.50. grad, McGuire's Tun |
| 1857-94 | Teater, David | carp 5½ da @ $1.65 - $9.05. repair bridges |
| 1857-55 | Teffery, David | lab 22 3/4 da @ $1 - $22.75. Rd Dept main stem 9th s-div |
| 1857-45 | Tegmeyer, John H. | asst mast of rd @ $125 per mo. Rd Dept 1st & 2d div |
| 1857-85 | Telherson, Patrick | lab 7 da @ $1.12 - $7.85. grad, Board Tree Tun |
| 1855-56 | Templeton, Patrick | lab 17 da @ $1 - $17.00. Rd Way Dept |
| 1857-57 | " | fore 26 da @ $1.25 - $32.50. Rd Dept main stem 11th s-div |
| 1855-83 | W. J. | app 23½ da @ $.55 - $14.90. Mach Dept |
| 1857-109 | Wm. | mach 31 da @ $1.50 - $46.50. Mach Dept, Balto |
| 1857-85 | Tennison, Oliver | bricklay 6½ da @ $2.25 - $14.60. grad, Board Tree Tun |
| 1857-17 | Terry, W. D. | tick agt 30 da @ $35 per mo - $35.00. Wheeling sta |
| 1857-139 | Tevedale, Daniel | lab 21 3/4 da @ $1.10 - $23.90. NW Va RR, Mach Dept, Parkersburg |
| 1855-78 | Tevis, Joseph | clk @ $50 per mo - $50.00. Mach Dept |
| 1857-108 | | timekpr @ $66.70 per mo - $66.70. Mach Dept, Balto |
| 1857-58 | Thaser, Barney | lab 25½ da @ $1 - $25.50. Rd Dept main stem 12th s-div |
| 1855-23 | Thayer, Arch'd. | fire 17¼ da @ $1.75 - $30.20. Trans Dept main stem |
| 1855-14 | S. | brak 17 da @ $40 per mo - $28.35. Trans Dept main stem |
| 1857-118 | Theiss, Herman | blksmith help 16 3/4 da @ $1 - $16.75. Mach Dept, Balto |
| 1855-83 | Theymice, Lewis | app 24 da @ $.65 - $15.60. Mach Dept |
| 1855-73 | Thilmeyer, F. | fore @ $65 per mo - $65.00. Rd Way Dept |
| 1857-124 | Thimall, Augustus | boil mkr help 22 da @ $1.10 - $24.20. Mach Dept, Martinsburg |
| 1855-73 | Thinsion, John | lab 25¼ da @ $1.25 - $31.55. Rd Way Dept |

| | | |
|---|---|---|
| 1855-92 | Thomas, Alfred | help 19¼ da - $22.95. Mach Dept |
| 1857-131 | " | mach 17 3/4 da @ $1.50 - $26.60. Mach Dept, Grafton |
| 1855-78 | B. F. | help 24 da @ $1 - $24.00. Mach Dept |
| 1855-30 | Bartley | prepar fuel 28 da @ $30 per mo - $30.00. Trans Dept main stem |
| 1857-126 | " | lab 30 da @ $1 - $30.00. Mach Dept, Martinsburg |
| 1855-92 | Edwin | app 21½ da @ $.55 - $11.80. Mach Dept |
| 1857-139 | " | mach 25½ da @ $1.35 - $34.40. NW Va RR, Mach Dept, Parkersburg |
| 1857-94 | Frank | carp 24½ da @ $1.75 - $42.90. repair bridges |
| 1855-14 | G. | brak 8 da @ $40 per mo - $13.35. Trans Dept main stem |
| 1857-20 | Gilbert | pass fire 1½ da @ $40 per mo - $2.00. 3d div |
| 1857-34 | " | ton fire 1 da @ $1.75 - $1.75. Board Tree Tun |
| 1857-34 | " | ton fire 20½ da @ $1.75 - $35.85. 4th div |
| 1857-14 | H. | watch 30 da @ $35 per mo - $35.00. Piedmont sta |
| 1855-30 | John | prepar fuel 23 da @ $1 - $23.00. Trans Dept main stem |
| 1857-100 | " | lab 20½ da @ $1 - $20.50. NW Va RR, Rd Dept 5th s-div |
| 1855-34 | John N. | watch 28 da @ $1 - $28.00. Trans Dept main stem |
| 1857-47 | Jonathan | lab 24½ da @ $1 - $24.50. Rd Dept main stem 2d s-div |
| 1857-24 | " | ton brak 19¼ da @ $40 per mo - $30.80. 1st div |
| 1857-118 | Joseph | blksmith help 16½ da @ $1 - $16.50. Mach Dept, Balto |
| 1857-57 | Lewis | lab 23¼ da @ $1 - $23.25. Rd Dept main stem 11th s-div |
| 1855-54 | Phillip | track lay 23 da @ $1.50 -$34.50. Rd Way Dept |
| 1855-11 | S. K. | conduc & brak 7¼ da @ $50 per mo - $15.10. Trans Dept main stem |
| 1857-21 | " " | ton conduc 20 da @ $50 per mo - $40.00. 1st div |
| 1855-49 | Serris | watch cuts 26 da @ $1 -$26.00. Rd Way Dept |
| 1855-55 | William | lab 18½ da @ $1 - $18.50. Rd Way Dept |
| 1857-16 | " | coop 25 da @ $30 per mo - $30.00. Benwood sta |
| 1857-128 | " | stat'ry eng'man @ $40 per mo - $40.00. Mach Dept, Piedmont |
| 1857-29 | Thompson, Buchrod | ton eng'man 15 da @ $2.50 - $37.50. 1st div |
| 1855-21 | Bushrod | fire 23½ da @ $1.75 - $41.10. Trans Dept main stem |
| 1857-16 | Calvin | mate 25 da @ $30 per mo - $25.00. transfer steam Brown Dick--Ohio Riv, bet Benwood & Bellaire |
| 1857-128 | David | boil mkr 19½ da @ $1.70 - $33.15. Mach Dept, Piedmont |
| 1857-18 | E. | pass train conduc 30 da @ $62.50 per mo - $62.50. Fred accom |
| 1855-7 | E. F. | pass conduc 28 da @ $40 per mo - $40.00. Trans Dept main stem |
| 1855-83 | F. | blksmith 12¼ da @ $1.25 - $15.95. Mach Dept |
| 1855-83 | " | mach 23½ da @ $1.60 - $37.60. Mach Dept |

B & O RR EMPLOYEES  319

| | | | |
|---|---|---|---|
| 1857-117 | Thompson, Francis A. | blksmith 16 3/4 da @ $1.35 - $22.60. Mach Dept, Balto |
| 1855-16 | G. W. | pass fire 2 da @ $40 per mo - $2.85. Trans Dept main stem |
| 1857-80 | George | lab 18 3/4 da @ $1 - $18.75. lay 2 d track |
| 1857-32 | George W. | ton fire 19½ da @ $1.75 - $34.10. 1st div |
| 1857-45 | H. | lab 9½ da @ $1 - $9.50. Rd Way Dept |
| 1857-16 | " | deck hand 30 da @ $20 per mo - $20.00. transfer steam Brown Dick--Ohio Riv, bet Benwood & Bellaire |
| 1857-49 | Hamilton | lab 23½ da @ $1 - $23.50. Rd Dept main stem 3d s-div |
| 1855-67 | J. G. | mason 20½ da @ $2 -- $41.00. Rd Way Dept |
| 1855-21 | J. W. | fire 21 da @ $1.75 - $36.75. Trans Dept main stem |
| 1855-33 | " | disp 28 da @ $40 per mo - $40.00. Trans Dept main stem |
| 1855-51 | James | lab 28 da @ $1 -$28.00. Rd Way Dept |
| 1857-29 | " | ton eng'man 4 da @ $3 - $12.00. 2d div |
| 1857-48 | " | watch 30 da @ $1 - $30.00. Rd Dept main stem 2d s-div |
| 1855-32 | John | tele oper 28 da @ $30 per mo - $30.00. Trans Dept main stem |
| 1855-36 | John D. | tele oper 30 da @ $15 per mo - $15.00. Harpers Ferry |
| 1857-13 | John W. | disp 30 da @ $40 per mo - $40.00. Martinsburg |
| 1857-21 | Joseph B. | ton conduc 25 da @ $50 per mo - $50.00. 1st div |
| 1855-55 | Matthew | lab 24 da @ $1 - $24.00. Rd Way Dept |
| 1855-57 | " | lab 24 da @ $1 - $24.00. Rd Dept main stem 11th s-div |
| 1855-75 | Michael | lab 21 da @ $1 - $21.00. Rd Way Dept |
| 1857-99 | N. M. | supv @ $60 per mo - $60.00. NW Va RR, Rd Dept 4th s-div |
| 1857-46 | Oliver | lab 22 da @ $1 - $22.00. Rd Dept main stem 1st s-div |
| 1857-113 | Otis | mach app 17 da @ $.45 - $7.65. Mach Dept, Balto |
| 1855-63 | P. | lab 21½ da @ $1 - $21.50. Mach Dept, Balto |
| 1857-68 | Patrick | lab 22 da @ $1 - $22.00. Rd Dept main stem 19th s-div |
| 1857-57 | Peter | lab 25 da @ $1 - $25.00. Rd Dept main stem 11th s-div |
| 1855-83 | R. T. | mach 21 3/4 da @ $1.65 - $35.90. Mach Dept |
| 1855-39 | S. | lab 24 da @ $1.25 - $30.00. Rd Way Dept |
| 1857-116 | Samuel | boil mkr help 17 3/4 da @ $1 - $17.75. Mach Dept, Balto |
| 1857-22 | Samuel J. | ton conduc 10½ da @ $50 per mo - $21.00. 2d div |
| 1857-49 | Smallwood | fore 25 da @ $1.25 - $31.25. Rd Dept main stem 3d s-div |
| 1855-78 | Thomas | help 24 da @ $1.15 - $27.60. Mach Dept |
| 1857-112 | Thomas N. | mach help 20½ da @ $1.15 - $23.55. Mach Dept, Balto |
| 1857-135 | Thornton | blksmith help 19 da @ $1 - $19.00. Mach Dept, Wheeling |
| 1857-40 | W. | ton brak 17 da @ $40 per mo - $27.20. NW Va rd, Parkersburg sta |

| | | |
|---|---|---|
| 1857-40 | Thompson, W. | ton conduc 10¼ da @ $50 per mo - $20.50. NW Va rd, Parkersburg sta |
| 1857-32 | W. H. | ton fire 24 da @ $33.33 per mo - $32.00. 1st div |
| 1855-57 | William | fore 24 da @ $1.25 - $30.00. Rd Way Dept |
| 1855-78 | " | help 25 da @ $1 - $25.00. Mach Dept |
| 1855-88 | " | help 9 da @ $1 - $9.00. Mach Dept |
| 1855-83 | " | mach 21 3/4 da @ $1.60 - $34.80. Mach Dept |
| 1857-109 | " | mach 18 3/4 da @ $1.65 - $30.95. Mach Dept, Balto |
| 1855-25 | Thomson, G. W. | clean eng 19¼ da @ $1.15 - $22.15. Trans Dept main stem |
| 1855-4 | " " | pass fire 6 da @ $40 per mo - $8.55. Trans Dept, Wash br |
| 1857-120 | Thorman, Henry | carp 18 da @ $1.50 - $27.00. Mach Dept, Balto |
| 1855-25 | Thorn, John | bur driv 13½ da @ $30 per mo - $16.85. Trans Dept main stem |
| 1855-24 | Michael | pass & bur driv 27 da @ $30 per mo - $33.75. Trans Dept main stem |
| 1855-71 | Thos. | smith 24 da @ $2 - $48.00. Rd Way Dept |
| 1855-27 | Thornton, D. | clean eng 4 da @ $1 - $4.00. Trans Dept main stem |
| 1857-17 | Daniel | lab 3 da @ $1 - $3.00. frt transfer force at Bellaire, opp Benwood |
| 1857-127 | Darby | mach help 21 da @ $1 - $21.00. Mach Dept, Piedmont |
| 1855-64 | Edw. | lab 24 da @ $1 - $24.00. Rd Way Dept |
| 1857-119 | T. H. | carp 17¼ da @ $1.50 - $25.85. Mach Dept, Balto |
| 1855-70 | Thrasher, Charles | lab 28 da @ $1 - $28.00. Rd Way Dept |
| 1857-36 | Joseph | tele oper 30 da @ $30 per mo - $30.00. Sir John's Run |
| 1855-11 | Thrift, John | conduc & brak 11 3/4 da @ $50 per mo - $24.45. Trans Dept main stem |
| 1857-29 | John H. | ton eng'man 24¼ da @ $2.50 - $60.60. 1st div |
| 1855-21 | Throgmorton, W. W. | fire 7 da @ $1.75 - $12.25. Trans Dept main stem |
| 1855-87 | Thuma, Charles | mach 28¼ da @ $1.25 - $35.30. Mach Dept |
| 1855-88 | Thumal, A. | help 30¼ da @ $1 - $30.25. Mach Dept |
| 1857-124 | Thumall, Charles | boil mkr 23 da @ $1.45 - $33.35. Mach Dept, Martinsburg |
| 1855-6 | Thumbert, J. E. | clk 28 da @ $58.65 per mo - $58.65. Trans Dept main stem |
| 1857-8 | Thumlert, J. E. | rec clk 30 da @ $58.35 per mo -$58.35. Camden sta |
| 1857-71 | Thurion, Jno. T. | lab 24 da @ $.75 - $18.00. Mt Clare, repair tracks in yd |
| 1855-18 | Tibbetts, Jno. | ton eng'man 9¼ da @ $3 - $27.75. Trans Dept main stem |
| 1855-18 | Ransom | ton eng'man 12 da @ $3 - $36.00. Trans Dept main stem |
| 1857-30 | " | ton eng'man 13½ da @ $3 - $40.50. 3d div |
| 1855-23 | Robert | fire 5½ da @ $1.75 - $9.60. Trans Dept main stem |
| 1857-30 | " | ton eng'man 13 da @ $3 - $39.00. 3d div |
| 1857-107 | W. | supv of mach on rd 3 div @ $83.35 per mo. Mach Dept |
| 1855-17 | Wm. | ton eng'man 9 da @ $3 - $27.00. Trans Dept main stem |

| ID | Name | Details |
|---|---|---|
| 1857-136 | Tice, Johnson | mast mech @ $83.35 per mo - $83.35. Mach Dept, Cumb |
| 1855-46 | Tidon, John | lab 22 da @ $1 - $22.00. Rd Way Dept |
| 1857-72 | Tiernan, James | lab 19½ da @ $1 - $19.50. Piedmont depot |
| 1855-27 | Tiernan, James | clean eng 28 da @ $1 - $28.00. Trans Dept main stem |
| 1857-122 | Tierney, Denis | lab 20 da @ $1 - $20.00. Mach Dept, Balto |
| 1857-73 | " John | lab 23 da @ $1.12 - $25.90. repair water sta, M.S. & P.B. |
| 1857-50 | " Martin | lab 24½ da @ $1 - $24.50. Rd Dept main stem 5th s-div |
| 1857-10 | Tilghman, Wm. | bur driv 27½ da @ $1.15 - $31.60. hp exp, Balto |
| 1855-11 | Tillan, N. | conduc & brak 2 da @ $40 per mo - $3.35. Trans Dept main stem |
| 1855-24 | Tillman, Wm. | pass & bur driv 26½ da @ $30 per mo - $33.10. Trans Dept main stem |
| 1857-13 | Tillow, Robert | haul wd 4 da @ $1 - $4.00. Martinsburg |
| 1857-102 | Timms, John | carp 26 da @ $1.65 - $42.90. NW Va RR bridges |
| 1857-32 | Tine, Alfred | ton fire 1 da @ $1.75 - $1.75. 1st div |
| 1855-28 | Tittow, James | reg eng 10 3/4 da @ $1.15 - $12.35. Trans Dept main stem |
| 1855-64 | Tobin, Cor. | lab 13 da @ $1 - $13.00. Rd Way Dept |
| 1857-93 | " Cornelius | smith help 21½ da @ $1 - $21.50. quarry & haul stone for Board Tree & Littleton Tun |
| 1855-41 | " Edward | lab 18 da @ $1 - $18.00. Rd Way Dept |
| 1857-74 | " Edward Jr | lab 21 da @ $1.12 - $23.65. repair bridges &c |
| 1857-74 | " Edward Sr | lab 22 da @ $1.12 - $24.75. repair bridges &c |
| 1855-41 | " James | lab 17 3/4 da @ $1 - $17.75. Rd Way Dept |
| 1857-27 | " John | ton brak 14½ da @ $40 per mo - $23.20. Board Tree Tun |
| 1855-41 | " " | ton brak 3 da @ $40 per mo - $4.80. 3d & 4th div |
| 1857-27 | " Patrick | lab 16 3/4 da @ $1 - $16.75. Rd Way Dept |
| 1857-73 | " " | lab 24 da @ $1.12 - $27.00. repair bridges &c |
| 1857-74 | " " | lab 25 da @ $1.12 - $28.15. repair bridges &c |
| 1857-37 | " W. | lab 25 da @ $30 per mo - $30.00. Wash br rd, Wash city sta |
| 1857-83 | Toblin, Patrick | lab 9½ da @ $1.12 - $10.70. grad, Board Tree Tun |
| 1857-36 | Todd, Amos | lab 5 da @ $1 - $5.00. J. R. Shrode's wd train 4th div |
| 1855-89 | R. T. | fore @ $66.65 per mo -$66.65. Mach Dept |
| 1857-132 | Samuel B. | fore blksmith @ $60 per mo - $60.00. Mach Dept, Grafton |
| 1855-30 | Toft, William | prepar fuel 28 da @ $30 per mo - $30.00. Trans Dept main stem |
| 1857-117 | Toler, William | blksmith 18 da @ $1.72 - $30.95. Mach Dept, Balto |
| 1855-32 | Toles, T. | lab 24 da @ $30 per mo - $30.00. Trans Dept main stem |
| 1855-25 | Tollot, Thomas | bur driv 24 da @ $40 per mo - $40.00. Trans Dept main stem |
| 1857-92 | Toney, Joseph | lab 17 da @ $1.12 - $19.10. grad, Littleton Tun |
| 1855-60 | Toney, Timothy | lab 21 da @ $1 - $21.00. Rd Way Dept |

| | | | |
|---|---|---|---|
| 1855-43 | Tonts, Wm. | lab 22 da @ $1 - $22.00. Rd Way Dept |
| 1855-78 | Tool, Richard | help 21 da @ $1.45 - $30.45. Mach Dept |
| 1855-69 | Tooley, Edward | lab 22 3/4 da @ $1 - $22.75. Rd Way Dept |
| 1857-28 | Toomey, Joseph | ton eng'man 13½ da @ $3 - $39.75. 1st div |
| 1855-21 | Toomy, Henry | fire 5 da @ $1.75 - $8.75. Trans Dept main stem |
| 1855-77 | Tooney, Henry | mach 18 da @ $1.72 - $30.95. Mach Dept |
| 1857-70 | Tooty, James | lab 29 da @ $1 - $29.00. Mt Clare sta, Balto |
| 1857-74 | Topp, Henry | lab 24 da @ $1.12 - $27.00. repair bridges &c |
| 1855-11 | Topper, A. J. | conduc & brak 10¼ da @ $40 per mo - $17.10. Trans Dept main stem |
| 1857-27 | " " | ton brak 27½ da @ $40 per mo - $43.60. 3d & 4th div |
| 1855-65 | " John A. | carp 19 da @ $1.50 - $28.50. Rd Way Dept |
| 1857-110 | Toucey, Henry | mach 17½ da @ $1.72 - $30.10. Mach Dept, Balto |
| 1857-13 | Toup, Luther | haul wd 6⅝ da @ $1 - $6.50. Martinsburg |
| 1857-117 | Townsend, Charles | blksmith 16½ da @ $1.35 - $22.35. Mach Dept, Balto |
| 1855-6 | W. M. | clk 28 da @ $11.65 per mo - $11.65. Trans Dept main stem |
| 1857-7 | " " | clk @ $50 per mo. Gen Tick agt Ofc |
| 1857-116 | Tracey, Daniel | boil mkr help 18 da @ $1 - $18.00. Mach Dept, Balto |
| 1857-112 | W. A. | mach help 18 da @ $1.15 - $20.70. Mach Dept, Balto |
| 1857-66 | Tracy, Bryan | lab 21½ da @ $1 - $21.50. Rd Dept main stem 18th s-div |
| 1857-64 | Hugh | lab 25 da @ $1 - $25.00. Rd Dept main stem 17th s-div |
| 1855-81 | Jarett | carp 20 da @ $1.50 - $30.00. Mach Dept |
| 1855-95 | Pat. | lab 21 3/4 da @ $1 - $21.75. Mach Dept |
| 1857-117 | Samuel | blksmith help 17 da @ $1 - $17.00. Mach Dept, Balto |
| 1855-27 | Trader, Alfred | clean eng 24 da @ $1 - $24.00. Trans Dept main stem |
| 1857-62 | Trainer, Owen | lab 24 3/4 da @ $1 - $24.75. Rd Dept main stem 15th s-div |
| 1857-92 | Travers, Hugh | lab 20⅝ da @ $1.12 - $23.05. grad, Littleton Tun |
| 1855-90 | Isaac | help 28 da @ $1.15 - $32.20. Mach Dept |
| 1855-59 | James | lab 10 3/4 da @ $1 - $10.75. Rd Way Dept |
| 1855-54 | John | lab 24 da @ $1 - $24.00. Rd Way Dept |
| 1855-62 | " | lab 12½ da @ $1 - $12.25. Rd Way Dept |
| 1857-67 | " | lab 22 da @ $1 - $22.00. Rd Dept main stem 19th s-div |
| 1855-50 | Patrick | watch cuts 30 da @ $1 - $30.00. Rd Way Dept |
| 1857-62 | " | lab 25 da @ $1 - $25.00. Rd Dept main stem 15th s-div |
| 1857-68 | " | lab 23 da @ $1 - $23.00. Rd Dept main stem 19th s-div |
| 1857-68 | Thomas | lab 20¼ da @ $1 - $20.25. Rd Dept main stem 19th s-div |
| 1857-133 | Travis, Isaac | lab @ $35 per mo - $35.00. Mach Dept, Fetterman |

| | | |
|---|---|---|
| 1857-91 | Travis, John | lab 23¼ da @ $1 - $23.25. grad, Welling Tun |
| 1855-51 | Travus, Patrick | watch cuts 16 3/4 da @ $1 - $16.75. Rd Way Dept |
| 1857-127 | Treakle, Edwin | mach 19 3/4 da @ $1.40 - $26.95. Mach Dept, Piedmont |
| 1857-110 | Treisor, Thomas | mach 19½ da @ $1.40 - $27.30. Mach Dept, Balto |
| 1855-27 | Trentor, Joseph | get out eng 15½ da @ $1.15 - $17.80. Trans Dept main stem |
| 1857-85 | Trien, Charles | blksmith 26 da @ $1.50 - $39.00. grad, Board Tree Tun |
| 1857-69 | Triford, Joseph | carp 18½ da @ $1.50 - $27.75. Mt Clare sta, Balto |
| 1855-46 | Trimble, Thomas | lab 21 da @ $1 - $21.00. Rd Way Dept |
| 1857-127 | Trinton, Joseph | mach help 26 da @ $1.15 - $29.90. Mach Dept, Piedmont |
| 1855-71 | Trogler, F. | help 24 da @ $1.15 - $27.60. Rd Way Dept |
| 1857-70 | " Frederick | help 14¼ da @ $1.15 - $16.40. Mt Clare sta, Balto |
| 1857-110 | Troll, Richard | mach 22¾ da @ $1.55 - $34.50. Mach Dept, Balto |
| 1857-95 | Trothingham, A. | fore 22 da @ $1.25 - $27.50. Wash br, Rd Dept |
| 1857-97 | Trough, Jacob | fore 11 da @ $1.25 - $13.75. NW Va RR, Rd Dept 2d s-div |
| 1855-72 | Trought, John | mach 10 da @ $1.73 - $17.30. Rd Way Dept |
| 1857-69 | " | mach 30 3/4 da @ $1.73 - $53.20. Mt Clare sta, Balto |
| 1857-110 | Trout, R. P. | mach 19½ da @ $1.35 - $26.30. Mach Dept, Balto |
| 1855-89 | Troutman, E. | blksmith 22 da @ $1.40 - $30.80. Mach Dept |
| 1857-54 | Troxall, George | lab 22 da @ $1 - $22.00. Rd Dept main stem 8th s-div |
| 1857-25 | Troxell, David | ton brak 2 da @ $40 per mo - $3.20. 2d div |
| 1857-76 | Troy, Lawrence | dril 22¾ da @ $1.10 - $21.45. ballast train for 2d track |
| 1855-77 | Trumbo, William | mach 10 3/4 da @ $1.50 - $16.10. Mach Dept |
| 1857-50 | Tryatt, Bath | fore 25 da @ $1.25 - $31.25. Rd Dept main stem 5th s-div |
| 1857-51 | " John | lab 25 da @ $1 - $25.00. Rd Dept main stem 5th s-div |
| 1855-36 | Tucker, Anthony | lab 24¼ da @ $25 per mo - $25.25. Trans Dept main stem |
| 1857-24 | " Frank | ton brak 16¼ da @ $40 per mo - $26.00. 1st div |
| 1857-122 | " Hanson | lab 17 3/4 da @ $1 - $17.75. Mach Dept, Balto |
| 1857-101 | " James | lab 17 3/4 da @ $1 - $17.75. NW Va RR ballast train |
| 1855-79 | " John | blksmith 25 da @ $1.50 - $37.50. Mach Dept |
| 1857-117 | " Michael | lab 25 3/4 da @ $1 - $25.75. NW Va RR, Rd Dept 5th s-div |
| 1855-74 | Tuel, Peter | lab 21 da @ $1 - $21.00. Rd Way Dept |
| 1857-95 | " | lab 23 da @ $1 - $23.00. Wash br, Rd Dept |
| 1857-130 | Tull, Owensy | clean eng 30 da @ $1 - $30.00. Mach Dept, Newburg |
| 1857-23 | Tunley, James | ton conduc 25 da @ $50 per mo - $50.00. 3d & 4th div |
| 1857-40 | Tunly, J. | ton conduc 2 da @ $50 per mo - $4.00. NW Va rd, Parkersburg sta |

324   B & O RR EMPLOYEES

| | | |
|---|---|---|
| 1857-83 | Tunnence, Michael | lab 17½ da @ $1.12 - $19.70. grad, Board Tree Tun |
| 1857-64 | Turbee, John | lab 21¼ da @ $1 - $21.25. Rd Dept main stem 17th s-div |
| 1857-21 | Turfield, P. T. | ton conduc 18 3/4 da @ $50 per mo - $37.50. 1st div |
| 1857-133 | Turner, Francis | mach 33¾ da @ $1.70 - $56.50. Mach Dept, Cameron |
| 1855-94 | George | app 21¼ da @ $.75 - $15.95. Mach Dept |
| 1857-122 | " | eng clean 28 3/4 da @ $1.15 - $33.05. Mach Dept, Balto |
| 1857-134 | " | mach @ $55 per mo - $55.00. Mach Dept, Wheeling |
| 1855-25 | James | clean eng 23 da @ $1.15 - $26.45. Trans Dept main stem |
| 1857-20 | John | pass fire 8 da @ $40 per mo - $10.65. 1st div |
| 1855-88 | " | help 24 da @ $1 - $24.00. Mach Dept |
| 1855-44 | " | lab 12 da @ $1 - $12.00. Rd Way Dept |
| 1855-68 | " | tend to masons 8¼ da @ $1 - $8.25. Rd Way Dept |
| 1857-92 | " | lab 21 da @ $1 - $21.00. grad, Littleton Tun |
| 1857-52 | " | lab 22 da @ $1 - $22.00. Rd Dept main stem 6th s-div |
| 1857-54 | " | lab 24 da @ $1 - $24.00. Rd Dept main stem 8th s-div |
| 1857-125 | John D. | wheel 17 3/4 da @ $1.25 - $22.20. Mach Dept, Martinsburg |
| 1855-42 | Joseph | lab 19½ da @ $1 - $19.50. Rd Way Dept |
| 1857-52 | " | fore 25 da @ $1.25 - $31.25. Rd Dept main stem 6th s-div |
| 1855-37 | M. | lab 25 da @ $1 - $25.00. Rd Way Dept |
| 1855-56 | Mart. | blksmith 21½ da @ $1.50 - $32.25. Rd Way Dept |
| 1855-71 | Richard | carp 23½ da @ $1.60 - $37.60. Rd Way Dept |
| 1855-73 | Thos. | carp 18 da @ $1.73 - $31.15. Mt Clare sta, Balto |
| 1857-132 | William | blksmith help 21 da @ $1.04 - $27.75. Rd Way Dept |
| 1857-11 | " | lab 23½ da @ $30 per mo - $21.85. Mach Dept, Grafton |
| 1857-69 | " | lab 17¼ da @ $1 - $28.20. Locust Pt |
| 1855-72 | Turney, Dennis | help 22 da @ $1 - $17.25. Mt Clare sta, Balto |
| 1857-71 | Jas. | cart driv 24 da @ $.54 - $12.95. Mt Clare, repair tracks in yd |
| 1855-67 | John | mason 22 3/4 da @ $2 - $45.50. Rd Way Dept |
| 1857-71 | Michael | lab 18 da @ $1 - $18.00. Mt Clare, repair tracks in yd |
| 1857-71 | Thos. | lab 18 da @ $1 - $18.00. Mt Clare, repair tracks in yd |
| 1857-55 | Twigg, John | lab 24 da @ $1 - $24.00. Rd Way Dept |
| 1857-120 | Tyler, Daniel | carp 30 da @ $1.50 - $45.00. Rd Dept main stem 9th s-div |
| 1857-115 | John | boil mkr 17½ da @ $1.50 - $26.25. Mach Dept, Balto |
| 1857-11 | Joseph | clk 25 da @ $30 per mo - $30.00. Locust Pt |
| 1855-67 | Tyrner, Patrick | lab 24 da @ $1 - $24.00. Rd Way Dept |

| ID | Name | Description |
|---|---|---|
| 1855-33 | Tyser, H. | watch 28 da @ $35 per mo - $35.00. Trans Dept main stem |
| 1857-18 | Henry | pass train conduc 30 da @ $41.65 per mo - $41.65. St car |
| 1857-9 | " | St car conduc 25 da - $41.65. hp exp, Balto |
| 1857-107 | Tyson, Henry | mast of mach, Ofc Camden sta, Balto @ $166.66 per mo. Mach Dept |
| 1857-110 | Uhorn, Frederick | mach 20¾ da @ $1.72 - $34.85. Mach Dept, Balto |
| 1855-45 | Ullman, John | fore 19 da @ $1.25 - $23.75. Rd Way Dept |
| 1857-65 | Ullom, H. | lab 15 da @ $1 - $15.00. Rd Dept main stem 17th s-div |
| 1855-52 | " Stephen | lab 28 da @ $1 - $28.00. Rd Way Dept |
| 1857-92 | Ulmes, Stephen | lab 20½ da @ $1.12 - $23.05. grad, Littleton Tun |
| 1857-120 | Ultyes, John | carp 18 da @ $1.50 - $27.00. Mach Dept, Balto |
| 1855-40 | Umberger, M. | lab 19 3/4 da @ $1 - $19.75. Rd Way Dept |
| 1855-71 | Umphreys, Edw. | smith 23½ da @ $1.40 - $32.90. Rd Way Dept |
| 1857-70 | Underwood, Alfred | blksmith 18 da @ $1.45 - $26.10. Mt Clare sta, Balto |
| 1857-21 | Unkles, Benjamin | ton conduc 18¾ da @ $50 per mo - $39.00. 1st div |
| 1855-71 | " | supt w sta @ $70 per mo - $70.00. Rd Way Dept |
| 1857-69 | " Benjamin Jr | supt w sta @ $75 per mo - $75.00. Mt Clare sta, Balto |
| 1855-71 | " | carp 22½ da @ $.50 - $11.10. Rd Way Dept |
| 1855-12 | Valiant, William | app 21 3/4 da @ $.60 - $13.05. Mt Clare sta, Balto |
| 1857-122 | Vance, Alfred | conduc & brak ½ da @ $40 per mo - $.85. Trans Dept main stem |
| 1855-88 | Van Cleve, N. | eng clean 23¼ da @ $.75 - $17.45. Mach Dept, Balto |
| 1857-109 | Vandiner, J. T. | carp 8 3/4 da @$1.40 - $12.25. Mach Dept |
| 1855-88 | Van Meter, A. | mach 20 da @$1.72 - $34.40. Mach Dept, Balto |
| 1857-24 | Vansant, William | help 25¼ da @ $1 - $25.25. Mach Dept |
| 1855-66 | Vanvactor, Daniel | ton brak 1¾ da @ $40 per mo - $6.80. 1st div |
| 1855-51 | Vanverth, Henry | repair cars &c 22 3/4 da @ $1.62½ - $36.95. Rd Way Dept |
| 1857-103 | Varley, Patrick | lab @ $30 per mo - $30.00. Rd Way Dept |
| 1855-25 | Vaughan, Patrick | lab 20 da @ $1 - $20.00. NW Va RR depot |
| 1857-122 | Vaughen, Patrick | clean eng 26¼ da @ $1.15 - $30.45. Trans Dept main stem |
| 1855-25 | Vee, Henry | eng clean 20 3/4 da @ $1.15 - $23.85. Mach Dept, Balto |
| 1855-73 | Vermilion, Nicholis | bur driv 24 da @ $40 per mo - $40.00. Trans Dept main stem |
| 1857-95 | " | fore 24 da @ $1.25 - $30.00. Rd Way Dept |
| 1857-36 | Vernetson, W. | fore 24 da @ $1.25 - $30.00. Wash br, Rd Dept |
| 1855-11 | Vernum, H. H. | tele oper 30 da @$30 per mo - $30.00. Monocacy |
| 1855-8 | " W. H. | conduc & brak 5¾ da - $9.05. Trans Dept main stem |
| 1857-130 | Vickroy, William T. | brak 3 da @ $33.35 per mo - $3.55. Trans Dept main stem |
| | | lab 15½ da @ $1.15 - $17.80. Mach Dept, Piedmont |

326	B & O RR EMPLOYEES

| | | | |
|---|---|---|---|
| 1857-61 | Viquesney, Augustus | pump water 30 da @ $1 - $30.00. Rd Dept main stem 14th s-div |
| 1857-38 | Virtue, Adam | ton fire 24 da @ $13.33 per mo - $32.00. Wash br rd, Wash city sta |
| 1857-29 | " David | ton eng'man 15¾ da @ $3 - $45.75. 1st div |
| 1857-38 | " " | ton eng'man 3 da @ $2.50 - $7.50. Wash br rd, Wash city sta |
| 1857-32 | " John J. | ton fire 19½ da @ $1.75 - $33.70. 1st div |
| 1857-120 | Voglesaing, Edward | carp 18½ da @ $1.50 - $27.75. Mach Dept, Balto |
| 1857-137 | Vogtman, Francis | carp @ $42 per mo - $42.00. Mach Dept, Cumb |
| 1855-84 | Voight, John | help 25½ da @ $1.15 - $29.30. Mach Dept |
| 1857-115 | " " | boil mkr 32¾ da @ $1.25 - $40.30. Mach Dept, Balto |
| 1855-90 | Voightman, F. | carp @ $42 per mo - $42.00. Mach Dept |
| 1855-11 | Volandt, William | conduc & brak 15 da @ $40 per mo - $25.05. Trans Dept main stem |
| 1855-78 | Volk, Charles | help 25 da @ $1.15 - $28.75. Mach Dept |
| 1857-111 | " " | mach help 21½ da @ $1.15 - $24.70. Mach Dept, Balto |
| 1855-73 | Volkman, David | tin 20 da @ $1.73 - $34.60. Rd Way Dept |
| 1857-69 | " " | tin 25 da @ $1.73 - $43.25. Mt Clare sta, Balto |
| 1855-73 | " Henry | tin 18 3/4 da @$1.73 - $32.45. Rd Way Dept |
| 1857-69 | " " | tin 14 da @ $1.73 - $24.20. Mt Clare sta, Balto |
| 1855-73 | " William | tin 22 da @ $1.73 - $38.05. Rd Way Dept |
| 1857-69 | " " | fore 14 da @ $1.73 - $24.20. Mt Clare sta, Balto |
| 1855-88 | Vollers, George | help 23 3/7 da @ $1 - $23.75. Mach Dept |
| 1857-36 | Voltz, Daniel | tele oper 30 da @$30 per mo - $30.00. Plane # 4 |
| 1855-33 | Vrooman, W. | clk 28 da @ $40 per mo - $40.00. Trans Dept main stem |
| 1857-39 | " " | clk 30 da @ $62 per mo - $62.00. NW Va rd, Parkersburg sta |
| 1857-25 | Wachter, Luther | ton brak 30½ da @ $40 per mo - $48.80. 2d div |
| 1857-134 | Waddle, William | storekpr @ $35 per mo - $35.00. Mach Dept, Wheeling |
| 1857-82 | Wagner, Frederick | brickley 12¾ da @ $2 - $24.50. grad, Board Tree Tun |
| 1855-81 | " John | lab 24 da @ $1.15 - $27.60. Mach Dept |
| 1855-39 | " " | nail 28 da @ $1.05 - $29.40. Rd Way Dept |
| 1857-49 | " " | nail 30 da @ $1.05 - $31.50. Rd Dept main stem 3d s-div |
| 1855-86 | " Joseph | help 24 da @ $1.10 - $26.40. Mach Dept |
| 1857-118 | " " | blksmith help 19 3/4 da @ $1.10 - $21.75. Mach Dept, Balto |
| 1857-82 | " " | brickley 20¼ da @ $2 - $40.50. grad, Board Tree Tun |
| 1855-38 | Wahan, John | lab 24 da @ $1 - $24.00. Rd Way Dept |
| 1855-37 | " Thomas | lab 22 da @ $1 - $22.00. Rd Way Dept |
| 1857-46 | " " | lab 16 da @ $1 - $16.00. Rd Dept main stem 1st s-div |
| 1857-27 | Wakeman, Gilbert L. | ton brak 4 da @ $1 - $6.40. 3d & 4th div |
| 1857-66 | Walch, A. | lab 22 da @ $1 - $22.00. Rd Dept main stem 18th s-div |

| | | |
|---|---|---|
| 1857-67 | Walch, Nicholas | lab 8 da @ $1 - $8.00. Rd Dept main stem 18th s-div |
| 1857-66 | William | fore 23 3/4 da @ $1.25 - $29.70. Rd Dept main stem 18th s-div |
| 1857-82 | Waldren, Patrick | lab 20 da @ $1.12 - $22.50. grad, Board Tree Tun |
| 1855-83 | Wales, John | lab 23 3/4 da @ $1 - $23.75. Mach Dept |
| 1855-96 | Waley, Ambrose | app 24 da @ $.45 - $10.80. Mach Dept |
| 1857-114 | " | iron mould app 21 da @ $.75 - $15.75. Mach Dept, Balto |
| 1855-15 | Walford, A. | brak 3½ da @ $40 per mo -$5.85. Trans Dept main stem |
| 1855-20 | Walker, David | ton eng'man 19 da @ $2.50 - $47.50. Trans Dept main stem |
| 1857-29 | " | ton eng'man 25 da @ $2.50 - $62.50. 2d div |
| 1855-38 | John | lab 24 da @ $1 - $24.00. Rd Way Dept |
| 1857-131 | Joseph | mach 9 3/4 da @ $1.70 - $16.55. Mach Dept, Grafton |
| 1857-89 | K. D. | tele oper @ $30 per mo - $30.00. grad, Welling Tun |
| 1855-78 | Peter | help 11 3/4 da @ $1 - $11.75. Mach Dept |
| 1857-111 | " | mach help 17¼ da @ $1 - $17.25. Mach Dept, Balto |
| 1855-35 | Wall, John F. | asst disp of trains 28 da @ $45 per mo - $45.00. Trans Dept main stem |
| 1857-14 | " " | disp 30 da @ $60 per mo - $60.00. Piedmont sta |
| 1855-96 | Joseph | lab 24 da @ $1.15 - $27.60. Mach Dept |
| 1857-114 | " | iron mould 23 da @ $1.25 - $28.75. Mach Dept, Balto |
| 1857-92 | Wallace, James | lab 24 3/4 da @ $1 - $24.75. grad, Littleton Tun |
| 1855-94 | Jarrett | carp 19 da @ $1.45 - $27.55. Mach Dept |
| 1855-90 | N. | app 26 da @ $.55 - $14.30. Mach Dept |
| 1857-130 | Thomas | lab 19¼ da @ $1 - $19.25. Mach Dept, Piedmont |
| 1857-113 | William | mach app 19 3/4 da @ $.55 - $10.85. Mach Dept, Balto |
| 1857-9 | " | watch 30 da @ $1.25 - $37.50. Mt Clare sta |
| 1857-98 | " | watch 29½ da @ $1 - $29.50. NW Va RR, Rd Dept 3d s-div |
| 1855-21 | Wallett, Henry | fire 16½ da @ $1.75 - $28.85. Trans Dept main stem |
| 1855-21 | John | fire 10½ da @ $1.75 - $18.35. Trans Dept main stem |
| 1857-21 | Walling, George | ton conduc 27¼ da @$50 per mo - $54.50. 1st div |
| 1857-21 | H. J. | ton conduc 25 da @ $50 per mo - $50.00. 1st div |
| 1855-11 | Henry | conduc & brak 19 da @$50 per mo - $39.60. Trans Dept main stem |
| 1857-21 | Joseph | ton conduc 19 3/4 da @ $50 per mo - $39.50. 1st div |
| 1857-101 | Walls, John | lab 22 da @ $1 - $22.00. NW Va RR ballast train |
| 1857-128 | Walraven, Wm. E. | boil mkr 19¾ da @ $1.60 - $30.80. Mach Dept, Piedmont |
| 1855-18 | Walrington, Wm. | ton eng'man 10½ da @ $2.50 - $26.25. Trans Dept main stem |
| 1857-96 | Walsh, Coleman | lab 17½ da @ $1 - $17.50. NW Va RR, Rd Dept 1st s-div |
| 1857-79 | Edward | lab 7 da @ $1 -$7.00. lay 2d track |

328                            B & O RR EMPLOYEES.

| | | | |
|---|---|---|---|
| 1857-96 | Walsh, John | fore 25 da @ $1.25 - $31.25. NW Va RR, Rd Dept 1st s-div |
| 1857-80 | " | lab 20½ da @ $1 - $20.50. lay 2d track |
| 1857-79 | Michael | lab 24¼ da @ $1 - $24.25. lay 2d track |
| 1855-66 | Patrick | lab 25½ da @ $1 - $25.50. Rd Way Dept |
| 1857-96 | Patrick 1st | lab 18 3/4 da @ $1 - $18.75. NW Va RR, Rd Dept 1st s-div |
| 1857-94 | Patrick 2d | lab 7¼ da @ $1 - $7.25. quarry & haul stone for Board Tree & Littleton Tun |
| 1857-94 | Peter | lab 4½ da @ $1 - $4.50. quarry & haul stone for Board Tree & Littleton Tun |
| 1857-77 | Richard | lab 18½ da @ $1 - $18.50. lay 2d track |
| 1857-80 | Wm. | lab 6¼ da @ $1 - $6.25. lay 2d track |
| 1855-4 | Walstrom, S. S. | lab 20 3/4 da @ $1.25 - $25.95. lay 2d track |
| 1855-11 | Waltemeyer, C. | brak 28 da @ $33.35 per mo - $33.35. Trans Dept, Wash br |
| 1857-12 | Waltemyer, Chas. | conduc & brak 15½ da @$50 per mo - $32.30. Trans Dept main stem |
| 1857-134 | Joseph | swit tend 30 da @$35 per mo - $35.00. swit abv Ellicotts Mills |
| 1855-81 | Walter, E. J. | mach app 19 da @ $.45 - $8.55. Mach Dept, Wheeling |
| 1857-133 | J. A. H. | coach mkr 23 da @ $1.65 - $37.95. Mach Dept |
| 1855-77 | James | carp 7 da @ $1.60 - $11.20. Mach Dept, Cameron |
| 1857-33 | PPhilip | quarry 7 da @ $1 - $7.00. ballast train for 2d track |
| 1855-8 | Walters, J. H. | ton fire 26 3/4 da @ $1.75 - $46.80. 3d div |
| 1857-18 | James H. | bag mast 28 da @ $45 per mo - $45.00. Trans Dept main stem |
| 1857-123 | John | pass train conduc 30 da @ $62.50 per mo - $62.50. thr mail & exp |
| 1857-83 | Patrick | mach 17 3/4 da @ $1.60 - $28.40. Mach Dept, Martinsburg |
| 1857-14 | Waltz, M. | lab 31¼ da @ $1.12 - $35.15. grad, Board Tree Tun |
| 1855-20 | Wane, Henry | lab 25 da @ $30 per mo - $30.00. Cumb |
| 1857-12 | Ward, Asa | ton eng'man 11 da @ $2.50 - $27.50. Trans Dept main stem |
| 1857-136 | Holmes | swit tend 30 da @ $35 per mo - $35.00. Plane # 1 |
| 1857-61 | J. E. | mach 18 3/4 da @ $1.60 - $30.00. Mach Dept, Cumb |
| 1855-58 | James | fire 5 da @ $1.75 - $8.75. Rd Dept main stem 14th s-div |
| 1855-45 | " | fore 24 da @ $1.25 - $30.00. Rd Way Dept |
| 1857-59 | " | lab 12 da @ $1 - $12.00. Rd Way Dept |
| 1857-33 | James E. | fore 26 da @ $1.25 - $32.50. Rd Dept main stem 13th s-div |
| 1855-81 | John | ton fire 28½ da @ $1.75 - $49.85. 3d div |
| 1855-45 | " | carp 26 da @ $1.65 - $42.90. Mach Dept |
| 1855-64 | " | lab 17½ da @ $1 - $17.50. Rd Way Dept |
| 1855-70 | " | lab 20 da @ $1 - $20.00. Rd Way Dept |
| 1855-39 | " | nail 28 da @ $1.05 - $29.40. Rd Way Dept |

| | | |
|---|---|---|
| 1857-120 | Ward, John | carp 18 3/4 da @ $1.65 - $30.95. Mach Dept, Balto |
| 1857-85 | " | lab 5½ da @ $1.12 - $6.20. grad, Board Tree Tun |
| 1857-87 | " | lab 18 3/4 da @ $1.12 - $21.10. grad, Welling Tun |
| 1857-55 | " | lab 18 3/4 da @ $1 - $18.75. Rd Dept main stem 9th s-div |
| 1857-49 | " | nail 30 da @ $1.05 - $31.50. Rd Dept main stem 3d s-div |
| 1855-64 | Michael | lab 21½ da @ $1 - $21.50. Rd Way Dept |
| 1857-93 | " | lab 25¼ da @ $1 - $25.25. quarry & haul stone for Board Tree & Littleton Tun |
| 1855-67 | Peter | tend to masons 21 3/4 da @ $1 - $21.75. Rd Way Dept |
| 1857-65 | " | watch 30 da @ $1 - $30.00. Rd Dept main stem 17th s-div |
| 1855-31 | Richard | saw wd 120 cords @ $.35 - $42.00. Trans Dept main stem |
| 1857-32 | " | ton fire 13½ da @ $1.75 - $23.60. 1st div |
| 1855-15 | T. E. | brak 13¼ da @ $40 per mo - $22.10. Trans Dept main stem |
| 1855-64 | Thomas | lab 21½ da @ $1 - $21.50. Rd Way Dept |
| 1855-68 | " | tend to masons 22½ da @ $1 - $22.50. Rd Way Dept |
| 1857-102 | " | paint 11 3/4 da @ $1.75 - $20.55. NW Va RR, rwy depot |
| 1857-85 | " | watch 29 da @ $1 - $29.00. grad, Board Tree Tun |
| 1857-70 | Wardell, Samuel | help 18½ da @ $1.12 - $20.80. Mt Clare sta, Balto |
| 1857-70 | Ware, Geo. W. | lab 19½ da @ $1 - $19.50. Mt Clare sta, Balto |
| 1857-29 | Henry | ton eng'man 27 da @ $2.50 - $67.50. 1st div |
| 1855-78 | James | help 23¼ da @ $1 - $23.25. Mach Dept |
| 1857-113 | " | mach app 24 da @ $.55 - $13.20. Mach Dept, Balto |
| 1857-111 | " | mach help 33½ da @ $1 - $33.50. Mach Dept, Balto |
| 1857-111 | Joseph | mach help 28½ da @ $1 - $28.50. Mach Dept, Balto |
| 1857-27 | Robert | ton brak 24½ da @ $40 per mo - $39.20. 3d & 4th div |
| 1855-81 | Thomas | carp 23 3/4 da @ $1.65 - $39.20. Mach Dept |
| 1857-120 | " | carp 23 3/4 da @ $1.65 - $39.20. Mach Dept, Balto |
| 1857-110 | Wm. H. | mach 25 3/4 da @ $1.65 - $42.50. Mach Dept, Balto |
| 1857-73 | Wareham, David | carp 25 da @ $1.65 - $41.25. repair water sta, M.S. & P.B. |
| 1855-94 | R. | app 28½ da @ $.60 - $17.10. Mach Dept |
| 1857-73 | Richard | mach 24 da @ $1.65 - $39.60. repair water sta, M.S. & P.B. |
| 1855-52 | Warfield, William | fore @ $50 per mo - $50.00. Rd Way Dept |
| 1855-12 | Warner, Charles | conduc & brak 15¼ da @ $40 per mo - $25.10. Trans Dept main stem |
| 1857-127 | Warren, Joseph | mach 16 da @ $1.60 - $25.60. Mach Dept, Piedmont |
| 1855-92 | W. C. | help 26¼ da @ $1 - $26.25. Mach Dept |
| 1857-86 | Warrick, John | bricklay 19½ da @ $2.25 - $43.85. grad, McGuire's Tun |
| 1857-21 | Warthan, B. H. | ton conduc 18½ da @ $50 per mo - $37.00. 1st div |

| | | |
|---|---|---|
| 1857-76 | Warthen, A. G. | dril 17 da @$1.10 - $18.70. ballast train for 2d track |
| 1855-15 | Washburn, L. | pass eng'man 29¼ da @ $3 - $87.75. Trans Dept main stem |
| 1857-19 | Libeus | pass eng'man 38 da @ $2.50 - $95.00. 3d div |
| 1857-131 | Washington, George | boil mkr 18¼ da @ $1.40 - $25.55. Mach Dept, Grafton |
| 1855-48 | Waters, Adw. | dril 18½ da @ $1.10 - $20.35. Rd Way Dept |
| 1857-113 | Amos | mach app 22 da @ $.45 - $9.90. Mach Dept, Balto |
| 1855-81 | E. D. | carp 17 da @ $1.50 - $25.50. Mach Dept |
| 1857-132 | E. J. | fore carp @ $50 per mo - $50.00. Mach Dept, Grafton |
| 1855-95 | George | mould 26¼ da @ $1.72 - $45.15. Mach Dept |
| 1855-8 | J. B. | St conduc 28 da @ $41.65 per mo - $41.65. Trans Dept main stem |
| 1857-97 | John | fore 26 da @ $1.25 - $32.50. NW Va RR, Rd Dept 2d s-div |
| 1855-64 | Pat. | watch 28 da @ $1 - $28.00. Rd Way Dept |
| 1857-10 | Peter | bur brak 15½ da @ $1.15 - $17.80. hp exp, Balto |
| 1857-47 | Stephen | lab 3 da @ $1 - $3.00. Rd Dept main stem 2d s-div |
| 1855-34 | Wath, Michael | lab 24 da @ $30 per mo - $30.00. Trans Dept main stem |
| 1855-95 | Watkins, James | mould 24 da @ $1.72 - $41.30. Mach Dept |
| 1855-25 | John | clean eng 26½ da @ $1.15 - $30.45. Trans Dept main stem |
| 1857-114 | William | iron mould 17 3/4 da @ $1.72 - $30.55. Mach Dept, Balto |
| 1857-118 | Watson, Watt | blksmith help 18 da @ $1.10 - $19.80. Mach Dept, Balto |
| 1857-95 | Watts, Nathaniel | lab 22 da @ $1 - $22.00. Wash br, Rd Dept |
| 1855-12 | Thomas | conduc & brak 11 3/4 da @ $40 per mo - $20.60. Trans Dept main stem |
| 1855-26 | Wattsbaker, John | clean eng 22¼ da @ $1 - $22.25. Trans Dept main stem |
| 1857-137 | " | eng clean 5¼ da @ $1 - $5.25. Mach Dept, Cumb |
| 1855-63 | Wattson, H. | blksmith 21 da @ $1.50 - $31.50. Rd Way Dept |
| 1857-56 | Waxler, John | lab 11 da @ $1 - $11.00. Rd Dept main stem 10th s-div |
| 1857-99 | Waxnery, Charles | lab 24½ da @ $1 - $24.50. N W Va RR, Rd Dept 4th s-div |
| 1855-32 | Ways, B. F. | tele oper 28 da @ $30 per mo - $30.00. Trans Dept main stem |
| 1857-36 | C. E. | tele oper 30 da @ $40 per mo - $40.00. Martinsburg |
| 1855-32 | Charles | tele oper 28 da @ $30 per mo - $30.00. Trans Dept main stem |
| 1855-20 | Jno. T. | ton eng'man 13 da @ $3 - $40.50. Trans Dept main stem |
| 1857-115 | Weaks, Samuel | pat mkr 17½ da @ $1.60 - $28.00. Mach Dept, Balto |
| 1857-56 | Wealsh, Thomas | lab 25 da @ $1 - $25.00. Rd Dept main stem 10th s-div |
| 1855-89 | Weaming, F. | app 23¼ da @ $.60 - $13.95. Mach Dept |
| 1857-123 | Weaning, Frank | mach 17 3/4 da @ $1.50 - $27.60. Mach Dept, Martinsburg |
| 1855-87 | J. A. | mach 4 da @ $1.60 - $6.40. Mach Dept |
| 1855-87 | J. O. | mach 21½ da @ $1.35 - $29.00. Mach Dept |
| 1857-123 | John A. | mach 17¼ da @ $1.60 - $27.60. Mach Dept, Martinsburg |

| | | | |
|---|---|---|---|
| 1857-123 | Weaning, Oliver | mach 16 3/4 da @ $1.50 - $25.10. Mach Dept, Martinsburg |
| 1855-83 | Weary, William | app 23 3/4 da @ $.75 - $17.80. Mach Dept |
| 1855-21 | Weaver, D. J. | fire 16¼ da @ $1.75 - $28.45. Trans Dept main stem |
| 1857-33 | " David J. | ton fire 27 da @ $1.75 - $47.25. 2d div |
| 1855-93 | " George | asst fore @ $60 per mo - $60.00. Mach Dept |
| 1855-74 | " Henry | lab 22 da @ $1 - $22.00. Rd Way Dept |
| 1855-77 | " J. J. | mach 22½ da @ $1.60 - $36.00. Mach Dept |
| 1855-85 | " John | blksmith 24 da @ $1.55 - $37.20. Mach Dept |
| 1855-21 | " " | fire 16½ da @ $33.35 per mo - $23.20. Trans Dept main stem |
| 1855-74 | " " | lab 9 da @ $1 - $9.00. Rd Way Dept |
| 1857-116 | " Robert | blksmith 17 3/4 da @ $1.55 - $27.50. Mach Dept, Balto |
| 1857-110 | " Thomas | mach 18¾ da @ $1.60 - $29.20. Mach Dept, Balto |
| 1857-32 | Webb, George | ton fire 17 da @ $1.75 - $29.75. 1st div |
| 1855-94 | " Jefferson | blksmith 22 3/4 da @ $1.80 - $40.95. Mach Dept |
| 1857-117 | " Jno. | blksmith 16¼ da @ $1.60 - $26.00. Mach Dept, Balto |
| 1857-109 | " Thomas | mach 17 3/4 da @ $1.50 - $26.60. Mach Dept, Balto |
| 1855-93 | Webbert, George | help 4 3/4 da @ $1 - $4.75. Mach Dept |
| 1855-20 | Webster, G. T. | ton eng'man 10 da @ $2.50 - $25.00. Trans Dept main stem |
| 1855-39 | " J. | lab 19½ da @ $1 - $19.50. Rd Way Dept |
| 1855-91 | " Richard | blksmith 22 da @ $1.30 - $28.60. Mach Dept |
| 1855-28 | " " | reg eng 27 da @ $1.75 - $47.25. Trans Dept main stem |
| 1855-88 | Weddle, Daniel | help 26½ da @ $1 - $26.50. Mach Dept |
| 1855-87 | Weeb, Thomas | blksmith 25 da @ $1.60 - $40.00. Mach Dept |
| 1857-124 | Weedman, George | blksmith 19½ da @ $1.65 - $32.15. Mach Dept, Martinsburg |
| 1855-88 | Weeks, Albert | help 23¾ da @ $1 - $23.25. Mach Dept |
| 1857-49 | Weible, John | lab 24 da @ $1 - $24.00. Rd Dept main stem 3d s-div |
| 1857-91 | Weigman, John | lab 16 da @ $1 - $16.00. grad, Welling Tun |
| 1857-112 | Weimer, G. | mach help 18 da @ $1.15 - $20.70. Mach Dept, Balto |
| 1857-14 | Weir, Jacob | watch 30 da @ $1.15 - $34.50. Cumb |
| 1857-55 | Weisermiller, Jacob | lab 24½ da @ $1 - $24.50. Rd Dept main stem 9th s-div |
| 1855-15 | " John | brak 21½ da @ $40 per mo - $35.85. Trans Dept main stem |
| 1857-33 | Weisgenber, Edward | ton fire 20½ da @ $1.75 - $35.85. 2d div |
| 1857-55 | Weishenny, C. | lab 23¼ da @ $1 - $23.25. Rd Dept main stem 9th s-div |
| 1857-55 | | lab 22½ da @ $1 - $22.50. Rd Dept main stem 9th s-div |
| 1857-134 | | mach app 33 da @ $.55 - $18.15. Mach Dept, Wheeling |
| 1855-45 | | lab 18 3/4 da @ $1 - $18.75. Rd Way Dept |

# B & O RR EMPLOYEES

| ID | Name | Record |
|---|---|---|
| 1857-116 | Welbert, George | blksmith 18 da @ $1.60 - $28.80. Mach Dept, Balto |
| 1855-59 | Welch, Edward | fore 12 da @ $1.12½ - $13.50. Rd Way Dept |
| 1855-57 | " | lab 20 3/4 da @ $1 - $20.75. Rd Way Dept |
| 1855-43 | James | lab 19½ da @ $1 - $19.50. Rd Way Dept |
| 1855-75 | " | lab 15 da @ $1 - $15.00. Rd Way Dept |
| 1857-83 | " | lab 6 da @ $1.12 - $6.75. grad, Board Tree Tun |
| 1857-51 | " | watch 30 da @ $1 - $30.00. Rd Dept main stem 5th s-div |
| 1857-35 | John | eng'man 18 da @ $2.50 - $45.00. Edwards' wd train 3d & 4th div |
| 1857-82 | " | lab 9 da @ $1.12 - $10.10. grad, Board Tree Tun |
| 1855-63 | M. | lab 18 da @ $1 - $18.00. Rd Way Dept |
| 1855-57 | Mike | lab 27½ da @ $1 - $27.50. Rd Dept main stem 11th s-div |
| 1855-42 | Pat. | lab 19 da @ $1 - $19.00. Rd Way Dept |
| 1855-55 | Peter | lab 7 da @ $1 - $7.00. Rd Way Dept |
| 1857-76 | Thomas | dril 22½ da @ $1.10 - $24.75. ballast train for 2d track |
| 1857-82 | " | lab 26½ da @ $1.12 - $29.80. grad, Board Tree Tun |
| 1857-99 | " | lab 28 da @ $1 - $28.00. NW Va RR, Rd Dept 4th s-div |
| 1857-59 | " | lab 26 da @ $1 - $26.00. Rd Dept main stem 13th s-div |
| 1857-49 | Welcome, Casper | lab 25 da @ $1 - $25.00. Rd Dept main stem 3d s-div |
| 1857-49 | John | fore 25 da @ $1.25 - $31.25. Rd Dept main stem 3d s-div |
| 1857-53 | Weldon, Andrew | lab 22½ da @ $1 - $22.50. Rd Dept main stem 7th s-div |
| 1357-29 | Weller, Joseph | ton eng'man 15½ da @ $3 - $46.50. 2d div |
| 1355-21 | Josiah | fire 16 da @ $1.75 - $28.00. Trans Dept main stem |
| 1857-39 | Welles, George A. | clk 30 da @ $58.35 per mo - $58.35. NW Va rd, Parkersburg sta |
| 1855-29 | Wellington, A. | haul & saw firewd 24 da @ $33.35 per mo - $33.35. Trans Dept main stem |
| 1857-14 | " | lab 25 da @ $33.35 per mo - $33.35. Cumb |
| 1855-25 | Wells, Chas. | clean eng 23 3/4 da @ $1.15 - $27.30. Trans Dept main stem |
| 1857-40 | F. M. | ton brak 19 da @ $40 per mo - $30.40. NW Va rd, Parkersburg sta |
| 1857-62 | John E. | watch 28 da @ $1 - $28.00. Rd Dept main stem 15th s-div |
| 1855-39 | Welsh, C. | lab 20 da @ $1 - $20.00. Rd Way Dept |
| 1855-11 | E. | conduc & brak 1 da @ $50 per mo - $2.10. |
| 1855-60 | Edward | lab 24 da @ $1 - $24.00. Rd Way Dept |
| 1857-62 | " | fore 24½ da @ $1.12 - $27.55. Rd Dept main stem 15th s-div |
| 1857-59 | " | lab 25½ da @ $1 - $25.50. Rd Dept main stem 12th s-div |
| 1857-92 | Henry | lab 19 da @ $1 - $19.00. grad, Littleton Tun |
| 1855-15 | Isaac | brak 18 da @ $40 per mo - $30.00. Trans Dept main stem |
| 1855-12 | James | conduc & brak 13 da @ $40 per mo - $21.65. Trans Dept main stem |

| | | | |
|---|---|---|---|
| 1855-60 | Welsh, James | fore 26¼ da @ $1 - $26.25. Rd Way Dept |
| 1857-90 | " | lab 12½ da @ $1.12 - $14.05. grad, Welling Tun |
| 1857-65 | " | watch 30 da @ $1 - $30.00. Rd Dept main stem 17th s-div |
| 1855-23 | John | fire 17 da @ $1.75 - $29.75. Trans Dept main stem |
| 1857-16 | " | deck hand 30 da @ $20 per mo - $20.00. transfer steam Brown Dick--Ohio Riv, bet Benwood & Bellaire |
| 1857-58 | Joseph | lab 26 da @ $1 - $26.00. Rd Dept main stem 12th s-div |
| 1855-38 | M. | lab 25½ da @ $1 - $25.50. Rd Way Dept |
| 1857-90 | Michael | lab 10 da @ $1.12 - $11.25. grad, Welling Tun |
| 1857-100 | " | lab 25¼ da @ $1 - $25.25. NW Va RR, Rd Dept 5th s-div |
| 1857-59 | " | lab 24 da @ $1 - $24.00. Rd Dept main stem 12th s-div |
| 1857-47 | Morriss | lab 27 da @ $1 - $27.00. Rd Dept main stem 1st s-div |
| 1857-104 | Owen | lab 25 da @ $1 - $25.00. N W Va RR Tun |
| 1855-60 | Patrick | lab 19½ da @ $1 - $19.50. Rd Way Dept |
| 1855-69 | " | lab 19 da @ $1 - $19.00. Rd Way Dept |
| 1857-89 | " | lab 23½ da @ $1.12 - $26.45. grad, Welling Tun |
| 1857-90 | " | lab 11½ da @ $1.12 - $12.95. grad, Welling Tun |
| 1857-46 | " | lab 27 da @ $1 - $27.00. Rd Dept main stem 1st s-div |
| 1857-25 | " | ton brak 6 da @ $40 per mo - $9.60. 2d div |
| 1857-61 | " | watch 30 da @ $1 - $30.00. Rd Dept main stem 14th s-div |
| 1857-89 | Patrick 2d | lab 11 da @ $1.12 - $12.35. grad, Welling Tun |
| 1855-44 | Peter | lab 23 da @ $1 - $23.00. Rd Way Dept |
| 1857-85 | " | lab 7 da @ $1.12 - $7.85. grad, Board Tree Tun |
| 1857-88 | " | lab 18½ da @ $1.12 - $20.80. grad, Welling Tun |
| 1857-90 | Richard | lab 6 da @ $1.12 - $6.75. grad, Welling Tun |
| 1855-38 | Thomas | lab 24 da @ $1 - $24.00. Rd Way Dept |
| 1855-55 | " | lab 24 da @ $1 - $24.00. Rd Way Dept |
| 1855-69 | " | lab 22¼ da @ $1 - $22.75. Rd Way Dept |
| 1857-63 | " | lab 22 da @ $1 - $22.00. Rd Dept main stem 16th s-div |
| 1855-36 | William | lab 25 da @ $25 per mo - $26.05. Trans Dept main stem |
| 1857-46 | " | lab 27 da @ $1 - $27.00. Rd Dept main stem 1st s-div |
| 1857-132 | Werner, George | cop'smith 22½ da @ $1.66 - $37.35. Mach Dept, Grafton |
| 1857-55 | Wener, John | lab 23¾ da @ $1 - $23.25. Rd Dept main stem 9th s-div |
| 1857-109 | Wentworth, John W. | mach 17½ da @ $1.50 - $26.25. Mach Dept, Balto |
| 1855-77 | Wentze, Charles | mach 15 3/4 da @$1.35 - $21.25. Mach Dept |
| 1857-72 | Werner, Lewis | lab 20 da @$1 - $20.00. Cumb depot |

334  B & O RR EMPLOYEES

| | | | |
|---|---|---|---|
| Wescoat, C. T. | 1857-101 | engr 25 da @ $3 - $75.00. NW Va RR ballast train |
| Wesley, James | 1855-74 | lab 24 da @ $1 - $24.00. Rd Way Dept |
| " | 1855-95 | fore 24 da @ $1.25 - $30.00. Wash br, Rd Dept |
| Joseph | 1855-74 | fore 24 da @ $1.25 - $30.00. Wash br, Rd Dept |
| " | 1857-95 | fore 24 da @ $1.25 - $30.00. Wash br, Rd Dept |
| Lewis | 1857-10 | bur brak 15 da @ $1.15 - $17.25. hp exp, Balto |
| West, Charles | 1857-20 | pass fire 38 da @ $40 per mo - $50.65. 2d div |
| John | 1857-127 | mach 4 da @ $1.75 - $7.00. Mach Dept, Piedmont |
| " | 1857-30 | ton eng'man 13 3/4 da @ $3 - $41.25. 3d div |
| Jos. | 1855-20 | ton eng'man 17 3/4 da @ $3 - $53.25. Trans Dept main stem |
| Westall, James | 1857-123 | nt fore mach @ $55 per mo - $55.00. Mach Dept, Martinsburg |
| Westbrook, C. | 1857-36 | supt tele oper 30 da @ $60 per mo - $60.00. whole line |
| Jestcott, C. F. | 1855-20 | ton eng'man 14 3/4 da @ $3 - $44.25. Trans Dept main stem |
| Westemberger, G. | 1855-72 | app 23½ da @ $.60 - $13.95. Rd Way Dept |
| Westerhaven, David | 1857-125 | carp 19 da @ $1.25 - $23.75. Mach Dept, Martinsburg |
| Westphal, Charles | 1855-87 | mach 22½ da @ $1.55 - $34.90. Mach Dept |
| Westphall, Chas. | 1857-123 | mach 21 3/4 da @ $1.60 - $34.80. Mach Dept, Martinsburg |
| Wetherall, Wm. | 1857-38 | pass fire 34½ da @ $40 per mo - $46.00. Wash br rd, Wash city sta |
| Wetherby, John | 1857-86 | lab 21 da @ $1 - $21.00. grad, McGuire's Tun |
| Weyl, Samuel | 1857-134 | clk @ $50 per mo - $50.00. Mach Dept, Wheeling |
| Whalen, John | 1857-56 | lab 25 da @ $1 - $25.00. Rd Dept main stem 10th s-div |
| Michael | 1855-24 | pass & bur driv 24 da @ $1 - $24.00. Trans Dept main stem |
| Pat. | 1857-10 | pass brak 25 da @ $30 per mo - $30.00. hp exp, Balto |
| S. | 1857-10 | bur brak 27 da @ $1.15 - $31.05. hp exp, Balto |
| W. | 1855-39 | lab 21 da @ $1 - $21.00. Rd Way Dept |
| Will | 1855-11 | conduc & brak 25 3/4 da @$50 per mo - $53.65. Trans Dept main stem |
| William | 1855-25 | bur driv 24 da @ $40 per mo - $40.00. Trans Dept main stem |
| " | 1855-86 | help 16 3/4 da @ $1 - $16.75. Mach Dept |
| " | 1857-10 | bur reg 25 da @$40 per mo - $40.00. hp exp, Balto |
| Whaling, Thomas | 1857-83 | lab 8 da @ $1.12 - $9.00. grad, Board Tree Tun |
| Whalley, George | 1857-135 | lab 30 da @ $1 - $30.00. Mach Dept, Wheeling |
| Whalling, John | 1857-22 | ton conduc 26 da @$50 per mo - $52.00. 2d div |
| Wharton, Isaac | 1855-93 | help 24 da @ $1 - $24.00. Mach Dept |
| Isaiah | 1857-53 | lab 24½ da @$1 - $24.50. Rd Dept main stem 7th s-div |
| " | 1857-52 | lab 25 da @ $1 - $25.00. Rd Dept main stem 6th s-div |
| Wheaney, Mike | 1857-121 | carp help 18 da @ $1.15 - $20.70. Mach Dept, Balto |

| Year-No | Name | Description |
|---|---|---|
| 1855-7 | Wheat, J. J. | bag mast 24 da @ $40 per mo - $34.30. Trans Dept main stem |
| 1855-23 | Wheeler, Andrew | fire 13½ da @ $1.75 - $23.60. Trans Dept main stem |
| 1855-7 | " C. H. | clk 28 da @ $41.65 per mo - $41.65. Trans Dept main stem |
| 1857-39 | " J. D. | clk 30 da @ $55 per mo - $55.00. NW Va rd, Parkersburg sta |
| 1857-8 | " John | rec clk 30 da @ $58.35 per mo - $58.35. Camden sta |
| 1857-41 | " John D. | lab 14 da @ $1 - $14.00. NW Va rd, Athey's wd train |
| 1855-6 | " Rich. | clk 28 da @ $62.50 per mo - $62.50. Trans Dept main stem |
| 1855-74 | " William E. | spik 28 da @ $1.05 - $29.40. Rd Way Dept |
| 1857-112 | | mach help 17¼ da @ $1 - $17.25. Mach Dept, Balto |
| 1857-94 | Whelan, James | lab 19½ da @ $1 - $19.50. quarry & haul stone for Board Tree & Littleton Tun |
| 1857-102 | Whetsell, Enoch | carp 17 da @ $1.65 - $28.05. NW Va RR bridges |
| 1857-24 | Whetter, Lewis J. | ton brak 10½ da @ $40 per mo - $16.80. 1st div |
| 1855-65 | Whipkey, J. | lab 19 da @ $1 - $19.00. Rd Way Dept |
| 1855-12 | Whisner, M. | conduc & brak 12 3/4 da @ $50 per mo - $26.55. Trans Dept main stem |
| 1857-110 | Whitbeck, James | mach 20 da @ $1.35 - $27.00. Mach Dept, Balto |
| 1855-27 | White, A. P. | clean eng 18 da @ $1 - $18.00. Trans Dept main stem |
| 1857-133 | " Alexander D. | fill tend 30 da @ $1 - $30.00. Mach Dept, Fetterman |
| 1855-33 | | lab 24 da @ $30 per mo - $30.00. Trans Dept main stem |
| 1857-137 | | carp 20¾ da @ $1.40 - $28.35. Mach Dept, Cumb |
| 1857-112 | | mach help 16 3/4 da @ $1 - $16.75. Mach Dept, Balto |
| 1855-93 | " George | pack 28 3/4 da - $42.05. Mach Dept |
| 1857-33 | " George W. | ton fire 28 3/4 da @ $1.75 - $50.30. 3d div |
| 1855-34 | " " | greas cars 28 da @ $1 - $28.00. Trans Dept main stem |
| 1857-133 | " H. L. | greas cars 30 da @ $1 - $30.00. Mach Dept, Fetterman |
| 1855-93 | " Henry L. | store kpr @ $35 per mo - $35.00. Mach Dept |
| 1855-89 | " J. S. | blksmith 24½ da @ $1.40 - $33.60. Mach Dept |
| 1855-48 | " James | watch cuts 28 da @ $1 - $28.00. Rd Way Dept |
| 1857-136 | " " | blksmith 18 da @ $1.50 - $27.00. Mach Dept, Cumb |
| 1857-96 | " " | lab 24 da @ $1 - $24.00. NW Va RR, Rd Dept 1st s-div |
| 1857-127 | " " | mach 20¼ da @ $1.50 - $30.35. Mach Dept, Piedmont |
| 1857-52 | " " | watch 30 da @ $1 - $30.00. Rd Dept main stem 6th s-div |
| 1855-78 | " John | help 22½ da @ $1 - $22.50. Mach Dept |
| 1857-111 | " " | mach help 20 3/4 da @ $1.25 - $25.95. Mach Dept, Balto |
| 1857-83 | " Joseph | app 23 3/4 da @ $.55 - $13.05. Mach Dept |
| 1857-109 | " Joseph J. | mach 19¼ da @ $1.60 - $30.80. Mach Dept, Balto |
| 1855-83 | " Joseph Jr | mach 25 da @ $1.72 - $43.00. Mach Dept |

| | | | |
|---|---|---|---|
| 1857-109 | White, Joseph Jr | mach 18 da @$1.80 - $32.40. Mach Dept, Balto |
| 1855-41 | M. | fore 23¾ da @ $1.25 - $27.80. Rd Way Dept |
| 1857-52 | Michael | fore 25 da @ $1.25 - $31.25. Rd Dept main stem 6th s-div |
| 1855-81 | O. G. | fire 19 da @ $2 - $38.00. Mach Dept |
| 1855-erratta | " " | "fore" instead of "fire" |
| 1857-121 | " " | car trim 18¼ da @ $2 - $36.50. Mach Dept, Balto |
| 1855-73 | Orlando | uphol 7½ da @ $2 - $15.00. Rd Way Dept |
| 1855-32 | P. | lab 24 da @ $30 per mo - $30.00. Trans Dept main stem |
| 1857-113 | Peter | mach app 23½ da @ $.45 - $10.55. Mach Dept, Balto |
| 1855-78 | Robert | storekpr @ $40.25 per mo - $40.25. Mach Dept |
| 1857-108 | " | asst storekpr @ $40.25 per mo - $40.25. Mach Dept, Balto |
| 1857-23 | " | ton conduc 3½ da @ $50 per mo - $7.00. Board Tree Tun |
| 1857-70 | Robert H. | app 21 3/4 da @ $.75 - $16.30. Mt Clare sta, Balto |
| 1855-27 | Thomas | clean eng 16 da @ $1 - $16.00. Trans Dept main stem |
| 1857-102 | William | carp 21 da @ $1.75 - $36.75. NW Va RR bridges |
| 1857-119 | Whitehurst, Henry | tin 22 da @ $1.65 - $36.30. Mach Dept, Balto |
| 1855-78 | Whiteley, J. | help 15 da @ $1 - $15.00. Mach Dept |
| 1855-23 | Whitford, J. S. | fire 9¾ da @ $1.75 - $16.20. Trans Dept main stem |
| 1855-70 | Whitman, Edward | 16 da @ $1.22 - $19.50. Rd Way Dept |
| 1855-93 | Joseph | help 25 da @ $1 - $25.00. Mach Dept |
| 1857-131 | Lewis | boil kpr 19¼ da @ $1 - $19.25. Mach Dept, Grafton |
| 1855-94 | M. | boil mkr 26½ da @ $1.50 - $39.75. Mach Dept |
| 1855-7 | Whitmeyer, E. | bag mast 24 da @$40 per mo - $34.30. Trans Dept main stem |
| 1855-29 | Whitmyre, Thomas | haul & saw firewd 18 da @ $1 - $18.00. Trans Dept main stem |
| 1855-88 | Whitson, Benjamin | carp 22½ da @ $1.30 - $29.25. Mach Dept |
| 1855-87 | William | mach 26¼ da @ $1.35 - $35.45. Mach Dept |
| 1857-124 | " | boil mkr 20 da @ $1.50 - $30.00. Mach Dept, Martinsburg |
| 1857-19 | Whittemore, E. M. | bag mast 30 da @$45 per mo - $45.00. w end |
| 1857-12 | Whitter, J. E. | watch 30 da @$30 per mo - $30.00. Fred sta |
| 1857-32 | Whittner, Wm. E. | ton fire 18 da @ $1.75 - $31.50. 1st div |
| 1855-64 | Whittner, S. | lab 20 da @ $1 - $20.00. Rd Way Dept |
| 1855-84 | Whitworth, Thomas | help 21½ da @ $1.15 - $24.70. Mach Dept |
| 1857-115 | " | boil mkr 19½ da @ $1.25 - $24.40. Mach Dept, Balto |
| 1857-19 | Wholey, Joseph | pass eng'man 27 da @ $3 - $81.00. 1st div |
| 1857-19 | Wm. | pass eng'man 30 da @ $3 - $90.00. 1st div |
| 1855-43 | Whorton, Wm. | lab 20 da @ $1 - $20.00. Rd Way Dept |

| | | | |
|---|---|---|---|
| 1855-86 | Wibber, Henry | help 23½ da @ $1.15 - $27.00. Mach Dept | |
| 1857-115 | Wicks, G. A. | pat mkr 17½ da @ $1.75 - $30.65. Mach Dept, Balto | |
| 1857-113 | " Thomas | mach app 22½ da @ $.75 - $16.90. Mach Dept, Balto | |
| 1855-84 | Wideman, John | help 20½ da @ $1.10 - $22.55. Rd Way Dept | |
| 1855-44 | Wiedermott, John | lab 20 da @ $1 - $20.00. Mach Dept | |
| 1857-73 | Wigginton, John J. | fore 25 da @ $2 - $50.00. repair water sta, M.S. & P.B. | |
| 1855-88 | Wigginton, Geo. | help 18 3/4 da @ $1.15 - $21.25. Mach Dept | |
| 1855-77 | Wiglesworth, John | mach 22½ da @ $1.72 - $38.70. Mach Dept | |
| 1855-46 | Wigman, John | lab 23 da @ $1 - $23.00. Rd Way Dept | |
| 1857-40 | Wigner, Wesley | ton brak 18½ da @ $40 per mo - $29.60. NW Va rd, Parkersburg sta | |
| 1857-27 | Wikoff, Matthew | ton brak 2 da @ $40 per mo - $3.20. 3d & 4th div | |
| 1855-87 | Wilckin, G. | mach 27½ da @ $1.40 - $38.15. Mach Dept | |
| 1855-39 | Wilcome, C. | lab 24 da @ $1 - $24.00. Rd Way Dept | |
| 1855-39 | " J. | lab 24 da @ $1 - $24.00. Rd Way Dept | |
| 1855-39 | " John | lab 26 da @ $1 - $26.00. Rd Way Dept | |
| 1857-85 | Wiles, John | stone mason 18 da @ $1.50 - $27.00. grad, Board Tree Tun | |
| 1857-134 | Wiley, T. A. | mach app 17 da @ $.55 - $9.35. Mach Dept, Wheeling | |
| 1855-8 | " " | bag mast 28 da @ $45 per mo - $45.00. Trans Dept main stem | |
| 1857-18 | " " | pass train conduc 30 da @ $50 per mo - $50.00. W end | |
| 1857-29 | Wilgar, Frank | ton eng'man 29½ da @ $3 - $88.50. 2d div | |
| 1857-22 | Wilger, William | ton conduc 27½ da @ $50 per mo - $55.00. 2d div | |
| 1857-115 | Wilhelm, A. | ton brak 18 da @ $40 per mo - $28.80. 3d & 4th div | |
| 1855-32 | Wilkerson, Barney | boil mkr 17¾ da @ $1.60 - $27.60. Mach Dept, Balto | |
| 1857-134 | Wilkinson, J. A. | tele oper 28 da @ $30 per mo - $30.00. Trans Dept main stem | |
| 1855-15 | " Wm. H. | mach 21 3/4 da @ $1.65 - $35.90. Mach Dept, Wheeling | |
| 1855-38 | Will, John | brak 5½ da @ $40 per mo - $9.15. Trans Dept main stem | |
| 1857-54 | Willhide, John | lab 23 da @ $1 - $23.00. Rd Way Dept | |
| 1857-122 | Williams, Alexander | lab 20½ da @ $1 - $20.50. Rd Dept main stem 8th s-div | |
| 1855-12 | " Benjamin | cart 21½ da @ $1 - $21.25. Mach Dept, Balto | |
| 1855-89 | " C. H. | conduc & brak 24 da @ $30 per mo - $30.00. Trans Dept main stem | |
| 1857-131 | " George | mach 31 3/4 da @ $1.80 - $57.15. Mach Dept | |
| 1855-64 | " " | asst mast mech @ $60 per mo - $60.00. Mach Dept, Grafton | |
| 1857-8 | " J. Jr | fore @ $50 per mo - $50.00. Rd Way Dept | |
| 1855-83 | " James | deliv clk 30 da @ $62.50 per mo - $62.50. Camden sta | |
| 1857-127 | " " | mach 27 da @ $1.65 - $44.55. Mach Dept | |
| | | mach 17½ da @ $1.60 - $28.00. Mach Dept, Piedmont | |

338   B & O RR EMPLOYEES

| ID | Name | Description |
|---|---|---|
| 1857-119 | Williams, James | tin 26 da @ $1.50 - $39.00. Mach Dept, Balto |
| 1857-109 | James E. | mach 18 da @ $1.65 - $29.70. Mach Dept, Balto |
| 1857-72 | James M. | lab 21 da @ $1 - $21.00. Locust Pt, load mat |
| 1855-21 | John | fire 13½ da @ $1.75 - $23.60. Trans Dept main stem |
| 1855-67 | " | mason 22 3/4 da @ $2 - $45.50. Rd Way Dept |
| 1857-136 | " | tin 29 da @ $1.50 - $43.50. Mach Dept |
| 1855-6 | " | mach 19 da @ $1.75 - $33.25. Mach Dept, Cumb |
| 1857-27 | John Jr | clk 28 da @ $50 per mo - $50.00. Trans Dept main stem |
| 1855-83 | Jonathan | ton brak 25 da @ $40 per mo - $40.00. 3d & 4th div |
| 1857-112 | Joseph | lab 24 da @ $1 - $24.00. Mach Dept |
| 1857-52 | " | mach help 18¼ da @ $1 - $18.25. Mach Dept, Balto |
| 1857-52 | Joshua | horse hire 48 da @ $.90 - $43.20. Rd Dept main stem 6th s-div |
| 1857-90 | Joshua P. | supv @ $45 per mo - $45.00. Rd Dept main stem 6th s-div |
| 1855-51 | Patrick | lab 11½ da @ $1.12 - $12.95. grad, Welling Tun |
| 1857-51 | S. M. | lab 28 da @ $1 - $28.00. Rd Way Dept |
| 1855-25 | Samuel | lab 25 da @ $1 - $25.00. Rd Dept main stem 5th s-div |
| 1857-67 | Thomas | bur driv 18 da @ $30 per mo - $22.50. Trans Dept main stem |
| 1855-90 | " | lab 18 3/4 da @ $1 - $18.75. Rd Dept main stem 18th s-div |
| 1855-64 | W. J. | help 22 da @ $1 - $22.00. Mach Dept |
| 1855-49 | William | fire 2½ da @ $1.75 - $4.35. Trans Dept main stem |
| 1857-29 | " | mason 24 da @ $1.75 - $42.00. Rd Way Dept |
| 1857-51 | " | watch cuts 28 da @ $1 - $28.00. Rd Way Dept |
| 1857-132 | " | ton eng'man 12 da @ $3 - $36.00. 2d div |
| 1855-9 | William J. | watch 30 da @ $1 - $30.00. Rd Dept main stem 5th s-div |
| 1857-32 | Williamson, D. | put away eng 30 da @ $1 - $30.00. Mach Dept, Grafton |
| 1857-135 | " | conduc 22½ da @ $50 per mo - $46.85. Trans Dept main stem |
| 1857-20 | David | ton fire 2 da @ $1.75 - $3.50. 1st div |
| 1855-9 | " | lab 1½ da @ $1 - $1.50. Mach Dept, Wheeling |
| 1857-23 | John | pass fire 2 da @ $40 per mo - $2.65. 2d div |
| 1855-15 | " | conduc 20½ da @ $50 per mo - $42.70. Trans Dept main stem |
| 1857-18 | S. | brak 14 da @ $40 per mo - $23.35. Trans Dept main stem |
| 1857-30 | Williard, J. P. | pass train conduc 30 da @ $62.50 per mo - $62.50. w end |
| 1855-35 | Julius | ton eng'man 17 3/4 da @ $3 - $53.25. 4th div |
| 1855-65 | Perry | disp of trains 28 da @ $50 per mo - $50.00. Trans Dept main stem |
| | Williman, D. | lab 14 da @ $1 - $14.00. Rd Way Dept |

B & O RR EMPLOYEES

| ID | Name | Description |
|---|---|---|
| 1857-36 | Willis, O. W. | tele oper 30 da @ $45 per mo - $45.00. Cumb |
| 1857-24 | Williur, Frederick | ton brak 28 da @ $30 per mo - $33.60. 1st div |
| 1855-51 | Willman, Frederick | lab @ $30 per mo -$30.00. Rd Way Dept |
| 1857-60 | Willmon, Frederick | watch 30 da @ $1 - $30.00. Rd Dept main stem 13th s-div |
| 1857-60 | " Wm. | watch 30 da @ $1 - $30.00. Rd Dept main stem 13th s-div |
| 1857-30 | Wills, John | ton eng'man 10 da @ $3 - $30.00. 3d div |
| 1857-109 | " Joseph | mach 18 da @ $1.55 - $27.90. Mach Dept, Balto |
| 1857-70 | " Walter | mach 16½ da @ $1.73 - $28.55. Mt Clare sta, Balto |
| 1857-14 | Willmore, Emory | clean pass rm 25 da @ $3 per mo - $3.00. Cumb |
| 1855-35 | Willmore, Emery | clean pass rm 28 da @ $5 per mo - $5.00. Trans Dept main stem |
| 1857-120 | Wilson, Allen | carp 18 da @ $1.55 - $27.90. Mach Dept, Balto |
| 1855-34 | " F. C. | watch 28 da @ $1 - $28.00. Trans Dept main stem |
| 1855-40 | " F. K. | ton brak 14½ da @ $40 per mo - $23.20. NW Va rd, Parkersburg sta |
| 1855-21 | " H. B. | fire 27 da @ $1.75 - $47.25. Trans Dept main stem |
| 1857-22 | " Henry B. | ton conduc 25 da @ $50 per mo - $50.00. 2d div |
| 1855-1 | " J. L. | asst mast of rd $1300 per annum - $108.33 |
| 1855-8 | " J. N. | brak 22 da @ $33.35 per mo - $26.20. Trans Dept main stem |
| 1855-24 | " James | pass & bur driv 15½ da @ $30 per mo - $19.35. Trans Dept main stem |
| 1855-18 | " " | ton eng'man 3 da @ $3 - $9.00. Trans Dept main stem |
| 1855-18 | " James B. | ton eng'man 21½ da @ $3 - $64.50. Trans Dept main stem |
| 1857-45 | " John L. | asst mast of rd @ $125 per mo. Rd Dept 3d & 4th div |
| 1857-86 | " Joseph | bricklay 20½ da @ $2.25 - $45.55. grad, McGuire's Tun |
| 1857-65 | " " | lab 14¼ da @ $1 - $14.25. Rd Dept main stem 17th s-div |
| 1855-24 | " Malcom | pass & bur driv 27 da @ $30 per mo - $33.75. Trans Dept main stem |
| 1857-118 | " Mat | blksmith help 18 da @ $1 - $18.00. Mach Dept, Balto |
| 1855-8 | " N. L. | brak 3 da @ $33.35 per mo - $3.55. Trans Dept main stem |
| 1855-9 | " " | conduc 6 da @ $50 per mo - $12.50. Trans Dept main stem |
| 1855-74 | " Stephen | fore 22½ da @ $1.25 - $28.10. Rd Way Dept |
| 1857-37 | " " | brak 30 da @ $33.33 per mo - $33.35. Wash br rd, Wash City sta |
| 1855-85 | " Thomas | blksmith 23¾ da @ $1.30 - $33.25. Mach Dept |
| 1855-81 | " Walter | carp 24 da @ $1.50 - $36.00. Mach Dept, Balto |
| 1857-120 | " Wm. S. | carp 20 da @ $1.60 - $32.00. Mach Dept, Balto |
| 1857-57 | Wilt, John H. | lab 22½ da @ $1 - $22.50. Rd Dept main stem 11th s-div |
| 1857-57 | " John W. | lab 26¼ da @ $1 - $26.25. Rd Dept main stem 11th s-div |
| 1857-57 | " T. | lab 18 3/4 da @ $1 - $18.75. Rd Dept main stem 11th s-div |
| 1857-61 | Wiltman, Deterick | lab 27 da @ $1 - $27.00. Rd Dept main stem 11th s-div |

339

| | | |
|---|---|---|
| 1855-66 | Wine, James | lab 23½ da @ $1 - $23.50. Rd Way Dept |
| 1857-86 | " | lab 22¼ da @ $1 - $22.25. grad, McGuire's Tun |
| 1855-26 | Winfield, William | clean eng 16¼ da @ $1 - $16.25. Trans Dept main stem |
| 1857-137 | " | eng clean 25½ da @ $1 - $25.50. Mach Dept, Cumb |
| 1855-81 | Wink, Saml. | lab 17½ da @ $1.15 - $20.10. Mach Dept |
| 1857-27 | Winkfield, M. | ton brak 21 da @ $40 per mo - $33.60. 3d & 4th div |
| 1857-23 | William | ton conduc 7½ da @ $50 per mo - $15.00. 3d & 4th div |
| 1855-35 | Winkleman, F. | coup 24 da @ $30 per mo - $30.00. Trans Dept main stem |
| 1857-29 | Winn, William | ton eng'man 23½ da @ $3 - $70.50. 1st div |
| 1855-89 | Winslow. P. | mach 15¼ da @ $1.65 - $25.15. Mach Dept |
| 1857-136 | Patrick | mach 25½ da @ $1.75 - $44.60. Mach Dept, Cumb |
| 1857-118 | Winter, Henry | blksmith help 17¼ da @ $1.10 - $18.95. Mach Dept, Balto |
| 1855-26 | Winters, Andrew | clean eng 13 da @ $1 - $13.00. Trans Dept main stem |
| 1857-124 | Frederick | sht iron work 18¼ da @ $1.25 - $22.80. Mach Dept, Martinsburg |
| 1855-9 | James | conduc 27 da @ $50 per mo - $56.25. Trans Dept main stem |
| 1855-56 | " | lab 13 3/4 da @ $1 - $13.75. Rd Way Dept |
| 1857-23 | " | ton conduc 23 da @ $50 per mo - $46.00. Board Tree Tun |
| 1855-20 | W. D. | ton eng'man 2 3/4 da @ $3 - $8.25. Trans Dept main stem |
| 1855-66 | Wise, Jacob | lab 24½ da @ $1.50 - $36.75. Rd Way Dept |
| 1857-89 | " | mason 8 da @ $2 - $16.00. grad, Welling Tun |
| 1857-9 | Wiseman, Charles | clk 30 da @ $54.15 per mo - $54.15. Mt Clare sta |
| 1857-118 | George | blksmith help 14 da @ $1 - $14.00. Mach Dept, Balto |
| 1857-27 | Jacob | ton brak 7 da @ $40 per mo - $11.20. 3d & 4th div |
| 1855-42 | Wisenburg, Geo. | lab 23 da @ $1 - $23.00. Rd Way Dept |
| 1855-41 | Wisendorf, Jos. | nail 27½ da @ $1.05 - $28.85. Rd Way Dept |
| 1855-65 | Wishart, William | supv @ $60 per mo - $60.00. Rd Way Dept |
| 1857-72 | " | fore @ $60 per mo - $60.00. Piedmont depot |
| 1857-123 | Wisong, George R. | clk @ $50 per mo - $50.00. Mach Dept, Martinsburg |
| 1855-88 | Wissenger, M. | help 14¼ da @ $1 - $14.25. Mach Dept |
| 1855-20 | William | ton eng'man 5½ da @ $2.50 - $13.75. Trans Dept main stem |
| 1857-27 | Witt, E. | ton brak 19½ da @ $40 per mo - $31.20. 3d & 4th div |
| 1855-75 | Wittman, Mart. | lab 20 da @ $1 - $20.00. Rd Way Dept |
| 1855-15 | Wolf, Adw. | brak 19 3/4 da @ $40 per mo - $32.90. Trans Dept main stem |
| 1857-27 | Andrew | ton brak 16½ da @ $40 per mo - $26.40. Board Tree Tun |
| 1857-27 | " | ton brak 4 da @ $40 per mo - $6.40. 3d & 4th div |
| 1855-15 | G. W. | brak 17 3/4 da @ $40 per mo - $29.60. Trans Dept main stem |

| | | |
|---|---|---|
| 1857-102 | Wolf, Henry | carp 22½ da @ $1.50 - $33.75. NW Va RR, rwy depot |
| 1857-60 | " | watch 27 da @ $1 - $27.00. Rd Dept main stem 13th s-div |
| 1855-53 | John | lab 18½ da @ $1 - $18.50. Rd Way Dept |
| 1857-56 | " | nail 28 3/4 da @ $1 - $28.75. Rd Dept main stem 10th s-div |
| 1855-83 | N. | app 19 da @ $.65 - $12.35. Mach Dept |
| 1855-68 | Peter | blksmith 22 da @ $1.50 - $33.00. Rd Way Dept |
| 1855-39 | William | lab 24 da @ $1 - $24.00. Rd Way Dept |
| 1857-123 | Wolfe, Lewis | mach 26¼ da @ $1.55 - $40.70. Mach Dept, Martinsburg |
| 1857-134 | Nicholas | mach 12 da @ $1.65 - $19.80. Mach Dept, Wheeling |
| 1857-49 | William | fore 25 da @ $1.25 - $31.25. Rd Dept main stem 3d s-div |
| 1857-34 | Wolff, George W. | ton fire 31 da @ $1.75 - $54.25. 4th div |
| 1855-87 | Louis | mach 31¼ da @ $1.55 - $48.45. Mach Dept |
| 1857-34 | Wolford, Adam | ton fire 2½ da @ $1.75 - $4.35. Board Tree Tun |
| 1857-33 | " | ton fire 14 da @ $1.75 -$24.50. 3d div |
| 1855-23 | Wollard, John R. | fire 21 da @$1.75 - $36.75. Trans Dept main stem |
| 1855-23 | William | fire 15¼ da @ $1.75 - $26.70. Trans Dept main stem |
| 1857-110 | Wollen, William | mach 19½ da @ $1.35 - $26.30. Mach Dept, Balto |
| 1855-16 | Wollenton, P. | pass fire 28½ da @ $1.75 - $49.85. Trans Dept main stem |
| 1855-86 | Wollett, George | asst fore @ $60 per mo - $60.00. Mach Dept |
| 1857-123 | " | asst mast mech @ $60 per mo - $60.00. Mach Dept, Martinsburg |
| 1857-29 | Henry | ton eng'man 19¼ da @$3 - $57.75. 2d div |
| 1855-5 | John | ton fire 1 da @ $33.33 per mo - $1.40. Trans Dept, Wash br |
| 1857-29 | " | ton eng'man 19 da @$2.50 - $47.50. 1st div |
| 1855-5 | Phillip | brak 24 da @ $30 per mo - $30.00. Trans Dept, Wash br |
| 1857-125 | William | app 28¼ da @ $.45 - $12.70. Mach Dept, Martinsburg |
| 1855-15 | Wolvington, W. | pass eng'man 11 da @ $2.50 - $27.50. Trans Dept main stem |
| 1857-31 | " | ton eng'man 12 da @ $3 - $36.00. Board Tree Tun |
| 1857-30 | William | ton eng'man 16 da @ $3 -$48.00. 4th div |
| 1855-93 | Wood, Edward | help 14¼ da @ $1 - $14.25. Mach Dept |
| 1855-12 | James | conduc & brak 11¼ da @ $40 per mo - $18.75. Trans Dept main stem |
| 1855-37 | John | lab 24 da @ $1 - $24.00. Rd Way Dept |
| 1857-50 | Oliver | lab 21¼ da @ $1 - $21.25. Rd Dept main stem 4th s-div |
| 1855-81 | Woodall, F. B. | carp 23½ da @ $1.60 - $37.60. Mach Dept |
| 1857-120 | " " | carp 18 da @ $1.60 - $28.80. Mach Dept, Balto |
| 1857-29 | John | ton eng'man 16 3/4 da @ $3 - $50.25. 1st div |
| 1855-33 | T. | ofcr 28 da @$41.65 per mo - $41.65. Trans Dept main stem |

342  B & O RR EMPLOYEES

| | | | |
|---|---|---|---|
| 1857-122 | Woodall, W. | put away eng &c 30¼ da @ $1.25 - $37.80. Mach Dept, Balto |
| 1855-25 | Walter | clean eng 25 da @ $1.15 - $28.75. Trans Dept main stem |
| 1855-86 | William | help 26 da @ $1 - $26.00. Mach Dept |
| 1855-20 | Woodcock, Chas. | ton eng'man 9 da @ $2.50 - $22.50. Trans Dept main stem |
| 1855-78 | T. | help 11 3/4 da @ $1 - $11.75. Mach Dept |
| 1857-114 | Theodore | iron mould 16 3/4 da @ $1.60 -$26.80. Mach Dept, Balto |
| 1857-41 | W. | ton fire 6¼ da @ $1.75 - $10.95. NW Va rd, Parkersburg sta |
| 1857-32 | Wm. | ton fire 17 3/4 da @ $1.75 - $30.65. 1st div |
| 1855-89 | Wooding, J. | blksmith 15¼ da @ $1.25 - $19.05. Mach Dept |
| 1857-41 | Woodring, W. | ton fire 17 da @ $1.75 - $29.75. NW Va rd, Parkersburg sta |
| 1855-7 | Woods, A. Q. | clk 28 da @ $52.50 per mo - $62.50. Trans Dept main stem |
| 1857-85 | Charles | bricklay 7½ da @ $2.25 - $16.85. grad, Board Tree Tun |
| 1857-87 | " | bricklay 18¼ da @ $2.25 -$41.05. grad, Welling Tun |
| 1855-38 | Charles L. | brak 12 da @ $30 per mo - $14.40. Wash br rd, Wash city sta |
| 1857-85 | David | bricklay 5½ da @$2.25 - $12.35. grad, Board Tree Tun |
| 1857-87 | " | bricklay 18¼ da @ $2.25 - $41.05. grad, Welling Tun |
| 1857-58 | John | watch cuts 27½ da @ $1 - $27.50. Rd Way Dept |
| 1855-49 | " | watch 30 da @ $1 - $30.00. Rd Dept main stem 11th s-div |
| 1855-86 | John B. | watch cuts 6½ da @$1 - $6.50. Rd Way Dept |
| 1857-110 | Philip | help 23½ da @ $1.10 - $25.85. Mach Dept |
| 1855-77 | William | mach 20 da @ $1.72 - $34.40. Mach Dept, Balto |
| 1855-77 | William Jr | mach 25 3/4 da @ $1.72 - $44.30. Mach Dept |
| 1857-3 | " | mach 23⅓ da @ $1.72 - $40.00. Mach Dept |
| 1857-7 | Woodside, Edmund L | clk @ $50 per mo. Gen Ofc |
| 1857-3 | W. S. | mast trans & paymast @ $250 per mo. Mast of Trans Ofc |
| 1855-1 | " | paymast @ $166.66 per mo. Gen Ofc |
| 1857-36 | Wm. S. | paymast $2000 per annum - $166.66. Ofc Hanover St |
| 1857-7 | Woodward, C. | tele oper 30 da @ $30 per mo - $30.00. C. Summit |
| 1855-71 | G. P. | clk @ $66.65 per mo. Gen Tick Agt Ofc |
| 1855-15 | Woolen, John | paint 16 da @ $1.75 -$28.00. Rd Way Dept |
| 1855-49 | Wooley, J. | pass eng'man 30 da @$3 -$90.00. Trans Dept main stem |
| 1857-53 | Woolford, Benjamin | watch cuts 28 da @ $1 - $28.00. Rd Way Dept |
| 1855-11 | John | watch 30 da @ $1 - $30.00. Rd Dept main stem 7th s-div |
| 1855-12 | Samuel | conduc & brak 15 3/4 da @$50 per mo -$32.80. Trans Dept main stem |
| 1855-50 | Woollard, William | conduc & brak 21½ da @$40 per mo -$39.35. Trans Dept main stem |
| | | watch cuts 23½ da @ $1 - $23.50. Rd Way Dept |

| | | |
|---|---|---|
| 1857-19 | Woollerton, P. H. | pass eng'man 36 da @ $2.50 - $90.00. 3d div |
| 1855-11 | Woollett, George T. | conduc & brak 19 da @ $50 per mo - $39.60. Trans Dept main stem |
| 1855-20 | Woolman, Geo. | ton eng'man 2 da @ $2.50 - $5.00. Trans Dept main stem |
| 1855-83 | Woolsey, William | mach 18 3/4 da @ $1.30 - $24.35. Mach Dept |
| 1855-93 | Work, Alex. | help 28½ da @ $1 - $28.50. Mach Dept |
| 1855-78 | Worman, William | help 26½ da @ $1 - $26.50. Mach Dept |
| 1855-44 | Worthen, John | lab 11½ da @ $1 - $11.50. Rd Way Dept |
| 1855-7 | Worthington, F. H. | clk 28 da @ $58.35 per mo - $58.35. Trans Dept main stem |
| 1857-63 | " J. | brak 12½ da @ $40 per mo - $20.40. Trans Dept main stem |
| 1855-88 | Wright, E. | watch 30 da @ $1 - $30.00. Rd Dept main stem 16th s-div |
| 1857-33 | " H. | help 18½ da @ $1 - $18.50. Mach Dept |
| 1857-8 | " Hamilton | ton fire 25 da @ $1.75 - $43.75. 2d div |
| 1855-91 | " J. B. | police ofcr 30 da @$41.65 per mo - $41.65. Camden sta |
| 1855-20 | " John | blksmith 23 3/4 da @ $36.95. Mach Dept |
| 1857-128 | " " | ton eng'man 10 3/4 da @ $2.50 - $26.85. Trans Dept main stem |
| 1857-120 | " Joshua J. | blksmith 19 da @ $1.65 - $31.35. Mach Dept, Piedmont |
| 1857-27 | " Josiah | carp 12½ da @ $1.50 - $18.35. Mach Dept, Balto |
| 1857-27 | " " | ton brak 24½ da @ $40 per mo - $39.20. Board Tree Tun |
| 1855-24 | " Nelson | ton brak 1 da @ $40 per mo - $1.60. 3d & 4th div |
| 1857-11 | " Thomas | pass & bur driv 24 da @ $35 per mo - $35.00. Trans Dept main stem |
| 1857-69 | " Thomas E. | lab 24½ da @ $1 - $24.25. Locust Pt |
| 1855-12 | " W. | lab 17 3/4 da @ $1 - $17.75. Mt Clare sta, Balto |
| 1857-11 | " William | conduc & brak 2 da @ $40 per mo - $3.35. Trans Dept main stem |
| 1857-50 | Writhrow, Martin | lab 24 da @ $30 per mo - $28.80. Locust Pt |
| 1857-27 | Wykoff, Mathew | lab 25 da @ $1 - $25.00. Rd Dept main stem 5th s-div |
| 1855-20 | Wyne, Geo. | ton brak 30½ da @ $40 per mo - $48.80. Board Tree Tun |
| 1857-64 | Yeany, Henry | ton eng'man 2 da @ $2.50 - $5.00. Trans Dept main stem |
| 1857-77 | Yearit, C. | lab 30 da @ $1 - $30.00. Rd Dept main stem 17th s-div |
| 1855-7 | Yingling, J. W. | quarry 20 da @ $1 - $20.00. ballast train for 2d track |
| 1857-124 | Yoh, Henry | pass conduc 28 da @ $62.50 per mo - $62.50. Trans Dept main stem |
| 1857-17 | Yost, Ely R. | blksmith 19 da @ $1.50 - $28.50. Mach Dept, Martinsburg |
| 1857-118 | " John | fore 30 da @ $50 per mo - $50.00. frt transfer force at Bellaire, opp Benwood |
| 1855-33 | Young, A. | blksmith help 17½ da @ $1 - $17.75. Mach Dept, Balto |
| 1855-77 | " Hiram | lab 24 da @ $1.60 - $38.40. Trans Dept main stem |
| 1857-109 | " " | mach 18 da @ $1.60 - $28.80. Mach Dept, Balto |

# B & O RR EMPLOYEES

| ID | Name | Description |
|---|---|---|
| 1855-8 | Young, James | bag mast 28 da @ $45 per mo - $45.00. Trans Dept main stem |
| 1855-21 | " | fire 4½ da @ $1.75 - $7.85. Trans Dept main stem |
| 1855-32 | " | lab 24 da @ $30 per mo - $30.00. Trans Dept main stem |
| 1857-13 | John | lab 13 3/4 da @ $.75 - $10.30. Rd Way Dept |
| 1857-61 | " | haul wd 1 da @ $1 - $1.00. Martinsburg |
| 1855-20 | Peter | lab 29 da @ $1 - $29.00. Rd Dept main stem 14th s-div |
| 1857-29 | " | ton eng'man 18½ da @ $2.50 - $46.25. Trans Dept main stem |
| 1857-121 | " | ton eng'man 28¾ da @ $3 - $84.75. 2d div |
| 1857-19 | W. A. | carp help 18¾ da @ $1.15 - $21.00. Mach Dept, Balto |
| 1855-12 | W. H. | bag mast 30 da @ $45 per mo - $45.00. thr mail & exp |
| 1857-116 | William | conduc & brak 17 3/4 da @ $40 per mo - $29.60. Trans Dept main stem |
| | " | boil mkr help 20 da @ $1.15 - $23.00. Mach Dept, Balto |
| 1857-65 | Youst, James | lab 3½ da @ $1 - $3.50. Rd Dept main stem 17th s-div |
| 1857-65 | Zeady, Leonard | lab 8 da @ $1 - $8.00. Rd Dept main stem 17th s-div |
| 1855-64 | Zeady, Wm. | lab 22¼ da @ $.87½ - $19.45. Rd Way Dept |
| 1857-118 | Zeighler, Conrad | blksmith help 18 da @ $1 - $18.00. Mach Dept, Balto |
| 1855-90 | Zeigler, Henry | help 23½ da @ $1.15 - $27.00. Mach Dept |
| 1857-137 | " | lab 22 3/4 da @ $1.15 - $26.15. Mach Dept, Cumb |
| 1857-137 | John H. | lab 22 da @ $1 - $22.00. Mach Dept, Cumb |
| 1857-136 | Zelch, Henry | mach 23 3/4 da @ $1.40 - $33.25. Mach Dept, Cumb |
| 1857-137 | John | eng clean 24 da @ $1 - $24.00. Mach Dept, Cumb |
| 1855-20 | Zellick, Henry | ton eng'man 11 da @ $2.50 - $27.50. Trans Dept main stem |
| 1857-47 | Zepp, Benjamin | lab 23½ da @ $1 - $23.50. Rd Dept main stem 2d s-div |
| 1855-39 | Ephraim | lab 19 da @ $1 - $19.00. Rd Way Dept |
| 1857-48 | " | lab 25 da @ $1 - $25.00. Rd Dept main stem 2d s-div |
| 1857-32 | George | ton fire 23½ da @ $1.75 - $41.10. 1st div |
| 1855-20 | Henry | ton eng'man 17 da @ $3 - $51.00. Trans Dept main stem |
| 1857-29 | " | ton eng'man 31 da @ $3 - $93.00. 2d div |
| 1855-20 | Jerry | ton eng'man 1 da @ $2.50 - $2.50. Trans Dept main stem |
| 1857-47 | John T. | ton eng'man 17¾ da @ $3 - $52.50. Trans Dept main stem 2d s-div |
| 1855-39 | P. | lab 24 da @ $1 - $24.00. Rd Dept main stem 2d s-div |
| 1857-48 | Presly | lab 22 da @ $1 - $22.00. Rd Way Dept |
| 1855-20 | Reuben | nail 25 da @ $1.05 - $26.25. Rd Dept main stem 2d s-div |
| 1855-4 | " | ton eng'man 15¼ da @ $3 - $45.75. Trans Dept main stem |
| 1857-19 | " | ton eng'man 1 da @ $2.50 - $2.50. Trans Dept, Wash br |
| | | pass eng'man 26½ da @ $3 - $79.50. 1st div |

| | | |
|---|---|---|
| 1855-74 | Ziglar, Christ. | lab 22 da @ $1 - $22.00. Rd Way Dept |
| 1857-95 | Zigler, Christian | lab 23½ da @ $1 - $23.25. Wash br, Rd Dept |
| 1855-43 | Ziler, George | lab 17½ da @ $1 - $17.50. Rd Way Dept |
| 1857-53 | " | lab 25 da @ $1 - $25.00. Rd Dept main stem 7th s-div |
| 1857-25 | Michael | ton brak 26 3/4 da @ $40 per mo - $42.80. 2d div |
| 1857-53 | Pendleton | lab 25 da @ $1 - $25.00. Rd Dept main stem 7th s-div |
| 1857-73 | Zimbro, William | carp 25 da @ $1.65 - $41.25. repair water sta, M.S. & P.B. |
| 1855-52 | Zimbroe, William | lab @ $45 per mo - $45.00. Rd Way Dept |
| 1857-132 | Zimmerman, Albright | carp @ $35 per mo - $35.00. Mach Dept, Grafton |
| 1857-7 | B. F. | clk @ $66.65 per mo. Gen Tick Agt Ofc |
| 1855-18 | D. | ton eng'man 12 da @ $3 - $36.00. Trans Dept main stem |
| 1857-71 | Fred. | fore @ $50 per mo - $50.00. Camden sta, repair tracks |
| 1857-71 | H. | track lay 22 da @ $1.37 - $30.25. Camden sta, repair tracks |
| 1855-8 | Zollickoffer, C. | brak 28 da @ $33.35 per mo - $33.35. Trans Dept main stem |
| 1857-108 | D. R. | oil house clk @ $40 per mo - $40.00. Mach Dept, Balto |
| 1855-70 | Zots, John | lab 13 da @ $1.75 - $22.75. Rd Way Dept |
| 1857-87 | Zotz, John | stone mason 24½ da @ $2 - $49.00. grad, McGuire's Tun |

ABBREVIATIONS

1855-70) identifies the List and page number on which the individual name appears (a copy of the List
1857-87) is in the Maryland Historical Society Library).

Error Ofc - Error's Office
Gen Frt Agt Ofc - General Freight Agent Office
Gen Tick Agt Ofc - General Ticket Agent Office
Mach Dept - Machinery Department
main stem

Rd Way Dept - Road Way Department
Trans Dept - Transportation Department
Trans Ofc - Transportation Office
Wash br - Washington branch

| | | | | | |
|---|---|---|---|---|---|
| & | - and | appt | - appointment | bag | - baggage | boil | - boiler |
| &c | - etcetera | arch | - architect | bag'man | - baggageman | br | - branch |
| abv | - above | asst | - assistant | Balto | - Baltimore | brak | - brakeman |
| accom | - accommodation | attend | - attendant | bet | - between | bricklay | - bricklayer |
| agt | - agent | | attending | bkkpr | - bookkeeper | bur | - burden |
| amt | - amount | audit | - auditor | blast | - blaster | build | - building |
| app | - apprentice | axe | - axeman | blksmith | - blacksmith | capt | - captain |

carp - carpenter
carr - carrier
carry - carrying
carter - carter
cast - castings
clean - cleaner
          cleaning
clk - clerk
co - company
collec - collecting
          collector
comm - commission
conduc - conductor
cons - construction
contrac - contractor
coop - cooper
cop'smith - coppersmith
counsel - counsellor
coup - coupler
Cumb - Cumberland
cut - cutter
da - day(s)
deliv - delivery
dept - department
disp - dispatcher
distrib - distributing
          distributor
doorkpr - doorkeeper
draft - draftman
draught - draughtsman
dril - driller
driv - driver
dry - drying
e - east
emig - emigrant
eng - engine

eng'man - engineman
engr - engineer
enter - entered
ex - extra
exam - examine
          examiner
          examination
exp - expense
          express
fill - filler
          filling
fin - finisher
fire - fireman
firewd - firewood
flag - flagman
fore - foreman
fr - from
Fred - Frederick
frt - freight
gasmkr - gasmaker
gather - gathering
gen - general
get - getting
grad - graduation
greas - greaser
          greasing
har - harness
haul - hauling
help - helper
hp - horse power
includ - including
inspec - inspecting
          inspector
junc - junction
kpr - keeper
lab - laborer

lay - layer
          laying
load - loading
loc - location
lock - locksmith
mach - machine
          machinery
          machinist
mak - making
manag - managing
mark. - marker
mast - master
mat - materials
mech - mechanic
          mechanical
mess - messenger
mkr - maker
mo - month
mould - moulder
Mt - Mount
nail - nailing
          nailor
no - number
nos - numbers
nt - night
NW - Northwestern
Oct - October
ofc - office
ofcr - officer
oil - oiler
omit - omitted
oper - operating
          operator
opp - opposite
ost - ostler
pack - packer

paint - painter
pass - passage
          passenger
pat - pattern
pav - paver
paymast - paymaster
plast - plasterer
plumb - plumber
pd - paid
polish - polisher
port - porter
prepar - preparing
pres - president
          president's
prev - previous
prin - principal
Pt - Point
pump - pumping
pur - purchaser
put - putting
quarry - quarrying
          quarryman
rd - road
rec - receiver
          receiving
rec'd - received
recheck - rechecking
reg - regulating
          regulator
repair - repairer
          repairing
          repairs
res - resident
rig - rigger
Riv - River
rm - room

B & O RR EMPLOYEES    347

| | | |
|---|---|---|
| RR - Railroad | stat'ry - stationary | thr - through | Va - Virginia |
| rwy - railway | steam - steamer | tick - ticket | vane - vaneman |
| s-div - sub-division | stonecut - stonecutter | timekpr - timekeeper | w - west |
| saw - sawing | storekpr - storekeeper | tin - tinner | wareh - warehouse |
| sawyer | Sun - Sunday | tinsmith | Wash - Washington |
| seal - sealer | supt - superintendent | ton - tonnage | watch - watching |
| secy - secretary | supv - supervisor | trans - transportation | watchman |
| sell - seller | swit - switch | trav - traveling | wd - wood |
| serv - service | swit'man - switchman | treas - treasurer | wheel - wheelman |
| sev - several | tak - taking | trim - trimmer | wi - with |
| sht - sheet | team - teamster | Tun - Tunnel(s) | wood - wooding |
| spik - spiker | tele - telegraph | turn - turning | work - worker |
| St - Street | tell - teller | unload - unloading | yd - yard |
| sta - station(s) | tend - tender | uphol - upholsterer | yr - year |
| stab'man - stableman | | | |

BIBLIOGRAPHY

A Citizen of Baltimore (Smith). A History and Description of the Baltimore and Ohio Rail Road; with an Appendix. Baltimore: John Murphy & Co., 1853.

Baltimore and Ohio Railroad Company. A Century of Progress 1827-1934.

———. Business Guide - Baltimore and Ohio Railway Company. 1860.

———. 1828 Then and Now 1880. Baltimore: John D. Lucas, 1880.

———. List of Officers and Employees in the Service of the Baltimore and Ohio R. Road Co. with Their Salaries, Duties, &c. September-1852. Baltimore: James Lucas, 1852.

———. List of Officers and Employees in the Service of the Baltimore and Ohio R. Road Co. with Their Occupation and Salary; as appearing on the company's pay rolls for the month of February 1855. Baltimore: James Lucas & Son, 1855.

———. List of Officers and Employees of the Baltimore and Ohio Rail Road with the Amount of Their Pay for the month of November 1857. Baltimore: John Murphy & Co, 1858.

———. List of Persons with Their Pay in the Service of the Baltimore and Ohio Rail Road Company April 1, 1842. Baltimore?: 1842.

———. Memorial of the Baltimore and Ohio Railroad Company to the Legislature of Virginia...1844. Baltimore?: 1844.

———. Table of Distances and Epitome of the Route by the Baltimore and Ohio Railroad, and its Connecting Lines, between Baltimore, Cincinnati, St. Louis, &c. Baltimore: Wiley, Printer, 1860.

Baltimore and Ohio Railroad Passenger Department. An Historical and Geographical Treatise on the Baltimore and Ohio Railroad. Baltimore?

Hungerford, Edward. The Story of the Baltimore and Ohio Railroad 1827-1927. New York: G. P. Putnam's Sons, 1928.

Latrobe, John H. B. The Baltimore and Ohio Railroad. Personal Recollections. A Lecture Delivered before the Maryland Institute, March 23d, 1868. Baltimore: The Sun Book and Job Printing Establishment, 1868.

Laws and Ordinances Relating to the Baltimore and Ohio Railroad Company. Baltimore: John Murphy & Co., 1850.

Letter written by Peter Arras from Friedrickstown dated November 7, 1831. (Furnished through the courtesy of Mr. Theron H. Arras, 2769 Shrewsbury Road, Columbus, Ohio 43221)

White, Roy Barton. At Baltimore on December 7, 1842--being extracts from a Railroad Minute Book...Princeton: 1943.

www.ingramcontent.com/pod-product-compliance
Lightning Source LLC
Chambersburg PA
CBHW050331230426
43663CB00010B/1819